The Theory of Hospitality & Catering

for Levels 3 and 4

David Foskett • Patricia Paskins

Consultant editors: Victor Ceserani • Neil Rippington

Contributors: Paul Hambleton • Andrew Pennington • Suzanne Weekes

DYNAMIC LEARNING

HODDER EDUCATION
AN HACHETTE UK COMPANY

Orders: please contact Bookpoint Ltd, 130 Milton Park, Abingdon, Oxon OX14 4SB.
Telephone: (44) 01235 827720. Fax: (44) 01235 400454. Lines are open from 9.00
to 5.00, Monday to Saturday, with a 24-hour message answering service. You can also
order through our website www.hoddereducation.co.uk

If you have any comments to make about this, or any of our other titles, please send
them to educationenquiries@hodder.co.uk

British Library Cataloguing in Publication Data
A catalogue record for this title is available from the British Library

ISBN: 978 1444 12376 0

Previous editions published as *The Theory of Catering*
First edition published 1964
Second edition published 1970
Third edition published 1974
Fourth edition published 1978
Fifth edition published 1984
Sixth edition published 1989
Seventh edition published 1992
Eighth edition published 1995
Ninth edition published 1999
Tenth edition published 2003
Eleventh edition published 2007
This edition published 2011
Impression number   10 9 8 7 6 5 4 3 2
Year   2015, 2014, 2013, 2012

Copyright © 2011 David Foskett and Patricia Paskins

Hachette UK's policy is to use papers that are natural, renewable and recyclable
products and made from wood grown in sustainable forests. The logging and
manufacturing processes are expected to conform to the environmental regulations of
the country of origin.

Cover photo © John Wang/Stockbyte/Getty Images.
Typeset by Fakenham Prepress Solutions, Fakenham, Norfolk NR21 8NN
Printed in Italy for Hodder Education, an Hachette UK company, 338 Euston Road,
London NW1 3BH.

Contents

Additional free material on the web at www.hodderplus.co.uk/catering: Chapter 15 Food and society; Chapter 16 Understanding molecular gastronomy and product development; Chapter 17 ICT in the hospitality industry.

Foreword

The *Theory of Hospitality and Catering* is a must-read. I remember in my university days reading textbooks by *the* authorities in their field – but that's all they are, memories. They, too, were must-reads at the time, but invariably grew dusty on the shelves after graduation.

The Theory of Hospitality and Catering, however, is a true necessity for any student of catering and hospitality anywhere in the world. It is a book you will keep with you throughout your career. Most importantly, it not only covers the theory of hospitality and catering, but also the practice. It is a comprehensive, authoritative book for everyone in the field. Whether back-of-house or front-of-house, this book is essential.

I know, having started a business from scratch, that ideas are useless on their own. It is ideas combined with action that make things happen. *The Theory of Hospitality and Catering* bridges the gap between idea and application, between theory and practice.

It was a privilege to work with Professor David Foskett MBE CMA in my capacity as former Chancellor of Thames Valley University (TVU, now The University of West London). David is truly one of the titans of the hospitality industry, and as Head of the London School of Hospitality and Tourism he has helped create a beacon of excellence, renowned not just across the UK but worldwide.

And with *The Theory of Hospitality and Catering*, David and his colleagues have produced a book that is itself a beacon of the industry – a work that is clear, and clearly useful, to people at all levels. Whether a student or a practitioner, this book is indispensable.

Lord Bilimoria of Chelsea CBE DL
Founder and Chief Executive, Cobra Beer

Acknowledgements

We are most grateful to Booker plc, in particular Ron Hickey and Niall Brannigan, for their support in the development of the book.

Special thanks to the Catering Equipment Suppliers' Association for valuable, up-to-date information, and to Keith Warren, its chairman.

We are also greatly indebted to the following people and organisations for their helpful advice and contributions to this edition:

- Lionel Benjamin for cost control
- John Cousins, Director, The Food and Beverage Training Company, London, for an overview of food and beverage service
- Joanne Tucker, Lecturer, University of West London
- Richard Fagan of Ebex
- Edward Griffiths for planning a function
- Peter Pelham, The University of West London
- Michael Stapleton, UK Corporate Affairs Director, Compass Group UK
- British Egg Information Services
- The British Hospitality Association
- The Dairy Council
- Food Service Intelligence
- The Sea Fish Authority
- Russums Catering Clothing and Equipment
- Bill Graney, Manager Client Services, Harrison Catering
- Alexia Chan, Rick Jackman, Deborah Edwards Noble, Lynn Brown, Laura DeGrasse and Melissa Brunelli at Hodder Education
- John Campbell, Director of Cuisine and Food and Beverage at Coworth Park, part of the Dorchester Collection
- The staff at The Vineyard at Stockcross
- Sam Bailey, photographer
- Barry Gregory, Chef Lecturer, Halesowen College
- Gary Hunter, Head of Culinary Arts, Westminster Kingsway College
- Steve Thorpe, Programme Manager Food and Beverage Curriculum, City College Norwich
- Tony Taylor, Deputy Director, Academy of Service Industries, Bournemouth and Poole College
- Harbour & Jones
- Baxter Storey.

About the contributors

Paul Hambleton is Deputy Dean of the Faculty of Professional Studies, University of West London.

Andrew Pennington is Lecturer in Food and Beverage Management and Hospitality Operations at the University of West London.

Suzanne Weekes is Senior Lecturer in Hospitality Management and Licensing Law at the University of West London.

Picture credits

Every effort has been made to trace and acknowledge ownership of copyright. The publishers will be glad to make suitable arrangements with any copyright holders whom it has not been possible to contact. The authors and publisher would like to thank the following for permission to reproduce copyright illustrative material:

Figs 1.5–1.8, 1.10–2.3 Compass; fig.3.1 © Stephan Gabriel/Imagebroker.net/Photolibrary.com; figs 3.3–3.12, 3.14–3.16 © EBLEX; figs 3.18–3.25, 3.27, 3.28 © BPEX; figs 3.30–3.43 © EBLEX; fig.3.96 © Kondor83 – Fotolia; fig.3.120 © karam miri – Fotolia; fig. 3.122 Compass; figs 3.127, 3.128 © Andrew Callaghan/Hodder Education; fig.4.11 Crown copyright; fig.4.12 Compass; figs 5.8, 5.10 Compass; figs 5.11, 5.18, 5.19 Russums; figs 5.20, 5.21 Compass; figs 5.23, 5.25 Russums; fig.5.26 Compass; fig.5.32 (left) © Silke Lorenz – Fotolia, (right) © Stepanov – Fotolia; fig.5.33 egg slice, cheese slice ©Tyler Olson – Fotolia, garlic press ©Thomas Brostrom – Fotolia, lemon squeezer © VRD – Fotolia; fig.5.34 ricer © Pefkos – Fotolia; masher © Silkstock – Fotolia; pestle and mortar © UgputuLf FT – Fotolia; fig.5.36 © Mario Beauregard – Fotolia; fig.5.37 Russums; fig.5.38 © Andrew Callaghan/Hodder Education; fig.5.39 Russums; fig.5.40 Lloyds; fig.6.5 Compass; fig.6.8 Russums; fig.7.8 The Ritz; fig.8.8 OPRL; figs 9.1, 9.2 Compass; fig.9.3 The Ritz; fig.9.4 © Kumar Sriskandan/Alamy; fig. 9.5 © Ilpo Musto/Rex Features; fig.9.6 © tomalu – Fotolia; fig.9.8 The Ritz; fig.9.11 © Cultura/Alamy; fig. 12.1 © Shariff Che'Lah – Fotolia; figs 12.2, 12.3 © Irving Bartlett/Alamy; fig.12.7 © Alex Segre/Rex Features; fig.12.10 © omicron – Fotolia; fig.12.14 © David Gilder – Fotolia; fig.12.18 © Fancy/Alamy; figs 12.28, 12.32 © Monkey Business – Fotolia; fig.13.8 Russums; figs 13.10, 13.11 Compass; fig.14.2 Russums; fig.14.4 © photo by Eric Erbe, digital colorisation by

Christopher Pooley – material produced by ARS is in the public domain; fig.14.8 © Martin Lee/Rex Features; figs 14.14, 14.15 Compass; fig.14.16 (left) © Ayupov Evgeniy – Fotolia, (right) © Bogdan Dumitru – Fotolia; fig.16.4 Compass.

Except where stated above, photographs are by Sam Bailey and illustrations by Barking Dog Art.

About CESA

The primary interest group for members of the food-service industry in the UK is the Catering Equipment Suppliers' Association (CESA).

The roots of CESA stretch back to 1938, when the first manufacturers' association was founded. This was enlarged in 1994, when the importers' association joined, and again when the Catering Utensils Association joined. Today, CESA has the largest membership of any UK association whose members are engaged in the manufacture, import or prime supply of foodservice equipment, including cooking, refrigeration, fabrication, utensils and after-sales service.

CESA is a member of the European Federation of Catering Equipment Manufacturers (EFCEM) and is pivotal within the Federation in working with its partners to influence pan-European legislation affecting the sector. CESA also has strong links with the North American Association of Food Equipment Manufacturers (NAFEM), and regularly exhibits at major trade exhibitions around the world, including in the UK, USA and Middle East.

Key goals and objectives for CESA include:

- Effective collaboration between all suppliers engaged in food service equipment manufacture and prime supply
- Active co-operation with other like-minded trade associations worldwide
- To further the interests and raise the standards of the industry and promote the welfare of its members
- Sustained representation on all matters affecting members to relevant government departments and regulatory authorities locally, nationally and internationally.

CESA has been an instrumental player in advancing the professionalism and industry awareness of all members and segments of the foodservice industry, and its members adhere to a code of practice that covers the range of support concerning manufacture, supply, installation and after-sales service that buyers can expect from members of the association.

Extracts from the Certified Food Service Professional (CFSP) programme are included in this book. This programme is operated under the auspices of CESA with the objective of improving the level of professionalism in the sector by creating a universally recognised and respected industry 'standard' for knowledge and experience. See www.cfsp.org.uk.

To successfully achieve the designation and the benefits that accrue from it, CFSP candidates must:

- Study for and pass a comprehensive written test
- Attend a half-day pre-test seminar
- Prove a certain level of experience in the industry
- Show personal development through the completion of recognised education or training programmes
- Demonstrate active involvement in the industry
- Maintain the above if they wish to continue to use the CFSP designation and receive regular communication from the programme.

Video credits

The authors and publishers would like to thank the following, whose expertise and kind help were instrumental in the making of the film clips for the accompanying Dynamic Learning resource:

- John Campbell and the staff at The Vineyard at Stockcross
- Andie Way, Robert Perry, Janet Rowson, Sue Montgomery, Sibel Roller and Elaine O'Sullivan at The University of West London
- Helen Evans, Gary Marshall and the Covent Garden Market Authority
- Adam Hands, Marigold Keylock and Winchcombe Abbey Primary School
- Andy Hazell, Mike Anthony and Gloucester RFC
- Dipna Anand and the staff at the Brilliant Restaurant, Southall
- Dr Claire Mills at IFR, Norwich
- The Loon Fung Superstore, Alperton
- Russ Timpson at The Fire Strategy Company.

Special thanks to Russell Hume Ltd for sponsoring the butchery videos, and in particular to Pat Herlihy, Operations Director, and Terry Connelly, Sales Account Manager. Russell Hume are meat, game and poultry specialists, and national suppliers of meat, game and poultry products to hotels, restaurants, pubs and event caterers. They are committed to quality and service nationwide and have 90 years' experience, with managers who have over 20 years' experience in the meat trade.

The films were produced and created by Adrian Moss of Instructional Design Ltd, Cheltenham.

Reasons to come to Booker the UK's biggest wholesaler

To find your nearest branch visit www.booker.co.uk

choice up

Huge range
The average branch carries over 10,000 lines in stock the whole time, with even more available to order.

New Lines
Our expert buyers are constantly sourcing great new lines for you.
Look for the 'New Line shelf' cards in branch, every week.

prices down

Catering Price check
Our catering price check service allows you to enter your current Brakes or 3663 prices and, with one click, instantly see if you can buy cheaper from Booker. Why not compare our prices for yourself by visiting www.booker.co.uk today!

Essentials - every day low price
We have lock down prices on a range of products that are essential to your business. From bread, milk, eggs and potatoes through to sugar, tuna, chips and peas we will give you a low price, every day to help you plan your menu and your budget.

better service

Internet ordering
The easiest way to place your order with your branch is via our website.
Simply log on to www.booker.co.uk, and register for online ordering.
Its so simple - start today!

Free, 7 days a week, delivery service*
All your fresh produce, frozen, wet and dry goods delivered to your door on the one vehicle - 7 days a week.

*Terms and conditions apply - see in branch for details.

Introduction to the 12th edition

As travel, tourism, recreation and hospitality become increasingly important in the economic life of the vast majority of countries, so the need for well-trained operatives and managers continues to grow.

This book is designed to meet the needs of those training for, or involved in, the hospitality and catering industry.

This 12th edition has been revised and updated to keep in line with the continuing changes both in industry and catering education. As in previous editions we have not attempted to write a completely comprehensive book, but rather have set out an outline as a basis for further study. In this way we hope to assist students at all levels and, for those who wish to study at great length, further references and websites are suggested where appropriate.

The qualification mapping grids on the next two pages show how the chapters of this book relate to a range of qualifications at Levels 2 and 3. This book also covers units/modules of Foundation degrees and BA(Hons) degrees in Hospitality Management, Event Management and Culinary Arts.

Qualification mapping grids

Level 2 NVQ and VRQ

Chapter	NVQ Food and Drink	NVQ Professional Cookery (Preparation and Cooking)	VRQ Diploma in Professional Cookery	NVQ Food Processing and Cooking	NVQ Hospitality
1 An overview of the UK and global hospitality industry			Unit 201		
2 Employment in the hospitality industry					
3 Food commodities		✓	Background knowledge: Units 208, 209, 210, 211, 212	✓	✓
4 Basic nutrition, diet and health		✓	Unit 204	✓	✓
5 Kitchen planning, equipment, services and energy conservation				✓	✓
6 Production systems		✓		✓	✓
7 Menu planning, development and structure			Unit 205		
8 Food purchasing, storage and control		✓	Unit 205	✓	✓
9 An overview of food and beverage service and food service design					
10 Managing resources	✓	✓		✓	✓
11 Marketing, sales and customer care	✓				✓
12 Accommodation management				✓	✓
13 Health, safety and security	✓	✓	Unit 203	✓	✓
14 Food safety and food safety legislation	✓	✓	Unit 202	✓	✓
15 Food and society					
16 Understanding molecular gastronomy and product development					
17 ICT in the hospitality industry					

Level 3 and BTEC

Chapter	NVQ Hospitality Supervision	NVQ Professional Cookery	BTEC Edexcel Extended Diploma (Certificate, Subsidiary Diploma or Diploma)
1 An overview of the UK and global hospitality industry			Unit 1
2 Employment in the hospitality industry		✓	Unit 20
3 Food commodities		✓	
4 Basic nutrition, diet and health			Unit 15
5 Kitchen planning, equipment, services and energy conservation	✓		Unit 14
6 Production systems			
7 Menu planning, development and structure	✓		
8 Food purchasing, storage and control	✓		Unit 4
9 An overview of food and beverage service and food service design	✓		Units 6 and 9
10 Managing resources	✓	✓	Units 5, 18, 19 and 20
11 Marketing, sales and customer care	✓		Units 2 and 3
12 Accommodation management	✓		Unit 23
13 Health, safety and security	✓	✓	
14 Food safety and food safety legislation	✓	✓	Unit 8
15 Food and society			
16 Understanding molecular gastronomy and product development			
17 Information and communication technology in the hospitality industry			Unit 17

An overview of the UK and global hospitality industry

Supporting material available on Dynamic Learning Online:

> Knowledge quizzes

> Activity worksheets: the industry; tourism

> Summary presentations

The UK hospitality industry

The largest sectors in the UK hospitality industry, in terms of numbers of outlets, are hotels and pubs – a microcosm of the catering industry itself since it comprises a wide variety of outlets, from sports clubs and stadia to theme parks, historic properties, cinemas and beyond. Indeed, many researchers are unsure whether to include the leisure sector within the catering market, since it consists of a large number of outlets, each of which serves only small quantities of food. However, this sector will be among those showing the fastest growth over the next few years.

Like hospitality and tourism, all leisure markets benefit from improving economic conditions. For many people, real disposable income has grown and the forecasts are that it will continue to grow. In wealthy markets, the leisure and pleasure sectors outperform the economy in general. It is usually the case that, as people become wealthier, their incremental income is not usually spent on upgrading the essentials but on pleasure and luxury items. However, whenever there is a downturn in the economy, the leisure sectors suffer disproportionately.

The leisure industry has been described as the biggest, fastest-growing industry in the UK. Within the leisure sector, some areas have slowed down, while others are consolidating and concentrating on core businesses. One of the most useful ways of categorising the leisure sector is to separate it into popular leisure activities – for example, theatre, ten-pin bowling and cue sports, casinos, bingo, and health and fitness.

Traditionally, catering activity has been divided into either profit or cost sector markets. The profit sector includes such establishments as restaurants, fast-food outlets, cafés, takeaways, pubs, and leisure and travel catering outlets; the cost sector refers to catering outlets for business and industry, education and health care. Recent developments have blurred the division between profit- and cost-orientated establishments.

The three main types of business

The industry can be divided into three main types of business: SMEs, public limited companies and private companies.

Small to medium-sized business enterprises (SMEs)

SMEs have up to 250 employees. In the UK as a whole, SMEs account for over half of all employment (58.7 per cent). These are usually private companies that may become public limited companies if they get very large.

Public limited companies and private companies

The key difference between public and private companies is that a public company can sell its shares to the public, while private companies cannot. A share is a certificate representing one unit of ownership in a company, so the more shares a person has, the more of the company they own.

Before it can start in business or borrow money, a public company must prove to Companies House (the department where all companies in the UK must be registered) that at least £50,000 worth of shares have been issued and that each share has been paid up to at least a quarter of its nominal value (so 25 per cent of £50,000). It will then receive authorisation to start business and borrow money.

Other types of business

The types of business in operation in the catering and hospitality industry can be further divided into sole traders, self-employed, partnership and limited liability companies. These are usually private companies.

Sole trader

A sole trader is the simplest form of setting up and running a business. It is suited to the smallest of businesses. The sole trader owns the business, takes all the risks, is liable for any losses and keeps any profits. The advantage of operating in business as a sole trader is that very little formality is needed. The only official records required are those for HM Revenue & Customs (HMRC), National Insurance and VAT. The accounts are not available to the public.

Self-employed

There is no precise definition of self-employment, although guidance is offered by HMRC. It is important to note that a mere agreement with an individual that he or she will be regarded as self-employed is insufficient for the purposes of HMRC and the Contributions Agency.

In order to determine whether an individual is truly self-employed, the whole circumstances of his or her work need to be considered. This may include whether he or she:

- is in control of their own time, the amount of work they take on and the decision making
- has no guarantee of regular work
- receives no pay for periods of holiday or sickness
- is responsible for all the risks of the business
- attends the premises of the person giving him or her the work
- generally uses her or his own equipment and materials
- has the right to send someone else to do the work.

Partnership

A partnership consists of two or more people working together as the proprietors of a business. Unlike limited liability companies, there are no legal requirements in setting up as a partnership. A partnership can be set up without the partners necessarily being fully aware that they have done so.

The partnership is similar to a sole trader in law, in that the partners own the business, take all the risks, stand any losses and keep any profits. Each partner individually is responsible for all the debts of the partnership. So, if the business fails, each partner's personal assets are fully at risk. It is possible, though not very common, to have partners with limited liability. In this case the partner with limited liability must not play any active part in the management or conduct of the business. In effect, he or she has merely invested a limited sum of money in the partnership.

The advantages of operating a business as a partnership can be very similar to those of the sole trader. Very little formality is needed, although everyone contemplating entering into a partnership should seriously consider taking legal advice and having a partnership agreement drawn up.

The main official records that are required are those for HMRC, National Insurance and VAT. The accounts are not available to the public. There may be important tax advantages, too, when compared with a limited company. For example, they might be able pay the tax they owe at a later date, or treat deductible expenses more generously. These are business expenses that can be claimed against tax – in other words, taken away from the business's income, so the amount of money taxed is less, which means the amount of tax owed is less.

Limited liability companies

These are companies that are incorporated under the

Companies Acts. This means that the liability of their owners (the amount they will have to pay to cover the business's debts if it fails or if it is sued) is limited to the value of the shares each shareholder (owner) owns.

Limited liability companies are much more complex than sole traders and partnerships. This is because the owners can limit their liability. As a consequence people either investing in them or doing business with them need to know the financial standing of the company. Company documents, which are listed below, are open to inspection by the public.

- The **Constitution**: this comprises two documents – the Memorandum of Association and the Articles of Association.
- The **Memorandum of Association**: this is the 'outer face' of the company, informing the outside world of its name and purpose.
- The **Articles of Association**: this is the 'inner face' of the company and is concerned with the detailed conduct of the company, including rules about general meetings, the powers of the directors, accounts, and so on.

The food service management industry

Food and service management covers providing a food service at work in business and industry, catering in schools, colleges and universities, hospitals and health care, welfare and local authority catering, and other non-profit-making outlets.

Despite its complexity, catering and hospitality represents one of the largest sectors of the UK economy and is fifth in size behind retail food, cars, insurance and clothing. It is also an essential support to tourism, another major part of the economy, and one of the largest employers in the country.

Number of contracted outlets, 1990 and 2009 (business and industry)

In terms of outlets, food and service management companies have taken their share of the business and industry (B&I) sector up to 49 per cent in 2009 at the expense of the self-operator; in terms of meals (see Table 1.1), contracting companies dominate the sector. This reflects their generally larger size of outlet.

Because they operate the largest outlets, food and service management (FSM) companies serve far more meals in the B&I sector than the self-operator, even though they operate only just over half the number of outlets.

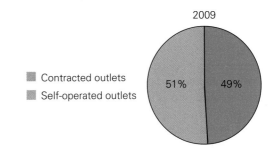

Figure 1.1 Meals served by food and service management companies, 2009 (business and industry)

Source: British Hospitality Association, *Food and Service Management Survey* 2009

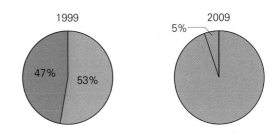

Figure 1.2 Total number of meals in the cost catering sector, 1999 and 2009

Source: British Hospitality Association, *Food and Service Management Survey* 2009

Horizons FS has estimated the number of outlets and meals served (excluding snacks) in the total food service management sector in 2009 as shown in Table 1.1.

This structure is not reflected in the food and service management market, where food service management companies have a greater share of business and industry than of any other sector.

Table 1.1 Number of outlets and meals served (excluding snacks) in the total food service management sector, 2009

	Outlets	Meals (m)
Business and industry	16,776	612
Education	34,455	1,136
Health and welfare	33,496	1,157
Other (inc. MoD)	4,513	339
TOTAL	89,240	3,244

Note: This data should be treated with caution as definition does vary.

Source: British Hospitality Association, *Food and Service Management Survey* 2009

World tourism

International tourism is likely to increase, with Europe attracting the major share of tourism arrivals and France the most popular destination – indeed, probably the most popular destination in the world, with the USA second and Spain third. However, in terms of receipts, Spain earns more and is second only to the USA. Spend per head in France is also less than in Spain, mainly because many arrivals in France are passing through to other destinations. China is emerging as a tourism destination having hosted the 2008 Olympics and because of its rapidly growing economy.

UK tourism

According to government statistics, the UK tourism and leisure market is estimated to be worth approximately £85 billion, but taking into account the full spectrum of the industry, the British Hospitality Association (BHA) suggests that this figure is estimated at around £109.7 billion. Tourism and hospitality is an important industry to the UK economy. The government has a target of £100 billion for the UK tourism industry by 2012; if leisure spend is included in the definition of tourism, this target has already been reached.

The principal change in source countries for UK tourism in recent years has been the inclusion of Poland in the list of ten leading visitor countries. Since 2004, the number of Polish visitors to the UK has almost trebled, with most of them likely to be seeking employment or visiting friends and relatives.

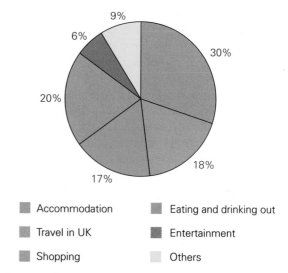

Figure 1.3 Tourism spend in the UK by UK residents

Source: British Hospitality Association, *Trends and Statistics* 2009

The travel balance

The travel balance is the difference between overseas visitor spending in the UK and spending by UK residents abroad. The imbalance has been rising continuously since the early 1990s and in 2008 stood at £20.2 billion. The expansion of budget airlines and the popularity of cheap overseas travel, as well as rising living standards, have contributed to this growth.

Up to 2009 fewer long holidays were being spent in Britain, while British residents spent far more on overseas holidays than they did on domestic holidays. This is a trend that is unlikely to be reversed in the

Table 1.2 Countries of origin of overseas visitors to the UK, 2000 and 2003–2008 by number of visits

		Visits (000s)						
Rank	**Country**	**2000**	**2003**	**2004**	**2005**	**2006**	**2007**	**2008**
1	USA	4096	3346	3616	3436	3896	3551	2959
2	France	3086	3073	3254	3333	3693	3404	3636
3	Irish Republic	2082	2488	2578	2824	2909	2970	3069
4	Germany	2757	2611	2968	3318	3411	3376	2905
5	Spain	848	1206	1465	1773	1981	2227	1977
6	Netherlands	1435	1549	1620	1729	1791	1823	1811
7	Italy	946	1168	1348	1189	1477	1615	1645
8	Poland	–	–	528	1027	1326	1294	1493
9	Belgium/Luxembourg	1047	978	1167	1171	997	1083	1031
10	Australia	776	723	787	915	956	941	959

Source: British Hospitality Association, *Trends and Statistics* 2009

long term, but in 2009 at least there were early indications that more people were planning to spend a holiday in Britain than in previous years.

Tourism and the UK economy

The impact of a sector of the economy is measured through gross value added (GVA). This measures the value of the output used less the value of the input used in the production of the output.

Gross domestic product (GDP) can be measured in three ways.

1 **Output measure:** this is the value of the goods and services produced by all sectors of the economy – agriculture, manufacturing, energy, construction, the service sector and government.
2 **Expenditure measure:** this is the value of the goods and services purchased by households and by government, investment in machinery and buildings; it also includes the value of exports minus imports.
3 **Income measure:** the value of the income generated mostly in terms of profits and wages.

In theory all three approaches should produce the same number.

In the UK the Office for National Statistics (ONS) publishes one single measure of GDP which, apart from the first estimate, is calculated using all three ways of measuring. Usually the main interest in the UK figures is in the quarterly change in GDP in real terms – that is, after taking account of changes in prices (inflation).

How is GDP calculated?

Calculating a GDP estimate for all three of the above measures is a huge undertaking every three months. The output measure alone – which is considered the most accurate in the short term – involves surveying tens of thousands of UK firms. The main sources used for this are ONS surveys of manufacturing and service industries. Information on sales is collected from 6000 companies in manufacturing, 25,000 service-sector firms, 5000 retailers and 10,000 companies in the construction sector. Data are also collected from government departments covering activities such as agriculture, energy, health and education, which is augmented by a wide range of sources to ensure that activity in the economy is well covered.

Tourism trips by UK residents

The main purpose of tourism trips by UK residents in the UK is for a holiday, which accounts for 81% of the total number of trips and 75% of total spend. Visiting friends and relatives remains the most popu-

lar type of accommodation enjoyed by almost half of those holidaying in the UK. Almost four trips out of ten are spent in a hotel or guest house.

UK residents: where they stay and how much they spend

The south-west, south-east and north-west are the most popular regions of the country for domestic visitors in terms of trips, nights and spend. London's popularity earns almost approximately £3 billion from the domestic visitor.

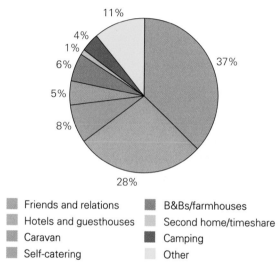

Friends and relations • B&Bs/farmhouses
Hotels and guesthouses • Second home/timeshare
Caravan • Camping
Self-catering • Other

Figure 1.4 Type of accommodation used by UK residents on holiday in the UK (%), 2008

Source: British Hospitality Association, *Trends and Statistics* 2009

Overseas visitors: where they stay and how much they spend

The distribution of overseas visitors to Britain is markedly different to that of domestic visitors. London is by far the favourite destination for overseas visitors, accounting for 50% of all their expenditure, followed – distantly – by the south-east of England and Scotland. The distribution of overseas visitors to the rest of the UK is evenly balanced although the north-east (with Northern Ireland) remains the least popular destination.

The size of the UK hotel industry

The UK hotel industry remains a significant sector of the UK economy, with an annual turnover of approximately £40 billion. There is no all-inclusive register of serviced accommodation in the UK. The approximate number of hotels and guest houses is 46,542 – a figure that has been declining despite new hotel openings. This is because of the closure

Table 1.3 Number of rooms and beds in serviced accommodation categories, 2009

	London	England	Scotland	Wales	Northern Ireland	Total rooms	Total beds
Hotel	63,130	216,300	67,880	21,000	4,950	373,260	769,000
Motor lodge/inn/ branded budget	20,250	64,000	8,950	4,000	800	97,700	210,000
Guest house/B&B	15,350	100,800	10,600	3,700	3,500	118,600	250,000
Inn	–	34,600	900	750	250	36,500	90,000
Farmhouse	–	9,500	250	500	100	10,350	20,000
Youth hostel	4,340	14,580	6,880	5,750	715	32,265	81,000
Total	**103,070**	**463,405**	**99,960**	**40,000**	**10,065**	**716,500**	**1,490,000**

Source: British Hospitality Association, *Trends and Statistics* 2009

of many small hotels and guest houses, particularly in coastal areas. The total number of rooms and beds in the UK serviced accommodation sector is very difficult to calculate because of the lack of definition and detailed statistics.

What is a hotel?

The definition of a hotel varies according to the source used. Basically, any establishment that calls itself a hotel is classified as a hotel.

Table 1.3 highlights the fragmented nature of the hotel industry. If the number of hotels and guest houses in the UK (which includes budget properties, private hotels and guest houses) is 46,000+ the average size of a hotel in the UK is approximately 11.5 rooms with the average-size budget hotel having 77 rooms.

Structure of the UK hotel industry

Whitbread, with its Premier Inn brand, is the largest hotel operator in the UK (in terms of number of hotel rooms), followed by InterContinental and Travelodge. Except for Premier Inn and InterContinental, all the leading hotel companies in the UK are foreign-owned. And, except for Premier Inn, Travelodge and Accor, expansion now takes place mainly through franchising.

The UK's ten largest hotel groups

Whitbread is the UK's largest hotel and restaurant group, operating in the budget hotel and branded restaurant sectors. It now has almost 600 Premier Inns with more than 40,000 rooms. Its restaurants include Beefeater, Brewers Fayre and Taybarns. Its Costa Coffee brand now has over 900 shops in the UK and over 400 internationally in 25 countries, second to Starbucks.

InterContinental Hotels Group (IHG)

InterContinental Hotels Group has more rooms than any other hotel company: approximately 620,000 in over 4300 hotels in approximately 100 countries. It has a portfolio of the following brands:

- InterContinental
- Hotel Indigo
- Crowne Plaza
- Holiday Inn
- Holiday Inn Express
- Staybridge Suites.

Travelodge (Dubai International Capital)

Travelodge was the first budget hotel brand to launch in the UK, in 1985, and now operates 380+ hotels (over 26,000 rooms) in the UK, Ireland and Spain.

Accor Hotels

Accor is the fifth largest hotel group by room numbers. It has more than 4000 hotels (500,000 rooms) in 90 countries. It operates 15 brands, with 138 hotels and almost 20,000 rooms. For example:

- Sofitel
- Novotel
- Mercure
- Ibis
- Etap
- Formule 1.

Hilton Hotels Corporation

Hilton now has more than 3300 hotels and 550,000 rooms in over 77 countries, and employs 135,000 people. It has ten brands.

Best Western

Best Western UK has 280+ independently owned hotels, operating 15,000 rooms. It is part of Best Western International, the world's largest hotel chain of independent operators, which has 4000 hotels with over 300,000 rooms in 80 countries.

Wyndham Worldwide

Wyndham is the second largest hospitality company in the world, with almost 7000 hotels offering 588,000 rooms in 66 countries, the majority franchised. The four major brands are:

- Wyndham Grand
- Ramada
- Ramada Encore
- Jurys Inn.

Marriott Hotels

Marriott is the world's third largest hotel company, with 3200+ hotels and 577,000 rooms in 67 countries. It operates and franchises ten hotel brands as well as extended-stay apartments and vacation ownership resorts. In the UK it operates nearly 60 hotels across five brands:

- JW Marriott
- Renaissance
- Marriott
- Grand Residences
- Courtyard.

Carlson Hotels

Based in Minneapolis, Carlson operates tour hospitality businesses and is the largest privately held company in the USA. It has five brands. The three operating in the UK are:

- Park Inn
- Park Plaza
- Radisson Hotels and Resorts, representing 42 hotels in the UK. With 7750 rooms worldwide it has over 1000 hotels in 72 countries.

The Rezidor Hotel Group

The Rezidor Hotel Group is based in Brussels. It has more than 380 hotels in operation, with approximately 81,000 rooms in 59 countries under five brands. In the UK it has over 50 hotels, operating Radisson and Park Inn Hotels.

The world's largest hotel groups

Table 1.5 lists the world's ten largest hotel groups. All but two are US-owned; only one company – IHG – is British-owned and Accor is French-owned. It should be noted that both Choice and Best Western are consortia of independent hotels, so are not groups under a common ownership. However, even hotels listed under other names are not necessarily owned or operated by that group, as the list includes all hotels operating under franchise agreements.

Food tourism

The experience of food and taste is an important element in tourism. In defining food tourism there is a need to differentiate between those tourists who consume food as a part of the travel experience and those whose activities, behaviours and even choice of destination are influenced by their interest in the food. Similar to these people are those who are interested in wine and visit the noted wine-producing areas of the world. For such people, vineyards, wineries, wine festivals, wine shows, wine tasting and/or experiencing the attributes of a wine region are the prime motivating factors. Similarly, food tourism refers to visits to food producers, food festivals, restaurants and specific locations renowned for a particular food, as well as food tasting and/or experiencing the attributes of specialist food production regions, or even visiting a restaurant to taste the dishes of a well-known chef; for food tourists, such factors provide the motivation for them to travel to a certain area. (Some people, for example, travel to Perigord in France to taste the foie gras and truffles, and sample the local Bergerac wine for which the area is renowned.)

The globalisation of the hospitality and tourism industries

Businesses today find themselves competing in a world economy for survival, growth and profitability. Managers working in the industry have to learn to adjust to change in line with market demands for quality and value for money, and increased organisational attention must be devoted to profitability and professionalism.

The globalisation of the hospitality and tourism industries has advanced under the pressures of increased technology, communication, transportation, deregulation, elimination of political barriers, sociocultural changes and global economic development, together with growing competition in a global economy. An international hospitality company must perform successfully in the *world's* business environment. There are a vast number of influences in the external international environment that greatly affect the multinational organisation. Some of these are as follows.

- Monetary and fiscal policies and exchange controls: some countries may limit the amount of money that can be withdrawn from their country, as well as impose large payments for international transactions (e.g. joint ventures, entry to the country).

- Financial and investment markets, individual consumer and corporate interest rates, the availability of credit, exchanges, and so on.
- Taxation and tariffs: taxes on individuals, corporations and imported goods, imposed by the host country/government.
- Trade/industrial factors: import/export measures of activity in commerce, and so on. These can serve as indices in determining the state of the economy (e.g. prosperity, depression, recession, recovery).
- Labour markets: the level of unemployment, welfare spending, and so on.

Travel, tourism and hospitality together make up the world's largest industry. According to the World Travel and Tourism Council (WTTC), the annual gross output of the industry is greater than the gross national product (GNP) of all countries except the United States and Japan. Worldwide, the industry employs over 112 million people. In many countries, especially in emerging tourism destinations, the hospitality and tourism industry plays a very important role in the national economy, being the major foreign currency earner.

As the world economy continues to become more interdependent, this will give rise to increasing amounts of business travel. With this in mind, it is clear that the global economic environment plays a significant role in the internationalisation opportunities available to hospitality and tourism companies, and that global economic policies and developments play a critical role in the hospitality and tourism industry.

One of the principal challenges confronting the industry of the future will result from the ongoing transition to the 'information age'. The convergence of computing, telecommunications and content will shape the way and pace at which people live and work. Above all, it will change the nature of the exchange process between providers and their customers – the latter will have more choice. The internet will offer numerous ways to find out whether a hospitality company or restaurant, say, delivers on its promises. Dissatisfied clients will be able to vent their feelings to an Internet-connected community of millions. Companies will in turn be expected to systematically accumulate information about their customers.

The effects of international tourism

As emerging markets such as China and India continue to grow, people with disposable income keen to spend it on travel will make the most of low-cost carriers and the easing of visa restrictions. While massive growth is forecast for these emerging markets, other regions around the world, particularly Europe and America, will remain among the most visited destinations.

China is investing heavily in travel and tourism. India's buoyant economy and its boom in business and leisure travel are driving a strong growth in tourism. To reduce the region's economic reliance on oil, many countries of the Gulf States are now focusing on tourism, capitalising on their natural assets, historic cultures and Islamic traditions: the Middle East is now the fourth most visited region in the world.

Investment in tourism in the Middle East is highest in the United Arab Emirates (UAE), followed by Saudi Arabia. Dubai's hotel market currently ranks among the world's best. International tourism is part of the wider move towards globalisation.

Airlines

Many people reach the hotel reception desk via an airline. Today, more than 2 billion passengers a year use the world's airlines for business and leisure travel.

People choose to fly for both business and leisure reasons. Some airlines, such as Aer Lingus, have only one class on all UK and European services. Food and drink has to be purchased on these flights as the carrier is trying to minimise the low-cost formula. The use of in-flight entertainment is slowly making its way to the low-cost sector.

Tier systems are used by airlines to describe the prestige of a passenger based on their frequent flyer programmes. A first, platinum or premium tier traveller will normally have travelled hundreds of thousands of miles with the carrier and will have access to its lounges and lots of other extras. Fierce competition between low-cost and traditional carriers, as well as cost-cutting by both airlines and corporate travel managers, have triggered this trend.

The major carriers are now offering all-business-class flights and are investing heavily to improve their products. The airlines' marketing highlights:

- increased comfort on board the aircraft, and the availability of gyms, shower facilities and massages
- increased technology – e.g. broadband, videoconferencing
- mood lighting to aid jet lag and assist sleep
- on-board entertainment, online gaming, etc.
- a range of reading materials, menu items, wines, etc.
- door-to-door service rather than gate to gate.

The hospitality industry: product and service

The hospitality product consists of tangible and intangible elements of food, drink and accommodation, together with the service, atmosphere and image that surround and contribute to the product.

The hospitality industry contains many of the characteristics of service industries with the added complications of the production process. It is the production process that is the complicated element as it focuses on production and delivery, often within a set period of time.

The need to provide the appropriate environment within which hospitality can be delivered means that most hospitality businesses need a substantial amount of investment in plant and premises. This creates a high fixed cost/low variable cost structure. The variable costs in servicing a room are minimal, although the hotel itself – particularly in the luxury hotel market – has a high fixed cost. In general, the financial break-even point for hospitality businesses is often fairly high. Exceeding this level will result in high profits, but low volumes will result in substantial losses.

Hospitality services suffer from fluctuations in demand: demand fluctuates over time and by type of customer. Forecasting business is therefore often difficult because of the mixture of patterns and variables that can affect demand, making planning, resourcing and scheduling difficult. Hospitality cannot be delivered without customers, who are involved in many aspects of the delivery of the hospitality service.

Achieving a satisfactory balance between demand patterns, resource scheduling and operational capacity is a difficult task for managers in hospitality. Managing customer demand to achieve optimum volume at maximum value is extremely complex. Too few customers could spell financial ruin; too many customers without the required capacity or resources, often means that the customers' experience suffers, leading to dissatisfaction. Scheduling of resources is also difficult, if too many staff are on duty to cover the forecast demand, then profitability suffers. Insufficient staffing creates problems – with servicing and staff morale. Forecasting is therefore a crucial function, which contributes to the successful operation of the hospitality business.

The ability to deliver a consistent product to every customer is also an important consideration. Staff must be trained in teams to deliver a consistent standard of product and service. This means being able to cater not just for individual customers but to the needs of many different groups of customers, all with slightly different requirements. The success of any customer experience will be determined at the interaction point between the customer and the service provider.

The service staff have an additional part to play in serving the customer: they are important in the future selling process, and therefore should be trained to use the opportunity to generate additional revenue.

From this analysis we are able to identify four characteristics of the hospitality industry that make it a unique operation.

1 Hospitality cannot be delivered without customers who provide the source of revenue for the continued financial viability of the operation. The customer is directly involved in many aspects of the delivery of the hospitality service, and is the judge of the quality of the hospitality provided.
2 Achieving a satisfactory balance between demand patterns, resource scheduling and operations is a particularly difficult task in the hospitality industry.
3 All hospitality operations require a combination of manufacturing expertise and service skill, in many cases 24 hours a day. To deliver a consistent product to each individual customer requires teams of people well trained to deliver to a set standard every time.
4 No matter how well planned the operation, how good the design and environment, if the interaction between customer and service provider is not right this will have a detrimental effect on the customer experience of the total product, and a missed opportunity to sell future products. Good interaction between customers and service providers can also increase present sales – for example, a waiter can 'up sell' by suggesting in a positive way additions to the meal, perhaps items the customer may not even have considered but is delighted by the recommendation or subtle persuasion.

Hotel catering

Hotel food and beverage strategy

Unlike in the past, when hotels typically operated food and beverage facilities merely to satisfy the demands of their guests, today's hoteliers are increasingly adopting a more proactive approach by using their food and beverage outlets as a means to generate not only profitability but also publicity, as well as to cultivate a loyal following. Traditionally, hotel restaurants have not been profitable enterprises for hotels, given that they were often considered to be only an essential value-added service for guests.

Mintel has identified four hotel catering formats, as follows.

1 **General:** hotels featuring restaurants that cater primarily for residents of the hotel and, second, for walk-in guests who are not residents. These often take the form of casual, all-day dining facilities. The most enterprising of these are attempting to attract different consumers at different times of the day.
2 **Signature:** hotels that have developed a restaurant as a brand that stands alone from the hotel, and is therefore primarily aimed at walk-in customers. Most of these restaurants are located in luxury or upscale establishments, a number of which are managed by celebrity chefs such as Giorgio Locatelli, Gary Rhodes, Gordon Ramsay, Brian Turner, Heston Blumenthal, Marcus Wareing and Alain Ducasse. Signature restaurants tend to operate independently of the hotel they are attached to. Establishments that fall into this category include Nobu (Metropolitan Hotel, London), Chino Latino (Park Plaza, Leeds and Nottingham), Locanda Locatelli (Hyatt Churchill, London) and Dinner (Mandarin Oriental, Hyde Park, London – Heston Blumenthal).
3 **Outsourced:** hotels that outsource the management and operation of their catering provision to a third party. The outsourcing of a hotel's food and beverage operations can take several forms: a lease contract, management contract or an agreement with a contracted caterer. An example of an outsourced food and beverage hotel operation is the Cumberland Hotel, London, which contracted Restaurant Associates, a division of the contract catering giant Compass plc, to operate all its bars and restaurants.
4 **Budget:** hotels that provide only a limited catering service, and sometimes no catering at all other than food from vending machines. The budget hotel sector in the UK is rapidly expanding, and consequently the vast majority of new hotels do not have any food and beverage facilities at all – in part this is due to lenders providing limited capital to developers in the accommodation sector.

Other developments include the following.

- Heston Blumenthal is running the restaurant at the Mandarin Oriental Hotel in London's Knightsbridge, called Dinner.
- Furthermore, many hotel chains that have come to rely upon the strength of their brand names have resorted to developing sub-brands designed to appeal to both guests and non-residents.

Conferences and business travel

Business travel is an important sector of the UK tourism industry. This sector is defined by the British Association of Conference Destinations (BACD), and includes tourists who attend conferences, trade fairs, exhibitions, incentive travel, corporate hospitality and business travel.

The UK is an important market for the global conference industry. As the international market continues to grow, the UK has to continue to become increasingly competitive in order to win lucrative conference business. London is one of the major capitals that attracts international conventions, hosting international exhibitions and conferences. Major exhibition centres are ExCeL, Olympia and Earls Court. London also attracts more meetings than most other capital centres. The reason why it is able to attract such international business are:

- It is easily accessible by mainland Europe and the rest of the world via the five international airports and the Channel Tunnel.
- It has a large number of old and modern landmarks – the O2, the London Eye, the Millennium Bridge, Shakespeare's Globe, and the Tate Gallery and Tate Modern, as well as, of course, the traditional landmarks – the Tower of London, Buckingham Palace, Palace of Westminster, and so on.
- Its superior facilities – e.g. purpose-built convention and exhibition centres, museums, theatres, livery halls, stately homes, hotels with meeting facilities.

However, there is competition from mainland Europe. Some conventions require larger conference facilities than London can offer. Larger exhibition space can be found in other European cities in Germany and France. Larger exhibition centres are in Milan, Frankfurt, Paris, Hanover and Düsseldorf.

Outsourcing

The contracting-out of food and beverage services to third parties will continue to be a major trend in the hotel catering sector over the next few years, although this will be much stronger in London than in the provinces. As many hotels continue to remain sluggish owing to evolving consumer demand for food and beverages and intense competition from the high street, the attraction of outsourcing food and beverage services will become increasingly appealing.

Vertical integration between many hotel and restaurant groups has meant that the outsourcing decision is often not such a radical step to take for many hoteliers, as costs and revenues remain within the group. Most outsourcing is agreed on either a flat fee or percentage basis and this is expected to remain unchanged.

Outsourcing is not always a straightforward option for hotels, however. To attract walk-in customers, a hotel ideally needs to be located where there is easy access to the restaurant itself, and the location of the hotel itself (city centre, countryside, etc.) needs to fit with the clientele that are being targeted – that is,

the product must be attractive to the passing trade. Despite these constraints, the number of outsourced restaurants is expected to increase considerably over the years to come.

Eating out in the UK

The eating-out market remains buoyant despite the difficulties experienced with the fluctuations in the economy. There remains big competition from supermarkets with their speciality meals. Many restaurateurs have had to make their offer more attractive and give better value for money. In times of difficulty, restaurateurs, pub operators and hoteliers have been forced to look at costs, and have 're-engineered' their menus using cheaper cuts of meat and smaller portions.

In-house catering development

With increased consumer interest in food and eating out, hotels are becoming more focused on developing attractive food and beverage facilities in-house.

Table 1.4 Leading restaurant groups in the UK, 2009

Owner	No. of outlets	Selected brands
Mitchell & Butler	775	Harvester, Browns, Toby, Vintage Inns, All Bar One
Gondola	585	Pizza Express, Ask, Zizzi
Whitbread	372	Beefeater, Brewer's Fayre
Punch Taverns	362	Chef and Brewer, Two for One, Miller's
Restaurant Group	350	Frankie & Benny's, Garfunkels
Tragus	270	Bella Italia, Café Rouge, Strada
Nando's	213	Nando's
Bay Restaurant Group	190	La Tasca, Slug & Lettuce, haha Grill
Little Chef	180	Little Chef
Famous Brands	176	Wimpy
Greene King	155	Loch Fyne, Hungry Horse
Prezzo	141	Prezzo, Ultimate Burger
Clapham House	79	Tootsie's, Gourmet Burger Kitchen
Paramount Restaurants	75	Groupe Chez Gerard, Caffe Uno
Town Centre Restaurants	57	Auberge, Café Giardino, Azzurro
Wagamama	56	Wagamama
Ispani Family	55	Ponti's, Caffe Alba
Carluccio's	42	Carluccio's
Yo! Sushi	41	Yo! Sushi
Orchid Pubs	40	Jim Thompson's, Country Carvery
Individual Restaurant Group	34	Piccolino, Zinc, Bank
Regent Inns	31	Old Orleans

Source: Horizons FS

Note: The table includes pubs whose food sales exceed 50 per cent of turnover.

The success of in-house catering development will depend on the willingness of hotels to deliver a product that will be attractive to the outside market, and to maintain this product so that it evolves with changing consumer tastes and trends. According to human resource specialists within the hotel sector, key factors holding back further development are that food and beverage managers in hotels tend to be hoteliers rather than restaurateurs, as well as the shortage of experienced culinary and service staff.

For the majority of the population, pub restaurants and gastropubs remain the most popular places to eat out.

Types of catering establishment

Commercial catering

Hotels and restaurants

The exact number of hotels in the UK is uncertain. The majority are group-owned. The presence of international chains is high in the five-star market. In the UK there are more hotel bedrooms in the mid-market, three-star, category than in any other category; the independent hotelier traditionally dominates this market.

In some cases special types of meal service – such as grill rooms or speciality restaurants, some with high-profile chefs – may limit the type of foods served (e.g. smörgasbord or steaks will be provided).

Wine bars, fast foods, takeaway: quick service

Customer demand has resulted in the rapid growth of a variety of establishments offering a limited choice of popular foods at a reasonable price, with little or no waiting time, to be consumed either on the premises or taken away.

Delicatessens and salad bars

These offer a service (usually lunch) based on a wide variety of bread and rolls (e.g. panini, focaccia, pitta, baguettes and tortilla wraps). Fresh salads, homemade soups and one hot 'chef's dish of the day' may be available.

A chilled food selection, from which customers can pick and mix, can provide the basis for a day-long service, including breakfast. A 'made to order' sandwich counter and a baked jacket potato bar with a good variety of fillings are very popular components of some of these establishments.

Private clubs

These are usually administered by a manager appointed by a management committee formed from club members. Good food and drink, often with an informal service in the 'old English' style, are required in most clubs, particularly in the St James's area of London. However, there is an increasing demand for more modern dishes and service, and members of these clubs also frequent the most prestigious hotels and restaurants.

Nightclubs and casinos usually offer the type of service associated with the restaurant trade. This provides another source of income to the business.

Chain catering organisations

There are many establishments with chains spread over wide areas and in some cases overseas. Prospects for promotion and opportunities are often considerable, whether in a chain of hotels or restaurants. These are the well-known hotel companies and restaurant chains, the popular type of restaurant, chain stores and shops with restaurants, which often serve lunches, teas and morning coffee, and have snack bars and cafeterias.

Licensed house (pub) catering

There are approximately 61,000 licensed houses in the UK and almost all of them offer food in some form. To many people the food served in public houses is ideal for what they want – that is, often simple, moderate in price and quickly served in a congenial atmosphere.

There is great variety of food on offer in such places, from the ham and cheese roll operation to the exclusive à la carte restaurant. Public-house catering can be divided into the following categories:

- the luxury-type restaurant
- gastropubs – there is a growing trend for well-qualified chefs to work in pubs and develop the menu according to their own specialities, making good use of local produce
- the speciality restaurant – e.g. steak bar, fish restaurant, carvery, theme
- 'fork dishes' served from the bar counter, where the food is consumed in the drinking areas
- finger snacks – e.g. rolls, sandwiches.

Beer and pub facts

Beer

- Around 90 per cent of the beer sold in the UK is produced in the UK.
- In the UK 28 million pints of beer are consumed every day, which equates to 100 litres per head each year – compared to 20 litres of wine per head.
- Beer is a traditional and wholesome produce made from natural ingredients.
- Over one-third of the UK barley crop is bought by UK brewers, who are also major users of English hops.
- There are over 2000 different beer brands available in the UK, and over 1.5 million pints a day are exported to over 120 different countries.
- UK brewers are industry leaders on environmental issues. Since 1976, energy usage per pint of beer produced has been reduced by 45 per cent, water consumption reduced by 40 per cent, and carbon dioxide (greenhouse gas) emissions reduced by over 40 per cent.

Pubs

- Over 80 per cent of pubs are small businesses run by tenants, licensees and owners.
- The average pub spends over £70,000 per annum on locally sourced goods and services.
- The pub food market continues to thrive; UK pubs now serve over one billion meals per year.
- Gastropubs remain popular in the UK.

Licensed retailing is a vast sector of the hospitality industry and is experiencing rapid change. Movements in organisations' structures and size, mergers and divestment ownerships, and management skills have been driven by two macro influences. First, the impact of 'Beer Orders', forcing restrictions on the linkages between brewing and licensed retail outlet ownership, has brought about substantial restructuring of the industry. Five types of pub operators or retailers have emerged as a result of Beer Orders:

1 national retailer with brewing interest
2 national retailer with no brewing interests (either demerged or fully independent)
3 regional or local retailer with brewing interests
4 regional or local retailer with no brewing interests
5 totally independent operator or free houses.

To find out more about the licensed trade, contact: The British Institute of Innkeeping, Wessex House, 80 Park Street, Camberley, Surrey GU15 3PT, or visit www.bii.org.

Secondly, pub food is the fastest-growing source of pub revenue and accounts for approximately 20 per cent of total sales.

Beer remains the cornerstone of the pub, but different beers, such as cask and speciality draught ales, stout and premium lagers, are driving sales. Sales of soft drinks, wines, tea and coffee continue to grow.

Successful pubs are now diversifying to become significant leisure and retail outlets using sophisticated management controls, technological systems and marketing skills. A wider range of customer needs will be catered for, alcohol will continue to play an important part but food, entertainment and leisure facilities will become an increasing trend. Many pubs will specialise in particular markets by developing brands or concepts to attract target groups. This reflects the modern concept of an all-day pub, not restricted to set drinking hours.

Speciality restaurants

Moderately priced speciality eating houses are in great demand and have seen a tremendous growth in recent years. In order to ensure a successful operation it is essential to assess customers' requirements accurately and to plan a menu that will attract sufficient customers to give adequate profit. A successful caterer is the one that gives customers what they want and not what she/he thinks the customers want. The most successful catering establishments are those that offer the type of food they can sell, which is not necessarily the type of food they would like to sell in an area with different levels of demand.

Country hotels

Country house hotels have been and are being developed in many tourist areas. Many are listed buildings, stately homes or manor houses. They normally have a reputation for good food, wine and service to reflect the ambience of the business and surroundings.

Consortia

A consortium is a group of independent hotels that

Table 1.5 The evolution of the pub

	Character of a pub	Consumer group	Products	Pub implementations
Up to late 1960s	Drinking place	Men	Bitter (mainly cask) Spirits Basic food	Downmarket Basic facilities of the community Home-grown entertainment 'Ordinary' to working-class men, not to other groups in society
Late 1960s to mid-1970s	The themed pub	Men Youth	Bitter Loss of cask Lager Spirits Basic food	Youth market Mass market Insensitive developments High-tech entertainment Jukeboxes Fruit machines Sound/light One-bar pubs
Mid-1970s to 1990	Targeted concept	Men Youth Women	Bitter Growth of cask Lager Soft drinks Wine Substantial growth in food	Retailing revolution Pub is the hero Targeted concepts Introduction of service standards
1990s on	Leisure experience	Men Youth Women Families Older people	Increasing low/non-alcohol products: beers; wines; spirits; soft drinks; coffee Increasing food sales Increasing premium/special products Greater range of packaged products More premium cask ales More premium lagers Increasing leisure facilities – games and accommodation Attractive, heated outside areas for smokers	Signage/branding revolution Concept types crystallise Greater customer recognition Opportunity to sign and label pubs better More open retail format The term pub becomes less relevant 'Pubs' become more ordinary to society as a whole The gastropub is established as a speciality brand

Source: Whitbread Market Research

purchase products and services such as marketing from specialist companies providing members of the consortium with access to international reservation systems. This enables the group to compete against the larger chains.

Motels/travel lodges

These establishments are sited near motorways and arterial routes. They focus on the business person who requires an overnight stop or the tourist who is on a driving holiday. These properties are reasonably priced, they consist of a room only with tea- and coffee-making facilities. Staffing is minimal and there

is no restaurant. However, there will be other services close by, often managed by the same company or group. The growth and success of the budget hotel sector has been one of the biggest changes to affect the hospitality industry in recent years.

Timeshare villas/apartments

A timeshare owner purchases the right to occupy a self-catering apartment, a room or a suite in a hotel or leisure club for a specified number of weeks per year over a set period of years, or indefinitely. These may be exchanged with the owners of timeshares in other locations.

Coffee shops

Coffee shops (both chain and independent outlets) are one of the most rapidly growing parts of the hospitality and leisure industries. By the end of 2012 there will be 12,500 outlets in the UK (predicted in *The Caterer*, December 2009).

Coffee shops provide a variety of good coffee based on the espresso, as well as a range of other drinks and snacks. Both comfortable seating and a take-away service are available.

Coffee shops may also be found within other establishments such as airports, department stores and hospitals.

Guest houses

Guest houses are to be found all over the UK. The owners usually live on the premises and let their bedrooms to passing customers. Many have regular clients. Guest houses usually offer bed, breakfast and evening meal, and are small privately owned operations.

Farms

Farmers, wishing to diversify and recognising the importance of the tourism industry in the countryside, formed a national organisation called the Farm Holiday Bureau. Most members have invested to transform basic bedrooms to meet the required standards. The National Tourist Board inspects every member property to ensure good value and quality accommodation. In most cases the accommodation is on or close to working farms.

Youth hostels

The Youth Hostels Association (YHA) runs hostels in various locations in England and Wales. These establishments cater mainly for single people and for those groups travelling on a tight budget. In some locations they also offer a number of sports facilities.

Airline services

Airline catering is a specialist operation.

Airports

Airports offer a range of hospitality services catering for millions of people every year. They operate 24 hours a day, every day of the year. Services include themed restaurants, speciality restaurants, coffee bars and seafood bars, as well as food courts, often supplemented with a general shopping arcade.

Spas

A spa is often part of a luxury hotel or country house hotel. The client can access a range of health and beauty treatments to promote health and well-being. Spa treatments are also an increasingly popular leisure activity.

The Gambling Act 2005

Who can provide gaming?

Those premises that have a licence to serve alcohol without having to do so as part of a meal may provide gaming. No licence or permit is required for pubs or other eligible premises to provide gaming under the exempt gaming provisions.

The Gaming Act

This allows pubs and other eligible premises to provide what the Act calls 'exempt gaming'. It must be 'equal choice' gaming (examples would be bingo, bridge and certain poker games). Stakes and prizes must comply with the limits prescribed in the regulations. No amount may be deducted or levied from amounts staked or won. No participation fees may be charged. The games played may take place only on one set of premises, i.e. there may not be any linking of games between premises. Children and young people must be excluded from participating.

Public-sector catering (cost sector)

This sector covers hospitals, universities, colleges, schools, prisons, the armed forces, police and ambulance services, local authority buildings, Meals on Wheels, and the like. It has been known for many years as 'welfare catering' and characterised by its non-profit-making focus, minimising cost by achieving maximum efficiency. However, with the introduction of competitive tendering, many public-sector operations have been won by contract caterers (often known as contract food service providers), which have introduced new concepts and commercialism to the public sector. This sector is more commonly known as the cost sector.

Prisons

Prison catering may be run by contract caterers or by the Prison Service. The food is usually prepared by prison caterers and inmates. The kitchens are also used to train inmates in food production, which can lead to useful qualifications and encourage them to seek employment on release. Prisons have now lost their Crown Immunity, which prevented prosecution for poor hygiene and negligence. There are also usually staff food service facilities in prisons for all the personnel who work there, such as administrative staff, prison officers and management.

The armed forces

Services here include feeding armed service staff in barracks, in the mess, and in the field or on ships. Much of the work involved is specialist, especially field cookery. However, the forces – like every other section of the public sector – are looking to reduce costs and increase efficiency. Consequently they too have initiated market testing and competitive tendering through the Ministry of Defence, resulting in contract caterers taking over many service operations at all the aforementioned locations.

Catering for the armed services is specialised and they have their own training centre; details of catering facilities and career opportunities can be obtained from career information offices. Contract caterers (contract food service management operators) are increasingly being used throughout the armed services.

Public catering

The fundamental difference between public catering and the catering in hotels and restaurants is that the hotel or restaurant is run to make a profit and provide a return on the investment capital. The aim of public catering is to minimise cost and cover overheads by achieving maximum efficiency. The standards of cooking should be equally good, though the types of menu may be different because of the specific nutritional needs of some parties, such as schoolchildren and soldiers. Hospital catering is sometimes classified as 'welfare catering', its objective being to assist the nursing staff to get the patient well as soon as possible. To do this it is necessary to provide good-

quality food that has been carefully prepared and cooked to retain the maximum nutritional value, and present it to the patient in an appetising manner and with hygiene of utmost importance.

Hospital food

In 2001 the government looked at how hospital food services could be improved. Research showed that a few changes could make a huge difference to patients' mealtime experience. A team of experts was brought together and the Better Hospital Food programme was launched in May 2001. The programme was designed to make effective changes to hospital food service country-wide. The Better Hospital Food programme's initial aims were to:

- produce a comprehensive range of tasty, nutritious and interesting recipes that every NHS hospital could use
- redesign hospital printed menus to make them more accessible and easier to understand
- introduce 24-hour catering services to ensure food is available night and day
- ensure hot food is available in hospitals at both midday and early evening mealtimes.

The Better Hospital Food Partnership Hospital Sites Club was formed from hospitals previously associated with the programme plus new hospitals that had made significant progress in implementing the 2001 Better Hospital Food targets. The club provided a forum in which NHS managers responsible for providing catering services could share ideas and information.

Other organisations involved

Environmental health officers worked in close association with the NHS to provide a forum of opinion about current food safety issues and a

Figure 1.5 Contract catering in a police canteen

Figure 1.6 Hospital catering

sounding board for the future. The Hospital Caterers Association attended meetings on a quarterly basis to discuss issues associated with the implementation of the Better Hospital Food programme. The NHS Menu Group included dietetic professionals nominated by the British Dietetic Association, caterers nominated by the Hospital Caterers Association and nurses who were nominated by the Chief Nursing Officer. The group gathered information about the most popular dishes currently used in the NHS. To ensure patients' views were taken into account when planning the NHS Menu programme a Patients Food Group was set up. This consisted of 14 patient representatives recommended by organisations including the Patients Association, the Patients Forum and the Multiple Sclerosis Society. The Vegetarian Society was involved in the development of recipes; its logo appears alongside dishes that are suitable for vegetarians.

24-hour catering

Hot food has not always been available to hospital patients who are admitted late in the day or who miss mealtimes due to treatment. With the introduction of 24-hour catering, patients can now ask a nurse or housekeeper for hot food, snacks and drinks at any time of the day or night. The 24-hour catering initiative comprises:

- light bite hot meals, including dishes such as cottage pie and cod in parsley sauce
- ward kitchen service of light refreshments such as tea or coffee with toast or fresh fruit
- snack boxes containing, for example, sandwiches, cheese and crackers, fruit and a drink.

The Flexi Menu

NHS menus traditionally change daily over one- to three-week cycles. This means that patients have a wide choice of dishes over a week but not so many to choose from each day. Better Hospital Food is trialling a new Flexi Menu system that would give patients a greater daily choice of meals. The Flexi Menu trials are designed to test the viability of offering the same fixed menu for both lunch and evening meals. This system would allow patients to select foods they enjoy and to have the same dish more than once. Limited early trials suggest this system would be popular with patients and result in less waste.

Nutrition

The delivery of adequate and appropriate nutrition to hospital patients is a key issue for caterers and dieticians. Intake of nutritious food is crucial for patients who are recovering from the effects of medical or surgical procedures. Patients who receive good nutrition may have shorter hospital stays, fewer post-operative complications and less need for drugs and other interventions. In order to ensure the effective delivery of good nutrition in health care facilities, a team-based approach is essential. Caterers, kitchen staff, dieticians, doctors, ward housekeepers and porters all have an important part to play.

A major challenge facing caterers and nutritionists is the number of patients entering health care facilities in a malnourished state. Studies show that up to 40 per cent of hospital patients are malnourished on admission. This means they have not been eating well enough to keep themselves healthy.

Sustainability

Health care catering service and other NHS organisations are being encouraged to develop sustainable food procurement policies. This means that the food they produce should do as little harm to the environment as possible. Sustainable food procurement includes sourcing fruit and vegetables locally to prevent transport pollution, and composting peelings and other preparation waste to keep landfill to a minimum. Other sustainable measures can include using organic or 'fairly traded' goods, energy efficiency measures and reducing food preparation waste.

Protected Mealtimes

Protected Mealtimes are periods on a hospital ward when all non-urgent clinical activity stops. During these times patients are able to eat without being interrupted and staff can offer assistance. Research shows that patients who are not interrupted and receive appropriate service and support during mealtimes are happier, more relaxed and eat more. The better nutrition a patient receives, the higher his or her chances of recovering.

In order to effectively implement Protected Mealtimes, Trusts should:

- conduct an observational audit of the meal delivery service
- discuss the results with relevant teams
- establish changes in practices required (times of ward rounds, visiting times, etc.)
- obtain agreement from those involved and set a start date
- provide information to patients, relatives, staff and other departments.

Figure 1.7 Hospital catering dietician

Dieticians

In many hospitals a qualified dietician is responsible for:

- collaborating with the catering manager on the planning of meals
- drawing up and supervising special diets
- instructing diet cooks on the preparation of special dishes
- advising the catering manager and assisting in the training of cooks with regard to nutritional aspects
- advising patients.

In some hospitals the food for special diets will be prepared in a diet bay by diet cooks.

Diets

Information about the type of meal or diet to be given to each patient is supplied daily to the kitchen. This information will give the number of full, light, fluid and special diets, and with each special diet will be given the name of the patient and the type of diet required.

Modern developments

As with all catering services, the health care sector seeks to continually improve the food and drink services to all stakeholders on hospital premises, whether they be patients, the personnel directly or indirectly dealing with them, or patients' visitors.

To find out more about NHS and hospital catering, visit the following websites.
- **NHS Estates Information Centre: www.nhsestates.gov.uk**
- **Hospital Caterers Association: www.hospitalcaterers.org**
- **British Dietetic Association: www.bda.uk.com.**

School meals

In September 2005, the government received recommendations from the School Meals Review Panel (SMRP) on school lunches and on a number of wider issues concerning food in schools. In response to that report – *Turning the Tables* – the newly established School Food Trust (SFT) was commissioned to advise ministers on standards for food in school other than lunch.

Nutritional standards for school lunches

There are two sets of standards for school lunches:

1 food-based, which will define the types of food that children and young people should be offered in a school lunch and their frequency, and
2 nutrient-based, which will set out the proportion of nutrients that children and young people should receive from a school lunch.

Table 1.6 sets out nutrient-based standards for school lunches from September 2008 (primary schools) or September 2009 (secondary and special schools). Table 1.7 sets out food-based standards for school lunches from September 2008 (primary schools) or September 2009 (secondary and special schools).

Figure 1.8 School meals

Table 1.6 Nutrient-based standards for school lunches from September 2008 (primary schools) or September 2009 (secondary and special schools)*

Energy	30% of the estimated average requirement (EAR)
Protein	Not less than 30% of reference nutrient intake (RNI)
Total carbohydrate	Not less than 50% of food energy
Non-milk extrinsic sugars	Not more than 11% of food energy
Fat	Not more than 35% of food energy
Saturated fat	Not more than 11% of food energy
Fibre	Not less than 30% of the calculated reference value *Note: calculated as non-starch polysaccharides*
Sodium	Not more than 30% of the SACN** recommendation
Vitamin A	Not less than 40% of the RNI
Vitamin C	Not less than 40% of the RNI
Folate/folic acid	Not less than 40% of the RNI
Calcium	Not less than 40% of the RNI
Iron	Not less than 40% of the RNI
Zinc	Not less than 40% of the RNI

Notes

This table summarises the proportion of nutrients that children and young people should receive from a school lunch. The figures are for the required nutrient content of an average lunch over five consecutive school days.

* Nutrient values, except for sodium, are based on Department of Health (1991).

** Scientific Advisory Committee on Nutrition (2003).

EAR = estimated average requirement – the average amount of energy or nutrients needed by a group of people. Half the population will have needs greater than this, and half will be below this amount.

RNI = reference nutrient intake – the amount of a nutrient that is enough to meet the dietary requirements of about 97% of a group of people.

SACN = Scientific Advisory Committee on Nutrition. For details of figures for the dietary reference values and derived amounts for nutrients for children and young people see Crawley (2005), with the exception that the derived reference value for fibre for boys aged 15–18 years should be capped at 18 g.

Standards for all school food other than lunches

The government has also decided that similar standards should apply to all school food other than lunches, as recommended by the School food Trust.
  This means that:

- no confectionery will be sold in schools
- no bagged savoury snacks other than nuts and seeds (without added salt or sugar) will be sold in schools
- a variety of fruit and vegetables should be available in all school food outlets; this could include fresh, dried, frozen, canned or juiced varieties
- children and young people must have easy access at all times to fresh drinking water in schools (NB: in guidance, it is made clear that it would be preferable for this drinking water to be chilled and for it to be located so that children do not have to depend on going to the lavatory to access it).

Table 1.7 Food-based standards for school lunches from September 2008 (primary schools) or September 2009 (secondary and special schools)

Fruit and vegetables – these include fruit and vegetables in all forms (whether fresh, frozen, canned, dried or in the form of juice)	Not less than two portions per day per child, at least one of which should be salad or vegetables and at least one fresh fruit, fruit tinned in juice or fruit salad (fresh or tinned in juice)
Oily fish	Oily fish shall be available at least once every three weeks
Manufactured meat products	Manufactured meat products may be served occasionally as part of school lunches, provided that they: 1 meet the legal minimum meat content levels set out in the Meat Products (England) Regulations 2003; products not specifically covered by these legal minima must meet the same minimum meat content levels prescribed for burgers 2 are not 'economy burgers' as described in the Meat Products (England) Regulations 2003, and 3 contain none of the following list of offal, except that mammalian large or small intestine may be used as a sausage skin (including chipolatas, frankfurters, salami, links and similar products): brains, lungs, rectum, stomach, feet, oesophagus, spinal cord, testicles, large intestine, small intestine, spleen, udder
Bread	Bread should be available on a daily basis
Deep-fried foods	Meals should not contain more than two deep-fried items in a single week; this includes products that are deep-fried in the manufacturing process
Drinks	The only drinks available should be: 1 plain water (still or fizzy) 2 milk (skimmed or semi-skimmed) 3 pure fruit juices 4 yoghurt or milk drinks (with less than 5% added sugar) 5 drinks made from combinations of those in points 1 to 4 of this list (e.g. smoothies) 6 low-calorie hot chocolate 7 tea 8 coffee NB: artificial sweeteners should be used only in yoghurt and milk drinks, or combinations containing yoghurt or milk
Water	There should be easy access at all times to free, fresh drinking water
Salt and condiments	Table salt should not be made available; if made available, condiments should be available only in sachets
Confectionery and savoury snacks	Confectionery, chocolate and chocolate-coated products (excluding cocoa powder used in chocolate cakes, or low-calorie hot drinking chocolate) shall not be available throughout the lunchtime; the only savoury snacks available should be nuts and seeds with no added salt or sugar

Sample menus for schools

You can see full sample menus with all the recipes at www.schoolfoodtrust.org.uk.

Further information on school meals policy may be obtained from the DfES, Sanctuary Buildings, Great Smith Street, Westminster, London SW10 3BT, Pupil Welfare and Opportunities Division Area 4E8. www.dfes.gov.uk/schoollunches.

Residential establishments

Under this heading are included schools, colleges, universities, halls of residence, nursing homes, homes for the elderly and hostels, where all meals are provided. It is essential in these establishments that the nutritional balance of food is considered, and it should satisfy all the residents' nutritional needs, as in all probability the people eating here will have no other food provision. Since many of these establishments cater for students, and the age group that leads a very energetic life, these people usually have large appetites and are growing fast. All the more reason that the food should be well prepared from good ingredients, nutritious, varied and attractive.

The contract food service sector

Contract food service management (often referred to as contract catering) covers such areas as feeding people at work in business and industry, catering in schools, college and universities, private and public health care establishments, public and local authority catering, and other non-profit-making outlets such as the armed forces, police and ambulance services, or the remote sector such as oil and gas exploration rigs. There is also a large market in this sector for catering in the executive dining rooms of many corporations and providing all their corporate hospitality needs.

Work in the traditional sectors – called cost or non-profit-making catering – continues but, because contractors are readily developing their interests in more commercial catering arenas such as stadia, general leisure venues and the like, the term food service management describes more accurately the total contract catering industry.

Definitions in this sector are becoming increasingly blurred as contract catering enterprises move into other areas, including catering for members of the public in such outlets as leisure centres, department stores and DIY stores, supermarket restaurants and cafés, airports and railway stations, as well as at public events and places of entertainment. Contractors are also providing a range of other support services such as housekeeping and maintenance, reception, security, laundry, bar and retail shops.

Catering for business and industry

The provision of staff dining rooms for industrial or business settings has allowed many catering workers employment in first-class conditions. Apart from the main meal services, beverage services, retail shops, franchise outlets and/or vending machines may be part of the service. In some cases a 24-hour, seven-day service is necessary, but generally the hours are more streamlined than in other sectors of the hospitality industry. Food and drink are provided for all employees, sometimes separately but increasingly together in high-quality restaurants and dining rooms. Training and career development potential are excellent, with an emphasis on personnel retention and people development.

Many industries have realised that output is related to the welfare of their employees. Satisfied workers produce more and better work, and because of this a great deal of money is spent on providing first-class kitchens and dining rooms, and improving the dining experience. This can also mean that the workers receive their food at a price lower than its actual cost, the rest of the cost being borne by the company. This is called a subsidy and contributes to the overall employment benefits of an employee.

However, many companies are increasingly competing within a global economy. Competition is fierce, and this has led them to cut costs, meaning that many organisations are moving towards a nil subsidy for meals consumed at the place of work.

Information on catering for business and industry can be obtained from the Association of Catering Excellence, Bourne House, Horsell Park, Woking, Surrey GU21 4HY, or by visiting www.acegb.org

Criteria for establishing a catering operation

A company is not committed to providing any catering facility if:

- there are suitable facilities available within easy access of the employee's place of work
- these facilities offer a reasonable choice of food
- the times of opening are suitable to employer and employees.

If the above criteria are not met and the demand for catering services exists then a catering facility should be established. Often, employers will provide a facility even if the above criteria exist, in order to provide better welfare and amenities for their people, so hoping to retain them as employees for longer.

Holiday centres

Holiday centres around the UK provide leisure and hospitality facilities for families, single people and groups. Many companies have invested large sums of money in an effort to increase the quality of the holiday experience. Center Parcs, for example, has developed subtropical pools and also offers other sporting facilities. Included in its complexes are a range of different restaurant experiences and food courts, bars and coffee shops. These centres are examples of year-round holiday centres, encouraging people to take breaks from home, at weekends or mid-week, throughout the year.

Motoring services

Many motoring services areas provide food court-type facilities for travellers, offering a comprehensive range of meals on a 24-hour, seven-day basis. These are becoming increasingly sophisticated, with baby changing, infant and pet feeding facilities, bathrooms and showers, extensive ranges of branded food outlets and often accommodation, fuel, convenience shops, and car washing and maintenance facilities. MOTO is one such an example; it operates across the country and makes most of the provisions above available in all of its outlets.

Table 1.8 Motorway service operators by number of outlets, 2009

Operators	Outlets
MOTO Hospitality	45
Welcome Break	28
RoadChef	27
Extra	9
First Motorway Services	1
Westmorland Motorway Services	2
Cairn Lodge Services	1
Stop 24	1

Drive-thru restaurants

Drive-thru restaurants are a relatively new concept in the UK. Drive-thrus are an American import – the most notable of these being the McDonald's Drive-thrus located in many parts of the UK. Customers stay in their vehicles and drive up to a microphone in order to place a request. This is then relayed to a fast-food service point and, as the car moves forward in the queue, the order is prepared and then presented to the driver at the service window. This type of facility is often part of the provision made in centres such as the motoring services described above.

Transport catering

Railway

Meals on trains may be served in restaurant cars and snacks from buffet cars. The space in a restaurant car kitchen is very limited and there is considerable movement of the train, which causes difficulty for the staff.

Two train services run by separate companies are running through the Channel Tunnel. One is Euro Tunnel's Le Shuttle train, which transports drivers and their vehicles between Folkestone and Calais in 35 minutes. Food and drink is limited to that bought before the train departs.

Foot passengers wishing to travel from London to Paris or Brussels may travel on Eurostar trains. Eurostar sees the airlines as its direct competition; therefore it provides airline catering standards on board the train for first- and premier-class passengers. Meals are served by uniformed stewards and stewardesses in an environment similar to an airline's club class. This food is included in the ticket price. Provision for economy travellers is usually via buffet carriages or trolley services along the aisles of the train. This is another area into which contract food service providers have expanded.

Marine

The large liner's catering is of a similar standard to that of the big first-class hotels, and many shipping companies are noted for the excellence of their cuisine. The kitchens on board ship are usually oil-fired, and extra precautions have to be taken in the kitchen in rough weather. Catering at sea includes the smaller ship, which has both cargo and passengers, and the cargo vessels, which include the giant tankers of up to 100,000 tonnes. Ferries serve routes such as the English Channel and the Irish Sea. The English Channel ferries are in direct competition with Eurostar and the Shuttle; in response to this, ferry operators have invested in leisure facilities and modern branded food outlets, sometimes in a food court arrangement, or in other cases in a buffet or carvery style.

Other aspects of catering

Food and service management

Contract catering is now generally referred to as food and service management. This takes into account cost sector catering. Food and service management now covers a much wider range of support services, such as reception, housekeeping, cleaning, estate and land management, laundry and waste management. This sector covers catering in business and industry, education, health care and the Ministry of Defence, and catering for members of the public in leisure outlets.

Food and service management companies are producing more meals than ever before due to new styles of food, and more attractive merchandising and presentation. The increase in grab-and-go menu items and more emphasis on healthy eating menus have given consumers a wider choice. More snack meals are being sold due to changing lifestyles, customer preferences and lunchtimes being shorter.

Table 1.9 Structure of the food and service management market by number of outlets, 2008

Sector	No. of outlets
Business and industry	8719
Health care	653
State education	5136
Independent schools	637
Local authorities	282
Ministry of Defence	421
Oil rigs	163
Catering for the public	972
TOTAL	**16,983**

Source: British Hospitality Association, *Food and Service Management Survey*, 2009

Table 1.10 Size of food and service management market by number of meals served (m), 2008

Sector	No. of meals served (m)
Business and industry	717
Health care	197
State education	266
Independent schools	88
Local authorities	23
Ministry of Defence	170
Oil rigs	18
Catering for the public	140
TOTAL	**1619**

Source: British Hospitality Association, *Food and Service Management Survey*, 2009

Food and service management covers feeding people at work in business and industry; catering in schools, colleges and universities; hospitals and health care; welfare and local authority catering and other non-profit-making outlets. Providing hospitality services in these traditional sectors is referred to as 'cost', non-profit-making, non-commercial catering or social catering. However, as many units in these sectors are now run by commercial contract caterers they are now forms of commercial catering in the public sector, but they are very much driven by costs. These definitions of the sectors are now included in the term food and service management as management companies are developing their interests in commercial catering. These describe more accurately the total contract catering market.

Today contract catering also covers leisure centres, department stores, public events and places of entertainment. It also covers housekeeping, maintenance, reception, security, laundry, bar and retail shops.

Outsourcing is now a key focus of many businesses as they look to cut costs, giving operators additional business from contractors previously in-house. There has also been an expansion of facilities management contracts, which have grown on the back of the growing need to outsource.

Contractors in the food and management sector have also had to respond to the demand for healthier menus. There is pressure from the Food Standards Agency to include calorie counts on menus so that consumers know how many calories they are eating. Some contract caterers have started to implement nutritional content information. However, this is not easy to achieve as food is cooked on-site for individual contracts, chefs are employed to use their skills and to be creative, so therefore asking them to provide nutritional information is difficult. This should be relatively easy using a software package, but it requires the chef to weigh all ingredients carefully. However, in some schools measuring of nutritional content has been achieved, where caterers' options are restrained by the nutritional guidelines laid down by the School Food Trust. These require caterers to provide an analysis of 14 specific nutrients in every recipe used over a three-week menu cycle, two fruit-based desserts each week, two portions of vegetables every day, red meats twice a week and fish once a week.

Sustainability

This has become a very important topic in recent years and part of a wider, greener strategy. The sourcing of fish and food in general is very much at the top of the sustainability agenda for all contract food service management caterers. Locally sourced food has also become a marketing and selling point.

Compliance

Another major focus for the food service sector is working towards compliance with ISO 14001, the internationally recognised standard for the environmental management of businesses. Companies are looking at reducing waste, addressing carbon emissions and reducing energy consumption.

Types of catering contract, 2007–2009

Significantly in a year of recession, the number of profit and loss contracts increased by over 75 per cent – contractors are being asked to take greater commercial risks than ever before. Cost plus/management fee contracts remain the least popular with clients, especially those wishing to abandon their catering subsidy, but they still represent almost a quarter of all contracts. The trend towards fixed price/performance guarantee contracts continues, though it lost some momentum during the year.

Number of outlets in which food and service management companies invested, 2009

Food and service management companies continue to invest in client premises – over £26 million in 2009, which is more than in the previous year (£16 million). A feature in 2009 is that investment in larger projects (i.e. over £250,000) is more pronounced, indicating that companies are willing to help finance larger as well as smaller projects.

A recent Eurest lunchtime survey suggested that the time taken by employees to eat at work is reducing annually and currently stands at a little over 20 minutes. Contract catering operators such as Compass have had to respond to this changing demand, and therefore branded retail outlets have become a growth area, which also reflects the commercial influence of contracting.

There are many catering concerns that are prepared to undertake catering for businesses, schools or hospitals, leaving these establishments free to concentrate on the business of educating, nursing, and so on. By employing contract caterers and using the services of people who have specialised in catering, organisations can thus relieve themselves of the worry of entering a field outside their province. Contract caterers are used by nearly every type of organisation, including the armed forces, business and industry in general, supermarkets, department stores and DIY chains, leisure centres, museums and galleries, and at sporting fixtures and events.

Contracts will vary considerably, but popular options are fixed price, cost plus, concession and profit and loss arrangements, or a mixture of these. Some arrangements will be subsidised and others won't. Contract permutations can be endless, but need to serve the interests of all stakeholders.

Contracts

No two services or clients' requirements are the same. For this reason, contracts differ from company to company. Some examples of the types of contract available are as follows.

Table 1.11 Types of catering contract, 2007–2009

	2009		2008		2007	
	Number	**%**	**Number**	**%**	**Number**	**%**
Cost plus/management fee (The client is billed for the cost of the operation, plus a management fee)	4,143	24.9	3,842	22.6	4,855	27.6
Fixed price/performance guarantee	10,553	63.7	12,070	71.1	12,035	68.4
Profit and loss/concession contracts and total risk contracts (The caterer and the client share the profit – or the loss; in total risk contracts, the caterer invests in the facility and earns all the revenue)	1,887	11.4	1,071	6.3	713	4.0
TOTAL	**16,583**		**16,983**		**17,603**	

Table 1.12 Number of outlets in which food and service management companies invested, 2009

	£0–£25k	**£26k–£50k**	**£51k–£100k**	**£101k–£500k**	**Over £501k**
Business and industry	81	30	13	36	8
Health care	–	1	–	1	1
Education	8	9	6	6	1
Ministry of Defence	–	2	2	2	2
Leisure	1	1	–	5	–
Other	–	–	–	4	7
TOTAL	**90**	**43**	**21**	**54**	**19**

Source (Tables 1.11 and 1.12): British Hospitality Association, *Food and Service Management Survey* 2009

- **Executive lease:** the contractor provides a senior executive who will direct the client's catering operation. Normally the whole operation remains the responsibility of the client and the staff are employed by the client. The aim is for the contractor and the executive to bring a level of expertise, which the client is unable to provide. The senior executive will be involved in implementing the systems managers and in the policy making. The contractor will provide a manager for the unit; all staff are employed by the client on their terms and conditions.
- **Management:** the client employs the contractor to supply a total catering service using the contractor's own on-site management and staff. The client also provides all the facilities and equipment. The contractor submits a monthly account to the client, which identifies all the expenditure and income associated with the operation. The difference between the expenditure and income, including the contractor's fee, will be payable to or from the contractor.
- **Fixed price:** the contractor works to an annual budget fixed with the client. If the contractor overspends, she/he pays. However, if she/he underspends she/he retains the difference.
- **Concession:** the contractor undertakes to manage an operation and rely for profit on his or her ability to maintain income levels over expenditure levels.

Contractor's charges

Contractors generally offset their administration costs, and they gain their profits from the following three sources:

1 fees charged
2 cash spent by customers
3 discounts from food and materials supplied to the client's operation.

The fees can be made up in a number of ways:

- a set annual figure charged on a weekly or monthly basis
- a percentage of takings or costs
- a combination of both with different percentages applying to various sections of costs
- a per capita or per meal charge.

With over 60 companies registered in the UK, contract catering is one of the biggest and most diverse sectors in the industry. Compass and Sodexho are two of the largest food organisations in the UK, with 8400 locations. These include Little Chef, Travelodge and motorway service stations. Other contract caterers include Harbour & Jones, Elior, Lexington and Initial Catering.

Partnership

This describes the situation where the client and customer are partners in the operations and share the costs and revenues.

Outside and event catering

When functions are held where there is no catering or where the function is not within the scope of the normal catering routine, then certain firms will take over completely. Considerable variety is offered to people employed on these undertakings and often the standard will be of the very highest order. A certain amount of adaptability, ingenuity and specialist equipment is required, especially for some outdoor jobs, but there is less chance of repetitive work. Greater flexibility is necessary on behalf of the personnel, often involving considerable travel, remote locations and outdoor venues. The types of function will include garden parties, agricultural and horticultural shows, the opening of new buildings, banquets, parties in private houses, military pageants and tattoos, and sporting fixtures such as horse racing, motor racing, football, tennis, rowing and rugby.

Franchising

Franchising is an agreement whereby one pays a fee and some set-up costs in exchange for the use of an established name or brand that is well known by potential purchasers and therefore likely to generate more business than an unknown or start-up brand. An example of this would be where the contract caterer Compass Group franchises the Burger King brand from its owner in exchange for a fee and a proportion of the turnover. There are normally strict guidelines, or 'brand standards', laid down for the franchisee (franchise user) to perform to, and these will govern which ingredients and raw materials are used and where they come from, together with portion sizes and the general product and service 'offer'. The franchisor (the franchise provider) will 'mystery shop' or check on the brand standards and operational standards regularly to ensure that the brand's reputation is not being jeopardised. The franchisor will normally also provide advertising and marketing support, accounting processes, help with staff training and development, and design provision for merchandising and display materials.

A form of franchising is also practised in the pub business in addition to other systems like the managed pub.

Many companies that supply caterers with products like soft drinks, ice cream and coffee distribute their products by means of purchased operators. Some suppliers providing food and drink to caterers have 'brand franchises', sometimes backing their product with appropriate equipment and advertising material to ensure that caterers prepare, present and promote the products in a consistent way.

Operating styles vary considerably, from pizzas, hamburgers, doughnuts and baked croissants to full-menu restaurants, coffee shops and pancake houses. Despite all the differences, all the franchise schemes work on the same basic principle: an established catering company offers a complete package of experience, operating systems and ongoing marketing support sufficient to enable outside operators to set up and operate their own units within the chain. The investor makes an initial franchise payment and then pays a continuing royalty or commission, which is often expressed as a percentage of gross turnover. All investment in property, buildings and equipment is borne by the franchise; in some cases the franchise might play some part in securing the property and assisting with design, building and fitting out so that a consistent look and feel are established.

Franchising has several advantages.

- First, it allows for many outlets to be set up nationally and, by doing so, maximises on economies of scale in purchasing promotional material in the development of the brand image.
- The franchisee gains because the opportunity is shared to invest in a pre-tested catering concept, backed by advertising, research and development, training and other resources that might otherwise be beyond their financial parameters.
- The banks also show an interest in franchising – in many ways they see it as a reasonably safe investment because of its established, tried-and-tested nature.
- The oldest franchising schemes in the UK are Wimpy, established in the mid-1950s, and KFC, which started in the early 1960s. Many of the most active franchise schemes are based on a fast-food style of menu and operating system. Now there is a growing market involving wider menus and medium-spend restaurants, mainly licensed. Examples include Pizza Hut, Delice de France, Marks & Spencer Simply Food, Krispy Kreme bakery products, TGI Friday's, and many others.

Cruises

Cruise companies are rapidly increasing their number of cruise liners and the size of their ships. This means the job opportunities and promotion prospects are excellent, and training is also provided. The benefits of travel all over the world, producing food and serving customers at the very highest standards make it a most interesting and worthwhile career. As an example of working conditions, staff may work for three months and then have, say, two months off. On-board hours of work could be ten hours a day, seven days a week. This appeals to many people who wish to be producing a wide variety of food at its best in excellent conditions. Figure 1.9 illustrates a Purser's Department F&B.

Cruise ships are floating luxury hotels, and more and more people are becoming interested in cruising as a leisure pursuit.

Food and beverage purchases on cruise liners

On cruises where the quality of the food is of paramount importance, other factors such as the dining room's ambience of refinement and elegance are also of great significance. Ship designers generally want to avoid Las Vegas-type glittery dining rooms, but also those that are too austere. Interestingly enough, the success of the dining operation is tied to the design of the ship.

Ship architects design cruise liners to provide quick and easy access to the kitchen areas, where food is prepared. In a sense, these architects design the ship around the galley and dining rooms. The food on most cruises can be described as excellent, quality banquet-style cuisine. Ships must be designed with easy access to the galley so waiters are able to get food quickly and with as little traffic as possible. A distinction can be made between traditional and modern eating on cruises, as shown in Table 1.13.

This set of polarities doesn't apply as much to the new giant ships that have many different dining rooms. On such ships passengers can eat in the dining room of their choice, more or less whenever they want, at tables of various sizes. This gives passengers maximum freedom, but they lose the opportunity to get to know people at their table.

Dining is one of the most important – and selling – points for cruise lines. People who take cruises want to dine well and generally they do, though cooking dinner for 800 people per sitting and giving people what they want takes skill and management.

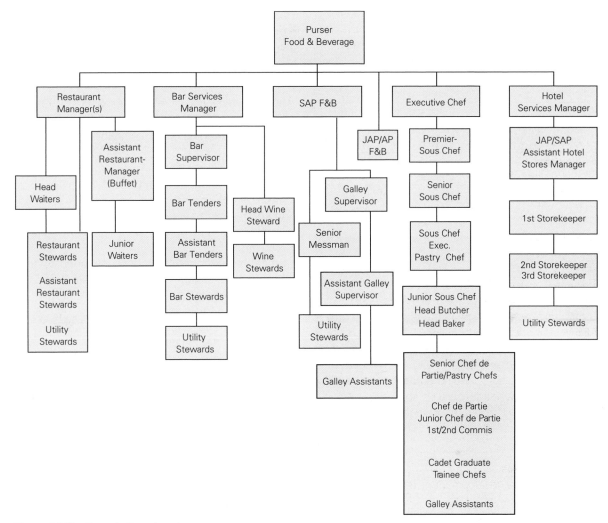

Figure 1.9 The Purser's Department

Cruise ship staff

The purser is much like a hotel front-desk manager or assistant manager. Unlike the hotel manager – who tends to larger operational issues – the purser administers day-to-day affairs. Some examples include management of passenger accounts, mail, messages, printing, the storing of valuables and immigration and customs requirements. On larger vessels, the purser has two assistants: the crew purser (who treats crew issues) and the hotel purser (who tends to passenger matters). The purser may have a large team of assistants who staff the purser's desk, coordinate publications, deliver messages and handle other concerns.

The shore excursion manager orchestrates the operation and booking of port-based packages. On certain lines, he or she is sometimes called the concierge, with broader responsibilities such as booking customised port experiences, changing flights, and so on. On larger ships a team of people attends to shore excursions, including an on-board travel agent who can book a passenger's future cruise needs. (If a sale is made, the passenger's travel agent will usually get the commission for that sale.)

The cruise director coordinates all entertainment and informational activities that take place as part of the cruise experience. Part host, part entertainer, gregarious and always gracious, the cruise director serves as a critical link between passengers and crew. He or she presides over many functions, including passenger orientation and disembarkation meetings. The cruise director also manages the musicians, entertainers, on-board lecturers (experts who provide their services in exchange for a free cruise), social hosts, health club staff, photographers and, in some cases, the shore excursion manager.

Table 1.13 The differences between traditional and modern eating on cruises

Traditional	Modern
Formal dining room	Choice of restaurants
Set times	Dine any time
Assigned tables	Choice of seating
Elaborate table settings	Self-serve, buffet or waiter service
Printed menu	Frequently changing menus
Social interaction	Wide variety of culinary styles

Figure 1.10 Self-service

The executive chef controls the preparation and serving of all food and beverages. He or she supervises the assistant or sous chef, the pastry chef and other kitchen staff.

The head housekeeper or chief steward manages all stateroom, public space and other shipboard cleaning. He or she supervises a squad of cabin or room stewards, who tend to the passengers' stateroom needs. (Cabin stewards have a much more active, personal and round-the-clock relationship with guests than do maids at hotels.)

The food and beverage manager oversees the serving of meals and drinks. (On smaller ships this may be handled by the executive chef.) The food and beverage manager watches over the dining room maitre d', table captains, waiters and busboys (general assistants). The food and beverage manager also oversees the bartenders, drink servers and wine steward.

Corporate hospitality

The purpose of corporate hospitality is to build business relationships and to raise corporate awareness. Corporate entertaining is also used as a means of thanking or rewarding loyal customers.

Companies are increasingly recognising the growing importance of relationship marketing and corporate reputation.

Reasons for spending money on corporate hospitality include:

- building relationships with potential customers
- to reward customers/thank them for loyalty
- as a marketing tool/raise company or product profile
- increase business/sales
- to achieve closer informal contact in a relaxed environment
- to keep ahead of competitors
- to raise and keep up the company's profile/public relations
- repeat business/retention of clients or customers
- keep the customers happy/to entertain them, act as a sweetener
- to talk about business/networking
- to achieve better communication interaction/ improved understanding
- to meet customer expectations
- to reward/boost staff or team morale
- social benefits/opportunity to relax.

Eventia is the professional association for the corporate and events industry. This industry is considered to be worth more than £700 million a year. A major new industry report commissioned by the World Tourism Organization (UNWTO), Meeting Professionals International (MPI) and Reed travel Exhibitions (RTE) strongly recommends adopting a form of 'tourism satellite accounting' to measure the economic global importance of the meetings industry, which is an important economic contributor.

The main reasons for the growth of this sector are company expansion and increased budgets for corporate hospitality. Those companies with increased budgets are generally committing to bigger or more superior events and increased spending per head, or holding events more frequently.

An emerging trend is for companies to use corporate hospitality in a more targeted way rather than taking a broad-brush approach. Companies are therefore being more selective about invitees and matching them to appropriate events.

A total of 90 per cent of corporate hospitality is aimed at current customers or clients. There is also a trend towards using corporate hospitality to motivate employees, in an increasingly competitive corporate environment that encourages companies to invest in their own workforce.

Recipients of corporate hospitality are more likely to accept invitations from current suppliers rather than from potential suppliers.

Using the Internet as a business tool

As in all areas of business, the Internet is playing an increasingly important role in corporate hospitality. It is used to source information, and bookings can also be made online.

Websites detail comprehensive corporate hospitality information on events throughout the year. Online services allow customers to book an event directly, offering real benefits to the customer. These include:

- official hospitality in official locations
- cost efficient by booking direct from source
- time efficient
- one-stop shop service from initial enquiry through the event.

Employment and qualifications

The hospitality, leisure, travel and tourism industry employs over 1.9 million people, but determining the exact number is complicated by the problems of defining the industry and of accurate data collection. Any comparison between different data sources should be treated with caution.

According to the ONS Labour Force Survey, the restaurant sector is the largest in terms of employment, with 567,600 people, while the industry in general has a mainly young workforce with 15 per cent of workers under 20 years of age and a further 20 per cent under the age of 30 (see Table 1.14).

In spite of the economic recession, the number of employees in the three principal sectors of the industry – hotels, restaurants and pubs – is rising, with the total number of workers in the hospitality industry increasing by just over 1 per cent compared with 2007. This is an unexpected and puzzling result.

In particular, the number of workers in the restaurant sector climbed from 526,700 to 567,700 (as noted above) – an increase of 7.7 per cent – while the number of workers in the pub and bars sector increased by over 5 per cent. There is also evidence to suggest that some workers from the EU Accession States have returned to their home country. This would further depress the total number of workers in the industry, as they represent a significant segment of the employment market – indeed, 11 per cent of workers in the industry are from ethnic minorities and 17 per cent are from overseas (60 per cent in London). Female workers represent 58 per cent of the total workforce.

A characteristic of the industry is that it is dominated by small businesses – over 80 per cent employ fewer than 50 people, although they account for only 42 per cent of the workforce. Indeed, taking the entire number of hotels and guest houses (Table 1.20), the average number of employees per hotel is just over five (nine in restaurants).

A further characteristic is that the industry is notable for its high level of labour turnover. It is estimated that this currently stands at 30 per cent, but many employers report a much higher figure. Some of this turnover is natural as many seasonal jobs are taken up by full-time students who are attracted to vacation work; they provide a

Table 1.14 Total employment in the tourism and hospitality industry in the UK by sector and age, 2008

	16–19	20–29	30–49	50–64	Over 65	TOTAL
Hotels	33,900	81,800	88,200	38,100	6,600	248,700
Restaurants	125,100	184,700	197,200	57,500	2,200	566,700
Pubs, bars and nightclubs	74,900	143,000	82,600	32,200	3,500	336,300
Food and service management	8,500	30,800	95,000	44,700	4,200	183,200
Travel and tourist services	5,600	31,500	52,400	20,600	1,200	111,300
Visitor attractions	3,800	4,400	1,300	1,200	-	14,100
Holiday parks and self-catering	4,100	9,800	19,200	19,900	6,200	59,200
Hospitality services	48,200	72,900	151,600	95,200	9,200	377,200
Other*	2,800	23,300	41,700	12,700	2,300	82,800
TOTAL	306,900	582,000	429,200	322,100	35,400	1,985,200

* Includes gambling and youth hostels.
Source: National Statistics website, www.statistics.gov.uk

Table 1.15 Numbers employed in the tourism and hospitality industry in the UK by gender, 2008

	Male	Female
Hotels	113,600	135,100
Restaurants	283,500	284,100
Pubs, bars and nightclubs	145,400	188,900
Food and service management	61,300	124,600
Travel and tourist services	42,000	69,700
Visitor attractions	8,100	6,000
Holiday parks and self-catering	22,600	36,600
Hospitality services	107,000	270,200
Other	38,500	47,900
TOTAL	**822,000**	**1,163,100**

Source: National Statistics website, www.statistics.gov.uk

* Includes self-catering and holiday centres, travel and tourist services, visitor attractions, gambling and youth hostels; sums may not add to totals due to rounding up.

flexible workforce, which suits both employer and employee. It can also be due to the transient population that occurs in some city populations, like London, where people move jobs to get experience. Nevertheless, turnover generally is higher in hospitality than in many other industries and, in some cases, staff shortages in the industry are caused more by problems of retention than recruitment, which could be solved by better management.

Some references to the hospitality industry elsewhere in this book:

- Accommodation providers.................................328
- Food and beverage providers.......................277

References

British Hospitality Association (2009) *Trends and Statistics*. London: British Hospitality Association.

Crawley, H. (2005) *Nutrition-Based Standards for School Food*. British Nutrition Foundation (also available at www.cwt.org.uk).

Deloitte/NYU (2006) *Hospitality 2010*. New York, NY: Deloitte Services/New York University (downloadable at www.nyu.edu/public.affairs/releases/detail/1116).

Department of Health (1991) *Dietary Reference Values for Food Energy and Nutrients for the United Kingdom*. London: HMSO.

Mancini, M. (2004) *Cruising: A Guide to the Cruise Industry*, 2nd edition. Florence, KY: Thomson Delmar Learning.

Scientific Advisory Committee on Nutrition (2003) *Salt and Health*. London: The Stationery Office.

Topics for discussion

1 Give your impressions of the food that was served at your previous schools, with suggestions for improvement.

2 Explain the importance of food for the hospital patient, with suggestions for the types of food to be offered.

3 Industrial catering (feeding people at work) is an important aspect of the catering industry; discuss why this is so and give examples of menus for three different dining rooms.

4 Discuss what you think persons travelling on aircraft would like to eat and explain how it may, or may not, be feasible to provide it.

5 How do you think changes in the industry will occur over the next ten years? Explain why you think they will happen.

6 Each student in the group to obtain a number of menus from each type of catering and pool for group discussion.

7 What impact, if any, do you think organic foods will have on menus?

8 What essential differences attract staff to the various aspects of the industry (consider, for example, pay, conditions of work, career prospects)?

9 Establishments such as motorway facilities should meet special needs; explain what they are and how they are met, then select another area of catering and state what those needs are and how they are achieved.

2

Employment in the hospitality industry

Supporting material available on Dynamic Learning Online:

> Knowledge quizzes

> Activity worksheets: employment law; industrial relations

> Summary presentations

DYNAMIC
LEARNING

To find out about jobs in the hospitality industry visit:
www.chefjobs.co.uk
www.hospitalityrecruitment.co.uk
www.hoteljobs.co.uk

Employment opportunities

For those employed in the hospitality industry it is important to understand that there is a considerable amount of legislation that regulates both the industry itself and employment in the industry. Employers who contravene the law or attempt to undermine the statutory rights of their workers – for example, paying less than the national minimum wage or by denying them their right to paid annual holidays – are not only liable to prosecution and fines but could be ordered by tribunals and courts to pay substantial amounts of compensation.

Workers and employees

An employee is a person who is employed under a contract of employment or service. An essential feature of a contract of employment is the 'mutuality of obligation'. The employer undertakes to provide the employee with work on specified days of the week for specified hours, and, if employed under a limited-term contract, during an agreed number of weeks or

months; while the employee undertakes to carry out the work in turn for an agreed wage or salary.

The only workers who can be characterised as not being employees are those engaged on an 'as and when required' basis – for example, from a list of casual workers who help out in banqueting, restaurant and bar when a member of the regular staff is ill or when extra staff are needed for a function. They are not 'employees' in the accepted sense of the word as there is no 'mutuality of obligation' between them and the employers who engage their services. These workers are free to reject work offered to them, if they wish. Unfair dismissal is exclusive to employees who have a 'Contract of Employment'.

Workers

Workers that are not necessarily employees have certain levels of protection. A worker is an individual who works under a contract of employment where the individual undertakes any work or services for another party to the contract whose status is not that of a client or customer.

Workers who are not employees nonetheless enjoy the protection afforded by:

- Health and Safety legislation
- anti-discriminatory laws
- National Minimum Wage Act 1998
- Part-time Workers (Prevention of Less Favourable Treatment) Regulations
- Working Time Regulations 1998
- Public Interest Disclosure Act 1998
- Equality Act 2010
- Data Protection Act 1998.

Recruitment and selection

When advertising for and recruiting new or replacement staff, employers in the hospitality industry should be mindful of the legislation in place, such as:

- Children and Young Persons Act 1933
- Licensing Act 1964
- Rehabilitation of Offenders Act 1974
- Data Protection Act 1988
- Immigration, Asylum and Nationality Act 2006
- National Minimum Wage Act 1998
- Working Time Regulations 1998
- Sex Discrimination Act 1975
- Race Relations Act 1976
- Disability Discrimination Act 1995
- Human Rights Act 1998
- Equality Act 2010.

Job advertisements

It is unlawful to discriminate against job applicants on grounds of:

- sex, marital status or gender
- colour, race, nationality, or national or ethnic origins
- disability
- sexual orientation
- religion or beliefs
- trades union membership or non-membership.

The following words should be avoided in a job advertisement:

- pleasing appearance
- articulate
- strong personality
- dynamic
- energetic
- no family commitments.

These could be construed, or misconstrued, as indicating an intention to discriminate on grounds of sex, race or disability.

Use of job titles with a sexual connotation (e.g.

'waiter', 'barmaid', 'manageress') will likewise be taken to indicate an intention to discriminate on the grounds of a person's sex, unless the advertisement contains an indication or is accompanied by an illustration to the contrary.

Job applications

Job application forms must be designed with care. A form should explain the need, if necessary, for 'sensitive personal information', to reassure the candidate that such data will be held in the strictest confidence and in keeping with the provisions of the Data Protection Act 1998.

Human Rights Act

Candidates must be informed at interview and when the application is sent out that they have to wear uniforms on duty, or protective clothing. Any surveillance monitoring the company is likely to carry out must also be disclosed to applicants.

Employment of door supervisors

Door supervisors or bouncers, whose job it is to deal with unruly behaviour and to screen people entering clubs and other licensed premises, are required to have a licence to do the job, issued by the Security Industry Authority (SIA). It is an offence under the Private Security Industry Act 2001 if a person works as a bouncer or door supervisor without this licence.

The Immigration, Asylum and Nationality Act 2006

An employer who negligently employs a person subject to immigration control, who does not have the legal right to live and work in the UK, is liable to a substantial fine. This is an offence under this Act and is liable to a conviction, unlimited fine and/or imprisonment for up to two years. To avoid unwittingly breaching the legislation, job application forms should clearly state that shortlisted candidates must produce documents confirming their right to take up employment in the UK. Every candidate should be interviewed regardless of sex, colour, race, nationality or ethic origin. The candidates should provide this evidence to avoid allegations of unlawful racial discrimination.

Job interviews

The purpose of the job interview is to assess the suitability of a particular applicant for the vacancy under consideration. The interviewer should ask questions designed to test the applicant's suitability for the job, covering qualifications, training and experience, and to elicit information about the individual's personal qualities, character, development, motivation, strengths and weaknesses.

If a job applicant resigned or was dismissed from previous employment, the interviewer may need to know why. Admitted health problems, injuries and disabilities may also need to be discussed in order to determine the applicant's suitability for employment – for example, in a high-risk working environment.

Employers may lawfully ask a job applicant if he or she has been convicted of any criminal offence, but must be aware of the right of job applicants, under the Rehabilitation of Offenders Act 1974, not to disclose details of any criminal convictions that have since become 'spent'.

The interview should not ask questions about sexuality or religion. Questions on religion may be asked if, for example, aspects of the job may directly affect the beliefs of an individual – an example would be the handling of alcoholic drinks.

Job offers

An offer of employment should be made or confirmed in writing and is often conditional on the receipt of satisfactory references from former employers. Withdrawing an offer of employment once it has been accepted could result in a civil action for damages.

Blacklists

Under the Employment Relations Act 1999 (Blacklists) Regulations 2010, it is unlawful to refuse to interview or employ someone whose name appears on a blacklist. A blacklist is a list of prohibited names of people who will be denied employment. The law applies whether recruiting new members of staff directly or through an employment agency.

Written statement of employment particulars

Every employee, whether full-time, part-time, casual, seasonal or temporary, has a legal right to be provided with a written statement outlining the principal terms and conditions of his or her employment. This must be issued within two months of the date on which the employee first starts work, but ideally on the employee's first day at work.

Any employee who is *not* provided with a written statement of employment particulars may refer the matter to an employment tribunal. If the employee's complaint is upheld the employer will be ordered

either to provide the statement or accept a statement written by the tribunal. An employer who presumes to discipline, dismiss or otherwise punish an employee for asserting his or her statutory rights, before an employment tribunal, may be ordered to pay that employee compensation.

Legislation affecting the employment of children, young persons and convicted persons

Employers, before recruiting staff, must be aware of the legislation that imposes restrictions on the employment of school-age children and young persons under the age of 18. They should also be mindful of legislation relating to the employment of persons with 'spent' criminal convictions (see below), and door supervisors or bouncers, who now need to be licensed.

Employment of school-age children

The employment of school-age children in hotels, restaurants and public houses at weekends and during the school holidays is regulated by the Children and Young Persons Act 1933 and by local authority by-laws. As a rule no child may be employed:

- if under age 14
- during school hours
- before 7.00 am or after 7.00 pm on any day
- for more than two hours in a school day or on a Sunday
- for more than eight hours (or, if under 15, for more than five hours) on any one day (other than a Sunday) that is not a school day
- for more than 12 hours in any week that is a normal school week
- for more than 35 hours (or, if under 15, for more than 25 hours) in any week in which the child is not required to be at school
- for more than four hours on any day without a rest break of at least one hour
- at any time in a year unless, at that time, he or she has had, or could still have, during school holidays, at least two consecutive weeks without employment
- to do any work other than light work (i.e. work of a kind that is unlikely to affect the safety, health or development of a school-age child or to interfere with the child's education, or regular and punctual attendance at school).

Before employing a school-age child, (or within seven days of doing so) an employer must apply to the relevant Local Education Authority for an Employment Certificate.

Most local authority by-laws prohibit the employment of school-age children in:

- hotel kitchens
- cook shops
- fish and chip shops
- restaurants
- snack bars and cafeterias
- any premises in connection with the sale of alcohol, except where alcohol is sold exclusively in sealed containers.

If an employee is under the age of 18, any other employee who works closely with the young person must be checked with the Criminal Records Bureau (CRB).

Employment of persons with criminal convictions

Under the Rehabilitation of Offenders Act 1974, a person applying for work in the hospitality industry need not admit or disclose any criminal conviction that has become 'spent' either when completing a job application form or when answering questions at an interview.

Figure 2.1 Outdoor catering

Employment of women

Save for duties imposed on all employers by the Management of Health and Safety at Work Regulations 1999 there is no health and safety legislation that prohibits the employment of women in any occupation within the hospitality industry.

Employment legislation

The meaning of 'pay'

Pay means any sums payable to a worker in connec-

tion with his or her employment, including any fee, bonus, commission, holiday pay or other emolument. It also includes statutory sick pay, statutory maternity pay, statutory adoption pay, statutory paternity pay, guaranteed payments, payments in respect of time off work, remuneration on suspension on medical or maternity grounds or under a protective award, and any sum payable in pursuance of a tribunal order for the worker's reinstatement or re-engagement.

Pay does not include any loan or advance on wages, payments in respect of expenses incurred by a worker in the carrying out of his or her employment, pension payments, or redundancy and severance payments.

Equal pay

Under the Equal Pay Act 1970, a woman engaged in like work, or work of a basically similar nature, or in work rated as equivalent, or in work of equal value to that undertaken by a man in the same employment is entitled to be paid the same as that man, and to enjoy equivalent terms and conditions of employment. The same rule applies if a woman is appointed or promoted to a job previously occupied by a man. In the absence of any express term, every contract of employment (and every collective agreement imported with an employee's contract) will be treated in law as containing an implied equality clause.

National minimum wage

Every UK worker, aged 16 and over, who is no longer of compulsory school age, must be paid no less than the appropriate national minimum wage (NMW). From 1 October 2010, the NMW for school leavers aged 16 and 17 is £3.64 an hour. For workers aged 18 to 20 inclusive, it is £4.92 an hour, and for workers aged 21 and over £5.93 an hour. There is also a minimum wage of £2.50 an hour for apprentices who are participating in government arrangements called Programme-led Apprenticeships and who are aged 19, or are over 19 but in the first year of their apprenticeship.

Of particular interest to hoteliers will be a publication entitled *The National Minimum Wage and the Hotel Sector* (URN 07/1337), which may be downloaded from the website www.berr.gov.uk/files/file41546.pdf or ordered from the BERR's Publications Orderline: 0845 015 0010.

Statutory Sick Pay

Employers in Great Britain are liable to pay up to 28 weeks' Statutory Sick Pay to any qualified employee who is incapable of work because of illness or injury.

Employers who operate their own occupational sick pay schemes may opt out of the Statutory Sick Pay scheme, so long as the payments available to their employees under such schemes are equal to or greater than payments to which they would otherwise be entitled under Statutory Sick Pay, and so long as these employees are not required to contribute towards the cost of funding such a scheme. Payments made under Statutory Sick Pay may be offset against contractual sick pay, and vice versa.

Meaning of 'incapacity for work'

An employee is incapacitated for work if he or she is incapable, because of disease or bodily or mental disablement, of doing work that he or she can reasonably be expected to do under the contract of employment. Under the Food Safety (General Food Hygiene) Regulations 1995, food handlers suffering from (or carriers of) a disease likely to be transmitted through food or while afflicted with infected wounds, skin infections, sores or diarrhoea must not be allowed to work in any food handling, even in any capacity in which there is a likelihood of directly or indirectly contaminating food with pathogenic microorganisms. In these circumstances, the worker is deemed to be incapacitated for work and, subject to the usual qualifying conditions, entitled to be paid Statutory Sick Pay until such time as the risk has passed.

Working Time Regulations

The Working Time Regulations apply not only to employees but also to every worker (part-time, temporary, seasonal or casual) who undertakes to do or perform work or service for an employer.

The 1998 Regulations are policed and enforced by employment tribunals (in relation to a worker's statutory rights to rest breaks, rest periods and paid annual holidays) and by local authority Environmental Health Officers.

Restrictions on working hours

The 1998 Regulations (as amended from 6 April 2003) impose a number of restrictions on working hours and periods of employment for workers aged 18 and over.

- Adult workers have the right not to be employed for more than an average of 48 hours a week.
- Adolescent workers may not lawfully be employed for more than eight hours a day or for more than 40 hours a week.
- Adult workers may not lawfully be employed at night for more than an average eight hours in any 24-hour period.
- Adolescent workers may not lawfully be employed at night between the hours of 10.00 pm and 6.00 am (or between 11.00 pm and 7.00 am if their contracts require them to work after 10.00 pm).
- Every worker is entitled to a minimum weekly rest period of 24 hours (or 48 hours in every fortnight); or, if under the age of 18, a minimum weekly rest period of 48 consecutive hours.
- Every worker is entitled to a daily rest period of a minimum 11 consecutive hours or, under the age of 18, a daily rest period of a minimum 12 consecutive hours.
- Every worker is entitled to a minimum 20-minute rest break during the course of any working day or shift lasting or expected to last for more than six hours or, if under the age of 18, a minimum 30-minute break during the course of any working day or shift lasting, or expected to last, for more than 4.5 hours.
- If an adult worker is content to work more than an average 48 hours a week, he or she must sign an agreement to that effect.

Holidays and holiday pay

From April 2009, every worker in the UK, whether full-time, part-time, temporary, permanent, seasonal or casual, is entitled to 5.6 weeks' paid holiday in every holiday year. For example, for a person who works a standard five-day week, 5.6 weeks translates into 28 working days' paid annual holiday. To calculate the holiday entitlement of workers pro rata, go to the website www.berr.gov.uk/employment/holidays.

Meaning of 'holiday year'

This will depend on the organisation and the employer – for example, some companies use 1 January to 31 December or 1 April to 31 March.

Part-time workers

Under the Part-time Workers (Prevention of Less Favourable Treatment) Regulations 2000, part-time workers, regardless of the number of hours they work, must not be treated less favourably than comparable full-time workers employed or engaged under the same type of contract and doing the same or similar work.

Fixed-term contracts

Under the Fixed-term Employees (Prevention of Less Favourable Treatment) Regulations 2002, employers who use the services of temporary employees, for short or long periods (for example, relief managers, to cover long-term sickness or maternity leave, or during busy operation periods such as summer or Christmas) must treat these employees in the same way as permanent employees.

Meaning of 'fixed-term' employees

'Fixed-term employee' means an employee who is employed under a fixed-term contract, which is a contract that terminates (ends) after a certain date, or at the end of a set project or task.

Parental leave

Under the Maternity and Parental Leave Regulations 1999, the employed parents of a child who is under the age of five (or under the age of 18, if adopted) have the legal right to take up to 13 weeks' unpaid parental leave during the first five years of the child's life or, if adopted, until the fifth anniversary of adoption or the child's 18th birthday.

Ordinary maternity leave

Providing an employee informs her employer, the pregnant woman may begin her ordinary maternity leave at any time on or after the beginning of the 11th week before her expected week of childbirth unless she gives birth prematurely. Then the leave starts the day after the birth occurs. On the other hand, an employee may choose not to start her leave until the very week her baby is due.

Rights during ordinary maternity leave

Unless the employee's contract states otherwise, an employee absent on maternity leave does not have the right to be paid her normal wages or salary during her period of leave. Her other terms and conditions remain the same, such as holiday entitlement, sickness benefits, seniority, pension rights, company car, mobile phone, etc.

Return to work after ordinary maternity leave

A woman returning to work at the end of her ordinary maternity leave has the right to return to the job she had before the period of leave, unless she wishes to return to work before the end of the 26 weeks.

Additional maternity leave

Every pregnant employee, regardless of her length of service, is entitled to a total of 52 weeks' maternity leave, comprising 26 weeks' ordinary maternity leave (OML) and 26 weeks' additional maternity leave (AML). An employee has no need to forewarn her employer of her intentions, so far as her entitlement to AML is concerned, nor is she under any legal obligation to give her employer advance notice of her intentions when that additional period of leave comes to an end.

Return to work after additional maternity leave (AML)

An employee who takes AML is entitled to return to work in the job in which she was employed before her OML began or, if that is not reasonably practicable, to another job that is both suitable for her and appropriate for her to do in the circumstances, and on terms and conditions no less favourable to her than those that would have applied to her but for her absence on maternity leave.

Adoption leave and pay

An employee's right to adoption leave is found in the Paternity and Adoption Leave Regulations 2002. Under adoption leave and pay legislation, an eligible employee with whom a child is to be placed for adoption is entitled to take up to 52 weeks' adoption leave, comprising 26 weeks' ordinary adoption leave (OAL) followed by up to 26 weeks' additional adoption leave (AAL).

Parental leave

Under the Maternity and Parental Leave etc. Regulations 1999, the employed parents of a child who is under the age of five (or under the age of 18 if adopted) have the legal right to take up to 13 weeks' unpaid parental leave during the first five years of the child's life or, if the child is adopted, until the fifth anniversary of adoption or until the child's 18th birthday, whichever occurs sooner.

Paternity leave or pay

Under the Paternity and Adoption Leave Regulations 2002, complemented by the Paternity and Adoption Leave Regulations 2003, an employee has the qualified right to one or two weeks' paid paternity leave to enable him or her to care for a child or to support the child's mother. That right applies if he is the child's biological father or the current spouse or partner of the child's mother. That same qualified right extends to an employee who has adopted a child or who is one of the couple who has jointly adopted a child. Paternity leave must be taken within 56 days of a child's birth or placement for adoption.

From 2012, employees who are fathers, or the spouses or partners of mothers on maternity leave, will enjoy the qualified right to take up to 26 weeks of additional paternity leave in the first year of the child's life. This is provided by the Additional Paternity Leave Regulations 2010, made under the Work and Families Act 2006.

Flexible working

Under the Flexible Working (Eligibility, Complaints and Remedies) Regulations 2002, eligible employees who are the parents (or adoptive parents) of children under the age of six, or of disabled children under the age of 18, and who wish to spend more time with their children, have the legal right to apply to their employers for a more flexible pattern of working hours.

The meaning of flexible working

Flexible working could involve shorter working hours or a shorter working week, a system of staggered or annualised hours, flexi-time, job-sharing, part-time work, term-time working, self-rostering, and so on.

Time off work

Employees have the legal right to be permitted a reasonable amount of paid or unpaid time off work to enable them to carry out their functions as public officials, shop stewards, members of recognised independent trades unions, safety representatives, pension schemes, trustees, and so on.

The legislation does not specify what constitutes a 'reasonable' amount of time off. A great deal will depend on the particular circumstances and a degree of common sense.

In summary, employees have the right to paid or unpaid time off work in the following circumstances:

- Having responsibilities for dependents – unpaid
- Having children under the age of 5 or adopted children under the age of 18 – unpaid
- For antenatal care during pregnancy – paid
- Acting as a justice of the peace or official of a public body – paid/unpaid
- Accompanying another worker at a disciplinary or grievance hearing – paid
- Acting as a pension scheme trustee – paid
- Redundant employees – paid
- Acting as an employee representative – paid
- Young employees in education or training – paid
- Acting as a safety representative – paid
- Acting as a trade union official (shop steward) – paid
- Trade union members – unpaid.

Time off work – trades union officials

Employees who are officials of an independent trades union that is recognised by their employer as having collective bargaining rights for the entire workforce (or for one or more groups within the workforce; this includes shop stewards or work convenors) have the right to be permitted a reasonable amount of paid time off work to enable them to carry out such of their duties as are concerned with pay and other terms and conditions of employment, working conditions, grievances, disciplinary matters affecting their members, etc. This will also include time off for training in industrial relations.

Time off for jury service

Section 1 of the Juries Act 1974 states that every UK resident aged 18 and over who is not otherwise ineligible or disqualified is liable to be summoned for jury service in the Crown Court, High Court and the County Courts.

Unlawful discrimination

It is unlawful for employers to discriminate against job applicants or existing workers by denying them access to opportunities for employment, promotion, transfer or tracking, or by victimising them, harassing them or subjecting to any other detriment because of their race, colour, nationality, national or ethnic origins, sex, disability, sexual orientation, religion or beliefs. It is also unlawful for employers – as the providers of goods, facilities and services to members of the public – to discriminate against would-be or existing customers or guests on any of the above grounds, either by denying them access to these facilities and services, or by treating them less favourably than they treat or would treat other members of the public.

In October 2007, a new non-departmental public body, the Commission for Equality and Human Rights (CEHR), came into being.

Sex Discrimination Act 1975

Under this Act it is unlawful to discriminate against a woman by refusing to interview her or offer her a job regardless of qualifications, skills or experience simply because she is a woman, or to treat her less favourably than a man.

Following amendments introduced by the Employment Equality (User Discrimination) Regulations 2005, sexual harassment is now specifically prohibited by the Sex Discrimination Act 1975. The amended Act states that a person subjects a woman to harassment if, on the grounds of her sex, he engages in unwanted conduct that violates her dignity or creates an intimidating, hostile, degrading, humiliating or offensive environment for her.

Harassment of staff by third parties

Under the Sex Discrimination Act 1975 (amendment) Regulations 2008, employers including pub landlords, restaurateurs, hoteliers and contract caterers, who do not take reasonably practicable steps to put to an end to any sexual or gender-based harassment directed at members of staff by third parties (i.e. customers, guests, visiting contractors or suppliers) are liable to be ordered to pay compensation (including damages for injury to feelings) to any member of staff whose complaints about such conduct have been largely ignored. An employer is required to act on such a complaint if the harassment has occurred on at least two previous occasions, whether by the same or by different person or persons.

Sexual harassment, whether in the workplace or in a public place, may amount to common assault, which could give rise to civil or criminal proceedings.

Victimisation

An employer is guilty of unlawful sex discrimination by way of victimisation if he or she treats the employee victimised less favourably that he or she treats or would treat other employees. Employees and other workers who are victimised by their employers (or who have action short of dismissal taken against them) for asserting certain of their statutory rights (or for bringing proceedings before an employment tribunal in order to enforce those rights, or for helping others to do so) have the right to complain (or complain yet again) to the employment tribunal and will be awarded appropriate and, at times, substantial compensation if their complaints are upheld. The relevant legislation is to be found in the:

- Employment Rights Act 1996
- Sex Discrimination Act 1975
- Race Relations Act 1976
- Disability Discrimination Act 1995
- Employment Equality (Sexual Orientation) Regulations 2003
- Employment Equality (Religion or Belief) Regulations 2003
- Employment Equality (Age) Regulations 2006
- Equality Act 2010.

By paying them less than other workers because of age, by victimising or subjecting them to harassment (or by failing to act when others do so), by unreasonably denying them an opportunity to continue working beyond normal retirement ages, by dismissing them or selecting them for redundancy, by subjecting them to any other detriment.

Age discrimination

Under the Employment Equality (Age) Regulations 2006, it is unlawful for employers, regardless of the size of their respective establishments, to discriminate against job applicants existing employees and in some instances, former employees, solely on grounds of age (e.g. by denying them access to job interviews, by refusing to employ them – because they are considered to be too young or too old for particular vacancies – by failing to promote them or provide them with opportunities for further training and development).

Racial discrimination

Under the Race Relations Act 1976, as amended in July 2003 by the Race Relations Act 1976 Amendment Regulations 2003, it is unlawful for any employer, regardless of the size of his or her business or undertaking, to discriminate against any person (job applicant, customer or member of the public) by denying that person access to employment, goods, facilities or services because of his or her colour, race, nationality, or national or ethnic origins.

The 1976 Act (as amended in 2003) identifies four types of discrimination in the field of employment that (unless shown to be justified irrespective of the colour, race, nationality, or national or ethnic origins of any person affected by such discrimination) could prompt a complaint to an employment tribunal or attract the attention of the Commission for Racial Equality (CRE). These are: direct discrimination; indirect discrimination; discrimination by way of victimisation; and discrimination by way of harassment.

1 Direct discrimination: this occurs when an employer discriminates against job applicants and existing employees on racial grounds by:
    - denying job interviews
    - refusing them access to employment
    - offering them less favourable terms and conditions of employment
    - withholding opportunities for promotion or transfer (or access to other benefits such as overtime or shift work)
    - segregating them from other members of staff
    - victimising or harassing them (or permitting others to do so)
    - dismissing them, selecting them for redundancy or subjecting them to any other

detriment (or, in the case of an employee on a fixed- or limited-term contract, refusing to renew that contract when it expires).

By 'racial grounds' is meant any of the following:
- colour
- race
- nationality
- national or ethnic origins.

2 Indirect discrimination: there is indirect racial discrimination when an employer deliberately or inadvertently applies a requirement or conditions to a candidate for employment, promotion or transfer etc., which although applied equally to every candidate competing for the same job, nonetheless puts a candidate of a particular racial group at a disadvantage relative to other candidates who are not of the same racial group. Such discrimination is unlawful:
- if the proportion of persons of the same racial group as that candidate who can comply with that requirement or condition is considerably smaller than the proportion of persons not of that racial group who can comply with it
- if the employer cannot show that requirement or condition to be justifiable irrespective of the colour, race, nationality or ethnic origins of the person to whom it is applied, and which is to the detriment of that other candidate because he or she cannot comply with it.

3 Discrimination by way of victimisation: an employer is guilty of unlawful racial discrimination by way of victimisation if he or she treats (or would treat) other employees more favourably, and does so because the employee in question:
- has brought (or is contemplating bringing) legal proceedings against the employer (or some other person acting on the employer's behalf) alleging a breach of his or her statutory rights under the 1976 Act
- has given (or proposes to give) evidence or information to the CRE or an employment tribunal in connection with proceedings brought by some other person (such as a fellow employee) under the 1976 Act, or has alleged (in good faith) that his or her employer (or some other person, such as a manager, supervisor, or member of the workforce) has committed an act that amounts to a contravention of the 1976 Act.

4 Discrimination by way of harassment: under the 1976 Act, as amended by the Race Relations Act 1976 Amendment Regulations 2003, employers are guilty of unlawful racial discrimination if they harass any existing or prospective employees for reasons connected with their race or ethnic or national origins. By 'harass' is meant engaging in unwanted conduct, which, in the perception of the employee in question, has the purpose or effect (or should reasonably be considered as having the effect) of violating his or her dignity, or creating for that person an intimidating, hostile, degrading, humiliating or offensive working environment.

Employers who fail to take steps to eliminate harassment in the workplace will, in most situations, be held vicariously liable for the activities of managers, supervisors and other members who themselves engage (or encourage others to engage) in such conduct.

Disciplinary and grievance procedures

Every employee must be issued with a written statement of employment particulars (or contract of employment) within eight weeks of starting work with a new employer. This rule applies to all employers regardless of the size of their establishments or the number of people they employ. Among other things the statement must include a note explaining the employer's disciplinary rules and the procedures to be followed should an employee choose to break one or other of these rules. Alternatively, the statement (or contract) must refer the employee to some other reasonably accessible document that explains these rules and procedures in more detail.

Disability discrimination

The Disability Discrimination Act 1995 cautions employers that it is unlawful to discriminate against disabled job applicants and existing employees either by refusing to contemplate employing, promoting or transferring any person who admits to being disabled (regardless of that person's suitability for appointment, promotion or transfer to the vacancy under consideration), or by offering any such candidate or employee less favourable terms and conditions than those offered to able-bodied persons appointed to (or already doing) the same job. By the same token, employers are not required to treat disabled job applicants more favourably than employees competing with them for appointment, promotion or transfer to the same job.

The meaning of 'disability'

For the purposes of the 1995 Act, a person has a disability if he (or she) has a physical or mental impairment that has a substantial and long-term adverse effect on his (or her) ability to carry out normal day-to-day activities. The term 'mental impairment' includes an impairment resulting from, or consisting of, a mental illness, but only if the illness is clinically well recognised.

An impairment is to be taken to affect a person's ability to carry out normal day-to-day activities if it has an effect on his or her mobility, manual dexterity, physical coordination, continence, concentration, perception of danger, speech, hearing or sight, or the ability to lift, carry or move everyday objects.

Any job advertisement that indicates, or might reasonably be understood to indicate, an intention to discriminate against disabled job applicants or that suggests a reluctance or inability on the employer's part to make appropriate adjustments to the workplace to accommodate the needs of people with particular disabilities, is admissible as evidence in any subsequent tribunal.

The employer's duty to make adjustments

Employers must take appropriate steps to accommodate a disabled person who might otherwise be at a disadvantage relative to able-bodied persons doing (or applying for) the same or similar work. These would include making adjustments to the premises, allocating some of the disabled person's duties to another person, altering his or her working hours, requiring or modifying equipment, providing supervision, and so on.

An employer's refusal to appoint a disabled person to a particular job may be justifiable on health and safety grounds, or because it is self-evident that the applicant would be quite incapable of doing that job – given the nature and extent of the applicant's disability, the type of work to be done and the conditions in which that work is to be carried out.

Chronically sick and disabled persons

The Chronically Sick and Disabled Persons Act 1970 (amended by the Chronically Sick and Disabled Persons (Amendment) Act 1976) imposes a duty on the owners and developers of new commercial premises (hotels, pubs, restaurants) to consider the needs of disabled persons when designing the means of access to (and within) these premises, including the means of access to parking facilities, toilets, cloakrooms and washing facilities.

Discrimination on grounds of sexual orientation

The Employment Equality (Sexual Orientation) Regulations 2003 state that it is unlawful for employ-

ers, regardless of the number of people they employ, to discriminate against job applicants and existing employees on grounds of their sexual orientation. This includes homosexuality, heterosexuality and bisexuality. The regulations envisage four types of discrimination on such grounds: direct discrimination; indirect discrimination; harassment; and victimisation.

Figure 2.2 Restaurant with wheelchair access

Figure 2.3 A modern staff restaurant

Discrimination on grounds of religion or belief

The Employment Equality (Religion or Belief) Regulations 2003 state that it is unlawful for any employer to discriminate against a job applicant or existing employee because of that applicant's or employee's religion or beliefs. The regulations prohibit discrimination, victimisation or harassment occurring after an employment relationship has come to an end.

The term 'religion or belief' means any religion, religious belief or similar philosophical belief.

Exceptions for genuine occupational requirements

The regulations allow that it is permissible in certain circumstances for an employer to discriminate against a job applicant (or a candidate for promotion or transfer) on the grounds of his or her religion or belief if being of a particular religion or having certain beliefs is a genuine and determining occupation or requirement for the vacancy in question.

A restaurant serving kosher or halal foods, for example, may be justified in its refusal to engage the services of cooks or waiting staff who are not of the Jewish or Islamic faiths, if certain foods have to be treated and prepared in a particular way before being served to customers.

Termination of employment (minimum notice periods and rights during notice)

Notice periods

Notice periods are the written statement of initial employment particulars necessarily issued to every employee, in compliance with the employment Rights Act 1996.

Notice to be given by employees

Unless the contract of employment specifies a longer period of notice, an employee who has worked for his or her employer for one month or more is required to give his employer at least one week's notice to terminate his or her employment. If an employee's contract specifies longer periods of notice than those prescribed by the 1996 Act, those longer notice periods take precedence. If the contract specifies a shorter period of notice, the statutory minimum periods of notice take precedence.

Notice to be given by employers

Under the 1996 Act, the statutory notice to be given by an employer to terminate an employee's contract of employment is determined by the employee's length of continuous service at the material time, as follows:

Length of service	Minimum notice
Less than one month	Nil
One month but less than two years	One week
Two years or more	One week for each year of service
12 years or more	Maximum 12 weeks

If an employee's contract states that he or she is entitled to longer periods of notice to terminate his or her employment (based on length of service, or whatever), those longer periods prevail. If the contract states that the employee is entitled to shorter periods of notice, the statutory minimum entitlement prevails.

Dismissal

Every employee has the legal right not to be unfairly dismissed. However, unless dismissed for a blatantly inadmissible or unlawful reason, the right to present a complaint of unfair dismissal to an employment tribunal is available to those employees only who have been continuously employed for one year or more at the effective date of termination of their contracts of employment.

Meaning of dismissal

Dismissal is when an employer terminates an employee's contract of employment with or without notice; when an employee resigns with or without notice in circumstances in which he or she is entitled to do so, without notice, because of the employee's unreasonable conduct; when a limited-term contract comes to an end without being renewed under the same contract.

Permitted reasons for dismissal and the issue of fairness

When responding to a complaint of unfair dismissal, it is the employer's responsibility to explain to an employment tribunal only if the employee was dismissed and to convince the tribunal that the employee had been dismissed for a permitted or legitimate reason. Examples deemed to be acceptable dismissal include the following.

The Employment Rights Act 1996 allows that it is prima facie acceptable to dismiss an employee for one or other of the following reasons, namely:

- incompetence, associated with a lack of qualifications, or of the skills or aptitude needed to do an efficient or satisfactory job of work
- sickness or a debilitating injury (often associated with a poor timekeeping record, or persistent or prolonged absenteeism).
- misconduct (including gross misconduct)
- redundancy
- Illegality of continued employment (e.g. being under the age of 18 if employed as a barman or barmaid), or
- for 'some other substantial reason' of a kind such as to justify the dismissal of an employee holding the position which that employee held (e.g. for unreasonably refusing to accept a change in working methods, the introduction of new technology and similar changes prompted by the need to improve business efficiency or profitability.

Dismissals and TUPE transfers

Under the Transfer of Undertakings (Protection of Employment) Regulations 2006, which came into force on 6 April 2008, (revoking the eponymous 1981 regulations commonly referred to as the TUPE Regulations 2006, or simply TUPE), an employer who purchases or acquires the lease on another employer's business as 'a going concern' (e.g. in a hotel, restaurant, pub) also inherits the contracts of employment of the people working in that business at the time the sale took place. In short, the new owner must honour those employees' existing terms and conditions of employment (including their rates of pay, holiday entitlements, etc.) even if (in the case of a purchaser expanding his or her business interests) those terms and conditions of employment are more generous than those enjoyed by his or her existing employees. To dismiss those inherited employees or any one of them, or to select them for redundancy simply to avoid having to honour their contracts is unfair and will inevitably lead to complaints of unfair dismissal, subject to the usual qualifying conditions relating to age and length of service.

Inadmissible and unlawful reasons for dismissal

An employee who is dismissed for an inadmissible or unlawful reason may present a complaint of unfair dismissal to an employment tribunal regardless of his or her age or length of service at the material time. The term 'inadmissible and unlawful' applies to a dismissal on grounds of an employee's age, sex, marital status, race, colour, nationality, national or ethnic origins, sexual orientation, religion or beliefs, disability, or trades union membership or non-membership. It is also unlawful and automatically unfair to dismiss employees (regardless of their ages or length of service when dismissed):

- for asserting their statutory employment rights, or for challenging or questioning their employer's refusal to acknowledge those rights (including the right to be paid the appropriate national minimum wage, the right to 5.6 weeks' paid annual holiday, the right not to be required to work more than an average 48 hours a week, the right to be provided with a written statement of employment particulars, and so on
- for exercising or presuming to exercise their rights to maternity leave and pay, adoption leave and pay, parental leave, paternity leave, time off for dependants, time off for ante-natal care, and other family-friendly rights

- for carrying out or proposing to carry out their functions as elected or appointed safety representatives, members of safety committees, or trustees of occupational pension schemes
- for performing or proposing to perform his or her functions as an employees' representative, a negotiating representative, an information and consultation representative, or a candidate in an election in which any person elected will, on being elected, be such a representative
- for leaving the workplace in circumstances of danger, which they reasonably believed to be serious and imminent (e.g. the possibility of a gas explosion) and which they could not reasonably have been expected to avert; or for refusing to return to the workplace until reassured that it was safe for them to do so
- for having made a 'protected disclosure' (i.e. for having disclosed information to the relevant enforcing authority – such as the Inland Revenue, HM Customs & Excise, the Environmental Health Department) concerning alleged breaches by their employers of legislation such as the Licensing Act 1964, the Food Safety Act 1990, the Environment Protection Act 1990, the Working Time Regulations 1998, the National Minimum Wage Regulations 1999, health and safety legislation, and so on.

Constructive dismissal

An employee will be treated in law as having been constructively dismissed if he or she is bullied, harassed, ridiculed or intimidated to the point where he or she is left with little choice but to resign, with or without notice. The same rule applies if an employer, without reasonable and proper cause, conducts himself or herself in a manner calculated or likely to destroy or seriously damage the relationship of confidence and trust that should exist between employer and employee.

Redundancy payments

Under the Employment Rights Act 1996 as amended by the Employment Equality (Age) Regulations 2006, any redundant employee with two or more years' service is entitled to be paid a statutory redundancy payment on the termination of his or her employment for each complete month of service beyond the employee's 64th birthday. A redundant employee with the required two or more years' service must be paid a statutory minimum redundancy payment equal to:

- one-and-a-half week's pay for each complete

year of service from the age of 41 to the effective date of termination of the employee's contract of employment

- one week's pay for each complete year of service between the ages of 22 and 41
- half a week's pay for each complete year of service below the age of 22.

Service in excess of 20 years (reckoned backwards from the effective date of termination of a redundant employee's contract of employment) may be ignored, as may average earnings in excess of £380 per week (which upper limit came into effect on 1 October 2009). It follows that (for 2009/10) the maximum statutory redundancy payment payable to an employee with 20 or more years' service is £11,400.

Dress codes

People applying for work in establishments with particular dress codes should be given to understand that their employment would be dependent on their adhering to these codes. The Equal Opportunities Commission (EOC) is unhappy about dress codes that require female workers to wear short or revealing skirts or low-cut blouses while at work. However, its view is that there is no breach of the Sex Discrimination Act 1975 or the Human Rights Act 1998 so long as the employer's policy on dress and appearance is made known to job applicants at employment interviews and employees are willing to accept it as part of their terms and conditions of employment.

Employers are not obliged to allow members of staff, whose religions require them to pray at certain intervals during the day, to take time off in order to comply with their religion's obligations.

The Data Protection Act

Most employers keep files containing information (or personal data) about the people they employ. In some cases this is stored on computer. Some is kept as paper-based information. Under the subject access provisions of the Data Protection Act 1998, workers have the right not only to see their personal files but also to be provided with hard copies or photocopies of most and, in some cases, all of the documents held in these files. They also have the right to know who within the organisation has access to these files.

Meaning of 'personal data'

In the field of employment, the term 'personal data' means information about an employee or worker who can readily be identified from that data, or from any other information or document held by a worker's employer in a computerised or paper-based filing system.

Examples of information held

The sort of information held is likely to include age, qualifications, marital status, health, attendance record, conduct and capabilities.

Data protection principles

The 1998 Act lists eight data protection principles relating to the 'processing' of personal data held on manual or computerised filing systems. Thus, personal data held in an employee or other worker's personnel file or in a computerised filing system:

- must have been obtained fairly and lawfully (see above)
- must not be held on file other than for a legitimate purpose (nor be used or made use of for any other purpose)
- must be adequate, relevant and not excessive in relation to the purpose or purposes for which it is kept
- must be accurate and, where necessary, kept up to date
- must not be kept for longer than is absolutely necessary
- must be held in compliance with a worker's rights of access to personal data; must not be processed in a way calculated (or likely) to cause damage or distress to a worker, and must be corrected, erased or destroyed if inaccurate or no longer relevant
- must be protected, by the best available means, against unauthorised access or disclosure, and against accidental loss, damage or destruction, and must be treated as confidential by the staff to whom they are entrusted
- must not be transferred to any country or territory (e.g. to a parent or controlling company) outside the European Economic Area (EEA) whose data protection laws or codes are non-existent or less than adequate – unless the worker agrees otherwise or the transfer is necessary for employment purposes (e.g. a proposed transfer or secondment overseas).

Disciplinary and grievance procedures

The written statement of initial employment particulars necessarily issued to all employees must include a note explaining the employer's disciplinary rules and procedures, or refer the employee to some other reasonably accessible document that explains them.

Although employers are under no strict obligation to develop their own rules and procedures for dealing with disciplinary issues within the workplace, the reasonableness of an employer's decision to dismiss an employee, for whatever reason, might very well be challenged before an employment tribunal, especially if the evidence before the tribunal reveals that the employer had failed to follow the best practice guidelines laid down in ACAS Code of Practice on Disciplinary and Grievance Procedures (see the ACAS website at www.acas.org.uk/dgcode2009/). This code of practice provides basic practical guidance for employers and employees. It sets out principles for handling disciplinary and grievance situations in the workplace.

Employment law from 6 April 2010

'Fit notes' have replaced the 'sick notes' formerly given by GPs when individuals are ill.

There is a new right for employees to request time off to undertake study or training where employees work in organisations with 250-plus people. All organisations are covered from April 2011.

In addition, whatever your employment status, whether you are an employee, worker or freelancer, you have rights at work that are protected by law. The information in the box offers a comprehensive summary of what you are entitled to.

Rights at work, protected by law

Reproduced with kind permission from www.freelanceadvisor.co.uk

The main legal rights of an employee:
- to a written statement – this must be provided within two months of beginning the employment
- maternity leave and pay, adoption leave and pay and paternity leave and pay
- ante-natal care
- parental leave
- time off to care for dependants
- the right to apply to work flexibly (in April 2010, the right to request time off to undertake study or training was introduced for employees working in companies of 250-plus employees (this will be introduced to all companies from April 2011); this will work in a similar way to the right to apply to work flexibly; employers will be obliged to consider requests seriously, but will be able to refuse a request where there is a good business reason to do so, but they must follow set procedures)
- the right not to be unfairly dismissed
- for your employer to operate a fair disciplinary and dismissal policy
- access to a grievance procedure at work
- statutory redundancy pay
- time off for public duties, e.g. magistrate duties; for trades union activities (where your employer recognises a trades union, union representatives have a statutory right to take paid time off to carry out trades union duties and training; a new ACAS Code of Practice was introduced on 1 January 2010 to reinforce this statutory right); to attend jury service
- a stakeholder pension – (if your employer has more than 5 employees)
- an itemised pay statement
- plus those rights that a worker has.

NB: Often employers will give benefits/terms to employees that are more generous than the legal minimum entitlements.

The main legal rights of a worker

Workers (including agency workers) and employees have the following rights:

- national minimum wage
- rest breaks and paid holiday under the Working Time Directive
- protection from unauthorised deductions of pay
- maternity and adoption pay (not leave) and paternity pay (not leave) – details as above
- protection against less favourable treatment if you are part-time
- statutory sick pay
- protection against less favourable treatment if you 'whistle-blow' (i.e. make a disclosure in the public interest)
- not to be discriminated against unlawfully on grounds of race, sex, marriage, disability, sexual orientation, age, religion or belief, and to receive equal pay (with members of the opposite sex if you can show they are doing similar work of equal value)
- protection under health and safety law; for details of the health and safety legislation in

the UK, please look at the official website, **www.hse.gov.uk**; with regard to appropriate temperatures for the workplace, there is no legal minimum temperature set – the law says that, during working hours, the temperature inside workplace buildings should be reasonable; however, the HSE's guidance recommends a minimum temperature of 16 degrees for workplaces where activity is mainly sedentary (e.g. offices) and 13 degrees for workplaces where work involves physical effort

- protection against discrimination for membership or non-membership of a trades union; since April 2010, the blacklisting of workers from employment as a result of their union membership or activities has been prevented – if a worker is blacklisted and suffers a detriment at work because of this (e.g. been refused employment, been subject to detriment or unfairly dismissed because of being on a blacklist) they can complain to a tribunal for damages and/or a restraining or prevention order against the blacklist
- agency workers will receive the right to equal treatment with permanent employees after 12 weeks; this legislation will be introduced by 2011.

The main legal rights of the self-employed (freelancer)

You do not have employment rights as such, as you are seen as your own boss and so can make decisions on fees, holidays, etc. You will *not* therefore be entitled to:

- company sick leave, company maternity pay or company pension provisions
- the legal right to protection under your company's internal disciplinary and grievance schemes
- the legal right not to be dismissed (always, however, read the contract of service you have agreed as this may contain clauses relating to termination of your agreement and time-periods).

There is however, legal protection so:

- you should not be discriminated against (as above)
- you are entitled to a safe and healthy working environment (as above); see www.hse.gov.uk
- you should be paid for the work that you have done; if you are having problems with late payments look at the comprehensive advice

from the NUJ at www.londonfreelancer.org/feesguide
- you may also be entitled to statutory maternity allowance if you are pregnant and have recently left an engagement.

Other information for freelancers

- On the occasion that you are classed as a 'worker' (for employment rights) but self-employed (for tax purposes), you may be entitled to the 'workers' rights as above, e.g. it is quite common in the film and TV industry for freelancers to be classed as 'workers' and receive paid holiday under the Working Time Directive legislation.
- Most self-employed individuals will pay class 2 National Insurance Contributions (NICs), which give them entitlement to the basic state pension and statutory maternity allowance. Class 2 NICs do not give you entitlement to Job Seekers Allowance, statutory sick pay or the additional state pension.
- If you are registered as a limited company and provide your services on a freelance basis to an organisation (as a provider) then you will not receive 'workers'' rights from this organisation. It is up to you to provide yourself with 'workers'' rights as you are employed by your own limited company.

What to do if you have a dispute with your employer about any of the rights listed above

- Try to resolve the problem first by talking to your manager or personnel/human resources department if you have one. Your organisation should have its own grievance procedure that, if you are an employee, you should have access to.
- Talk to your trades union or employee representative if you have one.
- Your local Citizens Advice Bureau (CAB) offers free and impartial advice on employment matters, see www.citizensadvice.org.uk.
- ACAS (the Advisory, Conciliation and Arbitration Service) offers free, confidential advice on all employment rights issues. Its helpline is 0845 7474 747, and its website http://www.acas.org.uk.
- If you cannot resolve the matter you may be able to make a claim at an employment tribunal – but this must be within three months of the dispute. The Employment Tribunal Service enquiry line is 0845 7959 775 and its website is www.employmenttribunals.gov.uk.

The Equality Act 2010

In 2010 the government introduced new equality laws to speed up issues of equality. Domestic discrimination law has developed over more than 40 years since the first Race Relations Act in 1965. Subsequently, other personal characteristics besides race have been protected from discrimination and similar conduct, sometimes as a result of domestic initiatives and sometimes through implementing European Directives.

The domestic law is now mainly contained in the following legislation:

- Equal Pay Act 1970
- Sex Discrimination Act 1975
- Race Relations Act 1976
- Disability Discrimination Act 1995
- Employment Equality (Religion or Belief) Regulations 2003
- Employment Equality (Sexual Orientation) Regulations 2003
- Employment Equality (Age) Regulations 2006
- Equality Act 2006 Part 2
- Equality Act (Sexual Orientation) Regulations 2007.

Stronger laws were needed because the old equality laws did not make equality happen fast enough.

The Equality Act brings together nine big equality laws and about 100 smaller laws. Bringing these laws together makes it a lot easier for employers and other people to know what they must do. It will also help everyone understand the law. The Equality Act is for people in England, Scotland and Wales. It became law in spring 2010.

What the Equality Act does

The Act tells some public bodies to do two new things to help make equality happen.

1 Some public bodies will have to think about how they can help to stop people doing less well than other people because of their family background or where they were born.
2 All public bodies must think about treating people from different groups fairly and equally.

These are things the law says someone must do:

- the Equality Act tells some public bodies that they will have to think about what they can do to make their services more helpful to poorer people
- treating people from different groups fairly and equally (The Equality Duty); this is a law for public bodies, telling them they must think about how

they can make sure their work supports equality – for example, in their services, through their jobs and through the money they spend

Public bodies already need to think about treating people of different races, disabled people, and men and women fairly and equally. The Act adds extra groups of people to the Equality Duty:

- people of different ages – younger and older people
- lesbian, gay and bisexual people
- the duty now fully covers people who have changed their sex or are in the process of doing so; people with a religion or belief, or people without a religion or belief
- women having a baby and women just after they have had a baby.

The Act will let civil partnerships for gay and lesbian couples be held in religious buildings.

Equal pay

If a company has 250 or more workers it may have to publish information about differences in men and women's pay. The Act also enables the government to tell public bodies to publish information about equal pay and how many workers it has who are disabled or people of different races. The government plans to do this for public bodies with 150 or more workers. The Act also stops employers telling workers they must not talk to each other about how much they get paid.

Diversity

The Act makes it easier for employers to use positive action and it lets them choose a person who will make their workers more diverse when choosing between people who are right for the job.

Extra powers for employment tribunals

Employment tribunals can suggest how an employer can put things right for a worker if they were treated unfairly. But most of the time this does not help the employer's other workers because most people who complain to employment tribunals have stopped working for the employer. The Equality Act allows the employment tribunal to tell the employer their advice should apply to all their workers even when the one who complained doesn't work there any more.

The Equality Act has several new rules to protect disabled people better. It makes the law on reasonable adjustments clearer.

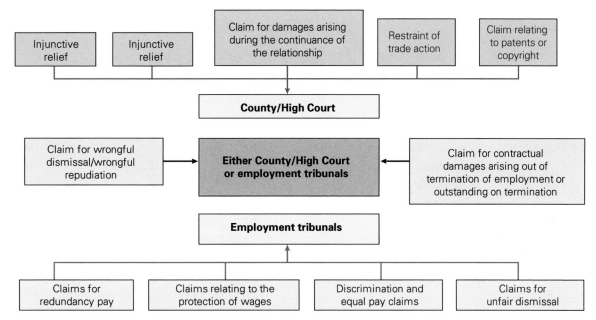

Figure 2.4 Jurisdiction of the courts and employment tribunals

Reasonable adjustments

These are changes an employer or someone providing a service has to make so that disabled people can do something like getting into shop or restaurant or a bank. Sometimes when an employer or someone providing a service makes a reasonable adjustment so that a disabled person can do something it will cost them extra money. The Equality Act says that most of the time they can't expect the disabled person to pay them that extra money back.

The Equality Act will make it harder for an employer to be unfair because it says they can only sometimes ask if a person is disabled. For example, an employer might need to know if a person is disabled so they can make changes to a test or a job interview.

The Act makes dual discrimination against the law. This is when someone is treated worse than other people because of a combination of two things:

- if they are a woman or a man
- if they are transsexual
- if they have a disability
- if they are heterosexual, lesbian, gay or bisexual
- their age
- their race
- their religion or belief.

Topics for discussion

1 Outline the function of an employment tribunal.
2 Discuss the reasons why the hospitality industry is poorly represented by trades unions.
3 Discuss some of the legislation that protects people from employment discrimination.
4 Why is it important to any organisation to develop good industrial relations?

5 Do you believe that the current employment legislation is adequate, inadequate or prohibits the development of the hospitality industry?
6 Why did the government introduce the Equality Act 2010 when there was already so much legislation governing equality?

Part 2 Food commodities and nutrition

3

Food commodities

Supporting material available on Dynamic Learning Online:

❯ Knowledge quizzes

❯ Activity worksheets: commodities; seasons

❯ Summary presentations

❯ Videos and worksheets: Asian and Oriental food commodities

❯ Videos: butchery

DL DYNAMIC LEARNING

The study of commodities

When studying commodities, students are recommended to explore the markets to get to know both fresh foods and all possible substitutes such as convenience or ready-prepared foods. Comparison should be made between various brands of foods, and between convenience and fresh unprepared foods. Factors to be considered when comparing should include quality, price, hygiene, labour, cost, time, space required and disposal of waste.

Students are advised to be cost conscious from the outset in all their studies and to form the habit of keeping up to date with the current prices of all

Figure 3.1 Purchasing fruit

commodities, equipment, labour and overheads. An inbuilt awareness of costs is an important asset to any successful caterer.

Further information about meat, poultry, fish, fruit and vegetables can be found in *Practical Cookery* and *Practical Cookery Level 3*.

Seasonality

The following are some of the reasons why eating seasonally is a good idea.

- Food tastes better in season.
- Food is better for you in season. Seasonal food is more likely to be local; and local food will have spent the minimum time in transit. So, sometimes, seasonal food is healthier.
- Seasonal food is better for the environment. If you believe that human activity contributes to climate change, then buying air-freighted French beans from Kenya in the winter is foolhardy, given the vast amount of greenhouse gas produced by such unnecessary trade – and especially when there are so many great local vegetables around in winter. Seasonal food fits into traditional systems of farming, which don't need the same energy-intensive inputs of pesticides, herbicides and artificial fertiliser as intensive systems.
- Seasonal food is cheaper. Crop permitting, almost anything that's in season will be plentiful and therefore cheaper.
- Seasonal food supports local agriculture. Whether it's from the farm down the road or a specialist producer a few hours away, seasonal food that suits our climate is more likely to have been grown closer to home. Buying locally offers another market for beleaguered food producers, who are often squeezed between the impossible demands of the supermarket buyers and cut-price competition from overseas.
- Seasonal food makes you think about preserving. Jams, chutneys, jellies, pickles preserves ... all of these were invented as ways of preserving a seasonal surplus.
- Finally, seasonal food brings variety into our lives. Who wants to eat the same things all year round? There is always a seasonal treat to look forward to in Britain, and once you know what they are, it will change the way you eat and shop – even the way you order in restaurants – and turn each month, even each week, into a gastronomic adventure.

Organic foods

Consumers are gradually becoming more interested in organic foods and more environmentally friendly. Although there are no nutritional reasons for using organic produce, organic foods are said to contain fewer contaminants. They have a lower content of pesticides, or none at all; however, global sources of contamination cannot be avoided by the organic farmer. Food inspection, particularly by the Department of Environment, Food and Rural Affairs (Defra), keeps a good check on the content of undesirable substances in conventional produce. The prospect of contamination, therefore, is not a good reason for using organically grown produce either. The main argument for using organic produce is that it supports environmentally sustainable development in farming. Caterers may thus consider using organic produce as a social priority. Some caterers have started using organic produce as they become more environmentally conscious.

Today's consumers, whether guests in a restaurant, staff in firms' restaurants or hospital patients, have a natural expectation that insensitive use of the environment or resources should be avoided. Staff in catering have a natural expectation with regard to a sensible working environment.

One of the problems for the organic market is the lack of a good distribution network. It is difficult to establish a distribution network as long as there are only a few catering kitchens that use organic vegetables. The solution to the problem is to distribute organic produce through traditional distribution channels, and this is being developed. The quality of organic produce is variable. The majority of caterers and food manufacturers at present take organic produce seriously. The trend for the future is likely to be towards environmentally friendly food products rather than organic food products.

'Organic' is a term defined by European law, and all organic food production and processing is governed by strict legislative standards. Catering operations preparing and selling organic menus must be certified with a UK certification body – for example, Soil Association Certification Ltd.

Environmentally friendly food products

These are foods that are produced under conditions that save on electricity and water as well as other environmental factors, or they can be products made using environmentally friendly technology. Products may be packed in environmentally friendly packaging and produce grown with a limited use of fertilisers and crop sprays, but not necessarily totally organic. In this way a trend may be expected in which industry slowly takes on the idea of organic production and increasingly begins to market environmentally friendly food products to the catering industry.

Meat

Cattle, sheep and pigs are reared for fresh meat. Tenderness and flavour are increased in beef and lamb if hung after slaughter. Pork and veal are hung for three to seven days, according to the temperature. Meat is generally hung at a temperature of 1°C.

Conversion of muscle to meat

Glycogen is a carbohydrate energy reserve stored in the muscle of animals. It is used to provide energy in the living animal, and is broken down to water and carbon dioxide. In muscle after slaughter there is no supply of oxygen and therefore the glycogen is converted to lactic acid. The build-up of lactic acid reduces the pH from about 7.0 to 5.6 (i.e. it makes the meat more acidic). This natural acidity is important for the keeping quality of meat.

Under some conditions this process cannot follow the normal pattern. In particular, if there is insufficient glycogen present in the muscle at slaughter the pH does not fall to the same extent and dark, firm, dry meat results. This is caused by insufficient feed prior to slaughter or a prolonged period of stress. Another condition, known as PSE (pale soft exudative), results if animals (especially pigs) are subjected to a period of acute stress prior to slaughter. This results in the pH fall occurring too rapidly, which gives rise to denaturation of the muscle protein.

Carcass hanging

The method of carcass hanging used can give rise to marked differences in eating quality. Hanging the carcase by the hip bone (aitch bone) instead of the traditional Achilles tendon puts tension on the important muscles of the hindquarter. This 'stretching' effect in some muscles makes them more tender. Traditionally carcasses were 'hung' (held as carcasses) for a period of several days. In fact, boning can take place as soon as 12 hours (pigs), 24 hours (sheep) or 48 hours (cattle) after slaughter, provided a period of ageing is allowed following butchery.

Ageing of meat

Like cheese and wine, meat benefits from a period of ageing, or maturation, before it is consumed. This gives an increase in both the tenderness and flavour. The increase in tenderness occurs as enzymes, naturally present within the meat, break down key proteins. The so-called calpain enzymes are important for the development of tenderness. Flavour may be increased by the release of small protein fragments with strong flavour. Minimum ageing periods of seven days from slaughter to consumption are often recommended for beef, lamb and pork. The flavour of meat is also dependent on the animal's diet, and the fat content dependent on species.

Storage

Raw meat should be stored separately from cooked meat or meat products. Chilled meat must be used by the 'use by' date.

The temperatures of chillers and freezers should be checked and recorded regularly. Regulations state that meat must be stored below 8°C but it is widely recognised as best practice to store it at 1–4°C, or even lower. High-risk meat products that do not need any further cooking must be stored in the 1–4°C range. Any vacuum-packed meat should be stored below 3°C.

Cuts and joints

For economic reasons of saving on both labour and storage space, very many caterers purchase meat by joints or cuts rather than by the carcass.

The Meat Buyer's Guide is a manual that has been designed to assist caterers who wish to simplify and facilitate their meat purchasing, and provides information and cutting guides.

Food value

Meat, having a high protein content, is valuable for the growth and repair of the body and as a source of energy. It is an important source of several vitamins, minerals and other nutrients (e.g. vitamins B, A and D, zinc and iron).

The fat content of meat varies according to the type and the cut. In some meats, the fat surrounds the lean muscle; in other meat, it appears as flecks of fat (marbling) in the lean tissue.

Preservation

- Salting: meat can be pickled in brine; this method of preservation may be applied to silverside, brisket and ox tongues. Salting is also used in the production of bacon, before the sides of pork are smoked. This also applies to hams.
- Chilling: this means that meat is kept at a temperature just above freezing point in a controlled atmosphere.
- Freezing: small carcasses, such as lamb and mutton, can be frozen; their quality is not affected by freezing. They can be kept frozen until required and then thawed out before use. Some beef is frozen, but it is inferior in quality to chilled beef.
- Canning: large quantities of meat are canned; corned beef is of importance since it has a very high protein content. Pork is used for tinned luncheon meat and in canned hams. Prepared meat products such as beef stew or beef pie filling are also available canned.
- Many cuts of meat are now sold in vacuum packs. This helps to preserve the freshness of the meat but the packs must be kept in the refrigerator at less than 3°C.
- Meat cuts and products are also sold in modified atmosphere packaging (MAP). The meat is placed in a clear container sealed with a clear film top. The meat is surrounded with a modified gas mixture that slows down deterioration. These packs must be kept in the refrigerator.

For further information about meat contact the Institute of Meat, on info@instituteofmeat.co.uk or visit www.instituteofmeat.co.uk.

Beef

The hanging or maturing of beef at a chill temperature of 1°C (34°F) for up to 14 days has the effect of increasing its tenderness and flavour and is essential as animals are generally slaughtered around the age of 18 to 24 months. Also, a short time after death, an animal's muscles stiffen – a condition known as rigor mortis. After a time chemical actions caused by enzymes and increasing acidity relax the muscles and the meat becomes soft and pliable. As meat continues to hang in storage rigor mortis dissipates, and tenderness and flavour increase. (Pork, lamb and veal are obtained from young animals, so toughness is not a significant factor.)

Large quantities of beef are prepared as chilled boneless prime cuts, vacuum packed in film. This process has the following advantages: it extends the storage life of the cuts; the cuts are boned and fully trimmed, thus reducing labour costs and storage space.

It is essential to store and handle vacuum-packed meat correctly. The storage temperature should be 1–4°C with the cartons the correct way up so that the drips cannot stain the fatty surface. A good circulation of air should be allowed between cartons.

When required for use, the vacuum film should be punctured in order to drain away any blood before the film is removed. On opening the film a slight odour is usually discernible, but this should quickly disappear on exposure to the air. The vacuum-packed beef has a deep-red colour, but when the film is broken the colour should change to its normal characteristic red within 20–30 minutes. Once the film has been punctured the meat should be used as soon as possible.

Quality

Lean meat should be bright red, with small flecks of white fat (marbled). The fat should be firm, brittle in texture, creamy white in colour and odourless. Meat of traceable origin is best.

Meat suppliers must be able to show the 'traceability' of the meat that they sell. This means that they can show where the meat came from and where it was slaughtered and butchered.

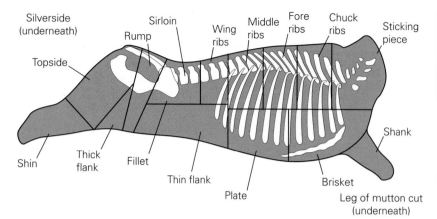

Silverside
(underneath)

Sirloin

Rump

Wing
ribs

Middle
ribs

Fore
ribs

Chuck
ribs

Sticking
piece

Topside

Shank

Shin

Thick
flank

Fillet

Thin flank

Plate

Brisket

Leg of mutton cut
(underneath)

Figure 3.2 Side of beef

Figure 3.3 Beef, silverside (rolled)

Figure 3.4 Rolled topside of beef

Figure 3.5 Boned shin of beef

Figure 3.6 Fillet and loin of beef

Figure 3.7 Forerib of beef

Figure 3.8 Beef, chuck steaks

Figure 3.9 T-bone steaks

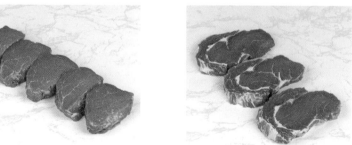

Figure 3.10 Sirloin steaks

Figure 3.11 Fillet steaks

Figure 3.12 Rib eye steaks

Veal

Originally, most top-quality veal came from Holland, but as the Dutch methods of production are now used extensively in Britain, supplies of home-produced veal are available all year round. Good-quality carcasses weighing around 100 kg can be produced from calves slaughtered at 12–24 weeks. This quality of veal is necessary for first-class cookery.

The flesh of veal should be pale pink and firm, not soft or flabby. Cut surfaces must not be dry, but moist. Bones in young animals should be pinkish white, porous and with a small amount of blood in their structure. The fat should be firm and pinkish white. The kidney ought to be firm and well covered with fat.

Welfare veal comes from calves that are loosely penned. The colour of the meat as a consequence is a deeper shade of pink.

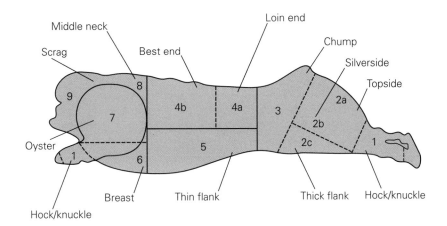

Figure 3.13 Side of veal

Figure 3.14 Veal kidneys

Figure 3.15 Veal escalopes

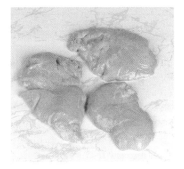

Figure 3.16 Veal sweetbreads

Pork

Lean flesh of pork is usually pale pink. The fat usually is white, firm, smooth and not excessive. Bones are usually small, fine and pinkish. The quality of the skin or rind depends on the breed. Suckling pigs weigh 5–9 kg dressed and are usually roasted whole.

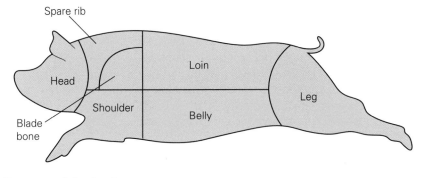

Figure 3.17 Side of pork

Figure 3.18 Leg of pork, boned and rolled

Figure 3.19 Boned leg of pork

Figure 3.20 Loin of pork

Figure 3.21 Pork chops

Figure 3.22 Gammon

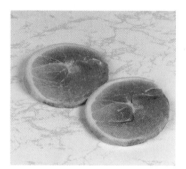

Figure 3.23 Gammon steaks

Boars

Boars are uncastrated male pigs. The meat of boars is available from specialist farms. It is better to obtain good-quality animals from suppliers using as near as possible 100 per cent pure breeding stock. Animals that are free to roam and forage for food may have a better flavour than farm-reared ones that have been penned and fed. Animals are best between 12 and 18 months old, and weighing 70–75 kg on the hoof. Slaughtering is best done during late summer when the fat content is lower. Recommended hanging time is between seven and ten days at a temperature of between 1 and 4°C. Marinating before cooking greatly improves the taste and texture of boar meat.

Bacon

Bacon is the cured flesh of a pig (60–75 kg dead weight) specifically reared for bacon because its shape and size yield economic bacon joints.

The curing process consists of salting either by a dry method and smoking, or by soaking in brine followed by smoking. Unsmoked bacon is brine cured but not smoked; it has a milder flavour but does not keep as long as smoked bacon.

There should be no sign of stickiness. There must be no unpleasant smell. The rind should be thin and smooth. The fat ought to be white, smooth and not excessive in proportion to the lean. The lean meat of the bacon should be deep pink in colour and firm, depending on the cure.

Bacon should be kept in a well-ventilated, preferably refrigerated, room. Joints of bacon should be wrapped in muslin. Sides of bacon are also hung on hooks. Cut bacon is kept on trays in the refrigerator or cold room. Bacon can also be vacuum packed ('vac packed').

Figure 3.24 Suckling pig

Pancetta is rolled slices of cured pork belly. Pancetta is salt cured, flavoured with herbs and spices and air dried. Lardo is an extremely fatty Italian bacon.

See also the section on hams (page 143).

Figure 3.25 Pig's trotters

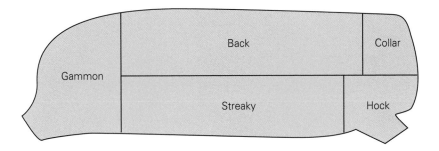

Figure 3.26 Side of bacon

Figure 3.27 Back bacon

Figure 3.28 Streaky bacon

Lamb and mutton

In Britain, more lamb and mutton are eaten than in any other European country. Lamb is generally meat from animals under one year old; mutton is the term for older animals.

The carcass should be compact and evenly fleshed. The lean flesh of lamb ought to be firm and of a pleasing dull-red colour, and of a fine texture or grain. The fat should be evenly distributed, hard, brittle, flaky and clear white in colour. The bones should be porous in young animals.

The factors influencing lamb composition, quality and value are essentially similar to those described above for beef.

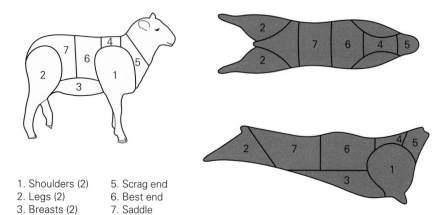

1. Shoulders (2)
2. Legs (2)
3. Breasts (2)
4. Middle neck
5. Scrag end
6. Best end
7. Saddle

Figure 3.29 Carcass of lamb

Figure 3.30 Saddle of lamb

Figure 3.31 Pair of best ends of lamb

Figure 3.32 Boned and rolled lamb shoulder

Figure 3.33 Shoulder of lamb

Figure 3.34 Double loin chops (Barnsley chops) of lamb

Figure 3.35 Lamb loin chops

Figure 3.36 Lamb cutlets

Figure 3.37 Best ends of lamb (racks, French trimmed)

Figure 3.38 Valentines of lamb

Figure 3.39 Leg chops

Figure 3.40 Lamb rosettes

Offal and other edible parts of the carcass

Offal is the name given to the parts taken from the inside of the carcass: edible offal includes liver, kidney, heart and sweetbread. Tripe, brains, oxtail, tongue and head are sometimes included under this term. Fresh offal (unfrozen) should be purchased as required and can be refrigerated under hygienic conditions at a temperature of −1°C (30°F), at rela- tive humidity of 90 per cent for up to seven days. Frozen offal should be kept frozen until required.

> **Further information on meats and offal can be found in** *Practical Cookery* **and** *Practical Cookery Level 3*, **and** *The Meat Buyer's Guide* **(for full details see the 'References' section on page 111).**

Figure 3.41 Lamb hearts

Figure 3.42 Lamb kidneys

Figure 3.43 Calves' liver

Tripe

Tripe is the stomach lining or white muscle of beef cattle. Smooth tripe comes from the first compartment of the stomach. Honeycomb tripe is from the second compartment of the stomach and is considered to be the best. Sheep tripe, darker in colour, is obtainable in some areas. Tripe may be boiled or braised.

Oxtail

Oxtails should be 1.5–1.75 kg, lean and with no signs of stickiness. They are usually braised or used for soup.

Suet

Beef suet should be creamy white, brittle and dry. It is used for suet paste. Other fat should be fresh and not sticky. Suet and fat may be rendered down for dripping.

Bones

Bones must be fresh, not sticky; they are used for stock, which is the base for soups and sauces.

Liver

Calves' liver is the most expensive and is considered the best in terms of tenderness and delicacy of fla- vour and colour. Lambs' liver is mild in flavour, tender and light in colour. Ox or beef liver is the cheapest and, if taken from an older animal, can be coarse in texture and strong in flavour. Pigs' liver is full- flavoured and used in many pâté recipes.

Quality

Liver should appear fresh and have an attractive colour. It must not be dry or contain tubes. It should be smooth in texture.

Food value

Liver is valuable as a protective food; it consists chiefly of protein and contains useful amounts of vitamin A and iron.

Kidney

Lambs' kidney is light in colour, delicate in flavour, and ideal for grilling and frying. Calves' kidney is light in colour, delicate in flavour and can be used in a wide variety of dishes. Ox kidney is dark in colour, strong in flavour and is generally used mixed with beef, for steak and kidney pie or pudding. Pigs' kidney is smooth, long and flat by comparison with sheep's kidney; it has a strong flavour.

Quality

Ox kidney should be fresh and deep red in colour. Lambs' kidney should be covered in fat, which is removed just before use; the fat should be crisp and the kidney moist.

Food value

Kidneys are a rich source of protein, vitamin A and iron.

Heart

Ox or beef hearts are the largest used for cooking. They are dark-coloured, solid, and tend to be dry and tough. Calves' heart, coming from a younger animal, is lighter in colour and more tender. Lambs' heart is smaller and lighter, and normally served whole. Larger hearts are normally sliced before serving.

Quality

Hearts should not be too fatty and should not contain too many tubes. When cut they should be moist.

Food value

Hearts have a high protein content and are valuable for growth and repair of the body.

Tongue

Tongues must be fresh. They should not have an excessive amount of waste at the root end. Ox tongues may be used fresh or salted. Sheep's tongues are used unsalted.

Sweetbreads

Sweetbreads is the name given to two glands, one is the pancreas, and is undoubtedly the best as it is round, flat and plump; the other is the elongated sausage-shaped thymus gland.

Quality

Sweetbreads should be fleshy, large and creamy white in colour.

Food value

Sweetbreads are valuable foods, particularly for hospital diets. They are very easily digested and useful for building body tissues.

For information on quality, types of poultry and their use see *Practical Cookery* and *Practical Cookery Level 3*. For further information on poultry in general, contact the British Poultry Council: www.poultry.uk.com.

Meat substitutes

Textured vegetable protein (TVP)

This is a meat substitute manufactured from protein derived from wheat, oats, cottonseed, soya beans and other sources. The main source of TVP is the soya bean, due to its high protein content.

TVP is used chiefly as a meat extender, varying from 10–60 per cent replacement of fresh meat. Some caterers on very tight budgets make use of it, but its main use is in food manufacturing.

By partially replacing the meat in certain dishes – such as casseroles, stews, pies, pasties, sausage rolls, hamburgers, meat loaf and pâté – it is possible to reduce costs, provide nutrition and serve food that is acceptable in appearance.

Myco-protein

This meat substitute is produced from a plant that is a distant relative of the mushroom. Myco-protein contains protein and fibre, and is the result of a fermentation process similar to that used in the production of yoghurt. It may be used as an alternative to chicken or beef, or in vegetarian dishes.

Quorn is the brand name for myco-protein.

Poultry

Poultry is the name given to domestic birds specially bred to be eaten and for their eggs. Poultry is Britain's most popular meat: almost twice as much poultry is consumed as beef.

Season

Owing to present-day methods of poultry breeding and growing, poultry is available all the year round either chilled or frozen.

Food value

The flesh of poultry is more easily digested than that of butchers' meat. It contains protein and is therefore useful for building and repairing body tissues, and providing heat and energy. Its fat content is low and it contains a high percentage of unsaturated fatty acids.

Storage

Fresh poultry must be hung by the legs under chilled conditions, otherwise it will not be tender; the innards are removed as soon as possible after slaughter.

Frozen birds must be kept in a deep-freeze cabi-net below −18°C until required. To reduce the risk of food poisoning, it is essential that frozen birds be completely thawed, preferably in a refrigerator, before they are cooked. Chilled birds should be kept at between 1 and 4°C.

Chicken

Chicken is probably the most popular type of poultry dish. It comes in various types, with different uses:

- spring chickens (poussin) – four to six weeks old
- broiler chickens – three to four months old
- medium and large roasting chickens
- capons (castrated cock birds)
- old hens – used in soups and sauces.

Quality

Fresh chicken should have a plump breast, a pliable breast bone and firm flesh. The skin should be white with a faint bluish tint and unbroken. The legs should be smooth with small scales and spurs.

Figure 3.44 Chicken: whole and prepared for cooking

Figure 3.45 Corn-fed chicken

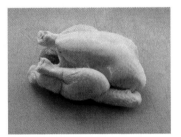

Figure 3.46 Poussin

Duck/duckling and goose/gosling

Goose is traditionally in season from Michaelmas (29 September) until Christmas.

Figure 3.47 Goose

Figure 3.48 Goose prepared for cooking

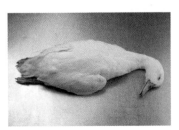

Figure 3.49 Duck: whole

Figure 3.50 Gressingham duck: prepared for cooking

Quality

The feet and bills should be bright yellow. The upper bill should break easily. The webbed feet must be easy to tear. Ducks and geese may be roasted or braised.

Turkey

Turkeys are usually roasted and served hot or cold. When the whole bird is not required, turkey cuts are also popular. These include crowns (breasts left on the bone), legs, boned legs, drumsticks, wings, escalopes and mince.

Quality

The breast should be large, the skin undamaged and with no signs of stickiness. The legs of young birds are black and smooth, the feet supple with a short spur. As the bird ages the legs turn reddish grey and become scaly. The feet become hard.

Guinea fowl

When plucked these grey and white feathered birds resemble a chicken with darker flesh. The young birds are known as squabs. The quality points relating to chicken (see page 59) also apply to guinea fowl.

Figure 3.51 Turkey

Figure 3.52 Turkey prepared for cooking

Figure 3.53 Guinea fowl: whole and prepared for cooking

Pigeon

Pigeon should be plump, the flesh mauve-red in colour and the claws pinkish. Tame pigeons are smaller than wood pigeons. Squabs are young, specially reared pigeons.

Ostrich

Ostrich is usually sold as a fillet (taken from the thigh) or leg steak. The neck or offal is also available and is cheaper. It is often compared to beef, but it has a slightly coarser texture with less fat and lower cholesterol.

Figure 3.54 Wood pigeon: whole and prepared for cooking

Figure 3.55 Squab: whole and prepared for cooking

Game

Game is the name given to certain wild birds and animals that are eaten. There are two kinds of game: feathered and furred.

Food value

As it is less fatty than poultry or meat, game is more easily digested, with the exception of water fowl, which has oily flesh. Game is useful for building and repairing body tissues, and for energy.

Storage

Hanging is essential for all game. It drains the flesh of blood and begins the process of disintegration that is vital to make the flesh soft and edible, and also to develop flavour. The hanging time is determined by the type, condition and age of the game, and the storage temperature. Old birds need to hang for a longer time than young birds. Game birds are not plucked or drawn before hanging. Venison and hare are hung with the skin on. Game must be hung in a well-ventilated, dry, cold storeroom; this need not be refrigerated. Game birds should be hung by the neck with the feet down.

Availability

Game is available fresh in season between the dates shown in Table 3.1, and frozen for the remainder of the year.

Table 3.1 Game in season*

Grouse	12 August–10 December
Snipe	12 August–31 January
Partridge	1 September–1 February
Wild duck	1 September–31 January
Pheasant	1 October–1 February
Woodcock	31 October–1 February

* Venison, hares, rabbits and pigeons are available throughout the year

Venison

Venison is the flesh from any member of the deer family, which includes elk, moose, reindeer, caribou and antelope. Red deer meat is a dark, blood-red colour; the flesh of the roe deer is paler and the fallow deer is considered to have the best flavour.

Meat from animals over 18 months in age tends to be tough and dry, and is usually marinated to counter-act this. Young animals up to 18 months produce deli-cate, tender meat that does not require marinating. Nowadays, venison is extensively farmed in the UK.

Venison contains 207 calories per 100 g, and young venison has only about 6 per cent fat (com-pared to beef, lamb and pork at around 20 per cent fat). It has the highest protein content of the major meats.

Venison is very suitable for a low-cholesterol diet because the fat is mainly polyunsaturated. The car-cass has little intramuscular fat; the lean meat con-tains only low levels of marbling fat.

Both farmed and wild venison are available. Joints should be well fleshed and a dark brownish-red colour. Venison is usually roasted or braised in joints, served hot or cold with a peppery/sweet type sauce. Small cuts may be fried and served in a variety of ways. Venison is available as: shoulder, boned and rolled; haunch, boned and rolled; prepared saddles and steaks; also as pâté, in sausages and burgers; and smoked.

Hare and rabbit

The ears of hares and rabbits should tear easily. In old hares the lip is more pronounced than in young animals. The rabbit is distinguished from the hare by its shorter ears, feet and body.

Hare may be cooked as a red wine stew thickened with its own blood, called jugged hare, and the saddle can be roasted.

Other meats

- Alligator is a white meat, with a veal-like texture and a shellfish-like flavour.
- Bison should be treated like a gamey, well-hung version of beef. However, because it is so lean it needs to be cooked quickly and served rare or medium rare.
- Camel is available as fillet, steak or diced. It comes frozen from Africa.
- Crocodile has a firm-textured, light-coloured meat with a delicate fishy taste, similar to monkfish, that absorbs other flavours well. It is surprisingly fatty.
- European wild boar has been reintroduced to

Figure 3.56 Venison

Figure 3.57 Rabbit and hare: furred

Figure 3.58 Rabbit and hare: skinned

British farms. It produces rich, dark-red meat with a dense texture.

- Kangaroo is similar to venison in flavour. It has a fine-grained meat that, once cooked, is similar in texture to liver; it is best served rare or medium rare.
- Kid usually comes from goats bred for their milk. However, the South African Boer goat, which is bred for its meat, has recently been introduced into this country. It has a rich yet delicate flavour with very little fat.
- Kudu is a breed of wild African antelope that is culled in a controlled way. The animals are very large and the meat has a stronger flavour than wild venison. It needs to be tenderised by marinating and cooking.

Game birds

The beak should break easily. The breast plumage should be soft. The breast should be plump. Quill feathers should be pointed, not rounded. The legs should be smooth.

- Grouse: A particularly famous and popular game bird is the red grouse, which is shot in Scotland and Yorkshire. Average weight is 300 g. Young birds have pointed wings and rounded soft spurs. Hang for five to seven days. Use for roasting.
- Partridge: The most common varieties are the grey-legged and the red-legged partridge. Average weight is 200–400 g. Hang for three to five days. Use for roasting or braising.

- Pheasant: This is one of the most common game birds. Average weight is 1.5–2 kg. Young birds have a pliable breast bone and soft pliable feet. They should be hung for five to eight days, and can be used for roasting, braising or pot roasting.
- Quail: These are small birds weighing 50–75 g, produced on farms and usually packed in boxes of 12. Quails are not hung. They are usually served roasted, grilled, spatchcock or braised.
- Snipe: Weight is about 100 g. Hang for three to four days. The heads and neck are skinned, the eyes removed; birds are then trussed with their own beaks. When drawing the birds, only the gizzard, gallbladder and intestines are removed. The birds are then roasted with the liver and heart left inside.
- Teal: The smallest duck, weighing 400–600 g. Hang for one to two days. Usually roasted or braised. Young birds have small pinkish legs and soft down under the wings. Teal and wild duck must be eaten in season otherwise the flesh is coarse and has a fishy flavour. Usually roasted or braised.
- Wild duck: Wild duck include mallard and widgeon. Average weight is 1–1.5 kg. Hang for one or two days. Usually roasted or braised.
- Woodcock: These are small birds with long, thin beaks. Average weight is 200–300 g. Prepare as for snipe. Usually roasted.

Figure 3.59 Grouse: whole and prepared for cooking

Figure 3.60 Red-legged and English partridge: whole and prepared for cooking

Figure 3.61 Male and female pheasants and one prepared for cooking

Figure 3.62 Snipe: whole

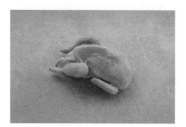

Figure 3.63 Quail: prepared for cooking

Figure 3.64 Wild duck: prepared for cooking

Fish

Fish have always made up a large proportion of the food we consume because of their abundance and relative ease of harvesting. However, because the fish supply is not unlimited, due to overfishing, fish farms (e.g. for trout, salmon, cod, halibut and turbot) have been established to supplement the natural sources. Overfishing is not the only problem: due to contamination by man, the seas and rivers are increasingly polluted, thus affecting both the supply and suitability of fish, particularly shellfish, for human consumption.

Fish are valuable, not only because they are a good source of protein, but because they are suitable for all types of menus, and can be cooked and presented in a wide variety of ways. The range of different types of fish of varying texture, taste and appearance is indispensable to the creative chef.

Table 3.2 Seasons for fish

Variety of fish	Season
Oily	
Anchovy	Imported occasionally June to December (home waters)
Common eel	All year, best in autumn
Conger eel	March to October
Herring	All year except spring
Kingfish	Check with supplier
Mackerel	September to July
Pilchard (mature sardine)	All year
Salmon (farmed)	All year
Salmon (wild)	February to August
Salmon trout	February to August
Salmon (Pacific)	July to November
Sprat	September to March
Sardines	All year
Trout	February to September
Trout (farmed)	All year
Tuna	All year
Whitebait	When available
White, flat	
Brill	June to February
Dab	March to December
Flounder	May to February, best in winter
Halibut	June to March
Megrim	April to February
Plaice	May to February
Skate	May to February
Sole, Dover	May to March
Sole, lemon	All year, best in sprin
Turbot	All year
Turbot (farmed)	When available
Witch	All year, best in spring

Variety of fish	Season
Round	
Barracuda	Check with supplier
Bass (wild/farmed)	June to September
Bream, fresh water	August to April
Bream, sea	June to December
Carp (mostly farmed)	Fluctuates throughout year
Cod	All year, not at best in spring
Dogfish (huss, flake, rigg)	All year, best in autumn
Grey mullet	May to February, best autumn and winter
Grouper	Check with supplier
Haddock	All year, best autumn and winter
Hake	June to February
John Dory	September to May
Ling	September to July
Monkfish (anglerfish)	All year, best in winter
Pike	All year
Perch	May to February
Pollock (yellow, green)	May to December
Redfish	All year
Red gurnard	All year, best from July to April
Red mullet	Imported best in summer, UK autumn
Sea bream	June to February
Smelt	Occasionally
Shark (porbeagle)	Occasionally
Snapper, red snapper	Check with supplier
Whiting	All year, best in winter

Types or varieties

Oily fish are round in shape (e.g. herring, mackerel, salmon). White fish can be round (cod, whiting, hake) or flat (plaice, sole, turbot). Shellfish and cephalopods are discussed on pages 69–72.

Purchasing unit

Fresh fish is bought by the kilogram, by the number of fillets or by whole fish of the weight required. For example, 30 kg of salmon could be ordered as 2 × 15 kg, 3 × 10 kg or 6 × 5 kg. Frozen fish can be purchased in 15 kg blocks. Fish may be bought on the bone or filleted in steaks or supremes. (The approximate loss from boning and waste is 50 per cent for flat fish, 60 per cent for round fish.) Fillets of plaice and sole can be purchased according to weight. They are graded from 45 g to 180 g per fillet, and go up in weight by 15 g.

Storage

Fresh fish are stored in a fish box containing ice, in a separate refrigerator or part of a refrigerator used only for fish at a temperature of 1–2°C. The temperature must be maintained just above freezing point.

Frozen fish must be stored in a deep-freeze cabinet or compartment at −18°C.

Smoked fish should be kept in a refrigerator.

Food value

Fish is as useful a source of animal protein as meat. The oily fish, such as sardines, mackerel, herrings and salmon, contain vitamins A and D in their flesh; in white fish, such as halibut and cod, these vitamins are present in the liver. Since all fish contains protein it is a good body-building food, and oily fish is useful for energy and as a protective food because of the vitamins it contains.

The bones of sardines, whitebait and tinned salmon, which can be eaten, provide calcium and phosphorus.

Owing to its fat content, oily fish is not so digestible as white fish and is not suitable for use in cookery for invalids.

Oily fish

- **Anchovies:** Anchovies are small, round fish used mainly tinned in this country; they are supplied in 60 g and 390 g tins. They are filleted and packed in oil. They are used for making anchovy butter and anchovy sauce, for garnishing dishes and for savouries, snacks and salads.
- **Common eel:** Eels live in fresh water and are also farmed, and can grow up to 1 m in length. They are found in many British rivers and considerable quantities are imported from Holland. Eels must be kept alive until the last minute before cooking and are generally used in fish stews.
- **Conger eel:** The conger eel is a dark-grey sea fish with white flesh, which grows up to 3 m in length. It may be used in the same way as eels, or it may be smoked.
- **Herring:** Fresh herrings are used for breakfast and lunch menus; they may be grilled, fried or soused. Kippers (which are split, salted, dried and smoked herrings) are served for breakfast and also as a savoury. Average weight is 250 g.
- **Kingfish** come from the Spanish mackerel family; their flesh is orangey-pink coloured.
- **Mackerel:** Mackerel are grilled, shallow-fried, smoked or soused, and may be used on breakfast and lunch menus. They must be used fresh because the flesh deteriorates very quickly. Average weight is 360 g.
- **Pilchards:** These are mature sardines and can grow up to 24 cm. They have a good, distinctive flavour.
- **Salmon:** Salmon is perhaps the most famous river fish; it is caught in British rivers like the Dee, Tay, Severn, Avon, Wye and Spey. It is also extensively farmed in Scotland and Norway. A considerable number are imported from Scandinavia, Canada, Germany and Japan. Apart from using it fresh, salmon is tinned or smoked. When fresh, it is used in a wide variety of dishes.

Figure 3.65 Herring

Figure 3.66 Kipper

Figure 3.67 Mackerel

Figure 3.68 Side of fresh salmon

Figure 3.69 Salmon

Figure 3.70 Side of smoked salmon

- **Salmon trout (sea trout):** Salmon trout are a sea fish similar in appearance to salmon, but smaller, and are used in a similar way. Average weight is 1.5–2 kg.
- **Sardines:** Sardines are small fish of the pilchard family, which are usually tinned and used for hors d'oeuvre, sandwiches and as a savoury. Fresh sardines are also available and may be cooked by grilling or frying.

Figure 3.71 Sardine

- **Sprats:** Sprats are small fish fried whole; they can also be smoked and served as an hors d'oeuvre.
- **Trout:** Trout live in rivers and lakes in the UK; they are cultivated on trout farms. Trout may be poached and served grilled or shallow-fried, and may also be smoked and served as an hors d'oeuvre. Average weight is 200 g.
- **Tuna:** Tuna has dark reddish-brown flesh that, when cooked, turns a lighter colour. It has a thin texture and a mild flavour. If overcooked it dries out, so is best cooked medium rare. It is used fresh for a variety of dishes or tinned in oil and used mainly as an hors d'oeuvre and in salads.
- **Whitebait:** Whitebait are the fry, or young, of herring; they are 2–4 cm long and are usually deep-fried.

Figure 3.72 Trout

Figure 3.73 Smoked trout

Figure 3.74 Whitebait

White flat fish

- **Brill:** Brill is a large flat fish, which is sometimes confused with turbot. Brill is oval in shape; the mottled brown skin is smooth with small scales. It can be distinguished from turbot by its lesser breadth in proportion to length; average weight is 3–4 kg. It is usually served in the same way as turbot.
- **Dab:** Dab is an oval-bodied fish with sandy brown upper skin and green freckles. Usual size is 20–30 cm. It has a pleasant flavour when fresh, and may be cooked by all methods.

Figure 3.75 Brill

- **Flounder:** This is oval, with dull brown upper skin (or sometimes dull green with orange freckles). Usual size is 30 cm. Flesh is rather watery and lacks flavour, needing good seasoning. It can be cooked by all methods.
- **Halibut:** Halibut is a long and narrow fish, brown, with some darker mottling on the upper side; it can be 3 m in length and weigh around 20–50 kg. Halibut is much valued for its flavour. It is poached, boiled, grilled or shallow-fried. It is also smoked.
- **Megrim:** Megrim has a very long slender body, sandy-brown coloured with dark blotches. Usual size is 20–30 cm. It has a softish flesh and an unexceptional flavour, so needs good flavouring. It is best breadcrumbed and shallow-fried.
- **Plaice:** Plaice are oval in shape, with dark-brown colouring and orange spots on the upper side. Used on all types of menus, they are usually deep-fried or grilled. Average weight is 360–450 g.
- **Skate:** Skate, a member of the ray family, is a very large fish and only the wings are used. It is usually served on the bone and either poached, shallow- or deep-fried, or cooked in a court bouillon and served with black butter.
- **Sole:** Sole is considered to be the best of the flat fish. Sole is cooked by poaching, grilling or frying (both shallow and deep). It is served whole or can be filleted and garnished in a great many ways.
  - The quality of **Dover sole** is well known to be excellent.
  - **Lemon sole:** This is related to Dover sole, but is broader in shape, and its upper skin is warm, yellowy-brown and mottled with darker brown.

Figure 3.76 Halibut

Figure 3.79 Skate

Figure 3.77 Smoked halibut

Figure 3.80 Dover sole

Figure 3.78 Plaice

Figure 3.81 Lemon sole

It can weigh up to 600 g, and may be cooked by all methods.

- **Turbot:** Turbot has no scales and is roughly diamond in shape; it has knobs known as tubercles on its dark skin. In proportion to its length it is wider than brill; 3.5–4 kg is the average weight. Turbot may be cooked whole, filleted or cut into portions on the bone. It may be boiled, poached, grilled or shallow-fried.
- **Witch:** This is similar in appearance and weight to lemon sole, with sandy-brown upper skin. It is best fried, poached, grilled or steamed.

Round fish

- **Barracuda:** A game fish with reddish flesh that, when cooked, turns pastel white. A mild-flavoured fish, it should be cooked as a supreme with the skin left on to prevent drying out.
- **Bass:** Bass have silvery grey backs and white bellies; small ones may have black spots. They have an excellent flavour, with white, lean, softish flesh (which must be very fresh). Bass can be steamed, poached, stuffed and baked, or grilled in steaks. Usual length is 30 cm but they can grow to 60 cm. Bass is usually farmed but sea bass is available (also called wild or natural) off the south coast of Britain. Farmed bass is also available from France and Greece.
- **Bream:** Sea bream is a short, oval-bodied, plump, reddish fish, with large scales and a dark patch behind the head. It is used on many less expensive menus; it is usually filleted and deep-fried, or stuffed and baked, but other methods of cooking are also employed. Average weight is 0.5–1 kg, size 28–30 cm. Bream are caught fresh or farmed.
- **Carp:** This is a freshwater fish, usually farmed. The flesh is white with a good flavour, and is best poached in fillets or stuffed and baked. The usual size is 1–2 kg.
- **Cod:** Cod varies in colour but is mostly greenish, brownish or olive grey. It can measure up to 1.5 m

in length. Cod is cut into steaks or filleted and cut into portions; it can be deep- or shallow-fried or poached. Small cod are known as codling. Average weight of cod is 2.5–3.5 kg.
- **Coley (saith, coalfish, blackjack):** Coley is dark greenish-brown or blackish in colour, but the flesh turns white when cooked. It has a coarse texture and a dry undistinctive flavour, so is best used in mixed fish stews, soups or pies. Average size is 40–80 cm.
- **Dogfish (huss, flake, rigg):** These are slender, elongated small sharks. The non-bony white or pink flesh is versatile, and is usually served shallow- or deep-fried. It has a good flavour when very fresh. Length is usually 60 cm and weight 1.25 kg.
- **Grey mullet:** This has a scaly, streamlined body, which is silver-grey or blue-green. Deep-sea or offshore mullet has a fine flavour, with firm, moist flesh. It may be stuffed and baked or grilled in steaks. Some people believe that flavour is improved if the fish is kept in a refrigerator for two to three days, without being cleaned. Length is usually about 30 cm, weight 500 g.
- **Grouper:** Types include brown, brown spotted, golden strawberry and red speckled. Grouper has a light pinkish flesh that cooks to a greyish-white, with a pleasant mild flavour.
- **Gudgeon:** Gudgeon are small fish found in continental lakes and rivers. They may be deep-fried whole. On menus in this country the French term 'en goujon' refers to other fish such as sole or turbot, cut into pieces the size of gudgeon.
- **Gurnard:** A large family of tasty fish with many culinary uses.
- **Haddock:** Haddock is distinguished from cod by the 'thumb mark' on its side and by its lighter colour. Every method of cooking is suitable for haddock, and it appears on all kinds of menus. Apart from fresh haddock, smoked haddock may

Figure 3.82 Turbot

Figure 3.83 Cod

Figure 3.84 Gurnard

Figure 3.85 Smoked haddock

Figure 3.86 Arbroath smokie (haddock smoked over hardwood)

be served for breakfast, lunch and as a savoury. Average weight is 0.5–2 kg.

- **Hake:** Owing to overfishing, hake is not plentiful. It is usually poached and is easy to digest. The flesh is very white and has a delicate flavour.
- **John Dory:** John Dory has a thin distinctive body, flattened from side to side, which is sandy-beige in colour and tinged with yellow, with a blue/silver-grey belly. There is a blotch on each side, referred to as the 'thumbprint of St Peter'. It has very tough sharp spikes. The flavour is considered superb, and the fish may be cooked by all methods, but is best poached, baked or steamed. The large bony head accounts for two-thirds of the weight. Usual size is 36 cm.
- **Ling:** This is the largest member of the cod family; it is mottled brown or green with a bronze sheen, and the fins have white edges. Size can be up to 90 cm. Ling has a good flavour and texture, and is generally used in fillets or cutlets, as for cod.
- **Monkfish:** Monkfish has a huge flattened head, with a normal fish-shaped tail. It is brown with dark blotches. The tail can be up to 180 cm, weight 1–10 kg. It may be cooked by all methods, and is a firm, close-textured white fish with excellent flavour.
- **Pike:** Pike has a long body, usually 60 cm, which is greeny-brown, flecked with lighter green, with long toothy jaws. The traditional fish for quenelles, it may also be braised or steamed.
- **Perch:** Perch has a deep body, marked with about five shadowy vertical bars, and the fins are vivid orange or red. Usual size 15–30 cm. It is generally considered to have an excellent flavour, and may be shallow-fried, grilled, baked, braised or steamed.
- **Pollock:** This is a member of the cod family, and has a similar shape and variable colours. Its usual size is 45 cm. It is drier than cod, and can

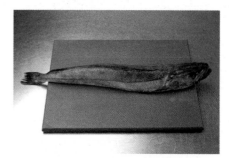

Figure 3.87 Hake

Figure 3.88 John Dory

Figure 3.89 Monkfish

Figure 3.90 Monkfish tail: prepared

be poached, shallow-fried or used for soups and stews.

- **Redfish:** This is bright red or orange-red, with a rosy belly and dusky gills. Usual size is 45 cm. It may be poached, baked or used in soups.
- **Red gurnard (grey and yellow gurnard may also be available):** This has a large 'mail-checked', tapering body with very spiky fins. Usual size is 20–30 cm. It is good for stews, braising and baking.
- **Red mullet:** Red mullet is on occasion cooked with the liver left in, as it is thought that this helps impart a better flavour to the fish. Mullet may be filleted or cooked whole, and the average weight is 360 g.
- **Rockfish:** Rockfish is the fishmonger's term for catfish, coalfish, dogfish, conger eel and the like, after cleaning and skinning. It is usually deep-fried in batter.
- **Shark:** The porbeagle shark, mako or hammerhead, fished off the British coast, gives the best-quality food. It is bluish-grey above with a white belly and matt skin. Size is up to 3 m. It may be cooked by all methods, but grilling in steaks or as kebabs is particularly suitable.
- **Smelt:** Smelts are small fish found in river estuaries and imported from Holland; they are usually deep-fried or grilled. Before grilling they are split open. The weight of a smelt is 60–90 g.
- **Snapper:** There are several kinds of snapper, all of which are brightly coloured. Deep-red or medium-sized ones give the best flavour. Snapper may be steamed, fried, grilled, baked or smoked.
- **Swordfish:** Swordfish is popular grilled, barbecued, roasted or shallow-fried.
- **Whiting:** Whiting is very easy to digest and is therefore suitable for use in cookery for invalids. It may be poached, grilled or deep-fried and used in the making of fish stuffing. Average weight is 360 g.

- **Wrasse:** Fish of variable colours, but usually tinged with red and blue, covered in white and green spots. Wrasse has a variety of culinary uses and can be baked and steamed.

Figure 3.91 Red mullet

Figure 3.92 Snapper

For further information on fish, visit: www.seafish.org.uk or contact the Seafish Industry Authority, 18 Logie Mill, Logie Green Road, Edinburgh EH7 4HG.

Shellfish

Shellfish are of two types:

1 crustaceans (lobster, crabs)
2 molluscs (oysters, mussels).

Shellfish is a good body-building food. As the flesh is coarse and therefore indigestible a little vinegar may be used in cooking to soften the fibres.

Crustaceans

- **Crabs:** Crabs are used in hors d'oeuvre, cocktails, salads, dressed crab, sandwiches and bouchées. Soft-shelled crabs are eaten in their entirety. They are considered to have an excellent flavour and may be deep- or shallow-fried or grilled.
- **Crawfish:** Crawfish are like large lobsters without claws, but with long antennae. They are brick-red in colour when cooked. Owing

Table 3.3 Seasons for shellfish

Shellfish	Season
Clams	All year
Cockles	All year, best in summer
Common crab	All year, best April to December
Spider crab	All year
Swimming crab	All year
King crab, red crab	Check with supplier
Soft-shelled crab	Check with supplier
Crawfish	April to October
Dublin Bay prawn	All year
Freshwater crayfish	Mainly imported, some farmed in the UK, wild have short season
Lobster	April to November
Mussels	September to March
Oysters	May to August
Prawn and shrimp	All year
Scallop	Best December to March
Sea urchin	All year

Figure 3.94 Crayfish

Figure 3.95 Lobster: raw

Figure 3.96 Lobster: cooked

to their size and appearance they are used mostly on cold buffets but they can be served hot. The best size is 1.5–2 kg. Menu examples include langouste parisienne (dressed crawfish Paris-style).

- **Crayfish:** Crayfish are a type of small freshwater lobster used for salads, garnishing cold buffet dishes and for recipes using lobster. They are dark brown or grey, turning pink when cooked. Average size is 8 cm.
- **Lobster:** Lobsters are served cold in cocktails, hors d'oeuvre, salads, sandwiches and on buffets. They are used hot for soup, grilled and served in numerous dishes with various sauces.
- **Prawns:** Prawns are larger than shrimps; they may be used for garnishing and decorating

Figure 3.93 Crab

fish dishes, for cocktails, canapés, salads, hors d'oeuvre and for hot dishes, such as curried prawns. Prawns are also popular served cold with a mayonnaise-type sauce.

- **Scampi, Dublin Bay prawns, langoustines:** Scampi are found in the Mediterranean. The Dublin Bay prawn, which is from the same family, is caught around the Scottish coast. These shellfish resemble small lobsters, about 20 cm long, and only the tail flesh is used for a variety of fish dishes, garnishing and salads.
- **Shrimps:** Shrimps are used for garnishes, decorating fish dishes, in cocktails, sauces, salads, hors d'oeuvre, potted shrimps, omelettes and savouries.

Figure 3.97 Langoustines

Molluscs

- **Clams:** There are many varieties; the soft or long-neck clams, such as razor and Ipswich, and small hard-shell clams such as cherrystones, can be eaten raw. Large clams can be steamed, fried or grilled and used for soups (chowders) and sauces.
- **Cockles:** These are enclosed in pretty cream-coloured shells of 2–3 cm. Cockles are soaked in salt water to purge and then steamed or boiled. They may be used in soups, salads and fish dishes, or served as a dish by themselves.
- **Mussels:** Mussels are extensively cultivated on wooden hurdles in the sea, producing tender, delicately flavoured, plump fish. British mussels are considered good; French mussels are smaller; Dutch and Belgian mussels are plumper. All vary in quality from season to season. Mussels are usually stored in their original packaging, in the refrigerator.
- **Oysters:** Oysters are produced from centres in England, Scotland, Ireland and Wales. Since the majority of oysters are eaten raw it is essential that they are thoroughly cleaned before hotels and restaurants receive them. Oysters must be alive; this is indicated by their firmly closed shells. They are graded in sizes, and the price varies accordingly. Oysters should smell fresh. They should be purchased daily. Oysters are in season in the UK from September to April (i.e. whenever there is an 'r' in the month). During the summer months oysters are imported from France, Holland and Portugal.

  Oysters are usually stored in their original packaging, in the refrigerator to keep them moist and alive. The shells should be tightly closed; if they are open, tap them sharply and, if they do not shut at once, discard them.

  The popular way of eating oysters is in the raw state. They may also be served in soups, hot cocktail savouries, fish garnishes, as a fish dish, and in meat puddings and savouries.
- **Scallops:** Great scallops are up to 15 cm in size, bay scallops up to 8 cm, queen scallops are small-cockle sized, and are also known as 'queenies'. Scallops may be steamed, poached, fried or grilled.
- **Sea urchin or sea hedgehog:** The sea urchin has a spine-covered spherical shell. Only the orange and yellow roe is eaten, either raw out of the shell or removed with a teaspoon and used in soups, sauces, scrambled eggs, and so on; 10 to 20 urchins provide approximately 200 g roe.
- **Winkles:** Winkles are small sea snails with a delicious flavour. They may be boiled for three minutes and served with garlic butter or on a dish of assorted shellfish.

Cephalopods and fish offal

Cuttlefish

Cuttlefish are usually dark with attractive pale stripes, and their size can be up to 24 cm. They are available all year by number and weight. Cuttlefish are prepared like squid and may be stewed or gently grilled.

Octopus

Octopus is available all year by number and weight. Large species are tough and need to be tenderised; they are then prepared as for squid. Small octopi can be boiled, then cut up for grilling or frying. When stewing, a long cooking time is needed.

Squid

The common squid has mottled skin and white flesh,

Figure 3.98 Clams

Figure 3.99 Mussels

Figure 3.100 Scallops

Figure 3.101 Octopus

Figure 3.102 Squid

Figure 3.103 Cod roe

two tentacles, eight arms and flap-like fins. Usual size is 15–30 cm. Careful, correct preparation (see below) is important if the fish is to be tender. It may be stir-fried, fried, baked, grilled or braised.

Preparation

- Pull head away from the body together with the innards.
- Cut off the tentacles just below the eye.
- Remove the small, round cartilage at the base of the tentacles.
- Discard the head, innards and pieces of cartilage.
- Scrape or peel off the reddish membrane that covers the pouch

Liver

An oil rich in vitamins A and D is obtained from the liver of cod and halibut. This is used medicinally.

Roe

The soft and hard roes of herring, cod, sturgeon and the coral from lobster are eaten. Soft herring roes are used to garnish fish dishes and as a savoury. Cod's roe is smoked and served as an hors d'oeuvre. The roe of the sturgeon is salted and served raw as caviar, and the coral of lobster is used for colouring lobster butter and lobster dishes, and also as a decoration for fish dishes.

Vegetables

Fresh vegetables and fruits are important foods, both from an economic and nutritional point of view. On average, each person consumes 125–150 kg per year of fruit and vegetables.

The purchasing of these commodities is difficult because the products are highly perishable, and supply and demand vary. The high perishability of fresh vegetables and fruits causes problems not encountered in other markets. Fresh vegetables and fruits are living organisms and will lose quality quickly if not properly stored and handled. Improved transportation and storage facilities can help prevent loss of quality. For more information on organic vegetables see page 00.

Automation in harvesting and packaging speeds the handling process and helps retain quality. Vacuum cooling – a process whereby fresh produce is moved into huge chambers, where, for about half an hour, a low vacuum is maintained, inducing rapid evaporation, which quickly reduces field heat – has been highly successful in improving quality.

Experience and sound judgement are essential for the efficient buying and storage of all commodities,

but none probably more so than fresh vegetables and fruit.

The grading of fresh fruit and vegetables within the EU

There are four main quality classes for produce:

1 Extra Class – for produce of top quality
2 Class I – for produce of good quality
3 Class II – for produce of reasonably good quality
4 Class III – for produce of low marketable quality.

Food value

- **Root vegetables:** useful in the diet because they contain starch or sugar for energy, a small but valuable amount of protein, some mineral salts and vitamins; also useful sources of cellulose and water.
- **Green vegetables:** no food is stored in the leaves, it is only produced there; therefore little protein or carbohydrate is found in green vegetables; they are rich in mineral salts and

vitamins, particularly vitamin C and carotene; the greener the leaf, the larger the quantity of vitamin present; chief mineral salts are calcium and iron.

Preservation

- **Canning:** certain vegetables are preserved in tins – artichokes, asparagus, carrots, celery, beans, peas (fine, garden, processed), tomatoes (whole, purée), mushrooms, truffles.
- **Dehydration:** onions, carrots, potatoes and cabbage are shredded and quickly dried until they contain only 5 per cent water.
- **Drying:** the seeds of legumes (peas and beans) have their moisture content reduced to 10 per cent.
- **Pickling:** onions and red cabbage are examples of vegetables preserved in spiced vinegar.
- **Salting:** French and runner beans may be sliced and preserved in dry salt.
- **Freezing:** many vegetables, such as peas, beans, sprouts, spinach and cauliflower, are deep frozen.
- **Modified atmosphere packaging (MAP):** prepared vegetable and salads are packed and surrounded by modified gases.

Types of vegetables

Roots

- **Beetroot** – two main types, round and long; used for soups, salads and as a vegetable.
- **Carrots** – grown in numerous varieties and sizes; used extensively for soups, sauces, stocks, stews, salads and as a vegetable.
- **Celeriac** – large, light-brown, celery-flavoured root, used in soups, salads and as a vegetable.
- **Horseradish** – long, light-brown, narrow root, grated and used for horseradish sauce.
- **Mooli** – long, white, thick member of radish family, used for soups, salads or as a vegetable.
- **Parsnips** – long, white root, tapering to a point; unique nut-like flavour; used in soups, added to casseroles and as a vegetable (roasted, purée, etc.).
- **Radishes** – small summer variety, round or oval, served with dips, in salads or as a vegetable in white or cheese sauce.
- **Salsify** – also called oyster plant because of similarity of taste; long, narrow root used in soups, salads and as a vegetable.
- **Scorzonera** – long, narrow root, slightly astringent in flavour; used in soups, salads and as a vegetable.

Figure 3.104 Root vegetables (left to right: parsnip, carrots, celeriac, horseradish, radishes, mooli)

- **Swede** – large root with yellow flesh; generally used as a vegetable, mashed or parboiled and roasted; may be added to stews.
- **Turnip** – two main varieties, long and round; used in soups, stews and as a vegetable.

Tubers

- **Artichokes, Jerusalem** – potato-like tuber with a bitter-sweet flavour; used in soups, salads and as a vegetable.
- **Potatoes** – many varieties are grown but all potatoes should be sold by name (King Edward, Desiree, Maris Piper); this is important as the caterer needs to know which varieties are best suited for specific cooking purposes. The various varieties fall into four categories: floury, firm, waxy or salad potatoes. Jersey royals are specially grown, highly regarded new potatoes. Purple Congo are a blue potato. Truffle de Chine are a deep-purple potato grown in France.
- **Taro** is the name used for several varieties of tuber found in tropical areas. Two common

Figure 3.105 Tubers (left to right: yam, sweet potato, potatoes, new potatoes, Jerusalem artichokes)

varieties of taro are eddo and dasheen. They are all a dark mahogany-brown with a shaggy skin, looking like a cross between a beetroot and a swede.

- **Sweet potatoes** – long tubers with purple or sand-coloured skins and orange flesh; flavour is sweet and aromatic; used as a vegetable (fried, puréed, creamed, candied) or made into a sweet pudding.
- **Yams** – similar to sweet potatoes, usually cylindrical, often knobbly in shape; can be used in the same way as sweet potatoes.

Bulbs

- **Fennel** – the bulb is the swollen leaf base and has a pronounced flavour. Used raw in salads and cooked.
- **Garlic** – an onion-like bulb with a papery skin inside of which are small individually wrapped cloves; used extensively in many forms of cookery; garlic has a pungent distinctive flavour and should be used sparingly.
- **Leeks** – summer leeks have long white stems, bright green leaves and a milder flavour than winter leeks; these have a stockier stem and a stronger flavour; used extensively in stocks, soups, sauces, stews, hors d'oeuvre and as a vegetable.
- **Onions** – there are numerous varieties with different-coloured skins and varying strengths; after salt, the onion is probably the most frequently used flavouring in cookery; can be used in almost every type of food except sweet dishes.
- **Shallots** – have a similar but more refined flavour than the onion and are therefore more often used in top-class cookery.

- **Spring onions** – are slim and tiny, like miniature leeks; used in soups, salads and Chinese and Japanese cookery. Ramp looks like a spring onion but is stronger.

Leafy

- **Chicory** – a lettuce with coarse, crisp leaves and a sharp, bitter taste in the outside leaves; inner leaves are milder.
- **Chinese leaves** – long white, densely packed leaves with a mild flavour resembling celery; make a good substitute for lettuce and can be boiled, braised or stir-fried as a vegetable.
- **Corn salad** – sometimes called lamb's lettuce; small, tender, dark leaves with a tangy nutty taste.
- **Cress** – there are 15 varieties of cress with different flavours, suitable for a large range of foods.
- **Culaboo** are leaves of the tero plant, poisonous if eaten raw, but widely used in Asian and Caribbean cookery.
- **Lettuce** – many varieties including cabbage, cos, little gem, iceberg, oakleaf, Webb's; used chiefly for salads, or used as a wrapping for other foods, e.g. fish fillets.
- **Mustard and cress** – embryonic leaves of mustard and garden cress with a sharp warm flavour; used mainly in, or as a garnish to, sandwiches and salads.
- **Nettles** – once cooked the sting disappears; should be picked young, used in soups.
- **Radicchio** – round, deep-red variety of chicory with white ribs and a distinctive bitter taste.
- **Red salanova** – a neat, tasty lettuce; very suitable for garnish.
- **Rocket** – a type of cress with larger leaves and a peppery taste.

Figure 3.106 Bulbs (left to right: leek, garlic, onion, shallots, spring onions)

Figure 3.107 Leafy vegetables (clockwise from top: cabbage, pak choi, spinach, watercress)

- **Sorrel** – bright-green sour leaves, which can be overpowering if used on their own; best when tender and young; used in salad and soups.
- **Spinach** – tender dark-green leaves with a mild musky flavour; used for soups, garnishing egg and fish dishes, as a vegetable and raw in salads.
- **Swiss chard** – has large, ribbed, slightly curly leaves with a flavour similar to but milder than spinach; used as for spinach.
- **Vine leaves** – all leaves from grape vines can be eaten when young.
- **Watercress** – long stems with round, dark, tender green leaves and a pungent peppery flavour; used for soups, salads, and for garnishing roasts and grills of meat and poultry.

Brassicas

- **Broccoflower** – a cross between broccoli and cauliflower.
- **Broccoli** – various types including calabrese white, green, purple sprouting; delicate vegetable with a gentle flavour used in soups, salads, stir-fry dishes, and cooked and served in many ways as a vegetable. Chinese broccoli is a leafy vegetable with slender heads of flowers.
- **Brussels sprouts** – small green buds growing on thick stems; can be used for soup but are mainly used as a vegetable, and can be cooked and served in a variety of ways.
- **Cabbage** – three main types including green, white and red; many varieties of green cabbage available at different seasons of the year; early green cabbage is deep green and loosely formed; later in the season they firm up, with solid hearts; Savoy is considered the best of the winter green cabbage; white cabbage is used for coleslaw;

green and red as a vegetable, boiled, braised or stir-fried.
- **Cauliflower** – heads of creamy-white florets with a distinctive flavour; used for soup, and cooked and served in various ways as a vegetable.
- **Chinese mustard greens** – deep green and mustard flavoured.
- **Kale and curly kale** – thick green leaves. The curly variety is the more popular.
- **Pak choi** – Chinese cabbage with many varieties.
- **Romanescue** – pretty green or white cross between broccoli and cauliflower.

Pods and seeds

- **Broad beans** – pale-green, oval-shaped beans contained in a thick fleshy pod; young broad beans can be removed from the pods, cooked in their shells and served as a vegetable in various ways; old broad beans will toughen and, when removed from the pods, will have to be shelled before being served.
- **Butter or lima beans** – butter beans are white, large, flattish and oval-shaped; lima beans are smaller; both are used as a vegetable or salad, stew or casserole ingredient.
- **Mangetout** – also called snow peas or sugar peas; flat pea pod with immature seeds that, after topping, tailing and stringing, may be eaten in their entirety; used as a vegetable, in salads and for stir-fry dishes.
- **Okra** – curved and pointed seed pods with a flavour similar to aubergines; cooked as a vegetable or in creole-type stews.
- **Peas** – garden peas are normal size, petits pois are a dwarf variety; marrowfat peas are dried; popular as a vegetable, peas are also used for soups, salads, stews and stir-fry dishes.

Figure 3.108 Brassicas (clockwise from top left: kale, broccoli, cauliflower, Brussels sprouts, kohlrabi)

Figure 3.109 Pods and seeds (clockwise from top left: okra, sweetcorn, runner beans, mangetout, peas, bean sprouts)

- **Runner beans** – popular vegetable that must be used when young; bright-green colour and a pliable velvety feel; if coarse, wilted or older beans are used they will be stringy and tough.
- **Sweetcorn** – also known as maize or Sudan corn; available 'on the cob', fresh or frozen or in kernels, canned or frozen; a versatile commodity and used as a first course, in soups, salads, casseroles and as a vegetable.

Stems and shoots

- **Asparagus** – the three main types are white, with creamy white stems and a mild flavour; French, with violet or bluish tips and a stronger more astringent flavour; and green, with what is considered a delicious aromatic flavour; used on every course of the menu, except the sweet course.
- **Bean sprouts** – slender young sprouts of the germinating soya or mung bean, used as a vegetable accompaniment, in stir-fry dishes and salads.
- **Cardoon** – longish plant with root and fleshy ribbed stalk similar to celery, but leaves are grey-green in colour; used cooked as a vegetable or raw in salads.
- **Celery** – long-stemmed bundles of fleshy, ribbed stalks, white to light green in colour; used in soups, stocks, sauces, cooked as a vegetable and raw in salads and dips.
- **Chicory** – also known as Belgian endive; conical heads of crisp white, faintly bitter leaves used cooked as a vegetable and raw in salads and dips.
- **Fallow wax beans** – similar to French beans.
- **Fiddlecoke fern** – also called ostrich fern; 5 cm long, a bit like asparagus and used in oriental dishes.
- **Globe artichokes** – resemble fat pine cones with overlapping fleshy, green, inedible leaves, all connected to an edible fleshy base or bottom; used as a first course, hot or cold; as a vegetable, boiled, stuffed, baked, fried or in casseroles.
- **Kohlrabi** – stem that swells to turnip shape above the ground; those about the size of a large egg are best for cookery purposes (other than soup or purées); may be cooked as a vegetable, stuffed and baked and added to stews and casseroles.
- **Palm hearts** – the buds of cabbage palm trees.
- **Samphire** – the two types are marsh samphire, which grows in estuaries and salt marshes, and white rock samphire (sometimes called sea fennel), which grows on rocky shores. Marsh samphire is also known as glass wort and sometimes sea asparagus.

Figure 3.110 Stems and shoots (left to right: globe artichoke, celery, fennel)

Figure 3.111 Fruiting vegetables (clockwise from top left: avocado, Italian aubergine, red pepper, yellow pepper, tomatoes)

- **Sea kale** – delicate white leaves with yellow frills edged with purple; can be boiled or braised, or served raw like celery.
- **Thai beans** – similar to French beans.
- **Water chestnuts** – common name for a number of aquatic herbs and their nut-like fruit; the best-known type is the Chinese water chestnut, sometimes known as the Chinese sedge.

Fruiting

- **Aubergine** – firm, elongated, varying in size with smooth shiny skins ranging in colour from purple-red to purple-black; inner flesh is white with tiny soft seeds; almost without flavour, it requires other seasonings, e.g. garlic, lemon juice, herbs, to enhance its taste; may be sliced and fried or baked, steamed or stuffed. Varieties include baby, Japanese, white, striped, Thai.
- **Avocado** – fruit that is mainly used as a vegetable because of its bland, mild, nutty flavour; two main types are the summer variety, which is

green when unripe and purple-black when ripe, with golden-yellow flesh; the winter ones are more pear-shaped with smooth green skin and pale green to yellow flesh; eaten as first courses and used in soups, salads, dips and as garnishes to other dishes, hot and cold.

- **Courgette** – baby marrow, yellow or light to dark green in colour, with a delicate flavour becoming stronger when cooked with other ingredients, e.g. herbs, garlic, spices; may be boiled, steamed, fried, baked, stuffed and stir-fried.
- **Cucumber** – a long, smooth-skinned fruiting vegetable, ridged and dark green in colour; used in salads, soups, sandwiches, garnishes and as a vegetable.
- **Gourds (exotic)** – include bottle gourds, chayotes (chow-chow), Chinese butter lemons.
- **Marrow** – long, oval-shaped edible gourds with ridged green skins and a bland flavour; may be cooked as for courgettes.
- **Peppers** – available in three colours, green peppers are unripened and they turn yellow to orange and then red (they must remain on the plant to do this); used raw and cooked in salads, vegetable dishes, stuffed and baked, casseroles and stir-fry dishes.
- **Pumpkins** – vary in size and can weigh up to 50 kg; associated with Halloween as a decoration but may be used in soups or pumpkin pie.
- **Squash** – many varieties e.g. acorn, butternut, summer crookneck, delicate, hubbond, kuboche, onion. Flesh firm and glowing; can be boiled, baked, steamed or puréed.

Figure 3.112 Mushrooms and fungi (clockwise from top left: girolles, chestnut, pieds du moutons, flat, button, chanterelle, shiitake)

- **Tomatoes** – along with onions, probably the most frequently used 'vegetable' in cookery; several varieties, including cherry, yellow, globe, large ridged (beef) and plum; used in soups, sauces, stews, salads, sandwiches and as a vegetable. Tomatoes are also sundried or semi-dried (sunblush) – these are now an important culinary ingredient.

Plantains

- **Ackee** – tropical fruit used in Caribbean-style savoury dishes.
- **Breadfruit** – fruit from a tropical tree found in the Islands of the South Pacific Ocean.

Mushrooms and fungi

All mushrooms, both wild and cultivated, have a great many uses in cookery, in soups, stocks, salads, vegetables, savouries and garnishes. Wild mushrooms are also available in dried form.

- **Mushrooms** – field mushrooms found in meadows from late summer to autumn; creamy white cap and stalk and a strong earthy flavour.
- **Cultivated mushrooms** – available in three types: button (small, succulent, weak in flavour), cap and open or flat mushrooms.
- **Ceps** – wild mushrooms with short, stout stalks with slightly raised veins and tubes underneath the cap in which the brown spores are produced.
- **Chanterelles or girolles** – wild, funnel-shaped, yellow-capped mushrooms with a slightly ribbed stalk that runs up under the edge of the cap.
- **Horns of plenty** – trumpet-shaped, shaggy, almost black wild mushrooms.
- **Morels** – delicate, wild mushrooms varying in colour from pale beige to dark brown-black with a flavour that suggests meat.
- **Oyster mushrooms** – creamy gills and firm flesh; delicate with shorter storage life than regular mushrooms.
- **Shiitake mushrooms** – solid texture with a strong, slightly meaty flavour.
- **Truffles** – black (French) and white (Italian) are rare, expensive but highly esteemed for the unique flavour they can give to so many dishes; black truffles from France are sold fresh, canned or bottled; white truffles from Italy are never cooked, but grated or finely sliced over certain foods (e.g. pasta, risotto).

Table 3.4 Seasons for home-grown vegetables

Spring		
Asparagus Cauliflower Cabbage Potatoes	Broccoli – white and purple New carrots	New turnips New potatoes Greens
Summer		
Artichokes, globe Turnips Asparagus Cauliflower Aubergine	Cos lettuce Beans, broad Peas Radishes Beans, French	Carrots Sea kale Sweetcorn
Autumn		
Artichokes, globe Parsnips Field mushrooms Artichokes, Jerusalem Aubergine Peppers	Beans, runner Cauliflower Red cabbage Broccoli Celery Shallots	Salsify Swedes Marrow Celeriac Turnips
Winter		
Brussels sprouts Chicory Cabbage Kale Celery	Parsnips Cauliflower Broccoli Red cabbage Savoy cabbage	Celeriac Swedes Turnips
All year round Although the following vegetables are available all year round, nevertheless at certain times – owing to bad weather, heavy demand or other circumstances – supplies may be temporarily curtailed. However, owing to air transport, most vegetables are now available all year round.		
Beetroot Tomatoes Spinach Onions	Mushrooms Leeks Watercress Lettuce	Cucumber Carrots

Fruit

For culinary purposes fruit can be divided into various groups: stone fruits, hard fruits, soft fruits, citrus fruits, tropical fruits and melons.

Food value

The nutritive value of fruit depends on its vitamin content, especially vitamin C; it is therefore valuable as a protective food. The cellulose in fruit is useful as fibre.

Storage

- Hard fruits, such as apples, are left in boxes and kept in a cool store.
- Soft fruits, such as raspberries and strawberries,

should be left in their punnets or baskets and refrigerated
- Stone fruits are best placed in trays so that any damaged fruit can be seen and discarded.
- Peaches and citrus fruits are left in their delivery trays or boxes, and can be refrigerated.
- Bananas should not be stored in too cold a place because the skins will turn black.

Quality and purchasing points

Soft fruits deteriorate quickly, especially if not sound. Care must be taken to see that they are not damaged or too ripe when bought. They should appear fresh; there should be no shrinking, wilting or signs of mould. The colour of certain soft fruits is an indication of ripeness (e.g. strawberries, dessert gooseberries).

Hard fruits should not be bruised. Pears should not be overripe.

Preservation

- **Drying** – apples, pears, apricots, dates, peaches, bananas and figs are dried; plums when dried are called prunes, and currants, sultanas and raisins are produced by drying grapes.
- **Canning** – almost all fruits may be canned; apples are packed in water and known as solid packed apples; other fruits are canned in syrup.
- **Bottling** – fruit is commercially preserved in this way; cherries are bottled in maraschino.
- **Candied, glacé and crystallised fruits** are mainly imported from France.
- **Jam** – some stone fruits and all soft fruits can be used.
- **Jelly** – jellies are produced from fruit juice.
- **Quick freezing** – strawberries, raspberries, loganberries, apples, blackberries, gooseberries, grapefruit and plums are frozen and must be kept below −18°C.
- **Cold storage** – apples are stored at temperatures of between 1–4°C, depending on the variety of apple.
- **Gas storage** – fruit can be kept in a sealed storeroom where the atmosphere is controlled; the amount of air is limited, the oxygen content of the air is decreased and the carbon dioxide increased, which controls the respiration rate of the fruit.

Fruit juices, syrups and drinks

Fruit juices such as orange, lemon and blackcurrant are canned. Syrups such as rosehip and orange are bottled. Fruit drinks are also bottled; they include orange, lime and lemon.

Uses

With the exception of certain fruits (lemon, rhubarb, cranberries) fruit can be eaten as a dessert or in its raw state. Some fruits have dessert and cooking varieties (e.g. apples, pears, cherries and gooseberries).

Stone fruits

Damsons, plums, greengages, cherries, apricots, peaches and nectarines are used as a dessert; stewed (compote) for jam, pies, puddings and in vari-

ous sweet dishes and some meat and poultry dishes. Peaches are also used to garnish certain meat dishes. Varieties of plums include Dessert, Victoria, Gamota, Mayoris, Burbank; for cooking, Angelina, Stanley, Beech Cherry and Reeves Seedling.

Figure 3.113 Stone fruits (clockwise from top: mango, plums, nectarines, dates)

Hard fruits

The popular English dessert apple varieties include Beauty of Bath, Discovery, Spartan, Worcester Pearmain, Cox's Orange Pippin, Blenheim Orange, Pink Lady, Laxton's Superb and James Grieve; imported apples include Golden Delicious, Braeburn and Gala. The Bramley is the most popular cooking apple. The William, Conference and Doyenne du Comice are among the best-known pears. Other varieties of Pear include: Anjou, Beurre-Beth, Beurre-Bose, Beurre-Hardi, Beurre-Supersin, Forelle, Morton Poirde, Onwaide, Rocha, Housi and Perry Tieatsin.

Apples and pears are used in many pastry dishes. Apples are also used for garnishing meat dishes and for sauce served with roast pork and duck.

Figure 3.114 Hard fruits (clockwise from top left: Comice pears, quinces, William pears, Braeburn apples, crab apples, Red Delicious apples)

Soft fruits

Raspberries, strawberries, loganberries and gooseberries are used as a dessert. Gooseberries, blackcurrants, redcurrants and blackberries are stewed,

Table 3.5 Different fruits and their seasons*

Fruit	Season	Fruit	Season
Apple	All year round	Greengage	August
Apricot	May to September	Lemon	All year round
Avocado pear	All year round	Mandarin	November to June
Banana	All year round	Melon	All year round
Blackberry	September to October	Orange	All year round
Blackcurrants	July to September	Peach	September
Cherry	June to August	Pear	September to March
Clementine	Winter	Pineapple	All year round
Cranberries	November to January	Plum	July to October
Damson	September to October	Raspberry	June to August
Date	Winter	Redcurrants	July to September
Fig	July to September	Rhubarb	December to June
Gooseberry	July to September	Strawberry	June to August
Grapefruit	All year round	Tangerine	Winter
Grapes	All year round		

*Modern transportation and storage methods mean that imported fruits may be available all year.

Figure 3.115 Soft fruits (clockwise from top: redcurrants, raspberries, blackberries, strawberries)

Figure 3.116 Citrus fruits (clockwise from top left: pink grapefruit, orange, lemons, limes, satsuma, white grapefruit)

used in pies and puddings. They are used for jam and flavourings, and in certain sauces for sweet, meat and poultry dishes. Other varieties of soft fruit include: dewberries, jam berries, young berries, boysenberries, sunberries, wineberries, blueberries and elderberries. Varieties of gooseberries include: Leveller, London and Golden Drop.

Citrus fruits

Oranges, lemons, limes and grapefruit are not usually cooked, except for use in marmalade. Lemons and limes are used for flavouring and garnishing, particularly fish dishes. Oranges are used mainly for flavouring and in fruit salads, also to garnish certain poultry dishes. Grapefruit are served at breakfast and as a first course generally for luncheon. Mandarins, clementines and satsumas are eaten as a dessert or used in sweet dishes. Kumquats look and taste like tiny oranges and are eaten with the skin on. Tangelos are a cross between tangerines and grapefruit, and are sometimes called uglis. Pomelos are the largest of the citrus fruits, predominantly round but with a slightly flattened base and pointed top.

Tropical and other fruits

- **Banana** – as well as being used as a dessert, bananas are grilled for a fish garnish, fried as fritters and served as a garnish to poultry (Maryland); they are used in fruit salad and other sweet dishes.
- **Bubaco** – hybrid of the papaya.
- **Cape gooseberry** – a sharp, pleasant-flavoured small round fruit, sometimes dipped in fondant and served as a type of petit four.

- **Carambola** – also known as starfruit, has a yellowish-green skin with a waxy sheen; the fruit is long and narrow and has a delicate lemon flavour.
- **Cranberry** – these hard red berries are used for cranberry sauce, which is served with roast turkey. Cranberry juice is also very popular.
- **Curuba** – also known as banana passion fruit; soft yellowish skin.
- **Custard apple** – heart-shaped or oval light tan or greenish quilted skin; soursops (prickly custard apples) have dark-green skins covered in short spines.
- **Date** – whole dates are served as a dessert; stoned dates are used in various sweet dishes and petits fours.
- **Dragon fruit** – yellow or pink; pink are large, about 10 cm long and covered with pointed green-tipped scales.
- **Durian** – large fruit that can weigh up to 4.5 kg; round or oval, have a woolly olive-green outer layer covered with stubby, sharp pikes, which turn yellow as they ripen; contains creamy white flesh with the texture of rich custard.
- **Feijon** – member of the guava family, resembles small slightly pear-shaped passion fruit, with a dark-green skin that yellows as the fruit ripens.
- **Fig** – fresh figs may be served as a first course or dessert; dried figs may be used for fig puddings and other sweet dishes.
- **Granadilla** – largest members of the passion fruit family; like an orange in shape and colour, light in weight and similar to a passion fruit in flavour.
- **Grape** – black and white grapes are used as a dessert, in fruit salad, as a sweetmeat and also as a fish garnish.
- **Guava** – vary in size between that of a walnut to that of an apple; ripe guavas have a sweet pink flesh and can be eaten with cream or mixed with other fruits.
- **Jackfruit** – related to breadfruit; the large, irregularly shaped oval fruits can weigh up to 20 kg; they have a rough spiny skin, which ripens from green to brown.
- **Jujube** – also known as Chinese jujubes, apples or dates; small greeny-brown fruit.
- **Kiwano** – also known as horned melon, horned cucumber or jelly melon; the oval fruits have thick, bright golden-orange skin covered with sharp spikes. The skin conceals a bright green, jelly-like flesh, encasing edible seeds, rather like a passion fruit.

- **Kiwi fruit** – have a brown furry skin; the flesh is green with edible black seeds that, when thinly sliced, gives a pleasant decorative appearance.
- **Loquat** – native to China and South Japan, also known as Japanese medlar. They have a sweet scent and a delicate mango-like flavour.
- **Lychee** – a Chinese fruit with a delicate flavour, obtainable tinned in syrup and also fresh.
- **Mango** – can be as large as a melon or as small as an apple; ripe mangoes have smooth pinky-golden flesh with a pleasing flavour; they may be served in halves sprinkled with lemon juice, sugar, rum or ginger; mangoes can also be used in fruit desserts and for sorbets.
- **Mangostine** – apple-shaped with tough reddish-brown skin, which turns purple as the fruit ripens; they have juicy creamy flesh.
- **Maracoya** – also known as yellow passion fruit. Vibrant green with a thick shiny skin, which turns yellow as it ripens. Inside orange pulp enclosing hard grey seeds.
- **Passion fruit** – the name comes from the flower of the plant, which is meant to represent the Passion of Christ; size and shape of an egg with crinkled purple-brown skin when ripe; flesh and seeds are all edible. Has many uses in pastry work.
- **Pawpaw (papaya)** – green to golden skin, orangey flesh with a sweet subtle flavour and black seeds; eaten raw sprinkled with lime or lemon juice. Served with crab or prawns and mayonnaise as a first course.
- **Pepino** – smooth golden skin heavily streaked with purple, sometimes called a tree melon. Native to Peru.
- **Persimmon** – a round orange-red fruit with a tough skin, which can be cut when the fruit is

Figure 3.117 Tropical fruits (clockwise from top left: pineapple, papaya, coconut, kiwis, passion fruit)

ripe; when under-ripe they have an unpleasant acid-like taste of tannin.

- **Pineapple** – served as a dessert; also used in many sweet dishes and as a garnish to certain meat dishes.
- **Pomegranate** – apple-shaped fruit with leathery reddish-brown skin, and a large calyx or crown. Inside is a mass of creamy-white edible seeds, each encased in a tiny translucent juice sac.
- **Prickly pear** – also known as 'Indian fig'. Fruit of the cactus. Skin is covered in prickles. Greenish-orange skin and orangey-pink flesh with a melon-like texture.
- **Rambutan** – related to the lychee, sometimes known as hairy lychees.
- **Rhubarb** – forced or early rhubarb is obtainable from January; natural rhubarb from April to June; used for pies, puddings, fools and compotes.
- **Sapodilla** – oval fruit from central America. Light brown skin, the flesh is sweet, with inedible hard black pips.
- **Sharon fruit** – a seedless persimmon tasting like a sweet exotic peach.
- **Snake fruit** – large member of the lychee family, the creamy flesh is divided into four segments each encasing a very large inedible brown stone.
- **Tamarillo** – known as the 'tree tomato', large egg-shaped fruits with thick, smooth wine-red skins. Each fruit has two lobes containing a multitude of black seeds.
- **Tamarind** – red, egg-shaped, flavour a mix of tomato, apricot and coconut, used in sweet dishes and salads.

For further information, visit the website of the Fresh Produce Consortium (www.freshproduce.org.uk).

Melons

There are several types of melon. The most popular are listed below.

- **Honeydew** – long, oval-shaped melons with dark green or yellow skins; the flesh is white with a greenish tinge.
- **Charentais** – small and round with a mottled green and yellow skin; the flesh is orange coloured.
- **Cantaloupe** – large round melons with regular indentations; the rough skin is mottled orange and yellow and the flesh is light orange in colour.
- **Ogen** – small round mottled green skins, each suitable for one portion (depending on size); mainly used as a dessert, hors d'oeuvre or in sweet dishes.

Figure 3.118 Melons (clockwise from top: watermelon, cantaloupe, honeydew, ogen)

Care must be taken when buying as melons should not be over- or under-ripe. This can be assessed by carefully pressing the top or bottom of the fruit and smelling the outside skin for sweetness. There should be a slight degree of softness to the cantaloupe and charentais melons. The stalk should be attached, otherwise the melon deteriorates quickly.

Nuts

Nuts are the reproductive kernel (seed) of the plant or tree from which they come. Nuts are perishable and may easily become rancid or infested with insects. Some people have an allergy to nuts, which can cause severe illness and possibly death.

Season

Dessert nuts are in season during the autumn and winter.

Food value

Nuts are highly nutritious because of their protein, fat and mineral salts. They are of considerable importance to vegetarians, who may use nuts in place of meat; they are therefore a food that builds, repairs and provides energy. Nuts are difficult to digest.

Storage

Dessert nuts, those with the shell on, are kept in a dry, ventilated store. Nuts without shells, whether ground, nibbed, flaked or whole, are kept in airtight containers.

Quality and purchasing points

Nuts should be of good size. They should be heavy for their size. There must be no sign of mildew.

Uses

Nuts are used extensively in pastry and confectionery work and vegetarian cookery, and also for decorating and flavouring. They are used whole or halved, and almonds are used ground, nibbed and flaked.

Types

- **Almonds:** Salted almonds are served at cocktail parties and in bars. Ground, flaked or nibbed almonds are used in sweet dishes and for decorating cakes.
  Marzipan (almond paste) has many uses in pastry work.
- **Brazil nuts:** Brazil nuts are served with fresh fruit as dessert and are also used in confectionery.
- **Chestnuts:** Chestnuts are used in certain stews, with vegetables (e.g. Brussels sprouts) and as stuffing for turkey. Chestnut flour is used for soup, and as a garnish for ice cream. Chestnut purée is used in pastries and gâteaux. Chestnuts are also available dried.
- **Coconut:** Coconut is used in desiccated form for curry preparations, and in many types of cakes and confectionery. Coconut cream and milk are also made and used in West Indian, Malaysian and Thai cookery.
- **Cob or hazel nuts:** These nuts are used as a dessert and in praline. Chopped or ground, they have many uses in pastry work.
- **Macadamia nuts:** These expensive nuts have a rich, delicate, sweetish flavour. They can be used in pasta dishes, savoury sauces for meat, game and poultry, and in ice cream, sorbets and puddings.
- **Pecans:** Pecan nuts are usually roasted and may be salted. Also used for desserts, various sweets and ice cream.
- **Peanuts and cashew nuts:** These may be salted and used as bar snacks. Also used in some stir-fry dishes. Peanuts are also used for oil and peanut butter.
- **Pine nuts:** Seeds of the stone pine, a native of the Mediterranean region. An important ingredient in pesto sauce.
- **Pistachios:** These small green nuts, grown mainly in France and Italy, are used for decorating galantines, small and large cakes and petits fours. They are also used in ice cream.
- **Walnuts:** Walnuts, imported mainly from France and Italy, are used as a dessert, in salads and for decorating cakes and sweet dishes. They are also pickled while green and unripe, and used for making oil.

 # Eggs

The term egg applies not only to those of the hen, but also to the edible eggs of other birds, such as turkeys, geese, ducks, guinea fowl, quails and gulls. Around 26 million hens' eggs are consumed each day in the UK and approximately 85 per cent of these are produced in the UK.

The British Egg Industry Council set up the British Egg Information Service in 1986. The British Egg Products Association (BEPA) introduced a strict Code of Practice in 1993, which covers all stages of production, from the sourcing of raw materials to packaging and finished production standards. Members of the BEPA can qualify to show a date stamp on their products, which signifies that the products have been produced to standards higher than those demanded by UK and European law. The aim of the date stamp is to reduce the risk of infection in hens, to monitor and take remedial action where necessary, and to ensure that eggs are held and distributed under the best conditions.

Food value

Eggs contain most nutrients and are low in calories: two large eggs contain 180 calories. Egg protein is complete and easily digestible, therefore it is useful for balancing meals. Eggs may also be used as a main dish; they are a protective food and provide energy and material for growth and repair of the body.

Production

Hens' eggs are graded in four sizes:

1 small − 53 g or under
2 medium − 53−63 g
3 large − 63−73 g
4 very large − 73 g and over.

The size of an egg does not affect the quality but does affect the price. The eggs are tested for quality, then weighed and graded. Under European law there are two classes of egg quality, A and B.

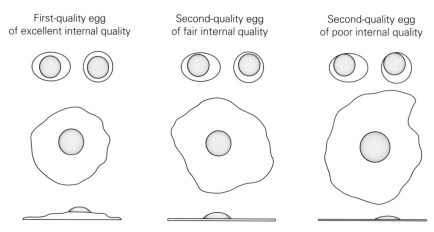

Figure 3.119 The quality of eggs

- Grade A – naturally clean, fresh eggs, internally perfect with intact shells and an air cell not exceeding 6 mm in depth; the yolk must not move away from the centre of the egg when it is rotated.
- Grade B – eggs of Grade B quality are broken out and pasteurised.

They are then packed into boxes. All egg boxes leaving the packing station are dated. Always buy eggs from a reputable retailer where they will have been transported and stored at the correct temperature (below 20°C).

All Class A eggs have to be marked with a code showing the country of origin and the farm or unit where they were produced. The code also includes a number to indicate the farming method used: 0 means organic, 1 free range, 2 barn and 3 cage. British eggs may also bear the Lion logo, a quality mark showing that the eggs were produced to the highest standards of food safety in the world: the hens are vaccinated against salmonella and the eggs are produced to a strict code of practice. Lion eggs also have a best-before date on the shell.

Raw eggs and salmonella

In a number of salmonella food poisoning cases, raw eggs have been suspected as being the cause. Most infections cause only mild stomach upsets but the effects can be serious in vulnerable people such as the elderly, the infirm, pregnant women and young children. Consumers, particularly the more vulnerable, are advised to avoid eating raw and lightly cooked eggs, uncooked foods made from raw eggs, and products such as mayonnaise, mousses and ice creams. Caterers are advised to use pasteurised eggs. Dishes with an obvious risk of passing on con-

tamination also include soft-boiled eggs, scrambled eggs and omelettes. The Department of Health has issued the following guidelines, which apply to raw eggs.

- Grade B eggs are always broken out and pasteurised.
- Look for the Lion quality mark on the egg shell and egg box – it shows that the eggs have been produced to the highest standards of food safety in the world, including a programme of vaccination against salmonella enteritidis.
- There does not appear to be a similar risk with eggs that are cooked thoroughly.
- Eggs should be stored in a cool dry place, preferably under refrigeration.
- Eggs should be stored away from possible contaminants such as raw meat.
- Stocks should be rotated: first in, first out.
- Hands should be washed before and after handling eggs.
- Cracked eggs should not be used.
- Preparation surfaces, utensils and containers should be cleaned regularly and always cleaned between the preparation of different dishes.
- Egg dishes should be consumed as soon as possible after preparation or, if not for immediate use, refrigerated.

Egg products

Most egg products are available in liquid, frozen or spray-dried form. Whole egg is used primarily for cake production, where its foaming and coagulation properties are required. Egg whites are used for meringues and light sponges where their foaming property is crucial.

Table 3.6 Composition of eggs (approximate percentages)

	Whole egg	White	Yolk
Water	73	87	47
Protein	12	10	15
Fat	11		33
Minerals	1	0.5	2
Vitamins			

Table 3.7 Uses of egg products

Pasteurised whole egg*†‡	Hard-boiled eggs*
Salted whole egg*†	Pickled eggs
Sugared whole egg*†‡	Chopped hard-boiled egg with mayonnaise*
Pasteurised yolk*†‡	Scrambled egg*†
Salted yolk*†	Omelettes†
Sugared yolk*†‡	Egg custard blend*‡
Pasteurised albumen*†‡	Quiche blend*†
Sugared albumen*	Egg/milk blends*†‡
Egg granules†	

* Chilled † Frozen ‡ Dried

For further information on eggs, visit: www.egginfo.co.uk.

Other types of eggs

Turkeys' and guinea fowls' eggs may be used in place of hens' eggs. The eggs of the goose or duck may be used only if they are thoroughly cooked. Quails' eggs are used in some establishments as a garnish, or as an hors d'oeuvre.

Availability

Table 3.7 shows the many egg products carrying the date stamp (see above) that are currently available. If you would like something a little different, it's worth talking to your supplier as he may be able to tailor the product to meet your specific needs.

Dairy products

Milk

Milk is a white, nutritious liquid produced by female mammals for feeding their young. The milk most used in this country is that obtained from cows. Goats' milk and ewes' milk can also be used.

Food value

Milk can make a valuable contribution to our daily eating pattern and can help to meet our nutritional needs as part of a balanced, varied diet. Milk is one of the most nutritionally complete foods available, containing a wide range of nutrients, which are essential for the proper functioning of the body. In particular, milk is a good source of protein, calcium and B group vitamins, and whole milk is a good source of vitamin A.

Storage

Milk is a perishable product and therefore must be stored with care. It will keep for four to five days in refrigerated conditions. Milk can easily be contaminated and therefore stringent precautions are taken to ensure a safe and good-quality product for the consumer.

Unless milk is supplied directly from the farm, it will be heat-treated in one of the ways described below. Heat treatment will bring any bacteria present down to a safe level or destroy them altogether.

- Fresh milk should be kept in the container in which it is delivered.
- Milk must be stored in the refrigerator (four to five days).
- Milk should be kept covered as it easily absorbs smells from other foods, such as onion and fish.
- Fresh milk should be ordered daily.
- Tinned milk should be stored in cool, dry, ventilated rooms.
- Dried milk is packaged in airtight tins and should be kept in a dry store.
- Sterilised milk will keep for two to three months if unopened, but once opened must be treated in the same way as pasteurised milk.
- UHT (ultra-heat-treated) milk will keep unrefrigerated for several months. Before using, always check the date stamp, which expires six months after processing, and make sure to rotate

stocks. Once opened it must be refrigerated and will keep for four to five days.

Packaging

Bulk fresh milk can be supplied in a variety of types of packaging. These come in the form of a plastic bag-in-box, which holds a capacity of between 12 and 20 litres. This should be placed in the appropriate refrigerated unit and the contents can be drawn off as required by fitting the correct tap device.

All packs contain fresh pasteurised homogenised milk and can be obtained in either whole, semi-skimmed or skimmed varieties.

Other types of packaging include:

- polybottles (large plastic bottles) of fresh milk available in 1-litre, 2-litre and 3-litre sizes
- cartons of fresh milk available in 0.5-litre and 1-litre sizes.

All the above milks are homogenised, and available whole, semi-skimmed or skimmed. Channel Island milk from the Jersey and Guernsey breeds of cow usually has a higher fat content than whole milk; it is often non-homogenised.

Milk heat treatment and types of milk

Milk is heat-treated in one of several ways to kill any harmful bacteria that may be present.

- Approximately 99 per cent of milk sold in the UK is **heat-treated**.
- **Pasteurised milk** – the milk is heated to a temperature of at least 71.7°C for 15 seconds and then cooled quickly to less than 10°C and refrigerated.
- **UHT (ultra-heat-treated) milk** – milk is homogenised (see below) and then heated to a temperature of at least 135°C for 1 second; the milk is then packed under sterile conditions.
- **Sterilised milk** – milk is pre-heated to 50°C, separated and standardised to produce whole, semi-skimmed or skimmed milk. Filled bottles are then passed through a steam pressure chamber at temperatures of between 110°C and 130°C for 10–30 minutes, and then cooled in a cold water tank.
- **Homogenised milk** – milk is forced through a fine aperture that breaks up the fat globules to an even size so that they stay evenly distributed throughout the milk and therefore do not form a cream line.
- **Whole milk** – comes pasteurised and homogenised, and has a fat content of an average 3.9 per cent.
- **Semi-skimmed milk** – comes homogenised and pasteurised and has a fat content of between 1.5 and 1.8 per cent.
- **Skimmed milk** – comes homogenised and pasteurised, and contains just 0.1 per cent fat.
- **Organic milk** – milk that comes from cows grazing on pastures with no chemical fertilisers, pesticides or agrochemicals, meeting the strict requirements of the Soil Association.
- **Channel Islands milk** – milk that comes from the Jersey and Guernsey breeds of cow, and has a particularly rich and creamy taste. It is not usually homogenised and has a distinct cream line; it contains, on average, 5.1 per cent fat.
- **Evaporated milk** – a concentrated sterilised product with a final concentration about twice that of the original milk.
- **Condensed milk** – concentrated in the same way as evaporated milk but with the addition of sugar; this product is not sterilised but is preserved by the high concentration of sugar it contains.
- **Dried milk powder** – milk produced by the evaporation of water from the milk by heat, or other means, to produce solids containing 5 per cent or less moisture; available as a whole or skimmed product; dried milk is skimmed milk powder to which vegetable fat has been added.
- **Soya milk** – can be offered as an alternative to vegans and people with intolerance to cows' milk.
- **Goats' milk** – nutritionally similar to cows' milk and can be useful for people with lactose intolerance.
- **Rice milk** – an alternative to dairy milk for vegans and those with an intolerance to lactose. It is heat stable, which makes it a good replacement for cows' milk in cooking although it tends to have a sweeter taste.
- **Coconut milk** – is high in saturated fats. It can be served as a drink but is more often used as an ingredient and a base for sauces.

Uses of milk

Milk is used in:

- soups and sauces
- the making of puddings, cakes and sweet dishes
- the cooking of fish and vegetables
- hot and cold drinks.

Cream

Cream is the lighter-weight portion of milk, which still contains all the main constituents of milk but in different proportions. The fat content of cream is higher than that of milk, and the water content and other constituents are lower. Cream is separated from the milk and heat treated. Cream is that part of cows' milk rich in fat that has been separated from the milk.

Other creams available include:

- extra thick double cream (48 per cent) homogenised and pasteurised – will not whip
- spooning cream or extra thick textured cream (30 per cent)
- frozen cream (single, whipping or double)
- aerosol cream – heat-treated by UHT method to give a highly aerated cream
- soured cream (18 per cent) cream soured by addition of a 'starter'
- crème fraîche – is a similar product with a higher fat content.

Table 3.8 Types of cream and their fat content

	Minimum butterfat content per cent by weight
Clotted cream	55
Double cream	48
Whipping cream	35
Whipped cream	35
Sterilised cream	23
Cream or single cream	18
Sterilised half cream	12
Half cream	12

Whipping of cream

For cream to be whipped it must have fat content of 38–42 per cent. If the fat content is too low there will not be enough fat to enclose the air bubbles and form the foam. Conversely, if the fat content is too high, the fat globules come into contact too easily, move against each other and form butter granules before the air can be incorporated to form the foam.

The addition of stabilisers to cream prevents seepage (particularly important when cream is used in flour confectionery). Cream substitutes are, in the main, based on vegetable fats or oils, which are emulsified in water with other permitted substances.

Storage

- Fresh cream should be kept in the container in which it is delivered.
- Fresh cream must be stored in the refrigerator until required.
- Cream should be kept covered as it easily absorbs smells from other foods, such as onion and fish.
- Fresh cream should be ordered daily.
- Tinned cream should be stored in cool, dry, ventilated rooms, and refrigerated after opening.
- Frozen cream should be thawed only as required and not refrozen.
- Artificial cream should be kept in the refrigerator.

Ice cream and other frozen dairy products

Ice cream is made by churning (stirring), while freezing, a pasteurised mix of one or more dairy ingredients – milk, concentrated fat-free milk, cream, condensed milk – sweetening agents, flavourings, stabilisers, emulsifiers, and optional egg or egg yolk solids or other ingredients.

Frozen custard (French ice cream, French custard ice cream) is similar to ice cream but contains a higher content of egg yolk solids.

Reduced-fat ice cream, low-fat ice cream, light (lite) ice cream and fat-free ice cream all contain less fat per serving.

Sherbet contains 1 to 2 per cent milk fat and 2 to 5 per cent total milk solids. Water, flavouring (e.g. fruit, chocolate, spices), sweetener and stabilisers are added. Sherbet has more sugar than ice cream.

Frozen yoghurt is made by freezing a mixture of pasteurised milk, with or without other milk products, flavourings, seasonings, stabilisers, emulsifiers and lactic acid cultures.

Nutritional information

Ice cream and frozen yoghurt can be nutritious foods providing high-quality protein, riboflavin (B2), calcium and other essential vitamins and minerals, The calorie and fat contents of these dairy foods vary depending on the type of milk used and the addition of cream, egg yolk solids or sweetening agents.

For further information, contact the Ice Cream Alliance – Tel: 01332 203333, Email: info@ice-cream.org.

Yoghurt

Yoghurt is a cultured milk product made from cows', ewes', goats' or buffalo milk. Differences in the taste and texture of the product depend on the type of milk used and the activity of the micro-organisms involved. A bacterial 'starter culture' is added to the milk, which causes the natural sugar 'lactose' to ferment and produce lactic acid. There are three types of yoghurt:

1 stirred yoghurt, which has a smooth fluid consistency
2 set yoghurt, which is more solid and has a firmer texture
3 Greek-style yoghurt, a smooth yoghurt that has been stirred to remove some of the water content, resulting in a thick, heavy yoghurt.

All yoghurt is 'live' and contains live bacteria that remain dormant when kept at low temperatures, unless it clearly states on the packaging that it has been pasteurised, sterilised or ultra-heat-treated. If stored at room temperature or above, the dormant bacteria become active again and produce more acid. Too high an acidity kills the bacteria, impairs the flavour and causes the yoghurt to separate. Yoghurt will keep refrigerated for 14 days.

To find out more, visit the Dairy Council's website at: www.milk.co.uk.

Yoghurt is available plain (natural) or in a wide variety of flavours; it often has pieces of fruit added during manufacture. Yoghurt beverages are available in a variety of flavours.

Food value

Yoghurt is rich in nutrients containing protein and a range of vitamins and minerals. It is particularly useful as a source of calcium.

Other fermented milk products

- **Cultured buttermilk** – this product is made from skimmed milk with a culture added to give it a slightly thickened consistency and a sharp taste; it contains less than 0.5 per cent fat and should be kept refrigerated.
- **Smetana** – this is a cultured product containing 10 per cent fat; it has a slightly sharp flavour and can be served chilled as a drink or used as an alternative to soured cream in recipes.

Table 3.9 The fat content of yoghurt

	% fat content per 150 g pot
Very low fat – plain (natural)/fruit	0.3
Low fat – plain (natural)/fruit	1.1–1.2
Whole milk/creamy	4.2
Greek, Greek style	13.7, 2 or 0
Bio or BA	percentage fat content as for very low fat, low fat and whole milk yoghurts

Cheese, fats and oils

Cheese

Cheese is made from milk protein coagulated by an enzyme such as rennet (an animal product). For vegetarian cheese a non-animal enzyme is used.

Cheese is made worldwide from cows', ewes' or goats' milk; it takes approximately 5 litres of milk to produce 0.5 kg of cheese.

There are many hundreds of varieties, and most countries manufacture their own special cheeses.

Quality

The skin or rind of cheese should not show spots of mildew, as this is a sign of damp storage. Cheese, when cut, should not give off an over-strong smell or any indication of ammonia. Hard, semi-hard and blue-vein cheese, when cut, should not be dry. Soft cheese, when cut, should not appear runny, but should have a delicate creamy consistency.

Hygiene

Cheese is a living product and should be handled carefully. It should always be wrapped in greaseproof or waxed paper or foil, or put in a closed container. Cheese stored in a refrigerator should have plenty of air circulating around it.

Natural rind can be exposed to air, so it can breathe, but cut surfaces should be covered with film to prevent drying out. Mould-ripened cheeses should be

Figure 3.120 Some cheeses

separated from other cheeses. Remove cheese from the refrigerator about an hour before serving to allow it to return to room temperature.

Recent scares about food poisoning included soft unpasteurised cheeses – this is because listeria can grow and multiply at a lower temperature than most bacteria; at 10°C or warmer, growth is rapid.

Storage

All cheese should be kept in a cool, dry, well-ventilated store and whole cheeses should be turned occasionally if being kept for any length of time. Cheese should be kept away from other foods that may be spoilt by the smell.

Food value

Cheese is a highly concentrated form of food. Fat, protein, mineral salts and vitamins are all present. Therefore it is an excellent body-building, energy-producing, protective food.

Preservation

Certain cheeses may be further preserved by processing. A hard cheese is usually employed, ground to a fine powder, melted, mixed with pasteurised milk, poured into moulds then wrapped in lacquered tinfoil (e.g. processed Gruyère, Kraft, Primula).

> **To find out more, visit the Dairy Council's website at: www.milk.co.uk.**

Uses

Soups, pasta, egg, fish and vegetable dishes, savouries.

Types

British cheese: some examples

- **Cheddar** – pale to golden colour with a close texture and a fresh mellow, nutty flavour, mild to mature.
- **Cheshire** – orange-red or white, loose crumbly texture and a mild mellow, slightly salty flavour.
- **Double Gloucester** – orange-yellow, a buttery open texture with a delicate creamy flavour.
- **Dunlop** – a Scottish equivalent of Cheddar, milder and lighter in colour and texture.
- **Leicester** – red in colour with a buttery open texture; a mellow medium strength.
- **Caerphilly** – a Welsh cheese, white in colour and flaky, with a fresh, mild, slightly salty flavour.
- **Lancashire** – white in colour, soft and crumbly with a fresh mild flavour.
- **Wensleydale** – white in colour, moderately close texture with a fresh, mild, slightly salty flavour; excellent with crisp apples or apple pie.
- **Stilton** – white with blue veins, soft and close texture, and a strong flavour.

French cheese: some examples

- **Brie** – white, round cheese with close, soft, creamy texture and delicate flavour.
- **Camembert** – white, round with soft, close, creamy texture and full flavour.
- **Chevre** – a generic name for a wide range of goats' cheeses.
- **Fourme d'Ambert** – sometimes called a French Stilton; salty, full flavour.
- **Roquefort** – blue cheese made from ewes' milk; rich, sharp flavour with salty aftertaste.

Italian cheese: some examples

- **Bel Paese** – round, firm, pearly-white texture and a fresh, creamy taste.
- **Gorgonzola** – blue vein with a rich, sharp flavour; Dolcelatte is a milder version.
- **Mascarpone** – rich, creamy, slightly acrid, used mainly in desserts.
- **Mozzarella** – traditionally made from buffalo milk; pale and plastic looking, sweet flavour with a little bite.
- **Parmesan** – hard, low-fat cheese; grated and used extensively in cooking.
- **Ricotta** – fresh, white, crumbly and slightly sweet, similar to cottage cheese.

Other cheeses: some examples

- Ireland – **Cashel blue:** a creamy rich blue cheese.
- Netherlands – **Edam:** round, full-flavoured with low-fat content; covered in red skin.
- Switzerland – **Gruyère:** firm, creamy-white with a full fruity flavour.
- Greece – **Feta:** white, moist, crumbly with a refreshing salty-sour taste.

Soft curd cheeses

- **Curd cheese** – made from pasteurised milk soured by the addition of a milk-souring culture and rennet; produce a soft, milk-flavoured, low-fat (11 per cent) cheese; made from either skimmed or medium-fat milk.
- **Cottage cheese** – a low-fat, high-protein product made from pasteurised skimmed milk; also available are very low-fat, sweet, savoury and flavoured varieties.
- **Fromage frais** – (fresh cheese) or fromage blanc is a fat-free soft curd cheese to which cream can be added to give richer varieties; also available in low-fat, medium-fat, savoury and fruit flavours.
- **Quark** – a salt-free, fat-free soft cheese made from skimmed milk.

Low-fat hard cheese

There is a range of hard cheese with half the fat of traditional cheese.

Vegetarian cheese

Traditional hard cheeses made using a non-animal rennet are also available.

Fats

Storage of all fats

Fats should be kept in a refrigerator.

Butter

Butter is a natural dairy product made by churning fresh cream. During the churning process, the butterfat globules in the cream coalesce to form butter, and the excess liquid – known as buttermilk – is drained off. A little salt is added, between 1 and 2.5 per cent, depending on the type of butter, to enhance its flavour and keeping qualities.

Food value

Butter contains 80–82 per cent fat and is therefore a high-energy food. The remaining constituents are water (approximately 16 per cent) and milk proteins. The fat-soluble vitamins A and D are present in butter, and there is a small amount of calcium. Each 100 g of butter supplies 733 kilocalories (3014 kilojoules).

Quality

The flavour of butter is rich, creamy and mellow. The colour of butter varies from a delicate pale yellow to a rich, bright colour; both are entirely natural, as explained below. Butter's texture is smooth and creamy, and remains firm when chilled. It should be kept refrigerated, below 5°C for optimum quality, where it can be kept for up to six weeks. Butter kept at room temperature soon deteriorates and exposure to light causes rancidity. As a recommendation, butter should be kept covered in a refrigerator, away from strong flavours or smells that could taint its delicate taste.

Production

Essentially, there are two types of butter: lactic and sweetcream.

In lactic, or 'continental taste', butter, the pasteurised cream is ripened before churning with a lactobacillus culture to produce a mildly acidic flavour. This mild acidity enhances the keeping properties, meaning that this type of butter can be purchased as unsalted or slightly salted, where 1–1.5 per cent salt is added.

In sweetcream butter – traditionally produced in the UK and the Republic of Ireland, and imported from New Zealand – the cream is not ripened before churning and therefore the salt content needs to be a little higher (between 1.5 and 2.5 per cent) to assist keeping qualities.

Apart from the salt, there are no additives in butter. The colour of butter is entirely natural, and varies slightly according to the type of butter, the breed of cow and the pastures on which they feed. Seasonal variations affect the colour of the butter slightly, as the cow's diet changes during the year.

Uses

The unique taste and texture of butter mean that it is ideal for spreading and using in all types of cooking, both professionally and in the domestic kitchen. It is the foundation of many classic recipes, as it improves the flavour and appearance of a great many foods.

Butter is used as a base for making soups, sauces, compound butters and for hard butter sauces like brandy butter. It is also used for making cakes and pastries, butter icings and frostings. Sometimes unsalted butter is chosen for these recipes.

Butter is ideal for shallow-frying foods, but it is not suitable for stir-frying or deep-frying, where higher temperatures would cause the butter to burn. Melted butter makes an ideal baste for brushing grilled foods, and can be combined with chopped fresh herbs, spices, grated citrus rind, and so on, to vary the flavour.

For finishing cooked foods, butter can be used as a glaze.

In sandwiches, butter acts as a protective layer, preventing moist foods from permeating the bread. The butter also gives the finished sandwich a delicious flavour.

Clarified butter can be made by gently heating butter until it has melted and separated. The milk solids can then be strained off. The resultant clarified butter can be used at higher temperatures. Ghee is a type of clarified butter, widely used as the basis of Indian cooking. A type of clarified butter known as concentrated butter is made by removing most of the water and milk solids. It is suitable for cooking and baking, but not for spreading or finishing foods.

Margarine

Margarine is produced from milk and a blend of vegetable oils emulsified with lecithin, flavouring, salt, colouring, and vitamins A and D.

Food value

Margarine is an energy-giving and protective food. With the exception of palm oil, the oils used in the manufacture of margarine do not contain vitamins A and D; these are added during production. Margarine is not inferior to butter from a nutritional point of view.

Quality

There are several grades of margarine: block (hard or semi-hard); soft (butter substitute); semi-hard for making pastry; and cake margarine, which creams easily and absorbs egg. Some margarines are blended with butter. Taste is the best guide to quality.

Uses

Margarine can be used in place of butter, the difference being that the flavour and aroma of nut brown (beurre noisette) or black butter (beurre noir) cannot satisfactorily be produced from margarine. The flavour of margarine when used in the kitchen is inferior to butter – it is therefore not so suitable for finishing sauces and dishes. It should be remembered, however, that it is equally nutritious and may be cheaper than butter.

Vegetable shortening and high-ratio fat are available. They are used extensively in bakery products.

To find out more, contact Unilever Ltd, Unilever House, Blackfriars, London EC4 or visit www.unilever.co.uk.

Animal fats

- **Lard:** Lard is the rendered fat from pigs. It has almost 100 per cent fat content. It may be used in hot water paste and with margarine to make short paste. It can also be used for deep- or shallow-frying.
- **Suet:** Suet is the hard solid fat deposits in the kidney region of animals. Beef suet is the best, and is used for suet paste and mincemeat.
- **Dripping:** Dripping is obtained from clarified animal fats (usually beef) and is used for deep- or shallow-frying.

Polyunsaturated fats and monounsaturated fats

Polyunsaturates, and to a lesser extent monounsaturates, have been shown to lower blood cholesterol levels and therefore help in reducing the risk of heart disease.

It is better to eat foods rich in monounsaturates (olive oil and rapeseed oil) and polyunsaturates (sunflower oil and soya oil), than foods rich in saturates.

Rapeseed oil, which, like olive oil, contains mostly monounsaturated fat, is a good and cheaper alternative to olive oil. Sunflower, soya bean and corn oil all contain mostly polyunsaturated fat so are also good choices.

Some oils are labelled as vegetable oil or blended oils. All of these are also low in saturated fat and are generally cheaper.

To find out more, contact the National Edible Oil Distributors' Association, see: www.fdf.org.uk.

Hydrogenated fats

Hydrogenation is the application of hydrogen to vegetable oils. It changes the unsaturated fatty acids to saturated, and changes the liquid oil into a solid or semi-solid fat. Hydrogenated fats are used in manufactured food products, but there is concern that they may be linked to heart disease. In many cases, food packaging will state whether hydrogenated fats are present, and in what proportion.

Oils

Choice of oil

The choice of an oil as a food ingredient or for cooking will usually involve a compromise. The factors that will need to be taken into account may include:

- price – variations will occur according to supply and demand
- intended use – some oils are versatile others are of limited use
- durability – in use and in storage
- nutritional and health concerns
- flash point – for frying purposes an oil must, when heated, reach a high temperature without smoking; food being fried will absorb the oil if the oil smokes at a low temperature; as oils are combustibles they can catch fire (known as the flash point); in some cases the margin between smoking and the flash point may be narrow (see *Practical Cookery* for further information).

Types of oil include:

- peanut (groundnut)
- cotton seed
- palm
- rapeseed
- olive
- coconut
- soya bean
- sunflower
- palm
- corn

- speciality (e.g. almond, grapeseed, hazelnut, walnut).

Herbal oils are available or can be made by adding chopped fresh herbs (e.g. tarragon, thyme, basil) to olive oil and keeping refrigerated in screw-top jars for about three weeks, then strained and rebottled. If fresh green herbs are used, blanching and refreshing them will enhance the colour of the oil, and kill any pathogens that may be present.

Food value

As oil has a very high fat content it is useful as an energy food.

Storage

Oil should be kept in a cool place. If refrigerated some oils congeal but will return to a fluid state when removed from the refrigerator. Oils keep for a fairly long time but may go rancid if not kept cool.

Uses

- Mayonnaise, vinaigrette and hors d'oeuvre dishes.
- Pasta, certain doughs and breads use olive oil.
- Deep-frying, lubrication of utensils and slabs.

Cereals

Cereals are cultivated grasses, but the term is broadened to include sago, rice and arrowroot. All cereal products contain starch. The following are the important cereals used in catering: wheat, oats, rye, barley, maize, rice, tapioca, sago and arrowroot. A wide variety of cereals are processed into breakfast foods (barley, wheat, rice, bran and corn).

Wheat

Source

Wheat is the most common cereal produced in the western world; it is grown in most temperate regions. Large quantities are home-grown and a great deal, particularly in the form of strong flour, is imported from Canada.

Food value

Cereals are one of the best energy foods. Wholegrain cereals provide vitamin B and are therefore protective foods.

Wheat and flour quality

Flours vary in their composition and, broadly speaking, are defined by the quality of wheats used in the grist prior to milling, and by their rate of extraction. The extraction is the percentage of whole cleaned wheatgrain that is present in the flour. A typical mill will produce hundreds of different types of flour using a wide range of home-grown and imported wheats.

Storage

Keep in airtight containers in a cool, dark, dry place. Whole grains can be stored for up to two years; flaked, cracked grains and flours should be used within two to three months of purchase.

Sprouting

Whole grains (e.g. wheat grains, raw buckwheat and barley) can be sprouted, which greatly enhances their nutritional value.

Cooking

To find out more, visit the Flour Advisory Bureau's website: www.fabflour.co.uk.

Cereals can be used in other ways, besides being ground into flour for bread, cakes, and so on. Whole grains can be added to stews and casseroles, or cooked until soft. Cracked or kibbled grains are cut or broken pieces of whole grains (e.g. kibbled wheat and bulgar wheat). Meal, a coarse kind of flour, can be used to make porridge or thicken soups, or mixed with wheat flour to add interesting flavours and textures to ordinary breads, biscuits, muffins, etc.

Whole grains should be washed thoroughly. Boil the required amount of water, add the washed grain, stir once, put a tight-fitting lid on the pan and simmer for the required cooking time or until the liquid is absorbed. Turn off the heat and leave to stand for five minutes before removing the lid.

Flour

Flour is probably the most common commodity in daily use. It forms the foundation of bread, pastry and cakes, and is also used in soups, sauces, batters and other foods.

- White flour contains 72 to 85 per cent of the whole grain (the endosperm only).
- Wholemeal flour contains 100 per cent of the whole grain.
- Brown flour contains 85–95 per cent of the whole grain.
- High-ratio or patent flour contains 40 per cent of the whole grain.
- Self-raising flour is white flour with the addition of baking powder.
- Semolina is granulated hard flour prepared from the central part of the wheat grain. White or wholemeal semolina is available. Semolina is used for couscous.
- Bulgar (steamed cracked wheat) is used in tabbouleh.

Storage of flour

- The storeroom must be dry and well ventilated.
- Flour should be removed from the sacks and kept in wheeled bins with lids.
- Flour bins should be of a type that can easily be cleaned.
- Rotate stock rather than adding new deliveries at the front.

Uses of flour products

- **Soft flour** – cakes, biscuits, all pastes except puff and flaky, thickening soups and sauces, batters and coating various foods.
- **Strong flour** – bread, puff, flaky, choux and hot water pastry, and pasta.
- **Wholemeal flour** – wholemeal bread and rolls, pastry and pasta.
- **Gnocchi**.

Rye

Rye flour is obtained from the cereal rye and is the most important European cereal after wheat.

Rye is the only cereal apart from wheat that contains gluten proteins. However, these gluten proteins are not of the same quality or quantity as those in flour produced from wheat. Dough produced from rye flour has a sticky, dense consistency. The baked product has a low volume. Rye flour is available as light, medium and dark rye. Likewise the colour and flavour of rye bread can range from light and mild to dark and strong, depending on the type of rye flour used. It should be stored in dry conditions at 10–16°C.

Rye flour must be weighed accurately to ensure that:

- the recipe remains balanced
- the correct yield is obtained
- a uniform product is obtained
- faults are prevented.

Oats

Oats are either rolled into flakes or ground into three grades of oatmeal: coarse, medium and fine.

Source

Oats are one of the hardiest cereals, and are grown in large quantities in Scotland and the north of England.

Food value

Oats have the highest food value of any of the cereals. They contain a good proportion of protein and fat.

Storage

Because of the fat content, the keeping quality of oat products needs extra care. They should be kept in containers with tight-fitting lids, and stored in a cool, well-ventilated storeroom.

Uses

- **Rolled oats** – porridge.
- **Oatmeal** – porridge, thickening soups, coating foods, cakes and biscuits, haggis.

- **Patent rolled oats** – nowadays largely displace oatmeal and have the advantage of being already heat treated, and consequently more quickly and easily cooked.

Barley

The whole grain of barley is known as pot or Scotch barley and requires soaking overnight. Pearl barley has most of the bran and germ removed, and it is then polished. These products are used for making barley water for thickening soups and certain stews.

Barley when roasted, is changed into malt and as such is used extensively in the brewing and distilling of vinegar. Barley needs the same care in storage as oats.

Buckwheat is the seed of the plant 'bran buck-wheat'. The grain is usually roasted before cooking, and is also ground into a strong savoury flour for pancakes and baking.

Maize

Maize is also known as corn, sweetcorn or corn on the cob, and besides being served as a vegetable is processed into cornflakes and cornflour. Maize yields a good oil suitable for cooking.

Cornflour

Cornflour is produced from maize and is the crushed endosperm of the grain, which has the fat and protein washed out so that it is practically pure starch.

Cornflour is used for making custard and blanc-mange powders, because on boiling with a liquid it thickens easily, and sets when cold into a smooth paste that cannot be made from other starches.

Custard powder consists of cornflour, colouring and flavouring.

Cornflour is used for thickening soups, sauces, and custards, and also in the making of certain small and large cakes.

Rice

Rice is the staple food of half the world's population and is second only to wheat as the world's most important food grain.

Three main types of rice are used in this country:

- **long grain** – a narrow, pointed grain, best suited for savoury dishes and plain boiled rice because of its firm structure, which helps to keep the rice grains separate (e.g. basmati, patna)
- **medium grain** – an all-purpose rice suitable for sweet and savoury dishes (e.g. arborio)
- **short grain** – a short, rounded grain, best suited

for milk puddings and sweet dishes because of its soft texture (e.g. carolina).

Types

- **Brown rice** – any rice that has had the outer covering removed but retains its bran and as a result is more nutritious, with a nutty flavour.
- **Wholegrain rice** – whole and unprocessed rice.
- **Thai fragrant rice (jasmine rice)** – used in Thai and Vietnamese dishes, this rice has a fragrant aroma; it is similar to basmati.
- **Basmati rice** – a thin, long grain rice which has a distinctive fragrance when cooking. The cooked rice is light and fluffy with the grains staying separate. Served with curries.
- **Wild rice** – seed of an aquatic plant related to the rice family. It has a nutty flavour and a firm texture.
- **Ground rice** – used for milk puddings.
- **Rice flour** – used for thickening certain soups (e.g. cream soups).
- **Rice paper** – a thin, edible paper produced from rice, used in the preparation of macaroons and nougat.
- Precooked instant rice, par-boiled, ready-cooked and boil-in-the-bag rice is also available.

Storage

Rice should be kept in tight-fitting containers in a cool, well-ventilated store.

To find out more about cereals, see www.vegsoc.org/info/cereals.html.

Tapioca

Tapioca is obtained from the roots of a tropical plant called cassava. Flake (rough) and seed (fine) are available. Tapioca may be used for garnishing soups and milk puddings.

Sago

Sago is produced in small pellets from the pith of the sago palm. It may be used for garnishing soups and for making milk puddings.

Arrowroot

Arrowroot is obtained from the roots of a West Indian plant called maranta. It is used for thickening sauces and is particularly suitable when a clear sauce is required as it becomes transparent when boiled. Arrowroot is also used in certain cakes and puddings, and is particularly useful for invalids as it is easily digested. It is easily contaminated by strong-smelling foods, therefore it must be stored in airtight tins.

Potato flour

Potato flour is a preparation from potatoes, suitable for thickening certain soups and sauces.

Raising agents

The method of making mixtures light or aerated may be effected in several ways.

Baking powder

Baking powder may be made from one part sodium bicarbonate to two parts of cream of tartar. In commercial baking the powdered cream of tartar may be replaced by another acid product (e.g. acidulated calcium phosphate).

When used under the right conditions it produces carbon dioxide gas; to produce gas, a liquid and heat are needed. As the acid has a delayed action, only a small amount being given off when the liquid is added, the majority of the gas is released when the mixture is heated. Therefore cakes and puddings when mixed do not lose the property of the baking powder if they are not cooked right away.

Uses

Baking powder is used in sponge puddings, cakes and scones, and in suet puddings and dumplings.

Yeast

Yeast is a fungus form of plant life available as a fresh or dried product.

Storage and quality points

- Yeast should be wrapped and stored in a cold place.
- It should have a pleasant smell.
- It should be ordered only as required.
- It should crumble easily.
- It must be perfectly fresh and moist.

Food value

Yeast is rich in protein and vitamin B. It therefore helps towards building and repairing the body, and provides protection.

Uses

Yeast is used in bread and bun doughs, cakes and batters.

Sugar

Sugar is produced from sugar cane grown in a number of tropical and subtropical countries and from sugar beet, which is grown in parts of Europe, including the UK. Syrups and treacle (for cooking and spreading) are liquid forms of sugar. It is also possible to buy organic sugar.

Food value

As sugar contains 99.9 per cent pure sugar, it is invaluable for producing energy.

Sugar in cooking

Sugar is not just a sweetener; it can be used in a number of different ways.

- As a preservative: at the right concentration sugar helps to stop micro-organisms growing and so prevents food spoilage (for example, in jams and other preserves). This is why reduced-sugar jams spoil much more quickly than traditional jams.
- It helps to produce subtle changes in flavour. Sugar offsets the acidity and sour flavour of many foods such as mayonnaise, tomato products, and tart fruits like gooseberries and grapefruit.
- As a bulking agent: sugar gives the characteristic texture to a variety of foods – including jams, ice cream and cakes.
- To raise the boiling point or lower the freezing point. This is essential in some recipes (for example, making ice cream).
- To speed up the process of fermentation (by yeast) in baking. This makes the dough rise (for example, bread and tea cakes).
- It makes cakes light and open-textured when it is beaten with butter or eggs in a recipe.

Types

- Refined white sugars: granulated, caster; cube; icing.
- Unrefined sugar: brown sugar.
- Partially refined sugar: demerara.
- Syrups and treacle.

Storage

Sugar should be stored in a dry, cool place. When purchased by the sack, the sugar is stored in covered bins.

To find out more, visit the website of British Sugar plc: www.britishsugar.co.uk.

Beverages (drinks)

The simplest, cheapest drink of all is water, which varies from place to place in taste and character according to the substances dissolved or suspended in it. Soft water has a low content of lime. Hard water has an abundance of lime (if the flavour of lime is too strong, the water may have to be softened to remove the excess of lime).

Water that has been artificially softened should not be used for coffee or tea making. The mineral content of water used for brewing can significantly affect the final taste of the coffee or tea. A blend of coffee or tea brewed in the very hard water of London has a completely different taste to the same blend brewed in Edinburgh, where the water is very soft. Water can also contain varying degrees of other substances (e.g. iron and sulphur), which in some instances are considered to be beneficial to health, and these are known as mineral waters.

Drink can be broadly classified into two categories: alcoholic and non-alcoholic (beverage or soft drink). Although the word beverage means a drink the generally accepted definition is a non-alcoholic liquid, e.g. chocolate, coffee, tea, cocoa, fruit drinks, mineral waters, milk.

Alcoholic drinks include cocktails, aperitifs, fancy drinks, wines, fortified wines, spirits, beers, cider, perry. Low-alcohol drinks are also available.

Non-alcoholic drinks

Coffee

Coffee is produced from the beans of the coffee tree, and is grown and exported from regions such as South America, India, the Middle East, the West Indies, Africa, Java and Sumatra. The varieties of coffee are named after the areas where they are grown, such as Mysore, Kenya, Brazil, Mocha and Java.

Purchasing units

Coffee beans – either unroasted, roasted or ground – are sold by weight. Coffee essence is obtained in bottles of various sizes.

Arab or Turkish coffee

Arab or Turkish coffee is very strong and thick. It is made with finely ground beans, sugar is added and it may be flavoured with cardamom seeds.

The filter method

In the drip, or filter, method, finely ground coffee is placed in a paper or reusable cone-shaped unit and nearly boiling water poured on top. The water filters through the coffee into the jug below. Individual one-cup filters are also available.

The plunger/cafetière

The cafetière pot is warmed, coarsely ground coffee is placed in the bottom, hot water is added to the grounds and stirred, then it is allowed to steep for three to five minutes before the plunger is pushed down to separate the coffee grounds from the coffee infusion. This is an efficient way to serve coffee to customers. Various sizes of cafetière are available, including single-serving pots.

Espresso and cappuccino

Today, espresso, which was invented in Italy, is the fastest-growing method of making coffee. Espresso machines force the hot water through very finely ground and compacted coffee and then into the cups below. Espresso may be consumed as it is, or diluted with boiling water. Cappuccino, latte and other popular coffees are based on the espresso, with varying quantities of steamed or frothed milk added.

The percolator

The percolator used to be a very popular way to make coffee, especially in the home. The percolator heats water to boiling point so that it bubbles and filters through ground coffee in the top of the unit. Percolators are now seen as old-fashioned.

Soluble, or instant, coffee

The quality and diversity of instant coffee have grown dramatically over the years, and we can make a good cup of coffee from today's products. Instant coffee has a number of advantages over fresh brewed coffee, including ease and convenience. It stays fresher longer, it is hard to damage the flavour, however hard you try, and most of all it is fast, cheap and clean.

Flavoured coffees

An interesting and fast growing area of the market is flavoured coffees. Today there are over 100 different flavoured varieties available. The growth in popularity of flavoured coffee is proof of coffee's versatility and strength. The flavours are added directly to the beans by roasting them, then spraying them with a carrier oil and then the particular flavouring. Another way to make a cup of flavoured coffee is to add a syrup to hot brewed coffee and popular coffee shops now offer a range of these syrups. By far the most important flavouring added to coffee over the world is milk. Although milk is not added to Arabian coffee, and coffee purists tend not to add milk, most people find coffee more palatable with its addition.

Caffeine content

The amount of caffeine in a cup of coffee can vary greatly, depending on its origin or the composition of the blend, the method of brewing and the strength of the brew. Instant, or soluble, coffee generally contains less caffeine than roast and ground coffee, but may be consumed in greater volume.

To find out more, visit the website of the Roast and Post Coffee Company: www.therealcoffeeco. com.

Tea

Tea is an evergreen plant of the camellia family, which is kept to bush size for easy plucking; only the two top leaves and bud on each stalk are plucked. There are more than 1500 blends of tea and tea grows in more than 31 countries.

Use a good quality loose leaf or bagged tea. This must be stored in an airtight container at room temperature. Always use freshly drawn boiling water. In order to draw the best flavour out of the tea the water must contain oxygen; this is reduced if the water is boiled more than once. Measure the tea carefully. Use one tea bag or one rounded teaspoon of loose tea for each cup to be served. Allow the tea to brew for the recommended time before pouring (see Table 3.10).

Blends

Blends of tea provide the widest possible choice of tea with many different characteristics and flavours. A popular brand-leading blend can contain as many as 35 different teas.

Speciality teas take their name from: the area or country in which they are grown; a blend of tea for a particular time of day; a blend of teas known after a person; a blend of teas to which fruit oil, flower petals

Table 3.10 Recommended brewing times for tea

	Type	Country of origin	Brewing time	Milk/black/ lemon	Characteristics
Darjeeling	Black	India	3–5 minutes	Black or milk	Delicate, slightly astringent flavour
Assam	Black	India	3–5 minutes	Black or milk	Full-bodied with a rich, smooth, malty flavour
Ceylon blend	Black	Sri Lanka	3–5 minutes	Black or milk	Brisk, full flavour with a bright colour
Kenya	Black	Kenya (Africa)	2–4 minutes	Black or milk	A strong tea with a brisk flavour
Earl Grey	Black	China or India/ Darjeeling	3–5 minutes	Black or lemon	Flavoured with the natural oil of citrus bergamot fruit
Lapsang souchong	Black	China	3–5 minutes	Black	Smoky aroma and flavour
China oolong	Oolong	China	5–7 minutes	Black	Subtle, delicate, lightly flavoured tea

Figure 3.121 Cafetière and filter machine

Figure 3.122 A modern coffee machine

or blossoms have been added or a 'made' processed tea.

Flavoured teas are real tea blended with fruit, herbs or spices. These should not be confused with tisanes and fruit infusions made from herbs, hibiscus leaves and fruits, which do not contain any real tea. Several varieties of green tea are also available, which research suggests has half the caffeine of black teas.

Buying

Tea comes in either tea bag or loose-leaf packs, which cover a wide variety of catering needs.

To find out more, visit the website of the UK Tea Council: www.tea.co.uk.

Cocoa

Cocoa is a powder produced from the beans of the cacao tree. It is imported mainly from West Africa.

Food value

As cocoa contains some protein and a large proportion of starch it helps to provide the body with energy. Iron is also present in cocoa.

Storage

Cocoa should be kept in airtight containers in a well-ventilated store.

Uses

For hot drinks, cocoa is mixed with milk, milk and water, or water. Hot liquid is needed to 'cook' the starch and make it more digestible. Cocoa can be used to flavour puddings, cakes, sauces, icing and ice cream.

Chocolate

Cocoa beans are used to produce chocolate, and over half of the cocoa bean consists of cocoa butter. To produce chocolate, cocoa butter is mixed with crushed cocoa beans and syrup. With baker's chocolate, the cocoa fat (butter) is replaced by vegetable fat thus giving a cheaper product that does not need tempering. For commercial purposes, chocolate is sold in blocks known as couverture. Pure chocolate couverture is made from cocoa mass, highly refined sugar and extracted cocoa butter. It is the additional cocoa butter that gives couverture its qualities for moulding, its flavour and therefore its higher price.

Uses

Chocolate or couverture is used for icings, buttercreams, sauces, dipping chocolates and moulding into shapes.

Drinking chocolate

This is ground cocoa from which less fat has been extracted and to which sugar and milk have been added. It can be obtained in flake or powder form.

Mineral waters and soft drinks

A wide range of mineral waters are available, both home produced and from overseas, and either natural (still or naturally carbonated) in character or treated with gas (carbon dioxide) to give a light sparkle or fizz. Examples of natural mineral waters are Buxton and Malvern. Manufactured soft drinks include grapefruit, lime juice (still) and tonic water, Coca-Cola, ginger beer (sparkling), and so on.

Spring water is bottled water which does not conform to the natural mineral water regulations. The important natural mineral elements in mineral water are regulated and must be present in consistent amounts. Spring water does not have to demonstrate this; it must meet the same regulations as tap water.

Squashes are concentrated, sweetened, fruit-flavoured drinks intended to be diluted with water. They may or may not contain natural fruit juice, and the amount of juice included varies.

Fruit syrups

Fruit syrups are concentrated fruit juices preserved with sugar or manufactured from compound colourings and flavours (orange, lime, cherry). A large range of compound flavourings is available.

Milk drinks

Milk can be offered plain, either hot or cold. Other milk drinks include:

- **milkshake** – a mixture of fresh milk, ice cream and a flavouring syrup, rapidly whisked and served in a tall glass
- **ice cream soda** – a combination of fruit syrup and fresh cream in a long glass filled with soda water and topped with ice cream
- other products from which beverages are made either by the addition of hot water or milk include Bournvita, Bovril, Horlicks and Ovaltine.

Alcoholic drinks

Wine

Wine has been made for over 6000 years and is produced in most parts of the world. It is the fermented juice of the grape and is available in many styles: red, white, rosé, sparkling, organic, alcohol-free, de-alcoholised and low alcohol. Wines may be dry, medium dry, or sweet in character, and according to the type and character they may be drunk while young (within a short time of bottling) or allowed to age (in some cases for many years).

Bottled wines should always be stored on their sides so that the wine remains in contact with the cork. This keeps the cork expanded and prevents air from entering the wine which, if allowed to happen, will turn the wine to vinegar. The exceptions to this are champagne and sparkling wines, which should be stored upright, and screw-top bottles.

Fortified wines

Fortified wines are those that have been strengthened by the addition of alcohol, usually produced from grape juice; the best known are port, sherry and Madeira.

Aromatised wines

Aromatised wines are produced by flavouring a simple basic wine with a blend of ingredients (fruit, roots, bark, peel, flowers, quinine, herbs). Vermouth and Dubonnet are two examples of aromatised wines popular as aperitifs.

Spirits

Spirits are distillations of fermented liquids that are converted into liquid spirit; they include whisky, gin, vodka, brandy and rum.

Liqueurs

Liqueurs are flavoured and sweetened spirits. A wide range of flavouring agents are employed (e.g. aniseed, caraway, peach, raspberry, violet, rose petals, cinnamon, sage, honey, coffee beans). Many different liqueurs are available (e.g. Cointreau, cherry brandy).

Cocktails and mixed drinks

Cocktails are usually a mixture of a spirit with one or more ingredients from liqueurs, fruit juices, fortified wines, eggs, cream, etc. Cocktails may be garnished with mint, borage, fresh fruit, olives, and so on.

Mixed drinks have an assortment of names that include flips, fizzes, nogs, sours and cups. Cocktails and mixed drinks can also be made from non-alcoholic ingredients.

Beer

Beer is a term that covers all beer-like drinks such as ale, stouts and lagers. Beer is made from a combination of water, grain (e.g. barley), hops, sugar and yeast. Types of beer include: bitter, mild, strong ale, barley wine, porter and lager. Reduced-alcohol beers are also available.

Beers are good sources of energy; they contain high levels of carbohydrates and protein. Beers are richer in minerals than wines, but lower in alcohol at only 3–5 per cent.

Cider

Cider is fermented apple juice. Also in this category are:

- pomagne – a sparkling cider
- scrumpy – strong, rough cider.

Perry

Perry is fermented pear juice.

Pulses

Pulses are the dried seeds of plants that form pods.

Types

- **Aduki beans** – small, round, deep-red, shiny beans.
- **Black beans** – glistening black skins and creamy flesh.
- **Black-eyed beans** – white beans with a black blotch.
- **Borlotti beans** – pink-blotched mottled colour.
- **Broad beans** – strongly flavoured beans, sometimes known as fava beans.
- **Butter beans** – available large or small, also known as lima beans.
- **Cannellini** – Italian haricots, slightly fatter than the English.
- **Chickpeas** – look like the kernel of a small hazelnut; the main ingredient of hummus.
- **Dhal** –the Hindi word for dried peas and beans.
- **Dutch brown beans** – light brown in colour.
- **Flageolets** – pale-green, kidney-shaped beans.
- **Ful mesdames or Egyptian brown beans** – small, brown, knobbly beans, also known as the field or broad bean in England.
- **Haricot beans** – white, smooth oval beans.
- **Lentils** – available in bright orange, brown or green.
- **Mung beans** – chiefly used for beansprouts.
- **Pinto beans** – pink-blotched mottled colour.
- **Puy lentils** – grey-coloured; do not require soaking and they hold their shape when cooked. Considered the finest of lentils.
- **Red kidney beans** – used in chilli con carne; a black variety is also available.
- **Soissons** – the finest haricot beans.
- **Soya beans** – the most nutritious of all beans.
- **Split peas** – available in bright green or golden yellow.

Food value

Pulses are good sources of protein and carbohydrate, and therefore help to provide the body with energy. With the exception of the soya bean, they are completely deficient in fat.

Storage

All pulses should be kept in clean containers in a dry, well-ventilated store.

Uses

Pulses are used extensively for soups, stews, vegetables and salads, as accompaniments to meat dishes and in vegetarian cookery.

Herbs

Of the 30 well-known types of herbs, approximately 12 are generally used in cookery. Herbs may be used fresh, but the majority are dried so as to ensure a continuous supply throughout the year. The leaves of herbs contain an oil that gives the characteristic smell and flavour.

Herbs have no food value but are important from a nutritive point of view in aiding digestion because they stimulate the flow of gastric juices. The most commonly used herbs are described below.

- **Basil:** Basil is a small leaf with a pungent flavour and sweet aroma. Used in raw or cooked tomato dishes or sauces, salads and lamb dishes.
- **Bay leaves:** Bay leaves are the leaves of the bay laurel or sweet bay trees or shrubs. They may be fresh or dried, and are used for flavouring many soups, sauces, stews, fish and vegetable dishes, in which case they are usually included in a faggot of herbs (bouquet garni).
- **Borage:** This is a plant with furry leaves and blue flowers that produces a flavour similar to cucumber when added to vegetables and salads.
- **Chervil:** Chervil has small, neatly shaped leaves with a delicate aromatic flavour. It is best used fresh, but may also be obtained in dried form. Because of its neat shape it is often used for decorating chaud-froid work. It is also one of the 'fines herbes' (see below) – the mixture of herbs used in many culinary preparations.
- **Chive:** Chive is a bright-green member of the onion family, resembling a coarse grass. It has a delicate onion flavour. It is invaluable for flavouring salads, hors d'oeuvre, fish, poultry and meat dishes, and chopped as a garnish for

Figure 3.123 Herbs (clockwise from top left: coriander, oregano, parsley, flat-leaf parsley)

Figure 3.124 Herbs (clockwise from top left: rosemary, bay, lemon thyme, thyme)

soups and cooked vegetables. It should be used fresh.
- **Coriander:** A member of the parsley family, coriander is one of the oldest flavourings used by man. It is both a herb and a spice. The leaves have a distinctive pungent flavour.
- **Dill:** Dill has feathery green-grey leaves and is used in fish recipes and pickles.
- **Fennel:** Fennel has feathery bright green leaves, and a slight aniseed flavour, and is used for fish sauces, meat dishes and salads.
- **Lemon grass:** Lemon grass is a tall plant with long, spear-shaped grass-like leaves with a strong lemon flavour. A natural companion to fish, also used in stir-fries and salads and widely used in Thai cookery.
- **Lovage:** Lovage leaves have a strong celery-like flavour; when finely chopped they can be used in soups, stews, sauces and salads.
- **Marjoram:** Marjoram is a sweet herb that may be used fresh in salads, and in pork, fish, poultry,

cheese, egg and vegetable dishes; when dried, it can be used for flavouring soups, sauces, stews and certain stuffings.
- **Mint:** There are many varieties of mint. Fresh sprigs of mint are used to flavour peas and new potatoes. Fresh or dried mint may be used to make mint sauce or mint jelly for serving with roast lamb. Another lesser-known but excellent mint for the kitchen is apple mint. Chopped mint can be used in salads.
- **Oregano:** Oregano has a flavour and aroma similar to marjoram but stronger. It is used in Italian and Greek-style cooking, in meats, salads, soups, stuffings, pasta, sauces, vegetable and egg dishes.
- **Parsley:** Parsley is probably the most common herb in Britain; it has numerous uses for flavouring, garnishing and decorating a large variety of dishes. Flat-leaf, or French, parsley is also available.
- **Rosemary:** Rosemary is a strong fragrant herb that should be used sparingly, and may be used

Figure 3.125 Herbs (clockwise from top left: chives, chervil, tarragon, marjoram)

Figure 3.126 Herbs: mint, sage

Figure 3.127 Bull's blood (right) and baby coriander (left)

Figure 3.128 A selection of micro-herbs

fresh or dried for flavouring sauces, stews, salads and for stuffings. It can also be sprinkled on roasts or grills of meat, poultry and fish during cooking and on roast potatoes.
- **Sage:** Sage is a strong, bitter, pungent herb that helps the stomach to digest rich fatty meat; it is therefore used in stuffings for duck, goose and pork.
- **Samphire:** Samphire is not really a herb, but the leaves of a low, branched bush found on salt flats. It has a mellow grassy sweetness that complements fish and shellfish dishes.
- **Tarragon:** This plant has a bright-green, attractive leaf. It is best used fresh, particularly when decorating chaud-froid dishes. Tarragon has a pleasant flavour and is used in sauces, one well-known example being sauce béarnaise. It is

one of the fines herbes and, as such, is used in omelettes, salads, fish and meat dishes.
- **Thyme:** Thyme is a popular herb in the UK; it is used fresh or dried for flavouring soups, sauces, stews, stuffings, salads and vegetables.

Fine herbs (fines herbes)

This is a mixture of fresh herbs – usually chervil, tarragon and parsley – that is referred to in many classical cookery recipes.

Other herbs

Balm, bergamot, fennel, savory, sorrel, tansy, lemon thyme and other herbs are used in cookery, but on a much smaller scale.

 ## Spices

Spices are natural products obtained from the fruits, seeds, roots, flowers or the bark of a number of different trees or shrubs. They contain oils that aid digestion by stimulating the gastric juices. They also enhance the appearance of food and add a variety of flavours. As spices are concentrated in flavour, they should be used sparingly, otherwise they can make foods unpalatable. Most spices are grown in India, Africa, the West Indies and the Far East.

- **Allspice or pimento:** This is so called because the flavour is like a blend of cloves, cinnamon and nutmeg. It is the unripe fruit of the pimento tree, which grows in the West Indies. Allspice is picked when still green, and dried when the colour turns

to reddish brown. Allspice is ground and used as a flavouring in sauces, sausages, cakes, fruit pies and milk puddings. It is one of the spices blended for mixed spice.
- **Anise:** This is also known as sweet cumin, and has a sweet aniseed flavour. It is used for fish, sweets, creams and cakes.
- **Anise (pepper):** A strong, hot-flavoured red pepper.
- **Anise (star):** Stronger than anise, this has a slight liquorice flavour. Used in Chinese cookery with pork and duck.
- **Asafoetida:** This is used in Indian cookery to add flavour to vegetarian dishes. Available in block or powder form.

Figure 3.129 Spices (clockwise from top left: tamarind, liquorice, red chilli, ginger, green chilli)

Figure 3.130 Spices (left to right: nutmeg, cloves, star anise)

- **Caraway:** Caraway seeds come from a plant grown in Holland, Germany, Russia and North America. The seeds are about 0.5 cm long, shaped like a new moon and brown in colour. Caraway seeds are used in seed-cake and certain breads, sauerkraut, cheese and confectionery. Also for flavouring certain liqueurs such as kümmel.
- **Cardamom:** Cardamom is frequently used in curry; it has a warm, oily sharp taste, and is also used in some sweets (e.g. rice pudding) and drinks (e.g. coffee and tea).
- **Cassia:** This comes in thicker sticks than cinnamon, is less delicate and more expensive. Used in spiced meats and curries.
- **Celery seed:** Slightly bitter, this should be used sparingly if celery or celery salt is not available.
- **Chillies and capsicums:** These are both from the same family and grow on shrubs. The large, bright-red type are capsicums; these are ground and known as paprika. There are many types of chillies; they vary in taste, colour, piquancy and heat (always test the heat by cutting off a small piece and tasting with the tip of the tongue). The seeds are one of the hottest parts of the chilli and they can be removed by splitting the chilli in half then scooping them out with the point of the knife. Hands should always be washed thoroughly after preparing chillies because the oils are exceptionally strong and will burn the eyes, mouth and other delicate areas of the body. Chillies are used in many dishes: pizzas, pasta and in Indian, Thai and Mexican cookery.
- **Chinese five spice powder:** Usually consists of: powdered anise, fennel, cloves, cinnamon and anise pepper. Used extensively in Chinese cookery.

- **Cinnamon:** Cinnamon is the bark of the small branches of the cinnamon shrub, which grows in China and Sri Lanka. The inner pulp and the outer layer of the bark are removed and the remaining pieces dried. It is a pale-brown colour and is obtained and used in stick or powdered form, mainly by bakeries and for pastry work.
- **Cloves:** Cloves are the unopened flower buds of a tree that grows in Zanzibar, Penang and Madagascar. The buds are picked when green, and dried in the sun until they turn a rich brown colour. They are used for flavouring stocks, sauces, studding roast ham joints and in mulled wine.
- **Coriander:** Coriander is a pleasant spice obtained from the seed of the coriander plant. It is a yellowish-brown colour and tastes like a mixture of sage and lemon peel. It is used in sauces, curry powder and mixed spice.
- **Cumin:** This is frequently used in curry, is powerful, warm and sweet, and has a slightly oily taste.
- **Dill seeds:** These are used for flavouring fish soups, stews and cakes.
- **Fennel seeds:** Fennel seeds have a sweet aniseed flavour; used in fish dishes and soups.
- **Fenugreek:** Fenugreek is roasted, ground and frequently used in curry; slightly bitter, with a smell of fresh hay.
- **Garam masala:** This literally means 'hot spices'; it is not a standardised recipe, but a typical mixture could include: cardamom seeds, stick cinnamon, cumin seeds, cloves, black peppercorns and nutmeg.
- **Ginger:** Ginger is the rhizome or root of a reed-like plant grown in the Far East. The root is boiled in water and sugar syrup until soft. Ground ginger is used mainly for pastry and bakery work and

Figure 3.131 Spices (clockwise from top left: black peppercorns, white peppercorns, juniper berries, pink peppercorns)

Figure 3.132 Spices (clockwise from top left: sesame seeds, cardamom, cumin, caraway seeds, poppy seeds)

for mixed spice. Whole root is used for curries, pickles, stir-fry dishes and sauces.

- **Juniper berries:** If these are added to game, red cabbage, pork, rabbit and beef dishes, they give an unusual background flavour.
- **Krachai:** A type of ginger with a slightly strange flavour.
- **Nutmeg and mace:** The tropical nutmeg bears a large fruit like an apricot that, when ripe, splits. Inside is a dark-brown nut with a bright-red net-like covering, which is the part that becomes mace. Inside the nut is the kernel or seed, which is the nutmeg. Although the two spices come from the same fruit, the flavour is different. Mace is more delicate and is used for flavouring sauces and certain meat and fish dishes. Nutmeg is used in sweet dishes (particularly milk puddings), sauces, soups, vegetable and cheese dishes. It is also used for mixed spice.
- **Poppy seeds:** Poppy seeds are used as a topping for bread, cakes, etc.
- **Saffron:** The stigmas from a crocus known as the saffron crocus (grown chiefly in Spain) are dried and form saffron, which is a flavouring and colouring spice. It is used in soups, sauces and particularly in rice dishes, giving them a bright-yellow colour and distinctive flavour. Saffron is very expensive as it takes the stigmas from approximately 4000 crocus flowers to yield just 30 g.
- **Sesame seeds:** These are used as a topping for bread and cakes, and in Chinese and vegetarian cookery. They are also crushed for oil and ground in preparations such as tahini.
- **Surmac seeds:** These are used in Middle

Figure 3.133 Spices (clockwise from top: cinnamon quills, saffron filaments, turmeric, allspice)

Eastern cooking for their acidic lemon/peppery flavour. Deep red-maroon colour.
- **Turmeric:** Turmeric grows in the same way as ginger and it is the rhizome that is used. It is without any pronounced flavour and its main use is for colouring curry powder. It is ground into a fine powder, which turns it yellow. Turmeric is also used in pickles, relishes and as a colouring in cakes and rice.

Others

There is a large number of other spices, and spice and herb mixtures available – for example, chermonla, curries, harissa and curry powders and pastes.

Some additional ingredients used in Asian and fusion cuisine

(Fusion cuisine is a mixture of food styles and ingredients from the cookery styles of East and West.)

- **Ajowan:** A native Indian plant used in Indian recipes. An ingredient of Bombay mix, and breads such as parathas, bean and pulse recipes.
- **Annatto:** Shrub indigenous to both the Caribbean and tropical America; has heart-shaped glossy leaves and pink flowers. The seeds are washed and dried separately for culinary use. An orange food colour is made from the husk.
- **Asafoetida:** Indigenous to Iran and Afghanistan and the north of India. Used in vegetable, fish, pulse and pickle ingredients.
- **Bamboo shoots:** Mild-flavoured, tender shoots of the young bamboo. Widely available fresh, or sliced or halved in cans.
- **Bengali five spices:** Bengali in origin, also known as panch phoron. Contains cumin seeds, fennel seeds, mustard seeds, fenugreek seeds and nigella seeds.
- **Berbera:** An Ethiopian blend of spices: dried red chillies, white cardamoms, allspice berries, black peppercorns, cumin seeds, coriander seeds, ajowan seeds, ground ginger, fenugreek seeds, cloves, ground nutmeg and salt.
- **Blackbean sauce:** Made from salted black beans, crushed and mixed with flour and spices (such as ginger, garlic or chilli) to form a paste. Sold in jars and cans.
- **Cajun spice mix:** Spice mixture used for fish, chicken and meat. Contains garlic, dried oregano, white mustard seeds, salt, black peppercorns, chilli powder, cumin seeds, paprika and dried thyme.
- **Cardamom pods:** Available both as small green pods and larger black pods containing seeds. They have a strong aromatic quality.
- **Chillies:** There are over 24 different types of chillies – for example, small green or red, garlic, and so on.
- **Chilli bean sauce:** Made from fermented bean paste mixed with hot chilli and other seasonings.
- **Chilli oil:** Made from fermented bean paste mixed with hot chilli and other seasonings.
- **Chilli powder:** Milder than cayenne pepper and more coarsely ground; prepared from a variety of mild and hot chillies.
- **Chilli sauce:** A very hot sauce made from chillies, vinegar, sugar and salt. Sold in bottles.
- **Chinese chives:** Also known as garlic chives.
- **Chinese rice wine:** Made from glutinous rice, also known as yellow wine huang jin or chiew because of its colour. The best variety is called shuo hsing or shuoxing, and comes from south-east China. Dry sherry may be used as a substitute.

- **Coconut milk and cream:** Not to be confused with the 'milk' or juice found inside the fresh coconut. The coconut milk used for cooking is produced from the white flesh of the coconut. If left to stand, the thick part of the milk will rise to the surface like cream.
- **Curry leaves:** Come from the tropical tree of the citrus-rue family, native to southern India and Sri Lanka. Strong, curry aroma. A classical way of using curry leaves is by frying mustard seeds in hot ghee, then adding a little asafoetida and several curry leaves for a few seconds, before stirring them into a plain dhal dish or dhal-based Indian soup.
- **Dashi:** Light Japanese stock, available in powder form. The flavour derives from kelp seaweed.
- **Dried shrimps and shrimp paste:** Dried shrimps are tiny shrimps that are salted and dried. They are used as a seasoning for stir-fry dishes. Shrimp paste, also known as terasi, is a dark, odorous paste made from fermented shrimps.
- **Galangal:** Fresh galangal, also known as lengkuas, tastes and looks a little like ginger, with a pinkish tinge to its skin.
- **Gram flour:** Made from ground chickpeas, this flour has a unique flavour.
- **Harissa:** Spice mix used in Moroccan, Tunisian and Algerian cooking. Used as a dip or accompaniment. Contains dried red chillies, olive oil, coriander seeds, garlic, cumin seeds and salt.
- **Hoi sin sauce:** A thick, dark brownish-red sauce that is sweet and spicy.
- **Juniper:** Grown in Hungary, southern Europe. An evergreen coniferous tree of the cypress family. The berries are used in the production of gin. A seasoning for some birds, venison, duck, rabbit, pork, ham and lamb.
- **Kaffir lime leaves:** These are used like bay leaves, to give an aromatic lime flavour to dishes.
- **La Kama:** Moroccan spice mix. Black peppercorns, ground ginger, ground turmeric, ground nutmeg, cinnamon stick.
- **Liquorice:** Native of the Middle East and south-east Europe. The root is the most important part; it sends out a deep and extensive network of rhizomes, which are grown for three to five years before they are harvested. The roots and rhizomes are cleaned, pulped, then boiled, and the liquorice extract is then concentrated by evaporation. Liquorice is best known as an ingredient in confectionery, also used in the making of Guinness and to flavour the Italian liquor sambuca.
- **Mahlebi:** Tree found only in the Middle East and

Turkey. This ground spice is used in breads and pastries.

- **Mango powder:** The unripe mangoes are sliced, sundried and ground to a powder, then mixed with a little ground turmeric. Used in vegetarian dishes, curries and chutneys.
- **Mirin:** A mild, sweet Japanese rice wine used in cooking.
- **Miso:** A fermented bean paste that adds richness and flavour to Japanese soups.
- **Nigella:** Grown in India. The seeds are held in a seed head similar to a poppy head. Sometimes used as a substitute for pepper. Nigella is one of the five spices in Bengali five spices. It is widely used in Indian cooking, in dhal and vegetable dishes, pickles and chutneys. The seeds are often scattered on naan bread.
- **Noodles:** There are several types of noodles:
  - cellophane noodles – also known as bean thread, transparent or glass noodles, made from ground mung beans
  - egg noodles – made from wheat flour, egg and water
  - rice noodles – made from ground rice and water
  - rice vermicelli – thin brittle noodles that look like white hair
  - somen noodles – delicate, thin white Japanese noodles made from wheat flour
  - udon noodles – Japanese noodles made of wheat flour and water.
- **Nori:** Paper-thin sheets of Japanese seaweed.
- **Oyster sauce:** Made from oyster extract.
- **Pak choi:** Also known as bok choi, this is a leaf vegetable with long, smooth milky-white stems and dark-green foliage.
- **Palm sugar:** Strongly flavoured, hard brown sugar made from the sap of the coconut palm tree.
- **Papaya seeds:** Seeds of the papaya fruit. Can be used fresh or dried. Rich in the enzyme papain, which is an efficient meat tenderiser of commercial value.
- **Pomegranate seeds:** Grown in Mediterranean countries, South America, the USA and parts of Africa. Grenadine is a syrup made from the juice of the pomegranate. Fresh pomegranate seeds are sprinkled on hummus.
- **Ras el hanout:** Moroccan spice mixture. Contains black peppercorns, coriander seeds, cumin seeds, cloves, green cardamoms, ground turmeric, cinnamon stick, ground ginger, salt nutmeg, dried red chillies and dried flowers.

- **Red bean paste:** A reddish-brown paste made from puréed red beans and crystallised sugar.
- **Rice vinegar:** There are two basic types:
  - red vinegar – made from fermented rice, has a distinctive dark colour
  - white vinegar – stronger in flavour, distilled from rice.
- **Sake:** A powerful fortified rice wine from Japan.
- **Sambaar powder:** Also known as sambar, used in south Indian dishes; made from red chillies, coriander seeds, black peppercorns, fenugreek seeds, urad dhal, channu dhal, mung dhal, ground turmeric and cumin seeds.
- **Sambal keeap:** Indonesian sauce used as an accompaniment or a dip. Dark soy sauce, lemon juice, garlic, red chilli, deep-fried onion slices.
- **Sambals:** Sambals is an accompaniment that is spooned directly on to the plate. Made from de-seeded red chillies puréed with salt.
- **Soy sauce:** A major seasoning ingredient in Chinese cooking, made from fermented soya beans, combined with yeast, salt and sugar. Chinese soy sauce falls into two main categories: light and dark. Light has more flavour than the sweeter dark sauce, which gives food a rich, reddish colour.
- **Spring roll wrappers:** Paper-thin wrappers made from wheat or rice flour and water.
- **Sumac:** Bush grown in Italy, Sicily and the Middle East. Its red berries are dried. Widely used in Lebanese, Syrian, Turkish and Iranian cuisines.
- **Szechuan peppercorns:** Also known as tarchiew; aromatic, best used roasted and ground. Not as hot as white or black peppercorns.
- **Tamarind:** The brown, sticky pulp of the bean-like seed pod of the tamarind tree. Used in Indian, Thai and Indonesian cooking.
- **Thai fish sauce (nam pla):** The most common flavouring in Thai food, in the same way soy sauce is used in Chinese dishes. It is made from salted anchovies and has a strong, salty flavour.
- **Thai nam prik sauce:** This is the most famous of the Thai sauces, it can be served on its own or used as a dip. Contains brown sugar, lemon juice, fish sauce, fresh red chillies, dried prawns, blanchan, cooked prawns, garlic and fresh coriander.
- **Thai parsley:** Similar in appearance to spring onion but without the bulb.
- **Thai red curry paste (krueng gueng phed):** Used for meat, poultry and vegetable dishes. Contains red chillies, groundnut oil, red onion, blanchan, lemon grass, salt, cumin seeds, citrus

peel, garlic, galangal, green chillies, white onion, fresh coriander and coriander seeds.
- **Toey leaves:** Also known as pandanus leaves, these are long, flat blades, bright green in colour.
- **Tofu:** Puréed, pressed soya beans, also known as bean curd. Rich in protein.
- **Wasabi:** Edible root used in Japanese cooking, to make a condiment with a sharp, pungent and fiery flavour. Similar to horseradish.
- **Water chestnuts:** Walnut-sized bulbs from an Asian water plant that looks like sweet chestnuts.

- **Wonton wrappers:** Small, paper-thin squares of wheat flour and egg dough.
- **Yard-long beans:** Long, thin beans similar to French beans but three or four times longer.
- **Yellow bean sauce:** A thick paste made from salted, fermented yellow soya beans crushed with flour and sugar.
- **Zedoury:** A member of the ginger and turmeric family, bright yellow in colour. Has a musky aroma with a hint of camphor.

Condiments

Salt

Food value

Salt (sodium chloride) is essential for stabilising body fluids and preventing muscular cramp. However, in general, too much salt is consumed. It should always be used in moderation as it has been proved that excess salt in the diet can be harmful to health, causing high blood pressure.

Storage

Salt must be stored in a cool, dry place as it readily absorbs moisture. It should be kept in airtight packets, drums or bins.

Uses

Salt is used for curing fish such as herrings and haddocks, and for cheese and butter making. Salt is also used for the pickling of foods, in the cooking of many dishes and as a condiment on the table.

Pepper

Pepper is obtained from black peppercorns, which are the berries of a tropical shrub. White peppercorns are obtained by removing the skin from the black peppercorn. White pepper is less pungent than black, and both may be obtained in ground form.

Green peppercorns are fresh unripe pepper berries, milder than dried peppercorns, available frozen or in jars or tins. Pink peppercorns are softer and milder than green peppercorns, available preserved in vinegar.

Ground pepper is used for seasoning many dishes and as a condiment at the table.

Cayenne pepper

Cayenne is a red pepper used on savoury dishes and in cheese straws. It is a hot pepper that is obtained from grinding chillies and capsicums.

Paprika

Paprika is a bright-red mild pepper used in Hungarian dishes, e.g. soups, stews (goulash). Smoked paprika is available in sweet, hot and bitter-sweet versions.

Mustard

Mustard is obtained from the seed of the mustard plant. There are three different types of seed: white, brown and black. It is sold in powder form and is diluted with water, milk or vinegar for table use, or sold ready mixed in jars. A large variety of continental mustards are sold as a paste in jars, having been mixed with herbs and wine vinegar.

Vinegar

Malt vinegar is made from malt, which is produced from barley. Artificial, non-brewed, pure or imitation vinegars are chemically produced solutions of acetic acid in water. They are cheaper and inferior to malt vinegar, having a pungent odour and a sharp flavour.

Spirit vinegars are produced from potatoes, grain or starchy vegetables, but they do not have the same flavour as malt vinegar. Red or white wine vinegars are made from grapes; they are more expensive and have a more delicate flavour than the other vinegars.

All vinegars can be distilled; this removes the colour. The colour of vinegar is no indication of its strength as burnt sugar is added to give colour.

Balsamic vinegar is a specially matured vinegar from Italy, with a distinctive flavour that varies in strength according to the age of the vinegar, which can be up to 30 years.

Other vinegars include chilli, sherry, cider, rice, herb (especially tarragon) thyme, oregano, sage, rosemary, and fruit such as raspberry and strawberry.

Uses

Vinegar is used as a preservative for pickles, rollmops and cocktail onions; and as a condiment on its own or with oil as a salad dressing; it is used for flavouring sauces such as mayonnaise and in reductions for sharp sauces (e.g. sauce piquante, sauce diable).

Colourings, flavourings and essences

Colourings

A number of food colourings are obtained in either powder or liquid form. Natural colours include the following.

- Cochineal: Cochineal is a red colour, produced from the cochineal beetle, used in pastry and confectionery work.
- Green colouring: This can be made by mixing indigo and saffron, but chlorophyll, the natural green colouring of plants, such as in spinach, may also be used. (Green pasta is coloured with dried spinach powder.)
- Indigo: Indigo is a blue colour seldom used on its own but, when mixed with red, it produces shades of mauve.
- Yellow colouring: A deep-yellow colour can be obtained from turmeric roots and is prepared in the form of a powder mainly used in curry and mustard pickles. Yellow colouring is also obtained by using egg yolks or saffron.
- Brown: Brown sugar is used to give a deep brown colour in rich fruit cakes; it also adds to the flavour.
- Blackjack or browning: Blackjack, or commercial caramel, is a dark-brown, almost black liquid; it is used for colouring soups, sauces, gravies, aspics, and in pastry and confectionery.
- Chocolate colour: This can be obtained in liquid or powder form, and is used in pastry and confectionery.
- Coffee colour: This is usually made from coffee beans with the addition of chicory.

Other colourings

A large range of artificial colours is also obtainable; they are produced from coal tar and are harmless. Some mineral colours are also used in foodstuffs. All colourings must be pure and there is a list of those permitted for cookery and confectionery use.

Flavourings and essences

Essences are generally produced from a solution of essential oils with alcohol, and are prepared for the use of cooks, bakers and confectioners. Among the many types of essence obtainable are:

- almond
- pineapple
- lemon
- raspberry
- orange
- strawberry
- peppermint
- vanilla.

Essences are available in three categories: natural, artificial and compound. The relative costs vary considerably and it is advisable to try all types of flavouring essence before deciding on which to use for specific purposes.

Natural essences

- Fruit juices pressed out of soft fruits (raspberries or strawberries).
- Citrus fruit peel (lemon, orange).
- Spices, beans, herbs, roots, nuts (caraway seeds, cinnamon, celery, mint, sage, thyme, clove, ginger, coffee beans, nutmeg and vanilla pod).

Artificial essences

Artificial essences (such as vanilla, pineapple, rum, banana and coconut) are produced from various chemicals blended to give a close imitation of the natural flavour.

Compound essences

Compound essences are made by blending natural products with artificial products.

Grocery, delicatessen

Delicatessen literally means 'provision store', but the name is commonly used to cover the place where a wide range of table delicacies may be bought.

- **Agar-agar:** This is obtained from the dried purified stems of a seaweed; it is also known as vegetable gelatine and is used in vegetarian cookery.
- **Anchovy essence:** This is a strong, highly seasoned commodity used for flavouring certain fish sauces and fish preparations such as anchovy sauce or fish cakes.
- **Aspic:** Aspic jelly is a clear savoury jelly, which may be the flavour of meat, game or fish. It may be produced from fresh ingredients or obtained in dried form. It is used for cold larder work, mainly for coating chaud-froid dishes, and may also be chopped or cut into neat shapes to decorate finished dishes.
- **Charcuterie:** Charcuterie is the name given to cold meat preparations usually pork (e.g. hams), galantines, black puddings, pâtés, salamis and a large variety of continental sausages and cured meats (e.g. bresaola).
- **Caviar:** Caviar is the uncooked roe of the sturgeon, which is prepared by carefully separating the eggs from the membranes of the roe and gently rubbing them through sieves of coarse hemp. It is then soaked in a brine solution, sieved and packed.
  Sturgeon fishing takes place in the estuaries of rivers that run into the Caspian or Black Sea, therefore caviar is Russian or Iranian in origin. The types normally obtainable in Britain are Beluga, Osetrova and Sevruga. These names refer to the type of sturgeon from which the caviar is taken. Caviar is extremely expensive, and needs to be handled with great care and understanding. It should be kept at a temperature of 0°C but no lower, otherwise the extreme cold will break the eggs down. Caviar must never be deep frozen. A red caviar (keta) is obtained from the roe of salmon. From the lumpfish a mock caviar is obtained. These are considerably cheaper than genuine caviar.
- **Extracts (meat and vegetable):** Extracts are highly concentrated forms of flavouring used in some kitchens to strengthen stocks and sauces (Bovril, Marmite, Maggi and Jardox are some examples).
- **Foie gras:** This expensive delicacy is obtained from the livers of specially fattened geese and is produced mainly in Strasbourg. It is available fresh and cooked in a variety of ways (e.g. terrine, pâté).
- **Gelatine:** Gelatine is obtained from the bones and connective tissue (collagen) of certain animals; it is manufactured in leaf or powdered form and used in various sweets, such as bavarois. (Vegetable gelatine is agar-agar.)
- **Haggis:** This traditional Scottish dish is made from the heart, lungs (lights) and liver of the sheep, mixed with suet, onion and oatmeal, and sewn up in a stomach bag. It is boiled and served with mashed potatoes.
- **Hams:** A ham is the hind leg of a pig cured by a special process, which varies according to the type of ham. One of the most famous English hams is the York ham, weighing 6–7 kg, which is cured by salting, drying and sometimes smoking. The Bradenham ham is of coal-black colour and is a sweet-cured ham from Chippenham in Wiltshire. Hams are also imported from Northern Ireland and Denmark. These are all cooked before use. Continental raw hams – Westphalian from Germany, Bayonne and Ardenne from France, Parma from Italy and Serrano from Spain – are cut into thin slices and served raw.
- **Horseradish:** Horseradish is a plant of which only the root is used. It is washed, peeled, grated and used for horseradish sauce and horseradish cream.
- **Panettone:** An Italian light-textured yeast bread containing sultanas and candied fruit.
- **Pickles:** These are vegetables and/or fruits preserved in vinegar or sauce and include red cabbage, gherkins, olives, onions, walnuts and capers. Mango chutney is a sweet chutney that is served as an accompaniment to curried dishes.
- **Smoked herring, anchovies and sardines:** These are preserved in oil and used as hors d'oeuvre.
- **Smoked salmon:** British, Scandinavian or Canadian salmon weighing between 6 and 8 kg are used for smoking. A good-quality side of smoked salmon (see Figure 3.70) should have a bright, deep colour and be moist when lightly pressed with the finger tip at the thickest part of the flesh. A perfectly smoked side of salmon will remain in good condition for not more than seven days when stored at a temperature of 18°C. This versatile food

is used for canapés, hors d'oeuvre, sandwiches, and as a fish course for lunch, dinner or supper.

- **Snails:** Edible snails are raised on the foliage of the vine. They are obtainable in boxes that include the tinned snails and the cleaned shells. The snails are replaced in the shells with a mixture of butter, garlic, lemon juice and parsley, then heated in the oven and served in special dishes. Snails are also farmed in Britain.

Confectionery and bakery goods

- **Cake covering:** This is produced from hardened vegetable fat with the addition of chocolate flavouring and colour.
- **Cape gooseberries:** A tasty, yellow-berried fruit resembling a large cherry. Cape gooseberries are often dipped in fondant and served as a petit four.
- **Chocolate vermicelli:** A ready-made preparation of small fine chocolate pieces used in the decorating of small and large cakes and some chocolate-flavoured sweets.
- **Cocktail cherries:** Bright-red cherries preserved in a syrup, often flavoured with a liqueur known as maraschino. In addition to being used for cocktails they are also used to give colour to grapefruit and grapefruit cocktails.
- **Fondant:** A soft, white preparation of sugar that has many uses in pastry and confectionery work, chiefly for coating petits fours, pastries and gâteaux.
- **Gum tragacanth:** A soluble gum used for stiffening pastillage; only a very clear white type of gum tragacanth should be used. It is obtained from the shrubs of the genus *Astragalus*.
- **Honey:** A natural sugar produced by bees working upon the nectar of flowers. It is generally used in the form of a preserve and in pastry work.
- **Ice cream:** A frozen preparation of a well-flavoured, sweetened mixture, which can be made in many ways and in many flavours. Ice cream may be bought ready prepared, usually in 5-litre containers that are suitable for deep-freeze storage. The storage temperature for ice cream should not exceed $-19°C$.
- **Jam:** A preserve of fruit and sugar obtainable in 28 g, 0.5 kg and 1 kg jars, and 3 kg tins. Raspberry and apricot jams are those most often used in the pastry.
- **Marmalade:** A preserve of citrus fruits and sugar, which is used mainly for breakfast menus and for certain sweets.
- **Marrons glacés:** Peeled and cooked chestnuts preserved in syrup. They are used in certain large and small cakes, sweet dishes and as a variety of petits fours.
- **Marzipan:** A preparation of ground almonds, sugar and egg yolks used in the making of petits fours, pastries and large cakes. Marzipan may be freshly made and is also obtained as a ready-prepared commodity.
- **Mincemeat:** A mixture of dried fruit, fresh fruit, sugar, spices, nuts, etc., chiefly used for mince pies. It can also be obtained in 0.5 kg and 1 kg jars, and 3 kg tins.
- **Pastillage (gum paste):** A mixture of icing sugar and gum tragacanth, which may be moulded into shapes for set pieces for cold buffets and also for making baskets, caskets, etc., for the serving of petits fours.
- **Piping jelly:** A thick jelly of piping consistency obtainable in different colours and flavours. It is used for decorating pastries and gâteaux and cold sweets. Piping jelly is obtainable in large tins.
- **Redcurrant jelly:** A clear preserve of redcurrants used as a jam as an accompaniment and also in the preparation of sauces.
- **Rennet:** A substance originally obtained from the stomachs of calves, pigs and lambs, but that can now be obtained in synthetic form. Rennet is prepared in powder, extract or essence form, and is used in the production of cheese and for making junket. Vegetable rennet, for vegetarians, is also available.
- **Vanilla:** This is the dried pod of an orchid used for infusing mild sweet flavour into dishes. After use rinse the vanilla stick, dry and store in a sealed jar of castor sugar ready for reuse.
- **Wafers:** Thin, crisp biscuits of various shapes and sizes usually served with ice cream. They are obtainable in large tins of approximately 1000, and half-tins of approximately 500 wafers.

References

Campbell, J., Foskett, D., Rippington, N. and Paskins, P. (2011) *Practical Cookery Level 3* (5th edn). London: Hodder Education.

Campbell, J., Foskett, D. and Ceserani, V. (2009) *Practical Cookery* (11th edn). London: Hodder Education.

North American Meat Processors Association (2006) *The Meat Buyer's Guide*. John Wiley & Sons, Inc.

Some references to commodities elsewhere in this book:

Topics for discussion

1 Factors that affect the quality of meat.
2 Pros and cons of using meat substitutes such as TVP and Quorn.
3 Purchasing of meat (by carcass, joints or portion-controlled cuts).
4 Much of today's poultry lacks flavour. How can this be remedied?
5 The popularity of fish compared to meat and poultry.
6 The best ways to purchase fish.
7 Buying policy for vegetables and fruit.
8 The importance of vegetables and fruit in the diet.
9 The importance of eggs to food production.
10 Compare the uses of butter, margarine or oil in cooking.
11 What is a sensible policy for selling cheese in a restaurant?
12 Is the average caterer sufficiently knowledgeable about the different types of flour and their suitability for specific purposes?
13 Should the caterer be offering a wider range of choice of teas and coffees?
14 The value of using pulses.
15 The value of using herbs, micro-herbs and spices.

Basic nutrition, diet and health

Supporting material available on Dynamic Learning Online:

DYNAMIC LEARNING

> Knowledge quizzes
> Activity worksheets: nutrition; food preservation
> Summary presentations
> Videos and worksheets: diets and food allergies

Food and nutrients

Nutrition is the science of food; it is the nutrients in food and the way in which they react in relation to our health. Nutrients are the substances in food that provide energy, promote growth and maintain the body. A diet is the selection of foods; a balanced diet provides all of the nutrients in sufficient quantities. People today are becoming more aware of food choices, therefore it is important for those involved in planning menus, purchasing foods, cooking and serving to have some nutritional knowledge.

Nutrients

Nutrients provide energy or kilocalories (kcals), and there are around 50 nutrients which are divided into six categories. 'Macro' nutrients such as protein, carbohydrates and fats provide the body with energy; the 'micro' nutrients do not provide energy but are essential for our health.

- **Proteins** provide 4 kcals per gram and are primarily responsible for growth and repair.
- **Carbohydrates** provide 4 kcals per gram and are the primary source of our energy. They are a large class of nutrients, which include starch, sugars and fibre.
- **Fats** provide 9 kcals per gram; they are a rich source of energy and essential to the structure of our cells.
- **Vitamins** do not provide any kcals, but are essential in small quantities for our health.
- **Minerals** do not provide any energy, and can be classed as either major or minor minerals; these again are required in small amounts, but perform important roles in our health such as transporting oxygen, making our bones and teeth strong, and regulating our heartbeat, to name but a few.
- **Water** is essential for our health.

Table 4.1 Foods containing the various nutrients and their use in the body

Nutrient	Food in which it is found	Use in body
Protein	Meat, fish, poultry, game, milk, cheese, eggs, pulses, cereals	For building and repairing body tissues; some heat and energy
Fat	Butter, margarine, cooking fat, oils, cheese, fat meat, oily fish	Provides heat and energy
Carbohydrate	Flour, flour products and cereals, sugar, syrup, jam, honey, fruit, vegetables	Provides heat and energy
Vitamin A	Oily fish, fish liver oil, dairy foods, carrots, tomatoes, greens	Helps growth; resistance to disease
Vitamin B1 – thiamin	Yeast, pulses, liver, whole grain, cereals, meat and yeast extracts	Helps growth; strengthens nervous system
Vitamin B2 – riboflavin	Yeast, liver, meat, meat extracts, wholegrain cereals	Helps growth, and helps in the production of energy
Nicotinic acid (niacin)	Yeast, meat, liver, meat extracts, wholegrain cereals	Helps growth
Vitamin C – ascorbic acid	Fruits such as strawberries, citrus fruits, green vegetables, root vegetables, salad	Helps growth, promotes health
Vitamin D (sunshine vitamin)	Fish liver oils, oily fish, dairy foods	Helps growth; builds bones and teeth
Iron	Lean meat, offal, egg yolk, wholemeal flour, green vegetables, fish	Building up the blood
Calcium (lime)	Milk and milk products, bones of fish, wholemeal bread	Building bones and teeth, clotting the blood, the working of the muscles
Phosphorus	Liver and kidney, eggs, cheese, bread	Building bones and teeth, regulating body processes
Sodium (salt)	Meat, eggs, fish, bacon, cheese	Prevention of muscular cramp

Most foods are a combination of a number of nutrients, but some foods – such as sugar – contain only one nutrient. Alcohol provides the body with 7 kcals per gram, but it actually has the same effect upon the body as a drug so is not classified as a nutrient.

Digestion

Digestion is the breaking down of food with the help of enzymes. Enzymes are proteins that speed up (catalyse) the breakdown processes. Digestion takes place:

- in the mouth, where food is mixed with saliva, and starch is broken down by the action of an enzyme in saliva
- in the stomach, where the food is mixed and gastric juices are added, and proteins are broken down
- in the small intestine, where proteins, fats and carbohydrates are broken down further and additional juices added
- in the large intestine, where bacteria attack undigested substances such as dietary fibre.

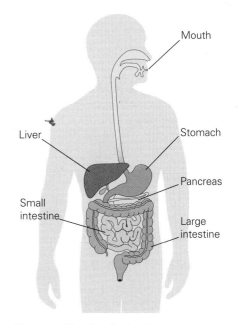

Figure 4.1 The digestive tract

Table 4.2 The main functions of nutrients

Energy	Growth and repair	Regulation of body processes
Carbohydrates	Proteins	Vitamins
Fats	Minerals	Minerals
Proteins	Water	Water

Absorption

To enable the body to benefit from food it must be absorbed into the bloodstream; this absorption occurs after the food has been broken down; the product then passes through the walls of the digestive tract and into the bloodstream. This occurs in:

- the stomach, where simple substances, such as alcohol and glucose, are passed through the stomach lining into the bloodstream
- the small intestine, where more of the absorption of nutrients takes place due to a further breakdown of the food
- the large intestine, where water is reabsorbed from the waste.

Food should smell, look and taste attractive in order to stimulate the flow of saliva and digestive juices. This will help the digestive process and ensure that most food is broken down and absorbed. If digestion and absorption are not efficient this could lead to a deficiency of one or more nutrients and a state of malnutrition.

Protein

Protein is an essential part of all living matter; it is therefore needed for the growth of the body and for the repair of body tissues.

There are two kinds of protein:

1 animal protein
2 vegetable protein.

Animal protein is found in meat, game, poultry, fish, eggs, milk and cheese: myosin, collagen (meat, poultry and fish); albumin, ovovitellin (eggs); casein (milk and cheese).

Vegetable protein is found mainly in the seeds of vegetables. The proportion of protein in green and root vegetables is small. Peas, beans and nuts contain most protein, and the grain of cereals such as wheat has a useful amount because of the large quantity eaten – for example, gliadin and glutenin forming gluten with water (wheat and rye).

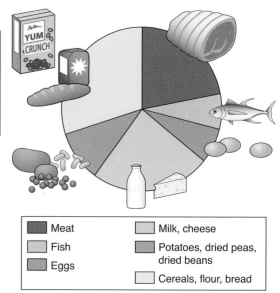

	Meat		Milk, cheese
	Fish		Potatoes, dried peas, dried beans
	Eggs		Cereals, flour, bread

Figure 4.2 Main sources of protein in the average diet

What is protein?

Proteins contain carbon, hydrogen, oxygen and nitrogen. They are made from long chains of amino acids, which are the building blocks of protein. The way that these amino acids are arranged or sequenced is how different proteins are formed, which is why the protein of cheese is different to the protein in meat. There are 20 different amino acids, of which eight are essential – which means that we have to obtain these from our diet as the body cannot make them – and there are 12 non-essential amino acids that the body can make from other amino acids. Proteins that contain all of the essential amino acids in the correct proportion are said to have a high biological value. It is preferable to take both animal and vegetable forms of protein so that we have a variety of the necessary amino acids available to us. Protein builds and repairs the body; it is part of many enzymes, hormones and antibodies. It is also involved in maintaining fluid, clotting the blood, and maintaining our acid and alkaline balance.

During digestion, protein is split into amino acids; these are absorbed into the bloodstream and used for building body tissues and to provide some heat and energy.

Table 4.3 shows the proportion of protein in some common foods. It shows that there is no such thing as a pure protein food (i.e. one containing 100 per cent protein). Foods with even the highest content do not contain more than 45 per cent.

It follows that, because protein is needed for growth,

Table 4.3 The proportion of protein in some common foods

Animal food	Protein (%)	Plant foods	Protein (%)
Cheese, Cheddar	26	Soya flour, low fat	45
Bacon, lean	20	Soya flour, full fat	37
Beef, lean	20	Peanuts	24
Cod	17	Bread, wholemeal	9
Herring	17	Bread, white	8
Eggs	12	Rice	7
Beef, fat	8	Peas, fresh	6
Milk	3	Potatoes, old	2
Cheese, cream	3	Bananas	1
Butter	<1	Apples	<1
		Tapioca	<1

Source: Fox and Cameron (1995) reproduced by permission of Hodder Education

growing children and expectant and nursing mothers will need more protein than other adults, whose requirements are mainly for repair. Any spare protein is used for producing heat and energy. In diets where protein intake is minimal, it is important that there is plenty of carbohydrate available so that protein is used for growth and repair, rather than for energy purposes.

Fats

What is fat?

Fats contain essential fatty acids that are essential to the diet. Edible fats are composed of glycerol with three fatty acids attached and are therefore called triglycerides.

There are three types of fatty acid:

1 monounsaturated

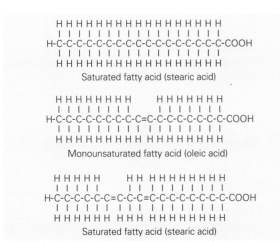

Figure 4.3 Types of fatty acid

2 polyunsaturated
3 saturated.

Saturated fats are, as the name indicates, saturated with hydrogen, which makes them straight and therefore heavy, so they produce solid fats such as butter and lard. Monounsaturated fats have one double bond, which means that they are not completely saturated with hydrogen. A monounsaturated fat such as olive oil can be liquid at room temperature but turn viscose when stored in the fridge. Polyunsaturated fats have two or more points that are not saturated with hydrogen; they are found in corn, sunflower, soybean and sesame oil.

These different types give different properties to different fats (e.g. butyric acid in butter, oleic acid in most oils, and stearic acid in solid fats such as beef suet).

Hard fats are mainly of animal origin and contain more saturated fatty acids, while, in comparison, oils and soft fats contain more polyunsaturated acids.

To be useful to the body, fats have to be broken down into glycerol and fatty acids so that they can be absorbed; they can then provide heat and energy. The food value of the various kinds of fats is similar, although some animal fats contain fat-soluble vitamins A and D. The function of fat is to protect vital organs of the body and to provide heat and energy; certain fats also provide vitamins and add flavour and texture to food.

There are two main groups of fats: animal and vegetable. Fats can be divided into:

- solid fat
- oils (fat that is liquid at room temperature).

Table 4.4 Percentage of saturated fat in an average diet*

Milk, cheese, cream	16.0
Meat and meat products	25.2
Other oils and fats	0.0
Other sources, including eggs, fish, poultry	7.4
Biscuits and cakes	11.4
The 25.2% for meat and meat products splits down into:	
Other meat products	9.1
Beef	4.1
Lamb	3.5
Pork, bacon and ham	5.8
Sausage	2.7

* A diet high in saturated fat is associated with an increased risk of heart disease

Table 4.5 Sources of saturated and unsaturated fats

High in saturated fats	Dairy products	Butter, cream, milk, cheese
	Meat	Liver, lamb, beef, pork
	Others	Coconut oil, palm kernel oil, palm oil, hard margarine, lard
High in polyunsaturated fats	Vegetable oils	Corn (maize) oil, soya bean oil, safflower seed oil, sunflower seed oil
	Nuts	Most, except coconut and cashew nuts
	Margarines	Many soft varieties especially soya bean and sunflower seed

Source: Fox and Cameron, 1995, reproduced by permission of Hodder Education

Fats are obtained from the following foods (see also Table 4.4):

- animal origin – dripping, butter, suet, lard, cheese, cream, bacon, meat fat, oily fish
- vegetable origin – margarine, cooking fat, nuts, soya beans.

Oils are obtained from the following foods:

- animal origin – halibut and cod liver oil
- vegetable origin – from seeds or nuts.

The contribution of animal fat in the western diet is gradually changing as healthy eating policies encourage a reduction in total fat intake, particularly animal fats. There has been a move towards skimmed milk, leaner cuts of meat, cooking with vegetable oils, and a reduced market for eggs, high-fat cheeses and butter.

Fats should be eaten with other foods such as bread, potatoes, etc., as they can then be more easily digested and utilised in the body.

Certain fish – such as herrings, mackerel, salmon and sardines – contain oil (fat) in the flesh. A type of fat that is increasingly popular as a dietary supplement is omega-3, which can be found in the flesh of oily fish. Other fish, such as cod and halibut, contain the oil in the liver.

Vegetables and fruit contain very little fat, but nuts and seeds have a considerable amount.

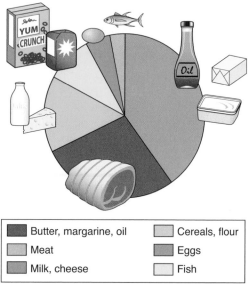

Figure 4.4 Main sources of fat in the average diet

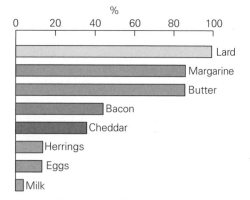

Figure 4.5 Proportion of fat in some foods

Carbohydrates

What are carbohydrates?

Carbohydrates are made by plants and then either used by plants as energy or eaten by animals or humans for energy. Carbohydrates are made up of sugar molecules.

There are three main types of carbohydrate:

1 sugar (saccharide)
2 starch (polysaccharide)
3 cellulose (fibre).

The function of carbohydrates is to provide the body with most of its energy. Starch is composed of a number of glucose molecules (particles), and during digestion starch is broken down into glucose.

Sugar

There are several kinds of sugar:

- glucose – found in the blood of animals and in fruit and honey
- fructose – found in fruit, honey and cane sugar
- sucrose – found in beet and cane sugar
- lactose – found in milk
- maltose – produced naturally during the germination of grain.

Sugars

Simple sugars are monosaccharides made of one unit, such as glucose, fructose and galactose. A disaccharide contain two monosaccharides joined together, such as sucrose from glucose and fructose, maltose from glucose, and glucose and lactose from glucose and galactose (they all contain a glucose); they all end in 'ose'.

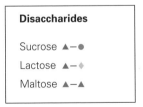

Monosaccharides	**Disaccharides**
Glucose ▲	Sucrose ▲—●
Fructose ●	Lactose ▲—♦
Galactose ♦	Maltose ▲—▲

Figure 4.6 Simple sugars are the building blocks: all carbohydrates are composed of single sugars, alone or in combination

Sugars are the simplest form of carbohydrate and the end products of the digestion of carbohydrates. They are absorbed in the form of glucose and simple sugars, and used to provide heat and energy.

Starch

Starch is present in the diet through the following foods:

- whole grains – rice, barley, tapioca
- powdered grains – flour, cornflour, ground rice, arrowroot
- vegetables – potatoes, parsnips, peas, beans
- unripe fruit – bananas, apples, cooking pears

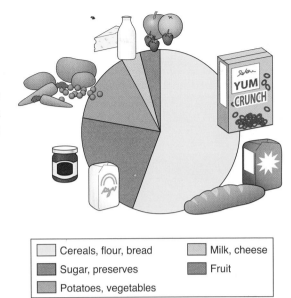

Cereals, flour, bread	Milk, cheese
Sugar, preserves	Fruit
Potatoes, vegetables	

Figure 4.7 Main sources of carbohydrates in the average diet

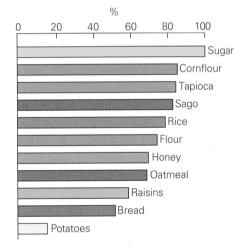

Figure 4.8 Proportion of carbohydrate in some foods

- cereals – cornflakes, shredded wheat, etc.
- cooked starch – cakes, biscuits, bread
- pastas – macaroni, spaghetti, vermicelli, etc.

Fibre

Fibre is found in plants, vegetables, whole grains, nuts, seeds and legumes. There are two types, which are classed as soluble and insoluble fibre. Soluble fibre swells in water to form a gel-like substance that slows digestion and helps to control the release of glucose into the bloodstream. It also binds with cholesterol in the gastrointestinal tract, so reducing cholesterol levels. Soluble fibres are found in fruits and vegetables, and grains such as oats. Insoluble fibre is the more tough, indigestible fibre such as the skin of fruits and vegetables, and the outer parts of seeds, wheat bran and brown rice. Insoluble fibre increases faecal weight, so assisting in the travel of waste, which prevents constipation.

Vitamins

What are vitamins?

Vitamins are chemical substances found in small amounts in many foods. They are vital for life, and if the diet is deficient in any vitamin, ill health results. As they are chemical substances they can be produced synthetically. Vitamins can be fat soluble (A, D, E and K) or water soluble (B and C).

General function of vitamins

Vitamins assist the regulation of the body processes:

- to help the growth of children
- to protect against disease.

Vitamin A

Vitamin A:

- assists in children's growth
- helps the body to resist infection
- enables people to see better in the dark.

Vitamin A is fat soluble; therefore it is to be found in fatty foods. It can be made in the body from carotene, the yellow substance found in many fruits and vegetables.

Dark-green vegetables are a good source of vitamin A, the green colour masking the yellow of the carotene. Carotene is gradually destroyed by light (hence the fading of orange-coloured spices and vegetables on prolonged storage).

At very high levels, vitamin A can be toxic.

Sources of vitamin A are:

- halibut liver oil
- milk
- cod liver oil
- herrings
- kidney
- carrots
- liver
- butter
- watercress
- spinach
- tomatoes
- cheese
- apricots
- eggs
- margarine (to which vitamin A is added).

Fish liver oils have the most vitamin A. The amount of vitamin A in dairy produce varies. Because cattle eat fresh grass in summer and stored feedstuffs in winter, the dairy produce contains the highest amount of vitamin A in the summer. Kidney and liver are also useful sources of vitamin A.

Vitamin D

Vitamin D controls the use the body makes of calcium. It is therefore necessary for healthy bones and teeth. Like vitamin A it is fat soluble.

An important source of vitamin D is from the action of sunlight on the deeper layers of the skin (approximately 75 per cent of our vitamin D comes from this source). Other sources include:

- fish liver oils
- egg yolk
- margarine (to which vitamin D is added).
- oily fish
- dairy produce

Vitamin B

When first discovered vitamin B was thought to be one substance only; it is now known to consist of at least 11 substances, the two main ones being:

1 thiamin (B1)
2 riboflavin (B2).

Others include folic acid and pyridoxine (B6), and cobalamin (B12). B6 and B12 aid the formation of blood, so can prevent anaemia.

Vitamin B is water soluble and can be lost during cooking; it is required to:

- keep the nervous system in good condition
- enable the body to obtain energy from the carbohydrates and amino acid metabolism
- encourage the growth of the body.

Vitamin C (ascorbic acid)

Vitamin C:

- assists in the healing of cuts and the uniting of broken bones
- prevents gums and mouth infection
- makes collagen – a protein that makes skin and bones strong.

Vitamin C is water soluble and can be lost during cooking or soaking in water. It is also lost through poor storage (keeping foods for too long, bruising or storing in a badly ventilated place) and by cutting vegetables into small pieces.

Table 4.6 Sources of vitamin B

Thiamin (B1)	Riboflavin (B2)	Nicotinic acid
Yeast	Yeast	Meat extract
Bacon	Liver	Brewers' yeast
Oatmeal	Meat extract	Liver
Peas	Cheese	Kidney
Wholemeal bread	Egg	Beef

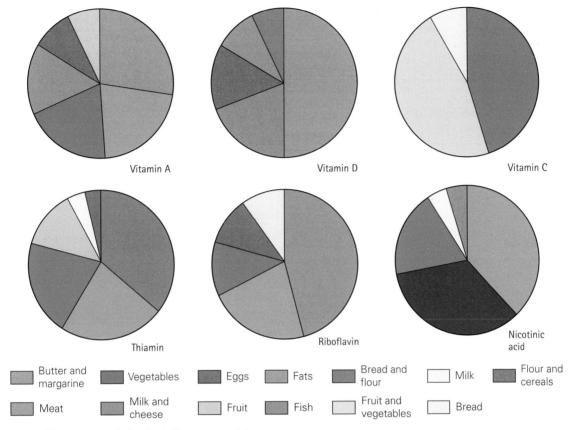

Figure 4.9 Main sources of vitamins in the average diet

Sources of vitamin C include:

- blackcurrants
- potatoes
- Brussels sprouts and other greens

- oranges
- grapefruit
- tomatoes

- strawberries
- lemons

- bananas
- fruit juices.

The major sources in the British diet are potatoes and green vegetables.

Table 4.7 Cooking times and vitamin C retention for some common foods

Cooking time (mins)	% retention of vitamin C during boiling			
	Brussels sprouts	Cabbage	Carrots	Potatoes
20	49	–	35	–
30	36	70–78	22	53–56
60	–	53–58	–	40–50
90	–	13–17		

Source: Fox and Cameron, 1995, reproduced by permission of Hodder Education

 Mineral elements

What are mineral elements?

There are 19 mineral elements, most of which are required by the body in very small quantities. The body has, at certain times, a greater demand for cer-tain mineral elements and there is a danger then of a deficiency in the diet. Calcium, iron and iodine are those most likely to be deficient.

Calcium

Calcium is required for:

- building bones and teeth
- muscle contraction
- transmission of nerve impulses.

The use the body makes of calcium is dependent on the presence of vitamin D.

Calcium can be found in:

- milk and milk products
- bones of tinned oily fish
- vegetables (greens)
- tofu
- wholemeal bread and white bread (to which calcium is added).

Note that it is still the practice to add calcium, iron, thiamin and nicotinic acid to flour despite the findings of DHSS Report No. 23 (1981) which recommended that this practice should be discontinued.

Although calcium is present in certain foods (spinach, cereals) the body is unable to make use of it as it is not in a soluble form and therefore cannot be absorbed.

Because of the need for growth of bones and teeth, infants, adolescents, expectant and nursing mothers have a greater demand for calcium.

Phosphorus

Phosphorus is required:

- for building bones and teeth (in conjunction with calcium and vitamin D)
- for fluid acid balance (acts as a buffering agent)
- as a component of ATP, which provides energy for our bodies.

Sources of phosphorus include:

- liver
- eggs
- bread
- kidney
- cheese
- tofu
- legumes
- nuts
- fish.

Iron

Iron is required for building haemoglobin in the blood and is therefore necessary for transporting oxygen and carbon dioxide round the body.

Sources of iron include:

- lean meat
- wholemeal flour
- offal
- green vegetables
- egg yolk
- fish.

Iron is most easily absorbed from meat and offal, and its absorption is helped by the presence of vitamin C.

Iron may also be obtained from iron utensils in which food is prepared.

As the haemoglobin in the blood should be maintained at a constant level, the body requires more iron at certain times than others (e.g. after loss of blood).

Sodium

Sodium is required in all body fluids, and is found in salt (sodium chloride). Excess salt is continually lost from the body in urine. The kidneys control this loss. We also lose sodium in sweating, a loss over which we have no control.

Sodium levels in processed foods have been highlighted in recent years by the government as being too high. Too much salt in the diet can lead to hypertension and heart disease. The Food Standards Agency (FSA) has now set salt targets for processed retail foods in order to control this area of health.

Many foods are cooked with salt or have salt added (bacon and cheese) or contain salt (meat, eggs, fish). Excess sodium can cause hypertension (high blood pressure) in middle age.

Iodine

Iodine is required for the functioning of the thyroid gland which regulates basal metabolism (see page 123).

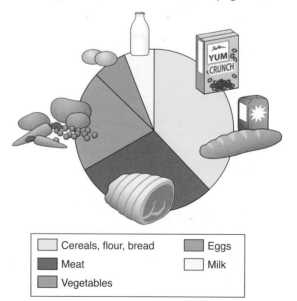

Cereals, flour, bread	Eggs
Meat	Milk
Vegetables	

Figure 4.10 Main sources of iron in the average diet

Sources of iodine include:

- sea foods
- iodised salt
- drinking water obtained near the sea
- vegetables grown near the sea.

Other minerals

Potassium, magnesium, sulphur and copper are some of the other minerals required by the body.

Water

Water is required for:

- regulation of body temperatures by evaporation of perspiration
- all body fluids
- metabolism
- digestion
- excretion
- absorption
- secretion.

Sources of water include:

- drinks of all kinds
- foods, such as fruits and vegetables, meat, eggs
- combustion or oxidation – when fats, carbohydrates and protein are used for energy, a certain amount of water (metabolic water) is produced within the body.

The effects of cooking on nutrients

Some foods are best eaten when freshly harvested, without further preparation or cooking. Fruit such as bananas, and vegetables such as tomatoes and lettuce fall into this category. Cooking and storage over prolonged periods reduces the nutritional value of these foods.

With the above exceptions, the digestibility of most foods is enhanced through cooking.

Protein

When protein is heated it coagulates and shrinks. Too much cooking can spoil the appearance of the food, such as scrambled eggs, as well as causing destruction of certain vitamins. On being heated, the different proteins in foods set, or coagulate, at different temperatures; above these temperatures shrinkage occurs; this is particularly noticeable in grilling or roasting meat. Moderately cooked protein is the most easy to digest: a lightly cooked egg is more easily digested than a raw egg or a hard-boiled egg.

Carbohydrate

Unless starch is cooked thoroughly it cannot be digested properly (e.g. insufficiently cooked pastry or bread). Foods containing starch have cells with starch granules, covered with a cellulose wall that breaks down when heated or made moist, making the starch digestible (this is called gelatinisation of starch).

When browned – for example, the crust of bread, toast, roast potatoes or the skin of rice pudding – the starch forms dextrins and these taste sweeter. This is known as the caramelisation of sugar.

On heating with water or milk, the starch gelatinises and causes the food to thicken (i.e. thickening of gravy).

Fat

The nutritive value of fat is not affected by cooking. During cooking processes a certain amount of fat may be lost from food when the fat melts, such as in the grilling of meat.

Mineral elements

There is a possibility of some minerals being lost in the cooking liquor, so diminishing the amount available in the food. This applies to soluble minerals, such as salt, but not to calcium or iron compounds, which do not dissolve in the cooking liquor.

Iron

Iron may be acquired from foods cooked in iron utensils. The iron in foods is not affected by cooking.

Calcium

Cooking foods in hard water may very slightly increase the amount of calcium in food.

Vitamins

- Vitamins A and D withstand cooking temperatures, and are not lost in the cooking.
- Vitamin B1 (thiamin) can be destroyed by high temperatures and by the use of bicarbonate of soda. It is soluble in water and can be lost in the cooking.
- Vitamin B2 (riboflavin) is not destroyed easily by heat, but bright sunlight can break it down.
- Vitamin C is lost by cooking and by keeping food warm in a hot place. It is also soluble in water (the soaking of foods for a long time and bruising are the causes of losing vitamin C). It is unstable and therefore easily destroyed in alkaline conditions (bicarbonate of soda must not be used when cooking green vegetables).

Table 4.8 Reference nutrient intakes (RNIs) for protein, vitamins and minerals

Age	Protein g/day	Vitamin A mg/day	Thiamin mg/day	Riboflavin mg/day	
0–3 months	12.5	350	0.2	0.4	
4–6 months	12.7	350	0.2	0.4	
7–9 months	13.7	350	0.2	0.4	
10–12 months	14.9	350	0.3	0.4	
1–3 years	14.5	400	0.5	0.6	
4–6 years	19.7	500	0.7	0.8	
7–10 years	28.3	500	0.7	1.0	
Males					
11–14 years	42.1	600	0.9	1.2	
15–18 years	55.2	700	1.1	1.3	
19–50 years	55.5	700	1.0	1.3	
50+ years	53.3	700	0.9	1.3	
Females					
11–14 years	41.2	600	0.7	1.1	
15–18 years	45.0	600	0.8	1.1	
19–50 years	45.0	600	0.8	1.1	
50+ years	46.5	600	0.8	1.1	
Pregnancy	+6	+100	+0.1*	+0.3	
Lactation	+11	+350	+0.2	+0.5	

Source: Gaman and Sherrington, 1998

Food requirements

Energy is required to enable the heart to beat, for the blood to circulate, the lungs and other organs of the body to function, for every activity such as talking, eating, standing, sitting, and for strenuous exercise and muscular activity.

Young and active people require a different amount of food than those who are elderly or inactive because they expend more energy; this energy is obtained from food during chemical changes that take place in the body.

The energy value of a food is measured by a term called a kilocalorie or Calorie (strictly speaking, this term should be written with a capital C, although popularly it is often written with a small c). This is the amount of heat required to raise the temperature of 1000 g of water from 15 to 16°C (59 to 61°F).

A new unit is now gradually replacing the Calorie. This is the joule. Since the joule is too small for practical nutrition, the kilojoule (kJ) is used:

1 Calorie = 4.18 kJ

(Both units will be given here and, for ease of conversion, 1 Calorie will be taken to equal 4.0 kJ.)

Foods contain certain amounts of the various nutrients, which are measured in grammes.

The energy value of nutrients is as follows:

- 1 g carbohydrate produces 4 Calories (16 kJ)
- 1 g protein produces 4 Calories (16 kJ)
- 1 g fat produces 9 Calories (36 kJ).

The energy value of a food, diet or menu is calculated from the nutrients it contains; 28 g of food containing:

- 10 g carbohydrate will produce 10 × 4 = 40 Calories (160 kJ)
- 2 g protein will produce 2 × 4 = 8 Calories (32 kJ)
- 5 g fat will produce 5 × 9 = 45 Calories (180 kJ)
- total – 93 Calories (372 kJ).

Foods having a high fat content will have a high energy value; those containing a lot of water, a low energy value. All fats, cheese, bacon and other foods with a high fat content have a high energy value.

Men require more Calories (kJ) than women; big men and women require more than small men and women; people engaged in energetic work require more Calories (kJ) than those with sedentary occupations.

Niacin mg/day	Folate mg/day	Vitamin C mg/day	Vitamin D mg/day	Calcium mg/day	Iron mg/day
3	50	25	8.5	525	1.7
3	50	25	8.5	525	4.3
4	50	25	7	525	7.8
5	50	25	7	525	7.8
8	70	30	7	350	6.9
11	100	30	–	450	6.1
12	150	30	–	550	8.7
15	200	35	–	1000	11.3
18	200	40	–	1000	11.3
17	200	40	–	700	8.7
16	200	40	**	700	8.7
12	200	35	–	800	14.8
14	200	40	–	800	14.8
13	200	40	–	700	14.8
12	200	40	**	700	8.7
+0	+100	+10	10	+0	+0
+2	+60	+30	1		

Basal metabolism

Basal metabolism is the term given to the amount of energy required to maintain the functions of the body, and to keep the body warm when it is still and without food. The number of Calories (kJ) required for basal metabolism is affected by the size, sex and general condition of the body. The number of Calories (kJ) required for basal metabolism is approximately 1700 per day.

In addition to the energy required for basal metabolism, energy is also required for everyday activities, such as getting up, dressing and walking; the amount required will be closely related to a person's occupation.

The approximate energy requirements per day for the following examples are:

- clerk – 2000 Calories (8000 kJ)
- carpenter – 3000 Calories (12,000 kJ)
- labourer – 4000 Calories (16,000 kJ).

Value of foods in the diet

Dairy products

Dairy products are a very important group of foods. Not only do they contain protein, carbohydrates and fat, but they are also a good source of calcium and vitamins.

Milk

Milk is designed by nature to be a complete food for young animals and humans. Cows' milk is almost the perfect food for humans due to its nutritional value.

When milk is taken into the body it coagulates in the same way as in the making of junket. This occurs in the stomach, when digestive juices (containing the enzyme rennin) are added. Souring of milk is due to the bacteria feeding on the milk sugar (lactose) and producing lactic acid from it, which brings about curdling.

Composition of milk

The approximate composition of milk is as follows:

- 87 per cent water
- 3–4 per cent proteins (mostly casein)
- 3–4 per cent fat
- 4–5 per cent sugar
- 0.7 per cent minerals (particularly calcium)
- vitamins A, B and D (the vitamin content varies from season to season, and according to breed of cow and preservation method).

In Channel Islands milk (Jersey and Guernsey) the percentage of fat must be 4 per cent; in all other milk the minimum is 3 per cent.

Milk contains protein, milk, sugar (lactose), fat, vitamins and minerals. Because of its high water content, while it is a suitable food for infants, it is too bulky to be the main source of protein and other nutrients after the first few months of life. It is also deficient in iron and vitamin C. However, it may be included in everyone's diet as a drink and can be used in a variety of ways.

Skimmed milk, which has had the cream layer removed, is increasing in popularity. Not only does it provide a lower calorie intake for those watching their weight, but also the potentially harmful animal fat has been removed.

Soya milk is a popular alternative, which is low in saturated fat and cholesterol. Nut milk, made from almonds, is also available.

Cream

Cream is the fat of milk; the legal minimum fat content of single cream is approximately 18 per cent, for double cream 48 per cent and clotted cream 60 per cent. Cream is therefore an energy-producing food, which also supplies vitamins A and D. It is easily digested because the fat is in a highly emulsified form (i.e. the fat globules are very small).

Butter

Butter is made from the fat of milk and contains vitamins A and D, the amount depending on the season.

Like cream, it is easily digested. It is a high-energy food.

Composition of butter

The approximate composition of butter is:

- 84 per cent fat
- 1 per cent salt
- 15 per cent water
- vitamins A and D.

Cheese

Cheese is made from milk; its composition varies according to whether the cheese has been made from whole milk, skimmed milk or milk to which extra cream has been added.

The composition of Cheddar cheese is approximately:

- 40 per cent fat
- calcium
- 30 per cent water
- vitamins A and D
- 25 per cent protein.

Hard cheese is high in saturated fat and can be high in sodium. Cheese provides protein, fat, and some vitamins and minerals.

The food value of cheese is exceptional because of the concentration of the various nutrients it contains. The minerals in cheese are useful, particularly calcium and phosphorus. Cheese is also a source of vitamins A and D.

It is a body-building, energy-producing and protective food because of its protein, fat and mineral elements, and vitamin content.

Cheese is easily digested, provided it is eaten with starchy foods and eaten in small pieces as when grated.

Margarine

Margarine, which is made from animal and/or vegetable oils, and skimmed milk, has vitamins A and D added to it. The composition and food value of margarine are similar to those for butter.

Table 4.9 The nutrient composition of creams per 100 g

Type	Energy (kJ)	Protein (g)	Fat (g)	Carbohydrate (g)	Sodium (mg)	Calcium (mg)
Half cream	568	2.8	12.3	4.1	55	96
Single cream	813	2.6	19.1	3.9	50	91
Whipping cream	1536	2.0	39.3	3.0	42	62
Double cream	1847	1.7	48.0	2.6	39	50

Source: Fox and Cameron, 1995, reproduced by permission of Hodder Education

Meat, poultry and game

Meat consists of fibres, which may be short, as in a fillet of beef, or long, as in silverside of beef. Generally, the shorter the fibre, the more tender and easily digested the meat. However, it is the cooking method that makes the most difference. Meat is carved across the grain to assist mastication and digestion of the fibres.

Hanging the meat helps to make the flesh more tender; this is because acids develop and soften the muscle fibres. Marinating in wine or vinegar prior to cooking also helps to tenderise meat so that it is more digestible. Expensive cuts of meat are not necessarily more nourishing than the cheaper cuts.

Meat is a very good source of protein and has variable amounts of fat, water, iron and thiamin, depending on the species and cut. Bacon and pork, in general, are particularly valuable because of their thiamin content. Red meat is a good source of iron, while poultry generally has a lower fat content, especially once the skin has been removed. Meat of all kinds is therefore important as a protein source.

Fish

Fish is a good source of protein.

The amount of fat in different fish varies: oily fish contain 5–18 per cent, white fish less than 2 per cent.

When the bones are eaten, calcium is obtained from fish (tinned sardines or salmon).

Oily fish is not so easily digested as white fish because of the fat content. However, oily fish is the best source of omega-3 – an essential fatty acid. It is recommended that we consume oily fish twice a week. Shellfish is not easily digested because of the coarseness of the fibres.

Eggs

The egg can store sufficient nutrients to supply a developing embryo with everything required for its growth.

Egg white contains protein called albumin (not to be confused with albumen, which is another name for the white of the egg itself) and the amount of white is approximately twice the amount of yolk.

The white is approximately one-eighth protein and seven-eighths water. In comparison the yolk is about one-third fats, half water, one-sixth protein, and a mixture of vitamins and minerals such as vitamins A and D, thiamin, riboflavin, calcium, iron, sulphur and phosphorus. All these factors make eggs a body-building, protective and energy-producing food. Eggs are also a rich source of cholesterol.

Fruit

The composition of different fruit varies considerably: avocado pears contain about 20 per cent fat, whereas most other fruits contain none. In unripe fruit the carbohydrate is in the form of starch, which changes to sugar as the fruit ripens. The cellulose in fruits acts as a source of dietary fibre.

Fruit is valuable because of the vitamins and minerals it contains. Vitamin C is present in certain fruits, particularly citrus varieties (oranges, grapefruit), blackcurrants and other summer fruits. Dried fruits such as raisins and sultanas are a useful source of energy because of their sugar content and fibre, but they contain no vitamin C. The vitamin C in fruit is lost during storage. Frozen fruit maintains its vitamin C content during freezing.

Composition of fruit

The approximate composition of fruit is:

- 85 per cent water
- 0.5 per cent minerals
- 5–10 per cent carbohydrate
- varying amounts of vitamin C
- 2–5 per cent cellulose.

Very small amounts of fat and protein are found in most fruits. Fruit is a protective food because of its mineral and vitamin content.

Nuts

Nuts are highly nutritious because of the protein, fat and minerals they contain, but much of the fat comes in monounsaturated or polyunsaturated form.

Nuts are not easily digested because of their fat and cellulose content.

Vegetables

Green vegetables

Green vegetables are particularly valuable because of their vitamin and mineral content; they are therefore protective foods. The most important minerals they contain are iron and calcium. Green vegetables are rich in carotene, which is made into vitamin A in the body.

The greener the vegetable, the greater its nutritional value. Vegetables that are stored for long periods, or that are damaged or bruised, quickly lose their vitamin C value, therefore they should be used as quickly as possible.

Green vegetables also act as a source of dietary fibre in the intestines. Onions and leeks are also green vegetables, and are an excellent source of fibre.

Root vegetables

Compared with green vegetables, most root vegetables contain more starch and sugar; they are therefore a source of energy. Swedes and turnips contain a little vitamin C, and carrots and other yellow-coloured vegetables contain carotene, which is changed into vitamin A in the body. They are an excellent source of fibre.

Potatoes

Potatoes contain a large amount of starch (approximately 20 per cent) and a small amount of protein just under the skin. Because of the large quantities eaten, the small amount of vitamin C they contain is of value in the diet.

Onions

Onions are oligosaccharides and aid the good bacteria in the gut. They are used extensively and contain some sugar, but their main value is to provide flavour.

Peas and broad beans

These vegetables contain carbohydrate, protein and carotene.

Cereals

Cereals include wheat and wheat products.

Cereals contain from 60 to 80 per cent carbohydrate in the form of starch and are therefore energy foods. They also contain 7–13 per cent protein, depending on the type of cereal, and 1–8 per cent fat.

The vitamin B content is considerable in stoneground and wholemeal flour, and B vitamins are added to other wheat flours, as are calcium and iron salts.

Oats contain good quantities of fat, protein and soluble fibre.

Of all cereals in the British diet, bread is by far the most important. The government fortifies flour (not wholemeal) with calcium, iron, thiamin and niacin to improve its nutritional value. However, wholegrain bread contains the greatest number of nutrients and white bread the fewest.

Sugar

There are several kinds of sugar, such as those found in fruit (glucose), milk (lactose), cane and beet sugar (sucrose).

Sugar, with fat, provides the most important part of the body's energy requirements.

Saccharin, although sweet, is chemically produced and has no food value.

Liquids

Water

Certain waters contain mineral salts; hard waters contain soluble salts of calcium. Some spas are known for the mineral salts contained in the local water. Bottled natural mineral waters are sold in many places (particularly supermarkets), and are being used more widely in the catering industry and in the home. Fluoride may be present naturally in some waters, and makes children's teeth more resistant to decay.

Fruit juices

In recent years there has been a tremendous increase in the consumption of fruit juices sold in cartons as a chilled drink or in 'long life' form, which will keep almost indefinitely before being opened. In addition, freshly squeezed orange juice is a popular alternative drink.

The nutritional value of fruit juices is very similar to that of whole fruit when freshly squeezed, but without the fibre. Fruit juices are high in sugars and low in fibre, and can dehydrate the body, so should be drunk in moderation.

Tea, coffee and cocoa

Tea and coffee have no food value in themselves, but the caffeine in them acts as a stimulant on the nervous system. Herb teas, green teas and rooibos teas are caffeine-free. Green tea is an excellent antioxidant.

Cocoa contains some fat, starch and protein, also some vitamin B and mineral elements.

When tea, coffee and cocoa are served with milk and sugar they do have some food value.

Alcoholic beverages

Alcohol must be considered as a foodstuff because it provides the body with energy. The energy value of wine is the same as that of milk, but without the nutritional benefit. Alcohol is a drug and affects the central nervous system. The effect of alcohol can range from mild stimulation to links with cancer of the liver, stomach and oesophagus.

Catering for health

Practical guidance on healthier catering

Concern that many catering courses include little information about nutrition led to the publication of guidance by the FSA and the Department of Health: *Catering for Health: A Guide to Teaching Healthier Catering Practices* (see the 'References' section for details of how to obtain a copy). However, in the newer VRQ courses, nutrition is part of the learning programme.

A balanced diet

Food intake needs to provide the vitamins, minerals, protein and fibre the body requires, without too much saturated fat, sugar and salt. The government recommends that all individuals should consume a diet that contains:

- plenty of starchy foods such as rice, bread, pasta and potatoes (choosing wholegrain varieties when possible)
- plenty of fruit and vegetables – at least five portions of a variety of fruit and vegetables a day
- some protein-rich foods, such as meat, fish, eggs, beans and non-dairy sources of protein, such as nuts and pulses

- some milk and dairy, choosing reduced-fat versions or eating smaller amounts of full-fat versions or eating them less often
- just a little saturated fat, salt and sugar.

The eatwell plate (Figure 4.11) is a pictorial representation of the contribution that different food groups should make to the diet. This representation of food intake applies to individuals over the age of five.

Caterers can assist customers to achieve a more balanced diet, within the parameters of their eating-out experience. When the customer base is all or mostly captive – in a home for the elderly, hospital, boarding school, the armed forces, workers on an oil rig, and so on – there are three meals a day, and a menu cycle that can be viewed over a week or fortnight. So, for example, the number of red meat main courses can be limited to two or three days a week, while fish is offered on one or two days a week, especially oily fish. A variety of fruit can be included in all meals, with perhaps a glass of fruit juice or fresh fruit at breakfast; so can starchy foods, with cereals and/or porridge at breakfast, and bread rolls. Vegetables and salads can feature more prominently for midday and evening meals. Dishes relatively high in fat and sugar can be limited to treats, perhaps once a week.

The eatwell plate

FOOD STANDARDS AGENCY
food.gov.uk

Use the eatwell plate to help you get the balance right. It shows how much of what you eat should come from each food group.

Fruit and vegetables

Bread, rice, potatoes, pasta
and other starchy foods

Flakes

Meat, fish, eggs, beans
and other non-dairy sources of protein

Foods and drinks high in fat and/or sugar

Milk and dairy foods

Figure 4.11 The eatwell plate

When the customer base is transient – as in most restaurants, pubs, wine bars, hotels, cafés, and so on – the menu choice can be varied to offer, say, a pasta dish, white meat and fish as well as red meat, dishes that are low in fat, interesting vegetables and salads, and imaginative, appealing dishes based on these. Alternatives might be offered to all-time favourites: a baked jacket potato with a salad garnish as an alternative to French fries with the main course.

Healthy catering by stealth has more chance of success than any attempt to corral customers into a better lifestyle, unless you are confident of reaching the quite specific market segment that wants only healthy dishes. Just as high-street retailers do with sandwiches and snacks aimed at the lunchtime market, it may work well to brand one or two dishes as healthy choices.

Bear in mind your customers' approach to food

Customers' approach to food is through experience, education, background, sophistication, travel, and so on. Some people enjoy experimenting, others don't. Some enjoy wholegrain pastas, rice and bread, for example, while others won't touch them. Healthy catering should not be introduced in such a way that it alienates people.

Even where there is quite strong customer resistance, subtle changes can be introduced over time, if necessary, to the content, presentation and service of favourite dishes.

Adapt recipes, preparation and cooking methods

With thought and skill, a substantial contribution can be made to a balanced diet without loss of flavour or texture, or restricting customer choice. Nor should it jeopardise operating margins. Indeed the process, by encouraging creativity, could lead to improved profits, with high added value yet less expensive ingredients.

There are many practical changes that can be made to the way food is prepared and cooked, which will lead to a healthier choice for your customers. To get the best results, some trialling and experimentation are recommended.

Possibilities include the following.

- **Adapt recipes:** use alternative flavourings to salt and proprietary products high in salt; reduce quantities of fat/oil; replace butter with olive oil or a mixture of butter and olive oil; thicken with purées of vegetables/fruit/pulses, or potatoes in place of a roux; use natural fruit juice to sweeten; use wholemeal with white flour for pastry.
- **Adjust preparation methods:** trim visible fat, remove poultry skin; leave skin on potatoes, vegetables and fruit (to increase fibre content and reduce vitamin loss); use chunky/thick cuts (to reduce fat absorption/vitamin loss).
- **Selected ingredients:** lean cuts and joints of meat; skinless poultry; fish rich in oils beneficial to health (e.g. salmon, mackerel, herring, trout); white fish (very little fat); prepared dishes that can be oven baked or grilled instead of fried; unsugared breakfast cereals; fruit juices and products in their natural juices/unsweetened; oils, fats and spreads that are high in monounsaturates or polyunsaturates; pre-prepared and convenience products that are low in salt/sugar/fat.
- **Change to low-fat cooking methods:** grill, bake, poach, microwave, stir-fry (quick cooking, minimum oil), shallow-fry in non-stick pans (to use less oil), steam chips to blanch. Keeping the temperature of oil low can protect its structure and therefore preserve its health properties.
- **For vegetables:** favour cooking methods that reduce vitamin loss – steam, microwave or stir-fry, cook in small batches (to reduce hot holding time).

Marketing and presentation

Describe dishes and menu choices in ways that will appeal to your customers. Avoid terms like 'health', 'low in fat', 'low in saturates', especially if your customers are eating out for enjoyment. Emphasise the positive: unusual flavours and combinations, freshly cooked, tasty, satisfying, interesting textures, colourful garnishes, exotic ingredients, associations with foreign travel, ethnic cuisines, and so on.

Feature as dishes of the day, special promotions, house specialities, and in counter and buffet display those dishes that have been prepared and cooked according to healthy catering guidelines. Expand the choice of accompaniments and sauces to give appealing, healthier alternatives to those that are high in fat or sugar. Choose garnishes that increase the starch, fibre, vegetable and/or fruit content.

Include healthy additions in the price, such as a granary or wholemeal roll with soup, fresh fruit with a sandwich or lunchtime snack, rice or naan bread with a curry. Select healthy choices for promotional offers.

Involve your staff: brief them on the dish content so that descriptions are appealing and accurate, and questions can be answered helpfully.

Take care not to use misleading or false descriptions, or terms that have a specific legal meaning under the food labelling regulations, such as 'low fat', 'reduced fat', 'low salt'.

Vegetarians

Some 10 per cent of 15–18-year-old girls claim to be vegetarian or vegan. Vegetarians, and vegans in particular, need to carefully balance their food intake to ensure that they do not go short of iron, vitamin B12, zinc, vitamin D and calcium. The less restricted the diet, the better. However, vegetarians have a lower risk of heart disease, stroke, diabetes, gallstones, kidney stones and colon cancer; they are also less likely to become overweight or to have raised cholesterol levels.

To find out more, contact the British Nutrition Foundation, High Holborn House, 52–54 High Holborn, London WC1V 6RQ (website: www.nutrition.org.uk) or the Nutrition Society, 10 Cambridge Court, 210 Shepherd's Bush Rd, London W6 7NJ (website: www.nutsoc.org.uk).

Pregnant and breastfeeding women

Foods to avoid: pregnant and breastfeeding women should not consume soft, mould-ripened cheese, pâté, raw or partially raw eggs, undercooked meat and poultry, tuna, swordfish or marlin, liver or liver-containing foods, alcohol or more than two portions of oily fish a week.

Special diets

There will be occasions when caterers will be asked to provide some special diets or to cater for a guest with special dietary needs.

Table 4.10 gives examples of some of the special diets that a caterer may have to produce. See also the section on food allergies, below.

Today there is a body of opinion within the medical profession which suggests that a regular diet of fresh fruit and vegetables can help to eliminate a number of diseases and certain types of cancers. Also it is advisable to reduce saturated fat intake, eat more fish, wholegrain breads, pulses and rice.

Practical steps to consider in order to achieve this are:

- accurate descriptions of dishes
- avoid general statements (e.g. 'all dishes may contain traces of nuts')
- choose suppliers that provide accurate information (e.g. ingredients labelling)
- choose and scrutinise the ingredients lists of convenience foods for any hidden components
- train staff on the content of dishes so they can provide helpful, accurate information to customers
- employ policies for segregation and prevention of cross-contamination in the kitchen.

Figure 4.12 A basic preparation area

Overweight and obesity

The challenge in the future will be to change the food culture in the UK to one that is more geared towards a healthy diet. It is now estimated that one-third of all cancers are the result of poor diet.

One of the biggest problems facing the UK and other developed countries is obesity.

Obesity

Obesity is a condition in which abnormal or excessive fat accumulation in adipose tissue impairs health. It is defined in adults as a body mass index (BMI) above 30. Obesity is one of the most visible and, until recently, most neglected public health problems. Body weight is influenced by energy intake (from food) and energy expenditure (needed for basal metabolism such as keeping the heart beating) and for physical activity. If a person regularly consumes more energy (calories) than they use, they will start to gain weight and eventually become overweight or obese. If a person regularly consumes less energy than they use they will lose weight. Extra energy is stored in the body as fat. Balancing energy intake and output to maintain a healthy weight has many benefits.

Table 4.10 Special diets

Diet	Foods to avoid
Vegetarian and other ethical diets	Meat or fish of any type, or dishes made with or containing the products of animals Check for 'vegetarians' who occasionally eat fish and/or meat (*semi-vegetarian* or *demi-vegetarian*), do not eat milk and dairy products (*ovo-vegetarian*), do not eat eggs (*lacto-vegetarian*), do not eat any food of animal origin, including honey, dairy products, egg (*vegan* – vegetables, fruits, grains, legumes, pasta made without eggs, soya products and other products of plants are acceptable to vegans), eat only fruit, nuts and berries (*fruitarian* or *fructarian*)
Religious diets	*Muslim:* pork, meat that is not halal (slaughtered according to custom), shellfish and alcohol (even when used in cooking) *Hindu:* meat, fish or eggs (orthodox Hindus are usually strict vegetarians); less strict Hindus may eat lamb, poultry and fish but definitely not beef as cattle have a deep religious meaning (milk, however, is highly regarded) *Sikh:* beef, pork, lamb, poultry and fish may be acceptable to Sikh men; Sikh women tend to avoid all meat *Jewish:* pork, pork products, shellfish and eels, meat and milk served at the same time or cooked together; strict Jews eat only kosher meat; milk and milk products are usually avoided at lunch and dinner (but acceptable at breakfast) *Rastafarian:* all processed foods, pork, fish without fins (eels), alcohol, coffee, tea
Therapeutic diets	*Diabetes:* dishes that are high in sugar and/or fat (low-calorie sweeteners can be used to sweeten desserts) *Low cholesterol and saturated fat:* liver, egg yolks and shellfish (which are high in cholesterol), beef, pork and lamb (which contain saturated fats), butter, cream, groundnut oil, margarine (use oils and margarines labelled high in polyunsaturated fats) *Low fat:* any food that contains fat, or has been fried or roasted *Low salt:* foods and dishes that have had salt added in cooking or processing (including smoked and cured fishes and meats, and hard cheeses), or that contain monosodium glutamate *Low residue:* wholemeal bread, brown rice and pasta, fried and fatty foods *Milk-free:* milk, butter, cheese, yoghurt and any pre-prepared foods that include milk products (check label) *Nut allergy:* nuts, blended cooking oils and margarine (since these may include nut oil; use pure oils or butter), and any dishes containing these (check label) *Gluten-free:* wheat, wholemeal, wholewheat and wheatmeal flour, wheat bran, rye, barley and oats (some doctors say oats are permitted; the Coeliac Society advises against), and any dishes made with these, including pasta, noodles, semolina, bread, pastries, some yoghurts (e.g. muesli), some cheese spreads, barley-based drinks, malted drinks, beer, some brands of mustard, proprietary sauces made with flour (use cornflour to thicken; rice, potato, corn and sage are also acceptable)

How common are overweight and obesity?

The latest NHS statistics on obesity show that, in 2008, almost a quarter of adults (24 per cent of men and 25 per cent of women aged 16 or over) in England were classified as obese with a BMI of over 30. A total of 42 per cent of men in comparison to 32 per cent of women in England were classified as overweight with a BMI of at least 25. A total of 16.8 per cent of boys aged 2 to 15, and 15.2 per cent of girls of the same age were classed as obese, with a steady increase since 1995. However, the overweight bracket remains constant.

Obesity is now a worldwide public health problem, affecting all age and socioeconomic groups. It is the most important dietary factor in chronic diseases such as cancer, cardiovascular disease and type 2 diabetes. It is second only to smoking as a cause of cancer. People who are overweight or obese are more likely to suffer from coronary heart disease, type 2 diabetes, gallstones, osteoarthritis (of the knees), high blood pressure and some types of cancer. Obese women are more likely to have complications during and after pregnancy. The World Health Organization (WHO) has predicted that one of the consequences of the global epidemic of obesity will be 300 million people with type 2 diabetes by 2025.

It is not just a problem of excess fat, but where that fat is deposited. People who have extra weight (fat) around their middle – 'apple shaped' – are at greater risk of some of these diseases than those who have most of the extra weight around their hips and thighs – 'pear shaped'. Because the health risks of obesity are compounded by the influence of fat distribution, waist-to-hip ratios or waist circumferences are now commonly measured. In general, men are at increased risk of obesity-related diseases when their waist circumference reaches 94 cm (37 inches). For women, risks increase at 80 cm (32 inches). The risks of disease become substantially increased at 102 cm (40 inches) for men and 88 cm (35 inches) for women.

Obesity and diabetes

Obese people also have a higher risk of developing diabetes. Diabetes develops when the body cannot use glucose properly. Around 1.4 million people in the UK have been diagnosed with diabetes, of whom around 1 million have type 2 diabetes. In addition, there are a large number of people who may have unrecognised diabetes.

Eating a healthy balanced diet, taking regular physical exercise, and maintaining a healthy body weight can help to prevent or delay the onset of type 2 diabetes. People with diabetes should try to maintain a healthy weight and eat a diet that is low in fat (particularly saturated fats) and salt, but that contains plenty of fruit and vegetables (at least five portions a day), and starchy carbohydrate foods such as bread, rice and pasta (particularly wholegrain versions).

Other health concerns

Yet another future challenge for the hospitality industry is to reduce the amount of salt used in cooking. It is now well recognised that there is a link between salt and hypertension (high blood pressure). High blood pressure often causes no symptoms but increases the risk of developing conditions such as heart disease and stroke.

Around a third of the adult population in the UK has been diagnosed with hypertension; it is most common in older people, those with a family history of the condition and in some ethnic groups.

A number of lifestyle factors can help to prevent or treat high blood pressure – for example, not smoking, being physically active, maintaining a healthy body weight, drinking alcohol in moderation (if at all), eating a balanced and varied diet that is low in fat (particularly saturated fats) and sodium (salt), and that includes low-fat dairy. A diet that is low in fat and includes low-fat dairy foods, and fruit and vegetables, has been shown to lower blood pressure in people with or without high blood pressure. This diet

reduced the amount of fat, saturates and cholesterol, and increased the amount of potassium, magnesium and calcium. Reducing the amount of salt in the diet also had a beneficial effect. The best effect was achieved when both approaches were combined. This highlights the importance of improving the diet overall rather than focusing on single nutrients. Eating a healthy, balanced diet will also help to maintain a healthy body weight.

Salt and health

A recent report by the Scientific Advisory Committee on Nutrition concluded that sodium intake is an important determinant of blood pressure, in part influencing the rise of blood pressure with age. As the main source of sodium in the diet is salt (sodium chloride), it has been recommended that people in the UK try to reduce their salt intake to a maximum of 6 g per day (about a teaspoon). For most people this will mean reducing their current intake by one-third.

Salt added at the table and during cooking contributes around 10–15 per cent of our total salt intake and naturally occurring salt in foods contributes another 10–15 per cent. Traditionally, salt has been used as a preservative and flavour enhancer. On average around 75 per cent of the salt in our diet comes from processed foods such as bread and cereal products, breakfast cereals, meat products, some ready meals, smoked fish, pickles, canned vegetables, canned and packet sauces and soups, savoury snack foods, biscuits and cakes. Spreading fats and cheese also make a small contribution to intake.

The cooperation and commitment of the food and hospitality industry are, therefore, required to develop lower-salt products to help people reduce their salt intake. The Food Standards Agency (FSA) is working closely with the food industry to explore ways to lower the sodium content of processed foods, and a number of manufacturers and retailers have already taken action to achieve the necessary reduction. However, such activities will be successful only if there is consumer acceptance of these products. The FSA is playing its part by raising public awareness of the dangers of high blood pressure and the need to reduce the amount of salt in our diets. People can do this by using food labels to select lower-salt/sodium products and by persevering so as to adapt their palates to less salty tastes.

Potassium, calcium and magnesium

An inadequate dietary intake of potassium may increase blood pressure. A high potassium intake may, therefore, protect against developing hyperten-

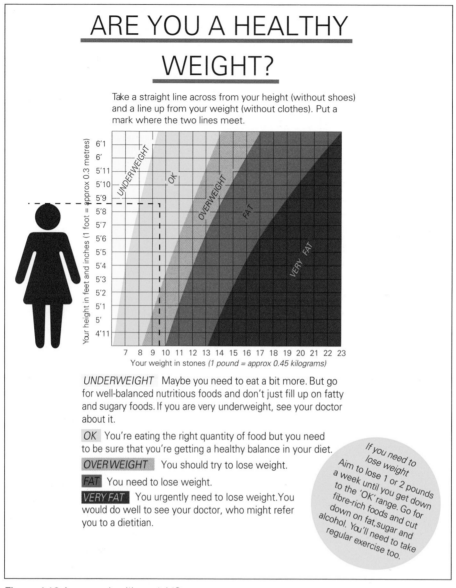

Figure 4.13 Are you a healthy weight?

sion and improve blood pressure control in patients with hypertension. There is also evidence to suggest that the effect of sodium (salt) on blood pressure may be related to the amount of potassium in the diet, and that the ratio of sodium to potassium in the diet might be more important than the absolute amount of either. Potassium is found in meat, milk, vegetables, potatoes, fruit (especially bananas) and fruit juices, bread, fish, nuts and seeds.

Studies have also suggested that ensuring an adequate amount of calcium and magnesium in the diet is important to protect against high blood pressure, as well as for general health. Sources of calcium include milk and dairy products, soft bones in canned fish, bread, pulses, green vegetables, dried fruit, nuts and seeds. Foods containing magnesium include cereals and cereal products, meat, green vegetables, milk, potatoes, nuts and seeds.

Diet and cancer

Approximately one-third of all cancers may be linked to diet.

What research tells us

Many of the early theories on the links between diet and cancer were tested in the laboratory and on animals. These provided helpful leads, but chemicals often react in quite different ways in humans than they do in animals or in a test tube. Also, it is not safe to assume that links found in animals equally apply to humans. The best information comes from studying human beings.

Types of study

Epidemiological studies look at what people eat, alongside the incidence of cancer; because dietary habits vary enormously these can produce a wealth of information on how diet may affect health.

- **Migrant studies** provide useful information on dietary and genetic factors. When Japanese people migrated to Hawaii, for example, their dietary patterns changed – and so did their risk of certain cancers. As the traditional Japanese diet has become more westernised so rates of breast and colon cancer have increased.
- **Case control studies** investigate the links that can be deduced by comparing the diets of cancer patients with similar people who do not have cancer. These tend to yield the best results when there is a big difference between the diets of those with and without cancer.
- **Cohort studies** follow the health and diet of healthy people over a long period of time to see if there is any difference in the diets of those who develop cancer and those who don't.
- **Intervention studies** track results from a particular diet or supplement, using a control group that is not given the diet or supplement. Ethically, of course, people should not be exposed to substances thought to increase the risk of cancer, so these studies are on particular nutrients thought to protect against cancer. 'Double blind' trials – when neither the researchers nor the individuals know which group they belong to – produce the most reliable results.

Some research may indicate a link between diet and cancer, while other research may provide more conclusive results. Where evidence is sufficiently strong, prestigious organisations such as the World Cancer Research Fund and the WHO publish guidance to help people make dietary changes.

Dietary influences

Studies over many years have shown a number of interesting correlations between different diets and cancers. The incidence of certain cancers, especially stomach and bowel, has increased as large-scale food processing has replaced many of the wholegrain cereals, pulses and roots in our diet with white flour and refined cereals and sugars.

Cancers of the stomach and oesophagus are much less common where the typical diet is high in cereals, tubers and starchy foods – often providing half of the dietary energy needs – but low in animal proteins (meat and dairy products). Diets in developed countries tend to be high in animal proteins, sugar and salt, but low in starches.

There is a greater incidence of stomach cancer in countries where traditionally a lot of salty foods are eaten – for example, Japan, China and Portugal.

In southern European countries, the consumption of fruit and vegetables is generally higher than in northern Europe, and the incidence of cancers of the mouth and throat, oesophagus, lung and stomach is lower in the south.

How can diet influence the development of cancer?

A damaged cell needs to replicate in order to grow into a group of cancer cells. Some substances in our diet may either encourage the replication process and promote cancer growth or slow it down, so protecting against cancer.

- **Carcinogenic agents:** These agents may directly influence DNA or protein in cells. Examples include alfatoxins, which are found in mouldy food, alcohol and certain compounds produced by some cooking and food-processing methods.
- **Tumour promoters:** Unlike carcinogens, tumour promoters do not act directly on DNA, but stimulate the genes and encourage replication. Some hormones may act in this way, and although the body produces these hormones naturally, diet can affect the level of, for example, oestrogens in the body. Other tumour promoters include alcohol and a high-fat or high-energy diet, which may promote the production of harmful substances, such as free radicals. Free radicals are thought to influence DNA disorganisation.

But, just as we may introduce harmful elements into our bodies through our diet, there are also nutrients that may protect us.

- **Protective nutrients:** Many foods contain protective substances that may reduce damage to tissues by free radicals, or potentially reduce cell growth.
- **Antioxidants:** Antioxidants are important constituents of the diet and are involved in DNA

Table 4.11 Protective nutrients: their sources and functions

Vitamins and mineral	Positive function	Sources
Carotenoids These are precursors of vitamin A; they include alpha-carotene, beta-carotene, xanthophylls (the main one is lutein), lycopene and cryptoxanthin	Antioxidant	Dark-green leafy vegetables, orange vegetables and fruit *Lutein:* kale, spinach, broccoli, corn *Lycopene:* tomatoes, watermelons, pink grapefruit, guavas *Cryptoxantin:* mangoes, papayas, persimmons, red peppers, pumpkins
Folate (folic acid)	Antioxidant; may affect division of cells in the colon	Beans, green leafy vegetables, liver, nuts, wholegrain cereals
Selenium	Stimulation of detoxification enzymes	Brazil nuts, bread, eggs, fish, meat
Vitamin C (ascorbic acid)	Antioxidant	Broccoli, cabbage and other green leafy vegetables, citrus fruit, mangoes, peppers, strawberries, tomatoes
Vitamin D	May control cell growth through its effect on calcium	Sunlight
Vitamin E	Antioxidant	Nuts, seeds, vegetables oils, wheatgerm, whole grains
Other bioactive compounds	**Positive function**	**Sources**
Allium compounds (contain sulphur)	Stimulate detoxification enzymes	Chives, garlic, onions
Flavonoids (e.g. quercetin)	Antioxidant function within the plant	Berries, broad beans, broccoli, onions, tomatoes
Isothiocyanates	Stimulate detoxifying enzymes	Broccoli, Brussels sprouts, cabbage and other brassicas
Phytoestrogens (isoflavones and lignans)	May alter steroid hormone metabolism	*Isoflavones:* beans, chickpeas, lentils, soya *Lignans:* oils seeds (e.g. flax, soya, rape), legumes and various other vegetables and fruit, particularly berries, whole grains
Plant sterols	May bind with hormones in the gut and influence hormone metabolism	Cereals, fruit, nuts, seeds, vegetables
Terpenoid (e.g. D-limonene)	Stimulate enzyme systems	Oil of lemons, oranges and other citrus fruits

Source: Dr Clare Shaw, Royal Marsden Hospital

and cell maintenance and repair. They may reduce the production of free radicals, preventing early damage to cells and so reduce the chance that they will become cancerous.

Antioxidants in the diet may be in the form of vitamins or minerals, such as vitamins C and E, beta-carotene and selenium, or they may be found in flavonoids in vegetables.

- **Phytoestrogens:** Phytoestrogens have properties similar to oestrogens, but they are much weaker than the oestrogens the body itself produces.

They can be divided primarily into two groups: isoflavones and lignans. Isoflavones are linked to the protein part of food and lignans to the fibre. Table 4.11 includes examples of sources of phytoestrogens.

- **Other bioactive compounds:** Many foods have functions beyond the vitamins and minerals they contain. Research is revealing that some of their chemicals and reactions may be beneficial to health. In laboratory experiments, for example, garlic extracts have killed *Heliobacter pylori*, a bacterium that can grow in the stomach and is known to increase the risk of cancer. Sulphur-containing compounds in garlic and onions may also reduce the formation of carcinogenic compounds that arise from the curing of meats.

> To find out more about catering for health, contact the Health Development Authority, Trevelyan House, 30 Great Peter Street, London SW1P 2HW.

Food allergies and intolerances

Estimates by the British Allergy Foundation and the Institute for Food Research put the proportion of the population with an allergy to at least one food at between 1 and 2 per cent, and the number is said to be growing each year by 5 per cent. The FSA has recently updated the food labelling regulations to incorporate more information on packaging about the type and level of allergens in supermarket foods. It is also strongly encouraging caterers to tell customers more and more about what is in their foods.

Food intolerances can be described as an adverse reaction to food. Intolerances fall into three groups:

1 intolerance to certain foods that cause a reaction – e.g. rashes, breathing difficulties and headaches
2 inability to digest certain foods – e.g. lactose intolerance, where there is not enough of the correct enzyme to digest the lactose

3 intolerance to certain chemicals – e.g. artificial colours, flavourings (as discussed on page 108).

Food allergies are a type of intolerance where the body's immune system sees the harmless food as harmful and therefore causes an allergic reaction. The allergic reaction that some people have to certain food items can sometimes be fatal.

Foods that may cause an allergic reaction in a very small number of people include milk and dairy products, fish, shellfish, eggs and nuts (particularly peanuts but also cashew, pecan, Brazil and walnuts). Peanuts are often commonly used in Bombay mix, peanut butter, satay sauce, nut-coated cereals, groundnut and arachide oils, salted peanuts, chopped nuts, vegetarian dishes, and salads that are a mixture of, say, nuts and fresh fruit.

Table 4.12 Special diets for those with food allergies and intolerances

Type of diet	Problems	Foods to avoid	Permitted foods
Coeliac	An allergy to gluten. Results in severe inflammation of the gastro-intestinal tract, pain and diarrhoea, and malnutrition due to inability to absorb nutrients	All products made from wheat, barley or rye; this includes bread; always check the label on all commercial products	Potatoes, rice and flours made from potatoes and rice; also cornflour, fresh fruit and vegetables
Food allergies	Individuals can suffer severe and rapid reactions to any food, which can be fatal; common allergies are to peanuts and their derivatives, sesame seeds, cashew nuts, pecan nuts, walnuts, hazelnuts, milk, fish, shellfish and eggs	Peanuts, chopped nuts, groundnut oil, satay sauce, arachide oil, peanut products and other nut products	
Low cholesterol	High levels of cholesterol circulating in the bloodstream are associated with an increased risk of cardiovascular disease	Liver, kidney, egg yolks, fatty meats, bacon, ham, pâté, fried foods, pastry, cream, full-fat milk, full-fat yoghurt, cheeses, salad dressings, biscuits, cakes	Lean meat and fish grilled or poached, fresh fruit and vegetables, low-fat milk, low-fat yoghurt, porridge, muesli
Diabetic	The body is unable to control the level of glucose in the blood	As above, plus high-sugar dishes; this can lead to comas and long-term problems such as increased risk of cardiovascular disease, blindness and kidney problems	As above plus wholemeal bread, pasta, rice, potatoes, pulses

The Anaphylaxis Campaign has warned caterers to be on the alert for foods containing flour made from lupin seeds as this can cause an allergic reaction similar to that of peanuts. Lupin flour is widely used as an ingredient in France, Holland and Italy because of its nutty taste, attractive yellow colour and because it is guaranteed GM free. Symptoms of anaphylactic shock include swelling of the throat and mouth, difficulty in swallowing and breathing, nausea, vomiting and unconsciousness. The fast administration of adrenaline will give relief.

Persons suffering an allergy to nuts need to know if and where they are used.

To find out more contact the British Allergy Foundation, St Bart's Hospital, London EC1A 7BE (website: www.allergyuk.org).
See also:
- **HCIMA Technical Brief No. 43**
- **www.foodallergy.com.**

Healthy cooking and eating

Different types of diet have different benefits. Try to increase the following foods in your menus, as they are beneficial for everyone.

- Fruit and vegetables contain potassium, magnesium and calcium, which control the movements of our muscles (including our heart) and help us to relax. They also contain antioxidants that protect us against high cholesterol and blocked arteries. The vitamin C in fruit and vegetables helps to keep our arteries supple and also regulates cholesterol levels.
- Onions and garlic help to lower cholesterol and blood pressure. Serve them raw for maximum benefit. Try red onion in salads, garlic in dressings, and add onion and garlic to soups, stews, stir-fries and roasted vegetables.
- Celery is a good source of potassium, which helps to keep the kidneys functioning efficiently; this in turn helps to lower blood pressure. Use it in salads, soups and stews or as crudités with hummus, guacamole or salsa.
- Cooked tomatoes provide more of the antioxidant lycopene than raw tomatoes. This helps to prevent furring (blocking due to cholesterol) of the arteries.
- Whole grains such as oats, rye, wholemeal bread and pasta contain fibre to help lower cholesterol and improve digestion. This helps to avoid re-absorbing the saturated fats that are bad for us. They also contain folic acid.
- Legumes such as beans and lentils, and pulses like chickpeas are good sources of low-fat protein (instead of high-fat red meat) and are high in B vitamins and fibre to help digestion.
- Nuts and seeds are good sources of heart-friendly essential fats, which lower blood pressure and keep arteries supple. They also contain magnesium for muscle relaxation, and the antioxidants vitamin E, selenium and zinc to protect against furring of the arteries. Provide these as snacks, or add them to cereal, salads and smoothies.
- Eggs, fish and lean poultry are good sources of protein, calcium and magnesium, plus B vitamins and zinc.
- Oily fish contain essential fatty acids. These are 'good fats' that help lower blood pressure. Everyone should aim to eat two to three portions of salmon, sardines, pilchards, mackerel, herrings, fresh tuna, trout or anchovies per week. Sardines are especially good as they reduce lipoprotein(a), a type of bad (LDL) cholesterol that can lead to heart disease if levels of it are too high.

The healthy heart

To help customers achieve or maintain heart health, decrease or avoid the following foods in your menus.

- Salt tells the body to retain water, which means that the heart needs to work harder to pump the increased volume of water through the blood vessels. This raises blood pressure. Avoid processed meats and cheeses, salted crisps and nuts, packaged foods and ready meals, and any food that contains more than 0.2 g of sodium per 100 g.
- Saturated fat can be found in red meat, processed foods, full-fat dairy products and fried foods. It can block arteries and is easily stored as fat.
- Hydrogenated/partially hydrogenated fat is added to processed foods and to some margarines to increase their shelf life. These block arteries and increase cholesterol.
- Sugar can cause weight gain, and can raise blood pressure if we eat too much of it.
- Alcohol contains a lot of calories and can

cause weight gain. We should limit our intake, particularly if we need to lose weight. Choose wine over spirits and beer, as evidence suggests that drinking a small amount of wine offers some protection to the heart.

People may also need to change some other aspect of their lifestyles to improve the health of the heart. Being overweight, smoking, not taking regular exercise and suffering from stress are all major contributors to heart problems.

The body needs a certain amount of cholesterol to function properly, for example, to make hormones. However, high levels of LDL cholesterol have been shown to increase furry deposits in the arteries, which causes them to narrow or block, making it hard for the blood to travel through them. HDL cholesterol can remove these deposits so, ideally, we want to raise our HDL cholesterol but reduce the total amount of cholesterol we eat. Anyone concerned about their cholesterol should see their doctor, who can monitor cholesterol levels.

Eating to detoxify

The liver is an extremely important organ. However, because you cannot see or feel it, it is easy to forget to look after it properly. One of the liver's major functions is to detoxify the body, removing harmful substances like alcohol, caffeine, sugar and waste such as old hormones.

The liver does have other functions, such as making hormones and helping digestion. However, if there are too many toxins in the body, the liver becomes so busy trying to detoxify that it neglects these other functions. Most of us could do with giving our liver a break from the constant onslaught of caffeine, alcohol, sugary and fatty foods, and too little sleep. The following suggestions of the 'top ten liver boosters' could help maintain a healthy liver .

1 Eat lots of garlic, onions, eggs, and vegetables like broccoli, cabbage, cauliflower and Brussels sprouts.
2 Eat detox-friendly fennel, artichoke, beetroot, lemon and parsley.
3 Eat good-quality protein (eggs, lean meat, fish, beans and pulses, nuts and seeds).
4 Eat brightly coloured fruits and vegetables in a range of colours, such as peppers, berries, squash and apples. Also eat dark-green leafy vegetables, which are rich in nutrients such as antioxidants.
5 Eat plenty of beans, pulses, lentils, and whole grains such as brown rice, oats and wholemeal

bread or rye bread. These have hormone-balancing properties.
6 Eat eggs, whole grains and nuts and seeds as these are rich in B vitamins, which again help hormone balance. This reduces the strain on the liver as it does not have to work so hard to regulate hormone levels.
7 Drink plenty of water (aim for two litres a day). Herbal teas, pure fruit juices and smoothies all count towards this.
8 Chew food thoroughly to improve your digestion.
9 Get enough sleep so that your liver can get on with its essential functions while you rest.
10 Try to relax, as stress produces hormones like adrenaline, which raise blood sugar levels. If this happens, the liver has to work hard to put the body back into balance.

We should avoid or limit the amount we eat of the following foods as they strain the liver:

- alcohol
- caffeine (in coffee, tea, cola, energy drinks and chocolate)
- sugar (including honey, syrup and sweeteners)
- saturated fats (red meat, fatty meat, full-fat dairy products, processed foods)
- hydrogenated fats (man-made fats added to processed food to increase their shelf life)
- preservatives and pesticides (in processed food and drinks, and non-organic fruit, vegetables and grains)
- processed meals and snacks (a toxic combination of sugar, saturated fat and chemical additives that places great strain on the liver).

Eating to boost energy, memory and concentration

What we eat can have a significant effect on your brain function, memory, concentration and energy levels. If you are under stress from work or exams, give your brain a boost by providing it with the right nutrients for the best performance.

The healthy brain

Blood sugar balance

If your blood sugar (the amount of sugar in your blood) is not at the right level (i.e. balanced) it can affect your energy levels and your ability to think straight. Sugar and caffeine make blood sugar levels rise rapidly. This gives a sudden burst of energy but it does not last long as your body quickly moves the excess sugar out of the blood before it can cause any damage.

Removing the sugar uses up energy so you end up feeling even more tired. To enjoy steady energy levels and good concentration it is important to eat carbohydrates that release their sugar more slowly. They will fill you up for longer without disturbing your blood sugar levels. Slow-release carbohydrates are usually fibre-rich whole foods like fresh fruit and vegetables, whole grains (such as brown rice, oats and wholemeal bread), and beans and lentils.

Vital vitamins and minerals

Vitamins and minerals do more than just ward off colds – they are also important in brain chemistry. We need them to turn glucose (a type of sugar) into energy and to turn the amino acids in protein into neurotransmitters (the parts of the brain that send messages to the body). Particularly important nutrients include:

- B vitamins in vegetables, beans and pulses, dairy products, fish, meat, eggs, whole grains, nuts and seeds
- vitamin C in fruit and vegetables, especially peppers, watercress, cabbage, broccoli, cauliflower, strawberries, citrus fruit, kiwi fruit, melon and tomatoes
- calcium in dairy products, nuts and seeds (especially almonds and pumpkin seeds), beans, soya, green leafy vegetables, sardines, anchovies and pilchards (fish where you are able to eat the bones), and prunes
- magnesium in whole grains, nuts (especially almonds, cashew nuts, Brazil nuts and pecans), potato skins, green leafy vegetables, peas, raisins, garlic and beans
- zinc in lamb, haddock, shrimps, oysters, egg yolk, rye, oats, wheat, nuts (especially pecans, Brazil nuts and almonds), peanuts, ginger, peas and turnips.

The human brain is up to 60 per cent fat. This is not just padding – it helps the brain to perform well. However, it is important to have the right type of fat in the brain. Essential fats help the brain to function, whereas hydrogenated fats and trans fats (produced in fried food when the fat is damaged by heat) block the brain function. We need to make sure that we eat essential fats as our body cannot make them itself.

There are two types of essential fats: omega-3 fats and omega-6 fats. Good sources of omega-3 fats include:

- oily fish – trout, salmon, fresh tuna (not canned), mackerel, sardines, anchovies, herring
- pumpkin seeds, walnuts, linseeds and flaxseeds.

Good sources of omega-6 fats include nuts and seeds, and their oils.

The brain-boosting diet

The following suggestions should help to increase your energy and concentration, and boost your performance.

- Eat more fruit and vegetables.
- Choose whole grains like brown rice, oats in porridge, muesli, oatcakes and rye bread.
- Eat foods that are rich in essential fats, like oily fish, and nuts and seeds. Aim for two to three portions of oily fish per week and a tablespoon of nuts or seeds per day as a snack or sprinkled on cereal or in smoothies.
- Avoid hydrogenated fats and partially hydrogenated fats. Check food labels carefully.
- Limit trans fats by avoiding fried food, and cooking with oils like medium (not virgin) olive oil or coconut oil from health food stores.
- Drink plenty of water.

Food additives

There is an increasing trend in the UK towards 'cleaning up' recipes and using as few artificial additives or as many natural ingredients as possible. For this reason, the use of some additives (such as monosodium glutamate) is increasingly frowned upon.

....

To find out more about additives, contact the Food Standards Agency, Room No. 213, Whitehall Place (East Block), London SW1A 2HH (website: www.food.gov.uk).

....

Additives can be divided into 12 categories and, except for purely 'natural' substances, their use is subject to certain legislation.

1 **Preservatives:** natural ones include salt, sugar, alcohol and vinegar; synthetic ones are also widely used.
2 **Colouring agents:** natural, including cochineal, caramel and saffron, and many synthetic ones.
3 **Flavouring agents:** synthetic chemicals

to mimic natural flavours (e.g. monosodium glutamate to give a meaty flavour to foods).

4 **Sweetening:** saccharin (an organic petroleum compound), sorbitol and aspartame.

5 **Emulsifying agents** (to prevent separation of salad creams, ice cream, etc.); examples are lecithin and glyceryl monostearate (GMS).

6 **Antioxidants:** to delay the onset of rancidity in fats due to exposure to air; examples are vitamin E and butylated hydroxy toluene (BHT).

7 **Flour improvers:** to strengthen the gluten in flour, such as vitamin C.

8 **Thickeners:** animal (gelatine); marine (agar-agar); vegetable (gum tragacanth – used for pastillage – and pectin; synthetic products.

9 **Humectants:** to prevent food drying out, such as glycerine (used in some icings).

10 **Polyphosphate:** injected into poultry before rigor mortis develops; it binds water to the muscle and thus prevents 'drip', giving a firmer structure to the meat.

11 **Nutrients:** vitamins and minerals added to breakfast cereals, vitamins A and D added to margarine.

12 **Miscellaneous:** anti-caking agents added to icing sugar and salt; firming agents (calcium chloride) added to tinned fruit and vegetables to prevent too much softening in the processing; mineral oils added to dried fruit to prevent stickiness.

Food spoilage

Unless foods are preserved they deteriorate; therefore, to keep them in an edible condition it is necessary to know what causes food spoilage. In the air there are certain micro-organisms called moulds, yeasts and bacteria, which cause foods to go bad.

There are two main types of spoilage:

1 chemical – i.e. over-ripening, breakdown of protein in meat leading to oxidation and rancidity

2 microbial – i.e. micro-organisms attack the food leading to spoilage and, in some cases, food poisoning.

Microbial spoilage

Moulds

These are simple plants that appear like whiskers on foods, particularly sweet foods, meat and cheese. To grow, they require warmth, air, moisture, darkness and food; they are killed by heat and sunlight. Moulds can grow where there is too little moisture for yeasts and bacteria to grow, and will be found on jams and pickles.

Although most of the time moulds are not harmful, they do cause foods to taste musty and to be wasted. There are a couple of types of moulds that are dangerous to health, so it is best not to eat them.

Correct storage in a dry cold store prevents moulds from forming.

Not all moulds are destructive. Some are used to flavour cheese (Stilton, Roquefort) or to produce antibiotics (penicillin, streptomycin).

Yeasts

These are single-cell plants or organisms, larger than bacteria, that grow on foods containing moisture and sugar. Foods containing only a small percentage of sugar and a large percentage of liquid, such as fruit juices and syrups, are liable to ferment because of yeasts. Although they seldom cause disease, yeasts do increase food spoilage; foodstuffs should be kept under refrigeration or they may be spoiled by yeasts. Yeasts are also destroyed by heat. The ability of yeast to feed on sugar and produce alcohol is the basis of the beer- and wine-making industries. Yeasts are also used in breadmaking and other fermented goods.

Bacteria

Bacteria are minute plants, or organisms, that require moist, warm conditions and a suitable food to multiply. They spoil food by attacking it, leaving waste products, or by producing poisons in the food.

Their growth is checked by refrigeration and they are killed by heat. Certain bacterial forms (spores) are more resistant to heat than others and require higher temperatures to kill them.

Pressure cooking destroys heat-resistant bacterial spores provided the food is cooked for a sufficient length of time, because increased pressure increases the temperature; therefore heat-resistant bacterial spores do not affect canned foods as the foods are cooked under pressure in the cans. Acids are generally capable of destroying bacteria, such as vinegar in pickles.

Dehydrated foods and dry foods do not contain

much moisture and, provided they are kept dry, spoilage from bacteria will not occur. If they become moist then bacteria can multiply – if dried peas are soaked and not cooked, for example, the bacteria present can begin to multiply.

Chemical spoilage

Food spoilage can occur due to other causes, such as by chemical substances called enzymes, which are produced by living cells. Fruits are ripened by the action of enzymes; they do not remain edible indefinitely because other enzymes cause the fruit to become over-ripe and spoil.

When meat and game are hung they become tender; this is caused by enzymes. To prevent enzyme activity going too far, foods must be refrigerated or heated to a temperature high enough to destroy the enzymes. Acid retards the enzyme action: lemon juice, for example, prevents the browning of bananas or apples when they are cut into slices.

Keeping up to date

Changes are occurring constantly regarding food production and manufacture, which may affect the use of foods in the kitchen. Consumers' reaction to reports of changes published in the press or seen or heard on the TV or radio may affect demand. Similarly, information about nutritional values can affect customers' preferences and thus cause trends and affect menu selection.

It is therefore essential to be aware of these reports and when necessary to act according to government recommendations. One example of research that has affected kitchen practice has been the use of eggs. In recent years, the rise in fatalities from bacteria such as BSE and E. coli has led to renewed concern and scrutiny of food production techniques.

Recommendations and contradictions produced by dietetic research can cause trends and affect consumer habits. The use of butter and margarine is one such example.

It is essential to keep up to date through the media and adopt a common-sense attitude to the comments made, but to take action when serious recommendations are made by valid research bodies.

Methods of preservation

In order to preserve food, it is important to kill the micro-organisms that cause the spoilage and then store the food in an environment where it cannot be re-infected, or in conditions where deterioration is slowed down or stopped.

Foods may be preserved by:

- removing the moisture from the food – drying, dehydration
- making the food cold – chilling, freezing
- applying heat – canning, bottling
- radiation, using X- or gamma-rays
- chemical means – salting, pickling, crystallising
- vacuum packing
- smoking
- chemical
- gas storage.

Drying or dehydration

Water is needed by micro-organisms to survive and reproduce. Therefore, by removing the water in foods below a critical value (this is a value that is specific for different types of foods) spoilage is reduced. In the past, this was done by drying foods (e.g. fruits) in the sun; today many types of equipment are used, and the food is dried by the use of air at regulated temperatures and humidity.

Advantages of drying

- If dried and kept dry, food keeps indefinitely.
- Food preserved by this method occupies less space than food preserved by other methods. Some dried foods occupy only 10 per cent of the space that would be required when fresh.
- Dried foods are easily transported and stored.
- The cost of drying and the expenses incurred in storing are not as high as those for other methods of preservation.
- There is no waste after purchase, therefore portion control and costing are simplified.

Foods preserved by drying

- Vegetables: peas, onions, beetroot, beans, carrots, lentils, cabbage, mixed vegetables, potatoes.
- Herbs, eggs, milk, coffee.
- Fruits: apples, pears, plums (prunes), apricots, figs, grapes (sultanas, raisins, currants).
- Meat, fish.

Vegetables

Many vegetables are dried; those most used are the pulse vegetables (beans, peas and lentils), which are used for soups, vegetable purées and many vegetarian dishes. Usually potatoes are cooked, mashed and then dried. The other dried vegetables are used as a vegetable (cabbage, onions).

Pulse vegetables may be soaked in water before use, then washed before being cooked. Vegetables that are dehydrated (having a lower content of water as more moisture has been extracted) are soaked in water.

Dehydrated potatoes are in powder form and are reconstituted with water, milk, or milk and water. They often have manufactured vitamin C added as dehydration results in a loss of this vitamin.

Herbs

Fresh herbs are tied into bundles and allowed to dry out in a dry place.

Fruits

Sultanas, currants and raisins are grapes that have been dried in the sun or by hot air. Figs, plums, apricots, apples and pears are also dried by hot air. Apples are usually peeled and cut into rings or diced and then dried.

All dried fruits must be washed before use, and fruits such as prunes, figs, apricots, apples and pears are cooked in the water in which they are soaked.

Little flavour or food value is lost when drying fruits, with the exception of loss of vitamin C.

Milk

Milk is dried either by the roller or spray process. With the roller method the milk is poured onto heated rollers, which cause the water to evaporate; the resulting powder is then scraped off. This method is not widely used now as it damages the milk proteins and results in a less soluble dried product, which is more difficult to reconstitute. With the spray process the milk is sent through a fine jet as a spray into hot air, the water evaporates and the powder drops down. The temperature is controlled so that the protein in the milk is not cooked.

Milk powder may be used in place of fresh milk, mainly for economic purposes (especially skimmed milk powder), and is used for making custard and white sauce.

Eggs

Eggs are dried in the same way as milk, and although they have a food value similar to fresh eggs, dried eggs do not have the same aerating quality. When reconstituted the eggs should be used at once; if they are left in this state in the warm atmosphere of a kitchen, bacteria can multiply and food poisoning may result; although pasteurised before drying, the mixture may be contaminated in the kitchen and it is a very suitable food for the growth of bacteria. Dried eggs are mainly used in the bakery trade.

Freeze drying

This is a process of dehydration whereby food requires no preservation or refrigeration yet, when soaked in water, regains its original size and flavour. It can be applied to every kind of food. The food is frozen in a cabinet, the air is pumped out and the ice vaporised. This is called freeze drying and is the drying of frozen foods by sublimation under conditions of very low pressure. (Sublimation is the action of turning from solid to gas without passing through a liquid stage; in this case it is ice to steam without first turning to water.)

When processed in this way, food does not lose a great deal of its bulk, but it is very much lighter in weight. When water is added the food gives off its natural smell.

Preservation by chilling and freezing

At low temperatures micro-organism growth is much slower. Therefore, refrigeration is used not to kill micro-organisms but to slow down their multiplication and their enzyme action. As a result, refrigeration prolongs the life of the food but not for long periods of time and, eventually, the food will go bad. Microbial and biochemical changes that affect the flavour, texture, colour and nutritional value of foods still take place and it is important to remember that the food must not be contaminated before chilling. Refrigerators are kept at a temperature of 1–4°C.

The lower the temperature the food is stored at, the longer the storage life. This is because the micro-organisms become inactive around −10°C and enzymes become inactive around −18°C. Most frozen foods can be kept at −17°C for a year and at −28°C for two years. Foods must be kept in deep freeze until required for use.

Cold chilled storage of fresh foods merely retards the decay of the food; it does not prevent it from eventually going bad. The aim of chilling is to slow down the rate of spoilage; the lower the chill temperature within the range 1°C to 5°C, the slower the growth of micro-organisms and the biochemical changes that spoil the flavour, colour, texture and nutritional value of foods. Lowering the temperature to this range also reduces food poisoning hazards, although it is important to remember that the food must not be contaminated before chilling.

If food is frozen slowly, large uneven crystals are formed in the cells. The water in each cell contains the minerals that give flavour and goodness to food; if food is frozen slowly, the minerals are separated from the ice crystals, which break through the cells; on thawing, the goodness and flavour drain away. Quick-freezing (see below) is more satisfactory because small ice crystals are formed in the cells of food; so, on thawing, the goodness and flavour are retained in the cells.

Meat

- **Chilling:** meat that is chilled is kept at a temperature just above freezing point and will keep for up to one month; if the atmosphere is controlled with carbon dioxide the time can be extended to ten weeks.
- **Freezing:** imported lamb carcasses are frozen; beef carcasses are not usually frozen because, owing to the size of the carcass, it takes a long time to freeze and this causes ice crystals to form which, when thawed, affect the texture of the meat; frozen meat must be thawed before it is cooked.

Quick-freezing of raw foods and cooked foods

During the cooking and freezing process, foods undergo physical and/or chemical changes. If it is found that these changes are detrimental to the product, then recipe modification is required. The following products require some modification: sauces, casseroles, stews, cold desserts, batters, vegetables and egg dishes.

Conventional recipes normally use wheat flour for thickening, but in the cook-freeze system this will not give an acceptable final product because separation of the solids from the liquids in the sauce will occur if the product is kept in frozen storage for more than

a period of several weeks. To overcome this problem it is necessary to use wheat flour in conjunction with any of a number of classically modified starches, such as tapioca starch or waxy maize starch. Many recipes prove successful with a ratio of 50 per cent wheat flour to 50 per cent modified starch.

Rapid freezing of foodstuffs can be achieved by a variety of methods using different types of equipment, for example:

- plate freezer
- blast freezer
- low-temperature immersion freezer
- still-air cold room
- spray freezer (using liquid nitrogen or carbon dioxide) – known as cryogenic freezing this is a method of freezing food by very low temperature; it also freezes food more quickly than any other method; the food to be frozen is placed on a conveyor belt and passed into an insulated freezing tunnel; the liquefied nitrogen or carbon dioxide is injected into the tunnel through a spray, and vaporises, resulting in a very rapid freezing process
- freeze flow – this is a system that freezes food without hardening it.

Foods that are frozen

A very wide variety of foods are frozen, either cooked or in an uncooked state.

- **Cooked foods:** whole cooked meals, braised meat, vol-au-vents, éclairs, cream sponges, puff pastry items.
- **Raw foods:** fillets of fish, fish fingers, poultry, peas, French beans, broad beans, spinach, sprouts, broccoli, strawberries, raspberries, blackcurrants.

With most frozen foods, cooking instructions are given; these should be followed to obtain the best results.

Fillets of fish may be thawed out before cooking; vegetables are cooked in their frozen state. Fruit is thawed before use and as it is usually frozen with sugar the fruit is served with the liquor.

Advantages of using frozen foods

- Frozen foods are ready prepared, therefore saving time and labour.
- Portion control and costing are easily assessed.
- Foods are always 'in season'.
- Storage is compact.
- Additional stocks are to hand.

- Quality is guaranteed.
- Very little vitamin C is lost from fruits and vegetables even after several months in a deep freeze.

Table 4.13 Storage of tinned foods

Type of tinned food	Advised storage time
Fruit	Up to 12 months
Milk	Up to 12 months
Vegetables	Up to 2 years
Meat	Up to 5 years
Fish in oil	Up to 5 years
Fish in tomato sauce	Up to 1 year

Table 4.14 Tin sizes

Size	Approx. weight	Use
	142 g	Baked beans, peas
	227 g	Fruits, meats, vegetables
A1	284 g	Baked beans, soups, vegetables, meats, pilchards
14Z	397 g	Fruits, vegetables
A2	567 g	Fruits, vegetables, fruit and vegetable juices
A2½	795 g	Fruits, vegetables
A10	3079 g	Fruits, vegetables, tongues

Preservation by heating

Canning and bottling

Bottled and canned food are sealed in airtight bottles or tins, and heated at a high enough temperature for a sufficient period of time to destroy harmful organisms. Spoilage does not occur over life because no micro-organisms can gain access to the food. Almost any type of food can be canned.

Dented cans that do not leak are safe to use, but blown cans – that is, those with bulges at either end – must not be used.

Some tinned hams are canned at a low temperature in order to retain their flavour and avoid excessive shrinkage in the can, and therefore should be stored in a refrigerator and consumed soon after purchase. Check the information on the can. Other tinned foods are kept in a dry, cool place; Table 4.13 indicates the recommended storage time.

Foods are canned in tins of various sizes (see Table 4.14).

The advantages of canned foods are similar to those of frozen foods, but a disadvantage is that, due to the heat processing, a proportion of the vitamin C and B1 (thiamin) may be lost. The quality and texture of the food may also be impaired.

Pasteurisation

Pasteurisation is a mild heat treatment, mainly used with milk and fruit juices. The food is taken to at least 72°C for a minimum of 15 seconds and then cooled rapidly.

In milk, over 99 per cent of the micro-organisms are killed and the rest are inactivated due to the rapid cooling and refrigerated conditions the produce is held in.

The loss in nutrients and effects on flavour and the quality of the products are minimal because the temperatures reached are not very high and are maintained for only a short period of time.

Sterilisation

This heat-treatment method employs much higher temperatures for a much longer period of time. The product is then packed in sterile containers. As a result, the product has a much longer shelf-life than its pasteurised counterpart and the cartons can be stored at ambient temperatures rather than chilled.

UHT (ultra heat treated) milk is an example of this and there is a more noticeable change in the flavour and quality of the finished product.

Preservation by salting and smoking

Salting

Micro-organisms cannot grow in high concentrations of salt. This method of preservation is used mainly to preserve meat and fish, and its advantage lies chiefly in the fact that a wider variety of dishes with different flavours can be put on the menu.

The salt added to butter and margarine, and also to cheese, acts as a preservative.

Meats

Meats that are salted or 'pickled' in a salt solution (brine) include brisket, silverside of beef, ox tongues and legs of pork.

Fish

Fish are usually smoked as well as being salted and include salmon, trout, haddock and herring. The amount of salting varies. Bloaters are salted more than kippers, and red herrings more than bloaters.

Smoking

There are two types of smoking:

1 hot smoking
2 cold smoking.

Smoking is mainly used nowadays to enhance the flavour and colour of the product, as its preservation effect is mainly limited to the surface of the product. Smoking does not allow long-term storage.

Smoke is a very complex material, with upward of 200 components that include alcohols, acids, phenolic compounds and various toxic, sometimes carcinogenic, substances. The toxic substances inhibit the growth of microbes, and the phenolics retard fat oxidation, and the whole complex imparts the characteristic flavour of burning wood to the meat, fish or vegetables.

Smoke substitutes are sometimes used in preference to real smoke to give the flavour and characteristics of traditionally smoked food. One smoke substitute is known as liquid smoke and does not contain carcinogenic substances.

The difference between smoke cooking and curing

Smoke cooking is done at higher temperatures in order to cook the meat. Smoke curing is really just smoking cured meat or sausage. Although smoking meat does provide some preservative effect, this alone is not sufficient to allow long-term storage.

The temperature of smoke when cooking meat

The temperature is very important. There are a variety of different smokes on the market, all with temperature guides; some recommend 93°C–104°C for hot smoking.

Temperature control is very important as excess heat will melt the fat and leave a dry product.

Examples of woods used for smoking

- **Alder:** the traditional wood for smoking salmon in the Pacific north-west, alder also works well with other fish. It has a light, delicate flavour.
- **Apple and cherry:** both woods produce a slightly sweet, fruity smoke that is mild enough for chicken or turkey, but capable of favouring a ham.
- **Hickory:** the king of the woods. The strong, hearty taste is perfect for pork shoulder and ribs, but also enhances any red meat or poultry.
- **Maple:** mildly smoky and sweet, maple mates well with poultry, ham and vegetables.
- **Mesquite:** great for grilling because it burns very hot, but below average for barbecuing for the same reason. Also, the smoke taste turns from tangy to bitter over an extended cooking time.
- **Oak:** if hickory is the king of barbecue woods, oak is the queen. The most versatile of hardwoods, blending well with a wide range of flavours.
- **Pecan:** burns cool and offers a subtle richness of character.
- **Grapevines:** very distinctive aroma, ideal for grilling food.

The smoking process

Before smoking commences, the raw meat or fish is either dry salted or soaked in brine. In hot countries salting is still used for the purpose of preservation, but in more temperate climates the salt is used only as a seasoning.

During smoking, weight loss occurs in the product, due to evaporation of water content from within the flesh of the meat or fish. This weight loss is essential to successful smoking. It follows that the greater the weight loss the greater the keeping qualities. Today, flavour tends to be more important than keeping qualities so it is better to create humid conditions to produce a succulent product.

Hot and cold smoking

Cold smoking flavours but does not cook the product. It is usually carried out at a temperature of between 10°C and 29°C. Some cold smoked products are eaten without further cooking (e.g. salmon, beef fillet, halibut and cod roe), whereas others – such as haddock, herring (kippers) and cod fillets – require a further period of cooking, although obviously not so much as a completely raw product as the cooking process has already been started.

Hot smoked products, after salting or brining, are first cold smoked to partially dry them out and to impart a smoked flavour. In the case of fish the temperature is then raised to 93–104°C and the fish are then cooked. Care must be taken during the initial cold smoking to see that the temperature does not exceed 26°C as this will harden the outside and stop further smoke penetration. Again, during hot smoking, temperatures must be monitored to see that the fish do not become overcooked. Herbs and spices may be incorporated into the smoking process.

Preservation by sugar

A high concentration of sugar prevents the growth of moulds, yeasts and bacteria. This method of preser-

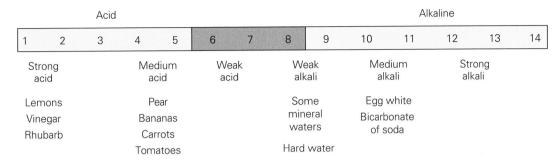

Figure 4.14 The pH range of some foods

vation is applied to fruits in a variety of forms: jams, marmalades, jellies, candied, glacé and crystallised.

- Jams are prepared by cooking fruit and sugar together in the correct quantities to prevent the jam from spoiling. Too little sugar means the jam will not keep.
- Jellies, such as redcurrant jelly, are prepared by cooking the juice of the fruit with the sugar.
- Marmalade is similar to jam in preparation and preservation, citrus fruits being used in place of other fruits.
- Candied fruit is made when the peel of such fruit as orange, lemon, grapefruit and lime, and also the flesh of pineapple, are covered with hot syrup; the syrup's sugar content is increased each day until the fruit is saturated in a very heavy syrup, then it is allowed to dry slowly.
- Crystallised fruit is made following candying. It is left in fresh syrup for 24 hours and then allowed to dry slowly until crystals form on the fruit. Angelica, ginger, violet and rose petals are prepared in this way.
- Glacé fruit, usually cherries, is first candied, then dipped in fresh syrup to give a clear finish.

Preservation by acids

The acidity and alkalinity of foods

The level of acidity or alkalinity of a food is measured by its pH value. The pH can range from 1 to 14, with pH7 denoting neutral (neither acid nor alkaline).

Most micro-organisms grow best at near neutral pH. Bacteria (particularly harmful ones) are less acid-tolerant than fungi, and no bacteria will grow at a pH of less than 3.5. Spoilage of high-acid foods, such as fruit, is usually caused by yeasts and moulds. Meat and fish are more susceptible to bacterial spoilage, since their pH is closer to neutral.

The pH may be lowered so that the food becomes too acidic (less than pH1.5) for any micro-organisms to grow, such as the use of vinegar in pickling. In the manufacture of yoghurt and cheese, bacteria produce lactic acid; this lowers the pH, and retards the growth of food poisoning and spoilage organisms.

Foods may be preserved in vinegar, which is acetic acid (ethanoic acid) diluted with water. In the UK, malt vinegar is most frequently used, although distilled or white wine vinegar is used for pickling white vegetables such as cocktail onions and also for rollmops (herrings).

Foods usually pickled in vinegar include gherkins, capers, onions, shallots, walnuts, red cabbage, mixed pickles and chutneys.

Preservation by chemicals

A number of chemicals in certain foods, such as sausages, meats and jams, are permitted by law, but their use is strictly controlled. (Campden preserving tablets can be used for domestic fruit bottling.)

Some of the more popular ones are:

- **sulphur dioxide and sulphites** – use in dried fruit and vegetables, sausages, fruit-based dairy products, cider, beer and wine, biscuit dough
- **sorbic acid** – soft drinks, fruit yoghurt, processed cheese
- **sodium and potassium nitrite/nitrate** – bacon, ham, cured meats, corn beef and some cheeses.

Preservation by radiation

What is irradiation?

Foods are exposed to ionising radiation, which transfers some of its energy as it passes through the food, killing the pathogenic bacteria, which would otherwise make the food unsafe to eat, or, at lower doses the spoilage bacteria, which cause food to rot. Ionising radiation is electromagnetic, like radio waves, infra-red light or ultraviolet light. It is similar to ultraviolet radiation but has a higher frequency and much greater energy. This is sufficient to protect food effectively, but not enough to make it radioactive.

Irradiation methods have other key advantages over heating, chilling and chemical preservation methods.

- Irradiation works well with frozen or heat-sensitive products, as it does not cause any significant increase in temperature.
- Packaged products can be sterilised in the final pack, thus preventing contamination.
- Irradiation has a minimal impact on the nutritional value of the food. Proteins and carbohydrates are unaffected.
- Irradiation processing is a clean technology. No chemical additives are used or residues left behind in the food, and the process does not contaminate or damage the environment.
- The chemical changes caused in the food by the ionising radiation are in general much less severe than those arising from other food-processing methods such as cooling and heating.

At present, 36 countries allow irradiation of about 30 individually specified foods. In 21 of these countries there are active commercial food irradiative plants.

The Food Labelling (Amendment) (Irradiated Food) Regulations 1990 came into force on 1 January 1991 in parallel with those regulations setting out the controls on irradiation. The regulations require all foods that have been irradiated to carry an indication of treatment using the specified words 'irradiated' or 'treated with ionising radiation'.

Preservation by gas storage

Gas storage is used in conjunction with refrigeration to preserve meat, eggs and fruit. Varying the gas composition surrounding the food increases the length of time it can be stored.

Vacuum packaging

There are two distinct methods in which vacuum packaging can be incorporated into kitchen procedures. The first process relates to preparation and preservation. The second is a process of cooking 'sous-vide': a process of preparation, sealing inside a pouch or bag, cooking at a low temperature, followed by rapid chilling and storage at no more than 2°C. (There is more on this in Chapter 6.)

Benefits to the caterer

- **Reduced dehydration and drip loss:** weight loss can be considerably reduced when meat is vacuum packed, and when this also cuts out the need to trim, financial benefits are significant.
- **Increased storage life:** 'use by' times can be extended on chilled items (3–5°C).
- **Increased hygiene and reduced cross-contamination:** vacuum pouches provide external barriers and will ensure food is protected in a hygienic condition, unaffected by any cross-contamination after packaging.
- **Improved workflow:** in any restaurant, there will inevitably be periods of time that are quiet. To spend that time vacuum packaging is not only an excellent use of your staff but also helps to relieve the workload when staff are busy. Vacuum packaging will make optimum use of all available time by helping to even out the workload.
- **Pre-packaging:** food may be pre-portioned and vacuum packed without the pressure of time; accurate weights and a reduction of waste should be obtained. The food can be kept chilled until needed. This also allows planning to take place for banquets, and can help overcome labour shortages at weekends and during holiday periods.
- **Reduced wastage:** vacuum packaging in advance can help minimise waste.
- **Satellite kitchens:** these can readily be supplied with vacuum-packed portions, eliminating the need for preparation in several areas.
- **Bulk buying:** many foods, like meat and fish, are affected by burn or dehydration in the freezer. The protective qualities of a vacuum pouch ensure this problem is eliminated.

Precautions

There are certain precautions that the chef has to be aware of when using vacuum packaging. The shelf-life of cooked foods should be kept to a minimum under chilled conditions. Cooked meats and fish should not be packed unless sous-vide techniques are used. Stock rotation must be strictly observed. All packs must be clearly labelled with the description of the contents, weight, date and 'use by' date. In the event of any pack becoming blown or leaking, the contents should immediately be opened, examined and repacked only if satisfactory. Strict hygiene, the immediate packing of foodstuffs, and accurate chill conditions are vital parts of the process.

Modified atmosphere packaging (MAP)

This is a flexible way of extending the shelf-life of

many kinds of fresh foods up to two to three times the normal levels. The method involves replacing the normal surrounding or 'dead space' atmosphere within food packages with specific mixtures of gases or single gases. Its objectives are to inhibit the growth of pathogenic bacteria and moulds, and to extend the shelf-life of chilled and certain ambient food products.

Originally the system was known as controlled atmosphere packaging, and was used for the retail portioning and packaging of red meat. The method was based on what is now known as the 'date of packaging + five days' system, using an 80 per cent oxygen/20 per cent carbon dioxide gas mixture. The gases used are carbon dioxide, nitrogen and oxygen. They are natural gases like those present in the air, but for MAP they are supplied purified and free of bacteria.

- Carbon dioxide (CO_2) inhibits the growth of pathogenic bacteria at temperatures not exceeding 8°C for a restricted period. CO_2 does not kill the bacteria but will restrict mould growth over long periods.
- Nitrogen has a neutral effect on foodstuffs

and is used in 100 per cent strength for dried and roasted foods, dairy cakes, cream and milk powders. The gas is also used in conjunction with CO_2 as a support gas.
- Oxygen sustains basic metabolism and prevents spoilage caused by anaerobic bacteria. It is also used in MAP gas mixtures for packaging red meats, where it preserves the red colour of the meat.

MAP effectively increases the length of time certain foods can be stored in the refrigerator. The gas mixtures used vary according to the product being packaged. MAP is particularly successful with bakery products where elevated CO_2 content permits high relative humidities with negligible mould growth.

Chefs employed in large food production operations and those employed as development chefs use MAP to aid food preparation and quality. Over the next few years we are likely to see further developments in this area as the catering industry becomes more involved in using gases to aid preservation of ingredients.

Table 4.15 Recommended gas mixture percentages (%) for MAP (based on refrigeration storage)

Product	Oxygen (%)	Nitrogen (%)	Carbon dioxide (%)	Shelf-life
Red meat	80	–	20	5–8 days
White fish	30	30	40	5–6 days
Fatty fish	–	40	60	5–6 days
Salmon	20	20	60	5–6 days
Poultry	–	75	25	17–18 days
Hard cheese	–	–	100	3 weeks
Bacon, cooked meats	–	65–80	20–35	3–4 days
Bread	–	30–40	60–70	3 weeks
Dairy cakes	–	100	–	3 weeks

References

Catering for Health: A Guide to Teaching Healthier Catering Practices is available from Food Standards Agency Publications, PO Box 367, Hayes, Middlesex UB3 1UT.

Fox, B.A. and Cameron, A.G. (1995) *Food Science, Nutrition and Health* (6th edn). Hodder Arnold.

Gaman, P.M. and Sherrington, K.B. (1998) *The Science of Food* (4th edn). Butterworth-Heinemann.

Henderson, L., Irving, K., Gregory, J. *et al.* (2003) *The National Diet and Nutrition Survey*. London: TSO.

Some references to nutrition elsewhere in the book:

For further information on methods of preservation refer to the following sources.

- *Eating for Health* (HMSO).
- Food (Control of Irradiation) Regulations 1990 (HMSO).
- Gaman, P.M. and Sherrington, K.B. (1996) *The Science of Food*. Pergamon.
- *Guidelines on Pre-cooked Chilled Foods* (HMSO).
- Kilgour, O.F.G. (1976) *An Introduction to Science for Catering and Homecraft Students*. Heinemann.
- Manual of Nutrition (HMSO).
- *McCance and Widdowson's The Composition of Foods* (HMSO).
- Education Department, Unilever Ltd, Unilever House, Blackfriars, London EC4
- Health Education Authority, Trevelyan House, 30 Great Peter Street, London SW1P 2HW
- Nutrition Society, 10 Cambridge Court, 210 Shepherd's Bush Road, London W6 7NJ

Topics for discussion

1 Why is a balanced diet desirable? What do you consider to be necessary to provide a balanced diet?

2 Why do you think trends, fads and fashions occur in our eating? Discuss how you could encourage a positive approach to having healthy eating habits.

3 How has presentation of foods changed and why have these changes come about?

4 What problems are associated with certain people's diets? What specific considerations are there for the diets of children, the elderly, nursing mothers and teenagers?

5 For what reasons may the nutritional value of foods be affected? Discuss examples of how this may occur and how such effects may be prevented.

6 What are the main sources of nutritional information?

7 Do you consider TV adverts and/or programmes affect people's diets?

8 Why do caterers need a good knowledge of nutrition and special diets?

Kitchen planning, equipment, services and energy conservation

Supporting material available on Dynamic Learning Online:

> Knowledge quizzes

> Activity worksheets: kitchen design; equipment

> Summary presentations

> Videos and worksheets: kitchen planning

Influencing factors on design

Factors that influence kitchen planning and design include:

- the size and extent of the menu and the market it serves
- services – gas, electricity and water
- labour, skill level of staff
- amount of capital expenditure, costs
- use of prepared convenience foods
- types of equipment available
- hygiene and the Food Safety Act 2005/2006
- design and decor
- multi-usage requirements.

The size and extent of the menu

Before a kitchen is planned, the management must know its goals and objectives in relation to market strategy. In other words, what markets are you aiming at and what style of operation are you going to operate? The menu will then determine the type of equipment you will require in order to produce the products that you know from the market research the customer is going to buy. You also need to know the target numbers you intend to service.

Services

The designer must know where the services are located and how efficient use can be made of them.

Labour and skill level

What kind of people does the company intend to employ? This will have an effect on the technology and equipment to be installed. The more prepared food used, the more this will affect the overall kitchen design.

Amount of capital expenditure

Most design has to work with a detailed capital budget. Often it is not always possible to design, then worry about the cost afterwards. Finance will very often determine the overall design and acceptability.

Because space is at a premium, kitchens are generally becoming smaller. Equipment is therefore being designed to cater for this trend, becoming more modular and streamlined and generally able to fit into less space. This is seen as a cost-reduction exercise. Labour is a significant cost factor, so equipment is being designed for ease of operation, maintenance and cleaning.

Use of prepared convenience foods

A fast-food menu using prepared convenience food will influence the planning and equipping very differently than for an à la carte or cook-chill kitchen. Certain factors will have to be determined.

- Will sweets and pastries be made on the premises?
- Will there be a need for larder or butcher?
- Will fresh or frozen food, or a combination of both be used?

Types of equipment available

The type, amount and size of the equipment will depend on the type of menu being provided. The equipment must be suitably sited. When planning a kitchen, standard symbols are used that can be produced on squared paper to provide a scale design. Computer-aided design (CAD) is now often used to do this.

Hygiene and the Food Safety Act 2005/2006

The design and construction of the kitchen must comply with the Food Safety Act 2005/2006. The basic layout and construction should enable adequate space to be provided in all food-handling and associated areas for equipment as well as working practices, and frequent cleaning to be carried out.

Design and decor

The trend towards provision of more attractive eating places, carried to its utmost perhaps by the chain and franchise operators, has not been without its effect on kitchen planning and design. One trend has been that of bringing the kitchen area totally or partially into view, with the development of back-bar type of equipment – for example, where grills or griddles are in full public view and food is prepared on them to order.

While there will be a continuing demand for the traditional heavy-duty type of equipment found in larger hotels and restaurant kitchens, the constant need to change and update the design and decor of modern restaurants means that the equipment's life is generally shorter – reduced perhaps from ten years to seven or five, or even less – to cope with the demand for change and redevelopment.

This has resulted in the generally improved design of catering equipment with the introduction of modular units.

Multi-usage requirements

Round-the-clock requirements such as in hospitals, factories where shift work takes place, the police and armed forces, have also encouraged kitchen planners to consider the design of kitchens with a view to their partial use outside peak times. To this end kitchen equipment is being made more adaptable and flexible, so that whole sections can be closed down when not in use, in order to maximise savings on heating, lighting and maintenance.

Front-of-house design

The 'front of house', better known by customers as the dining room, is one of the most critical components of any commercial food service operation. If the kitchen is the manufacturing plant, the dining area is the showroom where 'food meets customer'. The dining area is the 'stage' where good food, personal service and atmosphere come together to deliver a memorable dining experience.

Customer expectations of their 'dining experience' vary greatly by the type of restaurant. In the case of most restaurants and some venues, the customer has made a personal choice about the type and level of service desired, as well as the atmosphere in which they wish to dine. Sometimes speed of service is paramount. Sometimes they want a friendly sports bar with plenty of noise and lots of comfort food. On special occasions, they may want an intimate booth or table, a great wine list, impeccable service and classic cuisine. Regardless of the dining experience desired, there are base-level customer expectations for a clean dining area, with adequate seating, appropriate heating, air conditioning and lighting, plus clean plates and cutlery or service-appropriate disposables.

There are many factors that come into play when one is considering the design, equipment, furniture and supply items associated with any dining area. The following sections cover all the major factors critical to good front-of-house or dining room design. One of the most important elements is space.

Space considerations

Space allocation in any food service facility requires consideration of not only the building and construction costs but also the resulting operational costs. While smaller space allocations for some areas may reduce building costs, insufficient space can increase operating costs, impact efficient operations and hurt profitability.

Total space requirements are based on many factors. Some of the major decision criteria that any facilities designer or end-user/operator should consider include the following.

- How many individual customers are to be served, and over what period of time?
- What are the typical food requirements of these customers?

- How many customers will need service at any one time?
- What different types of food are to be offered and what kind of preparation methods will be used in the dining area, if any?
- What kind of service will be provided and on what schedule?
- What type and amount of storage space will be needed?
- What are the space requirements for maintenance, offices, employee facilities, toilets, etc.?
- Is there enough space allocated or left over for checkout, waiting, a cloakroom and service areas?

Dining room space requirements are usually based on the number of metres per person seated, multiplied by the number of persons seated at any one time. Space requirements should take into consideration the customers' size, comfort, and the type and quality of service. The amount of serving equipment to be used in the dining area, and in the case of a cafeteria the queuing space, will impact the space allocated for each seat. Space used for other than seating requirements is also included in the dining area requirements. This does not include waiting areas, cloakrooms, toilets and other on-service areas.

Table 5.1 provides some generally accepted 'space allowances per seat' for various types of food service operation.

Some of the other factors that should be taken into consideration when evaluating dining space requirements include those listed below.

- **The use of service stations:** service stations can be estimated based on one small unit for every 20 seats or a large central service station for every 50–60 seats. The advisability of having a central service station is influenced by the distance from the dining room to the service area. Service stations are important

Table 5.1 'Space allowances per seat' for various types of food service operation

Type of operation	Space allowance per seat (square metres)
Commercial cafeteria	1.5–1.7
College	1.1–1.4
School cafeteria	0.8–1.1
Counter service restaurant	1.7–1.9
Table service at a hotel, club or restaurant	1.4–1.7
Table service (minimum)	1.0–1.3
Banquet room	0.9–1.0

when the production area or kitchen and dining areas are on different floors or located at some distance.

- **Table size:** the size of tables and/or booths used will obviously have an influence on the comfort of the patron, as well as on the efficient utilisation of space. For example, in a cafeteria where patrons are more likely to dine directly off the trays, it is important that tables are large enough to accommodate the size and number of trays expected.
- **Aisle space:** carefully calculate the aisle space between tables and chairs to include passage area, plus the area occupied by the individuals seated at the tables. The size and configuration of the dining room or rooms will have a major impact on the room atmosphere and, ultimately, the dining experience. New facilities offer the maximum opportunity for control and creativity in the execution of the room layout. Existing buildings and room layouts are more of a challenge and often place fundamental limitations on seating capacity, seating type and room configuration. However, a good consultant or interior designer can often generate very creative solutions.

Lighting considerations

Lighting is a very important component of the overall dining room design. The amount of light required is dictated by the area and the activity that occurs there. Any design approach to lighting in a restaurant or commercial dining facility should encompass five basic principles, which are:

1 space relationships
2 perspective
3 contour
4 special details of intrinsic beauty
5 imaginative and subtle qualities.

These five principles apply to the three general types of illumination found in all food service facilities.

1 **Overall general illumination:** general lighting is designed to perform and function for both day and night time activity. It must achieve a perfect balance. If it doesn't, 'dark spots' or 'dead spots' will occur, creating a 'misreading' of the space. Sufficient general lighting/illumination is required so employees and patrons alike can see all the materials, furniture, etc., as well as the desired traffic patterns.
2 **Sparkle and excitement:** a burst of colour or a strategically placed light can enhance an otherwise monotonous lighting plan. Once the general illumination level has been established, these bursts of light can force certain areas to stand out. This kind of lighting treatment is appropriate for reception areas, windows, cathedral ceilings, partitions, special flooring or changes in flooring.
3 **Specific focal points:** the subtleties of light placement can direct the patron's eyes away from 'trouble spots' or create an illusion of extra space. Special-effect spots, uprights, indirect lights, etc., can be used for accenting artwork, a table, the patrons, a bar, a stairway, plants or the food. The repetition of focal lighting creates a general illumination and can create a visual relationship between specific focal areas as well. The various methods of achieving these qualities include:
   - silhouetting – objects having interesting or unusual lines or form can be emphasised
   - grazing light – is used to emphasise various textural qualities
   - modelling – this is designed to give depth and three-dimensional character to objects.

Kitchen design

Kitchens must be designed so that they can be easily managed. Managers must have easy access to the areas under their control and good visibility in the areas that have to be supervised. Large operations should work on separate work flows, for reasons of efficiency and hygiene:

- product – raw materials to finished product
- personnel – how people move within the kitchen;

for example, staff working in dirty areas (areas of contamination) should not enter areas of finished product, or where blast-chilling is taking place.
- containers/equipment/utensils – equipment should, where possible, be separated out into specific process areas
- refuse – refuse must be kept separated and should not pass into other areas in order to get to its storage destination.

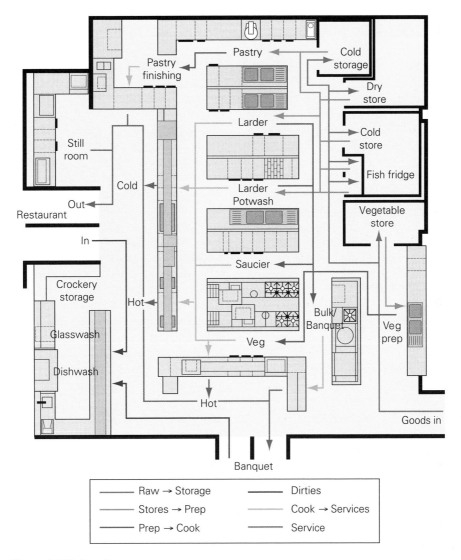

Figure 5.1 Kitchen design

Product flows

Each section should be subdivided into high-risk and contaminated sections. High-risk food is that which, during processing, is likely to be easily contaminated.

Contaminated food is that which is contaminated on arrival before processing – for example, unprepared vegetables, raw meat.

Back-tracking or cross-over of materials and product must be avoided.

Work flow

Food preparation rooms should be planned to allow a 'work flow' whereby food is processed through the premises from the point of delivery to the point of sale or service, with the minimum of obstruction. The various processes should be separated as far as possible, and food intended for sale should not cross paths with waste food or refuse. Staff time is valuable, and a design that reduces wasteful journeys is both efficient and cost-effective.

The overall sequence of receiving, storing, preparing, holding, serving and clearing is achieved by:

- minimum movement
- minimal back-tracking
- maximum use of space
- maximum use of equipment with minimum expenditure of time and effort.

Work space

Approximately 4.2 m² is required per person; too little space can cause staff to work in close proximity to stoves, steamers, cutting blades, mixers, and so on, thus causing accidents. A space of 1.37 m from equipment is desirable, and aisles must be of adequate size to enable staff to move safely. The working area must be suitably lit, and ventilated with extractor fans to remove heat, fumes and smells.

Working sections

The size and style of the menu and the ability of the staff will determine the number of sections and layout that is necessary. A straight-line layout would be suitable for a snack bar, while an island layout would be more suitable for a hotel restaurant.

Access to ancillary areas

A good receiving area needs to be designed for easy receipt of supplies with nearby storage facilities suitably sited for distribution of foods to preparation and production areas.

Hygiene must be considered so that kitchen equipment can be cleaned, and all used equipment from the dining area can be cleared, cleaned and stored. Still room facilities may also be required.

Equipment

The type, amount and size of equipment will depend on the type of menu being provided. Not only should the equipment be suitably situated but the working weight is very important to enable the equipment to be used without excess fatigue. When a kitchen is being planned, standard symbols are used that can be produced on squared paper to provide a scale design. Hand-washing facilities and storage of cleaning equipment should not be omitted.

Kitchen equipment manufacturers and gas and electricity suppliers can provide details of equipment relating to output and size.

The various preparation processes require different areas depending on what food is involved. In a vegetable preparation area, water from the sinks and dirt from the vegetables are going to accumulate, and therefore adequate facilities for drainage should be provided. Pastry preparation, on the other hand, entails mainly dry processes.

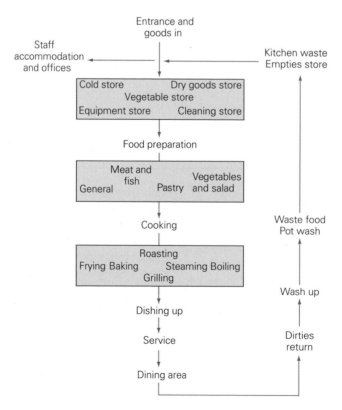

Figure 5.2 Work flow

Whatever the processes, there are certain basic rules that can be applied that not only make for easier working conditions but help to ensure that food hygiene regulations are complied with.

Food preparation areas

Proper design and layout of the preparation area can make a major contribution to good food hygiene. Staff generally respond to good working conditions by taking more of a pride in themselves, in their work and in their working environment.

Adequate work space must be provided for each process and every effort must be made to separate dirty and clean processes. Vegetable preparation and wash-up areas should be separate from the actual food preparation and service areas. The layout must ensure a continuous work flow in one direction in order that cross-over of foods and any cross-contamination is avoided. The staff should not hamper each other by having to cross each other's paths more than is absolutely necessary.

Actual worktop areas should be adequate in size for the preparation processes necessary, and should be so designed that the food handler has all required equipment and utensils close to hand.

Accommodation must be based on operational need. The layout of the kitchen must focus on the working and stores area, and the equipment to be employed. These areas must be designed and based on the specification of the operation.

Kitchens can be divided into sections; these must be based on the process. For example:

- **dry areas** – for storage
- **wet areas** – for fish preparation, vegetable preparation, butchery, cold preparation
- **hot wet areas** – for boiling, poaching, steaming; equipment needed will include atmospheric steamers, bratt pans, pressure steamers, steam jacketed boilers, combination oven
- **hot dry areas** – for frying, roasting, grilling; equipment needed will include cool zone fryers, salamanders, pressure fryers, induction cookers, bratt pans, halogen cookers, roasting ovens, microwave, charcoal grills, cook and hold ovens
- **dirty areas** – for refuse, pot wash areas, plate wash; equipment needed will include compactors, dishwashers, refuse storage units, glass washers, pot wash machines.

Size of kitchen and food preparation areas

Size is determined also by purpose and function.

- The operation is based on the menu and the market it is to serve.
- The design and equipment are based on the market the operation is to serve.
- Consideration must be given to the management policy on buying raw materials. Choice will determine kitchen plans on handling raw materials.
- Prepared food will require different types of equipment and labour requirements compared to part-prepared food or raw-state ingredients.
- Prepared food examples are sous-vide products, cook-chill, cook-freeze and prepared sweets. Part-prepared food examples are peeled and cut vegetables, convenience sauces and soups, portioned fish/meat. Raw-state food examples are unprepared vegetables, meat that requires butchering, and fish requiring filleting and portioning.

Consideration must also be given to the service policy on using all-plate service or a mixture of plate and silver service or self-service, and how all this will affect the volume and type of dishwashing required.

Planning and layout of the cooking area

Because 'raw materials' enter the cooking section from the main preparation areas (vegetables, meat and fish, dry goods), this section will be designed with a view to continuing the flow movement through to the servery. To this end, roasting ovens, for example, are best sited close to the meat preparation area, and steamers adjacent to the vegetable preparation area.

Layout is not, however, just a question of equipment siting and selection; much depends on the type of management policy on use of prepared foods and the operating cycle. Clearly the cooking section should contain no through traffic lanes (used by other staff to travel from one section to another). The layout should be planned so that raw foodstuffs arrive at one point, are processed in the cooking section and then despatched to the servery. There should be a distinct progression in one direction.

As with other areas, the cooking section should be designed with a view to making maximum use of the available area and providing economy of effort in use.

Island groupings

In an island arrangement, equipment is placed back to back in the centre of the cooking area. There will need to be sufficient space to allow for this, including adequate gangways around the equipment and space to place other items along the walls.

Wall siting

An alternative arrangement involves siting equipment along walls. This arrangement is possible where travel distances are reduced, and normally occurs in smaller premises (or sections thereof).

L- or U-shaped layouts

L- or U-shaped arrangements create self-contained sections that discourage entry by non-authorised staff; they can promote efficient working, with distances reduced between work centres.

When planning the layout of the cooking section the need to allow sufficient space for access to equipment such as ovens should be borne in mind. Opening doors creates an arc that cannot be reduced, and the operator must have sufficient room for comfortable and safe access. It is also likely that trolleys will be used for loading and unloading ovens, or rolling tables drawn into position in front of the oven.

The choice of layout

Selection of equipment will be made after detailed consideration of the functions that will be carried out within the cooking area of the kitchen. The amount of equipment required will depend upon the complexity of the menus offered, the quantity of meals served, and the policy of use of materials – from the traditional kitchen organisation using only fresh vegetables and totally unprepared items, to the use of prepared foods, chilled items and frozen foods, where the kitchen consists of a regeneration unit only.

Given, however, that a certain amount of equipment is required, the planner has the choice of a number of possible layouts, within the constraints of the building shape and size, and the location of services. The most common are the island groupings, wall siting and the use of an L- or U-shaped layout and variations upon these basic themes.

Siting of equipment

The kitchen operation must work as a system. It is advisable to site items of equipment used for specific functions together. This will help increase efficiency and avoid shortcuts.

Hand basins must be sited strategically to encourage frequent hand washing in all food preparation areas. One should be in evidence at each workstation.

The kitchen environment

- **Space:** The Office, Shop and Railway Premises Act 1963 stipulates 11.32 cubic metres (400 cubic feet) per person, discounting height in excess of 3 m.
- **Humidity:** A humid atmosphere creates side effects such as food deterioration, infestation risk, condensation on walls and slippery floors. Anything higher than 60 per cent humidity lowers productivity. Provision for the replacement of extracted air with fresh air is essential.
- **Temperature:** No higher than 20–26°C is desirable for maximum working efficiency and comfort, with 16–18°C in preparation areas.
- **Noise:** Conversation should be possible within 4 m.
- **Light:** The minimum legal level in preparation areas is 20 lumens per square foot with up to 38 lumens preferable in all areas.

Ventilation systems

There are three basic types of ventilation system.

1 **Extract:** this system only removes air, thereby creating a negative pressure in the space. Outside air will come into the space wherever it can, usually through doorways, window areas or specially prepared openings. It can be used to avoid contaminants spreading to other areas, as a negative pressure is created within the space in which the system operates
2 **Inlet:** this system is concerned only with the supply of outside air. In this case, the space is under positive pressure, with the air leaving through doorways or windows. This system is used mostly in clean spaces, thus preventing contaminants coming in from other areas. It is not a suitable system for a catering kitchen but may prove useful in areas such as storage rooms and larders, where it is desirable to prevent contaminants from reaching the foods stored.
3 **Combined:** this balances the flow of air into and out of the space.

All these systems use mechanical means of moving the air – that is, by electrically driven fans. In the first two cases, the replacement and displacement air, respectively, is virtually impossible to control, and there will always be draughts, particularly when the outside air is cold.

The ideal system, although more expensive, is the combined system, where the extract and supply of air can be controlled. It is especially suitable for kitchen ventilation, where large quantities of air are required to be removed from relatively small spaces.

The best and most effective way of removing contaminants is at source. This is normally by means of a purpose-made hood over the equipment that is producing heat, grease, smells, and so on. The following conditions relating to the hood must be satisfied:

- the hood should be made of non-corrosive material and so designed that it can be cleaned easily
- it must have a condensate channel around its bottom edge
- it must overhang the equipment underneath by 230–300 mm
- it must allow a sufficient velocity of air to pass over the edge of the hood.

Ventilation requirements for kitchens

There are three basic ways of determining these requirements.

1 **Air changes:** this method involves specifying an air change rate throughout the area. This is usually between 20 and 35 air changes per hour, but this method is only an approximation and, should there be more than one hood, then it would be difficult to apportion.
2 **Air velocity:** this system involves knowing the size of the hood over the equipment and allowing a certain velocity of air over the face area. Although this is a better method than the previous one, it is very difficult to obtain the correct velocity and reliance on experience is necessary. Velocity is usually between 0.3 and 0.8 mm per second.
3 **Air volume:** the most useful method is to allow a specific volume of air for each particular piece of equipment. Table 5.2 shows the air volumes that can be used for the different types of equipment.

For further information, consult IOH Technical Brief No. 30: Kitchen Ventilation.

It is important to note that the system will not necessarily function properly just by having the correct volume of air. Close attention must be paid to the design and installation of the hood, as indicated above, and, in addition, the trunking must (as far as

Table 5.2 Air volumes for the different types of equipment

Equipment	Cubic metres per second
Ranges (unit type) approx. 1 m^2	0.3
Pastry ovens	0.3
Fish friers	0.45
Grills	0.25–0.3
Boiling pans (90–135 litres)	0.3
Steamers	0.3
Sinks (sterilising)	0.25
Bains-marie	0.2
Stills boilers	0.15–0.25

possible) be constructed without sharp bends or long horizontal runs.

Special filters should be installed within the extract hood to collect contaminants, otherwise grease could build up and become a fire hazard.

Self-cleaning kitchen extracts

A system of self-cleaning ventilation equipment is available that can be adapted to operate either as a full extract system over kitchen equipment or be specially designed as part of individual items of equipment such as grills, deep-fat fryers and ovens.

The cleaning cycle is normally operated each day and requires that a supply of hot water is available to the ventilator, together with a facility for dosing with a suitable detergent. The extract fan must be switched off, an operation that, in itself, can be adapted to begin the cleaning operation.

Hot water, together with detergent, is then released into the ventilator for a predetermined period, controlled by an automatic timer. The deposits of grease and lint are washed out of the ventilator into drainage gutters, which need to be connected to the drainage system.

This timer shuts off the water supply at the end of the cleaning cycle and the ventilator is ready for reuse.

The ventilators can be fitted with automatic fire protection, which will result in baffles closing over the air inlet, shutting off the fan and operating the water supply to smother any fire.

Consultants

There are a number of specialist consultants involved in kitchen design. Consultants are often used by companies to provide independent advice and specialist knowledge. Their expertise should cover:

- equipment
- mechanical and electrical services
- food service systems and methods
- drainage
- architectural elements
- ventilation/air conditioning
- statutory legislation (Food Act, Health and Safety Act, fire regulations)
- energy conservation
- recycling
- green issues/legislation (waste management)
- refrigeration.

Consultants should provide the client with unbiased opinions and expertise not available in their company. Their aim should be to raise the standards of provision and equipment installation, while providing an efficient and effective food production operation that also takes into account staff welfare.

Maintenance

Planning and equipping a kitchen are an expensive investment. Therefore, to avoid any action by the Environmental Health Officer, efficient, regular cleaning and maintenance are essential. (The kitchens at the Dorchester hotel, Park Lane, London, are swept during the day, given soap/detergent and water treatment after service, and any spillages cleaned up immediately. At night, contractors clean the ceilings, floors and walls.)

Kitchen design: industry trends

In most cases, throughout the industry, companies are looking to reduce labour costs while maintaining or enhancing the meal experience for the customer. Some trends in various situations are as follows.

- Hotels: greater use of buffet and self-assisted service units.
- Banqueting: move towards plated service, less traditional silver service.
- Fast food: new concepts coming onto the market, more specialised chicken and seafood courts, more choices in ethnic food.
- Roadside provision: increase in number of operations, partnerships with oil companies, basic grill menus now enhanced via factory-produced à la carte items.
- Food courts: development has slowed down; minor changes all the time; most food courts offer an 'all day' menu.
- Restaurants/hotels: less emphasis on luxury-end, five-star experience.

- Theme restaurants: will continue to improve and multiply.
- Hospitals: greater emphasis on bought-in freezer and chilled foods; steam cuisine; reduced amount of on-site preparation and cooking; satellite kitchens; cook-chill; cook-freeze.
- Industrial: more zero-subsidy staff restaurants, increased self-service for all items; introduction of cashless systems will enable multi-tenant office buildings to offer varying subsidy levels.
- Prisons, institutions: little if any change; may follow hospitals by buying in more pre-prepared food; may receive foods from multi-outlet central production units, tied in with schools, meals on wheels provision, etc.
- University/colleges: greater move towards providing food courts; more snack bars and coffee shops.

Chefs and managers are often asked to assist in the design of food service systems. In these circumstances there are various issues that need to be taken into account. If possible, all designs should be market-led in the first place.

- Market expectations: type of customer demand (including price), type of menu, type of meal, type of establishment, 'product life' and possibility of 'product' changes, customer participation.
- Operational needs: amount of space available, expected throughput/seat turnover, type of operation (e.g. call order, traditional).
- Amount of basic preparation: amount of regeneration, storage needs, flows of materials, people and equipment, availability of supplies, frequency of delivery, need for storage, availability of services – gas, electricity, water, waste disposal, energy costs, ventilation, extraction and induction systems.
- Type and quantity of labour to be employed: e.g. unspecialised staff using pre-prepared materials, traditional 'partie' system using basic ingredients, room for future expansion.
- Finance: objective (e.g. to make a profit, to provide a service), cost of space (£s per square metre), amount and type of finance (e.g. purchase, leasing, hire purchase), whether to use second-hand equipment, depreciation policy, life of investment.

Towards the greener kitchen

Restaurants use about two to five times more energy per square foot than other commercial buildings.

Energy costs continue to rise. Investing in energy efficiency is therefore the best way to protect the business from rising energy costs.

Reducing energy costs

Sourced from *Caterer and Hotelkeeper* (October 2010), listed below are some ideas of ways to reduce energy costs.

- **The stores area:** use PIR (passive infrared) low-energy lighting. This reduces the risk of lighting being left on when the areas are not in use.
- Hand wash facilities: use sensor taps.
- **Refrigeration:** use drawer units in refrigerators – these can reduce the work of compressors and glass doors in upright cabinets as doors are opened less frequently. All refrigeration equipment should be checked against the Energy Technology List (ETL), which lists models that are 30 per cent more energy efficient than standard industry models.
- **Preparation sinks:** use pressure-reducing valves in taps, with inbuilt flow-limiting devices or aerators to reduce the volume of water used.
- **Cooking:** some ranges use pan sensors, which provide energy efficiencies, although energy is lost around the edge of the pan.
- **Fryers:** these burners only work when the range is being used. When the pan is removed from the cooking surface the flame is extinguished, leaving just the pilot light on, so no energy is used.
- **Induction hobs:** these also provide energy-saving benefits. Induction hobs are 50 per cent more efficient than halogen hobs, and 86 per cent more efficient than gas hobs.
- **Microwaves:** a combination of convection heat, impingement pressure and electromagnetic energy allows typical cook times from 15–90 seconds. A built-in catalytic converter eliminates the need for a ventilation hood so the oven can operate in any environment. This results in energy saving.
- **Combinations:** combinations of steam and convection can reduce energy costs by 50 per cent. A triple-glazed viewing door will save up to 40 per cent of energy compared to a single-glazed door.
- **Service pass:** use drawer warmers that have separate compartments, thermostat and humidity control to ensure food is held at the correct temperature and does not deteriorate. Each drawer is in its own separate compartment so when the drawer is open the temperature in the other drawers is not affected, and elements are

mounted in the cabinet interior rather than the wall, giving faster production and recovery.
- **Waste management:** many local authorities and water companies record the use of water disposal units as this passes the problem down the line.
- **Mechline GohBio:** this is a high-speed, high-volume food waste decomposition system, which introduces natural enzymes into a decomposition machine where organic waste is reduced to grey water that is safe for drains.
- **Bio-enzymatic fluid systems:** these break down fats, oils, and grease and starch, which can block kitchen drains. There are cost-effective solutions available to meet legislative demands.

Kitchen and restaurant areas

The calculation of the amount of space required is very complex as it is dependent on a mixture of influencing factors, including:

- volume of meals served, average time to consume a meal/product, seat turnover
- time over which the meals will be served
- size of menu
- complexity of individual menu items
- style of service (e.g. counter/plate/guéridon)
- mix of fresh and convenience food production
- number and type and size of dining facilities served by the kitchen (e.g. restaurants, floors)
- type of cooking methods to be used
- structural features of the building
- cost of floor space in the planned facility.

Kitchen equipment trends

- Refrigeration: more concentration on providing CFC-free equipment.
- Environmental: with an environmentally conscious society, energy conservation will feature higher in the development agenda; this will include heat recovery systems, recirculated air systems, improved working conditions and lighting systems.
- Cooking: more use of induction units, combination ovens, microwave and tunnel ovens.
- Servery counters: more decorative units being used.
- Dishwasher/potwash: greater economy of water, more mechanised and automated use of combination machines.
- Ventilation: moves towards integrated wash systems, recirculated air systems, integral air supply, integral fire suppression.

The general trend will be towards self-diagnostic equipment and automated service call-out. With the use of replacement components, there is less emphasis on repairs.

Linking equipment to computers

Head chefs and food and beverage managers will have PCs in their offices for jobs like recipe development, accounts, inventory and email. Electronic point of sale (EPOS) terminals in restaurant bars can interface directly with back-of-house computers. Some EPOS systems with kitchen monitor hook-ups can optimise meal preparation by telling chefs when to start cooking particular components, thus allowing all the items that make up an order to be completed at exactly the same time.

A growing range of kitchen equipment, from cookers and refrigerated storage to large ware-washing systems, come with on-board computer control, and several products can additionally be specified with extra hardware and software to permit continuous monitoring of the main equipment functions. Some appliances can also be specified with a two-way interactive link, enabling programs subject to frequent change (such as recipes) to be downloaded to the appliance from a computer directly via cable or wireless hook-up, or via modem connection to the Internet.

The temperature monitoring of all refrigerators and freezers within an establishment can be linked to a computer system. Several temperature readings are sent to the computer each day and it can also record temperature highs and lows, and any unusual trends. Temperatures outside the specified limits will be highlighted.

Water management

Legislation

Each country has its own laws governing the use of water. In the UK these include the Water Industry Act 1991, the Health & Safety at Work Act 1974 and the Water Supply Bylaw 1989.

The purpose of water law is to:

- discourage undue consumption of water
- prevent contamination of the water supply.

Substantial savings in water can be made through the renewal and replacement of wasteful, older water-using equipment. Self-closing taps, for example, reduce water consumption by as much as 55 per cent.

In many countries it is an offence for the owners or occupiers of buildings to intentionally or negligently allow any 'fitting to waste', or to unduly consume water. Examples:

- taps constantly dripping or left running
- overflows from storage and WC cisterns dripping
- water leaks not repaired.

There is evidence to show that the undertaking of a water-management audit can save money. Such an audit examines and quantifies possible savings.

Immediate practical action

- Water metering.
- Tap flow regulator – flow control.
- Urinals using less water.
- Shut-off devices and self-closing taps.
- Automatic or programmed mains shut-off device when buildings are not in use.
- Low-flow shower heads.

To find out more about water management, contact Water Training International, Burn Hall, Tollerton Road, Huby, Yorkshire YO6 1JB.

Equipment design

The Food Safety (General Food Hygiene) Regulations 1995, and subsequent regulations, 2006, require all articles, fittings and equipment with which food comes into contact to be kept clean and to be constructed of such materials and maintained in such condition and repair as to minimise risk of contamination, and to enable thorough cleaning and, where necessary, disinfection. Equipment must also be installed in such a way that the surrounding area is able to be cleaned.

Recommendations for equipment

The following equipment is preferable:

- tubular machinery frames
- stainless steel table legs
- drain cocks and holes instead of pockets and crevices that could trap liquid
- dials fitted to machines having adequate clearance to facilitate cleaning.

Preparation surfaces

The choice of surfaces on which food is to be prepared is vitally important. Failure to ensure a suitable material may provide a dangerous breeding ground for bacteria. Stainless steel tables are best as they do not rust, and their welded seams eliminate unwanted cracks and open joints. Sealed tubular legs are preferable to angular ones because, again, they eliminate the corners in which dirt collects. Tubular legs have often been found to provide a harbourage for pests.

Preparation surfaces should be jointless, durable, impervious, of the correct height and firm-based. They must withstand repeated cleaning at the required temperature without premature deterioration through pitting and corrosion.

Choosing cutting boards

Bear in mind the following aspects when choosing cutting boards:

- water absorbency – soft woods draw fluids into them and, with the fluids, bacteria are also drawn in
- wooden cutting boards made of hard wood, if cleaned and sterilised, are perfectly acceptable in catering premises
- resistance to stains, cleaning chemicals, heat and food acids
- toxicity – the cutting board must not give off toxic substances
- durability – the cutting board must withstand wear and tear
- cutting boards must not split or warp.

Appearances can be deceptive. Two researchers at the University of Wisconsin, Madison, USA, set out ways of decontaminating wooden kitchen surfaces and ended up finding that such surfaces are pretty good at decontaminating themselves. When working with wood from nine different species of tree and four sorts of plastic, the results were always the same. The researchers spread salmonella, listeria and E. coli bacteria over the various samples and left them for three minutes. The level of bacteria on the plastic remained the same, while the level on the wood plummeted, often by as much as 99.9 per cent. Left overnight at room temperature the bacteria on the plastic actually multiplied, while the wooden surfaces cleaned themselves so thoroughly that the researchers could not record anything from them. This is because of the porous structure of wood – previously thought to be a disadvantage in soaking up fluid with bacteria in it. Once inside, however, the bacteria stick to the wood's fibres and are 'strangled' by one of the many noxious anti-microbial chemicals with which living trees protect themselves.

Colour coding

To avoid cross-contamination, it is important that the same equipment is not to be used for handling raw and high-risk products without being disinfected. To prevent the inadvertent use of equipment for both raw and high-risk foods, it is recommended that, where possible, different colours and shapes are used to identify products or raw materials used.

Fixing and siting of equipment

Where practicable, equipment should be mobile to facilitate its removal for cleaning – that is, castor mounted and with brakes on all the wheels.

A guide for stationary equipment

To allow for the cleaning of wall and floor surfaces, stationary equipment must be positioned:

- 500 mm from the walls
- with 250 mm clearance between the floor and underside of the equipment.

Kitchen organisation

The purpose of efficient kitchen organisation is to produce the required quantity of food, of the best possible standard for the required number of people – on time, and by the most effective use of staff, equipment and materials.

Kitchen design and work flow

The kitchen should be designed not only to be suitable for the proposed menu(s), but also to be flexible enough to cope with any menu changes that may occur. (See also the section on kitchen design, pages 152–160.) To get ideas on effective kitchen design:

● visit existing kitchens with a critical eye

● ask staff for comments on the suitability, or otherwise, of layout, and its practicality
● seek professional advice from a number of manufacturers.

Working methods

Time and motion studies are essential for all tasks. Working in a hot environment – possibly against the clock, possibly leading to stress – it is necessary to conserve energy. A skilled craftsperson is one who completes the task in the minimum time, to the required standard and with the minimum effort.

Simplifying an operation

The objective is to make work easier; this can be achieved by simplifying the operation, eliminating unnecessary movements, combining two operations into one or improving old methods. For example, if you are peeling potatoes and you allow the peelings to drop into the container in the first place, the action of moving the peelings into the bowl and the need to clean the table could have been eliminated. This operation is simplified if, instead of a blunt knife, a good hand potato peeler is used, because it is simple and safe to use, requires less effort, can be used more quickly and requires less skill to produce a better result. If the quantity of potatoes is sufficient, then a mechanical peeler could be used, but it would be necessary to remember that the electricity used would add to the cost and that the time needed to clean a mechanical aid may lessen its work-saving value. If it takes 25 minutes to clean a potato-mashing machine that has been used to mash potatoes for 500 meals, it could be time well spent in view of the time and energy saved mashing the potatoes. It may not be considered worthwhile using the machine to mash potatoes for 20 meals, however. Factors such as this need to be taken into account.

Equipment and layout

Properly planned layouts with adequate equipment, tools and materials to do the job are essential if practical work is to be carried out efficiently. If equipment is correctly placed then work will proceed smoothly in proper sequence without back-tracking or criss-crossing. Work tables, sinks and stores, and refrigerators should be within easy reach in order to eliminate unnecessary walking. Equipment should be easily available during all working times.

The storage, handling of foods, tools and utensils, and the movement of food in various stages of production needs careful study. Many people carry out practical work by instinct and often evolve the most efficient method instinctively. Nevertheless careful observation of numerous practical workers will show a great deal of time and effort wasted through bad working methods. It is necessary to arrange work so that the shortest possible distance exists between storage and the place where the items are to be used.

When arranging storage see that the most frequently used items are nearest to hand. Place heavy items where the minimum of body strain is required to move them. Keep all items in established places so that time is not lost in hunting and searching for them. Adjustable shelving can be a help in organising different storage requirements. Only after all the pre-planning of the job is complete comes the actual work itself.

Careful preparation of foods and equipment (a good mise-en-place) is essential if a busy service is to follow and is to be operated efficiently so that orders move out methodically without confusion.

The work to be done must be planned carefully so that the items requiring long preparation or cooking are started first. Where fast production is required lining up will assist efficiency. Work carried out haphazardly, without plan or organisation, obviously takes longer to do than work done according to plan. There is a sequence to work that leads to high productivity and an efficient worker should learn this sequence quickly.

Kitchen supervision/management

The organisation under different industries varies according to their specific requirements, and the names given to people doing similar jobs may also vary. Some companies or organisations will require operatives, technicians and technologists; others need craftspeople, supervisors and managers. The supervisory function of the technician, chef de partie or supervisor may be similar.

The hospitality and catering industry is made up of people with craft skills. The craftsperson is involved with food production, the chef de partie may be the supervisor, supervising a section or sections of the food production system. The head chef will have both managerial and supervisory skills and he/she will determine kitchen policies.

Supervisors are involved with the successful deployment of money, material and people. The primary role of the supervisor is to ensure that a group of people work together to achieve the goals set by the business. Managing physical and human resources to achieve customer service goals requires planning, organising, staffing, directing and controlling.

Supervisors and head chefs need to motivate people, to persuade them to act in certain ways. In the kitchen/restaurant, as in any other department, staff must first be motivated to follow procedures. This can be done in a positive way by offering rewards, or in a negative way with catering staff who do not comply with requirements. Both methods can be effective, and can be used by supervisors to achieve their goals. One of the most effective ways is for a supervisor to build a team and offer incentives for good performance. However, staff can become indifferent to repeated schemes such as 'employee of the month'. A good supervisor will attempt to introduce novelty and fun into the reward system.

The supervisory function

Certain leadership qualities are needed to enable the supervisor to carry out his or her role effectively. These qualities include the ability to:

- communicate
- initiate
- make decisions
- coordinate
- mediate
- motivate
- inspire
- organise.

Those under supervision should expect from the supervisor:

- consideration
- understanding
- respect
- consistency.

In return the supervisor can expect:

- loyalty
- respect
- cooperation.

The good supervisor is able to obtain the best from those for whom he or she has responsibility, and can also completely satisfy the management of the establishment that a good job is being done.

The job of the supervisor is essentially to be an overseer. In the catering industry the name given to the supervisor may vary: sous-chef, chef de partie, kitchen supervisor or section chef. In hospital catering the name would be sous-chef, chef de partie or kitchen supervisor. The kitchen supervisor will be responsible to the catering manager, while in hotels and restaurants a chef de partie will be responsible to the head chef. The exact details of the job will vary according to the different areas of the industry and the size of the various units, but generally the supervisory role involves three functions: technical, administrative and social.

Technical function

Culinary skills and the ability to use kitchen equipment are essential for the kitchen supervisor. Most kitchen supervisors will have worked their way up through the section or sections before reaching supervisory responsibility. The supervisor needs to be able 'to do' as well as knowing 'what to do' and 'how to do it'. It is also necessary to be able to do it well and to be able to impart some of these skills to others.

Administrative function

The supervisor or chef de partie will, in many kitchens, be involved with the menu planning, sometimes with complete responsibility for the whole menu but more usually for part of the menu, as happens with the larder chef and pastry chef. This includes the ordering of foodstuffs (which is an important aspect of the supervisor's job in a catering establishment) and, of course, accounting for and recording materials used. The administrative function includes the allocation of duties and, in all instances, basic work-study knowledge is needed to enable the supervisor to operate effectively. The supervisor's job may also include the writing of reports, particularly in situations where it is necessary to make comparisons and when new developments are being tried.

Social function

The role of the supervisor is perhaps most clearly seen in staff relationships because the supervisor has to motivate the staff under his or her responsibility. 'To motivate' could be described as the initiation of movement and action, and having got the staff moving the supervisor needs to exert control. Then, in order to achieve the required result, the staff need to be organised.

Thus the supervisor has a threefold function regarding the handling of staff – namely to organise, to motivate and to control. This is the essence of staff supervision.

Elements of supervision

The accepted areas of supervision include:

- forecasting and planning
- organising
- commanding
- coordinating
- controlling.

Each of these will be considered within the sphere of catering.

Forecasting

Before making plans it is necessary to look ahead, to foresee possible and probable outcomes, and to allow for them. For example, if the chef de partie knows that the following day is her/his assistant's day off, s/he looks ahead and plans accordingly; when the catering supervisor in the hospital knows that there is a flu epidemic and two cooks are feeling below par, he or she plans for their possible absence; if there is a spell of fine, hot weather and the cook in charge of the larder foresees a continued demand for cold foods, or when an end to the hot spell is anticipated, then the plans are modified. For the supervisor, forecasting is the good use of judgement acquired from previous knowledge and experience. For example, because many people are on holiday in August fewer meals will be needed in the office restaurant; no students are in residence at the college hostel, but a conference is being held and 60 meals are required. A motor show, bank holidays, the effects of a rail strike or a wet day, as well as less predictable situations, such as the number of customers anticipated on the opening day of a new restaurant, all need to be anticipated and planned for.

Planning

From the forecasting comes the planning: how many meals to prepare; how much to have in stock (should the forecast not have been completely accurate); how many staff will be needed; which staff and when. Are the staff capable of what is required of them? If not, the supervisor needs to plan some training. This, of course, is particularly important if new equipment is installed. Imagine an expensive item, such as a new type of oven, ruined on the day it is installed because the staff have not been instructed in its proper use; or, more likely, equipment lying idle because the supervisor may not like it, may consider it is sited wrongly, does not train staff to use it, or for some similar reason.

As can be seen from these examples it is necessary for forecasting to precede planning, and from planning we now move to organising.

Organising

In the catering industry organisational skills are applied to food, to equipment and to staff. Organising in this context consists of ensuring that what is wanted is where it is wanted, when it is wanted, in the right amount and at the right time.

Such organisation involves the supervisor in the production of duty rotas, maybe training programmes and also cleaning schedules. Consider the supervisor's part in organising an outdoor function where a wedding reception is to be held in a church hall: 250 guests require a hot meal to be served at 2 pm and in the evening a dance will be held for the guests, during which a buffet will be provided at 9 pm. The supervisor would need to organise staff to be available when required, to have their own meals and maybe to see that they have got their transport home. Calor gas stoves may be needed, and the supervisor would have to arrange for these to be serviced and for the equipment used to be cleaned after the function. The food would need to be ordered so that it arrived in time to be prepared. If decorated hams were to be used on the buffet then they would need to be ordered in time so that they could be prepared, cooked and decorated over the required period of time. If the staff have never carved hams before, instruction would need to be given; this entails organising training. Needless to say, the correct quantities of food, equipment and cleaning materials would also have to be at the right place when wanted; and if all the details of the situation were not organised properly problems could occur.

Commanding

The supervisor has to give instructions to staff on how, what, when and where; this means that orders have to be given and a certain degree of order and discipline maintained. The successful supervisor is able to do this effectively, having made certain decisions and, usually, having established the basic priorities. Explanations of why a food is prepared in a certain manner, why this amount of time is needed to dress up food, say for a buffet, why this decision is taken and not that decision, and how these explanations and orders are given, determine the effectiveness of the supervisor.

Coordinating

Coordinating is the skill required to get staff to cooperate and work together. To achieve this, the supervisor has to be interested in the staff, to deal with their queries, to listen to their problems and to be helpful. Particular attention should be paid to new staff, easing them into the work situation so that they quickly become part of the team or partie. The other area of coordination for which the supervisor has particular responsibility is in maintaining good relations with other departments. However, the important persons to consider will always be the customers – for example, the patients, the schoolchildren – who are to receive the service, and good service is dependent on cooperation between waiters and cooks, nurses and catering staff, stores staff, caretakers, teachers, suppliers, and so on. The supervisor has a crucial role to play here.

Controlling

This includes the controlling of people and products, preventing pilfering as well as improving performance; checking that staff arrive on time, do not leave before time and do not misuse time in between; checking that the product, in this case the food, is of the right standard – that is to say, of the correct quantity and quality; checking to prevent waste, and also to ensure that staff operate the portion control system correctly.

This aspect of the supervisor's function involves inspecting and requires tact; controlling may include the inspecting of the bin to observe the amount of waste, checking the disappearance of a quantity of food, supervising the cooking of the meat so that shrinkage is minimised and reprimanding an unpunctual member of the team.

The standards of any catering establishment are dependent on the supervisor doing his or her job efficiently, and standards are set and maintained by effective control, which is the function of the supervisor.

Responsibilities of the supervisor

Delegation

It is recognised that delegation is the root of successful supervision; in other words, by giving a certain amount of responsibility to others, the supervisor can be more effective.

The supervisor needs to be able to judge the person capable of responsibility before any delegation can take place. But then, having recognised the abilities of an employee, the supervisor who wants to develop the potential of those under his or her control must allow the person entrusted with the job to get on with it.

Motivation

Since not everyone is capable of, or wants, responsibility, the supervisor still needs to motivate those who are less ambitious. Most people are prepared to work so as to improve their standard of living, but there is also another very important motivating factor: most people wish to get satisfaction from the work they do. The supervisor must be aware of why people work and how different people achieve job satisfaction, and then be able to act upon this knowledge. A supervisor should have been on a training course to attempt to understand what motivates people as there are a number of theories that s/he can use to stimulate ideas.

Symptoms of poor motivation

There are many symptoms of poor motivation. In general terms it reveals itself as a lack of interest in getting the job done correctly and within the required time. Although they may be indicators of poor motivation, lack of efficiency and effectiveness could also be a result of the staff overworking, personal problems, poor work design, repetitive work, lack of discipline, interpersonal conflict, lack of training or failure of the organisation to value its staff. An employee may be highly motivated but may find the work physically impossible.

Welfare

People always work best in good working conditions and these include freedom from fear: fear of becoming unemployed, fear of failure at work, fear of discrimination. Job security and incentives, such as opportunities for promotion, bonuses, profit sharing and time for further study, encourage a good attitude to work; but as well as these tangible factors people need to feel wanted and that what they do is important. The supervisor is in an excellent position to ensure that this happens. Personal worries affect individuals' performance and can have a very strong influence on how well or how badly they work. The physical environment will naturally cause problems if, for example, the atmosphere is humid, the working situation ill-lit, too hot or too noisy, and there is constant rush and tear, and frequent major problems to be overcome. In these circumstances staff are more liable to be quick-tempered, angry and aggressive, and the supervisor needs to consider how these factors might be dealt with.

Understanding

The supervisor needs to try to understand both men and women (and to deal with both sexes fairly), to anticipate problems and build up a team spirit so as to overcome the problems. This entails always being fair when dealing with staff, and giving them encouragement. It also means that work needs to be allocated according to each individual's ability; everyone should be kept fully occupied and the working environment must be conducive to producing their best work.

Communication

Finally, and most important of all, the supervisor must be able to communicate effectively. To convey orders, instructions, information and manual skills requires the supervisor to possess the right attitude to those with whom he or she needs to communicate. The ability to convey orders and instructions in a manner that is acceptable to the one receiving them is dependent not only on the words but on the emphasis given to the words, the tone of voice, the time selected to give them and on who is present when they are given. This is a skill that supervisors need to develop. Instructions and orders can be given with authority without being authoritative.

Thus the supervisor needs technical knowledge and the ability to direct staff and to carry responsibility so as to achieve the specified targets and standards required by the organisation; this he or she is able to do by organising, coordinating, controlling and planning but, most of all, through effective communication.

Skills for effective supervision

Robert L. Katz (1974) has suggested that there are three types of skills required for effective management:

1 technical
2 people
3 conceptual.

Technical skills

These are the skills chefs, restaurant managers and the like need in order to do the job. The supervisor must be skilled in the area they are supervising because they will be required in most cases to train other staff under them. Supervisors who do not have the required skills will find it hard to gain credibility with the staff.

People skills

Supervisors are team leaders, therefore they must be sensitive to the needs of others. They must be able to communicate effectively and be able to build a team to achieve the agreed goals – listening, questioning, communicating clearly, handling conflicts, and providing support and praise when praise is due.

Conceptual skills

A supervisor must be able to think things through, especially when planning or analysing why they are not going as expected. A supervisor must be able to solve problems and make decisions. For supervisors, conceptual skills are necessary for reasonably short-term planning. Head chefs and hospitality managers require conceptual skills for long-term strategic planning.

Henry Mintzberg (1975) suggested that the supervisor has three broad roles:

1 interpersonal – people skills
2 informational – people and technical skills
3 decision making – conceptual skills.

Supervisors and ethical issues

A supervisor must be consistent when handling staff, avoiding favouritism and perceived inequity. Such inequity can rise from the amount of training or performance counselling given, from the promotion of certain employees, and from the way in which shifts are allocated. Supervisors should engage in conversation with all staff, not just a selected few, and should not single out some staff for special attention.

Ethical treatment of staff is fair treatment of staff. A good supervisor will gain respect if they are ethical.

Confidentiality is an important issue for the supervisor. Employees or customers may wish to take the supervisor into their confidence, and the supervisor must not betray this.

Micromanagement

In business management, micromanagement is a management style where a manager closely observes or controls the work of his/her employees, generally used as a pejorative term. In contrast to giving general instructions on smaller tasks while supervising larger concerns, the micromanager monitors and assesses every step.

Micromanagement may arise from internal sources, such as concern for details, increased performance pressure, or insecurity. It can also be seen as a tactic used by managers to eliminate unwanted employees, either by creating standards they cannot meet, leading to termination of employment, or by creating a stressful workplace and thus causing the employee to leave.

Regardless of the motivation, the effect may be to demotivate employees, create resentment and damage trust.

Micromanagement can also be distinguished from management by worker-to-boss ratio. At any time when there is one worker being given orders by one boss, both people are rendered useless. When a boss can do a worker's job with more efficiency than giving the orders to do the same job, this is micromanagement.

Micromanagement is a counterproductive approach to dealing with the workforce and can be costly in many areas of the business.

Identifying recruitment needs

A supervisor must be able to identify what staff are required and where they are required in order to cope with the level of business. At the same time labour costs must be kept to a minimum. The supervisor must therefore ensure adequate staffing at the lowest possible cost.

An important aspect is to be able to carefully analyse projected business in order to adopt the best staffing mix.

Job design and the allocation of duties also have to be considered; where jobs are simple and require little training, employment of casual labour can be justified. For more skilled staff, full-time employment has to be considered with investment in staff development and training.

Often the supervisor has to write job descriptions. These documents are used for a number of purposes, which include:

- deciding on the knowledge, experience and skills required to carry out the duties specified
- allowing new staff to understand the requirements of their jobs
- allowing new staff to develop accurate expectation of the jobs
- identifying training needs
- assisting in the development of recruitment strategies.

Job descriptions allow supervisors and managers to monitor performance, and to manage discipline when performance is below standard. Job descriptions assist in allowing everyone to focus on the precise requirements of the job and ensure that everyone is clear about their expectations.

An example of a job description: Senior Sous Chef

Reporting to Head Chef

The Senior Sous Chef position reports to the Head Chef and is responsible for the day-to-day kitchen operation, overseeing the stores, preparation and production areas. The position involves supervising and managing the kitchen staff, with direct responsibility for rostering and scheduling production. In the absence of the Head Chef, the Senior Sous Chef will be required to take on the duties of the Head Chef and to attend Senior Management meetings in his/her absence.

Duties

- Monitor and check stores operation.
- Train new and existing staff in health and safety, HACCP (hazard analysis critical and control point), etc.
- Chair of the Kitchen Health and Safety Committee.
- Develop new menus and concepts together with senior management.
- Schedule and roster all kitchen staff.
- Maintain accurate records of staff absences.
- Maintain accurate kitchen records.
- Responsible for the overall cleanliness of the kitchen operation.
- Assist in the production of management reports.
- Establish an effective and efficient team.
- Assist with the overall establishment and monitoring of budgets.

Conditions

- Grade 3 management spine.
- Private health insurance.
- 5-day week.
- 28 days' holiday.

- Profit-share scheme after one year's service.

Personal specification: Senior Sous Chef

- Qualifications
  (i) Level 3 or 4 Professional Cookery

- Experience
  (i) Five years' experience in 4- and 5-star hotel kitchens; restaurant and banqueting experience

- Skills
  (i) Proficiency in culinary arts
  (ii) Microsoft Excel, Access, Word
  (iii) Operation of inventory control software
  (iv) Written and oral communication skills
  (v) Team-building skills

- Knowledge
  (i) Current legislation on health and safety
  (ii) Food hygiene

- (iii) HACCP
  (iv) Risk assessment
  (v) Production systems
  (vi) Current technology

- Other attributes
  (i) Honesty
  (ii) Reliability
  (iii) Attention to detail
  (iv) Initiative
  (v) Accuracy

- Essential
  (i) Basic computer skills
  (ii) High degree of culinary skills
  (iii) Good communication skills
  (iv) Supervisory and leadership skills

- Desirable
  (i) Knowledge of employment law
  (ii) Public relations profile

Induction programmes

Why induction?

Every establishment should have a detailed induction system. The induction process settles new employees into their new positions. It is important for the company to make a good impression as this will influence the person's attitude to the job. The new employee needs to be aware of their responsibilities. This will include not just their day-to-day procedures but also their role in legislation, food hygiene, health and safety.

Topics for induction

- Company procedures, policies.
- Tour of establishment and facilities.
- Fire drill procedures, health and safety procedures.
- Reporting procedures.
- Job description explained.
- Conditions of employment.
- Emergency procedures.
- Where to go for advice or assistance.

- Equal opportunities.
- Accident reporting.
- Dismissal procedures.

During the first few weeks of employment the following topics need to be explained to the new employee:
- organisational aims and objectives
- occupational health and safety
- performance appraisal
- job description explained
- grievance procedures
- quality standards
- staff development.

Where possible, new employees should be issued with an employee handbook with information on the company. The supervisor should take time to explain the contents of this handbook. Staff retention is an important issue in the hospitality and catering industry. Supervisors have a key role in developing teams to achieve effective working relationships that value people. These can help to reduce turnover. Staff turnover is extremely costly and every attempt should be made to reduce unnecessary turnover.

The cost of staff turnover to an establishment

- Replacement costs – advertising, training, etc.
- Overtime to existing staff.
- Extra pressure on existing staff.
- Time taken to recruit staff.

- Agency costs.
- Payroll and administration costs.
- Loss of business due to insufficient staff on duty to supply the required level of service.
- Loss of business through damage to reputation.

The supervisor and performance appraisal

Supervisors manage performance informally through instructions and advice, and by providing constructive feedback. The supervisor should give praise when it is due and reprimand an employee if necessary. Informal feedback takes place on a day-to-day basis but most large organisations operate a formal appraisal system. This involves the supervisor or the manager conducting a formal interview with the employee, examining past performance and assessing opportunities for the future. Overall performance may be ranked on a performance scale. During the interview, training needs and career development are analysed to establish the employee's performance objectives and plans for achievement.

Performance appraisal forms may cover efficiency, reliability, teamwork and working relationships. In service organisations this may also include customer relations. To be more specific the job description criteria may also be included in the form. Focusing on the job description promotes discussion about what is happening in the workplace and how hurdles to ineffective performance can be overcome. Performance objectives and training plans should also relate to the job requirements.

When a supervisor conducts a performance appraisal s/he should advise the employee in advance, explaining the purpose of the appraisal. In addition, sufficient time must be allocated to the process. The following should also be taken into account:

- creating an appropriate climate for the interview
- reviewing specific job performances against specific job targets
- openly discussing issues that may have an impact on performance
- agreeing on new performance targets
- giving positive constructive feedback.

Kitchen equipment

Cooking equipment provides the backbone of any busy catering operation. It is the key to catering success and quality. In terms of food safety it controls the most critical step in the food production process. A mistake at the cooking stage by undercooking of raw food is likely to result in a mass food-poisoning incident.

Kitchen equipment is expensive so initial selection is important, and the following points should be considered before each item is purchased or hired.

- Overall dimensions (in relation to available space).
- Weight – can the floor support the weight?
- Fuel supply – is the existing fuel supply sufficient to take the increase?
- Drainage – where necessary, are there adequate facilities?
- Water – where necessary, is it to hand?
- Use – if it is a specialist piece of equipment for certain foods or products, will there be sufficient use to justify the expense and investment?
- Capacity – can it cook the quantities of food required efficiently?
- Time – can it cook the given quantities of food in the time available?
- Ease – is it easy for staff to handle, control and use properly?
- Maintenance – is it easy for staff to clean and maintain?

- Attachments – is it necessary to use additional equipment or attachments?
- Extraction – does it require extraction facilities for fumes or steam?
- Noise – does it have an acceptable noise level?
- Construction – is it well made, safe, hygienic and energy efficient, and are all handles, knobs and switches sturdy and heat resistant?
- Appearance – if equipment is to be on view to customers does it look good and fit in with the overall design?
- Spare parts – are they and replacement parts easily obtainable?

Kitchen equipment may be divided into three categories:

1 large equipment – ranges, steamers, boiling pans, fish-fryers, sinks, tables
2 mechanical equipment – peelers, mincers, mixers, refrigerators, dishwashers
3 utensils and small equipment – pots, pans, whisks, bowls, spoons.

Manufacturers of all kitchen equipment issue instructions on how to clean and keep their apparatus in efficient working order, and it is the responsibility of everyone using the equipment to follow these instructions (which should be displayed in a prominent place near the machines).

Figure 5.3 Prover

Arrangements should be made with the local gas board for regular checks and servicing of gas-operated equipment; similar arrangements should be made with the electricity supplier. It is a good plan to keep a log book of all equipment, showing where each item is located when servicing takes place, noting any defects that arise, and instructing the fitter to sign the log book and to indicate exactly what has been done.

To find out more, see IOH Technical Brief No. 28, Purchasing Catering Equipment, or visit the website of the Catering Equipment Suppliers' Association (CESA): www.cesa.org.uk.

Legislation affecting equipment in the professional kitchen

(*This section is adapted from 'The law in your kitchen'*, Caterer and Hotelkeeper, *19 April 2006*.)

There is a large amount of legislation being imposed on professional kitchens. A great deal is concerned with how kitchen equipment is bought, operated and disposed of.

CE marking

All powered catering equipment sold in the UK and Europe must carry a small 'CE' badge. This means that the manufacturer has certified that it meets European Union safety, and in some cases performance, standards. The EU standards are among the strictest in the world and are drawn up to ensure that kitchen staff have the least possible risk of injury. Reputable brands of catering equipment bought from reputable dealers should always have the CE mark.

The regulation recognises that many kitchens have well-manufactured old equipment that predates the introduction of CE marking. That is why the legal requirement for kitchen equipment to be CE marked applies only to equipment manufactured after 1995.

When manufacturers sell kitchen equipment and offer a guarantee, it comes with conditions of servicing. Kitchen equipment is very technical, and needs a trained and accredited service engineer to keep it in working order and comply with the terms of the guarantee. If equipment breaks down and a chef calls on the guarantee for cost-free repairs, without evidence of accredited servicing the guarantee could be invalid.

When it comes to servicing and repairing kitchen equipment the law is clear. The only people who can install and maintain a gas-powered piece of kitchen equipment must be registered with the Gas Safe Register and be qualified to work with gas. They must carry a Register ID card. There are several levels of accreditation that an engineer can have. For example, a person working on a combination oven needs a different assessment from that needed to install a fryer; it is important to check that anyone servicing gas-powered equipment has the right accreditation for the equipment that they will be working on. The Gas Safe Register replaced the CORGI registration system.

For more information visit www.gassaferegister.co.uk.

Health and safety regulations

The Health and Safety Executive (HSE) makes the rules covering the safety of kitchen staff using machines or equipment. Some are guidance notes; some are law; but to go against either can result in both prosecution and compensation claims.

The regulations are complex, but no chef can ignore them.

To find out more, see IOH Technical Brief No. 28, Purchasing Catering Equipment, or visit the website of the Catering Equipment Suppliers' Association (CESA): www.cesa.org.uk.

Regulations affecting ventilation systems

The important issue here is interlocking. This means that, where there is a ventilation hood over the cooking area, there is a gas supply cut-out mechanism between the cooking equipment and the ventilation hood. If the extraction fan should fail, the gas supply to the kitchen equipment will automatically be turned off.

Interlocking regulations are not retrospective, meaning that in most existing kitchens they are strongly recommended, but not mandatory.

Any new kitchen using a fan-assisted extraction system must have this interlocking gas cut-out system. If more than half the appliances are replaced in existing kitchens then an interlocking gas cut-out system must be fitted.

PUWER

PUWER stands for the Provision and Use of Work Equipment Regulations. These regulations cover how chefs use kitchen equipment and are part of a European Directive that supplements regulations under the Health and Safety at Work Act. The aim is for kitchen management to accept responsibility for the use of equipment.

PUWER regulations say that, where there is machinery in the kitchen, management should have a risk assessment carried out, provide written instructions for operating it and provide adequate training to all staff that are going to use it. Under PUWER there is a legal obligation to maintain machinery properly, and if there is a service log book with the equipment, it has to be filled in.

WEEE

This is the Waste Electrical and Electronic Equipment Directive. This EU legislation's first aim is to achieve a sustainable Europe through recycling electrical equipment. Its second is to reduce the amount of waste material that goes into landfill. Historically with catering equipment, recycling has not been a problem due to the high value of the scrap materials – mainly stainless steel – which means the equipment has a history of being recycled responsibly.

To find out more, visit www.netregs.gov.uk/ netregs/legislation/380525/.

WRAS

The aim of the Water Regulations Advisory Scheme is to ensure that fittings, equipment or products that are connected to the mains supply, do not contaminate water.

Although WRAS regulations cover every industry, in commercial kitchens the main concern is the risk of contamination of pure drinking water through backflow. This is where dirty water, for whatever reason, accidentally passes back into the main water supply rather than going out to the drains. Every item of kitchen equipment that is connected to the mains must comply with the Water Supply (Water Fittings) Regulations.

Where badly contaminated water is discharged from an item of kitchen equipment, such as a dishwasher, the protection will be provided by an anti-syphonic backflow-preventing device or an air gap.

Most new equipment will come with the necessary fitting to comply with WRAS. Only engineers with a qualification to connect equipment to the water supply should fit kitchen equipment that needs a supply of water.

Large equipment

Ranges and ovens

A large variety of ranges is available operated by gas, electricity, solid fuel, oil, microwave or microwave plus convection.

Oven doors should not be slammed as this is liable to cause damage.

The unnecessary or premature lighting of ovens can cause wastage of fuel, which is needless expense. This is a bad habit common in many kitchens.

When a solid-top gas range is lit, the centre ring should be removed to reduce the risk of blowback, but it should be replaced after approximately five minutes, otherwise unnecessary heat is lost.

Convection ovens

These are ovens in which a circulating current of hot air is rapidly forced around the inside of the oven by a motorised fan or blower. As a result, a more even and constant temperature is created, which allows food to be cooked successfully in any part of the oven. This means that the heat is used more efficiently, cooking temperatures can be lower, cooking times shortened and overall fuel economy achieved.

Forced air convection can be described as fast conventional cooking: conventional in that heat is applied to the surface of the food, but fast since moving air transfers its heat more rapidly than does static air. In a sealed oven, fast hot air circulation reduces evaporation loss, keeping shrinkage to a minimum, and gives the rapid change of surface texture and colour that are traditionally associated with certain cooking processes.

There are four types of convection oven.

1 Where forced air circulation within the oven is accomplished by means of a motor-driven fan, the rapid air circulation ensures even temperature distribution to all parts of the oven.
2 Where low-velocity, high-volume air movement is provided by a power blower and duct system.
3 A combination of a standard oven and a forced convection oven designed to operate as either by the flick of a switch.
4 A single roll-in rack convection oven with heating element and fan housed outside the cooking area. An 18-shelf mobile oven rack makes it possible to roll the filled rack directly from the preparation area into the oven.

Combination ovens

Combination ovens (combi-ovens) have brought about a revolution in baking, roasting and steaming. There are now many varieties of combination ovens available on the market, fuelled by gas or electricity, and they are widely used in most sectors of the catering industry. They are especially used in large banqueting operations.

Ovens can be programmed easily to produce exact cooking times and the regeneration of chilled food, allowing chefs to produce consistent products every time.

The special features of combination ovens are:

- they reduce cooking times
- they are fully automatic – enable desired browning levels and exact core temperatures to be achieved
- they are self-cleaning

Figure 5.4 Deck oven

Figure 5.5 Forced air convection oven

- a combination oven system will allow more food to be produced in less space
- energy efficiency
- increased productivity.

A new type of combination oven has now been manufactured – it is a hybrid of fridge and oven, designed for use in cook-chill food systems for banqueting or industrial catering. The chilled food is held in chill until the predetermined moment when the chilling unit switches off and the oven facility kicks in, bringing the food safely up to eating temperature.

Rotary rack ovens

Rotary rack ovens resemble larger roll-in convection or combi-ovens, but they operate on a different principle and deliver even more production capacity. These ovens accept one or two full racks loaded with bake pans, which are rolled in to the oven compartment. Rather than relying on blowers to circulate hot air to even out browning, these ovens have either a mechanical lift system that suspends and rotates the rack during the cook cycle, or a floor-mounted platform that provides the rotation. Rack ovens are also equipped with a steam system, which provides the nice sheen to the crust required by many bread products.

Rotary rack ovens are available in both gas and electric heated models. Because of their size, they typically have a ventilation hood system integrated with the oven package. They are typically used in large institutional kitchens, hotels and banquet operations.

Mechanical ovens

Large mechanical ovens with trays evolved from conventional bake and roast ovens. Rather than having to

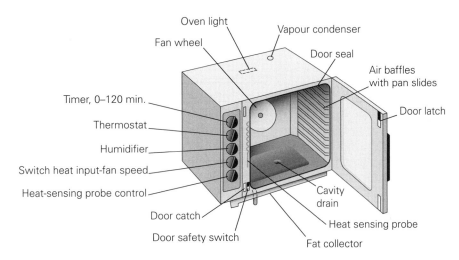

Figure 5.6 Hot air convection oven

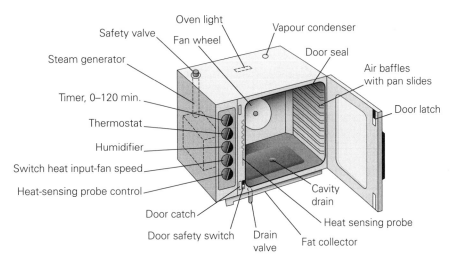

Figure 5.7 Hot air steamer oven

travel between ovens to load and unload product or check product being cooked, the chef or baker can do it all at one location. A convection oven has many operational and performance advantages, but it must be kept relatively small to control air movement. They are by design a *batch production* method. The moving tray oven has many of the benefits of a convection oven, but it is a *continuous production* method, with much higher production capabilities.

The revolving tray or *reel oven* (also known as the 'Ferris wheel' oven) has been the mainstay of many bakeries for more than 50 years. Like a Ferris wheel, pans are suspended from double wheels that revolve in a gas or electrically heated chamber. The pans are pivoted so that they remain level at all times, no matter what their position on the wheel. This type of oven has the reputation of turning out remarkably

Figure 5.8 A combination oven

good products at relatively low labour and energy costs.

For greater capacity in a mechanical oven, trays are attached to chains that move from the front to the rear, horizontally. They then circle around the wheel or transfer arm, to a lower level. From there they return to the loading area at the front of the oven. In some ovens, the product being baked merely goes from one end of the oven to the other, where it is unloaded. Then the tray or belt returns to the front for product reloading. At the front of the oven, the tray is raised to the unload-load position. An item that is to be baked may take several trips through this style of oven before it has finished baking. Other mechanical ovens move in a circular, horizontal path up to three and five levels. These types of oven are known as *rotary ovens*.

Although all of the ovens mentioned were originally designed for baking, they can be used for roasting as well. They are typically found in large institutional kitchens or commissaries, commercial and wholesale bakeries, and large restaurants that have separate baking areas.

The cooking process management system

This links the combi-oven to a PC, which monitors the cooking process to help with HACCP. The computer software monitors not just the combi-ovens, but other items of cooking equipment in the kitchen, such as pressure bratt pans, steamers and boiling kettles. The chef inputs into the software what the day's food production is to be, and the computer will work out the order in which the food should be cooked and in what pieces of equipment, to deliver the food just in time for freshness.

The HACCP management part of this system can track food from goods delivery to the plate by using probes – for example, a chilled or frozen chicken can be probed to monitor and record temperatures before the cooking process so that if a problem occurs in the food cycle, the kitchen manager can check to see if there were any discrepancies in the goods storage procedures.

During the cooking the probes will record any variations to the pre-set cooking programme. This means the software system can alert the kitchen management team not just that a problem has occurred during the cooking procedure, but where it occurred.

Combination ovens: cooking profile

Example: rationale

These are pre-programmed, offering ideal procedures for cooking different meats – in particular for roasts such as leg of lamb and roast pork. The special feature of these intelligent profiles is that they detect automatically the size of the meat and the volume of the food in the cooking cabinet. In addition, with the assistance of the internal quality temperature (IQT) sensor, they also determine the exact core temperature of the food, the remaining cooking time and the current level of browning. The profiles are self-regulating – that is, they adjust the cooking processes to the size of the meat and the load of food in the cooking cabinet.

IQT sensor: rationale

The sensor is inserted into the food to facilitate the detection of the core temperature. This prevents overcooking of joints and reduces weight loss.

Alto-shaam cook and hold ovens

These ovens reduce labour and product shrinkage, provide product consistency and increase holding life for banqueting service. Two items are available, one for holding and serve, the other for regeneration and serve.

Smoking ovens

Smoking certain foods is a means of cooking, injecting different flavours and preserving (there is more on the use of smoking as a method of preservation in Chapter 4). Smoking ovens or cabinets are well insulated with controlled heating elements on which wood chips are placed (different types of wood chips give differing flavours). As the wood chips burn, the heated smoke permeates the food (fish, chicken, sausages, etc.) that is suspended in the cabinet.

The microwave oven

Microwaves are common in most commercial kitchens, handling everything from defrosting to self-steaming and rapid rethermalisation. Solid-state programmable controls make them easy to use, and today's microwave ovens offer more power, better warranties and greater durability.

How do microwave ovens work?

A microwave is an invisible electromagnetic wave, which travels at the speed of light. That, by the way, happens to be 186,282 miles per second or, in terms of kilometres, almost 300,000 per second.

Microwave ovens operate in the 2450 megahertz frequency which is the only frequency currently used in microwave ovens. The microwaves are developed and introduced into the oven's cooking compartment by magnetron tubes. These tubes are designed

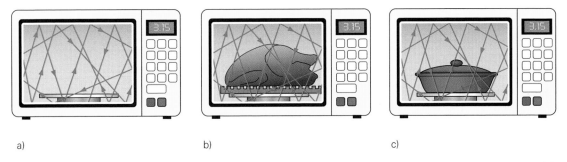

a)   b)   c)

Figure 5.9 (a) Microwave energy being reflected off cooking cavity walls; (b) microwave energy being absorbed by food; (c) microwave energy passing through cooking container material

specifically to convert electricity into microwaves. The microwaves, which themselves are not hot, leave the oven cool. The water and fat molecules that are found in food absorb the microwave energy. This energy causes these molecules to vibrate against each other (about 2.5 billion times per second), creating friction, which in turn creates heat, which in turn warms or cooks the food.

Microwave energy penetrates the food to a depth of 12.0 to 20.0 mm in most food products. The exception to this would be bread and pastry products, where the energy may go all the way through, because of the product's low density.

The reason that microwave energy cooks faster than conventional cooking is that a greater amount of heat is created in the outside portion of the food (the area 12.0 to 20.0 mm deep, which is penetrated by the microwave) so that the heat is transferred faster to the inside of the food.

A good example of how this works is the baked potato. In a conventional oven, the heat has to be passed on molecule by molecule, from the outside of the product to the centre. In a microwave oven, the outer 'sphere', which is approximately 20.0 mm deep, is penetrated by the microwave energy and cooked. From that point on, the potato cooks normally. The centre of a potato cooked in a microwave oven is cooked by conduction, the same as a conventionally cooked potato. The difference in speed occurs because the microwave energy cooks the outside 20.0 mm faster, allowing the heat to reach the centre of the potato faster.

Metal reflects microwave energy, which is why the sides of a microwave oven cavity are always made of metal. Microwave energy does not go through the oven's door screen because the holes in the screen are too small. The holes allow the light to go through, but not the much longer wavelength that is used for heating.

Metal dishes or aluminium foil should not be used in a microwave oven for exactly the same reason. The metal deflects the microwaves away from the food, preventing cooking and possibly overheating the magnetron. Paper, plastic, china, glass and ceramic are acceptable materials for use inside a microwave.

The technology that makes microwave ovens possible also creates a few disadvantages. For instance, standard microwave ovens do not brown foods. Food browns when amino acids and certain sugars are brought together under dry heat, at least 90°C, for a sustained period of time. Microwave cooking just does not create these conditions.

To solve this problem, combination convection/microwave ovens have been introduced to the commercial and consumer markets. These combination units introduce the dry heat and air movement of a convection oven, plus the speed of a microwave oven. The result is a cooking device with the advantages of both. This combination unit cooks up to 80 per cent faster than a standard convection oven, can accommodate metal cookware and delivers a fully browned product that looks good on the plate.

Microwave ovens have as many as four magnetrons, offering more cooking power. The magnetrons, which are air cooled and release a small amount of heat into the kitchen, use a transmitter or wave guide to direct the microwaves to the oven cavity. Wave stirrers are located at the point where the waves enter the oven cavity. They are designed to evenly distribute the waves throughout the cooking cavity, greatly reducing the hot spots and uneven cooking common in earlier microwave ovens.

A microwave oven's power input will determine what function it will have in a food service operation. The following is a brief description of the four basic types of commercial microwave ovens and their intended uses.

1 **Light-duty microwaves:** these units are generally rated in the 700- to 800-watt range. They are small and compact, and are most often used for quick point-of-service heating applications such as a food service station. They are also used in many low-volume restaurants where speed is not a critical factor.

2 **Heavy-duty microwaves:** most of these units are rated in the 900- to 2200-watt range. They all come with a stainless steel cavity and most, but not all, have a stainless steel exterior (dependent on the manufacturer). Most are also compact in their overall size.

3 **Bulk cookers and microwave steamers:** these large microwaves operate in the 2400- to 3700-watt range. Some of these units have been positioned to compete with countertop convection steamers. They rely on the water content of the food itself to generate some steam when heated by the magnetrons. These larger units are not normally used for single or small portion heating. However, they do work well for bulk applications, such as reheating and cooking products in cafeterias and other institutions.

4 **Convection microwave ovens:** these units are actually small convection ovens with built-in microwave assistance. They have now been available for quite a few years. Newer models are not as expensive as the first models introduced. They are also more versatile and require less space than the previous models.

To find out more, contact the Microwave Association (website: www.microwaveassociation. org.uk).

Figure 5.10 A microwave oven

Combination convection and microwave cooker

This cooker combines forced air convection and microwave, either of which can be used separately but that are normally used simultaneously, thereby giving the advantages of both systems: speed, coloration and texture of food. Traditional metal cooking pans may also be used without fear of damage to the cooker.

Induction cooking

Advantages of induction cooking hobs

- **Power savings:** the induction hob has a very high energy efficiency and only draws power when a pan is on the ring. Energy costs are substantially reduced.
- **Safety:** only the pan gets hot, therefore you cannot burn yourself on this type of hob.
- **Cool working environment:** as virtually all the energy is developed as heat directly in the pan, very little heat escapes to the atmosphere, therefore providing a cool working environment.
- **Less extraction:** because of the cool working environment the kitchen needs much less extraction, further reducing energy bills.
- **Hygiene:** the flat ceramic top provides a wipe-clean hygienic surface that remains cool, therefore spillage will not burn onto the cooking surface.
- **No combustion gases:** unlike gas hobs, induction hobs do not emit any combustion gases and are environmentally friendly.
- **Speed of cooking:** modern induction hob designs are faster than gas hobs.

History

Traditional ranges and ovens work because the energy source – for example, electricity – causes the burners to heat up. That heat is then transferred to the pan or pot placed upon the heated surface. In this method of creating heat, it is the burner that actually cooks the food. Conversely, an induction cooktop holds a series of burners called induction coils, which are based on magnetic principles. These coils generate magnetic fields that induct a warming reaction in steel-based pots or pans; it is the cooking vessels themselves that heat the food, not the stove elements. Because of this form of heat generation, the cooktops may feel slightly warm to the touch after they are turned off, but they remain relatively cool – and thus much safer.

Temperature, speed and control are additional benefits with an induction cooktop. This type of stove heats up faster than an electric range, allowing for faster cooking times – water will boil at half the time as on an electric cooking surface. Because of this reduced cooking time, energy savings can be substantial. Induction cooktops are 85–90 per cent more energy efficient than electricity-powered stoves and ovens, and use approximately half the energy of gas-sourced models.

Cleaning an induction cooktop is a breeze because the surface is flat and continuous; there are no nooks or crannies where food particles or spillovers can collect. Range-top mess is also reduced because the induction cooktops offer convenient safeguards; they turn themselves off if a pot has gone dry and, if there is a spillover, the cooking surface prevents the burning on and hardening of spilled food.

While induction cooktops will save money in the long run, there are some costly initial investments. The cooktops themselves, which range from a one-unit hotplate type to the traditional four-burner size, range in price from several hundred to several thousand pounds.

An additional expense can arise if you need to replace your current cookware. Induction cooktops induct energy only into ferrous metal-based pots and pans. If you are currently using cast iron, steel-plated or certain types of stainless steel pans, you should be able to continue to use the cookware you already own. However, you cannot cook with materials such as copper, aluminium or glass. Some makes of stainless steel pots and pans are conducive to cooking on an induction cooktop while others are not. If in doubt, test your present cookware with a magnet – if the magnet sticks to the pot, the pot will work with an induction cooktop.

Try to find an induction hob that works using normal pans. Beware of induction hobs that need special pans or do not give constant performance pan to pan.

Figure 5.11 An induction wok

To find out more, contact Induced Energy Limited, New Building, Westminster Road, Northamptonshire NN13 7EB (website: www. inducedenergy.com).

Halogen hob

This runs on electricity, and comprises five individually controlled heat zones, each of which has four tungsten halogen lamps located under a smooth ceramic glass surface. The heat source glows red, when switched on, getting brighter as the temperature increases.

When the hob is switched on, 70 per cent of the heat is transmitted as infra-red light directly into the base of the cooking pan, the rest is from conducted heat via the ceramic glass. Ordinary pots and pans may be used on the halogen hob, but those with a flat, dark or black base absorb the heat most efficiently.

The halogen range includes a convection oven, and the halogen hob unit is also available mounted on a stand.

Further information can be obtained by visiting the website of the Catering Equipment Suppliers' Association (CESA): www.cesa.org.uk.

Steam cooking equipment

Steam cooking equipment comprises many different and varied pieces of cooking equipment. Some of the major items that fall under this rather general category include compartment steam cookers (both pressure and pressureless steamers), combination oven steamers, boiling kettles/steam-jacketed kettles, and tilting braising pans or bratt pans. Under each of these general categories, there are numerous types, styles, models, power inputs, etc.

What is steam?

Steam is odourless, colourless, tasteless and invisible. It is water converted to the gas state. So why is it we think we can 'see' steam? What you are actually seeing when you think you are seeing steam is water vapour, which is very small droplets of water carried or entrained with the steam. Occasionally you will hear the terms 'dry steam' or 'wet steam' used in the kitchen. Wet steam is carrying significant water vapour. True dry steam carries little water vapour.

What makes steam so special? The secret to steam cooking is its efficiency as a heat transfer medium and its ability to give up that heat energy on contact with a cooler surface. In addition, steam expands in

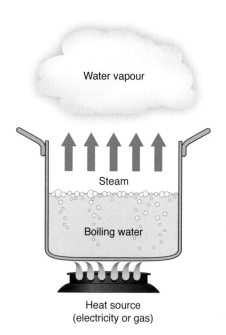

Figure 5.12 What is steam?

volume more than 30 times when it is converted from its liquid (water) state, which helps it move into and fill compartments, jackets and places where heat transfer can take place. These unique properties make steam an excellent medium for cooking and warming foods.

First steam was used within the confines of a (kettle) jacket, for the efficient conduction heating of products within a vessel. This method of indirectly cooking with steam is a refinement of the double boiler principle.

In addition, steam was introduced into a closed compartment, in direct contact with the food, resulting in the heating and cooking of those foods.

How steam cooking works

Steam is water that has been converted to its gaseous state by the application of heat energy. Heat

Figure 5.13 A pressureless steamer

energy is typically measured in British thermal units (BTUs). A BTU is defined as the amount of energy required to raise the temperature of 1 pound of water by 1 degree Fahrenheit, at sea level.

It takes only .05 kW/180 BTUs to raise the temperature of .45 kilograms/1 pound of water from 0°C to 100°C, the point at which it starts to boil. However, to evaporate and convert that same pound of water into steam requires .28 kW/970 BTUs. When water boils at 100°C and absorbs heat, the process is called the 'latent heat of vaporisation'. As a result, steam carries many times the energy of boiling water − six times as much, in fact.

Steam readily gives up that energy load when it condenses back into water (condensate) upon contact with food or any cooler surface. In the case of kettle cooking, that heat is transferred into the food by conduction, through the kettle wall.

Steamers

Steamers have been one of the fastest-growing equipment categories, driven by menu trends and the desire for healthier foods. There is a growing list of different models, sizes and steam-generation methods available in today's market. Here is a breakdown of the major categories and the key sub-categories:

- **pressureless steamers** (also known as convection or atmospheric steamers) − traditional convection steamers, connectionless steamers, 'boilerless' steamers
- **pressure steamers** − high-pressure steamers, low-pressure steamers
- **pressure/pressureless steamers**
- **speciality steamers**.

Pressureless steamers

In pressureless steamers, the heat transfer from steam to food is accomplished by forced convection, creating turbulence that reduces the insulating barrier of condensation on food. This 'forced convection' is achieved by using a fan wheel, steam ports or distribution manifolds to concentrate and accelerate the steam coming out of the boiler or steam generator.

When steam contacts the food's cooler surface, the steam transfers its energy load directly into the food. Because air and water diminish this heat transfer, a continuous venting system in pressureless steamers eliminates virtually all of the air from the cooking compartment, as steam expands and fills the compartment. This results in fast, gentle cooking at a relatively low temperature of 100°C, in a steamer at sea level.

Pressureless steamers are well suited to a wide variety of foods, including fresh or frozen seafood and vegetables, including loose individually quick frozen (IQF) pack frozen or frozen block vegetables. Because the cavity is continuously vented and condensate drained, unwanted flavour transfer from one food product to another is eliminated. Perforated gastronorm pans are recommended for cooking most food items, but some foods, such as rice, scrambled eggs, certain kinds of beef and pasta, are prepared in solid pans or a perforated pan nested in a deeper solid pan. These steamers are also effective for reheating vendor-prepared or cook-chill product.

Traditional cabinet base convection steamers can operate with direct steam from a central steam supply, a steam boiler that is remotely located or its own boiler mounted in the cabinet below the steamer compartments. Cabinet base boilers are most typical, and available in either gas or electric heated models.

Countertop units are most popular for their compact size and smaller power requirements. They typically have their own self-contained steam generators, and can be stacked or banked for additional capacity and cooking flexibility in the same footprint or hood space. The original models all had three-pan capacity but today are available with three-, four- or five-pan capacity. Traditional countertop steamers are electric or gas powered; they also require a water line and drain line connection.

Connectionless steamers

The amount of steam generated by countertop models makes them especially prone to hard water service problems and failures, unless regular deliming (descaling) and comprehensive water treatment and system maintenance is practised. In the mid-1990s a manufacturer introduced the first so-called 'connectionless' steamer and, by the end of the twentieth century, virtually all steam equipment manufacturers offered a version of a connectionless steamer.

Connectionless steamers don't have water or drain lines. They all generate steam inside, on the bottom of the steam compartment. The operator must pour 7–15 litres of water into the cook compartment. These units heat the compartment bottom or an adjacent open reservoir to generate steam in the cavity. These (all electric) models have heating elements clamped to the bottom of the compartment or reservoir and not immersed in the water. This design eliminates most water-related element failures, and the need for water treatment and regular deliming with caustic chemicals.

'Boilerless' steamers do require water and drain connections but eliminate the need for operators to manually fill the compartment with water or deal with hot, nutrient-rich waste water, which must be drained from connectionless steamers at close of day. In addition, they employ the same non-immersion heating elements or under-fired gas burner designs, which reduce water-related component failure and the need for heavy and frequent deliming or descaling.

Regardless of the type or style of pressureless steamers desired, proper sizing is important for timely and efficient food preparation and production. Actual requirements will depend on the menu, customer count and the availability of alternative equipment such as steam combination ovens. While most steamers accept 65–200 mm deep 1/1 gastronorm pans, 65 mm deep pans are most typically used. Here are some tips to convert pan capacity into menu portions.

- A 1/1, 65 mm deep gastronorm pan holds (72) 115 gram, (48) 170 gram or (36) 225 gram portions.
- A 1/1, 65 mm deep gastronorm pan is 2.54 cm full with 2.8 litres, 3.2 cm deep with 3.8 litres and 500 mm deep with 5.7 litres of liquid.
- A 1/1, 65 mm deep gastronorm pan comfortably holds 2.3 kg to 2.5 kg of frozen cut vegetables.

Large pans, boilers and fryers

Bratt pan

The bratt pan is one of the most versatile pieces of cooking equipment in the kitchen because it is possible to use it for shallow-frying, deep-frying, stewing, braising and boiling. A bratt pan can cook many items of food at one time because of its large surface area. A further advantage is that it can be tilted so that the contents can, quickly and efficiently, be poured out on completion of the cooking process. Bratt pans are heated by gas or electricity; several models are available incorporating various features to meet differing catering requirements.

Boiling pans

Many types are available in different metals – aluminium, stainless steel, etc. – in various sizes (10-, 15-, 20-, 30- and 40-litre capacity) and they may be heated by gas or electricity. As they are used for boiling or stewing large quantities of food, it is important that they do not allow the food to burn; for this reason the steam-jacket type boiler is the most suitable. Many of these are fitted with a tilting device to facilitate the emptying of the contents.

After use, the boiling pan and lid should be thoroughly washed with mild detergent solution and then rinsed well. The tilting apparatus should be greased occasionally and checked to see that it tilts easily. If gas fired, the gas jets and pilot should be inspected to ensure correct working. If a pressure gauge and safety valve are fitted these should also be checked.

Pasta cooker

This equipment is fitted with water delivery and drain taps, and can be used for the cooking of several types of pasta simultaneously. It is electrically operated.

Deep-fat fryers

A deep-fat fryer is one of the most extensively used items of equipment in many catering establishments. The careless worker who misuses a deep-fat fryer and spills food or fat can cause accidents and waste money.

Fryers are heated by gas or electricity and incorporate a thermostatic control in order to save fuel and prevent overheating. There is a cool zone below the source of heat into which food particles can sink without burning, thus preventing spoiling of other foods being cooked. This form of heating also saves fat.

Pressure fryers

Food is cooked in an airtight frying vat, thus enabling it to be fried a lot faster and at a lower oil temperature.

Conveyor fryers

Conveyor fryers are an excellent way to solve the high volume requirements of some commercial operations. They permit the operator to place the product in one end, typically in individual baskets attached to a conveyor system. The product is then carried through the oil-filled tank and dumped from the baskets at a collection station, after it has completed the cooking cycle. The conveyor holding the now empty fry baskets rotates back, in a continuous loop, for reloading.

The speed of the conveyor can be increased or decreased, permitting the operator to control the cooking process. As with the previous fryers covered, proper frying results depend on the temperature of the oil, the condition of the oil and the amount of time food is immersed in the oil.

Conveyor fryers are excellent units to have for high volume sites, such as theme parks, where concession stands need to produce a lot of product in a short period of time. Some conveyor fryers are capable of producing 45 kg of French fries per hour, from a compact countertop unit.

Air and speciality fryers

An air fryer is a small countertop unit that uses a small amount of oil in a rotating drum mounted inside a closed compartment to 'fry' single portions or small batches of product. They primarily use hot air convection heat transfer to cook fries and other fairly durable frozen product.

An advantage of these smaller units is that they typically don't require placement under a grease rated hood. They don't use or release significant amounts of grease-laden vapour, so they can be used in bars, snack shops, bowling alleys and other places without heavy-duty utilities and ventilation.

Hot cupboards

Commonly referred to in the trade as the hotplate, hot cupboards are used for heating plates and serving dishes, and for keeping food hot. Care should be taken to see that the amount of heat fed into the hot cupboard is controlled at a reasonable temperature. This is important, otherwise the plates and food will either be too hot or too cold, and this could obviously affect the efficiency of the service. A temperature of 60–76°C is suitable for hot cupboards and a thermostat is a help in maintaining this.

Hot cupboards may be heated by steam, gas or electricity. The doors should slide easily, and occasional greasing may be necessary. The tops of most hot cupboards are used as serving counters and should be heated to a higher temperature than the inside. These tops are usually made of stainless steel and should be cleaned thoroughly after each service.

Bains-marie

Bains-marie are open wells of water used for keeping foods hot; they are available in many designs, some of which are incorporated into hot cupboards, some

Figure 5.14 A waiter at the hotplate

in serving counters, and there is a type that is fitted at the end of a cooking range. They may be heated by steam, gas or electricity, and sufficient heat to boil the water in the bain-marie should be available. Care should be taken to see that a bain-marie is never allowed to burn dry when the heat is turned on. After use the heat should be turned off, the water drained and the bain-marie cleaned inside and outside with hot detergent water, rinsed and dried. Any drain-off tap should then be closed.

Food distribution equipment

In situations requiring mobile equipment (e.g. hospitals, banqueting) wheeled items are essential to facilitate service, particularly of hot foods.

Grills and salamanders

The salamander or grill heated from above by gas or electricity probably causes more wastage of fuel than any other item of kitchen equipment through being allowed to burn unnecessarily for long periods unused. Most salamanders have more than one set of heating elements or jets and it is not always necessary to have them all turned on fully.

Salamander bars and draining trays should be cleaned regularly with hot water containing a grease solvent such as soda. After rinsing they should be replaced and the salamander lit for a few minutes to dry the bars.

For under-fired grills (see Figure 5.18) to work efficiently they must be capable of cooking food quickly and should reach a high temperature 15–20 minutes after lighting; the heat should be turned off immediately after use. When the bars are cool they should be removed and washed in hot water containing a grease solvent, rinsed, dried and replaced on the grill. Care should be taken with the fire bricks if they are used for lining the grill as they are easily broken.

Figure 5.15 A water bath, used to cook delicate foods

Contact grills

These are sometimes referred to as double-sided or infragrills and have two heating surfaces arranged facing each other. The food to be cooked is placed on one surface and is then covered by the second. These grills are electrically heated and are capable of cooking certain foods very quickly, so extra care is needed, particularly when cooks are using this type of grill for the first time.

Fry plates, griddle plates

These are solid metal plates heated from below, and are used for cooking individual portions of meat, hamburgers, eggs, bacon, etc. They can be heated quickly to a high temperature and are suitable for rapid and continuous cooking. Before cooking on a griddle plate a light film of oil should be applied to the food and the griddle plate to prevent sticking. To clean griddle plates, warm them and scrape off any loose food particles; rub the metal with pumice stone or griddle stone, following the grain of the metal; clean with hot detergent water, rinse with clean hot water and wipe dry. Finally re-season (prove) the surface by lightly oiling with vegetable oil.

Figure 5.16 An under-fired grill

Figure 5.17 A bar grill

Griddles with zone heating are useful when demand varies during the day. These reduce energy consumption in quiet periods while allowing service to be maintained.

Mirror chromed griddles have a polished surface that gives off less radiated heat, which saves energy and makes for a more pleasant working environment.

Barbecues

Barbecues are becoming increasingly popular because it is easy to cook and serve quick, tasty food on them, and the outdoor location, smell and sizzle develop an atmosphere that many customers enjoy.

There are three main types of barbecue: traditional charcoal, gas (propane or butane) and electric. Remember that the charcoal-fired type takes about an hour before the surface is ready. With gas and electricity the barbecue is ready to cook on almost immediately.

Gas is more flexible and controllable than electricity. Propane gas is recommended because it can be used at any time of the year. Butane does not work when it is cold. Propane is, however, highly flammable and safety precautions are essential. Anyone connecting the gas container must be competent in the use of bottled gas. The supply pipe must be guarded to avoid accidental interference, and the cylinder must be placed away from the barbecue. The cylinder must be upright and stable, with the valve uppermost and securely held in position. Connections must be checked for leaks.

Sinks

Stainless steel is generally used for all purposes.

Tables

- Formica- or stainless steel-topped tables should be washed with hot detergent water then rinsed with hot water containing a sterilising agent – alternatively, some modern chemicals act as both detergent and sterilising agents. Wooden tables should not be used.
- Marble slabs should be scrubbed with hot water and rinsed. All excess moisture should be removed with a clean, dry cloth.
- No cutting or chopping should be allowed on table tops; cutting boards should be used.
- Hot pans should not be put on tables; triangles must be used to protect the table surface.
- The legs and racks or shelves of tables are cleaned with hot detergent water and then dried. Wooden table legs require scrubbing.

Butcher's or chopping block

A scraper should be used to keep the block clean. After scraping, the block should be sprinkled with a few handfuls of common salt in order to absorb any moisture that may have penetrated during the day.

Do not use water or liquids for cleaning unless absolutely necessary as water will be absorbed into the wood and cause swelling.

Storage racks

All types of racks should be emptied and scrubbed or washed periodically.

Figure 5.18 Storage rack

Mechanical equipment

(The Health and Safety Executive offers two publications on catering machinery, both obtainable from HMSO.)

If a piece of mechanical equipment can save time and physical effort and still produce a good end result then it should be considered for purchase or hire.

Figure 5.19 A hand-held liquidiser ('blitzer')

The performance of most machines can be closely controlled and is not subject to human variations, so it should be easier to obtain uniformity of production over a period of time.

The caterer is faced with two considerations:

1 the cost of the machine – installation, maintenance, depreciation and running cost
2 the possibility of increased production and a saving of labour costs.

The mechanical performance must be carefully assessed and all the manufacturer's claims as to the machine's efficiency checked thoroughly. The design should be foolproof, easy to clean and operated with minimum effort. Before cleaning, all machines should be switched off and the plug removed from the socket.

When a new item of equipment is installed it should be tested by a qualified fitter before being used by catering staff. The manufacturer's instructions must be displayed in a prominent place near the machine. The manufacturer's advice regarding servicing should be followed and a record book kept, showing what kind of maintenance the machine is receiving and when. The following list includes machines typically found in catering premises, which are classified as dangerous under the Provision and Use of Work Equipment Regulations 1998 (PUWER).

1 Power-driven machines:
   – worm-type mincing machines
   – rotary knife, bowl-type chopping machines
   – dough mixers
   – food mixing machines when used with attachments for mincing, slicing, chipping and any other cutting operation, or for crumbling
   – pie and tart making machines
   – vegetable slicing machines.

2 Potato peelers:
   – potatoes should be free of earth and stones before loading into the machine
   – before any potatoes are loaded, the water spray should be turned on and the abrasive plate set in motion
   – the interior should be cleaned out daily and the abrasive plate removed to ensure that small particles are not lodged below
   – the peel trap should be emptied as frequently as required.
   – the waste outlet should be kept free from obstruction.

3 Machines, whether power-driven or not:
   – circular knife slicing machines used for cutting bacon and other foods (whether similar to bacon or not)
   – potato chipping machines.

Dough preparation equipment

With the variety of baked goods produced today, it stands to reason that there are pieces of speciality equipment that have been designed to help the pastry chef/baker with all the repetitive but critical tasks.

- **Dough extruder:** a dough extruder is designed to dispense dough that has been prepared in bulk, into predetermined sizes and/or shapes. The dough is rammed or forced through die or openings of the desired shape and size.
- **Dough divider:** this piece of equipment is used to equally portion dough by size and weight. It can be either manually or hydraulically operated.
- **Dough divider/rounder:** similar to the dough divider, the dough divider/rounder is designed to divide and then shape bulk dough into equal portion-sized balls.
- **Dough/butter press:** a dough/butter press is a hydraulically run machine that is used to press and form bulk dough and/or butter into a shape that is suitable for use in sheeters, cutters and formers.
- **Former:** a former is a mechanical device that is designed to give a final length, size and/or shape to yeasted dough, before it is placed in pans.

- **Moulder:** a moulder, which is similar to a former, is a mechanical device that is designed to give a specific length and shape to yeasted dough before panning takes place.
- **Depositor:** a depositor is a machine that is designed to place pre-measured pieces of dough on or in bake pans.
- **Sheeter:** a sheeter is a machine that is used to flatten dough to the desired/required thickness and shape. It is also used to remove the gas from yeasted dough.
- **Sheeter/moulder:** this particular device is designed to sheet and mould dough pieces in one, simple process.
- **Sheeter/reversible sheeter:** a sheeter/reversible sheeter is a mechanical device that is used for rolling and layering dough into specific shapes and thicknesses. It is primarily used in the production of pastries and sweet goods.
- **Prover:** a prover is a very important piece of equipment found in every bakery. In essence, a prover is a cabinet that allows yeasted dough products to leaven (ferment) in an ideal temperature- and humidity-controlled environment, until the desired product volume is achieved. This process ensures the desired appearance and quality of the finished baked product. Leavening is a raising action that aerates dough or batters during mixing and baking, so that the finished product is greater in volume than the raw ingredients, with flavour characteristics that are superior to the same ingredients baked without leavening. Typical prover box temperatures range from 29°C to 46°C, with humidity levels ranging from 70 to 95 per cent. Provers are available in many sizes and often match the pan capacity of convection, rack and combi-ovens. Small provers are available for mounting below a half- or full-size convection oven, providing a compact baking centre in a small footprint. Large roll-in provers are sized by rack capacity, and can vary from one to 20 racks or more, depending on the size and number of ovens served.
- **Prover/retarder:** retarders are multi-function units. They are used to initially retard the rising of dough, then later prove the product, prior to bake-off.
- **Prover/quick thaw:** a prover/quick thaw is a prover that decreases the normal dough thawing time through the introduction of heat, then continues with the standard proving cycle. Obviously, it is used when frozen dough is employed.
- **Retarder:** a retarder is another important piece of equipment found in most bakery operations. In essence, a retarder is a speciality refrigeration unit that is designed to maintain a high level of humidity.

Food-processing equipment

Food mixer

This is an important labour-saving, electrically operated piece of equipment used for many purposes: mixing pastry, cakes, mashing potatoes, beating egg whites, mayonnaise, cream, mincing or chopping meat and vegetables.

- It should be lubricated frequently in accordance with manufacturer's instructions.
- The motor should not be overloaded, which can be caused by obstruction to the rotary components. For example, if dried bread is being passed through the mincer attachment without sufficient care the rotary cog can become so clogged with bread that it is unable to move. If the motor is allowed to run, damage can be caused to the machine.
- All components, as well as the main machine, should be thoroughly washed and dried. Care should be taken to see that no rust occurs on any part. The mincer attachment knife and plates will rust if not given sufficient care.

Food-processing machines

Food processors are generally similar to vertical, high-speed cutters except that they tend to be smaller and to have a larger range of attachments. They can be used for a large number of mixing and chopping jobs but they cannot whisk or incorporate air to mixes.

Liquidiser or blender

This is a versatile, labour-saving piece of kitchen machinery that uses a high-speed motor to drive specially designed stainless steel blades to chop, purée or blend foods efficiently and very quickly. It is also useful for making breadcrumbs. As a safety precaution food must be cooled before being liquidised.

Food slicers

Food slicers are obtainable both in manually and electrically operated versions. They are labour-saving devices, but can be dangerous if not used with care, so working instructions should be placed in a prominent position near the machine.

- Care should be taken that no material likely to damage the blades is included in the food to be sliced. It is easy for a careless worker to overlook a piece of bone that, if allowed to come into contact with the cutting blade, could cause severe damage.
- Each section in contact with food should be cleaned and dried carefully after use.

- The blade or blades should be sharpened regularly.
- Moving parts should be lubricated, but oil must not come into contact with the food.
- Extra care must be taken when blades are exposed.
- No one under 18 should complete these tasks.

Chipper

The electric chipper should be thoroughly cleaned and dried after use, particular attention being paid to those parts that come into contact with food. Care should be taken that no obstruction prevents the motor from operating at its normal speed. Moving parts should be lubricated according to the maker's instructions.

Figure 5.20 A gravity slicer

Figure 5.21 A vertical, variable-speed mixer

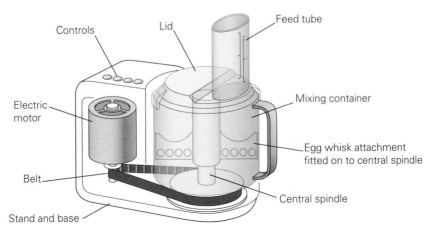

Figure 5.22 A belt-driven food processor

Figure 5.23 A high-speed food processor

Masher (hand or electric)

The hand type should be washed immediately after use, then rinsed and dried.

The electric masher should have the removable sections and the main machine washed and dried after use, extra care being taken over those parts that come into contact with food. The same care should be taken as with electric chippers regarding obstruction and lubrication.

Ice cream makers, juicers and mixers

Ice cream and sorbet machines are available from 1-litre capacity and enable establishments to produce home-made ice cream and sorbet using fresh fruit in season or frozen and canned fruits at all times of the year.

Juicers and mixers can provide freshly made fruit and vegetable juices, milk shakes and cocktails.

Figure 5.24 An ice cream machine

Figure 5.25 A portable ice cream machine

Boilers

Water boiling appliances for tea and coffee making

There are two main groups of water boilers: bulk boilers from which boiling water can only be drawn when all the contents have boiled, and automatic boilers, which provide a continuous flow of boiling water.

Bulk boilers

These are generally used when large quantities of boiling water are required at a given time. They should be kept scrupulously clean, covered with the correct lid to prevent anything falling in, and when not used for some time should be left filled with clean, cold water.

Automatic boilers

These boilers have automatic waterfeeds and can give freshly boiled water at intervals. It is important that the water supply is maintained efficiently, otherwise there is a danger of the boiler burning dry and being damaged.

Pressure boilers

This is the type that operates many still sets, consisting of steam heating milk boilers and a pressure boiler providing boiling water. Care should be taken with the pilot light to see that it is working efficiently. As with all gas-fired equipment it is essential that regular inspection and maintenance are carried out by registered gas fitters.

Coffee and milk heaters

Water-jacket boilers are made for the storage of hot coffee and hot milk, with draw-off taps from the storage chamber. Inner linings may be of glazed earthenware, stainless steel or heat-resistant glass. It is very important that the storage chambers are thoroughly cleaned with hot water after each use and then left full of clean, cold water. The draw-off taps should be cleaned regularly with a special brush.

Refrigerators, cold rooms, chill rooms, deep-freeze cabinets and compartments

Location

As adequate ventilation is vital, locate refrigeration equipment in a well-ventilated room away from:

- sources of intense heat – cookers, ovens, radiators, boilers, etc.
- direct sunlight – from window or skylights
- barriers to adequate air circulation.

In large establishments it is necessary to have refrigerated space at different temperatures. The cold rooms may be divided into separate rooms: one at a chill temperature for storing salads, fruits and certain cheeses; one for meats, poultry, game and tinned food, which have to be refrigerated; and one for deep-frozen foods. Frequently, the cold room storage is designed so that the chill room, the cold room and the deep-freeze compartment lead on from each other. Refrigerated cabinets, thermo-statically controlled to various desired temperatures, are also used in large larders. Deep-freeze cabinets are used where a walk-in, deep-freeze section is not required: they maintain a temperature of −18°C. Chest-type deep-freeze cabinets require defrosting twice a year. It is important to close all refrigerator doors as quickly as possible to contain the cold air.

Figure 5.26 Refrigerated food to go

Figure 5.27 A refrigerated gastronorm counter

Hygiene precautions

Refrigeration cannot improve the quality of foodstuffs; it can only retard the natural process of deterioration. For maximum storage of food and minimum health risk:

- select the appropriate refrigerator equipment for the temperature requirement of the food
- always ensure refrigerators maintain the correct temperature for the food stored
- keep unwrapped foods, vulnerable to contamination, and flavour and odour transfer, in separate refrigerators or in airtight containers and away from products such as cream, other dairy products, partly cooked pastry, cooked meat and delicatessen foods
- do not store foods for long periods in a good, general-purpose refrigerator because a single temperature is not suitable for keeping all types of food safely and at peak condition
- never keep uncooked meat, poultry or fish in the same refrigerator, or any other food that is not in its own sealed, airtight container
- never refreeze foods that have been thawed out from frozen
- always rotate stock in refrigerator space
- clean equipment regularly and thoroughly, inside and out.

Loading

- Ensure that there is adequate capacity for maximum stock.
- Check that perishable goods are delivered in a refrigerated vehicle.
- Only fill frozen food storage cabinets with pre-frozen food.
- Never put hot or warm food in a refrigerator unless it is specially designed for rapid chilling.
- Ensure that no damage is caused to inner linings and insulation by staples or nails in packaging.
- Air must be allowed to circulate within a refrigerator to maintain the cooling effect – do not obstruct any airways.

Cleaning

- Clean thoroughly inside and out at least every two months as blocked drain lines, drip trays and air ducts will eventually lead to a breakdown.
- Switch off power.
- If possible, transfer stock to available alternative storage.
- Clean interior surfaces with lukewarm water and a mild detergent. Do not use abrasives or strongly scented cleaning agents.
- Clean exterior and dry all surfaces inside and out.
- Clear away any external dirt, dust or rubbish that might restrict the circulation of air around the condenser.
- Switch on power, check when the correct working temperature is reached, refill with stock.

Further information can be obtained from the British Refrigeration Association, Henley Road, Medmanham, Marlow, Buckinghamshire SL7 2ER (website: www.feta.co.uk/bra/) and the Federation of Environmental Trade Associations Ltd, www.feta.co.uk.

Defrosting

This is important as it helps equipment perform efficiently and prevents a potentially damaging build-up of ice. Presence of ice on the evaporator or internal surfaces indicates the need for urgent defrosting; if the equipment is designed to defrost automatically this also indicates a fault.

Automatic defrosting may lead to a temporary rise in air temperature; this is normal and will not put food at risk.

For manual defrosting of chest freezers always follow the supplier's instructions to obtain optimum performance. Never use a hammer or any sharp instrument that could perforate cabinet linings – a plastic spatula can be used to remove stubborn ice.

Emergency measures

Signs of imminent breakdown include: unusual noises, fluctuating temperatures, frequent stopping and starting of the compressor, excessive frost build-up, absence of normal frost.

Prepare to call a competent refrigeration service engineer, but first check that:

- the power supply has not been accidentally switched off
- the electrical circuit has not been broken by a blown fuse or the triggering of an automatic circuit breaker
- there has been no unauthorised tampering with the temperature control device
- any temperature higher than recommended is not due solely to routine automatic defrosting, to the refrigerator door being left open, to overloading the equipment or to any blockage of internal passage of air
- there is no blockage of air to the condenser by rubbish, crates, cartons, etc.

If you still suspect a fault, call the engineer and be prepared to give brief details of the equipment and the fault. Keep the door of the defective cold cabinet closed as much as possible to retain cold air. Destroy any spoilt food.

Monitoring refrigeration efficiency

The Energy Technology Support Unit (ETSU) estimates that businesses could save 20–25 per cent of the energy currently consumed by refrigeration plants. Your local energy efficiency advice centre may be able to provide consultancy services at subsidised or no cost.

All types of refrigerators – walk-in, cabinet, with or without forced air circulation – should be fitted with display thermometers or chart recorders that will enable daily monitoring to check that the equipment is working correctly. Sensors that can set off available alarms must be placed in the warmest part of the cabinet.

Chilled display units include:

- multi-deck cabinets with closed doors, used for dispensing sandwiches, drinks and other foods; used if food needs to be displayed for more than four hours
- open and semi-open display cabinets where food

is presented on the base of the unit and cooled by circulating cooled air
- gastronorm counters (see Figure 5.27).

Because of surrounding conditions it is unsafe to assume that refrigerated display cabinets will maintain the temperature of the food below 5°C, which is why these units should never be used to store food other than for display periods of not more than four hours.

Maintenance and servicing should be carried out regularly by qualified personnel.

Basic operation of the dishwasher

The effective operation of the dishwasher plays a critical role in food service sanitation by providing the operator with visibly clean, sanitised and attractive tableware. A basic understanding of dishwasher operation will help ensure that clean and attractive tableware is always available. Most machines clean in a four-step process.

1 **Prewash stage:** in the prewash chamber of a dishwasher (not all dishwashers are built with prewash chambers), hot water sprays of around 45°C remove most of the 'easy' soil from the tableware. This soil is usually greasy and can't be effectively removed if the water is too cool. However, if the water is too hot, it may have a tendency to bake on other soils. For example, milk and fruit juice glasses should be prewashed in cold water. Dairy products bake on at high temperatures. A cool prewash is also necessary to remove fruit juice residues. If not properly removed, they may react with metal protecting agents in the wash water detergents, to form an insoluble film.

2 **Wash stage:** the heart of the dishwasher is the washing section. A solution of hot water of around 55°C and detergent is drawn into a powerful pump and then forced under pressure into pipes and either fixed or whirling arms above and below the dishes in racks or on conveyor belts. This solution is forced out of orifices in a heavy spray that has a flushing action, which first loosens the soil, then washes it down over perforated scrap trays designed to remove the gross soil. The water and detergent solution then returns to the wash tank. As it comes in contact with the tableware, the wash water should be a solid sheet, since drops of water in a spray do a poor job of soil removal. The temperature of the wash water should be in the 60°C to 65°C range. Temperatures in this range soften soils and melt greases so they can be effectively removed.

3 **Rinse stage:** during this cycle, hot water at 65°C to 75°C removes the detergent solution and any residual soils from the tableware. The action is similar to that described in the wash tank, using the same type of pump and spray assemblies, without the addition of detergent.

4 **Final rinse stage:** in the final rinse stage, all trace of the wash solution is removed. The water temperature should be 82°C to allow the sanitising action to take place. Fast surface drying will also occur at these temperatures. A

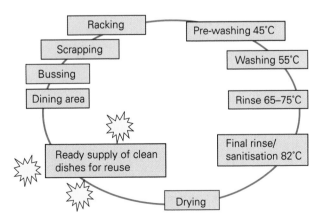

Figure 5.28 The dishwashing continuum

rinse additive is also injected into the final rinse water, to facilitate 'sheeting' and to prevent water spotting during this quick-dry stage.

Further information can be obtained from www.powersourcing.com/se/ dishwashingequipment.htm.

The servery area

There are several factors that affect the shape and size of serving lines:

- the volume or anticipated volume of sales
- the variety or complexity of the menu
- the size and shape of the available space, and
- the flow of traffic.

Simple, limited-choice menus may be served from either a permanently installed, continuous line cafeteria or one that is made up of mobile, modular units. This style of cafeteria is often referred to as an 'in-line' cafeteria.

Where there is a large number of people to be served within a relatively short period of time, or when there is a wide variety of food choices, a cafeteria with multiple counters and points of service may be the best layout. Cafeterias designed around these operating premises are referred to as a *hollow square* or *scrambled service* cafeteria.

The next stage in the evolution of cafeteria or buffet service layout was the *scatter system*. A scatter system provides multiple serving stations, easy access to beverages and condiments, and the grouping and physical separation of popular menu options, to reduce queues and hold-ups. This system lends itself to demonstration cooking areas, themed dining areas and more flexibility in changing menus to meet changing tastes.

Scrambled cafeteria plans and scatter systems are designed to speed up service by reducing the amount of time spent standing in line. Customers can pass others or go directly to the station that has their choice of food or beverage. During peak periods, short lines may form at some of the more popular service areas. Space allowance should be made for the movement of people passing each other with loaded trays. The layout should allow for easy re-supply of service stations with food and tableware. When a traffic area becomes crowded, it is difficult to supply food and replenish plates, flatware and disposables to centrally located stations.

Some key considerations when planning a scramble cafeteria layout include:

- what features would appeal to customers

- the ability to protect the quality of the food
- the ease and speed of supplying the food and dishes to various serving points
- the dishes that are to be promoted
- the selection habits of the customer base
- how to handle delay or back-up points in the service area
- the flow of traffic
- minimising hazards that could cause accidents
- the location of items that customers return for in the service area (e.g. sandwich condiments, flatware)
- the cost of labour
- the menu offerings – is it a simple, limited menu or is it complex, offering a wide variety of food?
- any service time limitations.

Achieving a smooth flow of cafeteria traffic requires anticipating the key items that will be sought by customers, then placing them at various stations within the cafeteria to achieve a good balanced flow. This is easier said than done. Food service design consultants can tap experience from previous cafeteria service operations and recommend alternative layouts. If fixed serving lines and service stations are to be used, a good people-flow plan is critical and subsequent changes costly.

The service-related equipment used in cafeterias is as varied as the food items offered. Some equipment needs are directly dependent on the type of cafeteria design being used (straight line vs scramble service), the complexity of the menu, anticipated traffic flow and the amount of available space. Some of the general service equipment categories frequently found in cafeteria line-ups include:

- sandwich prep tables
- salad bars
- dessert display case
- cold food tables
- hot food tables
- bains-marie
- beverage stations
- milk dispenser
- soft drink dispenser
- cup dispenser

- flatware dispenser
- grilled food unit
- menu boards
- cashier stand
- plate dispensers
- tray stands
- mobile dish racks
- sneeze guards
- heat lamps
- ice cream cabinets
- condiment stands
- tray rails.

Design of servery areas

Hygiene and food holding

Hygiene is a major issue in the design and operation of all cafeterias. The selection of appropriate equipment can certainly help. For example, the use of sneeze screens where foods are openly displayed is one method of promoting hygiene. Another is the use of serving utensils to discourage any hand contact with the food. However, one of the most critical hygiene issues is ensuring that proper food-holding temperatures are maintained. Proper food holding temperatures retard the growth of micro-organisms.

Hot food being held for service must be kept at or above 63°C; this is a legal requirement. Monitor and record the temperature of the food. Hot food that has been held below this temperature for two hours or more must be thrown away.

Chilled food that is on display or being held for service should be kept at between 1°C and 4°C, although the legal requirement is to keep it below 8°C. Chilled food that has been held at 8°C or above for four hours or more must be thrown away.

The service area of any food service facility should be designed with the following aims in mind:

- maintaining the quality and temperature of the food being served
- ensuring the microbial safety of the food
- presenting the food so that it is satisfying and attractive to the customers, and
- providing fast and efficient service.

In typical cook-serve operations, maintaining the quality of cooked foods calls for limiting holding time prior to being served to the customer. Equipment capacity needs to be planned around peak demand and how quickly food quality deteriorates for the various menu items being served. For example, meats are best served immediately after cooking. Vegetables under prolonged holding can lose their flavour, texture and

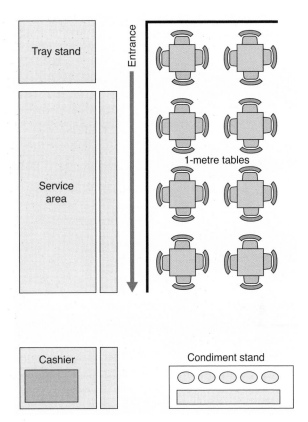

Figure 5.29 'In line' cafeteria service – a simple layout

important nutrients. When designing the service area, flexibility in holding capacity is desirable because different food items may be held in the serving area at different times. Different day-parts offering planned menu cycles and daily specials will require different holding times and conditions.

Larger kitchen operations often require advanced production and large batch production to even out the workflow, and to optimise the use of key cooking equipment such as ovens, steamers and steam-jacketed kettles. When key menu items are prepared far in advance of plating and service, safe and effective means of holding that production become critical.

Maintaining acceptable food quality and ensuring food safety require holding food at the proper temperature and humidity level. This will obviously vary, depending on the specific food item(s). Various methods and technologies are needed to maintain the desired holding environment. For example, infrared heaters may be used for a prime rib carving station, while soup may require a heated food well or self-serve display kettle that will maintain a higher temperature.

Some foods call for a fresh, moist appearance for presentation. In many cases this requires sufficient

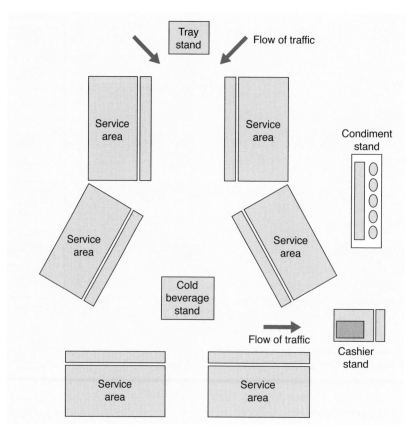

Figure 5.30 'Hollow square' or 'scrambled' cafeteria service

humidity in the holding and serving equipment to pre-vent drying and loss or change of colour. Vegetables should have a bright, natural colour while other items such as bread and rolls, should always have that 'just baked' texture and taste. Some items need moist air, while other items, such as fried foods, should be kept as dry as possible. Dry heat from an infrared heat lamp is best suited for these items. Many newer holding cabinets allow the humidity level inside the cabinet to be adjusted, to match the food being held.

Hot and cold food tables, salad bars and bains-marie

This holding and serving equipment is designed to merchandise and display food and ingredients, maintain safe holding temperatures, and provide easy access for both patrons and the cafeteria employees that replenish them. The design and heating or chill-ing methods vary, depending on whether the product is pre-plated or held in bulk containers for portioning and plating by staff or the customer.

Hot food tables and bains-marie are rectangular tables designed with heat wells or support frames

sized to hold steam table pans and other pan shapes. Typically a hot water reservoir is located under the pans. Electric heating elements or gas burners heat the water and provide the heat necessary to maintain a safe food serving temperature. For some products heat lamps or strip heaters are added above the food pans to provide additional dry heat, where needed.

Cold food tables and salad bars use a small, integrated refrigeration system or ice to maintain cold foods and salad components at safe holding temperatures.

The kitchen pass

One of the most popular pieces of equipment found in the service area of a table service restaurant is the *kitchen pass*, sometimes referred to as the hotplate. After the preparation and cooking of the food, the next stop is normally the pass. A kitchen pass can be as simple as a standard bain-marie unit with an attached worktable, or a large custom fabricated unit. Most kitchen passes are outfitted with some equip-ment. The equipment included is directly related to the type of food service operation and the operational

Important features of a food service area

- **Properly trained personnel:** the waiting staff have the primary contact with the dining public. Through their actions, responsiveness, knowledge of the menu, 'sales' ability and general demeanour, they leave a certain impression on the customer. The impression gained through personal contact with the waiting staff will colour the overall impression of the food service operation. A properly trained and empathetic waiter/waitress contributes significantly to the operational and financial success of a food service establishment.
- **Proximity of the service and kitchen areas to the dining room:** a shorter distance between these two functional areas (service area and kitchen area) can reduce labour costs and provide a higher-quality food product. It also reduces staff fatigue, which improves their attitude and the impression they make on the customer. A greater distance between these functional areas increases the cost of labour and makes it more difficult to deliver foods at an optimum serving temperature.
- **Proper equipment to maintain quality and temperature of food, and to ensure microbial safety:** as detailed in the text, both hot and cold foods must be held for service at the correct temperatures. In a properly designed and functioning service area, appropriate holding equipment should be used to ensure that these temperatures are maintained. Temperatures should be monitored and recorded.

needs of their service area. The type and placement of equipment provided on a kitchen pass are critical for effective table service.

Equipment that may be found in a kitchen pass area includes:

- refrigerated storage base
- ice bins
- refrigerated drawers
- refrigerated display case
- hot food drawers
- plate storage cabinets
- self-levelling plate racks
- hot food wells
- server call systems
- order holders
- soup warmers
- roll warmers
- toaster
- microwave oven
- heat lamps
- cutting/carving boards
- tray storage
- bread dispensers
- beverage dispensing equipment
- pan storage
- coffee makers/warmers.

Infrared strip heaters and heat lamps are commonly used for keeping plated meals hot for short periods. They may be installed above pass-through windows between the kitchen and service area or incorporated into the kitchen pass. These heaters have elements or lamps mounted directly above a shelf or plate landing area and typically are kept on. They provide instant radiated heat when a plate is placed under the warmer. They are available in a range of heat patterns, lengths and configurations designed to support all types of service method.

The use of refrigerated drawers and hot food drawers in both the service area and in the production kitchen is common. While a reach-in refrigerator is often just steps away, those steps add up and slow down meal component assembly. Locating small under-counter refrigerators or refrigerated drawers at the workstation below work/chef tables, and even under cooking equipment such as ranges and griddles, can speed up production, reduce staff fatigue, and help ensure safe holding of cooked product and raw ingredient storage.

The type of food service operation and the type of service offered will determine which beverages are offered and how those beverages are delivered to the customer. The availability of water, coffee, milk and carbonated beverages is almost universal. The service of wine, beer and spirits (straight and mixed drink service of whiskies, gin, vodka, tequila, etc.) requires an alcohol licence and operating decisions related to the importance of bar service and the target customer base desired.

While there are some equipment and supply items used in fine wine table service (racking, wine chillers, decanting gadgets, etc.) as well as full bar service (glass washers, refrigeration, bar sinks, glasses, mugs and more), the main focus in designing a beverage system is very often the provision of water, tea, coffee, other hot drinks and cold drinks.

Water service

Water is fundamental to life on earth and is often automatically set at the table, along with eating utensils, plates and the menu. The general environmental sensitivity has made it common to ask customers if they require water service. This step can also reduce dishwashing and glass inventory requirements. If water is desired, a source of ice and clean, clear water is needed in the primary (table) service area and/or remote wait-stations located closer to the customer/tables.

When bottled water is offered to customers, the only equipment required will be the necessary refrigerated storage space, if that water will be served chilled.

Miscellaneous equipment

Food waste disposers are operated by electricity and take all manner of rubbish, including bones, fat, scraps and vegetable refuse. Almost every type of rubbish and swill, with the exception of rags and tins, is finely ground, then rinsed down the drain. It is the most modern and hygienic method of waste disposal.

Care should be taken by handlers not to push waste into the machine with a metal object as this can cause damage.

Other pieces of equipment that may be found in a busy kitchen include an automatic pastry roller (see Figure 5.31) and toasters.

Figure 5.31 Automatic pastry roller (dough brake)

Figure 5.32 Sieve (left) and colander

Small equipment and utensils

Small equipment and utensils are made from a variety of materials such as non-stick coated metal, iron, steel, copper, aluminium and wood.

Iron

Items of equipment used for frying, such as movable fritures and frying pans of all types, are usually made of heavy, black, wrought iron.

Frying pans are available in several shapes and many sizes. For example:

- omelette pans
- oval fish-frying pans
- frying pans
- pancake pans.

Baking sheets are made in various sizes, of black wrought steel. The less they are washed the less likely they are to cause food to stick. New baking sheets should be well heated in a hot oven, thoroughly wiped with a clean cloth and then lightly oiled. Before being used, baking trays should be lightly greased with a pure fat or oil. Immediately after use and while still warm they should be cleaned by scraping and dry wiping. Hot soda or detergent water should be used for washing.

Figure 5.33 Clockwise from top left: egg slice, lemon squeezer, garlic press, cheese slice

Figure 5.34 Potato ricer, potato masher, pestle, mortar

Tartlet and barquette moulds and cake tins should be cared for in the same way as baking sheets.

Tinned steel

A number of items are made from this metal:

● conical strainer (chinois), used for passing sauces and gravies
● fine conical strainer, used for passing sauces and gravies
● colander, used for draining vegetables
● vegetable reheating container
● soup machine and mouli strainer, used for passing thick soups, sauces and potatoes for mash
● sieves.

Aluminium

(Note: minimum use of aluminium is recommended – stainless steel (see below) is to be preferred.)

Saucepans, stockpots, sauteuses, sauté pans, braising pans, fish kettles and large, round, deep pans and dishes of all sizes are made in cast aluminium. They are expensive, but one advantage is that the pans do not tarnish; also because of their strong, heavy construction they are suitable for many cooking processes.

A disadvantage is that in the manufacture of aluminium, which is a soft metal, other metals are added to make pans stronger. As a result certain foods can become discoloured (care should be taken when mixing white sauces and white soups). A wooden spoon should be used for mixing, then there should be no discoloration. The use of metal whisks or spoons must be avoided.

Water boiled in aluminium pans is unsuitable for tea making as it gives the tea an unpleasant colour. Red cabbage and artichokes should not be cooked in aluminium pans as they will take on a dark colour, caused by a chemical reaction. Acid foods react with aluminium pans, so avoid using them to cook foods such as rhubarb or Bramley apples.

Stainless steel

Heavy-duty stainless steel pans, incorporating an extra thick aluminium base that gives excellent heat diffusion, are available. They are suitable for all surfaces except induction hobs. Stainless steel is also used for many items of small equipment.

All-Clad cooking pans

All-Clad is a brand of cooking pan using a combination of materials designed to make the best use of the properties of them all. Each All-Clad pan is made of several layers of different metals and alloys (see Figure 5.35), permanently bonded together (clad). The designers paid attention to the thickness of each layer, and the order of the layers, with the goal of maximising:

● conductivity
● responsiveness
● non-reactivity
● consistency
● practicality
● durability.

The pans are designed to:

● heat evenly, with no hotspots, at a consistent rate
● cool evenly at a consistent rate
● be responsive to temperature changes
● not react with any foodstuffs or cleaning agents
● work equally well on any cooker type or in the oven.

No single metal or alloy meets these criteria, so the best cookware has always used layers of different metals.

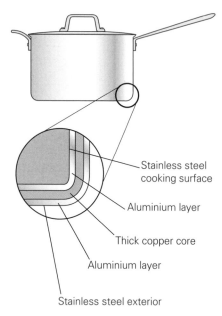

Figure 5.35 Diagram of a layered pan

Figure 5.36 Non-stick pans

using non-stick pans so that contact is not made to the surface with metal

● extra care is needed when cleaning non-stick surfaces; the use of cloth or paper is most suitable.

There are many small pieces of equipment made from metal of all types (see Figures 5.33 and 5.34).

Wood and compound materials

Cutting boards

These are an important item of kitchen equipment, which should be kept in use on all table surfaces to protect the table and the edges of cutting knives.

Wooden chopping boards

To comply with current regulations, wooden boards should not splinter or leak preservatives. They should be of close-grained hardwood, either in a thick, solid slab or separate pieces with close-fitting joints.

● Before using a new board, wash to remove any wood dust.
● After use, scrub with hot detergent water, rinse with clean water, dry as much as possible and stand on its longest end to prevent warping.
● Do not use for heavy chopping; use a chopping block instead.

Cutting boards of compound materials

There are several types available. When selecting compound cutting boards it is essential to purchase those with a non-slip surface.

One material used to make cutting boards is polyethylene.

Cutting boards are also made of hard rubber and rubber compounds (rubber, polystyrene and clay). These are hygienic because they are solid, in one piece and should not warp, crack or absorb flavours. They are cleaned by scrubbing with hot water and then drying or passing through a dishwasher.

All-Clad pans are used in a number of high-quality restaurants. They are available in several retail stores.

Stainless steel

The All-Clad Stainless range (an example of using layers of different metals) features a magnetic grade of stainless steel on the exterior for induction compatibility. It has an aluminium core and the same high-quality stainless interior layer as all of the other All-Clad products. The total thickness is 2.7 mm with 0.38 mm interior stainless and 0.38 mm exterior stainless.

Copper Core

The All-Clad Copper Core range is made of 60 per cent copper bonded with both aluminium and stainless steel, with the conductivity and heat retention of copper and aluminium.

Non-stick metal

An ever-increasing variety of kitchen utensils (saucepans, frying pans, baking and roasting tins) are available, and are suitable for certain types of kitchen operation, such as small scale or à la carte. Particular attention should be paid to the following points, otherwise the non-stick properties of the equipment will be affected:

● excessive heat should be avoided
● use plastic or wooden spatulas or spoons when

Plastic cutting boards

Plastic is the most popular material for cutting boards. It has the advantage of being able to be put through a dishwasher to clean and sterilise it, and can be colour coded so that high-risk foods are prepared only on the one cutting board, thereby reducing the risk of cross-contamination.

The accepted UK system is:

- **yellow** for cooked meats
- **red** for raw meats
- **white** for bread and dairy products (e.g. cheese)
- **blue** for raw fish
- **green** for salad and fruit
- **brown** for raw vegetables grown within the soil.

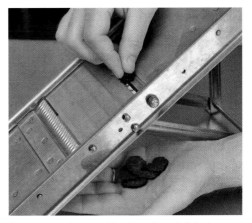

Figure 5.38 A vegetable slicer (mandolin) shown without the safety guard

Figure 5.37 Modern cutting boards

Rolling pins, wooden spoons and spatulas

These items should be scrubbed in hot detergent water, rinsed in clean water and dried. Rolling pins should not be scraped with a knife as this can cause the wood to splinter. Adhering paste can be removed with a cloth. Wooden spoons and spatulas are being replaced by a high-density plastic capable of withstanding very high temperatures. Wooden spoons/ spatulas are considered unhygienic unless washed in a suitable sterilising solution such as sodium hypochloride solution (bleach) or a solution of Milton. Metal piping tubes are being replaced by plastic; these can be boiled and do not rust.

Wooden sieves and mandolins

When these are being cleaned, care of the wooden frame should be considered, taking into account the previous remarks. The blades of the mandolin should be kept lightly greased to prevent rust (stainless steel mandolins with protective guards are available).

China and earthenware

Bowls and dishes in china and earthenware are useful for serving a variety of foods, and for microwaved dishes. They should be cleaned in a dishwasher with mild detergent and rinse aid, or by hand, using the appropriate detergent for hand washing.

Materials (cloths, etc.)

All materials should be washed in hot detergent water immediately after use, rinsed in hot, clean water and then dried. Tammy cloths, muslins and linen piping bags must be boiled periodically in detergent water. Kitchen cloths should be washed or changed frequently, otherwise accumulating dirt and food stains may cause cross-contamination of harmful bacteria/ germs on to clean food.

Muslin may be used for straining soups and sauces.

Piping bags are made from disposable plastic and are used for piping preparations of all kinds. Plastic piping bags are the most hygienic.

Figure 5.39 Examples of flameproof china dishes

Kitchen cloths:

- general purpose – for washing-up and cleaning surfaces
- tea towel (teacloth) – for drying up and general-purpose hand cloths
- bactericide wiping cloths – impregnated with bactericide to disinfect work surfaces; these cloths have a coloured pattern that fades and disappears when the bactericide is no longer effective; they should then be discarded
- oven cloths – thick cloths designed to protect the hands when removing hot items from the oven; oven cloths must only be used dry, never damp or wet, otherwise the user is likely to be burned.

Papers

- Greaseproof or silicone: for lining cake-tins, making piping bags and wrapping greasy items of food.

- Kitchen: white absorbent paper for absorbing grease from deep-fried foods and for lining trays on which cold foods are kept.
- General purpose: thick, absorbent paper for wiping and drying equipment, surfaces, food, etc.
- Towels: disposable, for drying the hands.

Foils

- Clingfilm: a thin, transparent material for wrapping sandwiches, snacks, hot and cold foods; clingfilm has the advantage of being very flexible and easy to handle and seal; due to risk of contamination, it is advisable to use a clingfilm that does not contain PVC or is plasticiser-free.
- Metal foil: a thin, pliable, silver-coloured material for wrapping and covering foods and for protecting oven-roasted joints during cooking.

Energy conservation and efficiency

The emphasis in coming years for chefs and managers will be to save energy. With the rising cost of fuel, pressure will be on all operations to look at efficient ways of saving money on fuel.

Climate change

Scientists predict that global warming will cause the earth's temperature to rise by between 1.5 and 5.8°C, and sea levels by between 10 and 90 cm over the coming 100 years. This will have severe implications, such as increased rainfall and more 'severe weather events', such as storms and flooding, worldwide.

Although the climate has always changed naturally, science shows that human activity is now the cause of major change: global temperatures have risen 0.6°C over the last 140 years (since the start of the Industrial Revolution), and the rate of warming is greater than at any time since the last Ice Age. Economic 'growth' and development remain dependent on the burning of fossil fuels, whose by-products (known as 'greenhouse gases') act as insulators in the atmosphere, inhibiting the earth's natural cooling mechanism.

However, if the world reduces its dependency on the use of fossil fuels then it is possible to ensure that the rise in the earth's temperature will be minimised.

Energy consumption in the hospitality industry

Statistics issued by the Building Research Establishment (BRE) indicate that the UK's hospitality sector remains a major consumer of fossil fuels, accounting for 16 per cent of all energy used in the service sector. Its consumption of electricity and fossil fuels is greater than that in education, government or the health service. The major cost sectors for energy use are heating, air conditioning, cooking and refrigeration, lighting and production of hot water. It is estimated that most hospitality businesses could, however, save between 20 and 40 per cent of energy.

The main uses of energy are for providing catering services and hot water.

Chefs and managers have to take responsibility for energy management. Fuel tariffs have to be checked to ensure the most competitive rates are achieved. Assess the current fuel costs and identify any wastage. All staff should be trained to save fuel and monitor use.

Energy and the environment

The burning of fossil fuels to generate energy releases gases into the atmosphere. These include sulphur dioxide, which gives rise to acid rain, and carbon dioxide, which is the main contributor to the threat of global warming.

Table 5.3 Energy efficiency measures and percentage savings

	Boilers, controls and hot water	Fossil saving %	Electricity saving %	Lighting, catering and other services	Fossil saving %	Electricity saving %
No cost	Ensure systems come on only when, where and to the extent they are needed	1	2	Switch off lights and other equipment whenever possible Label light switches	0	0.5
	Establish a daily routine for checking control settings, especially where they may have been overridden in response to unexpected circumstances	1	1	Make maximum use of daylight Place lights where they will be most effective Clean light fittings and use translucent shades Improve the reflection of light from walls and ceilings by using pale colours	0	0.5
	Use your existing equipment effectively Check that timers, programmers, optimum start controls and weather compensation controls are set up and operating correctly	3	1	Set illumination levels to the type of activity Reduce lighting levels where possible and remove surplus lamps (but do not compromise safety)	0	0.5
	Isolate parts of systems that are not in use – for example, seasonally Remove redundant pipework during refurbishment	1	0	Provide training for catering staff about energy costs and correct use of equipment Set energy targets for meals, monitor consumption and give feedback to staff	0.2	0.2
	Ensure plant is regularly and correctly maintained	0.5	0.5	Ensure regular maintenance of cooking utensils, all appliances, burners, timers, controls and taps Badly maintained equipment wastes energy	0.2	
	Review hot water thermostat accuracy and temperature settings periodically Reducing temperatures will save energy – but take precautions to avoid the risk of legionnaires' disease	1	0	Ensure optimum use of hot water, ventilation and lighting in the kitchen for various times of day and night Do not use hobs or ovens for space heating Run dishwashers only on full loads	0.2	0.2
Low cost	Fit draught stripping around windows and doors Fit heavy curtains to guest and public rooms	1	0	Where fittings allow, replace 38 mm fluorescent light tubes by 26 mm type, and install electronic starters and ballasts	0	0.5

Boilers, controls and hot water	Fossil saving %	Electricity saving %	Lighting, catering and other services	Fossil saving %	Electricity saving %
Check boiler efficiency periodically and make improvements as required	2	0	Consider replacement of tungsten lamps (including light fittings where necessary) by compact fluorescent types	0	6
Provide temperature and time controls for domestic hot water	1	0	Consider installation of timers, dimmers, photocells and sensors so lighting operates only when, where and to the extent needed	0	1
Install showers and flow restrictors where possible Reduce standing losses from hot water storage by lagging pipes and tanks	2	1	Consider installation of bedroom key fobs so lights and other electrical items operate only when rooms are occupied	0	1
Consider direct fired water heaters for hot water in place of boiler serving calorifier	3	0	When replacing catering equipment, review current developments in appliance design to select the most energy efficient	1	1
Establish a system for setting targets for energy consumption, monitoring actual consumption and assessing performance	1	2	If you have a swimming pool, provide and use a cover to reduce heat losses at night	0.5	0
Modernise heating and ventilation plant controls	6	1	Ensure enough linen is available so that laundry equipment is run at full load	0.5	0
Provide power factor correction, and consider load shedding to reduce maximum demand charges This will not save fuel but will reduce electricity charges	6	1	Use high-efficiency lights for all external lights, including car parking areas, controlled by timers and/or photocells	0	0.5

Factors to convert consumption of fuels to emissions of carbon dioxide, in kg of carbon dioxide produced per kWh of fuel used, are:

- gas – 0.21
- oil – 0.29
- electricity – 0.72.

See IOH Technical Brief No. 36, or contact the Department for Environment, Food and Rural Affairs (Defra) for information about energy efficiency (see www.defra.gov.uk).

A typical hotel releases about 160 kg of CO_2 per square metre of floor area annually, equivalent to about 10 tonnes per bedroom.

Who benefits from energy efficiency?

- Hotel owners and management benefit because efficiently run buildings cost less to operate.
- Guests benefit because an efficiently controlled hotel satisfies their needs and leads to repeat business.
- Staff benefit through improved morale and better motivation, which in turn increase productivity.
- The environment benefits because using energy efficiently reduces adverse effects on

the environment and preserves non-renewable resources for future generations.

Energy efficiency measures and percentage savings

The savings quoted in Table 5.3 are the minimum you can expect to achieve. Small percentage savings can mean appreciable cash benefits.

Services and energy

The supply of gas, electricity and water are of vital importance to the caterer. Any information required is best obtained from the appropriate local board so that it will be up to date.

Water

Water authorities are required, by law, to provide a supply of clean, wholesome water, free from suspended matter, odour and taste, all bacteria that are likely to cause disease, and mineral matter injurious to health.

Electrical safety

All electrical products must meet safety criteria laid out in European and national regulations.

Gas

Gas is a safe fuel, but like all fuels it must be treated with respect in order to remain safe.

What to do if you smell gas:

- Open all doors and windows.
- Check whether a gas tap has been left on, or if a pilot light has gone out. If so, turn off the appliance.
- If in doubt, turn off the gas supply at the meter and phone for emergency service.

Electricity

Electricity cannot be heard, tasted or smelled. Installed and used correctly, it is a very safe source of energy, but misused it can kill or cause serious injury. It is therefore essential that any electrical installation is undertaken by qualified engineers in accordance with British Standard 7671, and carried out by registered contractors of the National Inspection Council for Electrical Installation Contracting (NICIEC). A technical brief, 'Guide to Electric Lighting, No. 7/97', is available from HCIMA.

Comparison of fuels

Electricity and mains gas are most generally used in catering. Bottled gas (e.g. Calor) is also used in some catering operations. Before deciding on the fuel to use (if there is a choice) the following factors should be considered:

- safety
- constancy of supply
- cost
- cleanliness and need for ventilation
- efficiency
- cost of equipment, installation and maintenance.
- storage requirements.

Energy conservation

The costs of energy use in hotel and catering establishments vary widely according to the type of fuel used, the type and age of equipment, the way in which it is used and the tariff paid.

The basic principles of energy management are:

- obtain the best tariff available
- purchase the most suitable energy-efficient equipment
- reduce heat loss to a minimum
- match heat and cooling loads on environmental systems whenever possible to the demands
- maintain all equipment to optimum efficiency
- ensure that the operating periods of systems and equipment are set correctly
- use heat recovery systems
- monitor energy consumption
- train staff to be energy efficient.

Figure 5.40 A bank of modern equipment, with induction hobs built in

Table 5.4 Comparison of electricity and gas

Advantages	Disadvantages
Electricity	
Clean to use, low maintenance Easily controlled, labour saving Good working atmosphere Little heat loss, no storage space required Low ventilation requirements	Time taken to heat up in a few instances Particular utensils are required for some hobs, e.g. induction More expensive than gas
Gas	
Convenient, labour saving, no smoke or dirt Special utensils not required No fuel storage required Easily controllable with immediate full heat and the flames are visible Cheaper than electricity	Some heat is lost in the kitchen Regular cleaning required for efficient working For gas to produce heat it must burn; this requires oxygen, which is contained in the air, and as a result carbon dioxide and water are produced As a result, adequate ventilation must be provided for combustion and to ensure a satisfactory working environment

Some factors to be considered in energy conservation

- Always replace equipment with low-energy rating equipment, by referring to wattage and running costs.
- Ensure that all machinery is maintained at its optimum efficiency and that equipment needing regular cleaning is serviced in accordance with maintenance manual requirements. This particularly applies to filters on ventilation and on conditioning systems, refrigeration plant condensers, cooking equipment and dishwashing machines.
- When replacing equipment, it is an opportune time to review the contents of the menu, the cooking and storage methods that the menu requires. Can certain procedures be scaled down or omitted, or can alternative procedures be used?
- Check all pre-heating of equipment – overlong pre-heating wastes fuel.
- Constantly review all heating and cooking procedures.
- Is it possible to reduce operating hours?
- Regularly check ventilation systems.
- Regularly check that storage temperatures for hot water systems are not more than 65°C for central systems and 55°C for local units. Also ensure that this temperature is not less than 55°C to avoid the risk of legionnaires' disease.
- Regularly check all lighting systems; where possible use energy-efficient compact fluorescent bulbs.
- Train staff not to waste lighting or use lighting unnecessarily.

References

CESA, *An Introduction to the Food Service Industry* (hand-out to CFSP course delegates)
Katz, R.L. (1974) 'Skills of the effective administrator', *Harvard Business Review* 52(1).
Mintzberg, H. (1975) 'The manager's job: folklore and fact', *Harvard Business Review* 74.

Some references to planning and equipment elsewhere in this book:

Topics for discussion

1 Who should be responsible for planning a kitchen?

2 Discuss the worst organised kitchen that you have seen and how it could be improved.

3 Give good and bad examples of working methods.

4 Discuss the advantages and disadvantages of the straight-shift and split-shift systems from the point of view of the staff and the employer.

5 Compile a list of all the factors that affect the good design of a kitchen. Discuss why they are necessary to enable efficiency.

6 Poor design may cause accidents in the kitchen. Discuss the ways in which accidents can be prevented.

7 Discuss the reasons why organisation of staff needs to be considered in relation to a specific menu and the factors that influence the composition of the menu.

8 Discuss the qualities that go towards being a good (a) head chef, (b) chef de partie.

9 Organisational ability is a quality that is often quoted as an essential element to being successful in the kitchen. Discuss, with examples if possible, your understanding of organisational ability regarding (a) resources, (b) staff, (c) yourself.

10 Discuss the role of supervision and relate this, if possible, to an establishment you know.

11 As an employee, how do you like to be supervised?

12 What are the characteristics of a good supervisor?

13 List the essential requirements of kitchen equipment.

14 Discuss the respective advantages of a conventional oven, convection oven and a combination convection/steaming oven.

15 Compare induction cooking plates, halogen hobs and conventional cooking tops.

16 What are the advantages of pans made up of layers of different metals?

17 What are the benefits of the bratt pan?

18 What essential items of mechanical equipment are needed?

19 Discuss the importance of sufficient refrigeration.

20 What are the benefits of the food waste disposer or the advantages of a food compactor?

21 What is the argument for maintaining wooden chopping boards?

22 Discuss the design of equipment in relation to maintaining high standards of hygiene.

23 What factors should be considered by those designing kitchen equipment?

24 What faults, if any, do you wish to be remedied in any items of equipment?

25 What are the advantages and disadvantages of induction equipment?

26 The advantages of gas or electricity for kitchen equipment.

27 How to effect economy in the consumption of energy by catering equipment.

28 Why maintenance of all services is essential.

29 How water conservation can be achieved.

30 Why hot water is more costly than cold water, and how these costs can be reduced.

31 How could the sun and wind be used to reduce costs in small establishments?

32 Discuss how training could reduce wastage of water, gas and electricity.

6 Production systems

Supporting material available on Dynamic Learning Online:

> Knowledge quizzes
> Activity worksheets: production systems; hygiene
> Summary presentations

A strategic and methodical approach to food production and service

Every chef's challenge is to ensure that the production of food (mise-en-place) is as safe, efficient, cost effective and consistent as possible. This is only possible when the chef can analyse the full process using a critical path and identify all areas of work.

There is more evidence that today's young chef has the desire to achieve great things, which in itself is very admirable; however, this approach, if not tempered, is flawed and could cause frustrations when you are in a senior post within an organisation. The current desire to achieve, have the highest accolades with the biggest salary, and the best and most original food, detracts from the very foundation that supports the product that is so important to the organisation. This approach is partly driven by the media promoting the 'celebrity chef' and sometimes endorsing the taking of an 'unethical' approach in order to achieve stardom.

The 'progressive approach' is to establish a level of consistency in the building of knowledge where the trainee starts with the basics and progresses methodically, learning all areas of their craft. For example:

- health and safety
- communication with others
- personnel legislation
- delegation
- understanding facilities in the kitchen environment
- the welfare of others
- conceptual skills
- self-motivation
- recruitment and training
- working with others
- understanding the market

financial acumen
- understanding suppliers and their relationships
- making effective decisions
- kitchen administration and organisation.

This list identifies most of the areas that will support the food and beverage product, making it consistent and able to achieve longevity, with the capacity to maintain growth and gain the market edge. The list does not include food production and food styles, however, nor does it cover the scientific 'wow!' and bafflement factor.

However, the list is the essential foundation on which the food and beverage product should be based; without this foundation the product itself is prone to collapse, leading to heightened risk and ultimately placing the product/brand at risk.

Areas of 'risk'

Areas of risk include:

- heath and safety
- incorrect convergence of facilities
- financial loss
- suppliers
- the market
- cooking consistency
- the workforce
- non-compliance with food safety legislation.

All these areas hold potential risks that could devalue the product/brand by making the end result inconsistent, which will lead to a fall in profits and perhaps increase staff turnover. In extreme cases, businesses in hospitality that fail do so due to one or more of the above areas not being properly managed.

Quality in the management of food and beverage production systems

European Foundation for Quality Management Excellence Model (1999)

The European Foundation for Quality Management Excellence Model is a non-prescriptive framework, which recognises that there are many approaches to achieving sustainable excellence in all aspects of performance. The model is based on nine criteria. It emphasises that results for customers, people (employees) and society are achieved through leadership driving policy and strategy, people management, partnership and resources, and processes leading to business results.

Each of the nine elements shown in the model (Figure 6.1) is a criterion that can be used to appraise an organisation's progress towards total quality management. The four results criteria are concerned with what the organisation has achieved and is achieving. The five enablers criteria are concerned with how results are being achieved. The arrows shown are intended to emphasise the dynamic nature of the model. They indicate that innovation and learning help to improve the enablers and that this in turn leads to improved results. The overall objective of comprehensive self-appraisal and self-improvement is to regularly review each of the nine criteria and, thereafter, to adopt relevant improvement strategies.

British Standard EN ISO 9002: 1994

The British Standard scheme was introduced in 1979

with the aim of providing a method for organisations to assess the suitability of their suppliers' products. The scheme aimed to rationalise the many schemes of supplier assessment used by various purchasing firms and organisations.

The British Standard Quality Award BS EN ISO 9002: 1994, is a quality kitemark (standard or benchmark) in the fitness for purpose and safety in use sense, in the service provided and/or the products designed and constructed to satisfy the customer's needs. It is concerned primarily with evidence of systematic processes that are employed within an operation and which can demonstrate that there is a link between customer demand and the services and products on offer.

BS EN ISO 9002 identifies the systems, procedures and criteria that ensure that a product or service meets a customer's requirements. The key elements in quality management for most organisations in the hotel and catering (hospitality) industry include:

- management responsibility – policy, objectives, identification of key personnel
- quality system procedures – all functions must be covered
- auditing the system – it must be audited internally
- quality in marketing – honest promotional activities
- material control and traceability – supplies must be traceable
- non-conformity – ensuring that faulty products/ service do not reach the customer

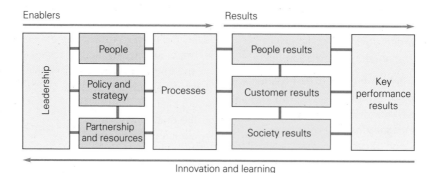

Figure 6.1 European Foundation for Quality Management Excellence Model

- corrective action – identifying reasons for faults, and subsequently implementing measures to correct them and records of the faults and measures, written and kept
- after-sales service – procedures for monitoring quality of after-sales service
- documentation and records – records of checks and inspections, action taken, audit reports
- personnel and training – identification of needs, provision and verification of training
- product safety and liability – procedures for handling, storing and processing materials (for example, foods).

BS EN ISO 9002 can be important to food service operations for two reasons. First, when purchasing goods and services, BS EN ISO 9002 indicates that a supplier operates a quality system of a high standard. Second, food service operators, such as contract caterers, may find that they will not be considered as potential tenderers if they have not achieved BS EN ISO 9002. Additionally, BS EN ISO 9002 may even provide useful evidence that due diligence had been exercised – for example, in the event of a food service operation being prosecuted under the Food Safety Act 1990/95.

In an increasingly competitive marketplace, and with increasing uniformity between operations, the level of service provided and its quality become ever more important. It is the front-line members of staff that offer this service – their training and development are crucial to the successful running of an operation. Total quality management (TQM) offers a framework by which members of staff are given the scope to treat guests as individuals, and thereby offer superior service.

However, the costs involved in attaining the standard can be high, and therefore the introduction of BS EN ISO 9002 needs to be carefully assessed before implementation takes place. On the other hand, the reviews from many of the organisations moving towards BS EN ISO 9002 have suggested that it is cost-effective.

Further information on quality matters can be obtained from the following sources.
- **European Foundation for Quality Management, Brussels Representative Office, Avenue des Pleiades 15, 1200 Brussels, Belgium (website: www.efqm.org).**
- **The complete documents on BS EN ISO 9002: 1994 are available from the British Standards Institution, Linford Wood, Milton Keynes MK14 6LE (website: www.bsi-global.com).**

 ## Problems

Food production systems, such as cook-chill, cook-freeze and sous-vide, have been introduced into certain areas of catering in order to increase efficiency and productivity; changes have been made to maximise the utilisation of equipment and to maintain high levels of output and viability.

The particular problems of the catering industry are as follows.

- **Staff:** unattractive work conditions, limited numbers of skilled staff, mobility of labour.
- **Food:** high cost, wastage.
- **Equipment:** high cost of replacement and maintenance, under-usage.
- **Energy:** wasteful high-cost traditional systems, availability.
- **Overheads:** wage increases, payments to National Insurance.

- **Space:** most kitchens and services must be adequate for comfortable working while using space efficiently; space is very costly.

The solution to these problems comes in the form of centralisation of production, using the skilled staff available to prepare and cook in bulk and then to distribute to finishing kitchens, which are smaller in size, employing semi-skilled and unskilled labour.

Cook-freeze and cook-chill systems have been developed to meet these requirements, each system having advantages over the other depending on the size and nature of the overall operation. For example, cook-freeze is not adaptable to very small units or to haute cuisine. Cook-chill can be adapted to any type of unit but cannot take advantage of seasonal, cheaper commodities.

Sous-vide, which is a method of working under vacuum-sealing, ice-water bath chilling and chilled storage, has also been developed as a production system.

Many catering operations face problems because of the growing shortage of skilled catering staff and the ever-increasing turnover of employees:

- It is essential that skilled staff are more fully utilised and given improved working conditions.
- Certain catering tasks require deskilling so as to be carried out by a greater proportion of unskilled staff.
- Better benefits and conditions of employment must be provided for fewer key staff in order to reduce levels of staff turnover and enhance job satisfaction.

Production

In order to ensure that high-quality, palatable food is produced at all times it is essential that working conditions are maintained to the highest possible standards, as laid down in the HMSO publication *Clean Catering* (ISBN 011 320 4833). For example:

- stringent personal hygiene precautions against infection of the food
- all working surfaces and utensils thoroughly cleaned to minimise spread of bacteria
- clean equipment and utensils separated from used items awaiting cleaning

- separation of raw and cooked foods at all times
- strict control of cooking times and temperatures
- staff training in food hygiene
- consultation with medical and public health officers when planning food production systems.

Equipment

The equipment used will vary according to the size of the operation, but if food is batch-cooked then convection ovens, steaming ovens, bratt pans, jacketed boiling pans, tilting kettles, and so on, may be used. Certain oven models are available in which a set of

Food	Preparation	Cooking	Holding	Regeneration	Presentation
Fresh	Weigh/measure	Blanch	Chill	Regithermic	Bain-marie
Fresh cooked	Clean/open	Warm	Sous-vide	Microwave	Service flats
Fresh prepared	Chop/cut	Simmer	Freeze	Convection	Plates
Canned	Combine/mix	Boil	Tray	Traditional	Trays
Frozen	Blend	Steam	Hot cupboard		Vending
Chilled	Shape/coat	Grill	Cold cupboard		Buffet
Vacuum	Form	Sauté			Trolley
Dehydrated		Brown			Dishes
Smoked		Bake			
Salted		Roast			
Crystallised		Fry			
Acidified		Microwave			
Pasteurised					
Bottled					
UHT					

Foods in ◄─────────── Process ───────────► Output

Figure 6.2 Elements of production

racks can be assembled with food and wheeled in for cooking.

The main difference between cook-freeze and cook-chill is the degree of refrigeration and the length of storage life. Other than these differences the information given in this chapter relates to both systems. (For details of cook-freeze, see page 215.)

We will now take a closer look at some of the methods of food production highlighted in Table 6.1.

Table 6.1 Methods of food production

No	Method	Description
1	Conventional	Term used to describe production utilising mainly fresh foods and traditional cooking methods
2	Convenience	Method of production utilising mainly convenience foods
3	Call order	Method where food is cooked to order either from customer (as in cafeterias) or from waiter; production area often open to customer area
4	Continuous flow	Method involving production-line approach where different parts of the production process may be separated (e.g. fast food)
5	Centralised	Production not directly linked to service; foods are 'held' and distributed to separate service areas
6	Cook-chill	Food production storage and regeneration method utilising principle of low temperature control to preserve the qualities of processed foods
7	Cook-freeze	Production, storage and regeneration method utilising principle of freezing to control and preserve the qualities of processed foods; requires special processes to assist freezing
8	Sous-vide	Method of production, storage and regeneration utilising principle of sealed vacuum to control and preserve the quality of processed foods
9	Assembly kitchen	A system based on accepting and incorporating the latest technological development in the manufacturing and conservation of food products

Cook-chill

Cook-chill is a catering system based on the normal preparation and cooking of food followed by rapid chilling storage in controlled low-temperature conditions above freezing point – 0–3°C – and subsequently reheating immediately before consumption. The chilled food is regenerated in finishing kitchens, which require low capital investment and minimum staff. Almost any food can be cook-chilled provided that the correct methods are used during the preparation.

The cook-chill system is used in volume catering, in hospitals, schools and in social services. It is also used for banquets, in conference and exhibition catering, in vending machines where meals are dispensed to the customer, and in factories, hospitals and services outside of main meal times.

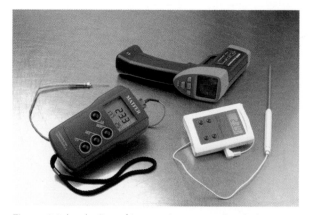

Figure 6.3 A selection of temperature measuring devices

Foods suitable for the cook-chill process

- Meats: All meat, poultry, game and offal can be cook-chilled. Meat dishes that need to be sliced, such as striploin of beef, are cooked, rapidly chilled, sliced and packaged for storage. The regeneration temperature must reach 70°C in the centre of the produce for two minutes. Therefore, it is not possible to serve undercooked meats.
- Fish: All precooked fish dishes are suitable for cook-chilling.
- Egg dishes: Omelettes and scrambled eggs are now commonly used in this process, especially on airlines. Omelettes are now manufactured by companies that are able to supply the airline with the chilled product. The quality of the end product has greatly improved and continues to do so as more and more money is invested in product development.
- Soups and sauces: Most soups and sauces can now be chilled successfully. Those with a high fat or egg yolk content do need a certain amount of recipe modification to prevent separation on regeneration.
- Desserts: There is a large number of desserts that chill well, especially the cold variety. Developments continue with hot sweets, especially those that require a hot base and a separate topping.

Recipe modification

Successful production of chilled food does require a certain amount of recipe modification. These modifications may have to be introduced during the preparation or cooking or both.

- Battered fish: The batter should be made thicker, using a mixture with a higher fat content. This type of batter does not easily break away from the fish and will give a crisper end product.
- Stewed/braised items: Cut meat into smaller portions to avoid undue thickness. Flour-based sauces must be thoroughly cooked otherwise they will continue to thicken during regeneration.
- Scrambled eggs: Cook until the egg begins to scramble, remove from heat and allow the product to continue to cook to a soft consistency. Chill immediately in shallow dishes and stir during chilling.
- Creamed and mashed potatoes: More liquid is added than normal, giving a loose and less dense product. This assists the chilling and regeneration stages as the potato absorbs more liquid when chilled.

The purpose of chilling food

The purpose of chilling food is to prolong its storage life. Under normal temperature conditions, food deteriorates rapidly through the action of micro-organisms and enzymic and chemical reactions. A reduction in the storage temperature inhibits the multiplication of bacteria and other micro-organisms, and slows down the chemical and enzymic reactions. At normal refrigeration temperatures reactions are still taking place but at a much slower rate, and at frozen food storage temperatures (−20°C approximately) all reactions nearly cease. A temperature of 0–3°C does not give a storage life comparable to frozen food, but it does produce a good product.

It is generally accepted that, even where high standards of fast chilling practice are used and consistent refrigerated storage maintained, product quality may be acceptable for only a few days (including the day of production and consumption). The storage temperature of 0–3°C is of extreme importance to ensure both full protection of the food from microbiological growth and the maintenance of maximum nutritional values in the food. It is generally accepted that a temperature of 10°C should be regarded as the critical safety limit for the storage of refrigerated food. Above that temperature, growth of micro-organisms may render the food dangerous to health.

In a properly designed and operated cook-chill system, cooked and prepared food will be rapidly cooled down to 0–3°C as soon as possible after cooking and portioning, and then stored between these temperatures throughout storage and distribution until required for reheating and service. Food prepared through the cook-chill system should be portioned and transferred to a blast chiller unit within 30 minutes. This will reduce the risk of the food remaining at warm incubation temperatures, and prevent the risk of contamination and loss of food quality.

The cook-chill process

- The food should be cooked sufficiently to ensure destruction of any pathogenic micro-organisms.
- The chilling process must begin as soon as possible after completion of the cooking and portioning processes, within 30 minutes of leaving the cooker. The food should be chilled to 3°C within a period of 90 minutes. Most pathogenic organisms will not grow below 7°C, while a temperature below 3°C is required to reduce growth of spoilage organisms and to achieve the required storage life. However, slow growth of spoilage organisms does take place at

these temperatures and for this reason storage life cannot be greater than five days.

- The food should be stored at a temperature of 0–3°C.
- The chilled food should be distributed under such controlled conditions that any rise in temperature of the food during distribution is kept to a minimum.
- For both safety and palatability the reheating (regeneration) of the food should follow immediately upon the removal of the food from chilled conditions and should raise the temperature to a level of at least 70°C.
- The food should be consumed as soon as possible and not more than two hours after reheating. Food not intended for reheating should be consumed as soon as convenient and within two hours of removal from storage. It is essential that unconsumed reheated food is discarded.
- A temperature of 10°C should be regarded as the critical safety limit for chilled food. Should the temperature of the chilled food rise above this level during storage or distribution, the food concerned should be discarded.

Cook-chill is generally planned within a purpose-designed, comprehensive, new central production unit to give small-, medium- or large-scale production along predefined flow lines, incorporating traditional catering/chilling/post-chilling packaging and storage for delivery to finishing kitchens. Within an existing kitchen, where existing equipment is retained with possible minor additions and modifications, chilling/post-chilling packaging and additional storage for cooked chilled food are added.

Finishing kitchens

These can consist of purpose-built regeneration equipment plus refrigerated storage. Additional equipment, such as a chip fryer, boiling table and pressure steamer for chips, sauces, custard, vegetables, and so on, can be added if required, to give greater flexibility.

Where chilled food is produced to supply a service on the same premises, it is recommended that the meals should be supplied, stored and regenerated by exactly the same method as used for operations where the production unit and finishing kitchens are separated by some distance.

Failure to adhere to just one procedure could result in disorganised production and reduced productivity. Once a decision is taken to sever production from service this method should be followed throughout the system.

Distribution of cook-chill

Distribution of the chilled food is an important part of the cook-chill operation. Fluctuations in storage temperature can affect the palatability and texture of food, and lead to microbiological dangers that require the food to be discarded. The distribution method chosen must ensure that the required temperature of below 3°C is maintained throughout the period of transport. Should the temperature of the food exceed 5°C during distribution the food ought to be consumed within 12 hours; if the temperature exceeds 10°C it should be discarded (Department of Health guidelines). Because of this, refrigeration during distribution is to be encouraged in many circumstances.

In some cases the cook-chill production unit can also act as a centralised kitchen and distribution point. Food is regenerated in an area adjacent to the cook-chill production area, and heat retention or insulated boxes are used for distribution. During transportation and service the food must not be allowed to fall below 63°C.

Know the legal requirements

Contravention of the Food Safety Act 1990/95, the amendment regulations, and lack of due diligence can be very costly if legal action is taken and proved against the caterer or food manufacturer. The labelling of food products, recording of temperatures, maintenance of hygiene standards and promotion of staff training is essential in defence of due diligence. For this defence to be successful, the caterer must convince the court that all the requirements under the law have been complied with and that the accepted customs and practices of the profession have been carried out. It is also of paramount importance that a caterer records that these systems have been adhered to by the submission of documentary evidence.

Avoiding the dangers of cook-chill

It is essential to:

- maintain and record the correct temperatures
- maintain high standards of hygiene
- use fresh, high-quality ingredients, avoiding raw materials that may contain excessive numbers of micro-organisms.

Deliveries

All food purchased must be of prime quality and stored correctly under the required temperatures.

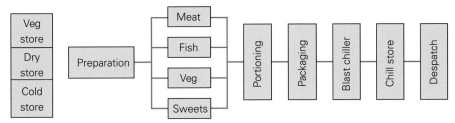

Figure 6.4 Production unit: planning for cook-chill

Preparation

All food must be prepared quickly under the appropriate conditions avoiding any possible cross-contamination and at the correct temperature.

Initial cooking and processing

During the cooking process the centre of the food must reach a temperature of at least 70°C; preferably this temperature should reach 75°C or even 80°C to achieve a greater safety margin.

Portioning

This should take place under appropriate conditions in a controlled environment, which is maintained to the highest hygiene standards. The depth of the food should be no more than approximately 5 cm. The containers must be labelled with the date of cooking, number of portions and reheating instructions.

Chilling

All food must be chilled within 30 minutes of cooking and reduced to a temperature of 0–3°C within 90 minutes.

Portioning after chilling

In some cook-chill systems the food is chilled in multi-portion containers then plated before reheating. The portioning process should be carried out in a controlled environment within 30 minutes of the food leaving the chilled store and before reheating commences at a temperature of 10°C. It is then transported under chilled conditions to the desired location – for example, the hospital ward – where it is reheated to at least 70°C but preferably 80°C on the plate on which it is to be served.

Storage

All chilled cooked food must be stored in its own special refrigeration area. Never store cooked chilled food under the same conditions as fresh products. Always monitor the temperature of the product regularly.

Reheating

All cook-chill food must be reheated as quickly as possible to a minimum temperature of 70°C, ideally 75°C but preferably 80°C.

Storage and quality of cook-chill foods

It has been found that, during the storage period before reheating and consumption, certain products deteriorate in quality.

- The flavour of certain meat dishes – in particular white meats, veal and poultry – deteriorates after three days.
- Chilled meats without sauces can develop acidic tastes.
- Fatty foods tend to develop 'off' flavours due to the fat oxidising.
- Fish dishes deteriorate more rapidly than meat dishes.
- Dishes containing meat tend to develop a 'flat' taste, and if spices have been used these can dominate the flavour of the meat by the end of the chilled storage period.
- Vegetables in general may discolour and develop a strong flavour.
- Dishes that contain large amounts of starch may taste stale after the chilled storage time.

Containers

The choice of containers must protect and in some cases enhance the quality of the product at all stages, it must assist in the rapid chilling, safe storage and effective reheating. Therefore the container must be:

- sturdy – to withstand chilling, handling and reheating
- safe – not made of a substance that will cause harmful substances to develop in the food, nor react with the food to cause discolouring or spoilage
- have an easy-to-remove lid – without damaging contents or causing spillage
- attractive – to enhance the appearance of the product

Figure 6.5 Testing food with a hand-held thermometer

- airtight and watertight – so that moisture, flavours or odours do not penetrate the food or escape during storage and transportation.

There are various types of container available.

Single-portion containers

These can be of cardboard laminated with plastic, aluminium foil (unsuitable for microwave heating), plastic compounds or stainless steel and ceramic, which are durable and reusable (stainless steel is, however, unsuitable for microwave ovens).

Multi-portion containers

These can be of strong plastic compounds, stainless steel, ceramic or aluminium foil. Gastronorm containers are shown in Figure 6.7.

Labelling

Labels must stick securely to containers and be easy to apply, clearly identifying the product. Colour coding is sometimes used to help identify the different day of production. For example:

- Sunday – white
- Monday – red
- Tuesday – yellow
- Wednesday – blue
- Thursday – orange
- Friday – green
- Saturday – purple.

Chilling equipment

Only specially purpose-built and designed equipment can take the temperature of cooked food down to safe levels fast enough.

Blast chillers or air blast chillers

These use rapidly moving cold air to chill the food evenly and rapidly. Some models have temperature probes so that the temperature of the food being chilled can be checked without opening the door.

Cryogenic batch chillers

These use liquid nitrogen at a temperature of $-196°C$; this is sprayed into the chilling cabinet containing the warm food. In the warmer temperature of the cabinet, the liquid nitrogen turns to super-cold gas, absorbing the heat from the food as it does so. Fans move the cold gas over and around the food. Once the gas has become warm it is removed from the cabinet. Some equipment uses carbon dioxide instead of nitrogen.

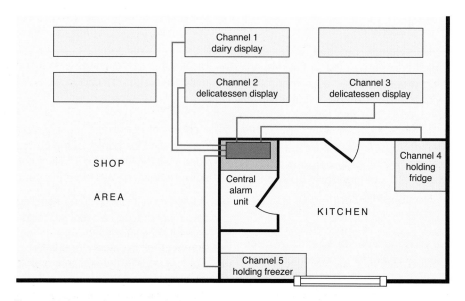

Figure 6.6 A central monitoring alarm unit and an example of the area it covers

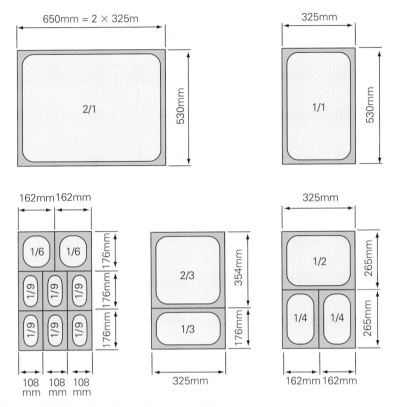

Figure 6.7 Module sizes for gastronorm containers

Figure 6.8 Labelling system

Reheating equipment

The caterer has the following choice of equipment for regenerating cook-chill products.

- Combination ovens: These are ideally suited for bulk production and can be used with steam, which is very effective in producing quality products.
- Steamers: These may be used for certain foods, especially vegetables.
- Microwave ovens: These are used for small amounts of food.
- Infra-red ovens: These may be used for small or large quantities of food.

Figure 6.9 A blast chiller

Points to remember to ensure a satisfactory product

- Time and temperature are crucial.
- The food should not wait longer than 30 minutes to be chilled.
- The food should not be above 3°C at the end of the chilling time. A higher temperature may be

due to the food being packed too deep in the containers; the food may have been covered; there may be a malfunction in the equipment.
- Food should not be stored beyond its 'use by' date.
- The temperature of the food rising above 3°C during transportation should be avoided. This may be due to: the journey taking too long using unrefrigerated transport; the refrigerated van not operating correctly; the insulated box (if used) not being precooled, or the lid not properly fitted. Whatever the cause, it must be recorded and the appropriate persons informed. If the temperature has not risen above 10°C and the food is going to be served within 12 hours, the food may be allowed through. This will obviously depend on the type of food. Outside these limits it should be discarded. If in doubt, throw it out.
- Food should not be overcooked after reheating. This may be due to the food being heated too long or the temperature being too high, or faulty equipment being used.
- Avoid food not reaching 70°C within the 30 minutes allowed for reheating. This may be due to: the label information not being followed correctly; the label information not being correct;

the lid being taken off when it should have been left on; faulty equipment. If the food temperature is unsafe, throw it away.
- Avoid damaged containers. This may be due to: mishandling during transportation; badly stacked storage containers.
- Observe high standards of personal hygiene and kitchen hygiene, to avoid product contamination or cross-contamination.
- Portions must be controlled when filling packages in order to: ensure efficient stock control; control costs; ensure that sufficient food is delivered to regenerating/finishing kitchens. Check that the standard regeneration procedures are safe to use.
- Food containers must be sealed correctly before storage in order to: protect the food from airborne contamination; enhance the presentation of dishes; prevent the evaporation of moisture when heated; reduce the dehydration effects chilling has on food; avoid finishing products being tampered with.
- All food products must be labelled correctly before storage to: identify the product and the day of production by the colour coding and 'use by' date; facilitate stock control; maintain stock rotation; enable visitors such as environmental health officers to check that the food safety laws have been and are being complied with; ensure that quality tracking can be carried out.
- Ensure that older stock is consumed before the new.
- Ensure the security of storage areas against unauthorised access in order to: prevent pilferage or damage by unauthorised persons; prevent unnecessary opening of store doors, which could destabilise storage temperature and thus may affect the temperature of the product, rendering it unsafe.

For further information, contact the Chilled Food Association, PO Box 14811 London NW10 9ZR (website: www.chilledfood.org).

Comparison of cook-chill and fast-food systems

The characteristics of each system are listed in Table 6.2.

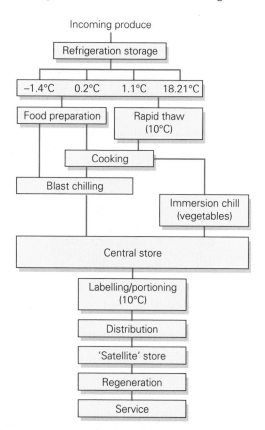

Figure 6.10 Refrigeration for cook-chill catering

Table 6.2 Characteristics of cook-chill and fast-food systems

	Cook-chill	**Fast food**
Types of equipment	Flexible, general purpose	Single purpose Single function
Design of process	Functional	Product flow
Set-up time	Variable	Long
Workers	Variously skilled, partie system, limited flexibility	Low skill Flexible
Inventories for start of process	Vary, depending on 'foods in' required Limited in time by planning and forecasting Limited by preplanning and forecasting	High to meet potential demand
Holding inventory	Five days max. Level forecasted	Ten mins max. Level controlled
Lot sizes	Small to large (multiples of ten)	Individual
Production time	Variable depending on menu requirements	Short or constant
Product range	Fairly wide but within constraints of three- or four-course meals, lunch or dinner	Very restricted
System structure	Stock/customer/operation	Stock/queue/operation
Capacity	Variable	Highly variable
Scheduling	Externally orientated	Externally orientated

Cook-freeze

Cook-freeze is a specialised food production and distribution system that allows caterers to take advantage of the longer life through blast freezing at −18 to −20°C and storage at that temperature until required for resale or consumption for up to three to six months. Blast freezers have increasingly been introduced with success into catering operations. The ability to freeze cooked dishes and prepared foods, as distinct from the storage of chilled foods in a refrigerator or already frozen commodities in a deep-freeze, allows a caterer to make more productive use of kitchen staff. It also enables economies to be introduced into the staffing of dining rooms and restaurants.

The cook-freeze process

Cook-freeze uses a production system similar to that used in cook-chill. The recipes used have to be modified, enabling products to be freezer-stable, and modified starches are used in sauces so that, on reheating and regeneration, the sauce does not separate. Blast freezers are used in place of blast chillers. The freezing must be carried out very rapidly to retain freshness and to accelerate temperature loss through the latent heat barrier, thus preventing the formation of large ice crystals and rupturing of the cells.

Blast freezing takes place when low-temperature air is passed over food at high speed, reducing food in batches to a temperature of at least −20°C within 90 minutes. Blast freezers can hold from 20 to 400 kg per batch, the larger models being designed for trolley operation.

Preparation of food

The production menu for a month is drawn up and the total quantities of different foods required calculated. Supplies are then ordered, with special attention given to their being:

- of high quality
- delivered so that they can immediately be prepared and cooked without any possibility of deteriorating during an enforced period of storage before being processed.

The dishes included in the menu must be cooked to the highest standards, with rigid attention to quality control and to hygiene. Deep-freeze temperatures prevent the multiplication of micro-organisms but do not destroy them. If, therefore, a dish were contaminated before being frozen, consumers would be put at risk months later when the food was prepared for consumption. The exact adjustment of recipes to produce the best result when the food is subsequently thawed and reheated is still in process of being worked out by chefs, using numerous variations of the basic system. The single change needed in cookery recipes involving sauces is the selection of an appropriate type of starch capable of resisting the effect of freezing. Normal starches will produce a curdled effect when subsequently thawed and reheated.

In order to achieve rapid freezing with a quick reduction of temperature to −18°C or below, the cooked food must be carefully portioned (close attention being paid to the attainment of uniform portion size). Portions, each placed into a disposable aluminium foil container, may conveniently be placed into aluminium foil trays holding from six to ten portions each, sealed and carefully labelled with their description and date of preparation.

Freezing

The food thus divided into portions and arranged in trays is immediately frozen. An effective procedure is to place the trays on racks in a blast-freezing tunnel and expose them to a vigorous flow of cold air until the cooked items are frozen solid and the temperature reduced to at least −5°C. The quality of the final product is to a significant degree dependent on the rapidity with which the temperature of hot cooked food at, say, 80°C is reduced to below freezing. The capacity of the blast freezer should be designed to achieve this reduction in temperature within a period of 60–90 minutes.

Storage of frozen items

Once the food items are frozen they must at once be put into a deep-freeze store maintained at −18°C. For a catering operation involving several dining rooms and cafeterias, some of which may be situated at some distance from the kitchen and frozen store, four weeks' supply of cooked dishes held at low temperature allows full use to be made of the facilities.

Transport of frozen items to the point of service

If satisfactory quality is to be maintained, it is important to keep food, frozen in the cooked state, frozen until immediately prior to its being served. It should therefore be transported in insulated containers to peripheral or finishing kitchens, if such are to be used, where it will be reheated.

If frozen dishes are to be used in outside catering, provision should be available for transporting them in refrigerated transport and, if necessary, a subsidiary deep-freeze store should be provided for them on arrival.

The reheating of frozen cooked portions

In any catering system in which a blast-freezing tunnel has been installed to freeze pre-cooked food, previously portioned and packed in metal foil or other individual containers, it is obviously rational to install equipment that is particularly designed for the purpose of reheating the items ready to be served. The blast-freezing system is effective because it is, in design, an especially powerful form of forced convection heat exchanger arranged to extract heat. It follows that an equally appropriate system for replacing heat is the use of a forced convection oven, especially for the reception of trays of frozen portions. Where such an oven is equipped with an efficient thermostat and adequate control of the air circulation system, standardised setting times for the controls can be laid down for the regeneration of the various types of dishes that need to be reheated.

Quality control

Adequate control of bacterial contamination and growth, which are hazards in any kitchen, can be achieved by a survey of the initial installation by a qualified analyst, and regular checks taken on every batch of food cooked. Very large kitchens employ a full-time food technologist/microbiologist. In smaller operations the occasional services of a microbiologist from the public health authority should be used.

How freezing affects different foods

Meat, poultry and fish

The tendency for the fat in meat to oxidise and go rancid, even in frozen storage, means that lean meat is better than fatty meat for freezing. Chicken fat contains a natural antioxidant (vitamin E), and this will react to prevent rancidity occurring.

Fresh meat must always be used for cook-freeze dishes. Never use meat that has previously been frozen. This is because each time meat is thawed, even in cool conditions, there is a chance for food-poisoning bacteria to multiply.

Some loss of flavour in fish is unavoidable and any surfaces left exposed can suffer from oxidation, thus producing a rancid taste. Deep-fried fish in batter has to be modified so that the batter does not peel off as a result of the freezing process. The batter should be made thicker or with a higher fat content.

Freezing does not stop the enzyme activity in the meat, poultry or fish that makes the fat present in the flesh go rancid. This particularly affects the unsaturated fats that are present in pork, poultry and fish. These items should therefore not be stored frozen for longer than two to three months. It is advisable therefore to trim off all fat before processing these items.

Fruit and vegetables

When fruit and vegetables turn brown, it is because of the action of enzymes present. These enzymes cause discoloration and gradually destroy the nutritive value of the fruit. Refrigeration slows this process down, and freezing will further slow it down but not stop it completely. Therefore, fruit and vegetables should be blanched or completely cooked prior to freezing, which will stop the enzymic processes.

The freezing process also has a softening effect on the texture of fruit and vegetables. This is acceptable for hard fruits such as apples, unripened pears and so on; it is not, however, suitable for soft fruits such as strawberries. Fruits like these are suitable for freezing only if they are later to be used as a filling or in a sauce, but not for decorative purposes.

Only exceptionally fresh vegetables should be used for freezing. Avoid bruised vegetables, which may produce the development of 'off' flavours. Blanch the vegetables to inactivate the enzymes, but avoid over-blanching, otherwise the vegetables will be overcooked. Blanch if possible in high-pressure steamers as this will help reduce vitamin C loss.

Recipe modification

Generally, recipes have to be modified for the cook-freeze process.

Sauces, batters, thickened soups, stews and gravies will break down and separate unless the flour used in the recipes has an addition of waxy starch. Colflo and Purity 69 are two commercially manufactured starches used in cook-freeze recipes.

Jellies and other products containing gelatine are unsuitable because they develop a granular structure in the cook-freeze process, unless the recipe is modified with stabilisers.

Packaging

Packaging is a very important consideration as it affects the storage and regeneration of the product. Containers must protect the food against oxidation during storage and allow for freezing and reheating. The containers must be:

- watertight
- non-tainting
- disposable or reusable
- equipped with tight-fitting lids.

Packaging materials

There are a number of packaging materials available, which include plastic compounds, aluminium foil and cardboard plastic laminates. These are available as single-portion packs, complete meal packs and bulk packs.

Choosing the container

Various factors affect your choice of container.

- **Menu choice:** single packs provide the greatest flexibility.
- **Food value:** the overheating of complete meal packs, or the edges of bulk packs, will damage the nutritional value.
- **Storage space:** large bulk packs make the best use of space.
- **Handling time:** after cooking, bulk packs are the quickest and easiest to fill, whereas complete packs are more difficult to fill. Bulk packs do, however, have to be portioned at the time of service and are therefore more time-consuming than if single packs are used.
- **Quality of the food:** freezing time is obviously affected by the depth of the food; therefore bulk packs, where the food is relatively deep, may not survive the freezing process as well as single-portion packs. Bulk packs also rely on trained service staff to present the food attractively and portion it accurately. Regeneration instructions can be complex if complete meal packs contain different food components that, in theory, may require different lengths of reheating time.

Freezing equipment

Specialist equipment is required in order to reduce the temperature of the food to the required storage temperature of −18°C.

- Air blast freezers or blast freezers: these take approximately 75–90 minutes to freeze food, depending on how it is packaged. Extremely cold air – between −32°C and −40°C – is blown by fans over the cooked food. The warm air is constantly removed and recirculated through the heat exchange unit to lower its temperature. In the larger cook-freeze units the food is pushed in on a trolley at one end and then wheeled out at the other end frozen.

- Cryogenic freezers: these use liquid nitrogen with the freezing time taking on average 25 minutes, depending on the food being frozen, provided the food is left uncovered. Liquid nitrogen at −196°C is sprayed into the freezing chamber. Fans circulate the nitrogen so that the foods freeze evenly. The warm gas is pumped out of the cabinet as more cold nitrogen is pumped in. Some freezers used liquid carbon dioxide.
- Plate freezers and tunnel freezers: these are used in food manufacturing and are less likely to be used in catering.

Transportation and distribution

Cook-freeze meals have to be delivered to finishing kitchens at the same temperature as they were held in storage. For short distances, insulated containers are used. These are cooled down before use. However, it is safer and more efficient to use refrigerated vans.

Finishing kitchen equipment

Thawing cabinets are similar to a forced air convection oven, but use a temperature of 10°C.

- Rapid thawing cabinet: These are used to defrost containers of frozen meals before they are placed in the oven; this has the effect of halving the reheating time. The temperature of the food is brought from −20°C to 3°C in approximately four hours, under safe conditions. Warming is kept at a steady controlled rate by a process of alternating low-volume heat with refrigeration.
- Combination ovens: These are suitable for large quantities of food.
- Microwave ovens: These are suitable only for small amounts of food.
- Dual-purpose ovens: These are microwave ovens that have a second heat source – for example, an infra-red grill – and a defrost control that switches the microwave power on and off.

Forced air convection ovens

These are suitable for large quantities of food.

Preparation

- Make sure that all preparation and cooking areas are clean and that the equipment is in working order.
- Never use previously frozen food.
- Avoid any delay between preparation and cooking.

Cooking

- Check on the cooking process for the food to ensure that it takes account of the overall effect on flavour, texture and nutritional value.
- Always use temperature probes to check that the centre of the food has reached a safe temperature before the final cooking is complete.

Portioning and packaging

- Make sure all areas are clean and hygienically safe.
- Ensure that all packaging is ready and that it is of the correct size and material.
- All reusable containers must be cleaned and sterilised thoroughly.
- Make sure that all assistants who portion and package wear food-handling gloves.
- Make sure that all general equipment used in this area is sterilised.
- Accurately portion the food according to the recipe.
- Do not pack the food to a depth greater than 5 cm (2 inches). For food that is to be microwaved the depth should be less.
- Portions must be controlled when filling in order to: standardise costs, control costs, facilitate stores control, assist in food service, standardise the thawing and reheating process, allow the sealing to be properly completed.
- Food containers must be sealed correctly before storage in order to: prevent spoilage due to contact with the cold air, prevent spillage prior to freezing, allow for safe stacking, helping to prevent damage to containers.
- Cover the food before blast freezing.
- Check and record the temperature of the food.

Labelling

- Label all food correctly.
- Ensure labels have the right information, which should include: production date, 'use by' date, name of dish, description of contents, storage life, number of portions, instructions for reheating/regenerating – including type of oven,

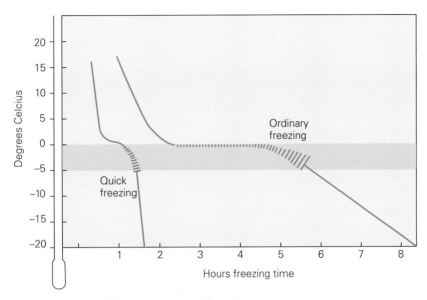

Figure 6.11 Speed of freezing and crystal formation

temperature, time, and whether lid should be on or off.

- Correct labelling will: accurately identify the contents of the container; enable quick and efficient stock-taking; indicate important information regarding the packaging, date and the 'use by' date; give information on the number of portions contained in the package.

Freezing

- Check all fast freezers are ready for use.
- Freezing should be done immediately after cooking.
- The foods must be frozen below −5°C within 90 minutes.
- There must be at least 2 cm air space between layers of containers in the freezer.
- Immediately after freezing the food must be transported to the deep-freeze storage.

Storing

- Store the food at the correct deep-freeze storage temperature of −20°C to −30°C and at least below −18°C.
- Monitor deep-freezer temperatures at all times and keep accurate records.
- Maintain the stock control rotation; keep all stock record systems up to date.
- Store the food in the accepted manner on shelves and racks above the floor, away from the door and with enough space around to allow the cold air to circulate.

- Always wear protective clothing when entering the deep-freeze store.
- Destroy any foods that have passed their 'use by' date.
- It is important to monitor and record food temperatures regularly in order to prevent contamination from incorrect storage conditions, and ensure flavour and texture is maintained.
- Stock rotation procedures must be followed in order to prevent damage or decay to stock, ensure that older stock is used before new stock.
- Storage areas must be secured from unauthorised access in order to prevent pilferage or damage by unauthorised persons, prevent injury to unauthorised persons, and prevent unnecessary opening of store doors, which would destabilise the temperature.

Distribution

- Maintain freezer temperatures during distribution.
- DHSS guidelines state that if the food is going to be regenerated within 24 hours, the permissible temperature range is between 0 and −18°C. Otherwise the temperature must be kept below −18°C.
- All documentation and control systems for checking delivery should be followed and implemented carefully.

Regeneration

- Check that the work area is ready for operation.

- Remove products from deep-freeze for regeneration; check the labels.
- Make sure equipment is at the correct temperature and in working order.
- Follow the regeneration instructions on the label.
- The foods must be reheated to at least 70°C but to 75–80°C immediately before service. Check temperature has been reached by using a sterilised calibrated temperature probe.
- Serve the food as soon as possible after regeneration.
- Food that has not been eaten within two hours should be thrown away. Food that has been allowed to cool must never be reheated.

General

- To avoid separated sauces, the recipe must be modified correctly using the appropriate starches.
- Meat and fish will taste rancid if badly prepared or kept for too long a storage period.
- Soggy, coated food will occur if the lid is not removed when regenerating.
- A backlog of food for freezing will occur with poor production planning.
- Freezer burn occurs due to badly packaged food or when food is stored for too long.
- Standards of personal hygiene and kitchen temperature are of paramount importance to maintain a clean and safe product.

Overall benefits of cook-chill/cook-freeze

To the employer:

- portion control and reduced waste
- no over-production
- central purchasing with bulk-buying discounts
- full utilisation of equipment
- full utilisation of staff time
- overall savings in staff
- savings on equipment, space and fuel
- fewer staff with better conditions – no unsociable hours, no weekend work, no overtime
- simplified, less frequent delivery to units
- solves problem of moving hot foods (EC regulations forbid the movement of hot foods unless the temperature is maintained over 65°C; maintaining 65°C is regarded as very difficult to achieve and high temperatures inevitably will be harmful to foods).

To the customer:

- increased variety and selection
- improved quality, with standards maintained
- more nutritious foods
- services can be maintained at all times, regardless of staff absences.

Advantages of cook-freeze over cook-chill

- Seasonal purchasing provides considerable savings.

- Delivery to units will be far less frequent.
- Long-term planning of production and menus becomes possible.
- Less dependence on price fluctuations.
- More suitable for vending machines incorporating microwave.

Advantages of cook-chill over cook-freeze

- Regeneration systems are simpler – infra-red and steam convection ovens are mostly used and only 12 minutes are required to reheat all foods perfectly.
- Thawing time is eliminated.
- Smaller capacity storage is required: three to four days' supply as opposed to up to 120 days'.
- Chiller storage is cheaper to install and run than freezer storage.
- Blast chillers are cheaper to install and run than blast freezers.
- Cooking techniques are unaltered (additives and revised recipes are needed for freezing).
- All foods can be chilled so the range of dishes is wider (some foods cannot be frozen). Cooked eggs, steaks and sauces such as hollandaise can be chilled (after some recipe modification where necessary).
- No system is too small to adapt to cook-chill.

Vacuum cooking (sous-vide)

This is a form of cook-chill, using a combination of vacuum sealing in plastic pouches, cooking by steam and then rapidly chilling in an ice-water bath, as this most effective way of chilling. The objective is to rationalise kitchen procedures without having a detrimental effect on the quality of the individual dishes.

To find out more, visit www.julabo-sous-vide.de.

The process

- Individual portions of prepared food are first placed in special plastic pouches. The food can be fish, poultry, meats, vegetables and so on, to which seasoning, a garnish, sauce, stock, wine, flavouring, vegetables, herbs and/or spices can be added.
- The pouches of food are then placed in a vacuum-packaging machine, which evacuates all the air and tightly seals the pouch.
- The pouches are next cooked by steam. This is usually in a special oven equipped with a steam control programme, which controls the injection of steam into the oven, to give steam cooking at an oven temperature below 100°C. Each food item has its own ideal cooking time and temperature.
- When cooked, the pouches are rapidly cooled down to 3°C, usually in an iced water chiller, or an air blast chiller for larger operations.
- The pouches are then labelled and stored in a holding refrigerator at an optimum temperature of 3°C.
- When required for service the pouches are regenerated in boiling water or a steam

combination oven until the required temperature is reached, then cut open and the food presented.

Vacuum pressures are as important as the cooking temperatures with regard to weight loss and heat absorption. The highest temperature used in sous-vide cooking is 100°C and 1000 millibars is the minimum amount of vacuum pressure used.

As there is no oxidation or discoloration involved, this method is ideal for conserving fruits, such as apples and pears (e.g. pears in red wine, fruits in syrup). When preparing meats in sauces the meat is pre-blanched then added to the completed sauce.

Sous-vide is a combination of vacuum sealing, tightly controlled en papillotte cooking and rapid chilling, which can be used by almost any type of catering operation.

Advantages

- Long shelf-life, up to 21 days, refrigerated.
- Ability to produce meals in advance means better deployment of staff and skills.
- Vacuum-packed foods can be mixed in cold store without risk of cross-contamination.
- Reduced labour costs at point of service.
- Beneficial cooking effects on certain foods, especially moulded items and pâtés. Reduces weight loss on meat joints.
- Full flavour and texture are retained as food cooks in its own juices.
- Economises on ingredients (less butter, marinade, etc.).
- Makes pre-cooking a possibility for à la carte menus.
- Inexpensive regeneration.
- Allows a small operation to set up bulk production.
- Facilitates portion control and uniformity of standards.
- Has a tenderising effect on tougher cuts of meat and matures game without dehydration.

Disadvantages

- Extra cost of vacuum pouches and vacuum-packing machine.
- Unsuitable for meats (e.g. fillet steak) and vegetables that absorb colour.
- All portions in a batch must be identically sized to ensure even results.
- Most dishes require twice the conventional cooking time.

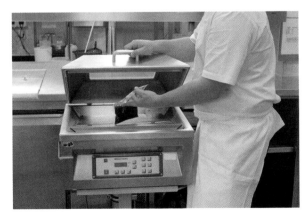

Figure 6.12 Vacuum packer

- Unsuitable for large joints as chilling time exceeds 90 minutes.
- Complete meals (meat and two vegetables) not feasible; meat component needs to be cooked and stored in separate bags.
- Extremely tight management and hygienic controls are imperative.
- Potentially adverse customer reaction ('boil-in-the-bag' syndrome).

Points to remember

- High standards of kitchen hygiene and personnel hygiene must be observed.
- Prime-quality ingredients should be used.
- All aspects of the Food Safety Act 1990/95 must be adhered to.
- Where possible, sous-vide should operate in a temperature-controlled environment.
- All the basic principles of cook-chill apply to sous-vide.

Centralised production

Why centralise?

Reasons for considering centralised production units are as follows.

- **Labour:** reduction of kitchen preparation staff in end units.
- **Food cost:** greater control over waste and portion sizes; competitive purchasing through bulk buying.
- **Equipment:** intensive central use of heavy equipment reduces commitment in individual units.
- **Product:** more control on product quality.
- **Labour strategy:** staff are employed at regular times (9 am to 5 pm), which can eliminate or lessen the difficulty of obtaining staff who will work shifts.

When considering a centralised production system it is essential that a detailed financial appraisal is produced and then looked at carefully, as each establishment has its own considerations. No general rule can be given as profitability depends on the product, the size of each unit, the number of units and the method of preserving food.

Design

Centralised production systems can be designed in two ways:

1 using existing catering (operations) unit and modifying, etc.
2 purpose-built.

Types of unit

Centralised production units are grouped into four types:

1 units preparing fresh cooked foods, which are then despatched
2 cook-freeze – food is partly prepared or cooked, then frozen and regenerated when required
3 cook-chill – food is cooked, then chilled and regenerated when required
4 sous-vide – food is sealed in a special casing, vacuum-sealed, cooked and chilled.

Food production and preparation

The profitability of the production system depends largely upon the content of the end-unit menus.

Meat

Careful purchasing is essential and the menu must be planned carefully.

- The cut of meat required must be clearly specified in order to produce the exact dishes.
- Strict portion control must be adhered to.
- Trimmings/by-products must be fully utilised: meat trimmings for cottage/shepherd's pie, bones for stock.

Vegetable preparation

Because of increasing labour costs and difficulty in obtaining staff, a number of establishments now purchase prepared potatoes, that are washed, peeled and in some cases shaped; prepared root vegetables; topped and tailed French beans; and ready-prepared salads.

Reception and delivery

It is desirable to have two loading bays: one for receiving and one for delivery. They should be adjacent to the relevant store to facilitate loading. The receiving bay should be adjacent to the prime goods store for purchased meat, vegetables, and so on, and the delivery bay near to the finished goods stores that contain items ready to go out to their end units.

Staff

Apart from a butcher, some of the staff may not be highly skilled. The various processes involved in meat production can be divided as follows and staff trained for each procedure.

- **Machine operators:** staff operating dicing machines, mincing machines, hamburger machines, to a strict procedure.
- **Trimmers:** staff who are taught to trim carcasses and prime cuts.
- **Packers:** pack goods into foil cans, operate vacuum-packing machines, and label or pack finished goods into containers; caterers will have to consider if it is economically viable to have a butchery or whether to buy in prepared meats (this very much depends upon the range of menu).

Frequently, staff who are employed to carry out specific functions within a centralised kitchen may not have catering qualifications but will be trained by the organisation.

Method of operation

There are two types of operation:

1 weekly production
2 daily total run.

Forecasts obtained from the end unit determine the quantity of the production run. This prepares items of a particular type on one occasion only. As soon as the run is completed the next run is then scheduled. The main advantage of this type of production is in the comparative ease with which a control system may be installed and operated.

A disadvantage is that, in the event of an error in production scheduling, it is wasteful and costly to organise a further production run of small volume. Another disadvantage is that the method leads to the building-up of stocks, both finished and unfinished, thereby affecting the profitability of the operation.

A daily total run is based upon the needs or items required by the end unit. A disadvantage is that the forecast gap is shorter, so the end units are not able to provide accurate requisitions.

Purchasing

Any organisation depending for its existence on the economics of bulk purchasing must pay particular attention to the process of buying.

The following are the main objectives of the buyer.

- Quality and price of goods must be equalled with the size of purchase order.
- All purchase specifications must be met.
- Buying practice must supplement a policy of minimum stock holding.

Transport

The distribution of goods, routing and the maintenance of vehicles are very important to a centralised production operation. The usual practice is for transport to be under the control of a senior manager, who also has the complicated job of batching up deliveries (normally weekly or bi-weekly). It is important that the senior manager has considerable administrative skill in order to prevent errors occurring.

Centralised production very often means that production is separated from the food service by distance, time, or both. An example is in hospital wards; here there are satellite kitchens or regeneration kitchens. Other examples exist in aircraft catering and banqueting. Banqueting houses that use cook-chill purchase from either their own production unit or an independent company.

Fast food

Fast food is characterised by a smooth operation. The principal control adopted is 'door time': $3\frac{1}{2}$ minutes is the control average, $1\frac{1}{2}$ minutes queuing and 1 minute serving. Capital costs are high for production equipment. The menu range is narrow, with the equipment often being specially developed to do one job. This is essentially one cell or family of related parts of one product.

Increases in volume required are met by increasing the speed of foods through the system. This is achieved by increasing labour and by duplicating the same cell. Workers are multi-functional but often of low skill. Staffing can be applied to a number of parts, depending on volume of throughput. This type of staffing can give high job satisfaction (although short term), similar to the rotation of chefs through the partie system.

This operation comes nearer to the continuous flow ideal and is often quoted as a classic just-in-time (JIT) system.

The principles of manufacturing exist in both fast-food and cook-chill systems. Other systems, such as cook-freeze and sous-vide, will take on a variety of cells relating to different parts of the meal. The fast-food system is primarily based upon one-cell systems. All systems use variations in the number of workers to control costs.

Small centralised operations

There are some very good examples of smaller centralised operations to be seen now in the catering industry. The purpose of installation is to provide ready-prepared goods that may be served to banquets or supplied to grills/coffee shops.

The preparation of the food takes place during the kitchen 'slack' period, principally after the luncheon service. The made-up items are put into polythene bags, which contain from one to six portions. The packed items are marked with the date of packing, and the name of the item, and then blast frozen prior to storage. They are kept in store from three to six months, and moved on a first-in, first-out basis. Some items have limited storage time so careful checking of dates is an important factor to consider. Refrigerators in the outlets are stocked up daily from the central code store.

When an item is ordered it is reheated by a simple boiling process operated by a timer. The cooked items are placed on the plate, with the garnish and vegetables being added separately. There are also, of course, many other refinements: carefully calculated production schedules and coloured photographs of the dishes to guide presentation, for example.

Ganymede dri-heat

This is a method of keeping foods either hot or cold. It is used in some hospitals as it ensures that the food that reaches the patients is in the same fresh condition as it was when it left the kitchens.

A metal disc or pellet is electrically heated or cooled, and placed in a special container under the plate. The container is designed to allow air to circulate round the pellet so that the food is maintained at the correct service temperature.

This is used in conjunction with conveyor belts and special service counters, and helps to provide a better and quicker food service.

Microsteam technology

Used for food production in hospitals and schools, microsteam is a fast, healthy cooking system, which maintains the freshness of food using steam cooking. It enables nutritious meals to be available in minutes without the need for full kitchen back-up.

It works with a broad range of raw ingredients, from fresh vegetables to chicken and seafood. The vacuum-packed polymer packaging allows cooking to near perfection, resulting in maximum flavour and minimal nutritional loss.

Microsteam is a unique value-control system that regulates the pressure throughout the cooking process. As soon as the pack goes into the microwave, energy waves create steam from the water in the raw ingredients, which gradually builds up in the container. The pack expands as it cooks, which is where the smart valve comes in – releasing the pressure gradually so that it stays at just the right level to cook the food perfectly. Each dish is ready in just a few minutes, with no preparation time involved.

The most important point about microsteaming is that it's not about reheating pre-cooked food: it's about cooking the freshest ingredients from raw – from chicken to couscous, fish to fresh vegetables. Steam cooking has long been recognised as one of the healthiest ways to prepare food, keeping nutritional loss to a minimum, and retaining much more vitamin C and chlorophyll than traditional or cook-chill methods.

The microsteam system is space saving. It reduces the need for bulky equipment. It allows kitchen systems to be simplified. If packages are kept sealed they will retain their heat at 75°C for 20 minutes.

With this system it is easier to manage the bulk production and cooking of fresh vegetables and other items for large-scale banqueting and industry events. The technology can also be used for vending machines, is suitable for people working off-peak hours, for airports, call centres, trains and any environment where it's difficult to have full kitchen back-up.

The scheme has been trialled by the NHS Better Hospital Food Programme, with favourable results – not just in terms of health benefits but also because it means patients and doctors are no longer restricted to set meal times.

The assembly kitchen concept

Research – quality – production – tradition – innovation. This is a system based on accepting and incorporating the latest technological developments in the manufacturing and conservation of food products. In the modern assembly kitchen, the chef does not automatically buy his or her ingredients. On the contrary, he will carefully choose from the 'five product types' (see the accompanying box) what is best for him or her by asking the following questions.

- Which fresh produce will I use?
- Which semi-prepared food bases will I use?
- Which finished products will I use?

The five product types

1 Fresh (raw product)
- meat with bones
- vegetables, potatoes, fruits, unpeeled
- whole fish
- milk

2 Shelf-stable
- sterilised, pasteurised – vegetables, potatoes, fruits; dairy products, meat products
- dehydrated products, partly elaborated – stocks, sauces; mousses, creams, custards; bouillons, soups, purées; culinary aids

3 Frozen
- meat, fish, vegetables, potatoes, fruits
- pastry products, ice cream

4 Chilled ('fresh' products, partly prepared)
- meat or fish, boned, cut into pieces or portioned
- washed, peeled and cut vegetables, potatoes, fruits, etc.

5 Chilled (products, normally cooked and packed or sous-vide)
- meat, fish, vegetables, desserts (with or without sauce)

The assembly kitchen still relies on skilled personnel. It requires a thorough understanding of how to switch over from the traditional labour-intensive production method to a more industrial type of production, with some of the principles of the cook-chill, cook-freeze or sous-vide production systems taken on board. It realises the existence and availability of modern kitchen equipment and new generations of high-quality convenience orientated food bases.

Thus, the concept includes:
- preparing the food component in an appropriate kitchen, respecting legislation
- arranging everything cold (even raw) on the plate
- regenerating (even cooking) on the same plate as served
- if necessary, serving the sauce.

Success requires:
- appropriate material and equipment
- very precise preliminary preparations (mise-en-place)
- support from a well-trained team (kitchen and service staff).
  Advantages include:
- fewer staff needed for arranging
- the regeneration can be done near the consumer

- different types of plate can be regenerated at the same time
- hygiene, and consequently safety, is guaranteed
- storage rooms needed for only five types of product (see above)
- large preparation areas disappear
- smaller equipment is needed.
  Inconveniences include:
- very hot plates
- some additional investments required (trolleys, etc.)
- some products cannot be prepared (French fries, etc.).

A planning schedule would envisage:
- 2 days   – cooking and chilling
              – storing at 3°C in labelled, dated gastronorm containers
- 12 hours   – arrange food on to plates
              – storage at 3°C on trolley
- 30 mins   – taking the trolley out of storage
              – setting of regeneration equipment
              – regeneration
- 2 mins   – taking out and finishing of plates
              – sauce, garnish
              – serving
              – cleaning of equipment.

The principal investments will be for:
- multi-purpose equipment, covering most of the cooking methods
- storage for dry, chilled, frozen products
- equipment to chill or freeze
- equipment to regenerate on plates, gastronorm pans.

The new-generation equipment must be:
- easy to handle
- gastronorm
- easy to clean
- easy to service.

References

The following sources were used as the basis for this chapter.

Food Standards Agency publications: *Safer Food Better Business* (England); *Safe Catering* (Northern Ireland); *CookSafe* (Scotland).
Visit www.food.gov.uk for advice and information.

Topics for discussion

1 The advantages and disadvantages of the cook-chill and cook-freeze systems.
2 Essential hygiene and food safety requirements for cook-chill and cook-freeze systems.
3 The reason for quality control, temperature control and microbiological control when producing cook-chill and cook-freeze foods.
4 Types of operation suitable for using cook-chill and cook-freeze foods.
5 For and against a centralised production system, with examples.
6 The food production system and its main advantages.
7 Discuss the importance of detailed specifications and traceability for cook-freeze and cook-chill products.

Menu planning, development and structure

Supporting material available on Dynamic Learning Online:

> Knowledge quizzes

> Activity worksheets: menu planning

> Summary presentations

DYNAMIC LEARNING

Evolution

Initially, menus were lists of food, in seemingly random fashion with the food being raw, prepared or cooked. Individual menus came into use early in the nineteenth century, and courses began to be formulated. For special occasions seven or so courses might be served, e.g. hors d'oeuvre, soup, fish, entrée, sorbet, roast, sweet, savoury.

With the formulation of menus, artistry and flair began to influence the various ways of cooking, and dishes were created after 'the style of' (e.g. à la Française) and/or given the names of important people for whom they had been created (e.g. peach Melba, a simple dish of poached fresh peach, vanilla ice cream and fresh raspberry purée created by Escoffier at the Savoy for Dame Nellie Melba, the famous opera singer).

As the twentieth century advanced, and people moved and settled around the world more, so began the introduction of styles of food and service from a wide variety of nations, resulting in the number of ethnic dishes and ethnic restaurants that abound today.

Eating at work, at school, in hospitals and institutions led to a need for healthy, budget-conscious food.

Rapid air transport made it possible for foods from all corners of the globe to be available which in the UK, together with domestic and European produce, gives those who compose menus a tremendous range of choice.

Essential considerations prior to planning a menu

- **Competition:** be aware of any competition in the locality, including prices and quality. It may be wiser to produce a menu that is quite different.
- **Location:** study the area in which your establishment is situated and the potential target market of customers.
- **Analyse:** the type of people you are planning to cater for (e.g. office workers in the city requiring quick service).
- **Outdoor catering:** are there opportunities for outdoor catering or takeaway food?
- **Estimated customer spend per head:** important when catering, for example, for hospital staff and patients, children in schools, workers in industry. Whatever level of catering, a golden rule should be 'offer value for money'.
- **Modern trends in food fashions:** these should be considered alongside popular traditional dishes.
- Decide the **range of dishes** to be offered and the **pricing structure**. Price each dish separately? Or offer set two- or three-course menus? Or a combination of both?
- **Space and equipment in the kitchens** will influence the composition of the menu (e.g. avoiding overloading of deep-frying pan, salamanders and steamers).
- **Number and capability of staff:** overstretched staff can easily reduce the standard of production envisaged.
- **Availability of supplies and reliability of suppliers:** seasonal foods and storage space.
- **Food allergies** (see page 135).
- **Cost factor:** crucial if an establishment is to be profitable. Costing is essential for the success of compiling any menu. Modern computer techniques can analyse costs swiftly and on a daily basis.

Types of menu

The main types of menu in use are as follows.

- **Table d'hôte or set-price menu:** a menu forming a meal, usually of two or three courses at a set price. A choice of dishes may be offered at all courses.
- **À la carte:** a menu with all the dishes individually priced. Customers can therefore compile their own menu, which may be one, two or more courses. A true à la carte dish should be cooked to order and the customer should be prepared to wait.
- **Special party or function menus:** menus for banquets or functions of all kinds.
- **Ethnic or speciality menus:** these can be set-price menus or with dishes individually priced, specialising in the food (or religion) of a particular country or in a specialised food itself – e.g. ethnic (Chinese, Indian, kosher, African-Caribbean, Greek), speciality (steak, fish, pasta, vegetarian, pancakes).
- **Hospital menus:** these usually take the form of a menu card given to the patient the day before service so that his or her preferences can be ticked. Both National Health Service and private hospitals cater for vegetarians and also for religious requirements.
- **Menus for people at work:** such menus vary in standard and extent from one employer to another due to company policy on the welfare of their staff and workforce. There may also be a call-order à la carte selection charged at a higher price. The food will usually be mainly British with some ethnic and vegetarian dishes. Menus may consist of soup, main course with vegetables, followed by sweets, cheese and yoghurts. According to the policy of the management and employee requirements, there will very often be a salad bar and healthy-eating dishes included on the menu. When there is a captive clientele who face the same surroundings daily and meet the same people, then no matter how long the menu cycle or how pleasant the people, or how nice the decor, boredom is bound to set in and staff then long for a change of scene. So, a chef or manager needs to vary the menu constantly to encourage customers to patronise the establishment rather than going off the premises to eat. The decor and layout of the staff restaurant plays a very important part in satisfying the customer's needs. The facilities should be relaxing and comfortable so that he or she feels that the restaurant is not a continuation of the workplace. Employees who are

happy, well nourished and know that the company has their interests and welfare at heart will tend to be well motivated and work better.

- **Menus for children:** in schools there is an emphasis on healthy eating and a balanced diet, particularly in boarding schools. Those areas with children of various cultural and religious backgrounds have appropriate items available on the menu. Many establishments provide special children's menus that concentrate on favourite foods and offer suitably sized portions.

Cyclical menus

These are menus that are compiled to cover a given period of time: one month, three months, etc. They consist of a number of set menus for a particular establishment, such as an industrial catering restaurant, cafeteria, canteen, directors' dining room, hospital or college refectory. At the end of each period the menus can be used again, thus overcoming the need to keep compiling new ones. The length of the cycle is determined by management policy, by the time of the year and by the different foods available. These menus must be monitored carefully to take account of changes in customer requirements and any variations in weather conditions that are likely to affect demand for certain dishes. If cyclical menus are designed to remain in operation for long periods of time, then they must be carefully compiled so that they do not have to be changed too drastically during operation.

Advantages

- Cyclical menus save time by removing the daily or weekly task of compiling menus, although they may require slight alterations for the next period.
- When used in association with cook-freeze operations, it is possible to produce the entire number of portions of each item to last the whole cycle, having determined that the standardised recipes are correct.
- They give greater efficiency in time and labour.

- They can cut down on the number of commodities held in stock, and can assist in planning storage requirements.

Disadvantages

- When used in establishments with a captive clientele, the cycle has to be long enough so that customers do not get bored with the repetition of dishes.
- The caterer cannot easily take advantage of 'good buys' offered by suppliers on a daily or weekly basis, unless such items are required for the cyclical menu.

Pre-planned and pre-designed menus

Advantages

- Pre-planned or pre-designed menus enable the caterer to ensure that good menu planning is practised.
- Before selecting the dishes that he or she prefers, the caterer should consider what the customer likes, and the effect of these dishes upon the meal as a whole.
- Menus that are planned and costed in advance allow banqueting managers to quote prices instantly to a customer.
- Menus can be planned to take into account the availability of kitchen and service equipment, without placing unnecessary strain upon such equipment.
- The quality of food is likely to be higher if kitchen staff are preparing dishes they are familiar with and have prepared a number of times before.

Disadvantages

- Pre-planned and pre-designed menus may be too limited to appeal to a wide range of customers.
- They may reduce job satisfaction for staff who have to prepare the same menus repetitively.
- They may limit the chef's creativity and originality.

The structure of menus

Length

The number of dishes on a menu should offer the customer an interesting and varied choice. In general, it is better to offer fewer dishes of good standard than a long list of mediocre quality.

Design

This should complement the image of the dining room and be designed to allow for changes (total or partial), which may be daily, weekly, monthly, etc. An inset for dishes of the day or of the week gives the customer added interest.

Language

Accuracy in dish description helps the customer to identify the food they wish to choose. Avoid over-elaboration and flowery choice of words. Wherever possible, use English language. If a foreign dish name is used then follow it with a simple, clear English version.

Presentation

Ensure the menu is presented in a sensible and welcoming way so that the customer is put at ease and relaxed. An offhand, brusque presentation (written or oral) can be off-putting and lower expectations of the meal.

Planning

Consider the following:

- type and size of establishment – pub, school, hospital, restaurant, etc.
- customer profile – different kinds of people have differing likes and dislikes
- special requirements – kosher, Muslim, vegetarian
- time of the year – certain dishes acceptable in summer may not be so in winter
- foods in season – are usually in good supply and reasonable in price
- special days – Christmas, Hogmanay, Shrove Tuesday, Eid, Chinese New Year, etc.
- time of day – breakfast, brunch, lunch, tea, high tea, dinner, supper, snack, special function
- price range – charge a fair price and ensure good value for money; customer satisfaction can lead to recommendation and repeat business
- number of courses
- sequence of courses
- use menu language that customers understand
- sensible nutritional balance
- no unnecessary repetition of ingredients from dish to dish
- no unnecessary repetition of flavours and colours
- be aware of the Trade Descriptions Act 1968 (see below) – 'Any person who in the course of a trade or business: applies a false trade description to any goods or supplies or offers to supply any goods to which a false trade description is applied shall be guilty of an offence'
- be aware of food allergies – provide useful information on the menu, and make sure staff are informed about the ingredients of each dish.

Menu policy: summary

- Provide a means of communication.
- Establish the essential and social needs of the customer.
- Accurately predict what the customer is likely to buy and how much he or she is going to spend.
- Purchase and prepare raw materials to pre-set standards in accordance with predictions and purchasing specifications.
- Skilfully portion and cost the product in order to keep within company profitability policy.
- Effectively control the complete operation from purchase to service on the plate.
- Customer satisfaction is all-important: remember who pays the bill.

Profitable menus

How chefs can make menus more profitable

Chefs must know the market and their customers. They must research the market for the best quality and the best price. Do not rule out part-prepared and fully prepared products – it is about creating a menu that appeals to customers at a price they are prepared to pay and that will give a good return. The right combination will vary from restaurant to restaurant, operation to operation, depending on the following.

- **Style of operation:** a fine-dining restaurant will use little in the way of convenience foods. Fine dining is often marked by skill in the variety of cooking, whereas a less skilled operation will very often use a high proportion of ready-prepared foods; this ensures a constant delivery of standards.
- **Volume:** where a chef is preparing for large numbers and with staff with limited skills, there is often a reliance on pre-prepared and fully prepared food.
- **Type of customer:** the market for food prepared fully from new materials is small – for the mass market, expectations are driven by the different situations in which they find themselves. Those dining at their place of work are not necessarily concerned if all the food is not prepared on site. However, when they are dining out for a special occasion they will probably expect something quite different.
- **Price:** customers have a sense of what they are willing to pay. This often depends on the occasion and the type of operation. For example, some people are prepared to spend more on a celebration dinner than a casual meal at the local

gastropub. The price must cover the costs of food and be calculated to take into account all the other variable and fixed costs.

- **Staff skills:** profitability will also depend on how you balance the level of skill in the kitchen, and the use of pre-prepared and fully prepared products.
- **Facilities – kitchen design:** where kitchens are

on the small size for the number of customers to be served, there may be very little space to prepare food from new materials. Therefore there may be much more of a reliance on pre-prepared and fully prepared foods. Likewise there will not be such a need for highly skilled staff requiring such high salaries.

Consumer protection

There is a comprehensive set of legislation concerned with protecting the consumer. This can be divided into that which is concerned with health and safety, economic protection such as weights and measures, and others that deal with unfair contract terms. Fundamentally, however, all consumer protection starts with the basic contract. If a supplier fails to supply what a consumer has contracted to purchase, the supplier may be in breach of contract. However, because breach of contract cases can be difficult to prove and expensive, the government over the years has introduced legislation to improve protection for the consumer.

The main consumer protection acts

Price Marking (Food and Drink on Premises) Order 1979

The wording and pricing of food and drink on menus and wine lists must comply with the law and be accurate. However, by offering dishes on the menu there is no legal obligation to serve the customer if he or she may cause a nuisance to other customers or because, due to demand, the dish has sold out and is 'off' the menu. But for establishments providing accommodation there is an obligation to provide refreshment providing the customer is able to pay and is in an acceptable state (e.g. sober).

Trade Descriptions Act 1968/1972

This act makes it a criminal offence to falsely describe goods or services, or to supply or offer for sale any goods or services to which a false description applies. It is also an offence to make reckless statements (i.e. statements without the knowledge to support the claims made about the goods or services). Examples of offences include describing pork as veal or frozen foods as fresh.

There are also offences under the Food and Safety Act 1990.

Sale of Goods and Services Act 1982

This act aims to ensure that goods sold are of satisfactory quality and fit for the purpose intended. This would especially apply to equipment as well as commodities. It applies to the *sale* of goods and services only. From the caterer's viewpoint this act works mainly to his or her advantage, whereas the Supply of Goods and Services Act 1982 (see below) works mainly to the customer's advantage. In essence, the act is concerned with ensuring that customers receive goods that are of satisfactory quality and are fit for the purpose.

Goods may be defined as of satisfactory quality 'if they are as fit for the purpose or purposes for which goods of that kind are commonly bought as it is reasonable to expect having regard to any description applied to them, the price (if relevant) and all the other circumstances'.

In addition to goods being of satisfactory quality they must also be fit for the purpose. This means that, if a purchaser makes known a specific purpose for their goods, then the goods should be able to satisfy that purpose.

Supply of Goods and Services Act 1982

This act is concerned with 'implied' terms in a contract.

Sale and Supply of Goods Act 1994

This is an amending act that mainly amends the Sale of Goods Act 1979.

Consumer Protection Act 1987

This act deals with three main areas: liability for defective products; consumer safety; misleading price indications. It contains recommendations in the form of a code of practice regarding a service charge. This should be incorporated in the inclusive price where practicable and indicated (e.g. 'price includes service'). Non-optional charges (e.g. cover charges or minimum charges) should be prominently displayed.

Code of Practice on Price Indications

The Code of Practice for Traders on Price Indication contains recommendations on service, cover and minimum charges in hotels, restaurants and similar establishments. It states:

> If your customers in hotels, restaurants or similar places must pay a non-optional charge e.g. a 'service charge':
>
> 1 incorporate the charge within the fully inclusive prices wherever practicable
> 2 display the fact clearly on any price list or priced menu whether displayed inside or outside (e.g. by using statements like 'all prices include service').

Do not include suggested optional sums, whether for service or any other item, in the bill presented to the customer.

The code concedes that it is not practical to include some non-optional extra charges – for example, cover charges or minimum charges – in a quoted price. In these cases the charge should be shown as prominently as other prices on any list or menu, whether displayed inside or outside.

Data Protection Act 1998

This act imposes specific duties on data users, and gives certain rights to individuals including employees on whom personal data is held. Subject to limited exceptions, data users must be registered with the Data Protection Registrar. The Registrar is empowered to refuse applications for registration if he/she has reason to believe data users will not abide by the data protection principles. In such circumstances enforcement notices, deregistration notices and transfer prohibition notices may be enforced.

Data protection principles

The data protection principles referred to above are as follows.

- The information to be contained in personal data shall be obtained and personal data shall be processed fairly and lawfully.
- Personal data shall be held only for one or more specified and lawful purposes.
- Personal data held for any purpose or purposes shall not be used or disclosed in any manner incompatible with that purpose or those purposes.
- Personal data held for any purpose or purposes shall be adequate, relevant and not excessive in relation to that purpose or those purposes.
- Personal data shall be accurate and, where necessary, kept up to date.
- Personal data held for any purposes shall not be kept for longer than is necessary for that purpose or those purposes.
- An individual shall be entitled at reasonable intervals and without undue delay or expense:
  - to be informed by any data user whether he holds personal data of which that individual is the subject
  - to access any such data held by a data user, and
  - where appropriate, to have such data corrected or erased.
- Appropriate security measures shall be taken against unauthorised access to or alteration, disclosure or destruction of personal data, and against their accidental loss.

Menu copy

Items or groups of items should bear names people recognise and understand. If a name does not give the right description, additional copy may be necessary. Descriptions can be produced carefully, helping to promote the dish and the menu. However, the description should describe the item realistically and not mislead the customer. Creating interesting descriptive copy is a skill; a good menu designer is able to illuminate menu terms and specific culinary terms, and in doing so is able to draw attention to them. Simplicity creates better understanding and endorses the communication process.

Some menus can be built around general descrip-tive copy featuring the history of the establishment or the local area in which the establishment is located. Descriptive copy can alternatively be based on a speciality dish that has significant cultural importance to the area or the establishment. In doing so the description may wish to feature the person responsible for creating and preparing the dish, especially if the chef is reasonably well known and has appeared on national or local television or radio. The chef may also have had his/her recipes featured in the local press. This too may be included in the menu to further create interest.

Menu copy should be set in a style of print that is

easily legible and well spaced. Mixing typefaces is often done to achieve emphasis; if overdone, however, the overall concept is likely to look a mess and therefore unattractive to the eye.

Emphasis may easily be achieved by using boxes on the menu. Also the paper used and the colour of the print can be chosen with care to make certain dishes stand out.

Some common mistakes in menu copy are:

- Descriptive copy is left out when it is required (confusing to the customer).
- The wrong emphasis is given.
- Emphasis is lost because print size and style are not correctly used.
- The menu lacks creativity (boring).
- The menu is designed for the wrong market.
- Much-needed information is omitted.
- Pricing is unclear.
- The menu sequence is wrong.
- Customers do not see valuable copy because added sheets such as 'dish of the day' or 'today's specials' cover up other parts of the menu, or obscure essential information.

Menu cover

The cover of the menu should reflect the identity or decor of the operation, and should ideally pick up the theme of the restaurant. A theme can be effective in creating the right image of the restaurant. The cover design must therefore reflect this overall image. The paper chosen must be of good quality, heavy, durable and grease-resistant.

Accurate food descriptions

In terms of the provision of accurate information on menus, it is important to be aware of the sort of problems that may be encountered with food descriptions. Some examples are listed below.

- **Scampi:** refers to products made from complete scampi. When using products which are made from pure scampi but using off-cuts of scampi, the products must be advertised as 'reformed scampi', as they are not of the same high quality.
- **King prawn:** king prawns can be called king prawns only where the prawns are of one of three specific species of prawn and are of the correct size.
- **Tiger prawn:** tiger prawns can be called tiger prawns only when they are of this species.
- **Chicken fillet and breast:** this term can be used only where the chicken is chicken flesh not chopped, shaped and reformed.
- **Smoked:** this means that the food must have been through a smoking process. If smoke flavour is used, it must state 'smoke flavoured'.
- **Fresh:** 'fresh' can be used only for fresh food, not canned or frozen.
- **Vegetarian dishes:** can be labelled vegetarian only when they have been produced without any contact or contamination with meat, fish or shellfish.

Menu flexibility

In times of inflation and recession, when prices rise or the amount of disposable income decreases, customer demands change and therefore menus become outdated and obsolete.

Some operations use the menu of the day on a wall board or chalk board to provide flexibility in items offered and pricing. This custom started in Paris. A neatly written wall board told customers as they entered the restaurant what was on offer that day. Some establishments change part of their menus daily or weekly, while the main core of the menu remains the same. Changes can be made on a paper insert and this can be added to the printed menu. Hors d'oeuvre, side dishes, salads, desserts and beverages do not change frequently; these dishes are printed on the main copy, while the speciality dishes, which do change more frequently, are placed on the paper insert.

Nothing becomes obsolete faster to the regular customer than the same menu. Menu fatigue sets in and you begin to lose customers. Even fast-food establishments, which have a basic menu on offer year in year out, still have to create interest by adding certain new products or new recipes to existing products in order to keep interest alive. Menus should change at least every three months.

Menu engineering

One approach to sales analysis that has gained some popularity is 'menu engineering'. This is a technique of menu analysis that uses two key factors of performance in the sales of individual menu items: the popularity and the gross profit contribution of each item. The analysis results in each menu item being assigned to one of four categories (see Figure 7.1).

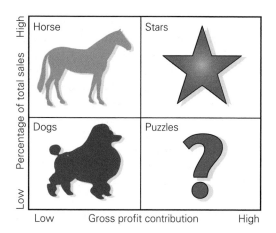

Figure 7.1 Menu engineering matrix (based on Kasavana and Smith, 1982)

1 Items of high popularity and high cash gross profit contributions. These are known as **Stars**.
2 Items of high popularity but with low cash gross profit contribution. These are known as **Plough horses**.
3 Items of low popularity but with high cash gross profit contributions. These are known as **Puzzles**.
4 Items of low popularity and low cash gross profit contribution. These are the worst items on the menu, and are known as **Dogs**.

Chefs and food and beverage managers operating in a competitive environment require a knowledge of menu engineering in order to maximise business potential. The advantage of this approach is that it provides a simple way of graphically indicating the relative cash contribution position of individual items on a matrix, as in Figure 7.1.

There is a variety of computer-based packages that will automatically generate the categorisation, usually directly using data from electronic point of sale (EPOS) control systems. The basis for the calculations is as follows.

In order to determine the position of an item on the matrix, two things need to be calculated. These are:

1 the cash gross profit
2 the sales percentage category.

The cash gross profit category for any menu item is calculated by reference to the weighted average cash gross profit. Menu items with a cash gross profit that is the same as or higher than the average are classified as high. Those with lower than the average are classified as low cash gross profit items. The average also provides the axis separating Plough horses and Dogs from Stars and Puzzles.

The sales percentage category for an item is determined in relation to the menu average, taking into account an additional factor. With a menu consisting of ten items one might expect, all other things being equal, that each item would account for 10 per cent of the menu mix. Any item that reached at least 10 per cent of the total menu items sold would therefore be classified as enjoying high popularity. Similarly, any item that did not achieve the rightful share of 10 per cent would be categorised as having a low popularity. With this approach, half the menu items would tend to be shown as being below average in terms of their popularity. This would potentially result in frequent revision of the composition of the menu. It is for this reason that Kasavana and Smith (1982) have recommended the use of a 70 per cent formula. Under this approach, all items that reach at least 70 per cent of their rightful share of the menu mix are categorised as enjoying high popularity. For example, where a menu consists of, say, 20 items, any item that reached 3.5 per cent or more of the menu mix (70 per cent of 5 per cent) would be regarded as enjoying high popularity. While there is no convincing theoretical support for choosing the 70 per cent figure rather than some other percentage, common sense and experience tend to suggest that there is some merit in this approach.

Interpreting the categories

There is a different basic strategy that can be considered for items that fall into each of the four categories of the matrix.

- **Stars:** these are the most popular items, which may be able to yield even higher gross profit contributions by careful price increases or through cost reduction. High visibility is maintained on the menu, and standards for these dishes should be strictly controlled.
- **Plough horses:** these, again, are solid sellers, which may also be able to yield greater cash profit contributions through marginal cost reduction. Lower menu visibility than Stars is usually recommended.
- **Puzzles:** these are exactly that – puzzles. Items such as flambé dishes or a particular speciality can add an attraction in terms of drawing customers, even though the sales of these items may be low. Depending on the particular item, different strategies might be considered, ranging from accepting the current position because of the added attraction that they provide, to increasing the price further.
- **Dogs:** these are the worst items on a menu

and the first reaction is to remove them. An alternative, however, is to consider adding them to another item as part of a special deal. For instance, adding them in a meal package to a Star may have the effect of lifting the sales of the Dog item and may provide a relatively low-cost way of adding special promotions to the menu.

The menu engineering methodology is designed to categorise dishes into good and poor performers. For dishes with high popularity and high contribution (Stars):

- do nothing
- modify price slightly – up or down
- promote through personal selling or menu positioning.

For dishes with high popularity and low contribution (Plough horses):

- do nothing
- increase price
- reduce dish cost – modify recipe by using cheaper commodities or reducing the portion size.

For dishes with low popularity and high contributions (Puzzles):

- do nothing
- reduce price
- rename dish
- reposition dish on menu
- promote through personal selling
- remove from menu.

For dishes with low popularity and low contribution (Dogs):

- do nothing
- replace dish
- redesign dish
- remove dish from menu.

Some potential limitations

- **Elasticity of demand:*** one of the practical difficulties with price-level adjustment is not knowing enough about the elasticity of demand. The effect of demand (number of covers) of any one change in the general level of menu prices is usually uncertain. Also, what applies to one menu item applies equally to the menu as a whole. There is an additional problem of cross-elasticity of demand, where the change in demand for one commodity is directly affected by a change in the price of another. Even less is known about the cross-elasticity of demand for individual menu items than is known about the elasticity of demand for the menu as a whole. Any benefit arising from an adjustment in the price of one item may therefore be offset by resultant changes in the demand for another item. Price-level adjustments must therefore be underpinned by a good deal of common sense, experience and knowledge of the particular circumstances of the operation.
- **Labour intensity:** in menu engineering the most critical element is cash gross profit. While this may be important, the aspect of labour intensity cannot be ignored. The cash gross profit on a flambé dish, for example, may be higher than on a more simple sweet; however, when the costs of labour are taken into account – especially at peak periods – it may well be that the more simple sweet is the more profitable overall.
- **Shelf-life:** the food cost of an item used to determine the cash gross profit may not take account of cost increases that are the result of food wastage through spoilage, especially at slack times.
- **Fluctuations in demand:** another factor is the consistency of the buying of the consumer. The approach assumes that changes can be made to promote various items and that this will be reflected in the buying behaviour of the customer. The approach will work well where the potential buying pattern of the consumer is fairly similar over long periods. However, where customers are continually changing, as for instance in the restaurant of a hotel, popularity and profitability can be affected more by changes in the nature of the customer and the resultant change in demand than as a result of the operation's attempting to manipulate the sales mix.

* Price elasticity of demand: this concept is explained on page 244.

Examples of different menus

Fruit Juice – Orange, Grapefruit or Tomato
Fresh Grapefruit or Orange Segments

Stewed Fruits – Prunes, Figs or Apricots

Fresh Fruit Selection, Fresh Fruit Salad

Yoghurts

Choice of Cereals, Porridge or Mix your own Muesli

Baker's Selection

Croissant, White and Wholemeal Rolls, Continental
Pastry

Your choice of White or Brown Toast

Marmalade, Preserve, Honey, Country Butter or Flora
Margarine

Assorted Cold Meats and Cheese

English Breakfast Tea with Milk or Lemon

Coffee – Freshly Brewed or Decaffeinated
with Milk or Cream

Hot Chocolate, Cold Milk

Chilled Ashbourne Water

Figure 7.2 Sample continental breakfast menu

À LA CARTE

FRUITS & JUICES

Fresh Orange or Grapefruit Juice £.... Large £....

Pineapple, Tomato or Prune Juice £.... Large £....

Chilled Melon £.... Stewed Prunes £.... Half
Grapefruit £....

Stewed Figs £.... Fresh fruit in Season £....

BREAKFAST FAVOURITES

Porridge or Cereal £....

Eggs, any style: One £..... Two £....

Ham, Bacon, Chipolata Sausages or Grilled Tomato £....

Omelette, Plain £.... with Ham or Cheese £....

Grilled Gammon Ham £.... Breakfast Sirloin Steak £....

A Pair of Kippers £.... Smoked Haddock with a Poached
Egg £....

Pancakes with Maple Syrup £....

FROM OUR BAKERY

Croissants or Breakfast Rolls £.... Brioche £....

Assorted Danish Pastries £.... Toast £....

BEVERAGES

Tea, Coffee, Sanka, Chocolate or Milk £....

Service Charge 15%

Figure 7.3 Sample English à la carte breakfast menu

Breakfast menu

Breakfast menus can be compiled from the following foods and can be offered as continental, table d'hôte, à la carte or buffet. For buffet service customers can self-serve the main items they require with assistance from counter hands. Ideally, eggs should be freshly cooked to order.

- Fruits, fruit juices, stewed fruit, yoghurts, cereals: porridge, etc.
- Eggs: fried, boiled, poached, scrambled; omelettes with bacon or tomatoes, mushrooms or sauté potatoes.
- Fish: kippers, smoked haddock, kedgeree.
- Meats (hot): fried or grilled bacon, sausages, kidneys, with tomatoes, mushrooms or sauté potatoes, potato cakes.
- Meats (cold): ham, bacon, pressed beef with sauté potatoes.
- Preserves: marmalade (orange, lemon, grapefruit, ginger), jams, honey.
- Beverages: tea, coffee, chocolate.
- Bread: rolls, croissants, brioche, toast, pancakes, waffles.

Points to consider when compiling a breakfast menu

- It is usual to offer three of the courses previously mentioned: fruit, yoghurt or cereals; fish, eggs or meat; preserves, bread, coffee or tea.
- As large a choice as possible should be offered, depending on the size of the establishment, bearing in mind that it is better to offer a smaller number of well-prepared dishes than a large number of hurriedly prepared ones.
- A choice of plain foods, such as boiled eggs or poached haddock, should be available for the person who may not require a fried breakfast.

Buffet breakfast – offers a choice of as many breakfast foods as is both practical and economic. Can be planned on a self-service basis or part self-service and assisted service (e.g. hot drinks and freshly cooked eggs).

Luncheon and dinner menus

Types of menu

- A set-price one-, two- or three-course menu with ideally a choice at each course.
- A list of well-varied dishes, each priced individually so that the customer can make up his/her own menu of whatever number of dishes they require.
- Buffet, which may be all cold or hot dishes, or a combination of both, either to be served or

	MONDAY	TUESDAY	WEDNESDAY	THURSDAY	FRIDAY
Soup of the day	Mushroom and chive (V) (L)	Roasted pepper (V) (L)	Parsnip and apple (V) (L)	Chilli and sweet potato (V) (L)	Leek and potato (V) (L)
Main meal 1	Aromatic chicken korma served with rice and poppadom (H)	Toad in the hole accompanied with onion gravy (H)	Roast turkey with bread sauce and cranberry (M)	Poached lemon and bay leaf chicken breast (L)	Breaded hake with chips and lemon (H)
Main meal 2	Boiled ham on the bone with a creamy parsley velouté (M)	Jambalaya with chorizo, prawns, rice and sweet peppers (M)	Beef and hoi sin with green peppers and noodles (M)	Pan-fried lambs' livers with redcurrant jus (M)	Hot chilli con carne with rice and sour cream (H)
Vegetarian meal	Vegetarian cottage pie with garden vegetables and a crusted potato topping (M)	Pesto roasted vegetables with chick pea couscous (M) (N)	Lightly spiced bean and tomato bruschetta (M)	Vegetable balti with coriander, cumin, mango and turmeric (M)	Sweet potato and mushroom pavé with tomato chutney (M)
Potatoes and vegetables	Rice or baby jackets Green bean Provençale	Mashed potato Sauté courgettes	Roast potatoes Vichy carrots	Parmentier potatoes Buttered cabbage	Chips or new potatoes Mushy peas
Hot dessert	Bread and butter pudding with custard sauce (H)	Banana sponge with toffee sauce (H)	Apple and cinnamon crumble with custard sauce (H)	Pineapple upside down cake with custard sauce (H)	Orange sponge with chocolate sauce (H)

Some of our foods may contain GM soya or maize; please ask our staff for details. N =Contains Nuts, L =low fat content, M =medium fat content, H =high fat content, V =vegetarian

Figure 7.4 Luncheon menu: staff restaurant

organised on a self-service basis. Depending on the time of year and location, barbecue dishes can be considered.

- Special party, which may be either: set menu with no choice; set menu with a limited choice, such as soup or melon, main course, choice of two sweets; served or self-service buffet.

Only offer the number of courses and number of dishes within each course that can be satisfactorily prepared, cooked and served.

A vegetarian menu may be offered as an alternative to or as part of the à la carte or table d'hôte menus (see Figure 7.7 for an example).

Tea menus

These vary considerably, depending on the type of establishment, and could include, for example:

- assorted sandwiches
- bread and butter (white, brown, fruit loaf)
- assorted jams
- scones with clotted cream, pastries, gâteaux

- tea (Indian, China, iced, fruit, herb).

The commercial hotels, tea rooms, public restaurants and staff dining rooms may offer simple snacks, cooked meals and high teas. For example:

- assorted sandwiches
- buttered buns, scones, cakes Scotch pancakes, waffles, sausage rolls, assorted bread and butter, various jams, toasted teacakes, scones, crumpets, buns
- eggs (boiled, poached, fried, omelettes)
- fried fish, grilled meats, roast poultry
- cold meats and salads
- assorted pastries, gâteaux
- various ices, coupes, sundaes
- tea, orange and lemon squash.

Light buffets (including cocktail parties)

Light buffets can include:

- hot savoury pastry patties of, for example, lobster, chicken, crab, salmon, mushrooms, ham

LUNCH

Galvin

Bistrot de Luxe

Entrées

Steak tartare

Soupe de poissons, rouille & croûtons

Salad of endive with Roquefort, chives & walnuts

Matjes Harengs marines, pommes à l'huile

Oak smoked salmon, fromage blanc & blini

Salad of Dorset crab, apple dressing

Half dozen Fines de Claire oysters

Salad of buffalo mozzarella & caponata

Escargots bourguignon

Parfait of foie gras & duck liver

Rillette of black boar

Plats Principles

Grilled Crottin de Chavignol, morels, peas & asparagus

Confit of organic salmon, Bayonne ham, beurre de tomate

Roast tranche of cod, crushed Jersey Royals, étuvée of leeks

Pot roast Landaise chicken, tagliatelle of asparagus & morels

Grilled calf's liver, shallots aigre-doux, lardoons & flat leaf parsley

Roast pork fillet, Bayonne ham, black pudding & caramelised apples

Roast rump of lamb, broad bean risotto

Braised veal's cheek, fresh pasta, baby spinach & Madeira sauce

Tête de Veau, sauce Ravigote

Desserts

Oeuf à la neige

Délice of milk and dark Valhrona chocolate

Crème brûlée, coconut mousseline

Gariguette strawberries, crème Chantilly

Apricot & chocolate soufflé

Prune & Armagnac parfait

Baba au rhum

Tarte au citron

Assiette de fromages with walnut & raisin loaf

Menu Prix Fixé

Gravadlax of organic salmon or velouté of broad beans

Grilled sea trout, petits pois à la Française or Confit duck, honey & rosemary
spring cabbage

Chocolate mousse, orange jelly or Brie de Meaux & walnut bread

Figure 7.5 Sample luncheon menu

DINNER

The Grill Room at The Dorchester

Appetisers

Oak-smoked wild Scottish salmon

Lobster soup with flamed Scottish lobster

Squab pigeon and spring vegetable consommé with black truffles

Crisp red mullet and spring vegetable salad with sundried tomato cream

Seared scallops with cauliflower purée, citrus vinaigrette and mimolette crisps

Foie gras and duck confit terrine with onion marmalade and toasted brioche

Caramelised endive with goats' cheese, honey and winter truffles

Ham hock ravioli with white beans, trompettes and parsley

Denham Estate venison burger with quail's egg, griottine cherries, parsnips and Port

Warm Gressingham duck salad with glazed root vegetables, chestnuts and meat juices

Baby spinach salad with cashel blue, spiced pears and walnuts

Main Courses

Roast sea bass fillet with olive oil mash, red pepper relish and aged balsamic vinegar

Dover sole grilled or pan fried with brown butter and capers

Seared tuna with fennel, cherry tomatoes and Jersey Royals

Ragoût of John Dory, lobster and mussels with crème fraîche and chives

Free-range chicken breast with creamed morels, asparagus and tarragon

New season rack of lamb with aubergine caviar, couscous and confit garlic

Roast rib of Aberdeen Angus beef with Yorkshire pudding and roast potatoes

Rabbit leg with calf's sweetbread, ceps, smoked bacon and Lyonnaise potatoes

Saffron risotto cake with stuffed tomato, grilled vegetables and Parmesan

Specialities from The Grill

Served with either hand-cut chips or olive mash, sauce béarnaise, sauce bordelaise, green
peppercorn sauce or rosemary butter

Veal chop

Rib eye steak

Calf's liver and bacon

Lobster (1 kg)

Desserts

Crisp apple tart with clotted cream and calvados

Lemon and blueberry millefeuille with blood orange sorbet

Hot ginger pudding with plums and crème fraîche sorbet

A plate of Valrhona chocolate desserts

Home-made vanilla and rhubarb yoghurt with churros

Strawberry ripple ice cream or mango sorbet

Honey roast pear with caramel sauce and cardamom custard

Iced passion fruit and bitter chocolate délice with chilli and coriander

Selection of Cheeses from the Board

***

Coffee and Petits Fours

Figure 7.6 Sample dinner menu

```
VEGETARIAN MENU

Iced Cucumber Soup

Flavoured with mint

Avocado Waldorf

Filled with celery and apple bound in mayonnaise,
garnished with walnuts

* * *

Vegetable Lasagne

Layers of pasta and vegetables with melted cheese,
served with salad

Mushroom Stroganoff

Flamed in brandy, simmered in cream with paprika
and mustard, served with rice

Chilli con Elote

Seasonal fresh vegetables in a chilli and tomato
fondue, served with rice

Poached egg Elizabeth

(Set on buttered spinach, coated in a rich cream sauce)
```

Figure 7.7 Sample vegetarian menu

Figure 7.8 Afternoon tea table

- hot chipolatas; chicken livers, wrapped in bacon and skewered
- bite-sized items – quiche and pizza, hamburgers, meatballs with savoury sauce or dip, scampi, fried fish en goujons, tartare sauce
- savoury finger toast to include any of the cold canapés; these may also be prepared on biscuits or shaped pieces of pastry
- game chips, gaufrette potatoes, fried fish balls, celery stalks spread with cheese
- sandwiches; bridge rolls, open or closed but always small
- fresh dates stuffed with cream cheese; crudités with mayonnaise and cardamom dip; tuna and chive Catherine wheels; crab claws with garlic

dip; smoked salmon pin wheels; choux puffs with Camembert
- sweets (e.g. trifles, charlottes, bavarois, fruit salad, gâteaux).

Fork buffets

All food for a fork buffet must be prepared in a way that enables it to be eaten with a fork or spoon.

Fast-food menus

Although some people are scornful of the items on this type of menu, calling them 'junk food', nevertheless their popularity and success are proven by the fact that, starting with the original McDonald's, which opened in Chicago in 1955, there are now many thousands of outlets worldwide. McDonald's offers customers a nutrition guide to its products, as well as information for diabetes sufferers.

Banquet menus

When compiling banquet menus, consider the following points.

- The food, which will possibly be for a large number of people, must be dressed in such a way that it can be served fairly quickly. Heavily garnished dishes should be avoided.
- If a large number of dishes have to be dressed at the same time, certain foods deteriorate quickly and will not stand storage, even for a short time, in a hot place.

A normal menu is used, bearing in mind the number of people involved. It is not usual to serve farinaceous dishes, eggs, stews or savouries. A luncheon menu could be drawn from the following and would usually consist of three courses. Dinner menus, depending on the occasion, generally consist of three to five courses.

- **First course:** soup, cocktail (fruit or shellfish), hors d'oeuvre, assorted or single item, a small salad.
- **Second course:** fish, usually poached, steamed, roasted or grilled fillets with a sauce.
- **Third course:** meat, poultry or game, hot or cold, but not a stew or made-up dish; vegetables and potatoes or a salad would be served.
- **Fourth course:** sweet, hot or cold.

Cheese may be served as an extra course.

The meal experience

If people have decided to eat out then it follows that there has been a conscious choice to do this in

Avocado filled with cream cheese and two fruit sauces

* * *

Seafood-filled fish mousse with crayfish sauce

* * *

Butter-cooked fillet of beef with sliced mushrooms and tongue in Madeira sauce

A selection of market vegetables

Potatoes fried with garlic and thyme

* * *

Light soft meringue topped with fruit

* * *

Coffee

Sweetmeats

Figure 7.9 Sample banquet menu (note: sweetmeats may also be called petits fours)

preference to some other course of action. In other words, the food service operator has attracted the customer to buy their produce instead of another product – for example, the theatre, cinema or simply staying at home. The reasons for eating out may be summarised under seven headings.

1 **Convenience:** for example, being unable to return home, as in the case of shoppers, people at work or those involved in some leisure activity.
2 **Variety:** for example, trying new experiences or as a break from home cooking.
3 **Labour:** for example, getting someone else to prepare and serve food, and wash up, or simply the impracticality of housing special events at home.
4 **Status:** for example, business lunches or people eating out because others of their socio-economic group do so.
5 **Culture/tradition:** for example, special events or because it is a way of getting to know people.
6 **Impulse:** a spur-of-the-moment decision.
7 **No choice:** for example, those in welfare, hospitals or other forms of semi- or captive markets.

People are, however, a collection of different types, as any demographic breakdown will show. While it is true that some types of food service operation might attract certain types of customer, this is by no means true all the time; for example, McDonald's is marketed

to the whole population, and customers are attracted depending on their needs at the time.

The decision to eat out may also be split into two parts: first, the decision to do so for the reasons given above, and then the decision as to what type of experience is sought. It is generally agreed that there are a number of factors influencing this latter decision. The factors that affect the meal experience may be summarised as follows.

● **Food and drink on offer:** this covers the range of foods, choice, availability, flexibility for special orders, and the quality of the food and drink.
● **Level of service:** depending on the needs people have at the time, the level of service sought should be appropriate to these needs. For example, a romantic night out may call for a quiet table in a top-end restaurant, whereas a group of young friends might be seeking more informal service. This factor also takes into account services such as booking and account facilities, acceptance of credit cards and the reliability of the operation's product.
● **Level of cleanliness and hygiene:** this relates to the premises, equipment and staff. Over the past decade this factor has increased in importance in customers' minds. The recent media focus on food production and the risks involved in buying food have heightened public awareness of health and hygiene aspects. Scores on the Doors and similar schemes have also increased awarness of hygiene standards.
● **Perceived value for money and price:** customers have perceptions of the amount they are prepared to spend and relate these to differing types of establishment and operation. However, many people will spend more if the

Figure 7.10 Taking orders

value gained is perceived to be greater than that obtained by spending slightly less.

- **Atmosphere of the establishment:** composed of a number of factors, such as design, decor, lighting, heating, furnishings, acoustics and noise levels, other customers, staff and the attitude of staff.

Identifying these factors is important because it considers the product from the point of view of the customer. All too often, food service operators can get caught up in the provision of food and drink, spend several thousand pounds on design, decor and equipment, but ignore the actual experience the customer might have. Untrained service staff are a good example of this problem. Operations can tend to concentrate on the core product and forget the total package. A better understanding of the customer's viewpoint or the nature of customer demand leads to a better product being developed to meet it.

Managing a function

A function can be described as the service of food and drink at a specific time and place, for a given number of people at a known price.

Examples of hospitality functions include:

- social functions – weddings, anniversaries, dinner dances
- business functions – conferences, meetings, working lunches, working dinners
- social and business functions – corporate entertaining.

Sometimes functions are called banquets; however, the word banquet is normally used to describe a large, formal occasion.

The variety of function events ranges from simply providing bar facilities in a conference reception area before a meeting, to the more formal occasion catering for 1500 to 2000 people. Many establishments concentrate and market themselves as specialist function caterers. The function business may be the company's sole business; on the other hand, it may be part of the product range – for example, in a hotel, you may well find rooms, restaurants, conferences facilities and banqueting.

The type of function facilities found in an establishment will also depend on the level of market for which it is catering. Function catering is found in the commercial and public sector of the hospitality industry. The types of function suites and variety of functions on offer in all establishments will often differ considerably.

Policy decisions relating to function catering are determined by a number of characteristics inherent to this type of catering. First, depending on where the establishment is located there will be a banqueting season; this is where the main business is concentrated – for example, from May to September (depending on the location) is known as the 'wedding season'.

A considerable amount of information is available to the caterer in advance of the function. This includes:

- number of guests
- price per head or cover
- menu requirement
- drink required
- type of menu.

This information allows the manager to assess the resource requirement. For example:

- staffing
- linen
- food and drink
- equipment.

The manager is then also able to assess the profit margins to be achieved. This will aid the control procedures and help to establish yardsticks against which the performance of a function may be measured.

Financial considerations

Function catering is most commonly associated with the commercially orientated sector of the hospitality industry. Gross profit margins in function catering tend to be higher than those achieved in hotel restaurants and coffee shops.

An average gross profit percentage of 65–75 per cent is usually required in function catering, depending on the type of establishment, types of customers, level of service, and so on.

The types of customers and their spending power can in most cases be determined in advance. The average spending power will comprise the cost of the meal and will generally include the beverages served during the function. Items that may not be included in the price of the meal are pre-dinner drinks, liqueurs and such like.

The financial policy will also determine the pricing structures of the different types of functions and different menus on offer. Some establishments will also make a separate charge for room hire.

The pricing structure for an establishment's function catering will be determined by its cost structure, with reference to its semi-fixed and variable costs. There are a variety of pricing structures that may be used for costing functions, the adoption of any one being determined by such factors as the type of establishment, the food and beverage product on offer, and the cost structure of the establishment.

Banquets and functions may generate additional income such as extra bar sales and overnight accommodations.

Marketing considerations

The marketing policy of a function establishment will focus on the market the business aims to capture, and how best to promote the special characteristics of the establishment. Different marketing techniques will be used to 'sell' the establishment.

An establishment's marketing policy should contain a review relating to the competition in the area in order to keep abreast of fashions and trends in the function market. To assist in this review it is important that information and quotations are obtained from other establishments. A manager must be constantly aware of the types of products and services on offer in the marketplace. Every consideration must be given to customers' needs and matching these needs to the establishment's facilities.

In the marketing of an operation's function facilities the function manager should be aware of who is buying the 'product' in a particular organisation being contracted. Arrangements should be made to show the client the facilities, and every effort should be made to create a good impression.

The function manager should devise a marketing plan based on the marketing policy for a given period. This plan should take into account the following factors.

- **Finance:** targets of turnover, profit for a given period.
- **Productivity:** targets of productivity and performance of the banqueting function department.
- **Promotions:** general – how to increase business and how this is to be achieved; special – specially devised promotions to be launched in a given period, often aimed at different groups, clubs, etc.
- **Facilities:** focused on selling certain facilities – for example, recently refurbished.
- **Development:** the promotion of a new development or concept; the launch of new conference/seminar rooms.
- **New product lines:** launch of weekend breaks for clubs, groups, etc., with special rates.
- **Research:** ongoing market research, project research, etc.

Every organisation needs to advertise and promote its functions. There are a number of ways in which an organisation can promote the business:

- special brochures
- photographs
- press releases about functions sent to local newspapers, magazines, etc.

Brochures have to be designed carefully using professional designers, printers, and so on. The menus should be clear and easily understood, with the prices stated. All photographs must be clear and accurate; they should be in no way misleading.

Brochures or folders should ideally contain the company logo. The pack should also contain the following:

- a letter from the banqueting manager to the client
- rates and prices
- wine lists
- details of all function rooms, with size and facilities on offer
- maps
- sample menus.

Any menus included will have been carefully constructed by the chef, with predetermined gross profits, recipe specifications and purchasing specifications in mind.

Pricing

Function menus are usually pre-listed with the desired profit margins added to them. These menus will generally have a standard set of purchasing and operational specifications added to them. However, there is normally a flexible element added to it. It is not unusual for a banqueting manager to offer additions to the menu at no additional cost to the client in order to capture the business in a competitive environment.

The relationship between price and value for money is an important aspect of pricing. Value for money extends far beyond the food to be served. It takes into account the whole environment in which the food is consumed: the atmosphere, decor and surroundings of the establishment, and the level of service.

In order to be successful and to obtain a satisfactory volume of sales, pricing has to consider three basic factors.

The nature of demand for the product

First, we have to think of the **elasticity of demand** (this means how sensitive demand is to the effects of pricing). Menus are said to have an elastic demand when a small decrease in the price brings about a significant increase in sales, and alternatively if an increase in price brings about a decrease in sales. Menus with an inelastic demand mean that a small increase or decrease in price does not bring about any significant increase or decrease in sales.

The level of demand for the product

Most catering operations experience fluctuations in demand for their products. The change in demand affects the volume of sales, which results in the under-utilisation of premises and staff. Fluctuation in demand makes it necessary to take a flexible approach to pricing in order to increase sales. For example, at certain times of the year it may be possible to obtain deals on functions.

The level of competition for the product

Competition is an important factor in pricing. Establishments commonly monitor the prices in competitors' establishments, recognising that customers have a choice. Monitoring competition is not just about examining price, however, but also the facilities, decor, services, and so on.

The specific method of pricing used by an establishment will depend on the exact market in which it is operating. The price itself can be a valuable selling tool and a great aid to achieving the desired volume of sales.

Every business, whatever its size, can choose to set its prices above its proper costs or at, or below, the prices of its competitors. More often establishments are forced to fix their price by the competition. This is the discipline of the marketplace. The challenge then is to get the costs below the price that has to be set. The danger here is that managers tend to subconsciously alter the costs. This happens when fixed costs such as wages, heating, and so on, are split over all the sales to arrive at the unit cost. It is always tempting then to overestimate the sales, thereby reducing the unit cost.

No one should attempt to sell anything until they have calculated the break-even point. This is the point the amount of sales (menus, portions) at a certain price have to reach to cover their variable costs and all the fixed costs. Profit only starts when the break-even point has been reached.

Pricing is as much about psychology as accounting. Establishments also need to market research price. Too low a price, although enabling them to produce profit on paper, may fail as customers may perceive the product to be cheap and of poor quality. Some people expect to pay high prices for some goods and services.

Planning a function

Collecting the function details

Customers are usually invited for a detailed view of the venue; in some establishments this will include a menu tasting. During the menu tasting the customer is encouraged to discuss their requirements; the food and beverage manager will gather this information. The customer will also be advised of the different options available. For example:

- different room layouts
- choice of menu, vegetarian or allergy requirements
- order of service
- flowers
- cloakroom requirements
- technical requirements, overhead projectors, public address system, etc.

The customer requirements are then summarised on a function sheet and divided into departmental responsibilities. The function sheet may be issued to the customer one week before the function.

Ideally, function sheets should be colour-coded for each department one week before the function. The date for confirmation of the final catering numbers is noted on the function sheet.

Internal communication procedures

Internal communication is especially important within any organisation. Frequent meetings are essential to inform staff of forthcoming events and the expected working hours for the following week. Often, more detailed and user-friendly internal function sheets are compiled so that the key people are aware of customer requirements.

Internal function sheets should be given to the relevant staff at least one week in advance of the function. It is then up to each department to assess its own responsibilities and needs relating to the event so that the work can be planned in advance. These sheets will determine the amount of staff required for the function, and how much linen, crockery, glassware, and so on, is required.

Such decisions will have to be made taking account of the price the customer is paying and the overall budget. Final attendance numbers should be confirmed with the client at least 48 hours before the event.

An example of costs and resources

Different services provided may be priced separately (e.g. menu price may comprise internal costs). For example:

- 30 per cent – food cost
- 30 per cent – labour
- 30 per cent – operational costs (e.g. linen, cleaning, etc.)
- 10 per cent – profit.

Usually each department has its own budget to reach. Resources for each department must be deployed and used effectively in order to maximise profitability.

All revenue earned and costs are summarised on a weekly basis in the form of a weekly cost-breakdown report. This is then passed on to the control office, manager or director.

Expenditure for each function is usually controlled on a daily basis. The head chef must be aware of the total food expenditure target for each function. All costs must be controlled through the careful management of resources. Staffing needs to be kept to a minimum without compromising quality.

The importance of timing

The accurate timing of functions is vital, for the following reasons.

- Each department needs time to prepare for the function. Some departments will require more time than others. For example, the kitchen needs the most time to prepare the menu, while a technician requires only a few minutes to prepare the video playback machine.
- The timing of deliveries is most important as late deliveries can cause severe problems for the kitchen. It is also important that deliveries meet the required specification.

- In high-quality banqueting houses much of the service and presentation is finished at the last minute.
- Any delays in the function will result in hourly paid staff being paid extra time, thus pushing up costs.
- Timing can affect the smooth running of the function, and whether it is possible to turn the room around in enough time for a second function (e.g. lunch, then dinner).

The importance of communication and information

Communication and flow of information in any organisation is of paramount importance to a successful organisation.

Information needs to be broken down and allocated to the appropriate departments, and it is vital that there is two-way communication between departments. Any changes to the function must be communicated to all those concerned immediately.

Information, first, is obtained by the first point of customer contact (i.e. the event organiser, the food and beverage manager, conference and function organisation). At a later stage more specialist information is gathered by the individual department heads, using various means of communication:

- telephone
- email
- fax
- meetings.

This information is recorded in different stages:

- telephone enquiry
- bookings diary
- hire contract
- function sheet
- internal function sheet
- invoice
- feedback form
- weekly report
- thank you letter.

Information may be presented in different ways, either formally or informally.

Formal correspondence

Information relating to a client's function must be professionally presented, accurate and reflect the company's image.

Internal information

This must also be accurate and well presented so that staff are able to understand clearly what is expected of them. All instructions should be in detail, leaving nothing to chance or guesswork.

Customer information

All information relating to the needs of the customers must be recorded throughout the booking process using appropriate documentation:

- hire contract
- function sheets, and so on.

Special requirements

In small establishments the services on offer can be tailored to the needs of the customer.

- Dietary needs must be catered for.
- It is important that, if wheelchair access is required, it is made available.
- Where it is difficult to accommodate certain special requirements, the customer should be given alternatives, where possible.

Food allergies

When planning menus for a large function the chef must think of the danger of any food allergies. All waiting staff must be informed of the contents of the dishes (e.g. shellfish, gluten, peanuts).

Legal requirements

All functions must be planned within the legal framework. Consideration must be given to the welfare of staff. Provide training in health, safety and hygiene. Employees must understand the fire regulations and evacuation procedures. Training is particularly important in risk assessment, handling dangerous equipment and handling chemical products.

Companies have a legal responsibility to the customer – for example, the customer needs to be aware of the maximum number of guests permitted in the building due to fire regulations and, similarly, whether or not a licence extension or evacuation procedures in the event of a fire or bomb threat are in place.

The issuing of a contract forms a legal bond between the customer and the venue.

The event

Staff are required to familiarise themselves with the function sheets, identifying any special requirements that are needed by the organiser. Staff also require a full briefing so that they understand exactly what is required of them and to reconfirm the function details. It is important that the client feels that they are being looked after and that they can feel at ease. The function must be executed as planned, in line with the client's needs.

At the end of the function it is essential to gain feedback from the client to ensure that, if the client was not satisfied, a follow-up letter apologising or offering some compensation can be sent. This client evaluation should then be passed on to the staff.

A final calculation of the costs incurred by each department needs to be done to check the efficiency of the budget management. Invoices are then raised.

Some companies will contact the client one to three days after the function to obtain constructive feedback, using a standard evaluation form for them to fill in.

Well-organised functions that give customer satisfaction can not only be profitable but may also lead to repeat business.

Figure 7.11 Briefing staff on the menu

Some references to menus elsewhere in this book:

Reference

Kasavana, M.L. and Smith, D.I. (1982) *Menu Engineering*. Haworth Press.

Topics for discussion

1 A sensible menu policy.
2 The advantages and disadvantages of a cyclical menu.
3 The advantages of using the English language in menus. When would you consider using another language?
4 The essentials of menu design and construction.
5 The various styles of buffet menus.
6 The implications of menu fatigue.
7 How would you promote your menu for a 50-seater high-street bistro in the centre of town?
8 Each member of the group to obtain a number of differing menus (e.g. breakfast, lunch, dinner, special party) from different types of catering area (e.g. school meals, industrial catering, small, medium and large hotels, and restaurants) for discussion and critique.
9 How have menus changed over the last 20 years? Discuss why they have changed.
10 What future menu changes do you envisage? Explain why you think they will occur.
11 Specify the essential menu requirements, and state your reasons, for children, teenagers and senior citizens.
12 The importance of using local produce on a menu.
13 How important to the customer is the traceability of the ingredients in the dishes?
14 Should a chef consider sustainability when planning a menu?

Food purchasing, storage and control

Supporting material available on Dynamic Learning Online:

> Knowledge quizzes

> Activity worksheets: purchasing; costing and control

> Summary presentations

> Video and worksheet: wholesale market

Liaising with food suppliers

There are certain important factors involved in a successful working relationship with food suppliers. Both parties have responsibilities that must be carried out to ensure proper food safety and quality. Food-borne illness incidents, regardless of their cause, have an impact on the reputation of caterers, and suppliers' business will be lost. A good working relationship and knowledge of each other's responsibilities is a major help in avoiding such incidents.

Suppliers must be aware of what is expected of the product. They must also make sure that the caterer is aware of any food safety limitations associated with the product. These are usually stated on all labelling. Such statements may simply say 'keep refrigerated' or 'keep frozen', others may well include a graph or chart of the projected shelf-life at different storage temperatures. The responsibility for meeting these specifications is an important factor in a successful catering operation.

Food purchasing

The purchasing cycle is pivotal to overall business performance, and a firm purchasing policy is the initial control point of the catering business.

Once a menu is planned, a number of activities must occur to bring it into reality. One of the first and

most important stages is to purchase and receive the materials needed to produce the menu items. Skilful purchasing with good receiving can do much to maximise the results of a good menu. There are six important steps to remember:

1 Know the market.
2 Design the purchase procedures.
3 Determine purchasing needs.
4 Receive and check the goods.
5 Establish and use specifications.
6 Evaluate the purchasing task.

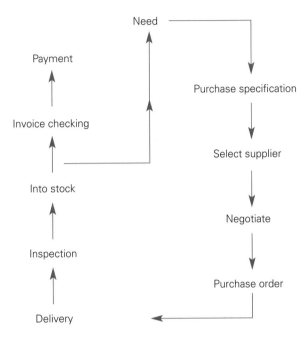

Figure 8.1 The purchasing cycle
Source: Drummond, 1998, reproduced by permission of Hodder Education

Knowing the market

Since markets vary considerably, to do a good job of purchasing a buyer must know the characteristics of each market.

A market is a place in which ownership of a commodity changes from one person to another. This could occur using the telephone, on a street corner, in a retail or wholesale establishment, or at an auction.

It is important that a food and beverage purchaser has knowledge of the items to be purchased, such as:

- where they are grown
- seasons of production
- approximate costs
- conditions of supply and demand
- laws and regulations governing the market and the products
- marketing agents and their services
- processing
- storage requirements
- commodity and product, class and grade.

The buyer

This is the key person who makes decisions regarding quality, amounts, price and what will satisfy the customers but also make a profit. The wisdom of the buyer's decisions will be reflected in the success or failure of the operation. The buyer must not only be knowledgeable about the products, but must have the necessary skills required in dealing with sales people, suppliers and other market agents. The buyer must be prepared for hard and often aggressive negotiations.

The responsibility for buying varies from company to company according to size and management policy. Buying may be the responsibility of the chef, manager, storekeeper, buyer or buying department.

A buyer must have knowledge of the internal organisation of the company, especially the operational needs, and be able to obtain the products needed at a competitive price. Buyers must also acquaint themselves with the procedures of production and how these items are going to be used in the production operations, in order that the right item is purchased. For example, the item required may not always have to be of prime quality − for example, tomatoes for use in soups and sauces.

A buyer must also be able to make good use of market conditions. For example, if there is a glut of fresh salmon at low cost, has the organisation the facility to make use of extra salmon purchases? Is there sufficient freezer space? Can the chef make use of salmon by creating a demand on the menu?

Buying methods

These depend on the type of market and the kind of operation. Purchasing procedures are usually formal or informal. Both have advantages and disadvantages. Informal methods are suitable for casual buying, where the amount involved is not large, and speed and simplicity are desirable. Formal contracts are best for large contracts for commodities purchased over a long period of time; prices do not vary much during a year once the basic price has been established. Prices and supply tend to fluctuate more with informal methods.

Informal buying

This usually involves oral negotiations, talking directly to sales people, face to face or using the telephone. Informal methods vary according to market conditions.

Formal buying

Known as competitive buying, formal buying involves giving suppliers written specifications and quantity needs. Negotiations are normally written.

Selecting suppliers

The selecting of suppliers is an important part of the purchasing process. First, consider how a supplier will be able to meet the needs of your operation. Consider:

- price
- delivery
- quality/standards.

Information on suppliers can be obtained from other purchasers. Visits to suppliers' establishments are to be encouraged. When interviewing prospective suppliers, you need to question how reliable a supplier will be under competition and how stable under varying market conditions.

Principles of purchasing

A menu dictates an operation's needs. Based on this the buyer searches for a market that can supply the company. After the right market is located, the various products available that may meet the needs are then investigated. The right product must be obtained to meet the need and give the right quality desired by the establishment. Other factors that might affect production needs include:

- type and image of the establishment
- style of operation and system of service
- occasion for which the item is needed
- amount of storage available (dry, refrigerated or frozen)
- finance available and supply policies of the organisation
- availability, seasonality, price trends and supply.

The skill of the employees, catering assistants and chefs must also be taken into account, as well as condition and the processing method, the ability of the product to produce the item or dish required, and the storage life of the product.

Three types of need

1 **Perishable:** fresh fruit and vegetables, dairy products, meat and fish; prices and suppliers may vary; informal needs of buying are frequently used; perishables should be purchased to meet menu needs for a short period only.
2 **Staple:** supplies that are canned, bottled, dehydrated or frozen; formal or informal purchasing may be used; because items are staple and can easily be stored, bid buying is frequently used to take advantage of quantity price purchasing.

3 **Daily use needs:** daily use or contract items are delivered frequently on par stock basis; stocks are kept up to the desired level and supply is automatic; supplies may arrive daily, several times a week, weekly or less often; most items are perishable, therefore supplies must not be excessive but only sufficient to get through to the next delivery.

What quantity and quality?

Determining the quantity and quality of items to be purchased is important. This is based on operational needs. The buyer must be informed by the chef or other members of the production team of the products needed. The chef and his or her team must establish the quality and they should be required to inspect the goods on arrival. The buyer with this information then checks out the market and looks for the best quality and best price. Delivery arrangements and other factors will be handled by the buyer. In smaller establishments the chef may also be the buyer.

When considering the quantity needed, the following factors should be borne in mind:

- the number of people to be served in a given period
- the sales history
- portion sizes (this is determined from yield testing a standard portion-control list drawn up by the chef and management teams).

The buyer needs to know about production, often to be able to decide how many portions a given size may yield. He or she must also understand the various yields. Cooking shrinkage may vary, causing problems in portion control and yield.

The chef must inform the buyer of quantities. The buyer must also be aware of different packaging sizes, such as jars, bottles, cans, and the yield from each package. Grades, styles, appearance, composition, varieties and quality factors must be indicated, such as:

- colour
- bruising
- texture
- irregular shape
- size
- maturity
- absence of defects.

Quality standards should be established by the chef and management team when the menu is planned. Menus and recipes may be developed using standardised recipes that relate directly to the buying procedure and standard purchasing specifications.

Buying tips

The following is a list of suggestions to assist the buyer.

- Acquire, and keep up to date, a sound knowledge of all commodities, both fresh and convenience, to be purchased.
- Be aware of the different types and qualities of each commodity that is available.
- When buying fresh commodities, be aware of part-prepared and ready-prepared items available on the market.
- Keep a sharp eye on price variations. Buy at the best price to ensure he required quality and also an economic yield. The cheapest item may prove to be the most expensive if waste is excessive. When possible, order by number and weight. For example, 20 kg plaice could be 80 × 250 g plaice, 40 × 500 g plaice, 20 × 1 kg plaice. It could also be 20 kg total weight of various sizes and this makes efficient portion control difficult. Some suppliers (e.g. butchers, fishmongers) may offer a portion-control service by selling the required number of a given weight of certain cuts. For example, 100 × 150 g sirloin steaks, 25 kg prepared stewing beef, 200 × 100 g pieces of turbot fillet, 500 × 100 g plaice fillets.
- Organise an efficient system of ordering with copies of all orders kept for cross-checking, whether orders are given in writing, verbally or by telephone.
- Compare purchasing by retail, wholesale and contract procedures to ensure the best method is selected for your own particular organisation.
- Explore all possible suppliers: local or markets, town or country, small or large.
- Keep the number of suppliers to a minimum. At the same time have at least two suppliers for every group of commodities, when possible. The principle of having competition for the caterer's business is sound.
- Issue all orders to suppliers fairly, allowing sufficient time for the order to be implemented efficiently.
- Request price lists as frequently as possible and compare prices continually to make sure that you buy at a good market price.
- Buy perishable goods when they are in full season as this gives the best value at the cheapest price. To help with the purchasing of the correct quantities, it is useful to compile a purchasing chart for 100 covers from which items can be divided or multiplied according to requirement. An indication of quality standards can also be incorporated in a chart of this kind.
- Deliveries must all be checked against the orders given for quantity, quality and price. If any goods delivered are below an acceptable standard they must be returned, either for replacement or credit.
- Containers can account for large sums of money. Ensure that all containers are correctly stored, returned to the suppliers where possible and the proper credit given.
- All invoices must be checked for quantities and prices.
- All statements must be checked against invoices and passed swiftly to the office so that payment may be made in time to ensure maximum discount on purchases.
- Foster good relations with trade representatives because much useful up-to-date information can be gained from them.
- Keep up-to-date trade catalogues, visit trade exhibitions, survey new equipment and continually review the space, services and systems in use in order to explore possible avenues of increased efficiency.
- Organise a testing panel occasionally in order to keep up to date with new commodities and new products coming on to the market.
- Consider how computer applications can assist the operation (see Chapter 17).
- Study weekly fresh food price lists.

Portion control

Portion control means controlling the size or quantity of food to be served to each customer. The amount of food allowed depends on the three following considerations.

1 **The type of customer or establishment:** there will obviously be a difference in the size of portions served, such as to those working in heavy industry or to female clerical workers. In a restaurant offering a three-course table d'hôte menu for £25 including salmon, the size of the portion would naturally be smaller than in a luxury restaurant charging £17.50 for the salmon on an à la carte menu.

2 **The quality of the food:** better-quality food

usually yields a greater number of portions than poor-quality food: low-quality stewing beef often needs so much trimming that it is difficult to get six portions to the kilogramme, and the time and labour involved also loses money. On the other hand, good-quality stewing beef will often give eight portions to the kilo, with much less time and labour required for preparation, and more customer satisfaction.

3 **The buying price of the food:** this should correspond to the quality of the food if the person responsible for buying has bought wisely. A good buyer will ensure that the price paid for any item of food is equivalent to the quality – in other words, a good price should mean good quality, which should mean a good yield, and so help to establish sound portion control. If, on the other hand, an inefficient buyer has paid a high price for food of indifferent quality then it will be difficult to get a fair number of portions, the selling price necessary to make the required profit will be too high and customer satisfaction can be affected.

Portion control should be closely linked with the buying of the food; without a good knowledge of the food bought it is difficult to state fairly how many portions should be obtained from it. To evolve a sound system of portion control, each establishment (or type of establishment) needs individual consideration. A golden rule should be: 'a fair portion for a fair price'.

Conveniently portioned items are available, such as individual sachets of sugar, jams, sauce, salt and pepper, individual cartons of milk and cream, and individual butter and margarine portions.

Portion control equipment

There are certain items of equipment that can assist in maintaining control of the size of the portions:

- scoops, for ice cream or mashed potatoes
- ladles, for soups and sauces
- butter pat machines, regulating pats from 7 g upwards
- fruit juice glasses (75–150 g)
- soup plates or bowls (14, 16, 17, 18 cm)
- milk dispensers and tea-measuring machines
- individual pie dishes, pudding basins, moulds and coupes.

The following real-life examples demonstrate how portion control can save a great deal of money.

- It was found that 0.007 litres of milk was being lost per cup by spilling it from a jug; 32,000 cups

= 5224 litres of milk lost daily; this resulted in a loss of hundreds of pounds per year.
- When an extra penny's worth of meat is served on each plate it mounts up to a loss of £3650 over the year when 1000 meals are served daily.

Portion amounts

The following is a list of the approximate number of portions obtainable from various foods.

General

- Soup: 2–3 portions to each half a litre.
- Hors-d'oeuvres: 120–180 g per portion.
- Smoked salmon: 16–20 portions to the kg when bought by the side; 20–24 portions to the kg when bought sliced.
- Shellfish cocktail: 16–20 portions per kg.
- Melon: 2–8 portions per melon, depending on the type of melon.
- Foie gras: 15–30 g per portion.
- Caviar: 15–30 g per portion.

Fish

- Plaice, cod, haddock fillet: 8 portions to the kg.
- Cod and haddock on the bone: 6 portions to the kg.
- Plaice, turbot, brill, halibut, on the bone: 4 portions to the kg.
- Herring and trout: 1 per portion (180–250 g fish).
- Mackerel and whiting: 250–360 g fish.
- Sole for main dish: 300–360 g fish.
- Sole for filleting: 500–750 g best size.
- Whitebait: 8–10 portions to the kg.
- Salmon (gutted, but including head and bone): 4–6 portions to the kg.
- Crab or lobster: 250–360 g per portion (a 500 g lobster yields about 150 g meat; a 1 kg lobster yields about 360 g meat).

Sauces

For each type, 8–12 portions to the half litre:

- hollandaise
- tomato
- custard
- jam
- béarnaise
- any demi-glace, reduced stock or jus-lié
- apricot
- chocolate.

For each type, 10–14 portions to the half litre:

- apple
- cranberry
- bread.

For each type, 15–20 portions to the half litre:

- tartare
- vinaigrette
- mayonnaise.

Meats

Beef:

- roast boneless – 6–8 portions per kg.
- boiled or braised – 6–8 portions per kg.
- stews, puddings and pies – 8–10 portions per kg.
- steaks – rump – 120–250 g per one portion, sirloin – 120–250 g per one portion, tournedos – 90–120 g per one portion, fillet – 120–180 g per one portion.

Offal:

- ox liver – 8 portions to the kg.
- sweetbreads – 6–8 portions to the kg.
- sheep's kidneys – 2 per portion.
- ox tongue – 4–6 portions per kg.

Lamb:

- leg – 6–8 portions to the kg.
- shoulder, boned and stuffed – 6–8 portions to the kg.
- loin and best end – 6 portions to the kg.
- stewing lamb – 4–6 portions to the kg.
- cutlet – 90–120 g.
- chop – 120–180 g.

Pork:

- leg – 8 portions to the kg.
- shoulder – 6–8 portions to the kg.

- loin on the bone – 6–8 portions to the kg.
- pork chop – 180–250 g.

Ham:

- hot – 8–10 portions to the kg.
- cold – 10–12 portions to the kg.
- sausages are obtainable 12, 16 or 20 to the kg.
- chipolatas yield approximately 32 or 48 to the kg.
- cold meat – 16 portions to the kg.
- streaky bacon – 32–40 rashers to the kg.
- back bacon – 24–32 rashers to the kg.

Poultry:

- poussin – 1 portion 360 g (1 bird), 2 portions 750 g (1 bird).
- ducks and chickens – 360 g per portion.
- geese and boiling fowl – 360 g per portion.
- turkey – 250 g per portion.

Vegetables:

- new potatoes – 8 portions to the kg.
- old potatoes – 4–6 portions to the kg.
- cabbage – 6–8 portions to the kg.
- turnips – 6–8 portions to the kg.
- parsnips – 6–8 portions to the kg.
- swedes – 6–8 portions to the kg.
- Brussels sprouts – 6–8 portions to the kg.
- tomatoes – 6–8 portions to the kg.
- French beans – 6–8 portions to the kg.
- cauliflower – 6–8 portions to the kg.
- spinach – 4 portions to the kg.
- peas – 4–6 portions to the kg.
- runner beans – 6 portions to the kg.

Methods of purchasing

There are three main methods for buying, each depending on the size and volume of the business.

1. **The primary market:** raw materials may be purchased at the source of supply (the grower, producer or manufacturer) or from central markets such as Smithfield (meat), Nine Elms (fruit and vegetables) or Billingsgate (fish) in London, or Rungis in Paris (the largest wholesale food market in the world). Some establishments or large organisations will have a buyer who will buy directly from the primary markets. Also, a number of smaller establishments may adopt this method for some of their needs (the chef patron may buy his fish, meat and vegetables directly from the market).

2. **The secondary market:** goods are bought wholesale from a distributor; the catering establishment will pay wholesale prices and obtain possible discounts.

3. **The tertiary market:** the retail or cash-and-carry warehouse is a method suitable for smaller companies. A current pass obtained from the warehouse is required in order to gain access. This method also requires the user to have his or her own transport. Some cash-and-carry organisations require a VAT number before they will issue an authorised card. It is important to remember that there are added costs:
   - running the vehicle and petrol used
   - the person's time for going to the warehouse.

Example of a standard purchasing specification

Tomatoes
- Commodity: round tomatoes.
- Size: 50 g, 47–57 mm diameter.
- Quality: firm, well formed, good red colour, with stalk attached.
- Origin: Dutch, available March–November.
- Class/grade: super class A.
- Weight: 6 kg net per box.
- Count: 90–100 per box.
- Quote: per box/tray.
- Packaging: loose in wooden tray, covered in plastic.
- Delivery: day following order.
- Storage: temperature 10–13°C at a relative humidity of 75–80 per cent.
- Note: avoid storage with cucumbers and aubergines.

Cash and carry is often an impersonal way of buying as there are no staff available with whom to discuss quality and prices.

For more information, visit the World Union of Wholesale Markets website, www.wuwm.org.

Standard purchasing specifications

Standard purchasing specifications are documents that are drawn up for every commodity describing exactly what is required for the establishment. These standard purchasing specifications will assist with the formulation of standardised recipes. A watertight specification is drawn up which, once approved, will be referred to every time the item is delivered. It is a statement of various criteria related to quality, grade, weight, size and method of preparation, if required (such as washed and selected potatoes for baking). Other information given may be variety, maturity, age, colour, shape, and so on. A copy of the standard specification is often given to the supplier and the storekeeper, who are left in no doubt as to what is needed. These specifications assist in the costing and control procedures.

Commodities that can be specified include the following.

- Grown (primary): butcher's meat; fresh fish; fresh fruit and vegetables; milk and eggs.
- Manufactured (secondary): bakery goods; dairy products.
- Processed (tertiary): frozen foods including meat, fish, and fruit and vegetables; dried goods; canned goods.

It can be seen that any food product can have a specification attached to it. However, the primary specifications focus on raw materials, ensuring the quality of these commodities. Without quality at this level, a secondary or tertiary specification is useless. For example, to specify a frozen apple pie, this product would use:

- a primary specification for the apple
- a secondary specification for the pastry
- a tertiary specification for the process (freezing).

But, no matter how good the secondary or tertiary specifications, if the apples used in the beginning are not of a very high quality, the whole product will not be of a good quality.

For most perishable items, rather than entering into a long-term contract, a daily or monthly quotation system is more common. This is essentially a short-term contract regularly reviewed to ensure that a competitive situation is maintained.

The standard recipe

The standard recipe is a written formula for producing a food item of a specified quality and quantity for use in a particular establishment. It should show the precise quantities and qualities of the ingredients, together with the sequence of preparation and service. It enables the establishment to have greater control over cost and quantity.

Objective

To predetermine the following:

- the quantities and qualities of ingredients to be used, stating the purchase specification
- the yield obtainable from a recipe
- the food cost per portion
- the nutritional value of a particular dish.

To facilitate:

- menu planning, purchasing and internal requisitioning, food preparation and production, portion control.

Also the standard recipe will assist new staff in the preparation and production of standard products, which can be facilitated by photographs or drawings illustrating the finished product.

Cost control

It is important to know the exact cost of each process and every item produced, so a system of cost analysis and cost information is essential.

The advantages of an efficient costing system are as follows.

- It discloses the net profit made by each section of the organisation and shows the cost of each meal produced.
- It will reveal possible sources of economy and can result in a more effective use of stores, labour, materials, and so on.
- Costing provides information necessary for the formation of a sound pricing policy.
- Cost records provide and facilitate speedy quotations for all special functions, such as parties, wedding receptions, and so on.
- It enables the caterer to keep to a budget.

No one costing system will automatically suit every catering business, but the following guidelines may be helpful.

- The cooperation of all departments is essential.
- The costing system should be adapted to the business, not vice versa. If the accepted procedure in an establishment is altered to fit a costing system then there is danger of causing resentment among staff and as a result losing their cooperation.
- Clear instructions in writing must be given to staff who are required to keep records. The system must be made as simple as possible so that the amount of clerical labour required is kept to a minimum. An efficient mechanical calculator or computer should be provided to save time and labour.

To calculate the total cost of any one item or meal provided it is necessary to analyse the total expenditure under several headings. Basically the total cost of each item consists of the following three main elements.

1 **Food or materials costs:** known as variable costs because the level will vary according to the volume of business; in an operation that uses part-time or extra staff for special occasions, the money paid to these staff also comes under variable costs; by comparison, salaries and wages paid regularly to permanent staff are fixed costs.

2 **All costs of labour and overheads:** regular charges that come under the heading of fixed costs; labour costs in the majority of operations fall into two categories: direct labour cost, which is salaries and wages paid to staff such as chefs, waiters, barstaff, housekeepers, chambermaids, and where the cost can be allocated to income from food, drink and accommodation sales; and indirect labour cost, which would include salaries and wages paid, for example, to managers, office staff and maintenance staff who work for all departments (so their labour cost should be charged to all departments). Overheads consist of rent, rates, heating, lighting and equipment.

3 **Cleaning materials:** an important group of essential items that is often overlooked when costing. There are over 60 different items that come under this heading, and approximately 24 of these may be required for an average catering establishment. These may include: brooms, brushes, buckets, cloths, drain rods, dusters, mops, sponges, squeegees, scrubbing/polishing machines, suction/vacuum cleaners, wet and wet/dry suction cleaners, scouring pads, detergents, disinfectants, dustbin powder, washing-up liquids, fly sprays, sacks, scourers, steel wool, soap, soda, and so on.

It is important to understand the cost of these materials and to ensure that an allowance is made for them under the heading of overheads.

Costing and profit

Pricing

There are several different approaches to pricing catering products and services. (There is more on pricing in Chapter 11.)

Table 8.1 Example breakdown

		Percentage of sales (%)
Food cost	£12,000	44
Labour	£6,000	25
Overheads	£3,000	18
	£21,000	
Net profit	£4,000	13
Sales	£25,000	

Competitive pricing

Using this method, prices are based on the prices charged by competitors for broadly similar products and services. The argument for this approach is that the consumer's choice is dependent largely upon price and that catering operations charging more than their competition price themselves out of business.

'Backward' pricing

This method bases prices on what market research indicates the consumer will be prepared and able to pay. Once the price has been determined, the cost of materials, labour and overheads is calculated in order to show a satisfactory profit. This method tends to be used by the more sophisticated operators.

Cost plus

This is the system used by many sectors of the industry. In order to arrive at the selling price, a percentage of ratio of cost price (e.g. 100 per cent) is added to cost of raw materials. This 'mark-up' should set a level that meets costs and, in commercial catering, makes a profit as well. There are variations on this cost-plus approach.

Gross profit – fixed percentage mark-up

The food cost of each dish is calculated and a fixed gross profit (e.g. 100 per cent) added. Gross profit refers to the difference between cost and selling price.

It is usual to express each element of cost as a percentage of the selling price. This enables the caterer to control profits.

Gross profit, or kitchen profit, is the difference between the cost of the food and the net selling price of the food. Net profit is the difference between

Table 8.2 Labour costs as a percentage of revenue

Type of outlet	% range (as a % of revenue) per annum	Factors that can affect labour %	
		Low %	**High %**
Hotels: 2–3 star	18–32%	Efficient design Limited menu	Inefficient design Extensive menus
Hotels: 4–5 star	25–35%	Living-in staff Limited services	High level of service, e.g. room service
Restaurants: waiter/waitress service	25–35%	As above	As above
Popular catering			
Waitress service	22–35%	As above	As above
Self-service	15–25%	As above	As above
Wine bars	12–22%	As above	As above
Fast food takeaway	11–18%	As above	As above
Kiosks, mainly confectionery and tobacco	Around 6%	Very high tobacco element	
Public houses	15–30%	Efficient design, e.g. one bar, mainly liquor sales, long turnover	High catering ratio, several bars/restaurants, low turnover

Note: These figures do not, however, accurately reflect work activity. Labour percentages do not indicate whether an employer employs a lot of low-paid staff or a few high-paid staff. In many other industries productivity is measured by measuring output against labour input, such as per full-time equivalent employee or per hour paid. Such measures can include covers per session for each type of operative.

Source: Croners Catering

Table 8.3 Calculating the selling price of a dish with food costs of £2.50 (before adding VAT)

Gross profit required (% of selling price)	Therefore, food costs are: (% of selling price)	Calculation	Selling price
70	30	$\dfrac{£2.50 \times 100}{30}$	£8.33
60	40	$\dfrac{£2.50 \times 100}{40}$	£6.25
50	50	$\dfrac{£2.50 \times 100}{50}$	£5.00
40	60	$\dfrac{£2.50 \times 100}{60}$	£4.17
30	70	$\dfrac{£2.50 \times 100}{70}$	£3.57

the selling price of the food (sales) and total cost (of food, labour and overheads). Here is an example:

Sales − Food cost = gross profit (kitchen profit)
Sales − total cost = net profit
Food cost + gross profit = sales

Example

Food sales for 1 week	= £25,000
Food cost for 1 week	= £12,000
Labour and overheads for 1 week	= £9,000
Total costs for 1 week	= £21,000
Gross profit (kitchen profit)	= £13,000
Net profit	= £4,000
Food sales − food cost	£25,000 − £12,000
	= £13,000 (gross profit)
Food sales − net profit	£25,000 − £4,000
	= £21,000 (total costs)
Food cost + gross profit	£12,000 + £15,000
	= £25,000 (food sales)

Profit is always expressed as a percentage of the selling price.

$$\text{Net profit} = \frac{£4000 \times 100}{£25,000} = 16\%$$

A breakdown reveals the figures shown in Table 8.1.

If the restaurant served 1000 meals, then the average amount spent by each customer would be:

$$\frac{\text{Total sales } £25,000}{\text{No of customers } 1000} = £25.00$$

As the percentage composition of sales for a month is now known, the average price of a meal for that period can be further analysed:

Average price of a meal = £25.00 = 100%
25p = 1%

which means that the customer's contribution towards:

Food cost	= 25 × 48%	= £12.00
Labour	= 25 × 24%	= £6.00
Overheads	= 25 × 12%	= £3.00
Net profit	= 25 × 16%	= £4.00
Average price of meal		= £25.00

A rule that can be applied to calculate the food cost price of a dish is: let the cost price of the dish equal 40 per cent and fix the selling price at 100 per cent.

$$\text{Cost of dish} = 400p = 40\%$$
$$\therefore \text{Selling price} = \frac{40 \times 100}{40} = £10.00$$

Selling the dish at £10, making 60 per cent gross profit (GP) above the cost price, would be known as 40 per cent food cost. For example:

Sirloin steak (250 g)
250 g entrecote steak at £10.00 a kg = £2.50

To fix the selling price at 40% food cost and 60% GP $= \dfrac{£2.50 \times 100}{40} = £6.25$

More examples are shown in Table 8.3.

If food costing is controlled accurately the food cost of particular items on the menu and the total expenditure on food over a given period are worked out. Finding the food costs helps to control costs, prices and profits.

An efficient food cost system will disclose bad buying and inefficient storing, and should tend to prevent waste and pilfering. This can help the caterer to run an efficient business, and enable her/him to give the customer adequate value for money.

Table 8.4 The food and beverage manager's guide to factors affecting the gross profit % (1)

Area	Causes	Method of detection	Remedies
Purchasing **1 Suppliers and specifications**	Poor specifications	Not fit for job in hand with regard to size, weight, standard, quality Goods disposed of or more used than necessary	Recheck all specifications against requirements
	Supplier unable to cope with volume or standard	As above	Change supplier
	Acceptance of minimum deliveries, which are in excess of daily requirements	Food wasted (kitchen bins checked)	Agree smaller deliveries or change supplier
	Not keeping close to agreed prices or checking market prices	Check market prices and competitors	Continually monitor suppliers' price lists
	Poor response following complaints	Items not changed immediately and credit note system not responsive	Change supplier
	Poor yields	Observation and physical checks	Carry out regular yield checks and introduce standard recipes
	Poor menu planning	Poor profitability Use of high-priced items out of season	Plan menus to take advantage of seasonal items Include realistic mix of high- and low-cost items
2 Ordering	Incorrect specification, quantity or price	Delivery note, visual check, invoice check	Increase control procedures Ensure orders are placed only by authorised staff Over-ordering, resulting in over-stocking
	Stock deteriorating Stock value high	Shortage of storage space	Closely monitor levels of business and establish trends Establish stock levels for non-perishable goods Eliminate standing orders Order as frequently as purchase contract allows to ensure lower stocks

The caterer who gives the customer value for money together with the desired type of food is well on the way to being successful.

Example

If a dish costs £2.80 to produce, what should its selling price be to achieve 60 per cent profit on sales?

GP 60% Food costs 40%

$$\text{Selling price} = \frac{£2.80 \times 100}{40}$$

$$= £7.00$$

Add VAT (£7.00 × .20) + £1.40

Final selling price = £8.40

Food cost and operational control

As food is expensive, efficient stock control levels are essential to help the profitability of the business. The main difficulties of controlling food are as follows.

- Food prices fluctuate frequently because of inflation and falls in demand and supply, through poor harvests, bad weather conditions, and so on.
- Transport costs rise due to wage demands and cost of petrol.
- Fuel costs rise, which affects food companies' and producers' costs.
- Any food subsidies imposed by governments could be removed.
- Changes occur in the amount demanded by the customer; increased advertising increases demand; changes in taste and fashion influence demand from one product to another.

- Media focus on certain products that are labelled healthy or unhealthy will affect demand; for example butter being high in saturated fats, sunflower margarine being high in polyunsaturates.

Each establishment should devise its own control system to suit its own needs. Factors that affect a control system are:

- regular changes in the menu
- menus with a large number of dishes
- dishes with a large number of ingredients
- problems in assessing customer demand
- difficulties in not adhering to or operating standardised recipes
- raw materials purchased incorrectly.

Table 8.5 The food and beverage manager's guide to factors affecting the gross profit % (2)

Area	Causes	Method of detection	Remedies
Materials lost during delivery **1 Receipts short on delivery**	Quantity not checked: • staff too busy • staff indifferent • staff unsuitable • staff untrained • insufficient time • staff failing to follow procedures • dishonesty • delivery times inappropriate Poor transportation of goods: • incorrect temperatures • incorrect packaging of goods • credit notes not checked	Inspection and observation of deliveries: • spot checks at delivery • unsigned delivery notes • staff shortages • observation • security checks • observation, goods arriving when stores unmanned • log temperatures of delivery vans • check condition of packaging • check credit notes	Establish procedures for checking orders on receipt of goods Constant spot checks Careful selection, training and monitoring of staff Report driver to supplier Visual checks Follow up on records
2 Change in source of supply and quantity	Inappropriate specifications issued Changes in supply standards not checked	Checking of material specifications against goods received	Establish appropriate purchase specifications
3 Poor stock rotation	Failure by staff Lack of training	Inspection and observation of storage areas and date-stamped goods Spot checks on stores Question staff on understanding of process	Establish stock rotation procedures (bin card system) Regular inspections Staff training Review stores layout
4 Hygiene	Failure of staff to carry out procedures Training update	Regular inspection of stores area	Establish procedures (HACCP) Instigate and maintain staff training

Factors assisting a control system include:

- Menu remains fairly constant (e.g. McDonald's, Harvester, Pizza Hut, Burger King).
- Standardised recipes and purchasing specifications used.
- Menu has a limited number of dishes.

Stocktaking is therefore easier and costing more accurate.

In order to carry out a control system, food stocks must be secure, refrigerators and deep-freezers should be kept locked, portion control must be accurate. A bookkeeping system must be developed to monitor the daily operation.

VAT (value added tax)

Calculating VAT

VAT is charged at the rate of 20 per cent, which has to be added to the value of any taxable sale.

VAT-inclusive price

The VAT-inclusive price is the price with VAT added. It may be calculated as follows:

Net VAT sale value £90.00

$$\frac{£90}{100} \times 120 = £108 \text{ or, more simply,}$$

$$£90 \times £1.20 = £108$$

Another way to calculate this is to take the selling price before tax and multiply it by 1 plus the rate of tax divided by 100. For example:

Selling price (SP) = £7.00

VAT = 20%

$$\frac{VAT}{100} = \frac{20}{100} = 0.2$$

$$1 + 0.2 = 1.2$$

$$SP \times 1.2 = £7.00 \times 1.2 = £8.40$$

If VAT changes, carry out the calculation in the same way. For example, if VAT is 17.5%:

Selling price (SP) = £7.00

VAT = 17.5%

$$\frac{VAT}{100} = \frac{17.5}{100} = 0.175$$

$$1 + 0.175 = 1.175$$

$$SP \times 1.175 = £7.00 \times 1.175 = £8.225$$

VAT-exclusive price

If a price is quoted including VAT, you might want to work out what it was before the tax was added: this is the VAT-exclusive price. In order to calculate the VAT-exclusive element of a VAT-inclusive price of £108, it is not correct to take 20 per cent of the value of the inclusive selling price of £108. This would result in a net price of £86.40. Instead, the correct calculation is:

$$£\frac{108}{100 + 20} \times 100 = £90.00 \text{ or, simply, } \frac{£108}{£1.20} = £90$$

Another way to calculate this is to take the selling price including tax and multiply it by 1 plus the rate of tax divided by 100. For example:

Selling price including tax (SP) = £8.40

VAT = 20%

$$\frac{VAT}{100} = \frac{20}{100} = 0.2$$

$$1 + 0.2 = 1.2$$

$$\frac{SP}{1.2} = \frac{£8.40}{1.2} = £7.00$$

Example

If a dish costs £2.80 to produce, what should its selling price be to achieve 60 per cent profit on sales?

£2.00 cost = £5.00 selling price
£0.80 cost = £2.00 selling price
Selling price = £7.00

Add VAT (£7.00 × .20) = £1.40

Final selling price = £8.40

The control cycle of daily operation

Purchasing

It is important to determine yields from the range of commodities in use, which will determine the unit costs. Yield testing indicates the number of items or portions obtained and helps to provide the information required for producing, purchasing and specification. Yield testing should not be confused with product testing, which is concerned with the physical properties of the food (e.g. texture, flavour, quality). In reality, tests are frequently carried out that combine these objectives.

Receiving

Goods must be checked on delivery to make sure they meet the purchase specifications.

Before items are delivered, it is necessary to know what has been ordered, both the amount and quality, and when it will be delivered. This is essential so that persons requiring items will know when foods will be available, particularly perishable items, and so that, on arrival, they can be checked against the required standard. It is also helpful for the storekeeper to know when to expect the goods so that he or she can plan the working day and also inform staff awaiting the arrival of items.

The procedure for accepting deliveries is to ensure that:

- adequate storage space is available
- access to the space is clear
- temperature of goods, where appropriate, is checked
- perishable goods are checked immediately
- there is no delay in transporting items to cold storage
- all other goods are checked for quantity and quality, and stored
- any damaged items are returned
- items past their 'use by' or 'best before' dates are not accepted
- receipts or amended delivery notes record returns
- one part of the delivery note is retained
- the other part is kept by the supplier
- a credit note is provided for any goods not delivered
- should there be any discrepancies, the person making the delivery and the supplier are informed.

Organisation of control

Control in every catering organisation is crucial: in small restaurants and tea shops, in hospital kitchens and in large hotels, in contract and airline catering, in school meals – in fact, in every establishment.

The role of potential managers and managers, whether they are called food and beverage manager or assistant food and beverage manager, executive chef, chef de cuisine, sous chef, head chef, chef de partie, or whatever, is to organise:

- themselves
- other people
- their time
- physical resources.

An essential factor of good organisation is effective control of oneself, of those responsible to you, and of physical resources, which often includes financial control. The amount and how it is administered will vary from establishment to establishment. However, successful control applies to all aspects of catering, namely:

- purchasing of food, etc.
- security
- storage of food, etc.
- waste
- preparation of food
- energy
- production of food
- first aid
- presentation of food
- equipment
- hygiene
- maintenance
- safety
- legal aspects.

Control of resources

The effective and efficient management of resources requires knowledge and, if possible, experience. In addition, it is necessary to keep up to date. This may require attending courses on management, computing, hygiene, legislation, and so on. Membership of appropriate organisations, such as HCIMA or former

Checklist for control

Goods inwards
- Are deliveries correct in terms of quality, quantity, hygiene, temperature?

Storage
- Items issued in rotation, accurate recording.
- Correct standards of hygiene: temperature, security, minimum wastage.

Food preparation **Production**	Proper standard of hygiene and safety
Presentation	Accurate portion control
Back door	Measures to prevent pilfering
Recording Monitoring Checking	Is it effective, adequate?

Figure 8.2 Organisation of resources

student associations, can also be valuable, as is attending exhibitions and trade fairs.

How the control of resources is administered will depend partly on the systems of the organisation but also on the way the person in control operates. Apart from knowledge and experience, respect from those for whom one is responsible is earned, not given, by the way staff are handled in the situation of the job. Having earned the respect and cooperation of staff, a system of controls and checks needs to be operated that is smooth-running and not disruptive. Training and delegation may be required to ensure effective control and, periodically, it is essential to evaluate the system to see that the recording and monitoring are being effective.

The purpose of control is to make certain:

- that supplies of what is required are available
- that the supplies are of the right quality and quantity
- that they are available on time
- there is the minimum of wastage
- there is no overstocking
- there is no pilfering
- that legal requirements are complied with.

Means of control

Checks need to occur spontaneously, without previous warning of the check being made, at regular intervals, which may be daily or weekly. These checks may involve one item, several items or all items. Records need to correspond with the physical items. For example, if records indicate 40 packets of sugar at 1 kilo, then those 40×1 kilo packets need to be seen. It is necessary to know to whom any discrepancies should be reported and what action should be taken. Therefore the policy of the establishment should be clear to all members of staff.

A system of authorisation regarding who may purchase and who may issue goods to whom, with the necessary suitable documents and records, needs to be established and inspected to see that it works satisfactorily.

The following topics, covered in other parts of this book, are essential reading:

- food purchase and control (see pages 248–251 in this chapter)
- energy conservation (Chapter 5)
- health (Chapter 4)
- legal aspects (Chapter 14)
- supervision (Chapter 10)
- computers (Chapter 17)
- hygiene (Chapter 14).

Introduction to the organisation of resources

Health and safety requirements

To comply with the regulations it is essential to observe the following good practice requirements, not only because of the legal requirement but for the benefit of all who use the storage areas of the premises.

- Receiving areas must be clean and free from litter.
- Waste bins, empty return boxes, and so on, should be kept tidy and safe.
- Waste bins (rubbish and swill) must be kept with lids on, emptied frequently and kept clean.
- All storage areas must be kept clean and tidy.
- Trolleys and stacking shelves should be suitable for heavy items.
- Trolleys should not be overloaded; accidents can occur due to careless loading, such as heavy items on top of light ones.
- Lifting of heavy items should be done in a manner to prevent injury.
- Cleaning equipment and materials must be available and kept separate from food items.
- All items should be stored safely, shelves not overloaded, heavier items lower than lighter items, with suitable steps to reach higher items.
- Stores should have a wash-hand basin, towel, soap and nail brush.
- Unauthorised persons should not have access to the stores or areas where goods are delivered.
- Be prepared for the unexpected; accidents can occur due to: delivery vehicles and trolley movement; breakages of containers, glass jars, etc.; undue waste left by delivery or storekeeping staff.
- Know where the first-aid box is.
- Know the procedures to follow in the event of an accident.

Temperature of food on delivery

Procedures must be laid down for checking the temperature of foods on arrival at the establishment. Delivery vehicles are subject to legislation and food should be at these temperatures when delivered.

Documentation of deliveries

Goods are ordered from the supplier for the amounts required and when needed. The quality and details of the foods will have been specified by the establishment so that when delivered the goods should comply with what was ordered.

Storing and issuing

Raw materials should be stored correctly under the right conditions, temperature, etc. A method of pricing the materials must be decided, and one of the following should be adopted for charging the food to the various departments. The cost of items does not remain fixed over a period of time; over a period of one year a stores item may well have several prices. The establishment must decide which price to use:

- actual purchase price
- simple average price
- weighted average price
- inflated price (price goes up after purchase)
- standard price (fixed price).

Weighted average price example (of dried beans)

$$5 \text{ kg} \times £0.80 = £4.00$$
$$10 \text{ kg} \times £1.00 = £10.00$$
$$\text{Total} \qquad £14.00$$
$$\therefore 14.00 \div 15 \text{ kg} = £0.93 \text{ per kg} = \text{weighted average price}$$

Preparing

This is an important stage of the control cycle. The cost of the food consumed depends on two factors:

1 the number of meals produced
2 the cost per meal.

In order to control food costs we must be able to:

- control the number to be catered for
- control the food cost per meal in advance of production and service by using a system of precosting, using standardised recipes, indicating portion control.

Sales and volume forecasting

This is a method of predicting the volume of sales for a future period. In order to be of practical value the forecast must:

- predict the total number of covers (customers)
- predict the choice of menu items.

Therefore it is important to:

- keep a record of the numbers of each dish sold from a menu
- work out the average spent per customer

- calculate the proportion, expressed as a percentage, of each dish sold in relation to total sales.

Forecasting is done in two stages.

1 **Initial forecasting:** this is done once a week in respect of each day of the following week. It is based on sales histories, information related to advance bookings and current trends, and when this has been completed, the predicted sales are converted into the food/ingredients requirements. Purchase orders are then prepared and sent to suppliers.
2 **The final forecast:** this normally takes place the day before the actual preparation and service of the food. It must take into account the latest developments, such as the weather and any food that needs to be used up; if necessary suppliers' orders may need to be adjusted.

Sales forecasting is not a perfect method of prediction, but it does help with production planning. Sales forecasting, however, is important when used in conjunction with cyclical menu planning.

Pre-costing of dishes

This method of costing is associated with standardised recipes, which give the total cost of the dish per portion and often with a selling price.

Summary of factors that will affect the profitability of the establishment

These include:

- overcooking food resulting in portion loss
- inefficient preparation of raw materials
- poor portion control
- too much wastage, insufficient use of raw materials; left-over food not being utilised
- theft
- inaccurate ordering procedures
- inadequate checking procedures
- no reference mark to standardised recipes and yield factors

- insufficient research into suppliers
- inaccurate forecasting
- bad menu planning.

Food labels

A great deal of information can be obtained from a food product by looking at the label. A number of regulations control what is permissible on a food product label:

- name of food
- list of ingredients
- conditions of use – special storage conditions
- indication of durability
- name and address of the manufacturer
- instructions for use, if necessary
- average weight of contents.

To find out more about food labelling, visit www.food.gov.uk/foodlabelling.

List of ingredients

If an ingredient is dehydrated or in a concentrated form, it may be positioned in the list according to its weight before dehydration (i.e. when fresh). Similarly, reconstituted foods may be listed after reconstitution.

Water and volatile products used as ingredients must be listed in order of their weight in the finished product. Mixtures of ingredients like nuts, vegetables and herbs can be put under the heading 'in variable proportions', provided no single one dominates.

Table 8.6 List of permitted titles for additives

Acided starch	Emulsifying salts	Preservation
Acidity regulator	Firming agent	Propellant gas
Anti-caking agent	Flavour enhancer	Raising agent
Anti-foaming agent	Flour treatment agent	Stabiliser
Antioxidant	Gelling agent	Sweetener
Bulking agent	Glazing agent	Thickener
Colour	Humectant	
Emulsifier	Modifi	

Table 8.7 Indication of durability*

Date to be declared	Period of durability
'Best before' – day/month	Within 3 months
'Best before end' – month/year	3–18 months
'Best before end' – month/year or year	18 months PLUS

* Minimum durability is indicated by 'best before' followed by the date up to which the food remains in first-class condition if stored correctly; the 'use by' date should be indicated by 'use by' followed by the date – day/month or, for longer periods, day/month/year; details of necessary storage conditions must be given

Table 8.8 Nutritional labelling

This must be in tabular form – for example:*	
Per serving (xg) and per 100g	
Energy	kJ and kcal
Protein	g
Carbohydrate of which sugars	g
Polyols	g
Starch	g
Fats of which saturates	g
Monounsaturates	g
Polyunsaturates	g
Cholesterol	mg
Fibre	g
Sodium	g
Vitamins*	Units as appropriate
Minerals	Units as appropriate

* Names of each vitamin and mineral to be given, and relevant units (e.g. vitamin C ascorbic acid 60 mg)

The naming of ingredients is important (e.g. 'fish' can be used for any species, 'fat' for any refined fat, 'sugar' for any type of sucrose).

Flavouring is identified by the word 'flavouring'; the word 'natural' may be added for naturally occurring products. Additives can be listed by either the principal function they serve, followed by the name or by their E-numbers (see Table 8.8).

Food labelling is strictly governed by law, and part of the role of the Food Standards Agency (FSA) is to prevent mislabelling or misdescription of foods.

Food authenticity is all about whether a food matches its description. If you, the buyer, are being deceived, then this deceit can be passed on to your customers by inaccurate wording on menus and/ or incorrect answers given to customers in reply to questions about ingredients in certain dishes.

Types of misdescription

- **Health and safety:** e.g. people with an intolerance of or allergy to certain foods may suffer severe or life-threatening reactions.
- **Not having the necessary composition for a legal name:** e.g. if named 'chocolate' the food must contain a certain amount of cocoa solids; a sausage must contain a certain amount of meat.
- **Substitution with cheaper ingredients:** e.g. diluting olive oil with lower-quality vegetable oil.
- **Incorrect origin:** e.g. misdescribing the meat species in a product or not declaring any other meat present; giving an incorrect county or country of origin of a food or wine.
- **Incorrect declaration of quantity:** e.g. giving the wrong amount of meat in a burger.

Storekeeping

A clean, orderly food store, run efficiently, is essential in any catering establishment for the following reasons.

- Stocks of food can be kept at a suitable level, so eliminating the risk of running out of any commodity.
- All food entering and leaving the stores can be properly checked; this helps to prevent wastage.
- A check can be kept on the percentage profit of each department of the establishment. (This control may be assisted by computer application, see Chapter 17.)

A well-planned store should include the following features.

- It should be cool and face the north so that it does not have the sun shining into it.
- It must be well ventilated, vermin-proof and free from dampness (dampness in a dry store makes

it musty, and encourages bacteria to grow and tins to rust).
- It should be in a convenient position to receive goods being delivered by suppliers and also in a suitable position to issue goods to the various departments.
- A wash-hand basin, soaps, nail brush and hand drier must be provided for staff; also a first-aid box.
- A good standard of hygiene is essential, therefore the walls and ceilings should be free from cracks, and either painted or tiled so as to be cleaned easily. The floor should be free from cracks and easy to wash. The junction between the wall and floor should be rounded to prevent the accumulation of dirt. A cleaning rota should clearly show daily, monthly and weekly cleaning tasks.
- Shelves should be easy to clean.

- Good lighting, both natural and artificial, is very necessary.
- A counter should be provided to keep out unauthorised persons, thus reducing the risk of pilfering.
- The storekeeper should be provided with a suitable desk.
- There should be ample, well-arranged storage space, with shelves of varying depths and separate sections for each type of food. These sections may include deep-freeze cabinets, cold rooms, refrigerators, chill rooms, vegetable bins and container stores. Space should also be provided for empty containers.
- Efficient, easy-to-clean weighing machines for large- and small-scale work should be supplied.
- Stores staff must wear clean overalls at all times, and suitable shoes to help prevent injury if a heavy item is dropped on the feet.
- Steps to help staff reach goods on high shelves and an appropriate trolley should be provided.

Store containers

Foods delivered in flimsy bags or containers should be transferred to suitable store containers. These should be easy to wash and have tight-fitting lids. Glass or plastic containers are suitable for many foods, such as spices and herbs, as they have the advantage of being transparent; therefore it is easy to see at a glance how much of the commodity is in stock.

Bulk dry goods (pulses, sugar, salt, etc.) should be stored in suitable bins with tight-fitting lids. These bins should have wheels so that they can be moved easily for cleaning. All bins should be clearly labelled or numbered.

Sacks or cases of commodities should not be stored on the floor; they should be raised on duck boards so as to permit the free circulation of air.

Some goods are delivered in containers suitable for storage and these need not be transferred. Heavy cases and jars should be stored at a convenient height to prevent any strain in lifting.

Special storage points

- Always comply with 'best before' or 'use by' dates.
- All old stock should be brought forward with each new delivery.
- Commodities with strong smells or flavours should be stored as far away as possible from those foods that readily absorb flavour; strong-smelling cheese should not be stored near eggs, for example.

- Bread should be kept in a well-ventilated container with a lid. Lack of ventilation causes condensation and encourages mould. Cakes and biscuits should be stored in airtight tins.
- Stock must be inspected regularly, particularly cereals and cereal products, to check for signs of mice or weevils.
- Tinned goods should be unpacked, inspected and stacked on shelves. When inspecting tins, the following points should be checked for: blown tins – this is where the ends of the tins bulge owing to the formation of gases either by bacteria growing on the food or by the food attacking the tinplate; all blown tins should be thrown away as the contents are dangerous and the use of the contents may cause food poisoning; dented tins – these should be used as soon as possible, not because the dent is an indication of inferior quality but because dented tins, if left, will rust and a rusty tin will eventually puncture; the storage life of tins varies considerably and depends mainly on how the contents attack the internal coating of the tin, which may corrode and lay bare the steel.
- Due to the use of fewer preserving additives, many bottled foods now need to be refrigerated once they are opened.
- Cleaning materials often have a strong smell; therefore they should be kept in a separate store. Cleaning powders should never be stored near food.

Table 8.9 Temperatures and storage times for freezers

Symbol	Maximum temperature	Safety storage time
*	−6°C	7 days
**	−12°C	1 month
***	−18°C	3 months
****	−18°C	3 months-plus

Storage accommodation

Foods are divided into three groups for the purpose of storage: perishable foods, dry foods and frozen foods.

- **Perishable foods** include meat, poultry, game, fish, dairy produce and fats, vegetables and fruit.
- **Dry foods** include cereals, pulses, sugar, flour, etc., bread and cakes, jams, pickles and other bottled foods and canned foods (cleaning materials can also be included in this section).
- **Frozen foods** must be placed immediately into a deep freeze at a temperature of −18°C to −20°C.

Storage of perishable foods

Meat and poultry

- Meat joints should be hung on hooks over a drip tray to collect any blood.
- The temperature of refrigerators should be between −1°C and 1°C.
- The humidity level should be approximately 90 per cent.
- Meat and poultry should ideally be stored in separate places.
- Cuts of meat may be brushed with oil or wrapped in oiled greaseproof paper, wrapped in clingfilm or vacuum packed.
- Drip trays and other trays used for meat or poultry should be cleaned daily.
- Frozen meat and poultry must be stored at between −18°C and −20°C.

Fish

- Store in ice in a fish refrigerator or fish drainer at between −1°C and 1°C.
- Keep different types of fish separated.
- Smoked fish should be kept separate from fresh fish.
- Frozen fish should be stored at −18°C.

Vegetables

- Ideally, have a cool, dry vegetable store with racks.
- As a safety precaution do not stack sacks too high.
- Leave potatoes in sacks.
- Place root vegetables on racks.
- Store green vegetables on racks.
- Store lettuce leaves as delivered in a cool environment.
- Remove any vegetables that show signs of decay.
- Leave onions and shallots in nets or racked.
- Place cauliflower and broccoli on racks.
- Leave courgettes, peppers, avocado pears and cucumbers in delivery containers.
- Leave mushrooms in containers.

Fruit

- Soft fruits should be left in punnets and placed in refrigeration.
- Hard fruits and stone fruits are stored in the cold store.
- Do not refrigerate bananas as they will turn black. If possible hang by the stems to slow down ripening.

Eggs

- Store refrigerated at 1−4°C.
- Keep away from other foods; their shells are porous and they can absorb strong smells.
- Keep in their delivery boxes; handle as little as possible.
- Use in rotation.

Milk and cream

- Store in the refrigerator below 5°C.
- Partially used containers should be covered.
- Use in rotation.

Cheese and butter

- Refrigerate at a temperature below 5°C.
- Cut cheeses should be wrapped.
- Use in rotation.

Bread, etc.

- Use in rotation: first in, first out.
- Store in a well-ventilated cool store.
- Avoid overstocking.
- Take care that biscuits are stacked carefully to avoid breaking.
- Frozen gâteaux should be kept frozen.
- Cakes containing cream must be refrigerated.

Sandwiches

- All sandwiches must be sold within four to 24 hours of preparation.
- They must be stored at a maximum temperature of 8°C.
- Sandwiches to be sold within four hours are not covered by this legislation.

Storage of dry goods

- Storage must be cool, well lit and well ventilated.
- Storage should be off the floor or in bins.
- Issue goods in rotation: first in, first out.
- Stack items so that stock rotation is simple to operate.
- Arrange items in such a way that they can easily be checked.

Storage of ice cream and frozen goods

- Store immediately on receipt.
- Storage temperature must be −20°C.
- Use in rotation.
- Keep chest lid closed as much as possible.

Cleanliness and safety of storage areas

High standards of hygiene are essential in the store.

- Personnel must:
  (a) wear clean clothing
  (b) be clean in themselves
  (c) be particular with regard to hand washing
  (d) have clean hygienic habits.
- Floors must:
  (a) be kept clear
  (b) be cleaned of any spillage at once
  (c) be in good repair.
- Shelving must:
  (a) be kept clean
  (b) not be overloaded.
- Cleaning materials must be:
  (a) kept away from foods
  (b) stored with care and marked dangerous if they are dangerous chemicals.
- Windows and, where appropriate, doors must be fly- and bird-proof.
- Walls should be clean and, where any access by rodents is possible, sealed.
- Equipment such as knives, scales, etc., must be:
  (a) thoroughly cleaned
  (b) stored so that cross-contamination is prevented.
- Cloths for cleaning should be of the disposable type.
- Surfaces should be cleaned with an antibacterial cleaner.
- All bins should have lids and be kept covered.
- All empties should be stacked in a safe area with care.
- Waste and rubbish should not be allowed to accumulate.
- Empty bottles, waste paper, cardboard and so on should be recycled.

The cold room

A large catering establishment may have a cold room for meat, with possibly a deep-freeze compartment where supplies can be kept frozen for long periods. The best temperature for storing fresh meat and poultry (short term) is between 4 and 6°C with controlled humidity (poultry is stored in a cold room). Fish should have a cold room of its own so that it does not affect other foods. Game, when plucked, is also kept in a cold room.

The chill room

A chill room is not the same as a walk-in refrigerator. It keeps food cold without freezing, and is particularly suitable for those foods requiring a consistent, not too cold, temperature, such as dessert fruits, salads and cheese. Fresh fruit, salads and vegetables are best stored at a temperature of 4–6°C with a humidity that will not result in loss of water from the leaves, causing them to go limp. Green vegetables should be stored in a dark area to prevent the leaves turning yellow. Certain fruits, such as peaches and avocados, are best stored at 10°C, while bananas must not be stored below 13°C otherwise they will turn black. Dairy products (milk, cream, yoghurt and butter) are best stored at 2°C. Cheese requires differing storage temperatures according to the type of cheese and its degree of ripeness. Fats and oils are best stored at 4–7°C – slightly higher than standard refrigeration – otherwise they are liable to go rancid. The chill room provides the optimum temperature to keep these commodities at their best.

Refrigeration

Because spoilage and food-poisoning organisms multiply most rapidly in warm conditions, there is a need for refrigeration through every stage of food delivery, storage, preparation, service and, in certain situations, onward distribution. Refrigeration does not kill micro-organisms but prevents them multiplying. Many cases of food poisoning can be tracked back to failure to control food temperatures or failure to cool food properly.

Temperature control is so important that statutory measures have been extended by the Food Hygiene Regulations whereby all food must be stored at or below 8°C and some foods at lower temperatures. Chilling at 0–3°C and freezing at −18 to −22°C are the easiest and most natural ways of preserving food and maintaining product quality because this:

- cuts down on wastage (reducing operating costs)
- allows a wider variety of food to be stacked
- gives flexibility in delivering, preparation and use of foods.

To maintain the quality and freshness of food, refrigeration at correct temperatures must be provided:

- at delivery
- for preparation
- for onward distribution
- for holding, display and service.
- for storage.

Types of refrigeration

- Mise-en-place – these are smaller refrigerators placed near to or under specific working areas. Some types have bain-marie-style containers that allow for the storage of the many small prepared food items required in a busy à la carte kitchen.
- Separate cabinets are essential for such foods as pastry, meat and fish, and cold buffets where food is displayed for more than four hours.
- Quick chillers – as the slow cooling of cooked food can allow rapid bacterial growth, rapid chillers are available.
- Display cabinets incorporating forced circulation of chilled air.

Temperature checks

In addition to the legal requirements for food to be stored at the correct temperature, the maintenance of correct temperature display should be specified on each cabinet and should be monitored regularly, with the use of probes, thermometers, etc. Temperatures and recommended storage times are listed on pages 266 and 267.

Points to note on refrigeration

- All refrigerators, cold rooms, chill rooms and deep-freeze units should be inspected and maintained regularly by qualified refrigeration engineers.
- Defrosting should take place regularly, according to the instructions issued by the manufacturers. Refrigerators usually need to be defrosted weekly; if this is not done, then the efficiency of the refrigerator is reduced.
- While a cold unit is being defrosted it should be thoroughly cleaned, including all the shelves.
- Hot foods should never be placed in a refrigerator or cold room because the steam given off can affect nearby foods.
- Peeled onions should never be kept in a cold room because their smell can taint other foods.

Vegetable store

This should be designed to store all vegetables in a cool, dry, well-ventilated room, with bins for root vegetables and racking for others. Care should be taken to see that old stocks of vegetables are used before new ones; this is important as fresh vegetables and fruits deteriorate quickly. If it is not convenient to empty root vegetables into bins they should be kept in the sack on racks off the ground.

Ordering of goods within the establishment

In a large catering establishment the stores carry a stock that, for variety and quantity, often equates to a large grocery store. Its operation is similar in many respects, the main difference being that requisitions take the place of cash. The system of internal and external accountancy must be simple but precise.

The storekeeper

The essentials that go to making a good storekeeper are:

- experience
- knowledge of how to handle, care for and organise the stock in his or her charge
- a tidy mind and sense of detail
- a quick grasp of figures
- possibly computer literate
- clear handwriting
- a liking for his or her job
- honesty.

There are many departments that draw supplies from these stores – kitchen, still room, restaurant, grill room, banqueting, floor service. A list of these departments should be given to the storekeeper, together with the signatures of the heads of departments or those who have the right to sign the requisition forms.

All requisitions must be handed to the storekeeper in time to allow the ordering and delivery of the goods on the appropriate day. Different-coloured requisitions may be used for the various departments if desired.

Duties of a storekeeper

- To keep a good standard of tidiness and cleanliness.
- To arrange proper storage space for all incoming foodstuffs.
- To keep up-to-date price lists of all commodities.
- To ensure that an ample supply of all important foodstuffs is always available.
- To check that all orders are correctly made out, and despatched in good time.
- To check all incoming stores – quantity, quality and price.
- To keep all delivery notes, invoices, credit notes, receipts and statements efficiently filed.
- To keep a daily stores issue sheet.
- To keep a set of bin cards.
- To issue nothing without receiving a signed chit in exchange.
- To check all stock at frequent intervals.

- To see that all chargeable containers are properly kept, returned and credited – that is, all money charged for sacks, boxes, and so on, is deducted from the account.
- To obtain the best value at the lowest buying price.
- To know when foods are in or out of season.

Types of records used in stores control

Bin card

There should be an individual bin card for each item held in stock. The following details are found on the bin card:

- name of the commodity
- issuing unit
- date goods are received or issued
- from whom they are received and to whom issued
- maximum stock
- minimum stock
- quantity received
- quantity issued
- balance held in stock.

BIN CARD				
UNIT (lbs, Tines, etc.) _____			PRICE	
			MAX STOCK ____	
COMMODITY _____			MIN STOCK ____	
DATE	RECEIVED	ISSUED	STOCK IN HAND	

Figure 8.3 Example of a bin card

In large catering operations, the traditional bin number system has been computerised. Beverages are managed through the Fidelio Food and Beverage system. This is a fully integrated software system with the following key features.

- Stock control – pricing, recipe function for cocktails, stock-take store values, variances are automated.
- Breakdowns are per outlet.
- Generates purchase orders.
- Interfaced with point of sale system (e.g. MICROS 8700, Fidelio Front Office for charging and Fidelio F&B for consumption).
- Invoice management – receiving and invoice control, invoice control is interfaced with a system (e.g. Oracle) for financial reporting.

Fidelio is one of the mainstay operating systems that is the backbone of all food and beverage control systems currently in use.

Stores ledger

This is usually found in the form of a loose-leaf file giving one ledger sheet to each item held in stock. The following details are found on a stores ledger sheet:

- name of commodity
- classification
- unit
- maximum stock
- minimum stock
- date of goods received or issued
- from whom they are received and to whom issued
- invoice or requisition number

Example of an operation

Stores Ledger/Departmental Requisitions
- Process – Outlets do a Fidelio requisition according to the outlet par stock and forecasted two-day expected levels of trading.
- Cellarman/stores supervisor allocates the request; this entails filling orders from stock, and managing par stock levels in accordance with outgoing requisition.
- Order requests are transferred to purchase orders and communicated to supplier for delivery.

- To minimise stock-holding values, and efficiently utilise space within the property, daily deliveries have been negotiated with main suppliers.
- One supplier is usually identified from whom it is compulsory for the entire estate to purchase 99 per cent of all beverages.
- Monthly stock-take and variance reports are produced.
- Value of the stock for recording on the balance sheet is automatically calculated.

Commodity	Unit	Stock in hand	Monday In	Monday Out	Tuesday In	Tuesday Out	Wednesday In	Wednesday Out	Thursday In	Thursday Out	Friday In	Friday Out	Total purchases	Total issues	Total stock
Butter	kg	27		2						3				5	22
Flour	Sack	2		1			1						1	1	2
Olive oil	Litres	8		1						1/2			1 1/2		6 1/2
Spices	30g packs	8		4			6						6	4	12
Peas, tin	A10	30		6						3				9	21

		_____ CANTEEN Week ending _____ No. meals served _____ Cost per meal _____															

| Commodity | Hand B/F | Stock received during week | | | | | | Stock used during week | | | | | | | | | In hand C/F |
		M	Tu	W	Th	F	Total	M	Tu	W	Th	F	S	Total	@*	Cost	
Apples, canned																	
Apples, dried Apricots, etc. – dried																	
Baking powder																	
Baked beans																	

* The cost of stock used can be checked by using two extra columns

Figure 8.4 Example of a daily stores issue sheet

BIN No   DESCRIPTION   CLASSIFICATION   CODE UNIT MAXIMUM MINIMUM

Date	DETAIL	Invoice or Req. No.	QUANTITY Recvd	QUANTITY Balance	QUANTITY Issued	UNIT PRICE	VALUE Received	VALUE Balance	VALUE Issued

Figure 8.5 Example of a stores ledger sheet

DEPARTMENTAL REQUISITON BOOK   267

Date _____   Class _____

Description	Quan.	Unit	Price per Unit	Issued if different	Quan.	Unit	Price per Unit	Code	£	

Figure 8.6 Example of a stores requisition sheet

- quantity received or issued and the remaining balance held in stock
- unit price
- cash value of goods received and issued, and the balancing cash total of goods held in stock.

Every time goods are received or issued the appropriate entries should be made on the necessary stores ledger sheets and bin cards. In this way the balance on the bin card should always be the same as the balance shown on the stores ledger sheet.

Departmental requisition book

One of these books should be issued to each department in the catering establishment that needs to draw goods from the store. These books can either be of different colours or have departmental serial numbers. Every time goods are drawn from the store a requisition must be filled out and signed by the necessary head of department – this applies whether one or 20 items are needed from the store. When the storekeeper issues the goods he or she will check them against the requisition and tick them off; at the same time the cost of each item is filled in. In this way the total expenditure over a period for a certain department can quickly be found. The following details are found on the requisition sheet:

- serial number
- price per unit
- issue number, if different
- quantity of goods required
- name of department
- cash column
- quantity of goods issued
- unit
- date
- signature
- unit
- price per unit.
- description of goods required.

Order book

This is in duplicate and has to be filled in by the storekeeper every time he or she wishes to have goods delivered. Whenever goods are ordered, an order sheet must be filled in and sent to the supplier, and on receipt of the goods they should be checked against both delivery note and duplicate order sheet. All order sheets must be signed by the storekeeper. Details found on an order sheet are as follows:

- name and address of catering establishment
- description of goods to be ordered
- name and address of supplier
- date
- serial number of order sheet
- signature
- quantity of goods
- date of delivery, if specific day required.

Stock sheets

Stock should be taken at regular intervals of either one week or one month. Spot checks are advisable about every three months. The stock check should be taken where possible by an independent person, thus preventing the chance of pilfering and 'fiddling' taking place. The details found on the stock sheets are as follows:

- description of goods

- price per unit
- quantity received and issued, and balance
- cash columns.

The stock sheets will normally be printed in alphabetical order.

All fresh foodstuffs, such as meat, fish and vegetables, will be entered on the stock sheet in the normal manner, but as they are purchased and used up daily, nil stock will always be shown on their respective ledger sheets.

Commercial documents

Essential parts of the control system of any catering establishment are delivery notes, invoices, credit notes and statements.

Delivery notes

These are sent with goods supplied as a means of checking that everything ordered has been delivered. The delivery note should also be checked against the duplicate order sheet.

Invoices

These are bills sent to clients, setting out the cost of goods supplied or services rendered. An invoice should be sent on the day the goods are despatched or the services are rendered or as soon as possible afterwards. At least one copy of each invoice is made and used for posting up the books of accounts, stock records, and so on (see Figure 8.7).

Invoices contain the following information:

- name, address, telephone numbers (as a printed heading), fax numbers, of the firm supplying the goods or services
- name and address of the firm to whom the goods or services have been supplied
- the word 'invoice'
- date on which the goods or services were supplied
- particulars of the goods or services supplied, together with the prices
- a note concerning the terms of settlement, such as 'Terms: 5% one month', which means that if the person receiving the invoice settles his or her account within one month he or she may deduct 5 per cent as a discount.

Credit notes

These are advice to clients, setting out allowances made for goods returned, or adjustments made through errors of overcharging on invoices. They should also be issued when chargeable containers such as crates, boxes or sacks are returned. Credit notes are exactly the same in form as invoices except that the words 'credit note' appear in place of the word 'invoice'. To make them more easily distinguishable they are usually printed in red, whereas invoices are always printed in black. A credit note should be sent as soon as it is known that a client is entitled to the credit of a sum with which he or she has previously been charged by invoice.

Statements

These are summaries of all invoices and credit notes sent to clients during the previous accounting period (usually one month). They also show any sums owing or paid from previous accounting periods and the total amount due. A statement is usually a copy of a client's ledger account and does not contain more information than is necessary to check invoices and credit notes.

Cash discount

This is a discount allowed in consideration of prompt payment. At the end of any length of time chosen as an accounting period (such as one month) there will be some outstanding debts. In order to encourage customers to pay within a stipulated time, sellers of goods frequently offer a discount. This is called cash discount. By offering cash discount, the seller may induce his or her customer to pay more quickly, so turning debts into ready money. Cash discount varies from 1.25 to 10 per cent, depending on the seller and the time: 2.5 per cent if paid in 10 days; 1.25 per cent if paid in 28 days, for example.

Trade discount

This is discount allowed by one trader to another, a deduction from the catalogue price of goods made before arriving at the invoice price. The amount of

---

INVOICE

Phone: 0208 574 1133 Fax: 0208 574 1123 Email: greend@veg.sup.ac.uk Website: http://www.greend.com Messrs. L. Moriarty & Co., 597 High Street, Ealing London, W5	No. 03957 Vegetable Suppliers Ltd., D. Green 5 Warwick Road, Southall, Middlesex Terms: 5% one month

Your order No. 67 dated 3rd September, 20...	£

Sept 26th	10 kg Potatoes bag 6.00 5 kg Sprouts, net 8.00	6.00 2.10 14.00

STATEMENT

Phone: 0208 574 1133 Fax: 0208 574 1123 Email: greend@veg.sup.ac.uk Website: http://www.greend.com Messrs. L. Moriarty & Co., 597 High Street, Ealing, London, W5	Vegetable Suppliers Ltd., D. Green 5 Warwick Road, Southall, Middlesex Terms: 5% one month

20...		£
Sept 10th	Goods	45.90
17th	Goods	32.41
20th	Goods	41.30
26th	Goods	16.15
		135.76
28th	Returns credited	4.80
		130.96

Figure 8.7 Example of an invoice and statement

trade discount does not therefore appear in the accounts. For example, in a catalogue of kitchen equipment, a machine listed at £250 less 20 per cent trade discount shows:

- catalogue price – £250
- less 20 per cent trade discount – £50
- invoice price – £200.

£200 is the amount entered in the appropriate accounts.

In the case of purchase tax on articles, discount is taken off after the tax has been deducted from list price.

Gross price is the price of an article before discount has been deducted.

Net price is the price after discount has been deducted; in some cases a price on which no discount will be allowed.

Cash account

The following are the essentials for the keeping of a simple cash account:

- all entries must be dated
- all monies received must be clearly named and entered on the left-hand or debit side of the book

- all monies paid out must also be clearly shown and entered on the right-hand or credit side of the book
- at the end of a given period – either a day, week or month or at the end of each page – the book must be balanced – that is, both sides are totalled and the difference between the two is known as the balance; if, for example, the debit side (money received) is greater than the credit side (money paid out), then a credit or right-hand side balance is shown, so that the two totals are then equal; a credit balance then means cash in hand
- a debit balance cannot occur because it is impossible to pay out more than is received.

An example is given in Table 8.10.

General rule

- Debit – monies coming in.
- Credit – monies going out.

Statement

Received monthly, and verified by cost control, who will ensure all invoices have been accounted.

Copy of invoices and credit notes are requested from the supplier.

Table 8.10 Cash account

DR.			First week			CR.
Date	**Receipts**	**£**	**Date**	**Payment**	**£**	
Oct 3 4 5	to lunches " teas " tax rebate	400 100 60	Oct 1 2 6	by repairs " grocer " butcher " balance c/fwd	80 100 120 260	
DR.			Second week			CR.
Date	**Receipts**	**£**	**Date**	**Receipts**	**£**	
Oct 9 11	to balance b/fwd " sale of pastries " goods	260 100 200 560	Oct 8 10 11 12	by fishmonger " fuel " tax " balance c/fwd	50 50 40 360 560	
DR.			Third week			CR.
Date	**Receipts**	**£**	**Date**	**Receipts**	**£**	
Oct 15 17 24 26 29	To balance b/fwd " teas " pastries " goods " goods " goods	360 120 110 60 80 60 790	Oct 19 21	By butcher " grocer " balance c/fwd	80 60 650 790	

Cash accounting

At hotel unit level, this is not applicable unless the hotel is privately owned – in which case, a cash flow reconciliation will be used similar to the example illustrated in Table 8.10.

Example

Make out a cash account and enter the following transactions:

Oct.	1	Paid for repair to stove £109.00	
	2	Paid to grocer	200.00
	3	Received for lunches	750.00
	4	Received for teas	200.00
	5	Received tax rebate	97.84
	6	Paid to butcher	120.00
Oct.	8	paid to fishmonger	72.60
	9	Received for sale of pastries	112.90
	10	Paid for fuel	80.00
	11	Paid tax	60.00
	11	Received for goods	500.00
	12	Paid to greengrocer	112.36
Oct.	15	Received for teas	150.20
	17	Received for pastries	150.00
	19	Paid to butcher	100.80
	21	Paid to grocer	95.00
	24	Received for goods	130.00
	26	Received for goods	150.00
	29	Received for goods	140.00

Example as used in a large hotel

Invoice statements

- Delivery notes received and checked in loading bay against delivery and purchase order – delivery note input into Fidelio on the basis of the purchase order, discrepancies are identified to supplier and purchasing.
- Delivery note and purchase order are transferred to Food and Beverages Accounts Payable, invoice will follow.
- Invoice checked against delivery note and purchase order, discrepancies will be corrected in Fidelio, outstanding credit notes will be requested from supplier.
- Invoice control – invoice details entered to Fidelio, this closes the purchasing and delivery process.
- Information is interfaced with Oracle for recording and payment.
- Oracle will automatically pay in line with pre-agreed payment terms, regardless of input date of data.
- On completion of input, statement is considered paid even though cheque or bank transfer may not have been expedited.
- From date of input statement recorded as a cost of sale on our ledger for the month.

Sustainability

A recent trend in the twenty-first century is the subject of sustainability. Further reference to this may be found in Chapter 15. In particular, great emphasis is now being placed on sustainable food that is purchased, consumed and prepared with as little impact on the environment as possible, for a fair price, and that makes a positive contribution to the local economy.

Caterers are now using more local, seasonal and available ingredients as a standard to minimise food transport, storage and energy use. This includes specifying produce from farming systems that minimise harm to the environment, such as certified organic. Livestock farming is one of the most significant contributors to climate change. Caterers are looking at ways to reduce meat on the menu, and promote vegetable dishes, pulses and nuts. When meat is purchased along with dairy products that these are produced to high environmental standards and animal welfare conditions. Fish species identified as at risk are not used. Only fish identified as being from sustainable sources are used. Bottled water is now being avoided in order to minimise transport and packaging waste. Tap water is perfectly safe and pure to offer. There is a growing trend among chefs to promote seasonal and local produce.

The key indications of success are:

- percentage of food sourced locally, nationally and abroad
- decrease in food waste
- reduction in food miles

- financial contribution to the local economy
- increase in recycling
- increase in food sales.

One of the key objectives is to reduce the food miles. This is the number of miles that food travels from producer to consumer. Food miles have implications for greenhouse gas emissions, and consequent effects on the climate.

Labelling

New types of labelling are being developed and introduced to the market in response to consumer demand for more information and as a tool to encourage behaviour change. One example is a label developed by the British Retail Consortium and the government's Waste and Resources Action Programme to signpost the recyclability of packaging.

Labels developed in response to consumer demand

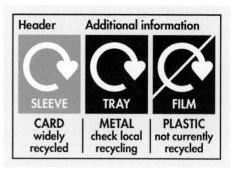

Figure 8.8 A new logo to explain the recyclability of food product packaging

are intended to drive up packaging recycling rates by signalling whether or not a product's packaging is collected for recycling. The Carbon Trust is also working with a number of companies, including food manufacturers and retailers.

Reference

Drummond, D. (1998) *Purchasing and Costing for the Hospitality Industry.* Hodder Arnold.

Some references to storage and control elsewhere in this book:

Topics for discussion

Food purchasing
1 A food-buying policy.
2 Is there a need for portion control?
3 The relationship between food quality and price.
4 The reasons for using standard purchasing specifications.
5 The use of standardised recipes.
6 How you would implement a cost control system.
7 The advantages of a computerised stock-keeping system.
8 How the role of the storekeeper may change in the future.

Storage and control
1 Why control of goods from receipt (delivery) to final destination (the customer) is essential.
2 What controls are needed regarding goods, staff and the preparation and service of food?
3 The need to be knowledgeable regarding the cost and quality of foods in relation to selling price.
4 The implication of setting the selling price too low, and also of setting it too high.
5 How do you consider a fair profit percentage is arrived at? Specify the establishment you have in mind.
6 What do you understand to be a 'suitable portion'? Give examples and explain your reasoning.

Part 3 Planning, production and service

9

An overview of food and beverage service, and food service design

Supporting material available on Dynamic Learning Online:

> Knowledge quizzes

> Activity worksheets: food and beverage service

> Summary presentations

> Videos and worksheets: food and beverage service

What is food and beverage service?

Food and beverage service is the essential link between the menu, beverages and other services on offer in an establishment, and the customers. People working in food and beverage service are the main point of contact between customers and an establishment. It is an important role in a demanding profession, with increasing national and international status. Skills and knowledge are transferable between establishments and sectors, and throughout the world.

For a particular food and beverage (or food service) operation, the choices on how the food and beverage service is designed, planned, undertaken and controlled are made taking into account a number of organisational variables. These include:

- customer needs
- level of customer demand
- the type and style of the food and beverage operation

- the nature of the customers (non-captive, captive or semi-captive)
- prices to be charged
- production process
- volume of demand
- volume of throughput
- space available
- availability of staff
- opening hours
- booking requirements
- payment requirements
- legal requirements.

Food and beverage service was traditionally seen as a delivery system, where only the requirements of the operation itself would determine how the service was designed, planned and controlled. This view has changed significantly as the customer is now seen as being central to the process and also as an active participant within it. It is also now recognised that food and beverage service actually consists of two separate systems, which are operating at the same time. These are:

1 the **service sequence**, which is concerned with the delivery of the food and beverages to the customer (see below)
2 the **customer process**, which is concerned with the experience the customer undertakes (see page 280).

The service sequence

The *service sequence* is essentially the bridge between the production system, the beverage provision and the *customer process* (or experience). The *service sequence* consists of, or may consist of, seven or more stages that can be summarised as:

1 preparation for service
2 taking food and beverage orders
3 the service of food and beverages
4 billing
5 clearing
6 dishwashing
7 clearing following service.

Within these seven elements, there is a variety of alternative ways of achieving the service sequence.

Preparation for service

Within the service areas, there is a variety of tasks and duties that need to be carried out in order to ensure that adequate preparation has been made for the expected volume of business and the type of service that is to be provided. These activities include:

- taking and checking bookings
- checking and ensuring the cleanliness of glassware, crockery, flatware and cutlery
- dealing with linen and paper items
- undertaking housekeeping duties
- arranging and laying up the service areas
- stocking hotplates, workstations, display buffets
- setting up bars and bar areas
- arranging and laying up lounge areas
- briefing of staff to ensure that they have adequate knowledge of the product and the service requirements.

Taking food and beverage orders

Taking orders from customers for the food and beverages they wish to have, takes time. The order-taking process is part of a longer process, which feeds

Figure 9.1 Feeding people at work

information to the food production or bar areas and provides information for the billing method. Whatever type of system is used — whether manual or electronic — it will be based on one of the three basic order-taking methods, listed below.

1 **Duplicate:** order taken and copied to supply point and second copy retained by server for service and subsequent billing.
2 **Triplicate:** order taken and copied to supply point and cashier for billing, third copy retained by server for service.
3 **Service with order:** taking order and serving to order, as used in, for example, bar service or takeaway methods.

Within the order-taking procedure there are many opportunities for exploiting the potential for personal selling that can be carried out by service staff. Personal selling refers specifically to the ability of the staff in a food and beverage operation to contribute to the promotion of sales, also known as *up-selling*. This is especially important where there are specific promotions being undertaken. Service staff must therefore be trained in selling and also be well briefed on special offers (see the section headed 'The customer process', page 280).

The service of food and beverages

The various service methods available are given in Table 9.2. The choice of service method will depend as much on the *customer service specification* (see page 286) as on the capability of the staff, the capacity of the operation and the equipment available. Differing service methods will also determine the speed of service and the time the customer takes to consume the meal, which in turn will have an impact on the throughput of customers.

Good food and beverage service is achieved where

management continually reinforces and supports service staff in the maintenance of good standards of achievement. Additionally the provision and maintenance of good service is primarily dependent on teamwork, not only among service staff but also among and between staff in other departments.

Billing

The various billing methods found in food service operations are as follows.

- **Bill as check:** second copy of order used as bill.
- **Separate bill:** bill made up from duplicate check and presented to customer.
- **Bill with order:** service to order and billing at same time, e.g. bar or takeaway methods.
- **Prepaid:** customer purchases ticket or card in advance either for specific meal or specific value.
- **Voucher:** customer has credit issued by third party, e.g. luncheon voucher or tourist agency voucher for either specific meal or specific value.
- **No charge:** customer not paying.
- **Deferred:** refers to function-type catering where bill is paid by organiser.

The actual choice of billing method will be dependent on the type and style of the operation. However, the billing system is also part of a longer process linked first to the order-taking method and second to the revenue-control procedures.

Clearing

The various clearing methods found in food service operations may be summarised as follows.

- **Manual 1:** the collection of soiled ware by waiting staff to dishwash area.
- **Manual 2:** the collection and sorting to trolleys by operators for transportation to dishwash area.
- **Semi-self-clear:** the placing of soiled ware by customers on strategically placed trolleys within dining area for removal by operators.
- **Self-clear:** the placing of soiled ware by customers on conveyor or conveyorised tray collecting system for mechanical transportation to dishwash area.
- **Self-clear and strip:** the placing of soiled ware into conveyorised dishwash baskets by customer for direct entry of baskets through the dishwashing machine.

The choice of clearing method, whether manual by staff or involving customers, will be dependent not only on the type of operation but also on the nature of the demand being met.

Dishwashing

The capacity of the dishwashing system should always be greater than the operational maximum required. This is because slow dishwashing increases the amount of equipment required to be in use at a particular time and increases the storage space required in service areas.

The various dishwashing systems are as follows.

- **Manual:** the manual washing by hand or brush machine of soiled ware.
- **Semi-automatic:** the manual loading by operators of a dishwashing machine.
- **Automatic conveyor:** the manual loading by operators of soiled ware within baskets mounted on a conveyor for automatic transportation through a dishwashing machine.
- **Flight conveyor:** the manual loading by operators of soiled ware within pegs mounted on a conveyor for automatic transportation through dishwasher.
- **Deferred wash:** the collection, stripping, sorting and stacking of ware by operators for dishwashing at later stage.

Essentially, the potential volume that can be accommodated increases, as does potential efficiency, from the manual method to the flight conveyor method, and the choice of method will be largely dependent on the scale of the operation. It is also often necessary to employ more than one method.

For hygienic washing-up the generally recognised requirements are a good supply of hot water at a temperature of 60°C for general cleansing followed by a sterilising rinse at a temperature of 82°C for at least one minute. Alternatively, low-temperature equipment is available that sterilises by means of a chemical: sodium hypochlorite (bleach).

Further information can be obtained from Lever Industrial, Lever House, St James Road, Kingston-upon-Thames, Surrey KT1 2BA.

Dishwashing machines take over an arduous job and save a lot of time and labour, ensuring that a good supply of clean sterilised cutlery, crockery and glassware is available. There are three main types of machine.

1 **Spray type:** the dishes are placed in racks that slide into the machines, where they are subjected to a spray of hot detergent water at 48–60°C from above and below. The racks then move on to the next section, where they are rinsed by a fresh hot shower at 82°C. At this temperature they are

sterilised, and on passing out into the air they dry off quickly.

2 **Brush type:** revolving brushes are used for the scrubbing of each article in hot detergent water; the articles are then rinsed and sterilised in another compartment.

3 **Agitator water machines:** baskets of dishes are immersed in deep tanks and the cleaning is performed by the mechanical agitation of the hot detergent water. The loaded baskets are then given a sterilising rinse in another compartment.

Dishwashing machines are costly and it is essential that the manufacturer's instructions with regard to use and maintenance are followed at all times.

Clearing following service

After the service periods, there is a variety of tasks and duties to be carried out, partly to clear from the previous service and partly to prepare for the next. The efficient management of the clearing stage can have a dramatic impact on the potential reuse of an area.

Included in this stage of the service sequence is the requirement for the management of cleaning programmes. Detailed cleaning schedules need to be developed to ensure that all cleaning activities are coordinated. These can be daily, weekly, monthly or for other periods. Alongside these cleaning schedules, it is desirable to incorporate maintenance checks. These, together with the operation of cleaning schedules, can help to ensure that equipment and facilities are always available and in working order.

The customer process

The customer receiving the food and beverage product is required to undertake or observe certain requirements – this is the *customer process*. If food and beverage service is viewed only as a delivery process, then the systems and procedures of an establishment tend to be designed only from the delivery perspective. However, for food and beverage service to work well then the customer has to be seen as being central to the process.

In food and beverage operations there are five basic processes that customers experience.

1 **Table service:** service at a laid cover. This type of service, which includes waiter service and bar counter service, is found in restaurants, cafés and in banqueting.

2 **Assisted service:** part service at a laid cover and part self-service. The customer is served part of the meal at a table and is required to obtain part

Figure 9.2 Self-service salad bar

through self-service from some form of display or buffet. This type of service is found in 'carvery'-type operations and is often used for meals such as breakfast in hotels.

3 **Self-service:** self-service by the customer. The customer is required to help him or herself from a buffet or counter. This type of service can be found in cafeterias and canteens.

4 **Service at a single point:** the customer orders, pays and receives the food and beverages at a single point – for example, at a counter, at a bar in licensed premises, in a fast-food operation or at a vending machine.

5 **Specialised service or service in situ:** the food and beverages are taken to where the customer is. This includes tray service in hospitals and

Figure 9.3 Fine dining

aircraft, trolley service, home delivery, lounge and room service.

In the first four of these customer processes, the customer comes to where the food and beverage service is offered, and then the service is provided in areas primarily designed for the purpose. However, in the fifth customer process, the service is provided in another location, and where the area is not primarily designed for the purpose. A summary of the five customer processes is shown in Table 9.1 and a full listing of all food and beverage service methods is given in Table 9.2.

Figure 9.4 Informal dining (brasserie)

Table 9.1 Simple categorisation of the customer processes in food and beverage service

Service method	Service area	Ordering/Selection	Service	Dining/Consumption	Clearing
Table service	Customer enters and is seated	From menu	By staff to customer	At laid cover	By staff
Assisted service	Customer enters and is usually seated	From menu, buffet or passed trays	Combination of both staff and customer	Usually at laid cover	By staff
Self-service	Customer enters	Customer selects items onto a tray	Customer carries	Dining area or takeaway	Various
Single-point service	Customer enters	Orders at single point	Customer carries	Dining area or takeaway	Various
Specialised or in situ service	Where the customer is located	From menu or predetermined	Brought to the customer	Served where the customer is located	By staff or customer clearing

Source: Cousins and Lillicrap (2010)

 ## Food and beverage service methods

(This section is adapted from Cousins and Lillicrap, 2010.)

There are 15 different service methods found in the hospitality industry and these fall into the five customer process groups identified in Table 9.1. The service methods are described in Table 9.2.

Table 9.2 Summary of the five food and beverage service customer processes

---

TABLE SERVICE

This is service of food and beverages to a customer at a laid cover.

1. **Waiter service**
   (a) *Silver/English service:* presentations and service of food to a customer by waiting staff from a food flat or dish.
   (b) *Family service:* main courses plated and with vegetables, placed in multi-portion dishes on tables for customers to help themselves. Any sauces are usually offered.
   (c) *Plated/American service:* service of pre-plated foods to customers, now widely used in many establishments and in banqueting.
   (d) *Butler/French service:* presentation of food individually to customers by food service staff for customers to serve themselves.
   (e) *Russian service:* table laid with food for customers to help themselves. (This is a modern interpretation, but may also be used to indicate guéridon or butler service.)
   (f) *Guéridon service:* food served on to a customer's plate at a side table or from a trolley. Also may include the preparation of salads and dressings, carving, cooking and flambé dishes.
2. **Bar counter service**
   Service to customers seated at a bar counter (usually U-shaped) on stools.

ASSISTED SERVICE

This is a combination of table service and self-service.

3. **Assisted**
   (a) Commonly applied to 'carvery'-type operations, some parts of the meal are served to seated customers; the customers collect other parts. Also used for breakfast service.
   (b) Buffets where customers select food and drink from displays or passed trays; consumption is either at tables, standing or in lounge area.

SELF-SERVICE

4. **Cafeteria service**
   (a) *Counter:* customers line up in a queue at a service counter and choose the menu items they require at different points. The customer places her items on a tray. Some establishments use a 'carousel' – a revolving, stacked counter saving space.
   (b) *Free flow:* selection as in a counter service. Customers move at will to random service point, exiting via a payment point.
   (c) *Echelon:* this is a series of counters at angles to customer flow within a free-flow area, thus saving space.
   (d) *Supermarket:* island service points within a free-flow area.
   Note: call order cooking may also feature in some cafeterias.

SINGLE-POINT SERVICE

This is the service of customers at a single point where they consume on the premises or they take away.

5. **Takeaway**
   Customer orders are served from a single point, usually at a counter, hatch or snack stand; customer normally consumes the food off the premises, although some takeaway establishments provide limited seating. This service method is commonly used for *fast-food* operations; this also includes *drive-thrus* where the customer drives a vehicle past order, payment and collection points.
6. **Vending**
   Automatic retailing of food and beverage products.
7. **Kiosks**
   Service provided by outstations during peak demand in specific locations.
8. **Food court**
   A group of autonomous counters where customers may either order and eat or buy from a number of counters and take away or eat in a central eating area.
9. **Bar**
   A selling point for the consumption of intoxicating liquor in licensed premises.

SPECIALISED (OR IN SITU) SERVICE
Service to customers where they are located and in areas not primarily designed for service.

10. **Tray service**
    Service of a meal or part of a meal in a tray to the customer in situ, e.g. in hospitals or in an aircraft.
11. **Trolley**
    Service of food and beverage from a trolley away from dining areas to customers – for instance, at their seats or desks. Used, for example, on an aircraft, on trains and in offices.
12. **Home delivery**
    Food and beverage delivered to a customer's home or place of work, e.g. pizza delivery, meals-on-wheels, or sandwiches to offices.
13. **Lounge service**
    Service of food and beverages in a lounge area, e.g. hotel lounge.
14. **Room service**
    Service of food and beverages in hotel guest rooms, or in meeting rooms.
15. **Drive-in**
    Customers are served food and beverages to their vehicles.

Note: banquet/function catering is a term used to describe food and beverage operations that are providing service for a specific number of people at specific times in a variety of dining layouts. Service methods also vary. The term banquet/function catering therefore refers to the organisation of service rather than a specific service method.

Source: adapted from Cousins and Lillicrap (2010)

Food and beverage service staff

In food and beverage establishments today, there are many different ways of using and deploying staff. In addition, differing terminology is used to describe what people do.

For food and beverage service staff the four key requirements are:

1 sound product knowledge
2 competence in technical skills
3 well-developed social skills, and
4 the ability to work as part of a team.

While there have been changes in food and beverage service, with less emphasis on the high-level techni-cal skills in some sectors, these four key requirements remain for all staff. However, the emphasis on these key requirements varies according to the type of establishment and the particular service methods being used.

Food and beverage staff play an important role in the overall customer meal experience. As well as being trained in knowledge of the product and technical service skills, service staff must be trained in customer service skills. They must have the ability to respond to customer needs and to observe the overall dynamics of a restaurant. Good food and beverage staff should, through experience, be

Figure 9.5 Gastropub dining

Figure 9.6 Fast food

able to anticipate the individual needs of customers and read their body language. Customers want individual attention; good service professionals should be able to anticipate the individual needs of the customer.

Roles in food and beverage service

The various types of job roles in food and beverage service are identified below. In smaller operations a number of these job roles may be combined. In addition, different terminology can be used for the various job roles in differing types of establishment.

Food and beverage manager

Depending on the size of the establishment, the food and beverage manager is either responsible for the implementation of agreed policies or for contributing to the setting of the food and beverage policies. The larger the organisation the less likely the manager is to be involved in policy setting. In general, food and beverage managers are responsible for:

- ensuring that the required profit margins are achieved for each food and beverage service area, in each financial period
- updating and compiling new wine lists according to availability of stock, current trends and customer needs
- compiling, in liaison with the kitchen, menus for the various food service areas and for special occasions
- purchasing of all materials, both food and drink
- ensuring that quality in relation to price paid is maintained
- determining portion size in relation to selling price
- ensuring staff training, sales promotions and maintenance of the highest professional standards
- employing and dismissing staff
- holding regular meetings with section heads to ensure all areas are working effectively, efficiently and are well coordinated.

Restaurant manager/supervisor

The restaurant manager or supervisor has overall responsibility for the organisation and administration of particular food and beverage service areas. These may include the lounges, room service (in hotels), restaurants and possibly some of the private function suites. It is the restaurant manager who sets the standards for service and is responsible for any staff training that may be required, either on or off the job. They may make out duty rotas, holiday lists, and

hours on and off duty, and contribute to operational duties (depending on the size of the establishment) so that all the service areas run efficiently and smoothly.

Reception headwaiter

The reception headwaiter is responsible for accepting any bookings and for keeping the booking diary up to date. S/he will reserve tables and allocate these reservations to particular stations. The reception headwaiter greets guests on arrival, takes them to the table and seats them.

Headwaiter/maître d'hôtel/supervisor

The headwaiter has overall charge of the staff team and is responsible for seeing that all the pre-preparation duties necessary for service are efficiently carried out and that nothing is forgotten. The headwaiter will aid the reception headwaiter during the service and will possibly take some orders if the station headwaiter is busy. The headwaiter also helps with the compilation of duty rotas and holiday lists, and may relieve the restaurant manager or reception headwaiter on their days off.

Figure 9.7 Serving wine

Station headwaiter/section supervisor

For larger establishments the restaurant area is broken down into sections. The station headwaiter has the overall responsibility for a team of staff serving a number of stations within a section of the restaurant area. Each of the sets of tables (which may be anything from four to eight in number) within the section of the restaurant area is called a *station*.

The station headwaiter must have a good knowledge of food and wine and its correct service, and be able to instruct other members of staff. He or she will take the food and beverage orders (usually from the host) and carry out service at the table with the help of the chef de rang, who is in command of one of the stations within the section.

Station waiter/chef de rang

The chef de rang, or station waiter, provides service to one set of tables (between about four and eight) known as a station within the restaurant area. The chef de rang will normally have had less experience than a station headwaiter.

Assistant station waiter/demi-chef de rang

The assistant station waiter or demi-chef de rang is the person next in seniority to the station waiter and assists as directed by the station waiter.

Waiter/server/commis de rang

The waiter or commis de rang acts by instruction from the chef de rang. This person mainly fetches and carries, may do some of the service of either vegetables or sauces, offers rolls, places plates upon the table and so on, and also helps to clear the tables after each course. During the pre-preparation period, many of the cleaning and preparatory tasks will be carried out by the commis de rang.

Trainee/commis/debarrasseur/apprentice

The trainee, commis or debarrasseur is the apprentice or learner, having just joined the food and beverage service staff, who wishes to take up food service as a career. During the service this person will keep the sideboard well stocked with equipment and may help to fetch and carry items as required. The debarrasseur will carry out some of the cleaning tasks during the pre-preparation periods. They may also be given the responsibility of looking after and serving hors d'oeuvres, cold sweets and assorted cheeses from the appropriate trolleys.

Carver/trancheur

The carver, or trancheur, is responsible for the carving trolley and the carving of joints at the table as required. The carver will plate up each portion and serve with accompaniments as appropriate. Very few establishments use this style of service.

Floor or room service staff/chef d'étage/ floor or room waiter

Floor or room service staff are often responsible for a complete floor in an establishment or, depending on the size of the establishment, a number of rooms or suites. Room service of all meals and beverages

throughout the day is normally offered only by a first-class establishment. In smaller establishments room service may be limited to early-morning teas and breakfasts with the provision of in-room mini bars, and tea and coffee facilities.

Lounge staff/chef de salle

Lounge service staff may be employed only for lounge service within larger establishments. In a smaller establishment it is usual for members of the food service staff to take over these duties on a rota basis. The lounge staff are responsible for the service of morning coffee, afternoon teas, aperitifs and liqueurs before and after both lunch and dinner, and any coffee required after meals. They are responsible for setting up the lounge in the morning, and maintaining its cleanliness and presentation throughout the day.

Wine butler/wine waiter/sommelier

The sommelier is responsible for the service of all alcoholic drinks and non-alcoholic bar drinks during the service of meals. The sommelier must also be a sales person. This employee should have a thorough knowledge of all drink to be served, of the best wines and drinks to go with certain foods, and of the liquor licensing laws in respect of the particular establishment and area.

The sommelier will advise on the wines to be stocked and the appropriate level of stock. This staff member will also train colleagues in dealing with wine and other drinks.

Figure 9.8 Bar

Bar staff/bar tender/mixologist

The people working within bar areas must be responsible and competent in preparing and serving a variety of wine, drinks and cocktails. They should have a thorough knowledge of all alcoholic and non-alcoholic drinks being offered within the establishment, and the ingredients necessary for the making of cocktails; they should also have knowledge of the requirements of the liquor licensing laws, to ensure legal compliance. A mixologist is an employee who mixes and serves alcoholic beverages at a bar; this is also often used as a name for people who are creators of new mixed drinks, and can also mean a cocktail maker or cocktail bar person, or simply bar tender. Mixology is the art of making mixed drinks.

Barista

The word *barista* is of Italian origin. In Italian, a barista is a male or female bar tender who typically works behind a counter, serving both hot and cold beverages as well as alcoholic beverages. Barista does not mean specifically a coffee maker, although it is now often used as such. The plural in English is baristas.

Buffet assistant/buffet chef/chef de buffet

The chef de buffet is in charge of the buffet in the room, its presentation, the carving and portioning of food and its service. This staff member will normally be a member of the kitchen team.

Cashier

The cashier is responsible for billing and taking payments or making ledger account entries for a food and beverage operation. This may include making up bills from food and drink checks or, in a cafeteria for example, charging customers for their selection of items on a tray.

Counter assistants

Counter assistants are found in cafeterias where they will stock the counter and sometimes serve or portion food for customers. Duties may also include some cooking of call-order items.

Table clearers

Table clearers can be found in seating areas where the service is not waiter service. These people are responsible for clearing tables using trolleys specially designed for the stacking of crockery, glassware, cutlery, etc.

Function catering/banqueting staff/events staff

In establishments with function catering facilities there will normally be a certain number of permanent staff. These will include the banqueting and conferencing manager, one or two assistant managers, one or two headwaiters, a dispense bar person and a secretary to the banqueting and conferencing manager. All other banqueting, conferencing and events staff are normally engaged as required on a casual basis. In small establishments, where there are fewer events, the manager, the assistant manager and the headwaiter will undertake the necessary administrative and organisational work.

Customer service specification

Increasing competition within the industry has meant that the quality of the service, and the perceived value of the experience had by the customers, have become the main differentiators between operations that are seeking to attract similar customers. Therefore understanding the customer's involvement in the process, and identifying the experience they are likely to have, and should expect, have become critical to the business success of food service operations.

Like the food, beverages and other product specifications, there must also be a *customer service specification*. For food and beverage operations, the customer service specification is focused as much on identifying the procedures that need to be followed (as summarised in the notes on the service sequence, pages 278–279, and the *customer process*, pages 280–281) as they are on the way they are carried out. This is because food and beverage is more than a delivery system – it also requires customers to be assisted in following various procedures, such as being seated at a table, and also to enable a positive interaction between staff and customers.

However, a customer service specification cannot be achieved if it does not take account of both the infrastructure supporting the specification as well as the ability to implement standards within the interactive phase. A customer service specification can be defined taking account of a combination of the following five key characteristics.

1 **Service level:** the method of service and the extent of the individual personal attention that is given to customers.
2 **Availability of service:** e.g. the opening times, the variation in the menus and wine and drinks lists on offer.
3 **Level of standards:** e.g. food quality, decor, equipment cost, staffing professionalism.
4 **Reliability of the service:** the extent to which the product is intended to be consistent in practice.
5 **Flexibility of the service:** the provision of alternatives, or variations in the standard product on offer.

In designing a food service operation to meet a customer service specification, care is taken to ensure the profitability of the operation by considering the efficiency of the use of resources. The resources used in food service operations are as listed below.

- **Materials:** commodities and equipment
- **Labour:** staffing and staff costs
- **Facilities:** the premises and the volume of business that the premises are physically able to support.

The management of the operation must therefore take account of the effect that the level of business has on the ability of the operation to maintain the service, while at the same time ensuring a high productivity in all the resources being used.

The operation must be physically capable of supporting the customer service specification. Otherwise limitations in the physical capabilities of the operation to meet the requirements of the customer service specification will always be the cause of difficulties. In addition, the staff must be capable of supporting the intended customer service specification. This takes account of the technical and interpersonal skills, product knowledge and team-working capability of the staff.

As well as the interaction with customers, service staff also are interacting with staff outside of the service areas, e.g. kitchen staff, bill office staff, dispense bar staff, still room staff. It is important that the provision of the food and beverage product within an establishment is seen as a joint effort between all departments, with each department understanding the needs of the others in order to meet customers' demands.

In order to minimise problems with customer relations, there has to be equal concern over the physical aspects of the service, the way in which the service is operated, and with the interpersonal interaction between customers and staff. Knowing what the potential for customer satisfaction is from the food and beverage product can help to ensure that there are procedures in place for dealing with any difficulties that might arise. The potential for satisfaction should already have been built in to the design of the product so that it meets the needs the customers have at the time. There is, though, also the potential for dissatisfaction. Potential dissatisfactions fall into two categories: *tangible* (those that are controllable by the establishment, such as scruffy, unhelpful staff or cramped conditions); and *intangible* (those that are uncontrollable, such as the behaviour of other customers, the weather or transport problems). Being able to identify all of these possibilities provides an operation with the potential to have procedures in place to deal with them when they occur.

Restaurant planning

Restaurant planning needs to focus on the market the establishment is aiming to attract, its customers, the theme the restaurant will take, and the type of food and service it is going to offer. In any establishment a customer's first impressions on entering the service area are of great importance. A customer may be gained or lost on these impressions alone. The creation of atmosphere, by the right choice of decor, furnishings and equipment, is therefore a major factor that contributes to the success of the food service operation. A careful selection of items in terms of shape, design and colour enhances the overall decor or theme, and contributes towards a feeling of total harmony. The choice of layout, furniture, linen, tableware, small equipment and glassware will be determined by considering:

- the type of clientele expected
- the site or location
- the layout of the food and beverage service area
- the type of service offered
- the funds available.

There are many service areas behind the scenes, or what may be termed *back of house*. These areas are usually between the kitchen and food and beverage

Figure 9.11 Restaurant receptionist

service areas. They are important parts of the design of a food service operation, acting as the link between kitchen or food preparation areas and the restaurant or food and beverage service areas. These areas are also meeting points for staff of various departments as they carry out their duties, and therefore there must be close liaison between these various members of staff and between the departments to ensure the smooth running of the operation.

In general, especially in large operations, five main back-of-house service areas can be identified. These are:

1 still room (the area directly between the food production area and the food service area, and where food and beverage items are prepared for the service of a meal that are not catered for by the other major departments in a food

service operation, such as the kitchen, larder and pastry)
2 silver or plate room (for the storage of all metal service equipment)
3 wash-up (usually adjacent to the still room area)
4 hotplate (often called the pass, where orders are given in and collected from the food production area by service staff)
5 spare linen store (used for paper and linen).

A well-designed layout of all these areas is important to ensure an even flow of work by the various members of staff. However, the layout itself may vary with different establishments, depending on the type of operational needs.

The general considerations for the planning of the back-of-house service areas are:

- appropriate siting and logical layout of equipment
- ease of delivery access
- ease of service
- meet hygiene, health and safety requirements
- ease of cleaning
- sufficient storage space for service equipment and food items
- security.

The *front-of-house* areas are used by both customers and staff, and include:

- food service area(s)
- reception – the place for taking bookings, receiving customers and processing the bills
- licensed bar
- coffee lounge
- customer cloakroom facilities.

Table 9.3 Examples of space allocation in different types of food and beverage service areas

Restaurant and hotel dining areas	
Style	**Space per cover (m²)**
Traditional restaurant	1
Banqueting	0.9
High-class restaurants	2
(Note: for safety reasons all aisles should be 1 metre wide)	

Cafeteria – square metres per meal served/hour:			
Meals	Up to 200	200–500	500+
m²	0.45–0.70	0.35–0.45	0.25–0.35

Fast-food outlets: the average overall size of most fast-food outlets is currently around 1000–1500 m²

Note: space allocation includes sideboards, aisles, etc.

Source: adapted from Cousins, Foskett and Gillespie (2002)

The general considerations for the planning of the areas used by both customers and staff include first the general considerations for staff-only back-of-house areas as above, and then taking into account the consideration of:

- decor and lighting
- heating and ventilation
- noise level
- the size and shape of the areas.

In most food service operations the back-of-house and front-of-house areas are quite separate so that customers cannot see into the back-of-house areas, especially the kitchen. More recently, food service operations are making a feature of the cooking area; this is in full view of the customer and contributes to their meal experience. In this case the kitchen is a central feature with some of the cooking smells and noise going into the food service area.

Space

The amount of space required per customer depends on the type of standard expected from the style and theme of the operation. Consideration has to be given to comfort versus the maximum number of customers you are trying to fit into the restaurant. The more upmarket the restaurant, the more comfortable and spacious it should be. Examples of the space allocation for different types of food and beverage service areas are given in Table 9.3.

Liquor and other licensing

The sale of alcoholic liquor is subject to the Licensing Act (2003) requirements, which have four key objectives:

1 the prevention of crime and disorder
2 public safety
3 the prevention of public nuisance
4 the protection of children from harm.

The usual requirements of the Act are:

- the display of a summary of the premises licence, including the days and times of opening, the name of the registered licence holder, the licence number and a valid date
- drinks price lists to be displayed

- restrictions on under-aged persons being served alcohol and employed to serve alcohol
- the need for an authorised person (or the personal licence holder) to be on site at all times.

Other types of licence may include, for example, licences for music (live or pre-recorded), dancing, gambling, theatrical performance and television display. In all cases the supervisor and the staff should be aware of the provisions and limitations of the licences to ensure compliance. Further information regarding licensing in England and Wales should be sought from the local Licensing Authority covering the area of the establishment.

Matching food to wine/drinks

Food and its accompanying wine/drink should harmonise well, with each enhancing the other's performance. However, the combinations that prove most successful are those that please the individual.

Wine and food

When considering possible food and wine partnerships there are no guidelines to which there are not exceptions; however, general guidelines on matching wine and food are summarised in Table 9.4.

Some general guidelines when selecting and serving wines are given below.

- Dry wines should be served before sweeter wines.
- White wines should be served before red wines.
- Lighter wines should be served before heavier wines.
- Good wines should be served before great wines.
- Wines should be at their correct temperature before serving.
- Wine should always be served to customers before their food.

Table 9.4 General guidelines for matching wine and food

Characteristic	Food Considerations
Acidity	Can be used to match, or to contrast, acidity in foods – for example, crisp wines to match lemon or tomato, or to cut through creamy flavours
Age/maturity	As wine ages and develops it can become delicate, with complex and intricate flavours; more simple foods, such as grills or roasts, work better with older wines than stronger-tasting foods, which can overpower the wines
Oak	The more oaked the wine, the more robust and flavoursome the foods need to be; heavily oaked wines can overpower more delicate foods
Sweetness	Generally the wine should be sweeter than the foods or it will taste flat or thin; sweet dishes need contrast for them to match well with sweeter wines – for example, acids in sweeter foods can harmonise with the sweetness in the wines; savoury foods with sweetness (e.g. carrots or onions) can match well with ripe fruity wines; blue cheeses can go well with sweet wines, also sweeter wines can go well with salty foods
Tannin	Tannic wines match well with red meats and semi-hard cheeses (e.g. Cheddar); tannic wines are not good with egg dishes and wines with high tannin content do not work well with salty foods
Weight	Big, rich wines go well with robust (flavoursome) meat dishes, but can overpower lighter-flavoured foods

Source: Cousins and Lillicrap (2010)

Beers and food

Recently there has been an increasing trend to offer beers with food, either alongside or as an alternative to wines. As with wines it is a question of trial and error to achieve harmony between particular beers and foods. Generally the considerations for the pairing of beers and foods are similar to those for matching wines with foods, as shown in Table 9.4, and in particular, taking account of acidity, sweetness/dryness, bitterness, tannin, weight and the complexity of the taste.

Making recommendations to customers

A few general pointers are set out below that may be followed when advising the customer on which beverage to choose to accompany a meal. However, customers should at all times be given complete freedom in their selection of wines or other drinks.

- Apéritifs are usually alcoholic beverages that are drunk before the meal. If wine will be consumed with the meal, then the aperitif selected should be a grape (wine-based) rather than a grain (spirit-based) aperitif, since the latter can potentially spoil or dull the palate.
- The aperitif is usually a wine-based beverage. It is meant to stimulate the appetite and therefore should not be sweet. Dry and medium dry sherries, dry vermouths and Sercial or Verdelho Madeira are all good examples of aperitifs.
- Starter courses are often best accompanied by a dry white or dry rosé wine.
- National dishes should normally be complemented by the national wines of that country – for example, Italian red wine with pasta dishes.
- Fish and shellfish dishes are often most suited to well-chilled dry white wines.
- Red meats such as beef and lamb blend and harmonise well with red wine.
- White meats such as veal and pork are acceptable with medium white wines.
- Game dishes require the heavier and more robust red wines to complement their full flavour.
- Sweets and desserts are served at the end of the meal, and here it is acceptable to offer well-chilled sweet white wines that may come from the Loire, Sauternes, Barsac or Hungary. These wines harmonise best with dishes containing fruit.
- The majority of cheeses blend well with port and other dry, robust red wines. Port is the traditional wine that harmonises best with Stilton cheese.
- The grain- and fruit-based spirits and liqueurs all harmonise well with coffee.

The nature of alcohol and how it affects the body

Alcohol is classed as a drug because, when consumed, it alters the physical, mental and emotional state of the drinker. Where the alcohol by volume (ABV) is over 0.5 per cent, the drink is classed as alcohol for the purpose of licensing law.

Strength of alcoholic drinks

The strength of an intoxicating drink depends on how much alcohol it contains. The amount of alcohol contained is expressed as percentage of alcohol by volume: 'ABV' for short. The formula for expressing ABV on labels is alc % vol or % vol. So a fortified wine, such as sherry or vermouth, labelled as alc 18% vol means that 18 per cent of any given quantity is pure alcohol.

Examples

- Whisky labelled as alc 40% vol or 40% vol means 40 per cent of any given quantity is pure alcohol. Most spirits are around 40 per cent ABV.
- Wines labelled as alc 12% vol or 12% vol means that 12 per cent of any given quantity is pure alcohol. Wines vary from 8 per cent to 16 per cent ABV.
- Beer labelled as alc 3.2% vol or 3.2% vol means that 3.2 per cent of any quantity is pure alcohol. Beers range from 3 per cent to 9 per cent ABV. Ciders range from 3 per cent to 8.5 per cent ABV.

Alcohol-free and low-alcohol drinks

To be classified as alcohol-free, a drink must contain no more than 0.05 per cent ABV; to be classified as low alcohol, no more than 1.2 per cent ABV. Both must be labelled accordingly.

Units of alcohol

A unit is 8 grams (g) or 10 millilitres (ml) of alcohol. Any quantity of drink that contains 8 g or 10 ml of alcohol is said to contain one unit. Half a pint of beer of 3.6 per cent ABV contains about 8 g of alcohol, hence one unit. One 25 ml measure of whisky of 40 per cent ABV also contains 8 g of alcohol; therefore in alcohol intake terms, half a pint of beer 3.6 per cent ABV 8 g of alcohol is equivalent to one measure of whisky.

Recommended safe limits of alcohol

Moderate drinking can be beneficial to health; excessive drinking can be detrimental to health. Recommended safe limits of alcohol, as recommended by the government and other organisations such as the Portman Group, are as follows:

- men should drink no more than three to four units a day and no more than 21 units per week
- women should drink no more than two to three units a day and no more than 14 units per week.

Alcohol in the body

When drunk, alcohol is absorbed into the blood and reaches all parts of the body. Most of the alcohol is absorbed rapidly into the bloodstream. Nearly all

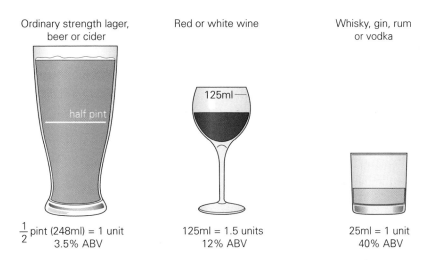

Ordinary strength lager, beer or cider

Red or white wine

Whisky, gin, rum or vodka

125ml

half pint

$\frac{1}{2}$ pint (248ml) = 1 unit
3.5% ABV

125ml = 1.5 units
12% ABV

25ml = 1 unit
40% ABV

Figure 9.10 Popular drinks and their units

the alcohol has to be burned up by the liver and the rest is disposed of either in sweat or urine. A person becomes drunk because he/she drinks alcohol faster than his/her body can eliminate it, to a point where it affects the body. The amount of alcohol in the bloodstream is measured by the blood alcohol concentration (BAC). BAC varies according to a person's sex, weight, body composition and speed of drinking.

BAC is measured in milligrams (mg) of alcohol in millilitres of blood. A BAC of 80 mg of alcohol in 100 ml of blood is the level above which it is an offence to drive. This measurement has an equivalent in terms of micrograms in ml of breath (35 micrograms in 100 ml of breath). This can be measured using a breathalyser.

The amount of alcohol that gets into the bloodstream and the speed with which it does, depends on the following factors.

- **Quantity:** how many drinks a person consumes and how strong the drinks are.
- **The size of a person:** the amount of alcohol will produce a higher BAC in women than men.

- **Food eaten:** the presence of food in the stomach slows down the rate at which alcohol enters the bloodstream.

Usually about 20 minutes after the last drink, BAC starts to fall. Some alcohol is lost through the lungs, some in the urine but most is removed by the liver as the blood circulates through it. As a rough guide, it takes one hour to remove one unit of alcohol from the body.

What is a sensible limit?

People must keep to the recommended sensible limits to avoid damaging their health. As noted above, the recommended sensible limit is up to 21 units for men and up to 14 units a week for women, with one or two drink-free days (see Figure 9.11). Remember, there are times when even one or two drinks can be too much – for example, if you are going to drive or operate machinery. It can be dangerous to drink alcohol if you are taking certain types of medicine.

Designing a food service system

The process of designing a food service facility is complex and dynamic. It encompasses the many facets of business planning, right through to the development of facility layout drawings, interior designs and equipment specifications. It is certainly not unusual for an operator to consider opening a new restaurant or actually open a restaurant without knowing what type of facility will have the best chance of success. A potential operator may have sufficient money to invest, a location or a theme in mind, and a great amount of enthusiasm to make it work – but they may not have adequately considered the total concept of the operation.

Concept development in the food service industry means planning the menu, developing a theme for the decor and developing a method of serving food to an identified target market to achieve an acceptable level of profit from the operation. Concept development should also encompass a strategy for growth and for a reasonable financial return on investment.

The 'five Ms'

In order to have a successful food service operation, an operator must combine the following elements into a comprehensive and cohesive plan:

- the **M**enu

- the **M**arket
- the **M**oney needed
- competent **M**anagement
- a **M**ethod of execution.

The menu

One can't overemphasise the importance of the menu in the design of any food service facility, and its ultimate success or failure. From a design and layout perspective, the following are some of the major operational and design factors influenced or driven by the menu:

- the selling price of the food
- the type of cooking equipment that will be needed
- the production capacities of the various pieces of cooking equipment that will be used
- the size of refrigeration and storage areas required
- the size of the dishwashing area, as well as the capacity of the machines
- the total amount of floor space that will be needed
- the type and capacity of seating
- the design and type of service area(s)
- the total financial investment that will be needed.

The market

Conducting market research studies prior to proceeding with the construction of a food service facility is an important component of any concept development plan. Some of the basic marketing questions that should be addressed include those listed below.

- To whom is the food service operation being marketed? In other words, what is the target market or potential customer base?
- Is the identified market large enough to generate acceptable levels of sales and profits?
- What are the tastes, preferences and motivations of the target market?
- What are the best methods of marketing communication to reach the target market or customer base?
- What are the appropriate messages that will influence and motivate the target audience to listen and act?
- Will the target audience need or want the food items that are being planned or the facility?
- Will the operation's internal marketing efforts be successful in selling the customer additional products and services after they have arrived at the food service facility?

One of the classic marketing mistakes made by operators is not acting on the marketing data that have been obtained. Instead, decisions are made based on a 'gut' feeling. Many gut-feeling decisions have resulted in failed operations and subsequent ulcers for owners.

The money

One of the primary causes of the high failure rate of food service operations is lack of money – in particular, lack of money set aside for working capital. Often, an operator or prospective operator has access to sufficient funds to get the proposed food service venture off the ground. Unfortunately, these individuals fail to plan for the day-to-day cash requirements of product purchases and payroll demands. As a result, they quickly find themselves in a working capital deficit position.

In addition to the need for sufficient working capital, the proper capitalisation of a food service facility must include sufficient funds for:

- professional planning and design
- new building construction or the renovation of an existing building
- professional interior design and decorating

- the purchase of various pieces of equipment and supply items, and
- the purchase of furniture and fixtures.

Funds for these items must be identified and committed before any serious planning can begin. However, in the early concept development stage of the design process, such commitments may not be made simply because all of the costs are not known. Therefore, the planning process for capital funds should be considered a two-phase process.

In the initial phase, the financial needs of the operation are estimated and, if the prospective operator or owner does not have sufficient personal funds to cover all of the expenses, then sources of financial support should be contacted to determine the possibility of obtaining necessary funds.

Next, lenders and investors make firm financial commitments after the concept development has taken place, preliminary designs and construction estimates have been made and market research has been completed.

Management

The quality and style of management in any food service operation are the most important elements in achieving success. The following questions need to be addressed by any owner and investor.

- Who will actually run the day-to-day affairs of the food service facility? Will it be the owner or majority shareholder, or will an outside 'professional' manager be hired to run the operation?
- What kind of educational background and food service experience must the manager and management team have?
- What level of assistance will be available to the manager? In other words, who will assist the general manager in covering the long hours often required to operate a food service facility?
- What kind of level of remuneration will the manager and his/her assistants receive?
- Will the remuneration package contain an incentive for performance?
- How will operational policies be established?
- How will these policies be communicated to the management team?
- How will the management team communicate with the rest of the operation's employees?

The answers to these and related questions will help determine the organisational structure of the operation and the kind of management team needed to operate the facility in an effective and efficient manner.

Many successful restaurants are owned and operated by one individual whose personality becomes a part of the guests' dining experience. On the other hand, the management of the food and beverage department of a large hotel, or the food service director in a large hospital or university, may be under the control of more than one person and is usually part of a more complex organisational team. In these cases, the policies and procedures of the food service facility should be laid out in an operations manual, to ensure consistent implementation of management policies.

Method of execution

This last step in the concept development process is centred on operational issues. Three of the primary areas that need to be addressed deal with methods of production, control systems and various personnel issues.

Methods of food production raise questions such as: 'Will pre-prepared foods be used or will the more traditional "from scratch" methods of cooking be used?' This particular decision will have a major influence on the size of refrigerated and dry storage areas, and on the size of the kitchen. The chosen production method will also greatly influence the number of employees in the kitchen, as well as the skill levels of these employees.

Food and beverage control systems involve many different areas and individuals within a food service facility. Planning for these controls before the project has been completed, or even before it is under construction, is highly recommended. Specific areas that should be looked at, and control procedures that should be established include:

- cash control
- sales analysis
- control of the guests' bills and receipts
- food production forecasting
- control over the various storage areas, including refrigeration
- purchasing and receiving control
- portion control
- quality control.

Operators significantly increase their chances of success when all of these areas have been critically examined and sufficient controls have been established.

How management deals with key personnel issues can significantly affect the success of any operation. Areas that should be addressed include:

- determining the amount of required labour
- the establishment of employee work schedules
- the determination of operating hours
- staffing patterns
- the various benefits that will be offered to employees
- the varying skill levels that will exist among employees
- the level of supervision that will be required
- issues that are centred on the remuneration package.

These, plus many other closely associated issues, must be addressed as part of the concept development process.

The feasibility study

Once the concept development process has been completed, it is time to move on to the next phase, which focuses on assessing the feasibility of the concept. Many terms are commonly used within the food service industry to describe the process of determining whether or not a proposed operation is likely to return a profit to its owner(s) or investors. But the term that is most frequently used and best describes this process is 'feasibility study'.

The primary goal of a feasibility study is to determine a food service facility's potential to generate sales and profits. This will in turn have a direct impact on the ROI (return on investment) analysis, which is critical to each investor in the operation.

A comprehensive feasibility study consists of many components. One of these components is the *market feasibility* study. This phase deals with all the issues associated with the marketplace, including those listed below.

- A comprehensive analysis of the demographics of the proposed geographical area to be served. This would include but not be limited to: age, sex, income level, size of household, occupation, ethnicity, etc.
- An analysis of the buying and eating-out habits of the individuals in the area under study. This sort of information could be obtained through a questionnaire or survey process.
- An analysis of the traffic patterns of the area, including an assessment of roadway access, future street development, availability of public transportation, etc.
- An analysis of general economic factors, such as employment statistics, industry growth, future economic development plans, tax structure and commercial growth in the area.

- A detailed competitive analysis, to include size (number of seats), estimated customer counts, menu items, pricing, decor or theme, and professionalism of the staff at existing food service operations within the potential service area.
- A projection of sales. This would be based on a 'guesstimated' customer count over a specific period of time, as well as on an estimation of what the average bill amount might be.

Understanding and properly responding to the target market are two of the keys to success, for any food service operation. Another critical component that needs to be tackled is the *financial feasibility study*. Typically required by lending institutions, as well as by private investors, the financial feasibility study should paint a financial picture of the proposed operation, based on the information obtained in the market feasibility study. This study should include the following.

- A pro forma profit and loss statement. This should be supported by a sales analysis, an analysis of the cost of goods sold, plus a fixed and variable cost analysis.
- A pro forma balance sheet, detailing all assets and liabilities.
- A projected cash flow analysis. This document is critical. If done properly, it will provide the operator with valuable information on the short- and long-term cash requirements of the organisation.

These projections should cover a three-year time frame. Of course, the further one goes out into the future, the more difficult it becomes to forecast accurately. However, it does force the operator to look at the long-term picture and not just focus on the immediate or short-term needs of the proposed facility.

Once the comprehensive feasibility study is complete, it is up to the prospective operator and/or investors to make the critical 'go or no-go' decision. If, after a careful analysis of the findings and projections, the project looks financially sound, the market is identified and can be reached easily, a need for the proposed food service facility exists, and sufficient funding and working capital is available, the decision to proceed can be made with confidence.

However, if one or more of the critical elements associated with the decision process is uncertain, there are a few alternatives to explore. One of the first options is modification of the proposed concept to address the problem area or areas identified. For instance, the facility may be too large. (Downsize the facility.) The labour cost estimates may have been too

high. (Change the service concept.) The menu may be wrong for that particular market. (Change the menu.) The originally proposed menu prices may be too high based on the customer demographic information obtained. (Change the price structure and menu.) Finally, the local competition may be stronger than originally assumed. (Consider an alternative location or concept.)

The second option is to abandon the project altogether. If the projections and conclusions drawn in the feasibility study do not paint a positive picture, then there is no point in trying to 'force' the numbers.

The third option is to procrastinate and delay the go/no-go decision until a later date. This is the least desirable option. It may cost the operator just to keep the proposed project alive.

Assuming that a 'go' decision is made, the design process moves into an entirely new phase: the hiring of a professional food service facility designer or a food service design consultant, as they are frequently called.

Today's modern food service facilities are very complex systems, made up of numerous interrelated sub-systems. They are also very expensive. In order for a food service operation to function smoothly and at the optimum level of efficiency and effectiveness, it has to be designed properly, taking into consideration numerous factors, such as energy, labour, space, equipment requirements, traffic flow and menu, to mention a few. This type of complexity requires the services of a professional who has been educated and trained in the intricacies of food service operations. Thus, most operators or prospective operators today rely on the services of food service design consultants to help them through the critical stages of the overall design process, equipment selection, construction and even project start-up.

The benefits from using a professional food service facility design consultant include:

- potential savings in operational costs as a result of efficiencies in physical layout and design
- potential savings in equipment costs, the result of proper selection
- construction cost savings from more efficient utilisation of space
- review and synchronisation of construction and installation
- savings on the purchase prices of equipment and supplies from properly written specifications and bid documents

- operator or owner peace of mind in knowing that the planning and design of their facility was provided by a trained professional.

There are other professionals who may be involved in the overall planning and design process. They range from interior designers who will help guide and coordinate the theme of the facility, to accountants, lawyers, architects and bankers. The services of these necessary members of the team should be viewed as a good financial investment. Proper use of their services will help increase the facility's chances of success.

Now it's time to begin the actual design process …

The design process

The design process should be very interactive in nature. The professional design consultant should always be 'listening' to his/her client to ensure that the decisions assumed at the initiation of the project are still in place and that, if any other variables have come into play, they are accounted for in the overall design and layout process. Conversely, the operator should have a constant dialogue with the food service design consultant to ensure that requests are being

handled to their satisfaction and in a professional manner.

The design function normally follows a nine-phase process. Each phase is critical to both the design consultant and client/operator. In addition, each stage is totally interdependent on each of the other stages. The following model outlines the natural sequence of events that takes place between the design consultant and the food service facility operator/owner.

Phase 1: initial contact and proposal

At this initial phase in the design continuum, the client is encouraged to explore with the consultant which services they can provide, and the costs of those services. This initial phase is designed to establish the ground rules and future working relationship between the design consultant and their client.

Phase 2: feasibility study

The importance of the feasibility study was discussed in some detail earlier in this chapter. One of the roles of the food service design consultant is to assist the prospective operator/client in conducting a proper feasibility study. The results of this study greatly

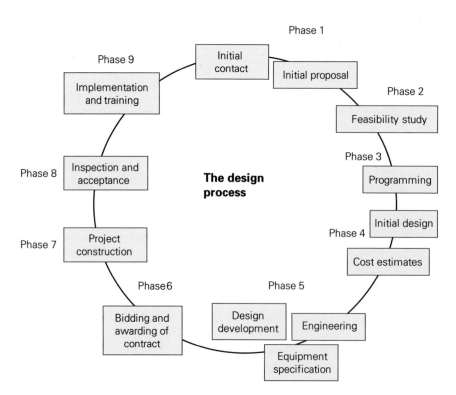

Figure 9.11 The sequence of events between design consultant and food service facility operator/owner (source: CESA)

assist the design consultant with various aspects and phases of the work.

Phase 3: programming

A programme for a food service facility describes in words the function of each area in the building, how that particular space will be most frequently used, and the number of square metres required to serve the stated needs. A typical food service facility's programme includes the following categories of information:

- the room number
- the name of the room (i.e. the kitchen)
- the relationship of this room (the kitchen) to the other rooms in the design
- a description of use
- the amount of square metres required, and
- the finishes (this includes the types of materials and finishes to be used on the floors, walls, ceilings, etc.).

The key element in the programming phase is the establishment of space relationships among the functional areas of the facility. After the space relationships are established and the programme summarised, the total square metre space requirements are discussed with the client. It is at this point that, if changes need to be made (for example, a reduction in the total square metres in the proposed facility) because of financial constraints or for any other reason, they are initiated.

Phase 4: initial design and cost estimates

The primary purpose of the initial design or schematic drawings is to show the shape of the building, the various entrances and flow patterns, plus the location of the dining room, kitchen and all the other functional areas within the proposed facility. These drawings will show elevations of the outside of the building (if applicable), site plans for the building lot, and the location of roads, parking areas, etc. In addition, and if required, schematic drawings are often used to gain preliminary approval from local authority planning departments. Formal acceptance of the building and/or food service facility floor plan should be in writing, by the owner and the architect (if one is involved in the project), as well as by the food service design consultant.

Phase 5: design development, equipment specification and engineering

It is during this phase that the food service design consultant, along with the engineers and architect, begins the detailed work. Working drawings – the detailed plans that will guide and be used by contractors who actually build the facility – are developed during this phase of the process. The selection of all the equipment to be used in the facility, the assembly of equipment literature, writing performance specifications and the development of utility schedules will be accomplished.

During this phase it is extremely important for the design consultant and the client to maintain a high

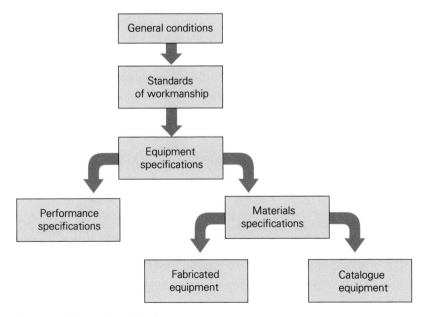

Figure 9.12 Types of specification

level of contact and communication. Many important project decisions are made. All parties should be involved in this process.

Equipment specification is one of the most important components of the design development process. These specifications can be written in several different ways, but the most important thing is to ensure the exact requirements for the equipment are clearly written. The equipment must be described in such a manner that the bidder is in no doubt about the required specification of the equipment and that he quotes accordingly. From a design consultant's perspective, the 'best' piece of equipment is the piece that matches the specification exactly.

Phase 6: bidding and awarding the contract

The bidding and awarding of the contract is a process that can vary in length of time, depending on the complexity and size of the project under consideration.

Phase 7: project construction

During the construction phase of the overall process, the role of the food service design consultant is primarily to:

- work closely with the general contractor and architect, and answer any questions as to the design work the consultant has done
- inspect the fabricated equipment to make sure it has been built to specification and that it meets all of the requirements written into the specification documents.

Phase 8: inspection and acceptance

The new food service facility will be inspected at least twice by the design consultant, owner/operator, equipment dealer and all other constituents in the process.

Phase 9: implementation and training

Demonstration of all the equipment found in the faculty, along with thorough training sessions designed to explain the layout and design of the equipment to all employees, is an important function that should not be overlooked.

The basic principles of design

Although there are significant differences in the physical layout, menu and method of service between the various types of food service facility, there are some underlying design principles that are consistently followed by all food service design consultants. Every food service project design should:

- have flexibility and modularity built in to it
- be designed for simplicity
- be designed so that there is an efficient flow of material and personnel
- facilitate the ease of sanitation
- make it easy to supervise the employees of the facility, and
- make efficient use of the space that is available.

The flow of materials and people

The movement of food through a food service facility should follow a logical sequence starting with receiving and storage functions and continuing through to the disposal of waste products and waste.

> **Detailed information on all aspects of food and beverage service can be found in Cousins and Lillicrap (2010).**

> **Some references to food and beverage service elsewhere in this book:**
> | | |
> |---|---|
> | Beverages | 96 |
> | Customer care | 321 |
> | Establishments | 12 |
> | Managing people | 306 |
> | Marketing | 314 |
> | Menus | 227 |

References

CESA: *An Introduction to the Food Service Industry* (hand-out given to CFSP course delegates).

Cousins, J. and Lillicrap, D.R. (2010) *Essential Food and Beverage Service*. London: Hodder Education.

Cousins, J., Foskett, D. and Gillespie, C. (2002) *Food and Beverage Management* (2nd edn). Pearson Education.

Topics for discussion

1 Discuss the relationship between kitchen staff and waiting staff. Explain how good relations may be developed.

2 Discuss the merits of six different methods of service and the kind of establishment for which they would be suitable.

3 Why should food service staff be knowledgeable about the food dishes they will serve?

4 Why should the kitchen staff appreciate the role of the waiting staff?

5 Explain your reasons for what you consider to be a suitable selection for a wine/drink list. State the kind of establishment you have in mind.

6 Discuss the following statement: 'Every chef should serve as a waiter and every waiter work as chef for a period of time.'

7 What is your opinion of the kitchen being on view to the customers? What do you think is the opinion of customers?

8 Discuss how the food service design process should be implemented.

10 Managing resources

Supporting material available on Dynamic Learning Online:

> Knowledge quizzes

> Activity worksheet: managing people

> Summary presentations

Assessing yourself as a manager

To effectively manage people and resources it is first essential to have the ability to manage yourself; to do this, it is essential to analyse yourself truthfully, assess your weaknesses and take positive action to improve. This is necessary so that self-development improves.

'Know yourself and to yourself be true' is a maxim that assists the potential manager to develop and earn the respect of those he or she will manage. It is not easy to assess one's own personality, nor is it easy to improve or change it. The following self-analysis guide may be helpful.

● Having assessed your strengths and weaknesses, what need or needs do you require to be self-fulfilled or self-satisfied in order to develop into a successful manager? In catering, because of the variety of roles, most people's needs can be met. These include the need: to achieve; to be friendly; to show off; to be tenacious; to be free of controls; to have power; to have sympathy; to seek knowledge; to be orderly; to show care.

● Having concluded the kind of person you think

you are (which may not be the same as others see you) list your qualities and your failings, and endeavour to change those you think should be changed. To be successful in achieving this it is essential to be positive and really want to improve. Be clear about the benefits of what you hope to gain. Know what you want and, when things do not go as expected, have other options and seek the advice and help of others.

Key skills for management

These include:

● self-management
● resource management
● communication
● decision making.
● time management

We will now take a closer look at some of these.

Self-management

Effective management starts with how you see yourself, how superiors see you and how those you are responsible for see you. First and subsequent impressions are vital to successful development as a manager. First, what constitutes a good manager: what qualities, attitudes and values are desirable to form the basis from which to improve?

- Honesty and integrity.
- Orderly and of neat appearance.
- Loyalty and conscientiousness.
- Able to lead and set an example.
- Willingness and cooperativeness.
- Enthusiastic and punctual.
- Courteous and caring.

Direction

To progress it is essential to be able to clarify roles, to focus on key issues and to specify targets and standards – that is, to know in what direction you are going and how you intend to get there.

Teamwork

When working in a team it is essential to plan, to use the ideas of the team members so that you can be effective.

Actions

Actions need to be taken. Prevarication, hesitancy and lethargy do not help decision making (see below). However, before acting, ensure that priorities are right, and use resources, manpower, finances, equipment and commodities efficiently.

Results

Analyse problems, give and receive feedback and use the information to persuade others, thus improving your own performance.

Positive balanced management

To improve performance, clear positive thinking and the ability to generate enthusiasm may be helpful. A flexible approach, sensitive to others' feelings and expectations and capable of inspiring them may well develop confidence in one's own ability.

Decision making

1 Define the aim.
2 Collect the information.
3 List possible courses of action.
4 Evaluate the pros and cons, examine the consequences and make the decisions.
5 Act on the decision, monitor and review it.

Table 10.1 Different types of people as managers

Category or type of person		Management skills that may need improving
Confident Bold Arrogant	Self-centred Authoritative Independent	May be too bossy and aggressive, needs to develop patience
Optimistic Cheerful Enthusiastic	Sociable Articulate Persuasive	May be too friendly and require greater self-discipline in difficult management situations
Relaxed Patient Laid back	Stable Passive Calm	May be unwilling to change and lacks any sense of urgency to change
Careful Neat Perfectionist	Self-disciplined Accurate Aggressive	May find difficulty in delegating, worry too much and be defensive
Agreeable Self-effacing Frustrated	Peaceful Unassuming Easily discouraged	May find leadership hard and become discouraged in difficult situations
Reserved Quiet Pessimistic	Distant Imaginative Remote	May be shy and unsociable, and not good at dealing with people
Restless Erratic Tense	Impetuous Quick Highly strung	May be seen as impatient, intolerant and aggressive, may need to learn to calm down
Independent Stubborn Argumentative	Informal Uninhibited	May be an effective delegator but unreliable and not good at making decisions

First, know why a decision has been made and consider the situation and possible solutions. Evaluate how the aim will be achieved, how long it will take and what is its cost. Moreover, is it acceptable? If it is not acceptable, reconsider.

Thinking requires the following aspects to make it effective.

- **Analysing:** breaking the whole into small parts and the complex into simple elements.
- **Holistic thinking:** thinking of the entirety, the opposite to analysing.
- **Valuing:** the judgemental and critical aspect.

To make decisions fully effective it is necessary to use all three of these thought processes. Decisions based on intuition, instinct or emotion will not produce logical decision making.

Before making a decision, ensure you have the facts and then decide what to do. Value judgements are effective only if you are aware of any prejudices you have that may affect your decision, acknowledge them and learn not to be prejudiced. Also you need to know of any codes of values that are needed by the establishment, such as legal requirements, and any social behaviour codes and company procedures.

Decision-making styles

- **Autocratic:** the manager solves the problem based on the information he or she has.
- **Information finding:** when a manager does not have enough information or skill, he or she asks other people, then makes a decision.
- **Consultation:** the situation is explained to the group, who generate and evaluate solutions and make recommendations. The leader makes the decision.
- **Negotiation:** the group is provided with information. The group members then negotiate a solution that is acceptable.
- **Delegation:** responsibility for the decision rests with a group or an individual. The manager may guide the discussion that leads to the decision, which is then implemented.

Implementation of the decision

Having made a decision, determine clear objectives and consider what can be delegated, to whom, the time needed and whether further training is necessary. To action the decision, define it in writing, set details of progress and when to report back.

Time management

To organise yourself efficiently so as to be an effective manager requires attention to controlling your time. Determining priorities is an essential step to this end and can be aided by producing lists and categorising jobs to be done, as well as using a diary effectively.

Time needs to be allocated for tasks such as thinking and planning, as well as using a diary effectively. A good organiser plans both for the expected and the unexpected. Be prepared for problems but allow time to prevent them if possible, and allot time for solving them.

It is important to realise that good managers need adequate-quality sleep and exercise, so as to be healthy and alert at work. Time is also needed for leisure, and self-development. Control of good eating and drinking habits may not be easy in the catering industry, but they require time to be allocated sensibly – not too long, too short or erratic.

Time is the substance life is made of; time is money, time past has gone for ever, today's newspaper is history tomorrow. You cannot buy time, but an efficient manager can organise his or her own time and that of those for whom he or she is responsible advantageously.

Unfortunately a lot of time is wasted by being punctual because others are not on time. Always be punctual and expect others to be so. Be well organised before a meeting, know what you expect from it and what others expect from you. Set objectives that are:

- clear
- attainable
- specific
- challenging
- measurable
- timed
- worthwhile.

If no time limit is stated then time could be wasted. Ideally, agree with the person the objectives that apply to them, as well as the time required to fulfil these objectives.

- Plan each day, and decide on priorities.
- Identify immediate, short-term and long-term goals, and organise office and paperwork.
- Avoid distractions, prevent interruptions.
- Delegate, make lists and delete things as they are done.
- Be organised, develop routines.
- Do important jobs when you are at your best. Set time limits and keep to them.
- Do not put off unpleasant or difficult tasks. Let others know when you are having quiet time.
- Do one thing at a time and finish it if possible; plan phone calls.

- Arrange breaks; keep a notebook for ideas.
- Learn to say no, and think before acting.

Communication and information

To develop managerial skills it is important to communicate effectively with senior management and other departmental managers, and with those for whom you are responsible. It is essential to ensure that what is communicated is understood in the way it is intended. Likewise it is very important that information, suggestions, commands, decisions, requests, and so on, are clear, cannot be misconstructed and are unambiguous. Listening is an art that needs particular attention as it is a vital aspect of effective communication.

Information may be communicated by oral or visual means, depending on the establishment's policy, personal preference and the matter to be conveyed. The advantage of speech is that questions and discussions can clarify the issues immediately, and intonation and emphasis convey more accurately what is intended. While the telephone is invaluable, there is no eye contact, which makes face-to-face communication more effective. Body language conveys much to both communicators, which naturally can occur only in direct contact situations.

Written instructions, reports and so on have the advantage that there is tangible evidence of what is communicated. However, care must still be taken that what is written is understood by the recipient: that which is written may be clear to the person writing the instructions, but it is essential that it is specific, unambiguous and not too wordy, so that there are no misunderstandings.

Although emails are a popular modern form of communication, they also bring with them the risk of losing the value of face-to-face contact and oral skills.

Self-assessment

In order to improve performance it is desirable to review one's current situation and how to develop into the future. Appropriate others, such as colleagues in the establishment, and comparison with people in similar situations in other organisations, members of professional associations, tutors at colleges and those who have experience of management in catering, may all provide constructive advice. Keep abreast of developments by reading journals and visiting trade fairs.

Balanced organisation

Evaluate responsibilities objectively so that you understand, appreciate and can act effectively in an efficient but balanced style.

- Assess your responsibilities for: people, finance, development, administration and communication.
- People to consider are: yourself, your subordinates, your family and your department.
- Finance: your own, the department's, budgeting, authorisation of expenditure and control of expenditure.
- Development in: the organisation, the department, your own and new ideas.
- Administration may include: an office, secretary, your department, other departments and customers.
- Communication: ensure it is effective – to others and from others.

Developing trust and support with managers

Trust and support with one's immediate manager will simply not appear in an ad hoc fashion. For a chef this person may be the food and beverage manager or the general manager. Serious attention has to be paid to developing a communication channel with one's immediate manager in order to encourage an effective relationship that will help to achieve departmental or organisational goals. The better the communication, the more likely that the relationship will become better and more efficient.

It is important that the departmental head consults with his or her line manager on a regular basis to genuinely seek his or her views, ideas and feelings, which may improve the quality of decisions. This will stimulate better cooperation between managers.

Conflict with your immediate line manager can be very damaging. However, one of the main areas in which conflict can and does take place is at work. Section heads may often feel dissatisfied with their line manager, perhaps in connection with pay, working conditions and the like. Another issue may be one of communication between the section head and the line manager. The section head should take time to find out about his/her line manager by discussing, observing and talking to him/her and other managers in the organisation.

It also helps if a close relationship is developed with the manager and a good understanding of all the issues the organisation is faced with. Provide the manager with ideas, give definitions of problems and your views on solutions.

A manager will generally have:

- another, or alternative, view on things
- more information on the overall picture
- advice on difficult issues
- guidance on appropriate policies.

They will be able to offer support and protection (through consultation with him or her).

The departmental head must in turn provide:

- clear documentation
- clear definition of issues
- identified courses of action and views on the various strategies available
- reasoned arguments on how/why he or she has arrived at the recommendations
- predictions about likely outcomes and contingencies if a recommendation he or she actions is unsuccessful
- information on his or her team's progress.

Your line manager is expecting you to produce results and to organise your team. This will strengthen your relationship with the line manager. Your manager will often, in turn, take a certain amount of credit for what you do well.

Consider also your own relationship with your sub-ordinates. If the relationship works well, then what are the reasons for this? Are these relevant to establishing a working relationship with your line manager?

Assess your line manager

- Understand what she or he wants for her/himself.
- What are his or her values?
- Is she or he able to accept criticism?
- Is he or she ambitious?
- How does she or he measure herself/himself?
- Who are the people that he or she admires?
- Does the manager like open, frank discussion?
- Does the manager take risks? Or is she or he a protector?
- Is the manager an autocratic leader, expecting you to do as he or she says? Or intuitive, expecting you to follow broad, informal indications or signs?

Try to analyse why situations produce conflict or stalemate. Is it because your views differ or because you both manage the situations badly? Does this help you to decide if you have the qualities she or he values? What does your manager expect from you? Do his or her goals match yours? If not, can you live with the resulting difficulties?

Learn to understand your manager's strengths and weaknesses

- Does the manager need time and lengthy explanations?
- Is the manager good at one-to-one communication?
- Is the manager able to see essentials, and keen to resolve issues?
- Does the manager contribute to good ideas?
- Is he or she able to see practical solutions?
- Is the manager able to handle conflict, or does she or he seek to avoid it?

Once these strengths and weaknesses have been identified you should seek to complement them. You may need to modify your behaviour to ensure your relationship with him/her is legitimate, not a sellout, and can be productive – taking care not to go too far in compromising.

Analyse his or her style

- Does your manager prefer written, detailed reports? If so, you should provide them and check them thoroughly.
- He or she may prefer verbal briefings. If so, provide them but follow up with a memo or email.
- He or she may prefer formal meetings with itemised agendas.
- Assess the circumstances within the environment you are both working in.
- What are the pressures on you both?
- What are her or his own dealings with her or his peers and more senior managers?
- What is expected of your manager? Where does he or she look for success?
- What are the rewards for succeeding? Salary increase? Promotion? Bonus? Could this reflect on your relationship?
- How are you contributing to what she or he is trying to achieve?
- How do people view the manager in the organisation?

Making decisions

Decision making is a very important part of the management process. No matter how good you are as a section manager, how well you motivate your staff or how good your ideas, you will be judged by your manager and your staff on the quality of the decisions you make.

Quantity can be no substitute for quality. An excess of bad or short-term decisions will lead to a serious backlog of niggling problems.

Decisions are your judgement choices between alternative courses of action. To be effective, this often means keeping decision making to a minimum, but ensuring the decisions that have to be made are timed correctly, after taking into account all the facts and information at our disposal.

Managing the team and its performance in a regular series of tasks and a number of various projects involves decisions relating to routine, individuals and the team.

- Different strategies and styles of working/ interaction that encourage effective working relationships with senior staff.
- Range of methods to keep the immediate manager informed and how to select an appropriate method according to a range of issues and contexts.
- The types of emerging threats and opportunities about which the manager needs to be informed, and the degree of urgency attached to this.
- How to develop and present proposals in a way that is realistic, clear and likely to influence the immediate manager's decision making positively.
- Handling disagreements positively. Assess the likely reaction from both the team and individuals.
- Avoid making decisions on impulse.
- Collect all information, not just the material that supports your view.
- Discuss decisions with more experienced senior staff, but retain responsibility for the final decision.
- Do not take premature or unnecessary decisions.

Routine decision making is often delegated by a departmental head to a junior. This encourages and develops them in the decision-making process and allows the head to concentrate on more strategic issues.

Certain decisions remain with the departmental manager:

- those that focus on overall direction
- staff resourcing
- organisation structure in the section to achieve objectives and cope with the workload
- skills, forecasting
- planning to achieve operational objectives.

Avoid using one style to deal with everything. Use 'unswerving flexibility'.

Managing projects means making hard decisions about money, materials, time and staff.

- All team members must know their roles.
- Progress must be reviewed frequently in order to spot potential problems and to note what time and resources are available.
- Continually feed back to your line manager to avoid misunderstandings or conflict if things go wrong.
- Consult experts when necessary before any emergency.
- Refer any decisions to your line manager that fall outside your sphere of authority, responsibility or flexibility. Referrals should be accompanied by a clear statement of possible choices, together with your recommendations.

Steps to effective decision making

Classify the problem

If it is generic, it is probably one of those everyday problems that has to be solved by adapting the appropriate generic rule, policy or principle. If it is extraordinary, the problem must be dealt with on its individual merits.

Define the problem

State precisely the nature of the problem and check your definition against all the observable facts. Beware the plausible but incomplete definition that does not embrace all the known facts.

Specify the conditions

Clarify exactly what the decision must accomplish. These are the so-called boundary conditions, or specifications, that must be satisfied by the solution to the problem.

Decide on the right action

Decide first of all what it is right to do rather than what is acceptable in the circumstances. Make the decision that satisfies all the specifications.

Compromise the decision

In reality there usually has to be some form of compromise, so make the best decision possible by adapting it to the circumstances.

Implement the decision

Assign the responsibility of carrying out the decision to those staff who are capable of doing so. Inform everyone who needs to know about the decision and the effects of the decision.

Review the effectiveness of the decision

The implementation process should involve feedback and monitoring. Receive reports on the results of the decision – how does the decision measure up to expectations? All positive facts should be incorporated into the classifying, defining and specifying process of making decisions.

Managing people

This involves developing the trust and support of colleagues and team members.

As individuals working within an organisation, we can achieve very little, but working within a group we are able to achieve a great deal more. Good, effective teamwork is an important feature of human behaviour and organisational performance.

Each member in a group must:

- regard themselves as being part of that group
- interact with one another
- perceive themselves as part of the group
- share the purpose of the group.

This will help build trust and support, and will result in an effective performance. Cooperation is therefore important.

People in groups will influence one another; within the group there may be a leader and/or a hierarchical system. The pressures within the group may have a major influence over the behaviour of individual members and their performance. The style of leadership within the group has an influence on the behaviour of members within the group.

Groups help shape the work pattern of organisations, and the attitudes and behaviour of members to their jobs.

Two types of team can be identified within an organisation.

- The **formal team** is the department or section created within a reorganised structure to pursue specified goals.
- The **informal team** deals with a particular situation; members have fewer fixed organisational relationships and the team is disbanded after performing its function.

Both groups have to be developed and led. Thought has to be given to relationships, and to the tasks and duties the team has to carry out.

Selecting and shaping teams to work within a department is a very important task. This is the job of the departmental head. It requires management skills. Matching each individual's talent to the task or job has to be considered. A good, developed team will be able to:

- analyse problems effectively and create useful ideas
- communicate with each other and get things done
- show good leadership, which will result in skilled operations with technical precision and ability
- evaluate logically and equate control systems.

The group will never become a team unless the personalities involved are able to relate to and communicate with one another, and value the contribution that each employee or team member makes.

The team leader has a strong influence on his or her team or brigade, and is expected to set examples that have to be followed, particularly when under pressure, dealing with conflict, personality clash, change and stress.

People's behaviour is affected by many factors. For example, individual characteristics, cultural attributes and social skills: the head must lead rather than drive, and encourage the team to practise reasonable and supportive behaviour so that any problems are dealt with in an objective way and the team's personal skills are harnessed to achieve their full potential.

Every team has to deal with:

- the egos, and the weaknesses and strengths of the individuals
- the self-appointed experts within the group
- relationships/circumstances constantly changing.

The head is able to manage the team successfully by pulling back from the task in hand. He or she must examine the processes that create efficient teamwork, finding out what it is that makes it greater than the sum of its parts. To assist this process the following attributes are necessary:

- have a consistent approach to solving problems
- take into account people's characters as well as their technical skills
- encourage supportive behaviour in the team

- create an open, healthy climate
- make time for the team to appraise its progress.

Supportive team practices

Listening skills

- Pay attention, responding positively.
- Look interested, avoid interrupting.
- Build on proposals, asking for clarity on questions.
- Summarise to check your understanding.

Cooperating

- Encourage others to give their views.
- Compliment good ideas.
- Avoid coercion and acrimony.
- Give careful consideration to different proposals.
- Offer new ideas openly.

Challenging

- Any assumptions are questioned in a reasonable manner.
- Continually refer back to the problem-solving process and aims.
- Review the progress of objectives and aims, in relation to the team and time taken.

Motivation and the team

An understanding of what motivates staff is crucial to the creation of productivity and the realisation of profits. People's needs and wants are complex and often difficult to define.

Money and status are important but they cannot be relied upon exclusively. Behavioural scientists have provided useful ways of thinking about people's needs and wants.

F. W. Taylor (1911) established a scientific management approach that involved breaking jobs into simple but repetitive tasks, providing training, isolating individuals from distractions and each other, and paying good wages, which included bonuses for productivity over target levels.

In the short term, productive gains were significant; in the long run, these gains were less than significant as people reacted against the idea of being treated like a machine.

The scientific approach may have been discredited because some managers give too much attention to pay and too little to personal needs, and the needs of groups and teams.

Abraham Maslow (1954) concentrated on human needs, which he defined as a fivefold hierarchy.

1 **Physiological needs:** the need for food and shelter.

2 **Safety needs:** the security of home and work.
3 **Social needs:** the need for a supportive environment.
4 **Esteem needs:** gaining the respect of others.
5 **Self-fulfilment:** the need to realise your own potential.

As each goal is achieved, the next is sought. Thus, at different stages of career development, each individual has different values, depending on their progress through this 'hierarchy of needs'.

In 1959 Frederick Herzberg (see Herzberg *et al.*, 1959) added to Taylor's and Maslow's work by introducing the idea of 'hygiene factors'. If these hygiene factors are absent they will lead to dissatisfaction and will prevent effective motivation. The hygiene factors can be identified as follows.

1 The organisational policy and rules.
2 The management styles and controls.
3 Retirement and sickness policies.
4 Pay and recognition of status.

- Hygiene factors, although considered important, do not have lasting effects on motivation, as other positive motivating factors must be present.
- Money obviously plays an important role in motivation. There are a number of non-financial motivators, and these are considered to be highly important, to achieve the organisational goals.
- Most people want to achieve – those in charge of teams must recognise this and provide opportunities for others to attain levels of achievement that celebrate ability.
- People also want recognition. Praise and feedback spur people on to achieve even more.
- People generally want to move on to more challenging situations. The team should aim to challenge its members.
- Certain workers (e.g. chefs) want to practise their skill and use their intelligence to maintain interest.
- Most workers want to accept responsibility and authority.

Motivating a team

A leader must motivate his or her team by making their work interesting, challenging and demanding. People must also know what is expected of them and what the standards are. Rewards are linked to effort and results.

Unless these factors go towards fulfilling the organisational needs and the expectations of team members, if pay and prospects within the establishment are bad, the system should be improved and performance should be recognised. Therefore, the leader should attempt to intercede on behalf of his or her staff. This, in turn, will help to increase their motivation and their commitment to the team.

For the leader to manage his or her staff effectively, it is important to get to know them well, understand their needs and aspirations, and help them achieve their personal aims.

Communication

Successful communication is vital when striving to build working relationships. Training and developing the team are about communicating. In work, the quality of our personal relationships depends on the quality of the communication system.

- The speaker must know what he or she wishes to convey.
- He or she must find visible symbols, gestures, words, body movements, to externalise the internal thoughts.
- The listener must be receptive to these visible symbols, know the language and terminology, and understand the non-verbal symbols being demonstrated.
- The listener must translate all these symbols into thought.

Communication requires a transmitter and a receiver, and therefore it is a shared responsibility. Speaking in a meeting you have several potential listeners; a memo you send to staff may have multiple copies. Many staff receive messages, commands, notices and so on – but they don't give them. Therefore the communication system may imply only a transmitting process.

The greatest scope for quantitatively improving your communication skills is to improve your listening, observing, reading and watching abilities, as a priority over speaking and writing. The most effective transmissions are those that are able to fit into the receiving processes of the recipients.

Hearing and understanding the content of the instruction or the message are not sufficient for full communication. There has to be a match between the 'intent' and the 'effect' the instruction or message has on the individual. Breakdowns in communication can be identified by looking at the 'intent' and the 'effect' as two separate realities. Sometimes, the intent is not translated into the effect. Such breakdowns can adversely affect staff and team relationships. Good relationships depend on good communication.

Awareness of the potential gap between intent and effect can help clarify and prevent any misunderstanding within the group.

By bridging the gap between intent and effect you can begin to change the culture of the working environment – the processes become self-reinforcing in a positive direction. The staff begin to respect each other in a positive framework; they listen more carefully to each other, with positive expectations, hearing the constructive intent and responding to it.

As a manager, the art is in achieving results through the team, with communication being the key to the exercise. A great deal of time will be taken up with communicating in one way or another.

Planning communication

Communication can be planned in a systematic way with clarity about the objectives and methods to be used. Not every communication needs to be planned, as many trivial or routine transmissions can go through automatic channels. The significant communication lines are those that recur frequently and/or take up a great deal of time, or that carry substantial rewards or penalties for success or failure.

First, the manager must define his or her job objectives, then he or she must identify the communication strategy to achieve these objectives.

Planning the communication will cover the subject and the method content and process.

The **content** means:

- collecting the data
- getting your thoughts in order
- formulating information.

The **process** means:

- alternative ways communication may proceed and achieve objectives.

The **medium** can be:

- face to face, meeting, phone call, fax, email, memo.

A major factor in the quality of any communication system is the climate in which it takes place. The climate refers to the prevailing attitudes and habitual behaviours of the team within which the communication is being attempted. The degree of friendliness and/or hostility that exists between the transmitters and receivers will affect the communication outcome.

The climate for communication is greatly influenced by the leader. The leader sets the tone in the way he or she interacts with the team. Do not patronise staff as this causes resentment, which results in sullen silence

Table 10.2 The predominant communication component in each category of meeting

Purpose of meeting	Predominant communication component
Information exchange	Facts and opinions
Problem solving	Ideas and goal wishes
Briefing	Facts
Consultation	Opinions
Conflict resolution	Ideas and goal wishes
Morale building	Feelings and goal wishes

or overt hostility. Being dogmatic, with a closed mind, results in others being dogmatic in return.

Accept disagreement as an interesting alternative view that is worth exploring, demonstrating how you are able to learn from it. This provides a climate of open-mindedness. Staff very often respond to the expectations communicated to them, either directly or indirectly.

Meetings

Any hospitality manager must ask her/himself what is the purpose of meetings, what they are trying to achieve by holding the meeting. The purpose needs to be expressed in specific terms. We are able to identify the predominant communication component in each category of meeting (see Table 10.2).

Work–life balance

It is increasingly being recognised by employers of all sizes and in all industry sectors that it makes good business sense to create a better work–life balance for their workers. Where this has been successfully organised, it has resulted in increased morale and employee loyalty, better productivity and effectiveness at work, and improved adaptability in the face of change.

Research shows that, when employees are better able to integrate their needs outside work into their daily lives with no detriment to their work, there are considerable benefits to the business.

Leading the team

- Look at tomorrow's problems and issues today to detect signs of changes and pitfalls.
- Learn to adapt to change, to embrace it and turn it to positive advantage.
- Set high standards and clear objectives.
- Think clearly, allowing intuition to influence rationality.
- Create a sense of value and purpose in work, so that team members believe in what they do and do it successfully.
- Provide a positive sense of direction in order to give meaning to the lives of team members.
- Act decisively, but ensure decisions made are soundly based and not just on impulse.
- Set the right tone by your actions and beliefs,

thus creating a clear, consistent and honest model to be followed.
- Choose the right time to make decisions and take action.
- Create an atmosphere of enthusiasm in which individuals are stimulated to perform well, find fulfilment, gain self-respect and play an integral role in meeting the organisation's overall goals.
- Be sensitive to individual team members' needs and their expectations.
- Define clear responsibilities and structures, so collective effort is enhanced not hindered.
- Recognise what motivates each team member and work with these motivations to achieve standards and objectives.
- Determine boundaries within which team members can work freely.

Most good managers do one of the following:

- make a decision the team accepts
- 'sell' a decision before trying to have it accepted
- present decisions but respond to the team's questions
- present a tentative decision, subject to change after team input
- present problems, ask the team for input, then make a decision
- define the limits within which the team can make a decision
- ensure that chef and team make a joint decision.

Managing diversity

The world of work, especially the hospitality industry, is becoming more diverse. Increasing numbers of women are entering the labour force, who expect to progress to senior management; the ethnic mix is becoming wider and the population in western economies is ageing. In the case of multinational companies, domestic diversity is compounded by the diversity that is introduced through the movement of people around the globe. The mobility of labour is further encouraged by regional mechanisms such as arrangements for the free movement of people in the European Union. All these changes (and more) are affecting the nature of customers and their needs.

What is diversity?

Diversity recognises that people are different. It includes some of the more obvious and visible differences – such as gender, ethnicity, age and disability – and also the less visible differences – such as sexual orientation, background, personality and work style. Diversity management is about recognising, valuing and celebrating these differences. It is about harnessing difference to improve creativity and innovation, and is based on the belief that groups of people who bring different perspectives together will find better solutions to problems than groups of people who are the same.

Why is diversity management important?

The markets served are constantly changing (e.g. women and older people have more spending power, minority ethnic groups are an important market segment, disabled people and their carers want accessible holidays) and, in order to meet the needs of these diverse markets, the same groups need to be represented in the workforce. Taking a proactive approach to diversity management can achieve the following:

- access the best people from the widest labour pool available
- develop the creative talents of all employees
- motivate all staff
- reduce labour turnover
- improve quality and customer service.

Minimising interpersonal conflict

Interpersonal conflict is a fact of life. It starts with children in school, who in most cases are able to resolve their disagreements quickly and often make friends again. With adults this ability to resolve conflict tends to fade away as we become older. In an organisational context a whole range of things can get in the way, which makes handling conflict even more difficult. A conflict with the manager or with colleagues can easily get entangled with issues about work and status – both of which can make it difficult to approach the problem in a rational and professional way.

- One of the skills of all front-line managers is the need to identify conflict, so that plans can be put in place to minimise it.
- Conflict arises where there are already strained relations and personality clashes between members of your team.
- Conflict often occurs in a hospitality business when the brigade is understaffed and under pressure, especially over a long period. Pressure can also come from, for example, restaurant reviews and guides, where a chef is, say, after a Michelin star or special accolade.
- Conflicts damage working relationships and upset the team; eventually this will show in the finished product.

The chef and manager must also be aware of the insidious conflict that may be going on around them, in less obvious places. Covert conflicts are those that take place in secret, and can be very harmful. This type of conflict is often difficult to detect. A new person joining the team may have no idea that the conflict is taking place. This type of conflict will also undermine the team's performance. Such conflict may happen when a person has been passed over for promotion and has never received feedback as to why. In other words, they have been ignored. The resentment, anger and bitterness can bubble away beneath the surface.

Many conflicts start with misunderstandings or a small upset that grows and develops out of all proportion. The manager or chef should attempt to:

- stop it getting worse
- make the individuals confront their own problems
- manage the situation to avoid any escalation.

Destructive and constructive conflicts

It is important to reflect on and analyse the nature of conflict and individual attitudes to it. While conflicts can be very damaging and upsetting, there can also be some positive outcomes. Conflict can also be a learning curve that a chef or manager has to enter into; this then has to be handled properly and focused to achieve the desired outcome.

Conflict is destructive when it:

- produces name calling
- makes people feel angry and let down with each other
- causes people to close off and withdraw.

Conflict is constructive when it:

- acts as the first stage towards negotiating
- clears the air
- helps staff to talk to each other.

Some common physical reactions when we are threatened by conflict are sweaty palms, a rise in pulse rate, dry mouth, trembling.

Flight

This is an unsatisfactory way of dealing with conflict at work or, indeed, in other social situations. Much of the time, you can't just run away and, if there is no escape, it can turn into a demonstration of submission, a form of passive behaviour. Don't be so intent on pleasing others that you fail to please yourself. The emotional aftermath of submitting often results in guilt and feeling that you have let yourself down.

Examples of flight reaction and passive behaviour include:

- withdrawing eye contact, looking down, hiding behind hair
- withdrawing body language, hiding
- continual agreement.

Fight (aggressive behaviour)

Aggressive behaviour is equally unsatisfactory. This can be demonstrated by:

- a raised voice, clipped or sarcastic tone
- pointing a finger, clenched fist, banging the table and waving the arms
- staring and invasive eye contact – glaring

- moving closer to someone, standing up to tower over someone else
- not listening, talking so much there is no space to respond.

Why does conflict arise?

The chef/manager needs to be aware within which areas interpersonal conflict can arise in order to put strategies in place to manage it. He/she should act positively, rather than simply react to a conflict when it breaks out.

If people feel that they do not have a chance to discuss their problems and difficulties with someone this could also lead to conflict. It could also lead to:

- a breakdown in trust
- misunderstandings about standards
- failing to communicate with one another correctly
- dealing with complex personal problems that should have been passed to an expert.

Other reasons for conflict can be:

- racism, sexism, differences in opinion
- inappropriate personal habits, non-compliance with organisational norms/values
- discriminatory behaviour, working conditions
- unrealistic work expectations, personal antagonism.

In some cases conflicts that arise from these issues may result in formal grievances, or even disciplinary matters. Formal procedures can often be helpful in containing conflict to a standard approach. This depersonalises it and stops the manager or chef taking it personally, converting it into a standard work-role approach that spells out who is to do what by when.

Conflict between the chef and the manager, the supervisor and the manager, or the staff and the supervisor

This can be very damaging and leads to feelings of dissatisfaction. Often it may be the result of poor communication in either direction, about activities, progress results and achievements.

The main issues include:

- failing to communicate accurately or promptly – on problems, opportunities and activities
- going it alone – taking decisions that require the approval of the manager or another party
- coming up with problems rather than solutions,

and neglecting to put forward proposals for action at the appropriate level of detail

- feeling hurt when ideas are rejected, instead of coming up with other proposals
- allowing some disagreements to grow without limiting the damage
- failing to do what the job requires and not meeting expectations without good reason
- balancing the expectations of the kitchen/restaurant team, and trying to live up to your manager's expectations and demands.

Therefore, there is a need to continue to find ways of improving and maintaining relationships with line managers and the team. Relationships have to be worked on, they need constant nurturing.

Turning the situation round

Here are nine steps that will help to enhance working relationships with your immediate manager.

1 Keep the manager well informed on what you and the team are doing, by means of regular progress reports that clearly identify achievements.
2 Inform him or her of problems and opportunities. Give information at the right stage.
3 Ask for advice when you need it. Use your manager as a resource.
4 Make proposals for action clearly and at the right time, giving the right level of detail.
5 Not all proposals will be accepted by your line

manager. If a proposal is rejected, wait for a while, then put forward an alternative proposal.
6 Deal with disagreements with your line manager in a positive way. Avoid falling out and so damaging the relationship.
7 Continue to find ways to improve your relationship.
8 Check you have completed everything you are required to do in your job.
9 Carry out your activities positively, willingly and in a helpful way.

Sometimes there may be a member of staff who keeps calm, gets everyone listening and talking sensibly, and comes up with a reasonable compromise that gets everyone out of a hole. This person should be the chef or the manager.

Some references to management elsewhere in this book:	
Computer use	Ch. 17
Conservation	198
Cost control	255
Functions	244
Kitchen organisation	161
Portion control	251
Supervision	163
Working methods	162

References

DTI (2001) *A Good Practice Guide for the Hospitality Industry* (produced by the Insitute of Hospitality's Managing Diversity Working Group in conjunction with the DTI's Work–Life Balance Team). Free copies available from DTI Publications, tel: 0870 1502 500, website: www.dti.gov.uk/publications.

Herzberg, G.F., Mausner, B. and Snydeman, B.B. (1959) *The Motivation to Work.* New York: Wiley.
Insitute of Hospitality, May 1999.
Maslow, A. (1954) *Motivation and Personality.* New York: Harper & Row.
Taylor, F.W. (1911) *The Principles of Scientific Management.* New York: Harper Bros.

Topics for discussion

1 Ways in which conflict can be resolved in a kitchen and restaurant.

2 The importance of acquiring management skills when working as a head chef or restaurant manager.

3 Why trust in the management process is important.

4 Which is more important: gaining accolades and Michelin stars, good reviews or operating a successful kitchen and restaurant/hotel where managers and staff feel comfortable and the product is successful?

5 The importance of developing teams.

6 Why good communication in the organisation is important.

7 What are the qualities of a good manager?

8 What does the employee expect of the manager?

9 What does the manager expect of the employee, and what does the employee expect of the management?

10 Discuss what makes a successful organisation/company. Name two different companies that you consider to be successful, and explain why.

Marketing, sales and customer care

Supporting material available on Dynamic Learning Online:

› Knowledge quizzes

› Activity worksheets: marketing; promotion; customer care

› Summary presentations

Marketing

Operating a successful business in today's competitive environment means that an establishment has to gain an advantage over its competitors. A hospitality establishment has to carefully predict customers' wants, needs and desires, and translate these into a product that people will want to purchase.

This chapter primarily focuses on promotion and selling. Marketing is necessary for the long-term survival of any business. It is not just about selling, however: it is the whole complex of business behaviour that identifies customer needs and trends in buying behaviour, and carefully monitors and interprets the business environment in which the establishment or organisation is operating. Factors include the amount of disposable income people have, the economic environment and exchange rates. There are also political factors, such as the change in the VAT rate and legislation such as the impact of the Food Safety Act on an establishment's hygiene costs.

Market research relies on a systematic approach, and there are a number of different approaches to researching a particular market. The SWOT analysis is a well-known example. SWOT stands for Strengths,

Weaknesses, Opportunities and Threats. When a SWOT analysis is carried out it is useful to take into account the so-called '7 Ps' of marketing:

1 product
2 process
3 place
4 physical environment
5 price
6 promotion
7 people.

Strengths refer to the positive aspects of the establishment. For example:

- good reputation
- good location
- attractive environment
- comfortable restaurant.

Weaknesses could refer to:

- declining market
- lack of staff training
- lack of investment
- no parking spaces.

Opportunities could include:

- economic environment – people with high disposable incomes
- geographical – good attractive area, good parking facilities

- attractive area
- good transport links
- demographic – increasing numbers of young professional people moving into the area
- technological – availability of new equipment, good control systems available
- competition – little competition in the area.

Threats could include:

- technological – out-of-date equipment
- competition
- decline in demand for product
- geographical – area becoming run-down, poorly kept area, difficult parking
- legislation – impact of new legislation, which means more bureaucracy.

It is important for any manager to know the market, and this is done by carrying out detailed market research. Some companies will do their own market research, while others will bring in consultants. This research will assist the company in knowing the potential and current customers, the competition and the business pattern, and will bring the company closer to knowing its own product, strengths, weaknesses and specific characteristics.

Pricing

Once it is clear from the research what the business is, where the profits should be coming from and what the competition is, then decisions on pricing can be made. There are a number of different pricing policies that can be adopted.

Competitive pricing

This looks carefully at what the competition is charging and aims to price at the same level, or sometimes at a slightly lower price. It is vital that the prices charged and the cost structure are compatible.

Backward pricing

This requires an accurate estimate of what people are likely to spend in the future. The product and services are then designed to match what the market will bear – in other words, what the customer is prepared to pay for the product or service within that particular market segment.

Cost plus

This is where a set mark-up or a set percentage is added to basic costs.

This approach is reasonably high risk. For example, if the price of the raw materials rises, then a cost-plus approach will mean that the price of the product or service will also have to rise – in some cases beyond the reach of the customer. For this reason many organisations adopt the backward-pricing approach.

Marginal pricing

This takes into account the actual costs a customer incurs in using the product or service; these costs include materials and energy costs. These are the direct costs. The customer is charged just over the direct costs, and so a contribution is made to the overhead costs. Overheads such as capital, insurance and staff costs have to be incurred whether or not the customer used the product or service. This pricing is used often at weekends and off season to sell hotel rooms, in the hope that the customer will purchase other products at the realistic price.

Discounts

Discounting is used to sell hotel rooms and hospitality products. It is used to maintain customer loyalty, increase the business, to attract repeat business, increase demand in off-peak periods and to encourage the prompt settlement of accounts.

Why some restaurants fail

Location

- The basic attributes of location are missing, such as footfall, access, visibility, parking, neighbouring complementary activity. The neighbourhood profile has permanently changed but this has not been recognised by the owners/operators. For example, if office businesses have closed in an area; this means that new office populations and customers have to be generated.
- Onerous operating conditions enforced by local agencies: delivery times, dining constraints, environmental health officer checks, noise and nuisance controls. Some local authorities are strict on enforcement, which can affect trade.
- Locations with permanently high base rents and rates with large annual and five-year increases, particularly if an area is dominated by absentee institutional landlords as this drives up break-even to an unsustainable level.
- Misunderstanding and misreading of traffic flows; some ostensibly high-volume sites suffer from having mixed markets: office workers, domestic and overseas tourists, day trippers. With no one market segment strong enough to sustain business, it becomes difficult for the operator to know whom to target.

The catering cycle

Caterers running a business should attempt to understand and apply the catering cycle principle (Figure 11.1).

Food and beverage (or food service) operations are concerned with the provision of food and a variety of beverages within business. The various elements that comprise food and beverage operations can be summarised in the catering cycle. Food and beverage operations are concerned with the following factors.

1 The markets served by the various sectors of the food service industry, and consumer needs.
2 The range and formulation of policies, and the business goals and objectives of the various operations, and how these affect the methods adopted.
3 The interpretation of demand, and decisions to be made on the food and beverages to be provided, as well as the other services.
4 The planning and design to create a convergence of facilities required for food and beverage operations, and making decisions about the plant and equipment required.
5 The development of appropriate provisioning methods to meet the needs of the production and service methods used within given operational settings.
6 Operational knowledge of technical methods and processes, and ability in the production and service processes and methods available to the food service operator, understanding the varying resource requirements (including staffing) for their operation, as well as decision making on the appropriateness of the various processes and methods to meet operational requirements.
7 Controlling the costs of materials as well as the costs associated with the operation of production and service, and controlling the revenue.
8 The monitoring of customer satisfaction.

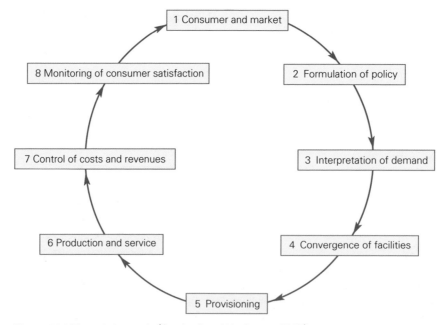

Figure 11.1 The catering cycle (Cracknell and Kaufmann, 2002)

Aspects of promotion and selling

Once a catering establishment has been planned, the process has to be generated whereby the buyer and seller come together. Through promotion, customers are made aware of the establishment, persuaded to make a visit and encouraged to return. Promotion is concerned with the product. This product constitutes a total package on offer, and includes some of the following concepts:

- the image of the establishment
- the prices charged
- the quality of the product and service
- the environment, facilities and services
- the style of management and staff.

Promotion should inform customers of the establishment, make them aware of its existence, persuade them to buy, and convince them of the image and quality of the product. This is done through:

- personal selling
- merchandising
- advertising
- public relations
- sales promotion
- agents.

Promotion is an activity that must be carefully planned and controlled. Usually, the main objective of the promotional campaign is to stimulate demand by using persuasive messages to attract new customers and past users of the establishment. Such messages must convince prospective customers that the product on offer represents good value for money.

Defining the market

The manager or chef should establish the best potential market. This will determine the type of messages to project in order to influence customer behaviour. It will also indicate the best form of media relevant to the age, sex, social class, income level and location of the target customer. It is important for these messages to emphasise the benefits of the product to the customer.

Promotion timing

Promotion timing depends on the objectives and when the decision to purchase is to be made by the customer.

Personal selling

Personal selling is done through contacts with local organisations and committees, for example, or, more directly, through senior restaurant staff talking to clients. All employees who are in contact with customers must be made aware of the importance of selling the products to increase profits and provide a satisfactory experience for the customer.

All staff must therefore gain a good knowledge of the company's products and services, and develop good social skills with an ability to promote and sell. Showing concern for customers not only makes them feel comfortable, but also promotes sales and increases the effectiveness of the establishment.

Advertising

This should convey messages that will influence consumer attitudes and behaviour favourable to the seller. Advertising should:

- increase sales immediately
- create greater public awareness of the location and existence of the establishment
- persuade the public that the product and services offer good value for money
- concentrate on the benefits of using the establishment and consuming the product
- focus on the product differences from those of competitors.

Advertising can be done via the following media:

- posters
- television
- radio
- newspapers
- magazines
- direct mail
- the Internet (including Facebook and Twitter)*
- email.

The selection depends on finance and desired target audience.

* Advertising and promoting on Facebook and Twitter: with the expansion and wider use of these and other social networking sites, companies are increasingly using them to promote their products and services.

Direct mail

The advantages of direct mail include:

- the ability to select potential customers who are likely to buy the product – target groups can be broken down into geographical location, leisure interest and socio-economic groups, to name but a few
- the ability to express a personal message to each customer
- the ability to time the promotion
- the ability to gauge the level of response from various segments of the market and evaluate the cost-effectiveness of the exercise.

Sales promotion

Sales promotion is a day-to-day operation relating to discount offers, price reductions and special offers, such as a free bottle of wine with every meal for two.

They are designed to appeal to a certain section of the market: weekend promoting, gastronomic evenings, gastronomic weekends, golfing weekends and food festivals.

Food festivals are held to promote the cuisine and beverages of a particular region or country. A themed promotion may help the business and promote sales in the following ways:

- increase sales during off-peak periods by attracting new customers
- gain publicity in local press and on local radio
- stimulate and keep the interest of regular customers.

Competing with other establishments and creating a new type of trade, such as conferences, are two other examples of sales promotion activities.

Merchandising

To be a successful caterer, it is important to have a knowledge of merchandising. The object of merchandising is to sell more and to reassure customers about the quality of what is being offered – for example, the quality of the cooking, fresh produce being used and persuading customers to return to the establishment.

Merchandising is the art of displaying products attractively in order to promote sales. This is done to great effect in supermarkets. For example, on the fresh fish counter they display a very small selection of rare or expensive fish and shellfish. This has the effect of making the fish counter interesting, drawing customers' attention and encouraging them to buy – not necessarily the specialist items, but more generally the everyday species. An example of merchandising in a fast-food restaurant is the illustrated fascia above the counter, showing what is available with the help of coloured photographs. Such a display may also be used in a luxury restaurant where a display of exotic fruits and vegetables helps to promote sales.

In a staff restaurant, tent cards and displays are used at various points on the counter to promote certain dishes. These areas are commonly known as hotspots, and are where the customer is encouraged to buy either an additional item or an item that yields a higher profit margin.

Menus and wine lists are important merchandising tools and should be at the forefront of the merchandising strategy.

The customer

First, profile the groups of customers and consider their preferences. Before you decide what you are going to display, first define:

- type of customer (age, background, social class, income groups, gender)
- the people and organisations that use your establishment
- the frequency of their custom
- their use of other catering services
- how they use their time
- how they use their disposable income.

The product

Consider the product profile; this will define the context of your merchandising policy. You must consider all aspects of the product and products, particularly those that relate to:

- the appearance of food and beverage – for example, preparing dishes in front of the customer, such as salads, grilling meat and fish or flambé dishes; this may be suitable in some situations but not others
- how customers see the service you offer
- how the product can be further developed with appearance in mind
- how the product may be promoted using posters, tent cards, illustrated menu cards, sending emails, using social networking sites (Facebook, Twitter, etc.).

Many of the major supermarkets can give caterers good ideas on how to develop merchandising.

What and how to display

When the marketing context has been established, the next stage is to consider how to show services and products to their best advantage and to develop aspects of them that will provide additional attractions. The caterer may like to focus on:

- the quality and freshness of ingredients
- the use of specialist lighting
- the use of fresh flowers and fruits for display
- using a selection of finished dishes for display; this is done to great effect when displaying a choice of plated sweets on a tray
- assessing how displayed food on a self-service buffet will look after customers have taken portions from the various dishes
- how dishes deteriorate in presentation and flavour when they have been standing for too long
- assessing how the smell of cooking is an advantage or disadvantage; supermarkets often

pump out the smell of freshly baked bread and this encourages people to buy bread products
- how the menu is displayed and the language that is used to describe dishes (do the layout and language encourage sales?)
- the provision of essential information about ingredients, sources of wine, vintages and prices in menus and wine lists.

Where to display

In any restaurant thought must be given to the space required for merchandising and the strategic points where a display will give maximum effect. Consider:

- customer flow
- position of check-in and cash desks
- entrances and exits
- use of lounges and bar areas
- use of displays outside restaurants (for example, in the street or windows)
- hotel bedrooms for a hotel restaurant
- the facilities of agents or business associates.

When to display

Timing is important both as an opportunity and as a means of getting the best from a merchandising project. Opportunities on many occasions present themselves at short notice and projects need not be long-lasting.

Special evening events may be held where key clients or customers are invited to sample food. Major department stores invite storecard holders to special evenings, pre-sales events or special Christmas shopping events. These account customers feel special and are encouraged to buy. If special events are to be held, the caterer must consider:

- the season
- the weather
- the event – whether it is to be local or national.

The meal experience

People who eat out do so because they want to satisfy a need. Reasons for eating out may be summarised as follows.

- For convenience – at work or near home.
- For variety – to make life more interesting.
- To avoid preparing food at home.
- Status – hosting business lunches, to feel important.
- To attend social events.
- Impulse – spur-of-the-moment decision.
- Captive market – where there is no choice (for example, hospital patients, prisoners).

The decision to eat out may be split into two parts.

1 the decision to do so for the reasons given above
2 the decision as to what type of experience is to be undertaken.

A number of factors influence the latter decision. The factors that affect the meal experience are as follows.

- **Food and drink:** the range of foods, choice availability, flexibility of the restaurant to cope with special orders, quality of the food and drink.
- **Level of service:** depending on the needs people have at the time – the level of service must be suitable to the needs. For example, a romantic night out may call for a quiet table in a luxury restaurant, whereas a group of friends may well be seeking a more informal service. This factor also takes into account services such as booking and account facilities, acceptance of credit cards, and also the reliability of the operation's product.
- **Level of cleanliness and hygiene:** this relates to the premises, equipment and staff. These days, people are concerned about food safety and are prepared to pay for it.
- **Perceived value for money and price:** people have perceptions of the amount they are prepared to spend in different establishments, and in different operations.

Merchandising administration

Ideas have to be developed and implemented. All relevant material relating to food and drink must reflect the style and service of the product on offer.

- Descriptive terms used in menus and displays must be appropriate to the aims of the catering establishment. Accuracy and spelling are very important. Remember the menu and wine list are selling tools and should help the customer understand what you have to offer.
- All themes should be carefully researched; ambition must not exceed capability.
- Point-of-sale notices should be in keeping with the overall style of the restaurant. Wording must be positive and friendly. Notices should be presented with style and confidence.
- Avoid handwritten notices; these give a very amateurish impression of your establishment.
- Items displayed in generous quantities can assist sales. For example, when supermarkets are running special offers, they sometimes stack the product so it gives the impression that it is plentiful; this has the effect of encouraging the

customer to buy not one but at least two of the items on special offer.

- Consider combined presentations: port with Stilton, dessert wine with the sweet course.
- All display material must be maintained in good order, otherwise it will have the adverse effect of discouraging sales. For example, the sweet tray should be replenished. Menus and wine lists should be replaced before they become shabby.

Automatic vending

The automatic vending market has developed in the last 20 years. The quality of the products has improved enormously. There are approximately 1.2 million machines in operation in the UK.

Applications

Vending/automatic retailing has applications wherever people gather to work, rest, play or study, and where there is a common need for refreshment or the provision of a facility for casual purchase:

- factory
- office
- school, college, university
- hospital – staff dining room, visitors' waiting room, patients' rest room
- recreation centre, swimming pool, sports ground
- ferry terminal, bus/railway station, airport
- exhibition centre, amusement park, tourist site, zoo
- hotel, holiday camp, camping site, caravan park
- motorway service station, garage forecourt
- shopping centre.

Cashless systems: the money card or key reader and revaluator

This is a completely cashless system of vending. Basically this is a plastic-type credit card or key with a magnetic strip that carries an identification code and money balance. When the card is used in the machine the value of the vend is automatically subtracted from the money balance on the card. When the spending power runs out, the card may be topped up to a desired value by the customer inserting the card in a revaluator unit.

Vending operation

The vending operating company will source and site the machine for you, and be able to provide a service/maintenance contract for cleaning, filling and cash collecting, as well as any necessary maintenance.

Why vending?

- **Convenience:** vended goods are available 24 hours a day and machines can be sited just where they are wanted.
- **Time/money saving:** vending machines are not only convenient, they are time saving too. As noted above, research conducted by NOP showed that an average-size business with 50 staff could be spending more than £85,000 of its annual wages bill on time spent by employees making their own tea and coffee.
- **Hygiene:** with vending you get a clean cup every time and avoid the chore of washing up china cups or, worse still, having dirty crockery hanging around all day.
- **Recycling:** the SaveaCup scheme provides a ready way to recycle used vending cups into durable items for the office.
- **Variety:** vending machines offer a whole range of different products and beverages. Drinks vending machines can offer not just black and white coffee and tea, but can also make the drink weak or strong according to taste. Fresh brew, cappuccino and chocolate drinks are also available. Then there are confectionery, savoury snacks, ice cream, sandwiches, snack foods and meals.

Types of equipment

The main types of refreshment machine are:

- beverage – traditional or in-cup
- can or carton
- glass-fronted merchandisers for confectionery and snacks
- refrigerated food
- confectionery and ambient foods
- ice cream.

Beverage machines are available to suit all sizes of operation, from table-top machines suitable for a small office environment to fully automatic high-volume machines.

Manual dispenser-type machines are either

plumbed into mains water or have a built-in water tank for filling by hand. There are two types: in-cup, where the ingredients are pre-packed in the cup, and dispenser, where customers place an empty cup under the ingredient-dispensing point.

Most dispensers are mounted on cabinets and can have payment systems fitted if required. Single product dispensers are dedicated to one drink, such as leaf tea, ground coffee, hot chocolate or cappuccino. They are sited primarily at counter service areas.

To find out more, visit the website of the Automatic Vending Association: www.ava-vending.org.

Vending equipment

The type of machine and its exact location will depend on the likely demand. Before deciding on equipment consider the following questions.

- How many people will be using the machine and during what hours?
- What products will they want?
- How much will they be prepared to pay for the drinks?
- Will there be long periods when the machine is not in use (for example, school holidays)?
- What other sources of supply are available locally? What do they charge and what do they offer?
- Where will the machine be located?
- Is it readily accessible to all those who want to use it?
- Is there a convenient supply of potable water and electricity nearby?
- Do you want users to pay by cash, token or card, or are you providing free drinks?
- What is your budget for the machine?

Customer care

Many staff may have the opportunity of direct contact with consumers or customers in most types of establishment. For some it will be a regular aspect of their job, for others it may be for irregular events or special occasions. Waiters/waitresses and food service personnel called upon to serve customers need to be aware of how to provide customer satisfaction.

Catering staff serving at food service counters directly to customers may be employed in canteens, refectories, dining halls, and so on, in schools, hospitals, industrial establishments, offices and other premises. Other food outlets include fast-food establishments such as crêperies, baked potato houses, McDonald's, fish and chip shops and takeaways, buffets at all kinds of functions (including outdoor catering, wedding receptions and carveries). The following information is intended to assist catering employees at all levels not only to provide customer satisfaction but to obtain job satisfaction when caring for customers. The first thing to remember is that a smile gets both the customer and you off to a good start; however, it is important to realise that excellent food served from the kitchen is only the first essential to satisfy the customer: the finest food produced for a meal can be completely spoiled if served by uncaring staff. Technical skills and technique are very important, but equally (or perhaps more) important are sincere caring attitudes and manners, with the food served in an environment that has an atmosphere that makes the customer feel at ease, wanted and welcome.

Customer care is, therefore, caring for customers. Remember:

- put the customer first
- make them feel good
- make them feel comfortable
- make them feel important
- make them want to return to your restaurant or establishment.

It is important that you adjust your behaviour to suit certain customers and to treat all customers equally as if they were special. Give them your time and full attention. Use body language to put customers at ease.

Concentrate on:

- your appearance
- using the phone correctly
- a clean and tidy environment
- writing to customers
- answering the phone within three rings
- finding out what makes customers happy
- achieving positive results
- ensuring that what you give is what the customer wants.

The customer needs to be kept informed. You yourself should take responsibility and not pass the buck, and achieve results if people complain. You must show the customer empathy and be able to discuss things from their point of view. They expect good customer care. This is an important concept: getting customers and keeping them creates revenue (income). All other activities create costs.

Emotional factors surround the products that people buy; these include after-sales service, speed of delivery and ambience, especially in a restaurant. Customer satisfaction or dissatisfaction comes more and more from the way people are treated. Customers buy a total package. Customer care gives the caterer the opportunity to be 'special', to stand above the competition, winning customers and keeping them loyal. When a customer comes into contact with you, the caterer, your image is being exposed to the customer. The staff of the company are perceived as representing not themselves but the company that they are working for.

Customer perceptions are often emotional, idiosyncratic and sometimes irrational, often based on narrow observations. When a restaurant manager remembers a customer's name, that customer will be delighted, but if staff treat customers badly, they will be unhappy. Often customers will then react in a way that makes staff unhappy, thus affecting the business. If staff make the customers happy they will respond in kind:

$$\text{Happy staff} \leftrightarrow \text{Happy customers}$$
$$\downarrow$$
$$\text{Good profits}$$

Staff can benefit from good customer care training. Dealing with people is a highly complex skill; we train people to use complicated machinery but we do not often consider training staff to deal with the most complex machinery of all: the human being.

The caterer must first:

- set standards for customer care
- measure performance
- set up training schemes
- reward accordingly.

Staff must know:

- what the company stands for, what its mission is
- what behaviour the company values highly
- that cutting costs is not more important than customer care
- that all guarantees must be honoured
- that the restaurant or establishment is in business to keep the customer happy
- that happy customers can lead to repeat business and recommendations to friends and colleagues.

How to win commitment from staff

Staff will be happier and feel more committed by:

- good leadership
- avoiding unnecessary stress (remove the causes, if they are under your control)
- knowing the fundamental importance of the customer; seek ideas from your staff on how to improve customer care
- receiving good customer care training
- building pride in their work performance
- having their training reinforced periodically.

Training aspects in customer care

When you are training staff the following points can be used as a guide.

- Identify what the staff should know in caring for the customer.
- Know what the customer may ask them.
- Know what's on the menu and the composition of the dishes.

- Know what the special dishes of the day are.
- Know what the chef's specialities are.

Examples of good customer care phrases you may hear in a restaurant or service area include:

- 'I'll take care of that for you right away.'
- 'I'll go and get it for you myself.'
- 'Is there anything else I can help you with?'
- 'I'll be glad to help you.'
- 'I don't know, but I'll find out now. Please take a seat for a moment.'
- 'I'm sorry to hear about that. Let's find out what went wrong and I'll put it right.'
- 'I'm sorry for the delay. I'll check with the kitchen to see how long your order will be.'

Good communication within the organisation assists in the development of customer care. It is important that the staff are constantly kept informed of what is going on otherwise they will feel that they are not part of the organisation. They must have a sense of 'ownership' or responsibility, since well-motivated staff are good for the organisation and will assist in the progressive development of the business, helping to avoid the 'it's not my job' attitude.

If staff are expected to work hygienically and treat the customer well, you must likewise treat the staff with respect and care for their well-being. Good staff welfare aids the process of customer care. Staff must have good, clean changing rooms, washing and/or showering facilities, quality facilities for refreshments, and medical provision.

Staff, too, must treat each other with respect, cooperating and supporting each other. Good team spirit will ultimately rub off on the customer. Remember that behaviour begets behaviour, so if one member of staff treats another badly, they in turn may treat the customer badly.

Customer care is a team game. It is about all the staff working towards the same aim: getting the customers on their side.

Define standards of performance

The starting point is a clear analysis of what should happen at each of the points of contact that a customer might have with the restaurant. It can become a checklist, as in the following example.

- A customer enters the restaurant or service area:
  (a) the entrance should be clean and tidy
  (b) the doors could be marked 'welcome'.
- The customer is then greeted by the head waiter, restaurant manager or receptionist:
  (a) the reception area is clean and tidy, perhaps decorated with fresh flowers
  (b) menu sample and drinks list on display
  (c) all staff smartly dressed and well groomed
  (d) staff smile when greeting customers
  (e) if possible head waiter, restaurant manager or receptionist use customer's name
  (f) customer is escorted to the table, assisted into the seating position
  (g) if there is any delay, staff apologise and explanation is given to the customer
  (h) waiter introduces him/herself to the customer.
- At the end of the meal, head waiter or restaurant manager escorts customer to the door, smiles and exchanges pleasantries: 'Good day'/'Good night'.

When defining standards of performance, use numbers: for example, answer the phone within three rings; if there is a delay, update the caller every 20 seconds with 'Sorry, the line is still engaged, do you still wish to hold?'

Staff must have a sense of identity with the company or organisation. McDonald's, for example, has a 700-page Operations and Training Manual, which explains every stage of the cooking process and the correct behaviour to be used when dealing with customers.

Disney requires all new staff to go through an induction programme called 'Traditions', which explains about Walt Disney, the characters, what it is like to work at Disneyland, and their role. It stresses that all visitors are not 'customers' but 'guests', so they must be treated that way. Although on most days there will be more than half a million 'guests', they must be dealt with as individuals, not as a crowd. These individuals look to the staff to help them enjoy their day; staff therefore have a crucial role to play. Disney explains to all its staff that they:

- are part of showbusiness
- are performers in a live show
- must make sure that nothing spoils the perfect picture the guests see
- must make a clear distinction between 'on stage' and 'off stage' – off stage they are able to relax, on stage they must play the perfect role; they must never be seen 'with their mask off'.

It may be said that caterers, too, are part of showbusiness, that waiters are performers in a live show. TGI Friday's restaurants have further developed this concept, and waiters and food service staff are interviewed on the basis of their personality. They become actors as part of a large show. Traditionally waiters that perform flambé dishes 'live' in front of a customer show off their flair and skill. Such staff develop a sense of importance and pride in their job.

Figure 11.2 Greeting guests in the restaurant

Measure and monitor performance

The defined standards of performance must be monitored and measured. You need to measure success in terms of your promises to customers. Measuring the right thing helps staff understand what is important to customers and how to act accordingly.

Staff who look after customers and provide the service and care they expect, deserve reward. Good positive feedback to staff is important. You may:

- just say 'Well done', which goes a long way
- make a payment of a bonus
- give an increment on their annual pay increase
- give a promotion.

Continuing customer care

Keep in touch with customers through mailshots, advertising, and so on (see page 317).

Customer care skills

Attitude and behaviour

If a customer is rude or aggressive to a waiter (e.g. blames a waiter for the chef's mistake), the waiter should not be rude or aggressive in return. If the waiter can remain calm and use his/her skills of patience, the customer will often apologise for their anger. Behaviour is a choice; you should select the behaviour that is appropriate to the customer.

When dealing with customers, behaviour should be:

- professional
- understanding – customers in a restaurant want a service and are paying for it; learn to understand their needs
- patient – learn to be patient with all customers
- enthusiastic – it can be contagious
- confident – it can increase a potential customer's trust in you
- welcoming – it can satisfy a customer's basic human desire to feel liked and be approved of
- helpful – customers warm to helpful staff
- polite – good manners are always welcomed
- caring – make each customer feel special
- empathy – understanding what it is like to be a customer.

Appearance

Remember, you never get a second chance to make a first impression. What you wear and how you look are part of how potential customers judge your organisation. You are part of the company's image.

Body language

Body language includes:

- how you dress
- posture
- your distance from others
- stance
- how you sit
- facial expressions
- movements
- eye contact
- gestures
- eye movements.

Body language includes unconscious signals that tell us what people really think/feel. If someone is telling a lie, for instance, their body language will usually give them away. By focusing on other people's body language you can discover their true feeling towards you and what they think of what you are saying. It has a clear value in business situations and is therefore very important in customer care.

Learn to:

- look for what is important
- recognise other people so you are able to 'read' them better
- recognise how to use body language
- control it and use it to your advantage, so that you give the right positive message to people.

Remember that body language is universal but does mean different things in different cultures.

Signs and meanings

A gesture doesn't always reveal exactly how a person is thinking. For example, arms folded may mean that:

- the person is being defensive about something
- the person is cold
- the person is comfortable.

Some gestures are open, expansive and positive. For example, leaning forward with open palms facing upwards shows interest, acceptance and a welcoming attitude, while leaning backwards, arms folded, head down says closed, defensive and negative, uninterested, rejection.

Using plenty of gestures usually indicates warmth, enthusiasm and emotion, while using gestures sparsely may indicate that a person is cold, reserved and logical.

Distance

Each person has around them an area that they regard as their personal space. Beware of intruding into a customer's personal space. Although some customers may regard it as friendliness, you may make others feel uncomfortable.

Placing people at a table for a meeting or for lunch

or dinner is an art. The way people sit round a table sends messages.

- Formal meeting: people sit opposite each other.
- Teamwork: sitting people side by side is stressful.

Eyes

Eye contact should be used as a way of acknowledging customers, making them feel welcome and as the foundation of building a good relationship. Eye contact should be used to show the customer you are listening.

Ears

Really listening is the highest form of courtesy.

- Look at the customer.
- Ignore any negative thoughts you have about them.
- Lean towards them.
- Think at the pace they are talking.
- Listen to every word.
- Try not to interrupt.
- Use facial expressions and body language to show you understand.
- Stick to the subject.
- Use their name wherever possible.

Greeting people

If you are already dealing with another customer in the restaurant, acknowledge the new customer and reassure them that you will help them as soon as possible. Try to greet people with a smile that is genuine. You may even get one in return – after all, smiles are free! Remember that good manners are important.

Use people's names: it holds their attention, and demonstrates recognition and respect. Their name is probably the most important word in the world to them. Always use their surname until they give permission for you to use their first name.

Asking the customer questions will demonstrate:

- you have properly understood what they want
- you have time for them to talk
- interest on your part
- that you feel the customer is important
- you are able to find out how they feel
- you can keep control of the conversation
- you can understand their needs, their complaints
- you know how to make them feel better.

'Stroking'

This is defined as giving any kind of attention. Humans need 'stroking'. A prolonged absence of it can cause serious adverse effects. How good a customer feels about your restaurant or catering establishment is directly connected to the amount and types of 'strokes' (attention) they have received.

Stroking can be both positive or negative, it can be physical, verbal and non-verbal. Some examples of positive stroking include:

- greetings
- compliments
- laughing.

Some examples of negative stroking include:

- unpleasant greeting
- adverse criticism
- pushing
- swearing
- sarcastic remarks
- snatching
- absence of praise
- unpleasant hand gestures.

Pacing

Pacing is speaking in a way that is compatible with your customers. Match their speed, tone and volume. Do not talk above their heads.

Assertiveness

Remember that customers are human beings; you may have to handle them when they shout at you, interrupt you, are rude to you, criticise you or blame you for something you have not done. The answer is for you to be assertive, standing up for your rights.

Being assertive means:

- stating your views while showing that you understand their views
- enhancing yourself without diminishing them
- speaking calmly, sincerely and steadily.

Advantages of assertive behaviour

There are some advantages to be gained.

- It gives you greater self-confidence.
- You will be treating others as equals, recognising the abilities and limitations of others, rather than regarding them as superiors.
- It gives greater self-responsibility.
- It gives greater self-control; your mind is concentrated on achieving the behaviour you want.
- It can produce a win-win situation; opinions on both sides are given a fair hearing, so each side feels it has 'won'.

Telephone

A badly handled telephone call can destroy the effect of good advertising. Remember: when using the telephone, give all your attention to the customer; get their name, write it down and use it. Take note of all the other details the customer is wanting. Listen and use your voice correctly. Summarise what you have agreed with the customer at the end of the conversation.

How to handle customer complaints

Here are some statistics on complaints and customer satisfaction:

- 96 per cent of dissatisfied customers do not go back and complain, but they do tell between 7 and 11 other people how bad your restaurant or service is
- 13 per cent will tell at least 20 other people
- 90 per cent will never return to your restaurant
- it costs roughly five times as much to attract a new customer as it does to keep an existing one.

Therefore, encourage customers to complain on the spot. If they are unhappy about anything that is served to them, they should be encouraged to inform the member of staff who served them. This will give the establishment the opportunity to rectify the fault immediately. Ask them about their eating experience; this information will be vital for future planning. Treat any customer who complains well; offer them a free drink or a free meal. Make the complainant your ambassador. Show them empathy, use the appropriate body language, show concern, sympathise. Always apologise. If you handle the complaint well you will make the customer feel important. Remember:

Don't:

- say 'It's not my fault'
- say 'You're the fifth today to complain about that'
- interrupt – it will only add to their wrath
- jump to conclusions
- accept responsibility until you are sure it's your firm's fault
- be patronising
- argue
- lose your temper
- blame others.

Do:

- show empathy and use appropriate body language (e.g. show concern on your face, nod)
- use their name, when possible
- shut up and listen, and use body language to show that you are listening (e.g. use eye contact)
- take notes
- let them make their case, they will lose their head of steam
- ask questions to clarify the details
- recapitulate; confirm with them that you've got it right.
- sympathise (regardless of where the blame lies)
- gather together your version of the facts before replying
- phone back if necessary – on time!
- apologise profusely if your company is at fault
- tell them what you propose to do
- give them alternatives to choose from, if your company is at fault

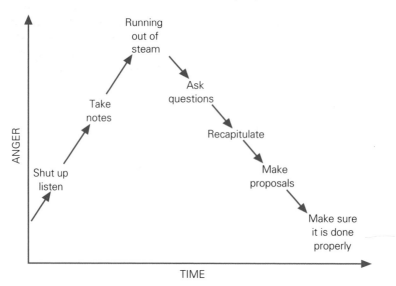

Figure 11.3 Let them make their case

- offer more than the bare minimum (e.g. make some concession on 'future business')
- get their full agreement that this will resolve the issue
- make sure that it is done properly and that they are kept fully informed
- contact them very soon afterwards to make sure that they are happy
- see it as an opportunity to cement the relationship and encourage more business.

Customer care
↓
Happy customers
↓
Profit
↓
Jobs

If you handle a customer complaint well, you will make the customer feel important. They will want to praise your company to their friends. Then they may well be prepared to deal with you again. So ask open questions to discover their future wants. For example:

- 'How often do you come to this establishment?' and 'How often do you order this from the menu'?
- 'How do you think your requirements will change in the future?'
- 'What will you be looking for then?' and 'What other services or meal items will you be looking for in the future?'

> **Some references to marketing elsewhere in this book:**
>
> - The Internet .... Ch. 17
> - Menu planning 227

Reference

Cracknell, H.L. and Kaufmann, R.J. (2002) *Practical Professional Catering Management.* Thomson Learning Vocational.

Topics for discussion

1 Your ideas for promoting a 100-seat industrial catering restaurant in an office block.
2 Examples of advertising and promotion.
3 What you understand by good public relations.
4 The advantages of cafeteria service.
5 The popularity of takeaways and what you think the changes will be in takeaway services in the future.
6 When is the use of vending machines worthwhile? Discuss where and how.
7 Can advertising increase sales? Explain how it could be used for a restaurant or any food service facility.
8 Making contact with local media to promote your business.
9 State the advantages of 'theatre' cookery (open-style kitchens, which enable the customer to see the food being cooked), with particular reference to customer service.
10 List six of the most important points you need to get across to staff when designing a training poster for customer care.

12 Accommodation management

Supporting material available on Dynamic Learning Online:

> Knowledge quizzes

> Activity worksheets

> Summary presentations

To accompany high-quality food and beverage, a high standard of accommodation management is vital to any hospitality operation. Although not all hospitality operations will provide room accommodation, a warm welcome and clean, safe and well-maintained premises are imperative in attracting and retaining guests.

Accommodation can be categorised into either private or public, or commercial or non-commercial operations.

- Private:
  - hotels
  - motels
  - serviced apartments
  - public houses
  - guest houses
  - private clubs
  - youth hostels
  - caravan parks
  - transport
  - time-share apartments.

Figure 12.1

- Public:
  - welfare (hospitals and residential establishments)
  - university halls of residence
  - military accommodation
  - prisons.

Classifications of accommodation

For details of the classifications used in private accommodation, see Table 12.1.

Tables 12.4 to 12.7 describe other types of accommodation.

Table 12.1 Private accommodation

Type	Description
Five-star hotels	Can be part of a large hotel chain, consortia or independent. Deluxe facilities may include several food and beverage outlets, conference and banqueting, leisure facilities and retail outlets. Accommodation categories in most cases include suite, executive and standard rooms, to meet the needs of different customer segments. Rooms are spacious, comfortable, well equipped and designed to a high standard. Front-office operations are extensive, providing a wide range of personal services from check-in to check-out. Typical guests would include head office corporate executives, business executives, government officials and celebrities.
Four-star hotels	Can be part of a large hotel chain, consortia or independent. A high standard of facilities may include restaurant, bar, coffee shop, conference and banqueting, leisure and retail outlets. The majority of accommodation would consist of standard rooms followed by executives and a few suites. Rooms are comfortable and well equipped.
Boutique hotels	Anhar (2001) defines a boutique hotel as follows: 'Style, distinction, warmth, and intimacy are key words in the architecture and design of boutique hotels. Boutique hotels are not boxed into standards; the definition and expression of a theme is a crucial path to success. Many boutique hotels introduce different themes in each guestroom, making every single stay unique, even for their repeat guests.' A relatively new concept, the key characteristics of boutique hotels include: • in most cases independent but can also be part of a small chain • four- or five-star • located in buildings that have been refurbished (i.e. car parks, office blocks or old buildings) • small in nature, ranging from 20–150 rooms • many rooms feature different internal decor and design • public areas are stylish and trendy • restaurant and bar are of high quality • highly personalised service.
Serviced apartments	A relatively new concept that emerged as an alternative for long-stay executives. Most large hotels, particularly in Asia and the Middle East, allocate a small percentage of their accommodation to serviced apartments. In some cases in the USA, whole properties consist of exclusively serviced apartments. The main difference between a serviced apartment and a normal hotel room is that its facilities will in most cases include a dining area, fully equipped kitchen, washing facilities and TV relaxation area. Operators achieve satisfaction from guests due to having a larger space that is more flexible and the opportunity to self-cater.
Budget hotels	The British Hospitality Association (BHA) defines a budget hotel as a strongly branded offer with generally compact rooms, a small food and beverage operation, and limited facilities and services. The UK has seen a rise in the growth of budget hotels in the past ten years. The characteristics of a budget hotel are: • often chained • in city-centre or motorway locations • two-or three-star standard • rates are competitive • food and beverage services are limited (breakfast buffet and maybe a bar) • internal decor has a common theme throughout • services are limited with 'no frills' • services are highly standardised, little flexibility • rooms are compact and feature the basics (some feature no baths, only showers) • front office features only a reception (no concierge, guest relations) – some self-check in terminals • in many cases support services such as housekeeping and maintenance are for the most part outsourced.

▶

Type	Description
Private clubs	Some private members' clubs will provide some accommodation within the club. These rooms would consist of basic facilities and may be used by members from affiliate clubs who are travelling to the location.
Guest house or bed and breakfast (B&B)	Typically operated by the owner, who deals with most of the front-office procedures during arrival and departure. These small businesses provide limited but comfortable room accommodation. Rooms would be cleaned by a small team of in-house cleaning personnel. Facilities are limited, with the exception of a small area provided for breakfast and in some cases a small bar area is also available.
Motels	Motels are in most cases situated close to motorways and are normally in the budget category. Their main purpose is to provide a place for motorists to rest.
Public house or inn	Pubs' core focus is to provide food and beverage in a relaxed environment. In some cases pub landlords also provide basic accommodation at a reasonable price on the same premises. Some large pubs will also have a function room where weddings or social get-togethers can be provided. Guests travelling to or through an area may also find pubs a good low-budget alternative. The preparing and cleaning of the rooms would be carried out by in-house cleaning personnel. Pub operators can look at the sales of accommodation for additional revenue opportunities in a challenging and competitive marketplace.
Youth hostel	Budget accommodation centrally located in most cities. Prices are low and rooms can be provided in different configurations, i.e. single, double or shared dormitories. Rooms are very basic and fittings may include a wardrobe and TV. In most cases bathroom facilities are separate.
Time-share	Tourists pay for access to an apartment or villa for a specific period over a number of years.

Table 12.2 Hotel sub-segments

Hotel	Description
Resort hotels	The main purpose of resorts is for rest, relaxation and recreation. Resorts can be subdivided into two main types: country resort and holiday centre. • Country resort hotels are in most cases situated in rural locations with natural surroundings. Resorts in hot climates can provide extensive facilities that may include swimming pools, tennis courts, spas, miniature golf, and gardens. Resorts normally occupy more land, which requires lots of maintenance. Rooms are spacious and comfortable. • Holiday centres offer for the most part self-contained villas, chalets or apartments. Facilities are extensive and include restaurants, leisure and entertainment. A growing trend is in the area of eco resorts, where the central theme is to provide accommodation in a natural setting with a sustainable operation. Seth (2006) explains eco tourism as 'environmentally friendly travel that emphasises seeing and saving natural habitats and archaeological treasures.'
City-centre hotels	City-centre hotels are located in central, city locations. Due to space being at a premium, these hotels are normally high-rise structures, and leisure and recreation facilities such tennis courts, swimming pools and gardens are less prominent.
Airport hotels	Located in close proximity to airports, these hotels are normally large, with between 200 and 1000+ rooms. Guests are transient and range from air crew and passengers to delegates attending meetings. In some cases, guests may rent room for just a few hours to freshen up and rest between flights.
Casino hotels	These hotels act as support for the casino, which is the main focus. Many hotels (such as those in Las Vegas and Macao) are very large, with over 1000 rooms. In addition, there is a large space allocated to retail outlets, dining, recreation and entertainment. Rooms are luxurious and spacious.
Conference hotels	Conference hotels provide conference and banqueting facilities to delegates or visitors attending an event. They are normally located on the periphery of a city.

AA star ratings

The UK Automobile Association (AA) provides a star rating system to classify hotels. This assists guests in selecting accommodation and provides standards for hotel operators. See Table 12.3.

Figure 12.2 The Venetian Macao: a casino hotel

Figure 12.3 Virgin Airlines Upper-Class accommodation

Table 12.3 AA star ratings

★	Courteous staff provide an informal yet competent service. The majority of rooms are en suite, and a designated eating area serves breakfast daily and dinner most evenings.
★ ★	All rooms are en suite or have private facilities. A restaurant or dining room serves breakfast daily and dinner most evenings.
★ ★ ★	Staff are smartly dressed and professionally presented. All rooms are en suite, and the restaurant or dining room is open to residents and non-residents.
★ ★ ★ ★	Professional, uniformed staff respond to your needs or requests, and there are usually well-appointed public areas. The restaurant or dining room is open to residents and non-residents, and lunch is available in a designated eating area.
★ ★ ★ ★ ★	Luxurious accommodation and public areas, with a range of extra facilities and a multilingual service available. Guests are greeted at the hotel entrance. High-quality menu and wine list.

Source: AA (2010)

Table 12.4 Non-serviced accommodation

Type	Description
Caravan park or campsite	Individuals provide their own accommodation (tents, caravans or mobile homes) as a means of accommodation while on vacation. (Some campsites provide caravans for rent.) Customers pay a small fee for a space on the site. Communal bathrooms, cafés, and leisure and entertainment venues may be provided.
Villas or apartments	These are privately owned by individuals or companies. Fully furnished, they feature bedroom, living, kitchen and outdoor spaces. Guests rent for vacation and self-cater. In most cases cleaning does not take place until the guests vacate, when the company's cleaning personnel clean and prepare for the next guests.

Table 12.5 Transport and accommodation

Type	Description
Cruise ship	Cruise ship passengers enjoy a large range of facilities while on board. These can range from restaurants, bars and nightclubs to conference rooms, gymnasiums and spas, to name a few. Sleeping accommodation (cabins) can range from deluxe to basic. Different cruise companies' standard cabins can be of a range of sizes, however the average cabin is around 150 square feet. Cabins feature beds (berths), bathroom and in some cases balconies.
Rail	Some trains in Europe provide beds (berths) for sleepers on long train journeys. These beds can in some areas of Europe be referred to as 'couchettes'. In most cases this accommodation is communal, with travellers sleeping up to six berths per cabin. Blankets and pillows are provided in most cases.
Air	Most international airlines now offer some kind of sleeping facility for 'upper class' passengers. Virgin Airlines' Upper Class offers passengers seats that convert into fully flat beds (see Figure 12.3). In-flight cabin crew (stewards) ensure passengers have a comfortable flight.

Table 12.6 Accommodation within the non-commercial sector

Type	Description
Hospitals	Accommodation for patients who require to stay in overnight can vary. Public-sector hospitals provide 'wards' where patients share accommodation. In private hospitals, patients in most cases are provided with single (or twin) roomed accommodation, which is very comfortable, featuring own bathroom, refrigerator and television. To minimise the risk of infection the standard of hygiene is paramount in any hospital, so cleaning is carried out frequently by a well-trained team of cleaning personnel. Matrons or persons of a similar standing have personal responsibility and accountability for delivering a safe and clean care environment.
Military	Accommodation can vary for military personnel depending on the rank and situation of the individual. For personnel who are with their families, fully furnished accommodation would be provided on or close to the military base. Single living accommodation (or barracks) is also provided on or close to base and would in most cases consist of fully furnished en suite accommodation. For new recruits, multi-occupancy barracks are commonly used. This style of accommodation is non-private and can accommodate up to 20 personnel at one time. Each individual has a single bed and wardrobe. Bathing facilities are communal. Depending on rank, military personnel in most cases would be responsible for maintaining the cleanliness of their accommodation on a day-to-day basis.
Prisons	Prisoners are accommodated, for most of the time, in cells. Cells are 6 × 8 feet in size and in most cases accommodate two inmates on a vertical-standing 'bunk bed'. Furniture and fixtures are limited apart from a lavatory, which may be provided. Shower facilities are separate. The prison provides cleaning personnel to clean cells as and when required.
University halls of residence	Most universities provide halls of residence in close proximity to the university for students. Student rooms are small and would feature in most cases a single bed, desk, television and shower. Communal kitchens are provided where students can prepare meals. The university would in most cases outsource the cleaning of rooms and public areas to a specialised cleaning company.
Welfare	Many residential homes provide private comfortable rooms for all residents. Homes are in most cases developed as a single-storey unit so all rooms are easily accessible. Rooms feature pleasant views, double beds, own bathroom, television and air conditioning/heating. Residents dine together in in-house restaurants. Rooms and public areas are cleaned on a daily basis by in-house staff.

Table 12.7 International examples of accommodation specific to a particular country/area

Country	Type	Description
Spain	Paradors	State-run hotels located throughout Spain, which are in most cases located in old buildings, castles or monasteries.
Portugal	Posadas	Small family-run guest houses.
Japan	Ryoken	Small, friendly, owner-operated inns with authentic Japanese design. Rooms are equipped with tatami mats and futon beds, and are in most cases situated close to a hot spring bath.
Japan	Capsule	High-rise accommodation located in central city areas. Rooms are around 6 feet long by 3 feet wide (and high). Guests access through a hatch-like door with room only for lying down. Guests check in via a vending machine and leave their luggage in a locker. Capsules include a television, mattress, bedding and light control.

Demand for accommodation

The demand for accommodation is closely linked to tourism activity. Individuals require accommodation for different reasons, such as business, attending conferences, vacationing, visiting friends and family, studying and health care.

Different data are collected on accommodation users, for example:

- type of accommodation used (e.g. hotel, motel, B&B)
- length of stay
- domestic or overseas
- nationality of guest
- age
- gender
- reason for visit.

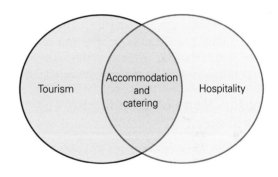

Figure 12.4

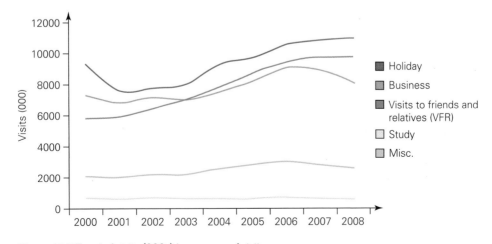

Figure 12.5 Trend of visits (000s) by purpose of visit

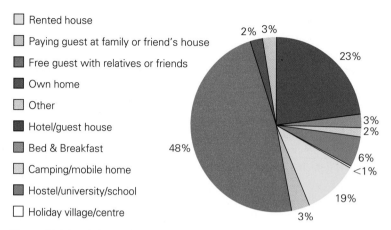

- ☐ Rented house
- ☐ Paying guest at family or friend's house
- ☐ Free guest with relatives or friends
- ☐ Own home
- ☐ Other
- ☐ Hotel/guest house
- ☐ Bed & Breakfast
- ☐ Camping/mobile home
- ☐ Hostel/university/school
- ☐ Holiday village/centre

Figure 12.6 Breakdown of accommodation type used by tourists visiting UK (Visit Britain, 2009)

Quality management

It is imperative that hospitality managers ensure that each guest has a pleasant experience during their visit. When customers are satisfied, they are more likely to return, and will pass on their positive experiences to friends and colleagues. This will in turn result in many benefits for accommodation operators.

Core functions of accommodation management

Quality tools that can be used in accommodation management include:

- completed 'customer questionnaires' for every customer
- speak to customers face to face throughout their visit
- mystery guests to evaluate the accommodation product and services
- effective 'service recovery' and complaint handling
- good leadership and supervision
- the ongoing review and utilisation of internal management information
- focus groups with customers
- conduct external surveys with target customers
- implement, monitor and review service standards
- conduct internal surveys with employees
- the ongoing monitoring of competition
- research industry academic literature
- employ external consultants to evaluate product, service and systems

- adopt quality programmes (e.g. Hospitality Assured, Investors In People)
- recruit good people and invest in training and development
- source good products.

Customers' evaluation of service delivery is essential to improve the operation and remain competitive.

Table 12.8 Contrasts in quality management

High quality	Low quality
Happy customers	Unhappy customers
Retain customers	Lose customers
Meet budgets	Under budget
Positive word of mouth	Negative word of mouth
Good image	Poor image
Market growth	Market decline
Retain employees	Lose employees
Attract customers	Difficult to attract
Easy to attract employees	Struggle to attract
No discounts	Frequent discounts
Open	Closed

The continual desires to meet the core functions are essential to the success of the accommodation product. The link to the market mix details the main areas that need to be carried out in order to successfully sell your product.

Table 12.9 The market mix's link to accommodation

Market mix	Linkage
Product	Both the tangible and intangible products need to be aligned to continuously meet the needs of the target customer at all times. Tangible products can include the exterior, the interior furnishings, bedrooms, restaurants and bathrooms, to name a few. Examples of intangible elements could include the lighting, air temperature, music and service. The product is managed by accommodation managers through ongoing research with guests, employee training, monitoring of service standards and external scanning.
Price	Price is of great importance in service industries due to the high perishability of the product. In most cases the revenue generated from rooms yields the greatest profitability of all departments within the hotel. Therefore it is imperative that the price is positioned correctly to meet the demands of the guests and cover operational expenses. To achieve and set the correct price, accommodation managers need to consider a wide range of internal and external information that will guide their decisions. If prices are too high managers risk losing guests, while pricing too low can result in loss of profits.
Place	Place is 'where' the organisation distributes or 'sells' its room product. For example, if a guest wants to book a room in a four-star branded hotel, this can in most cases be purchased through various channels, including a travel agent, the hotel's website, group's central reservations office (CRS), a third-party website or over the counter, to name a few. Alternatively, a small bed and breakfast operation may distribute its rooms only over the counter or on its website. Therefore, the key is for accommodation operations to increase the amount of channels available where individuals can purchase rooms. The more distribution channels, the more opportunities to sell your accommodation. This, however, requires careful management to ensure the best returns are achieved from each channel.
Promotion	Once a good standard of accommodation has been achieved, the operator needs to create awareness to attract buyers and effectively sell its product. As most hospitality businesses operate in a seasonal environment, they often create promotions during the 'low season' to attract demand.

Characteristics

In this section, hotel accommodation will be investigated, focusing on the rooms division department.

At the core of the rooms division department are front office and housekeeping, with maintenance and security acting as valuable support departments. Rooms division and food and beverage are in most cases the two main revenue-generating departments within the hotel. It is often the case that rooms provide more profit than food and beverage due to lower operating costs. The size and scope of the rooms division can depend on the type of the hotel.

Front office is a revenue-generating department, while housekeeping is a support department.

The front office department

The hotel's front office is in most cases the busiest area within the hotel, attracting the most traffic and activity. It is the visitor's first impression on arrival and their last on departure. It is a hub of activity where individuals may be arriving, checking in or out, attending meetings, requesting information from the concierge, having refreshments, shopping, waiting for taxis, or just sitting in the lobby reading newspapers.

Individuals that come into contact with front office personnel may include guests staying in the hotel,

Figure 12.7 The hotel lobby

Table 12.10 Characteristics

Characteristic	Description	Solutions
Intangibility	A large part of the hospitality product is made up of intangible elements such as service, ambience and other guests. These elements can provide many challenges for the operator as they are hard to standardise and can create inconsistencies.	Regular employee training Develop service standards and monitor
Simultaneous production and consumption	The uniqueness of the hospitality product is that it is produced and consumed simultaneously in most cases. This means limited time for quality control.	Standardise tasks Simplify tasks Supervision Empowerment
Heterogeneity	Each service experience is different; service delivery can vary in the same organisation due to different producers, and different consumers with different needs and wants.	Understand target market's needs and wants Standardise tasks Flexibility
Consistency	Due to the intangible element of the accommodation product, consistency is a challenge, which is what most consumers demand. For example, as humans our moods can change easily due to a combination of factors such as illness, bad news and difficult guests.	Job specifications Job descriptions Effective recruitment Standardise tasks Supervision
Perishability	The accommodation product, as in most service industries, is highly perishable. This means that certain products, such as bedrooms, cannot be stored. If a bedroom is not sold tonight, the revenue will be lost. Unused hospitality services cannot be returned, claimed or resold.	Sales-orientated employees Internal budgeting External monitoring Revenue management Yield management
Ownership	When purchasing a hospitality product the consumer owns that product only for that period of time. Bedrooms are rented not owned.	Customer care Customer retention
No guarantees	As with most other industries there is little post-consumption aftercare or service.	Loyalty schemes Customer care Follow-up evaluation
Imitation is easy	The service process is easily observed by competitors. No patents.	External monitoring Differentiate
Seasonality	Many hospitality businesses operate in a seasonal marketplace, which creates many challenges for operators in relation to staffing and expenses.	Market research Forecasting Budgeting Yield management
External variables	The industry is faced with many external variables that can impact the running of the business. Examples include weather, competitors and PESTLE factors,	PESTLE analysis (Political, Economic, Social, Technological, Legal and Environmental) Contingency
No pre-trial	According to Jones and Paul (1996), unlike many other products on sale, accommodation cannot be sampled or tried out before purchase.	Accurate and effective brochures and websites

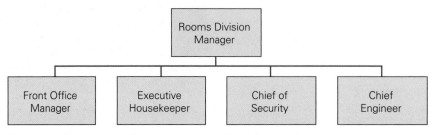

Figure 12.8 Typical rooms division structure in a large four-star hotel

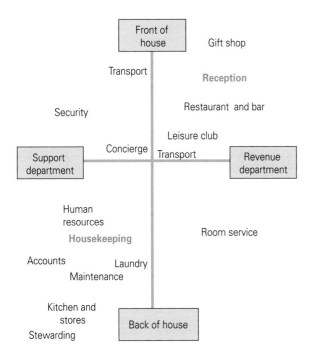

Figure 12.9 Revenue and support centres in a typical four-star hotel

Figure 12.10 A doorman

guests of guests, non-residents visiting the hotel's restaurants, conference and banqueting attendees, and individuals meeting with hotel executives.

The times with the heaviest footfall tend to be the morning, when guests are checking out, and late afternoon, when arrivals are due.

The objectives of the front office are to:

- maximise profits through the effective management of room inventory
- ensure that at each stage of the customer cycle consumer expectations are met
- effectively channel and process information between the front office and stakeholders.

In order to achieve the front office objectives there are many challenges and variables that need to be managed and overcome.

Table 12.11 Key challenges in the front office

Challenge	Meeting the challenge
Achieving financial control	The front office deals with a large number of financial transactions each day. These could include receiving cash from guests or selling the correct rooms to the correct guests. Therefore, front office managers must place a great emphasis on financial control. This entails the correct planning and selling of room inventory, coupled with the monitoring and maintaining of departmental expenses.
Communication	With front office acting as the main communication hub that channels information throughout the hotel, it is essential that processes are in place to ensure that effective communication is achieved between front office and all its stakeholders.
Complex distribution network	Guests need to be reassured that they are buying at a fair price, and that the information on availability and price is consistent regardless of the distribution channel they have used. They look for integrity in that system. The distribution channel is the method used to purchase the hotel room, i.e. website, travel agent, tour operator. The management of various distribution channels is a complex and demanding task for managers. This is compounded by the fact that supply and demand patterns can change quickly. The front office manager must be able to assimilate a great deal of information quickly and make appropriate decisions while maintaining consistency across the distribution network.

▶

Challenge	Meeting the challenge
Fixed capacity	The hotel has a maximum quantity of rooms that it can sell. On occasions, demand exceeds supply and the hotel fails to meet those demands due to a fixed quantity of rooms. This fixed capacity sometimes places limits on opportunities to sell more rooms and achieve greater sales. It is therefore important for front office managers to be aware of demand trends and to capitalise on them when they arise.
Diversity	With an increase in numbers of international travellers the front office needs to be able to meet their needs and expectations, to ensure satisfaction is achieved. Hotel diversity and intercultural training is essential to achieving this aim.
Legal framework	To protect the hotel, its assets, employees and guests, the hotel's front office is required to work within a legal framework.
Major guest interface	The front office department is a highly visible and busy department with lots of activity. It is for this reason that it is essential that all employees working in this area are well trained and able to meet the myriad of demands that confront them in their day-to-day exchanges with guests, managers and partner departments.
Perishability	The aim of the accommodation department is to sell rooms. When rooms are not sold they cannot be stored and sold another time, as products in other industries can (e.g. manufacturing). Unsold rooms equate to lost revenue. The high perishability of rooms is one of the greatest challenges for accommodation managers.

Staffing and structures

Front office structures and staffing

The organisational structure of a hotel front office can depend on many factors. These may include those listed in Table 12.12.

Table 12.12 Factors affecting the organisational structure of a hotel front office

Factor	Example
Star rating or standard	A budget hotel's front office may consist only of a reception manager, receptionist and luggage porter. While, in contrast, a five-star hotel may have staff including door attendants, lobby hosts, guest services and concierge.
Size of hotel	The quantity of personnel is also a factor in front office structure. If a hotel has 50 rooms or 5000 rooms this will require different manning levels.
Management structure	Management requiring close control may have a centralised, tight structure that will require more employee positions. Alternatively, a more open decentralised management approach may require fewer employees, but who are cross-trained and more flexible.
Target customer	The type of customer can also be a factor in some circumstances. Some hotels that cater to business clientele may provide separate executive check-in desks. Hotels attracting business guests may also require a higher staff-to-customer ratio.
Location	Some resort hotels will have more transport personnel to transport guests around the facilities. Many hotels in China still feature the role of cashier as a separate position.

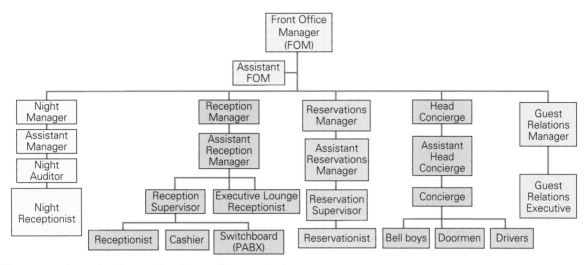

Figure 12.11 A standard four-star hotel front office organisation

The role of the front office manager

The front office manager is the leader of the team and responsible for the day-to-day running of the front office department. They oversee all front office sub-departments in their operations and ensure that each customer's needs are met throughout the guest cycle.

Job title: Front Office Manager
Report to: General Manager

Key functions

Key management functions include maximising sales, minimising costs and maintaining standards simultaneously at all times.

Major responsibilities and duties

- Be responsible for the smooth, effective, efficient and professional operations of all front office areas
- Conduct daily briefings, outlining daily targets, areas for improvement and VIPs
- Ensure all front office personnel comply with hotel's standard guidelines
- Attend daily management morning briefing, sales strategy meeting and other meetings as required; prepare all relevant reports to managers
- Ensure all daily VIPs are pre-registered and greeted, and escorted to their rooms on arrival
- Ensure all VIP room allocations are checked prior to guests' arrival
- Train all front office staff to be fully acquainted with the property management system (PMS)
- Coordinate with the housekeeping department to ensure that there is a maximum number of rooms available for sale at all times
- Develop a close and effective working relationship with all other department heads

- Plan and hold meetings with employees and department managers
- Ensure that costs are minimised at all times
- Ensure that customer satisfaction is achieved, through constant monitoring
- Implement systems to minimise and manage customer complaints
- Manage and monitor room occupancy and average room rates throughout the day
- Recruit and select front office personnel
- Motivate employees and set incentives
- Plan, organise and deliver training
- Constantly evaluate service standards
- Write and monitor budgets
- Train and develop staff to the quality and consistency of service standards
- Ensure that all front office employees are fully conversant with all hotel facilities, activities, and points of interests and attractions in the city
- Train all front office staff how to identify frequent guests, to know their preferences, ensuring all guests' needs are met
- Train all front office employees to understand and be familiar with cultural differences of gusts
- Be fully conversant with all emergency procedures and train all front office staff to know how to act upon them.

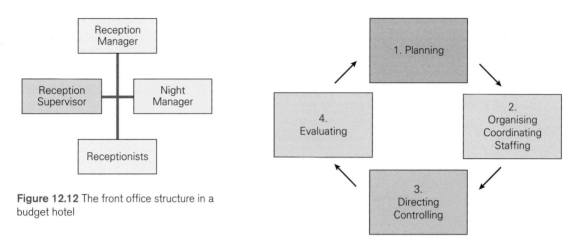

Figure 12.12 The front office structure in a budget hotel

Figure 12.13 The management process

Table 12.13 Front office managers: application to disciplines

Discipline	Front office application
Planning	Planning of staffing to ensure there is sufficient manpower on duty to deal with demand Planning of departmental budgets to set financial targets for room revenues and expenses Planning of departmental training to ensure standards are met consistently Planning of departmental stocks to ensure all resources are in place for employees to complete their work successfully
Controlling	Controlling of room inventory, ensuring the right price is allocated to the right customer at the right time Controlling of departmental assets (cash and equipment) Controlling of guests' assets (safety deposit boxes) Controlling of guests' details (Data Protection Act) Controlling of departmental service standards, ensuring these are being met consistently at all times
Coordinating	Coordinating of monthly departmental meetings to discuss front office issues and performance
Organising	Organising of employee social events and activities Organising of room promotions
Staffing	Screening and interviewing potential new front office personnel Recruitment and selection of front office personnel Assisting new personnel with a smooth induction and departmental orientation Carrying out departmental training Setting employee incentive programmes Motivating and encouraging employees continuously in their work Guiding and correcting employees continually in their work Issuing disciplinary warnings as and when required
Directing	Directing employees to perform duties Directing employees on new guidelines or standards
Evaluating	Evaluating the recruitment of front office personnel Evaluating the performance of all front office personnel both daily and in the conducting of employee appraisals Evaluating rooms performance against daily room financial targets Evaluating customer satisfaction Evaluating service standards against service audits Evaluating competitors' performance against the hotel's (benchmarking) Evaluating own performance through 360-degree appraisal

Front office managers communicate through their staff, feelings of warmth, care, safety and efficiency to each front office guest.

(Bardi, 2007)

Employees working in the front office department require a myriad of skills to deal with a challenging, fast-paced and diverse environment (see Table 12.14). Competent employees will be rewarded with opportunities to develop personal communication skills, problem solving, decision making and progression, to name but a few.

Table 12.14 Requirements of front office personnel

Challenges	Requirements
24-hour, fast-paced operation	Stamina Personal fitness
Continuous guest contact	Communicative Adaptive Reactive Ability to read people Confident Outgoing General enthusiasm to meet people
Demanding guests	Patient Good composure Ability to solve complaints
Highly automated work environment	Computer literate Ability to use email, intranet and Internet systems Knowledge of front office software (e.g. Fidelio, Opera, Micros, Remanco, Galileo, Amadeus) Ability to use property management system (PMS)
Highly visible	Excellent personal presentation Good posture Good body language
International client base	Multilingual Culturally aware
Large work team	Ability to work in a team Excellent communication skills
Revenue department	Ability to sell Product knowledge Jones and Paul (1996) explain, 'A sales orientation or awareness should be an integral part of the operations culture, particularly where there is a continuous need to increase occupancy and revenue levels.'

The relationship developed by personnel may or may not impress the customer, may or may not encourage the customer to sample the facilities and services available, may or may not encourage the customer to return or recommend the hotel to other potential guests.

(Jones and Paul, 1996)

Table 12.15 lists brief descriptions of the roles and responsibilities of front office personnel. These can differ from property to property.

Figure 12.14 Working front of house involves continuous guest contact

Table 12.15 Roles and responsibilities of front office personnel

Position	Responsibilities
Receptionist	Welcoming, checking in and registering guests Carrying out cashiering duties and exchanging currency Allocating customer rooms, and cutting and issuing room keys Checking room status with housekeeping departments Fulfilling any guest requests Upselling room categories Informing guests of hotel facilities and of any special events taking place within the hotel Following departmental operating standards of performance Carrying out any bill adjustments Carrying out customer check-outs Assisting with any room reservations Communicating with other departments as and when required Dealing with customer complaints Operating hotel point-of-sale (POS) system
Concierge	Being aware of the hotel facilities, locations and hours of operation Providing details of local information to guests – should have knowledge of local areas, e.g. social, cultural and physical attractions, and their hours of operation Having awareness of local restaurants and their hours of operation Assisting with the booking of local tours and attractions Booking of onward transport, flights and accommodation
Reservationist	Dealing with calls, emails and fax enquiries Checking room availability Providing hotel information Providing, negotiating and confirming rates Using revenue and yield management to manage supply Sending out reservation confirmations Maintaining reports Regular communication with front office and sales managers
Guest relations officer (GRO)	Making guests feel welcome Reviewing arrivals list Organising VIP amenities for rooms Greeting VIP guests, assisting with guest check-in and escorting guests to rooms Dealing with customer enquiries Conducting guest tours Escorting sick or unwell guests to the hospital
'Executive lounge' receptionist	Checking in guests for executive rooms Informing guests of executive lounge facilities Checking guest satisfaction throughout stay Assisting with the service of food and beverage in the executive lounge Checking out executive guests
Switchboard operator (PABX)	Ensuring all calls are answered promptly and courteously Transferring incoming calls to guests, employees and managers Taking messages Providing guidance on dialling codes Assisting guests with outgoing calls Dealing with any emergency calls as per hotel standard
Luggage porter/ bell boy	Storing, tagging and transferring luggage Guiding guests as required – should have a good knowledge of hotel layout, rooms, facilities and hours of operation Promoting hotel facilities and restaurants whenever possible Delivering mail, faxes, messages and packages to guest rooms Performing light housekeeping duties in lobby area Delivering newspapers to rooms

Position	Responsibilities
Night manager	Bardi (2004) details the six steps involved in preparing a night audit: • posting room and tax charges • assembling guest charges and payments • reconciling departmental financial activities • reconciling the accounts receivable • running the trail balance • preparing the night audit report.
Hotel driver	Ensuring hotel vehicle is clean internally and externally at all times, is well maintained and has passed the appropriate roadworthiness checks Ensuring vehicle is equipped with newspapers, magazines and hotel literature Receiving and delivering guests to and from airport Providing a comfortable, friendly and informative travel experience to guests Being prompt in collection of guests The safe loading and unloading of guests' luggage
Doorman	Greeting all guests in a friendly, attentive manner (using name wherever possible) Bidding farewell and 'bon voyage' to departing guests Some general cleaning duties of external arrival area Providing directions to guests as and when required Calling of taxis and opening doors of taxis for guests Keeping external forecourt free of traffic build-up and illegal parkers
Cashier	Ensuring sufficient change in float to deal with guest transactions The accurate completion of transactions Dealing with foreign currency exchange Processing cheques, credit/debit and cash transactions efficiently Reconciling all transactions at end of shift and completing the appropriate reports Dealing with any 'petty cash' transactions Keeping all cash assets safe at all times through added vigilance Ensuring all stationery, till rolls and printer cartridges are in stock
Valet parker (in some deluxe properties)	The safe parking of guests' personal cars/vehicles The storage of guests' keys while in the hotel Some very general cleaning/polishing of vehicles The safe retrieval of guests' cars/vehicles

Operations (front office, housekeeping and facilities)

The front office process

The front office exchange moves through four main phases – more commonly termed the 'guest cycle' (Figure 12.15). The guest cycle details the different stages that most consumers go through when dealing with the front office. Although most consumers advance through the cycle, this can change in certain situations – for example, when hotels receive 'walk in' guests who have not pre-booked. From a management perspective, each stage of the cycle provides opportunities and challenges. It is the front office manager's responsibility to ensure that all departmental objectives are met and this process is free from defects.

In addition to these core guest cycle functions, more specific functions are included for different

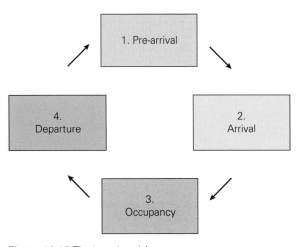

Figure 12.15 The 'guest cycle'

customer types such as business guest, leisure, international, family, disabled and groups.

Throughout the cycle, front office personnel carry out specific functions (as shown in Figure 12.16) to ensure guests have a positive experience.

Market segmentation

Different types of accommodation target different types of customer. The type of customer drives the establishment's product design, level of service and overall mission.

Meeting the needs of guests in the front office

While they are in the hotel, it is imperative that the customer's needs are met. When these needs are not met then dissatisfaction occurs.

All consumers are different, and have different needs and requirements; it is the goal of the hotel to ensure that these specific needs are met, not only during their stay but *before* they arrive. Using past experience and information on consumer trends, hotels are able to meet the customer's needs on arrival. For example, a business guest may require a limousine pick-up from the airport, express check-in, a particular room of their choice and a particular newspaper. If their needs are anticipated then there is a greater opportunity to achieve satisfaction.

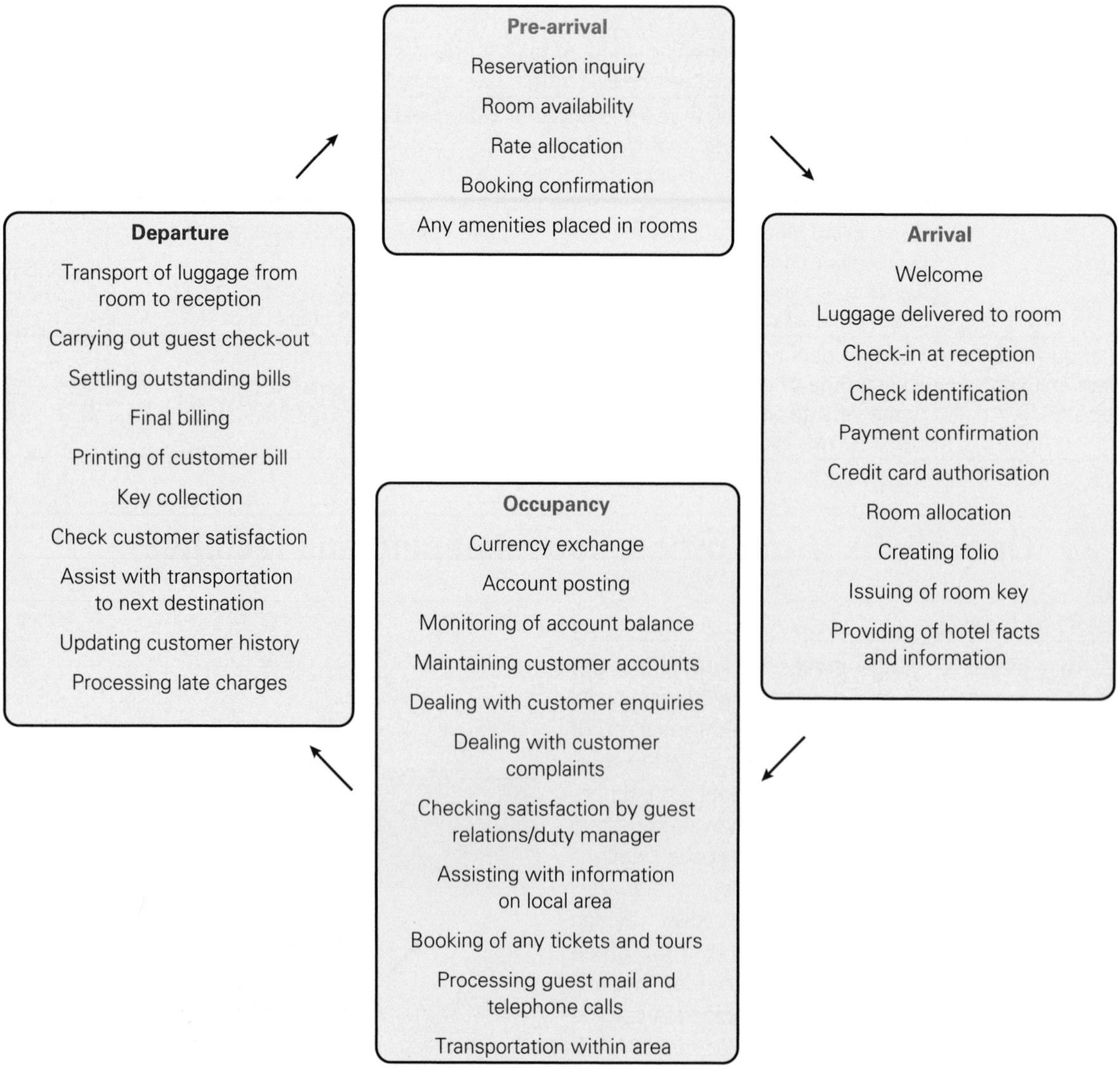

Pre-arrival

Reservation inquiry

Room availability

Rate allocation

Booking confirmation

Any amenities placed in rooms

Departure

Transport of luggage from room to reception

Carrying out guest check-out

Settling outstanding bills

Final billing

Printing of customer bill

Key collection

Check customer satisfaction

Assist with transportation to next destination

Updating customer history

Processing late charges

Occupancy

Currency exchange

Account posting

Monitoring of account balance

Maintaining customer accounts

Dealing with customer enquiries

Dealing with customer complaints

Checking satisfaction by guest relations/duty manager

Assisting with information on local area

Booking of any tickets and tours

Processing guest mail and telephone calls

Transportation within area

Arrival

Welcome

Luggage delivered to room

Check-in at reception

Check identification

Payment confirmation

Credit card authorisation

Room allocation

Creating folio

Issuing of room key

Providing of hotel facts and information

Figure 12.16 Key functions and interactions during the guest cycle

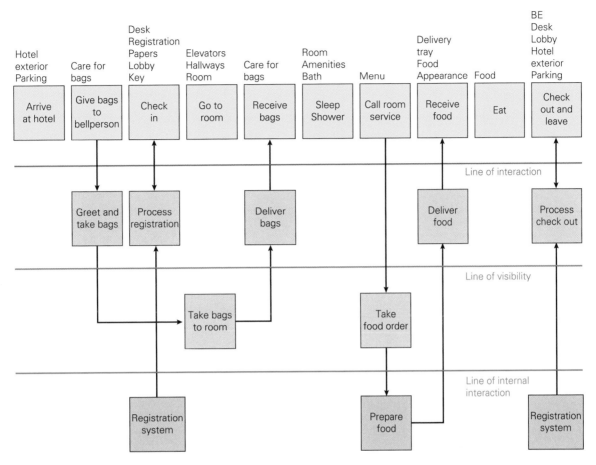

Figure 12.17 The flow of guest activity from arrival to departure

Figure 12.18 Transporting luggage to the room

Customer expectation ————→←———— Service delivery

Expectations
exceeded

Customer expectation ————→←———— Service delivery

Expectations
met

Customer expectation ——→ GAP ←—— Service delivery

Expectations
not met

Figure 12.19 Customer satisfaction

Another method to ensure guests receive a better service is to use 'guest histories', provided that they have stayed previously. Each time a guest stays at a hotel, data are collected on their prefer- ences, which can be used to enhance satisfac- tion on their return. For example, a customer who stays quarterly at the hotel always prefers a room with a view and the *Financial Times* newspaper,

Table 12.16 Specific functions of front office personnel

Employee	Pre-arrival	Arrival	Occupancy	Departure
Receptionist	Checking room arrivals list Checking room status information Preparing resources	Welcoming guest Completion of registration form Completing financial transactions Briefing on facilities Issuing of key	Posting room charges Dealing with any enquiries Updating room status Moving rooms Checking room balances Dealing with lost keys	Printing invoice Making any adjustments Collecting payment and settling room bill Printing receipt Collecting key card or room key Checking satisfaction Updating customer history
Concierge	Checking arrival information Considering any specific needs or wants Communicating with transport personnel Updating information on external events and activities	Greeting, assisting where necessary	Assistance with: • guidance on places of interest in local area • where to shop • recommending restaurants • maps and how to get around • tourist attractions • making onward hotel reservations • booking and travel arrangements • booking theatre tickets	Assisting with any onward hotel or transport reservations
Bell boy	Identifying customer peaks in arrival times Preparing luggage trolleys for expected guests Ensuring sufficient manpower available to greet guests and transport luggage	Tagging luggage Transporting luggage to rooms In-room guidance (how to use aircon, TV, etc.)	Delivering newspapers to rooms Delivering mail, faxes or messages to rooms Helping with any guest shopping bags Running any emergency errands for guests	Transporting luggage from room to reception Assisting with transport of luggage to taxi or other transport
Reservationist	Receiving reservation Confirming reservation details	Dealing with reservations as required	Dealing with reservations as required	Dealing with reservations as required
Guest relations	Preparing welcome letters for rooms Confirming any in-room guests amenities (fruit basket, wine, champagne, etc.)	Meeting guests Escorting to rooms in some cases Dealing with any immediate enquiries	Checking customer satisfaction Dealing with any customer enquiries Solving customer complaints	Checking satisfaction

Table 12.17 Examples of accommodation segmentation (can differ from property to property)

Accommodation	Target guests
Four- and five-star city hotels	*Monday to Friday* Corporate CEOs and executives Business travellers Frequent independent travellers (FITs) Conference attendees Airline crew Some leisure business Corporate groups Leisure groups (off-season) *Weekends* Leisure guests (families, shoppers, weekend visitors) Guests attending banqueting functions (wedding party guests)
Four- and five-star resort hotels	Vacationers Conference and banqueting guests Incentive guests
Airline hotels	Short-stay travellers in transit (half-day let) Passengers of cancelled/delayed flights Airline crew Conference attendees
Conference hotels	Conference delegates Banquet attendees
Casino hotels	Gamers Tourists Pre-wedding parties (stag and hen)
Budget	Budget-conscious travellers Independent businessmen
Bed and breakfast (B&B)	Budget-conscious travellers Independent businessmen Tourists
Youth hostel	Students Tourists

and always requests extra hangers. This information would be flagged when the customer makes another booking, and these preferences put in place. The key is reducing the customer's opportunity 'to ask' for services or products by anticipating and fulfilling their needs.

Reservations

Guests have the opportunity to reserve rooms in a variety of ways. These may include travel agent, tour operator or hotel website. Accommodation operators use these reservation channels in different ways depending on different factors, which may include room demand, season, rate of commission and overall customer strategy. Kotler *et al.* (2003) describe

distribution channels as 'a set of interdependent organisations (intermediaries) involved in the process of making a product or service available for use or consumption by the consumer or business user'.

It is good practice for accommodation managers to regularly evaluate the performance of each distribution channel, to achieve overall efficient performance within the rooms department. For example, you may be receiving a high quantity of bookings through travel agents at a low commission, but the type of customer is not your target market and requires more work. Alternatively, research from customers details that they found it difficult to book online through the hotel's website, a channel that is relatively cost-effective.

Table 12.18 Meeting customers' specific needs

Customer type	Particular needs	Front office
Large group	Organisation Communication	Rooms allocated and group rooms located together Keys cut before arrival and rooms allocated Separate check-in area Pre-registration If on package, tables reserved, and menus and dining times given to group members on check-in Additional bell boys scheduled to deal with high volume of luggage
Business guests	Efficient service Recognition	Express check-in Information on Wi-Fi and business centre Club lounge information Mobile phone adaptor Newspaper Information on hotel's meeting rooms Registration form completed and ready just for signature
Female guests	Safety Comfort	Non-interconnecting room
Families	Safety Entertainment	Interconnecting rooms Low-level floor Information on babysitting service Rollaway bed
Tourists	Information on local area	Currency exchange Local maps Sightseeing information
Older guests	Safety	Low-floor room Room with a pleasant view Assistance with luggage

Table 12.19 Appraisal of distribution channels

Channel	Explanation	Advantages	Disadvantages
Central reservations	The central reservations system (CRS) is in most cases used by large hotel chains Reservationists are off-site and deal with reservations for hotels within a particular region	Guests have access to knowledgeable, efficient sales personnel Lower space costs as most CRSs are located off-site, thus freeing up space in the hotel Reservationists have up-to-date room availability for all properties in region	Can be costly to develop and staff
Airport desk	Airports feature hotel desks to advertise hotel rooms to individuals arriving at destination without a reservation	Opportunity to sell unsold rooms inventory throughout the day	Fee to airport representative Net profit is not always high
Third-party websites (e.g. Expedia, lastminute.com)	Hotels sell rooms to third-party websites, which then sell to consumers booking through the websites	Hotels can advertise and reach growing number of consumers booking through websites Increase in market share	Highly competitive May impact brand image No personal contact for guests
Travel agents	Hotel uses agents to sell rooms on its behalf	Hotels can use multiple agents around the globe Can target agents for specific demographic and geographic segments	Percentage of final rate paid to agent Rates are cheap Lack of full control over clients

Channel	Explanation	Advantages	Disadvantages
Company/hotel website	Most hotels develop their own websites to attract guests	No commission Can change/update Consumers can view all hotel facilities online	Not always most competitive rate May be slow for guests
Over the counter	Guests have no prior booking and arrive to purchase room	Consumer can view facilities before purchase Negotiation is possible	If hotel is full, may lead to disappointment
Corporate travel agents	Large corporate companies develop corporate travel agents to book reservations for their employees	Sales department can create contracts with companies based on quantity of rooms booked per year	Tension is created at periods when demand is high as rooms could be sold at a higher rate
Marketing consortia	Groups of independent hotels form a coalition and develop a CRS to compete with chains	Cross-marketing New distribution channel More competitive	Share costs of CRS and marketing
Competitors' 'overflow'	Agreements can be formed between competing hotels to send overflow guests to each other when capacity is exceeded	An opportunity for the overflow hotel arises as new guests could switch loyalty and become loyal to overflow hotel	Percentage of room fees paid to full-capacity hotel for overflow customer

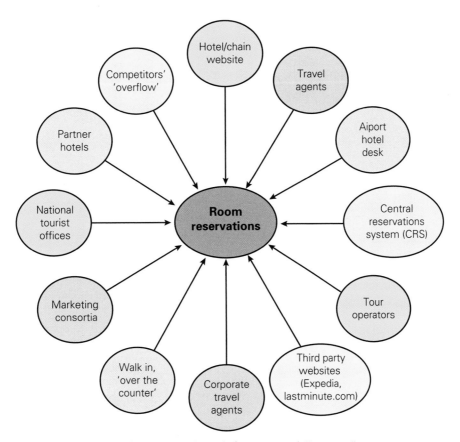

Figure 12.20 Examples of distribution channels for accommodation operations

Technology in the front office

In the hotel the front office is the core for technology. The technology links the front office with the hotel's other departments, its guests and external intermediaries. The property management system (PMS) acts as the hub interfacing with different systems to serve the guest.

Computer applications are central to front office operations in today's modern hotels.

(Bardi, 2007)

The benefits of using a central reservations system (CRS) include:

- agents are 'sales' orientated
- maintains statistical information (call volume, talk time, conversion rates, denial rates)
- maintains data on customer relationship management (loyalty programmes)
- provides properties with necessary technologies
- communicates room availability to e-distribution channels
- agents have up-to-date hotel information at hand to assist caller's enquiry
- delivers reservations to properties
- in most cases, the CRS offers a toll-free or 0800 number
- bills properties for handling reservations
- maintains demographic information about callers
- CRS offices are 'off-site', allowing for cost savings
- sales agents are in most cases multilingual.

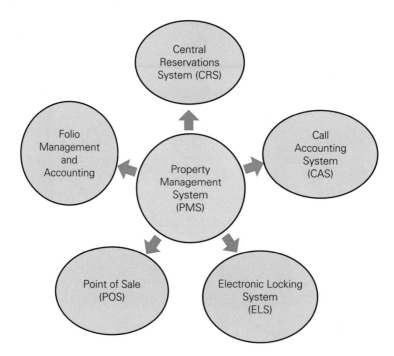

Figure 12.21 A property management system

Table 12.20 Technology in the front office

Technology	Description
Property management system (PMS)	The PMS is the central hardware hub that interfaces with all other hotel systems. According to Bardi (2007), 'The property management system gives the front office manager an unlimited opportunity for managerial control.'
Central reservations system (CRS)	A service developed by chains and consortia. Customers can call toll-free numbers and speak to a reservations agent 24 hours a day. Agents are trained in sales techniques and knowledgeable on any of the properties, products and services within the organisation. Travellers in various market segments depend on a well-organised reservation system that is easily accessible through toll-free numbers, the Internet or at a few hours notice (Bardi, 2007).
Call accounting system (CAS)	Software that captures telephone charges for in-room guests calling numbers outside the hotel. The system captures rate per minute, minutes called and number called; this charge then appears on the guest's folio.
Electronic locking system (ELS)	Many hotels now feature electronic locks on hotel room doors, offices and storage areas. The locks provide additional security for guests and capture data on when the room was accessed and by whom.
Point of sale (POS)	According to Bardi (2004) the point-of-sale option allows the front office computer to interface with the computers in other departments. In a hotel, when a front office interfaces with the restaurant, the front office computer terminal accepts and automatically costs charges made in the restaurant (the point of sale) to a guest's folio.
Folio management and billing	Software that captures and manages all guest billing information

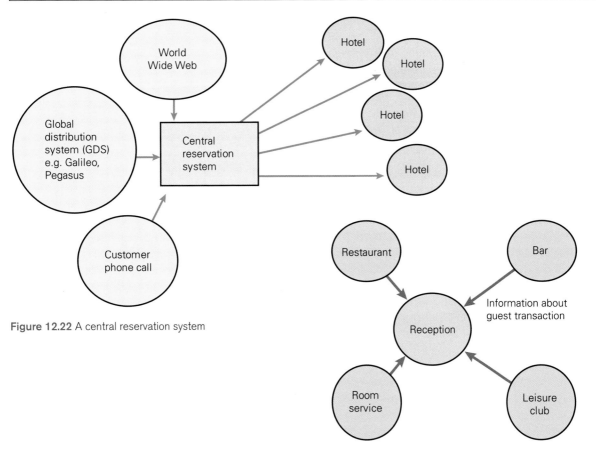

Figure 12.22 A central reservation system

Figure 12.23 Central reservation: benefits

Revenue management

For hotels and other providers of room accommodation, it is imperative that they develop strategies to effectively sell their rooms inventory. Room sales are important in terms of:

- meeting budgeted financial targets and achieving a return on investment
- avoiding wasted capacity and space
- providing owners with financial returns
- remaining competitive
- reducing expenses
- achieving a vibrant environment
- utilising stocks
- maintaining satisfaction among employees
- improving operational performance
- avoiding loss of profits and closure
- attracting and retaining customers
- attracting potential investors.

Front office managers are required to invest lots of time in research and forecasting to achieve these financial objectives. Possibly the most important planning function is the development of the room's budget. Budgeting is a management tool that forecasts departmental revenues, expenses and profit. Each manager with their individual teams prepares their department and these are collated to produce a 'hotel budget'. This takes place once a year and is a very critical task, which can be time consuming due to its importance.

Considerations when planning a budget include the following.

- What rates shall we charge for our rooms?
- How much demand will we have for our rooms on each day?
- How much profit is required?
- What will our operational costs be?
- What prices are our customers prepared to pay?
- What events will create demand?
- What is our room supply on each day?
- What are our strengths and weaknesses within our rooms operation?
- How much supply and demand will our competitors have?

- How can we create additional demand through room promotions?
- What are our competitors' strengths and weaknesses?
- What strategies and tactics can we use to sell more rooms?
- How can we get a competitive advantage with our rooms?
- How can we leverage our rooms product to achieve the highest rate possible?
- What is our current position within the marketplace?
- Which customers yield the most profit?
- What changes in external forces will impact how we deliver our rooms products?
- Which reservation channels yield the most profit?
- Are there any ways in which we can increase supply?
- Is this budget realistic and achievable?

A SWOT analysis is a valuable business analysis technique which can be used to build up a picture of the reality of the business and identify strengths, weaknesses, opportunities and threats to the accommodation product.

(Jones and Paul, 1996)

Yield management

A modern approach, commonly used in large international hotel operations is yield management (YM). The concept of this approach is to maximise profitability with careful forecasting tactics – more simply, selling the right room to the right customer at the right time. Through studying past history and future demand, reservation managers can use this information to determine whether room rates should be increased or decreased, or if a booking should be accepted or declined to achieve the greatest profit on the room sale.

YM is based on supply and demand. Prices tend to rise when demand exceeds supply; conversely, prices tend to fall when supply exceeds demand.

Internal audit	SWOT anaysis (Strengths, Weaknesses, Opportunities and Threats)	PESTLE analysis (Political, Economic, Social, Technological, Legal and Environmental)	Competitor analysis	Strategic response

Figure 12.24 Process and models used in room forecasting

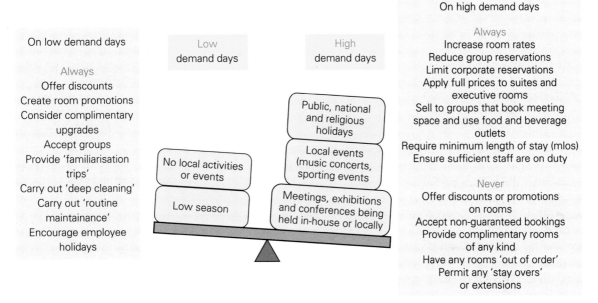

On low demand days

Always
Offer discounts
Create room promotions
Consider complimentary upgrades
Accept groups
Provide 'familiarisation trips'
Carry out 'deep cleaning'
Carry out 'routine maintainance'
Encourage employee holidays

Low demand days

No local activities or events

Low season

High demand days

Public, national and religious holidays

Local events (music concerts, sporting events)

Meetings, exhibitions and conferences being held in-house or locally

On high demand days

Always
Increase room rates
Reduce group reservations
Limit corporate reservations
Apply full prices to suites and executive rooms
Sell to groups that book meeting space and use food and beverage outlets
Require minimum length of stay (mlos)
Ensure sufficient staff are on duty

Never
Offer discounts or promotions on rooms
Accept non-guaranteed bookings
Provide complimentary rooms of any kind
Have any rooms 'out of order'
Permit any 'stay overs' or extensions

Figure 12.25 Examples of yield management strategies

Performance indicators

It is essential that front office managers evaluate the performance of resources within their department. This ongoing measurement will assist in improving profits and the hotel's positioning overall within the marketplace.

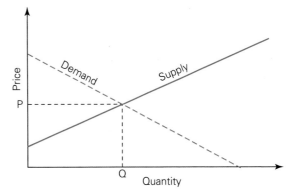

Figure 12.26 Key performance indicators in the front office

Table 12.21 Key performance indicators in the front office

Measure	Formula	Considerations
Rooms occupancy and average room rate (ARR)	Rooms occupancy = total number of rooms occupied/total number of rooms available for sale × 100 ARR = total rooms revenue/total rooms sold *or* total rooms revenue/ total number of rooms occupied	Rooms occupancy measures the quantity of rooms occupied in the hotel. Although it measures total capacity of room stock, this formula has a number of weaknesses. On its own it is ineffective as a hotel can have 99% occupancy, but if the hotel's average room rate is $1 its performance is poor. Therefore, it is really effective only when combined with the average room rate formula. In addition, if room occupancy is 80% one might also consider this to be relatively good. However, if the target daily occupancy of the hotel was 95% on that same day, it has failed to meet the target. Therefore, it is important to always measure against the target occupancy. Another consideration with this formula is that one should consider who is occupying the rooms. If the rooms are being occupied by individuals on a complimentary basis – for example, employees, managers and travel agents – then no sales are being achieved. Therefore as a financial measure a more accurate formula to be used is total number of rooms *sold*, as opposed to rooms occupied: total number of rooms sold/total number of rooms available × 100
Performance per room type or category	Suite occupancy = total suites occupied/total suites available for sale × 100 and suite ARR = total suite revenue/total suites sold	In many hotel properties there are several different room categories that may include suite, executive and standard rooms. It is therefore important for front office managers to measure the performance of these categories individually. This breakdown of room category performance will also help in identifying any particular weaknesses in occupancy and ARR.
Bed or sleeper occupancy and double occupancy	Total number of beds occupied/total number of beds available for sale × 100 doubles/twins let as doubles/twins/doubles/ twins available for sale × 100	To evaluate how well you are utilising your beds is to consider the number of sleepers per room. Many hotel rooms have a configuration of two beds per room (twin) and if only one sleeper is allocated to the room this may be considered poor utilisation. Although, the room price may be the same if either one or two sleepers occupied the room one should consider the potential for spend on other facilities within the hotel – for example, food and beverage.
Revenue per sleeper	Total rooms revenue/ total sleepers	This formula is slightly different from ARR as it looks at room revenue per individual and not per room.
Room yield Revenue per available room (REVPAR)	Yield = rooms realised/ rooms potential (rack rate × 100% occupancy) Rooms actual (ARR × actual occupancy/rooms potential (rack rate × 100% occupancy)	The room yield formula looks at how well you are managing your total room capacity. It investigates how well your rooms performed (actual) in relation to how well they could have performed (potential). For example, a hotel has 100 rooms for sale and the rack rate (published rate or highest rate) is $100. Therefore if the hotel sold all rooms (100%) and each room was sold at the highest rate $100 the total yield is 100 rooms × $100 = $10,000 revenue. Consider this, if the hotel achieved total daily room revenue of $7,100 the room yield percentage would be 76%. Hence, from a management perspective only 76% of your total potential has been realised. Therefore, both occupancy and ARR would have to be looked at in more depth to identify where the problem was. Another name for this formula is REVPAR.
Gross operating profit per available room (GOPPAR)	Gross operating profit/ total rooms available for sale	This measure is the only formula that evaluates the cost management of rooms. The one weakness with many other rooms performance indicators is that they do not measure profit. For example, the hotel can achieve high occupancies and ARRs, but if management is failing to maintain costs then, ultimately, profit is reduced. The gross operating profit per available room (GOPPAR) formula assists front office managers in measuring this. Accommodation managers need to ensure that a strict eye is kept on operating costs, such as staffing and cleaning, to ensure that profit is achieved. This formula is used less frequently due to the difficulties in measuring costs on a daily basis.

Design

When designing a front office area there are many factors to consider to achieve a functional and appealing environment. According to Jones and Paul (1996), 'Although the psychological aspects of design, such as ambience created and the initial impact of the total design scheme of this area on the arriving customer, are very important design issues, the practicalities of designing for functional efficiency are also important.'

Table 12.22 Key considerations in front office design

Considerations	Rationale
Aesthetic appeal	To enhance the appearance of the area, careful attention should be given to the coordination of colours, textures and fabrics of furniture, fittings and interior.
Atmosphere	To achieve the desired atmosphere, attention must be given to layout of furniture, lighting, foliage and background music. Four- and five-star hotels may use chandeliers, fountains, aquariums, and flora and fauna to achieve this experience.
Branding	In some chain hotels (particularly budget) the colours of the brand are introduced into the overall design to maintain theme and brand image. This may include lighting, fabric colour, carpets and employee uniforms, to name a few.
Comfort	Comfort can be achieved through the use of soft furnishings, appealing furniture, art, background music, carefully positioned televisions, and air temperature control.
Communication	To increase access for customers and efficiency for employees it is important to locate the sub-departments of reception, concierge and bell desk as close together as possible. Effective telecommunication is essential for the exchange of information between employees and to guests. This can be enhanced with front office areas being supplied with email, intranet, facsimile, Internet, touch-dial telephones and pagers.
Cleaning	The cleaning requirements need to be considered when purchasing furniture and equipment. Furniture should be easy for housekeeping personnel to move.
Environmental	Energy-reducing design considerations can include natural light, energy-efficient equipment, energy management systems (EMSs), air blowers and revolving doors.
Legislation	Legislation should be considered. For example, in accordance with Disability Discrimination Act (DDA) legislation, the front office entrance should have a ramp for wheelchair access and a lowered desk to allow for easy check-in.
Fashion	To remain contemporary, hotels should attempt to integrate modernity into design. This may include fashionable colours, art or technological advances – for example, Wi-Fi.
Flow	Traffic flow is important when designing a front desk operation. Outside there needs to be sufficient room for vehicles to arrive, drop off and depart without causing any queues. Similarly, queuing should be avoided on check-in, therefore sufficient check-in counters should be available.
Health and safety	The safety and security of guests, employees and the hotel's assets need to be considered. Ergonomic workstations, CCTV, safety deposit boxes and task lighting are some examples.
Sales opportunity	The opportunity for the hotel to maximise sales should not be missed. Examples include gift shop, window boxes, posters of partner hotels, and clear signage to other facilities and services.
Storage	Sufficient storage for guest luggage and hotel inventory items.
Technology	Technology to be integrated to improve guest service, financial control and communication (POS, self check-in, Wi-Fi, pagers).

Departmental communication

While the guest is in-house a large amount of information is communicated between the front office and other departments. Although the front office communicates with many departments, the department with which it has the closest relationship is housekeeping. The availability of rooms as guests check out and check in requires constant communication to ensure that guests receive a clean, ready-prepared room on check-in.

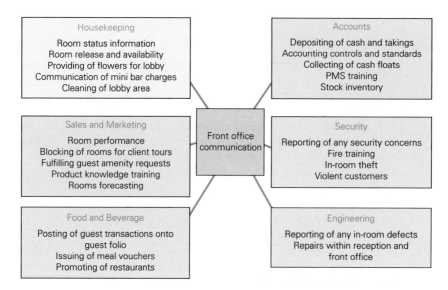

Figure 12.27 Front-office communication

Housekeeping

Efficiently managed housekeeping departments ensure the cleanliness, maintenance, and aesthetic appeal of lodging properties. The housekeeping department not only prepares clean guestrooms on a timely basis for arriving guests, it also cleans and maintains everything in the hotel.

(Kappa, Nitschke and Schappert, 1997)

Challenges for the housekeeping department include:

- responsibility for the largest volume of area within the hotel
- the largest department in the hotel in terms of staffing
- in most cases, has the largest departmental staff count in the hotel
- hard to attract skilled employees
- hard to motivate and retain employees.

The responsibility for cleaning an operation can vary depending on its size, standard and type of operation. Small independent restaurants and bars may employ

Figure 12.28

a part-time cleaner, whereas a hotel may employ a whole team of cleaning staff. Many operations now outsource their cleaning to improve quality and reduce expenses.

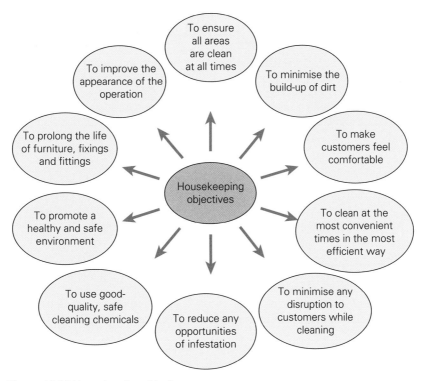

Figure 12.29 Housekeeping objectives

The importance of cleaning

Clean facilities are critical to the success of any hospitality operation. A clean environment can attract and retain guests and employees, and reduce sickness and accidents, thus avoiding waste and legal claims. Tools for achieving a high standard of cleanliness include:

- cleaning schedules
- checklists
- standards of performance – 'how to clean'
- ongoing training
- provide cleaning personnel with the right tools

- good-quality chemicals and equipment
- productivity standards
- follow cleaning principles
- good leadership and supervision
- comply with the law
- correct scheduling of cleaning personnel
- continually speak with customers.

Hotel housekeeping

Within a hotel, the housekeeping is managed by the executive housekeeper, who manages a large team of employees to achieve a high standard of cleanliness.

Table 12.23 Housekeeping structures and services: accommodation

Organisation	Employee structure	Housekeeping services offered
Five-star hotel	Large team of employees, to include executive housekeeper, floor housekeepers, room maids, housekeeping porters, public area cleaners, butlers, valet, and linen and laundry personnel	High standard of cleanliness Large team of skilled employees Longer room cleaning times Evening turndown service Good-quality linen and furniture Luxury internal design Butler and valet services provided in some cases Public area cleaners more visible Own florist Toilet attendants Less likely to outsource room cleaning
Four-star hotel	Similar to a five-star, but butlers may not be used	Room cleaning Turndown service Public area cleaning
Budget hotel	Room attendants may be outsourced to minimise costs and keep in line with main mission of hotel No in-house laundry, therefore linen is outsourced	Room cleaning during guest occupancy and departure Cleaning of entrance and public areas, bar and restaurant
Bed and breakfast (B&B)	Owner carries out most cleaning; may employ part-time staff to assist when busy Linen may also be cleaned in-house	Room cleaning during occupancy and on departure Cleaning of entrance and public areas
Independent food service operator	Independent catering outlets in most cases employ a part-time cleaner or carry out general cleaning by themselves	General cleaning of facilities after service periods and at night
Non-commercial operation (e.g. hospital, school, university)	In most cases outsourced to a large cleaning company	Daily cleaning of facilities Deep cleaning

Job description
Executive housekeeper

- Ensure that all areas are kept clean and as per standard at all times
- Have in place an inspection programme that checks rooms, corridors, public areas, back-of-house areas, laundry and external surroundings
- Ensure each area has cleaning specifications and that these are adhered to at all times
- Ensure through efficient employee rostering that there are always the correct quantity of employees on duty at all times in relation to business demand
- Create housekeeping budget detailing forecast consumption of each housekeeping item, and ensure budget is met each month
- Ensure all employees follow health and safety legislation at all times
- Ensure employees follow maintenance 'work order' system and keep rooms free from defects at all times
- Successfully recruit all new housekeeping employees and carry out departmental inductions
- Implement strategies to retain employees and reduce labour turnover
- Motivate and guide employees at all times
- Be visible throughout hotel and meet with customers as often as possible
- Implement systems to collect feedback on housekeeping products and performance
- Liaise with other department heads and communicate effectively
- Ensure that par levels of housekeeping supplies and equipment are maintained
- Constantly be proactive in looking for ways to improve the housekeeping product

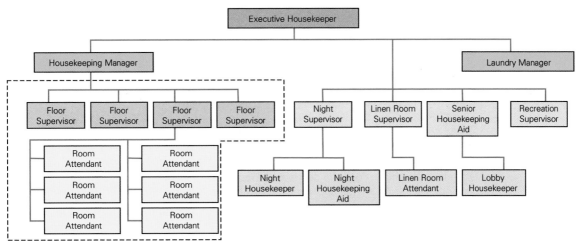

Figure 12.30 Typical organisation chart for housekeeping in a large four- or five-star hotel

Table 12.24 Examples of employees within the housekeeping department

Position	Responsibilities (may differ depending on property)
Assistant manager	Deputises for executive housekeeper
Floor supervisor	Quality checks rooms Checks rooms prior to arrival, during occupancy and after departure Releases clean rooms to reception Conducts shift briefings Reviews guest lists and VIP reports Organises and schedules rooms and suites maintenance – for example, spring clean, wall and ceiling washing, dusting, high dusting and under-bed vacuuming Hands over the shift and all information regarding their floor to the evening housekeepers Communicates any issues regarding their rooms and suites with the housekeeping office coordinator and senior housekeepers Carries out weekly and monthly stock-takes to maintain par levels Ensures all keys (master and floor) are controlled tightly Motivates and monitors staff accordingly Reviews 'out of order' rooms Ensures all storage rooms are clean and stocked at all times
Room attendant	Attends daily briefings Stocks service trolleys Cleans rooms and suites to the highest standards Completes turndown service Maintains maid service and pantry areas Communicates with floor housekeeper Reports any broken and missing items in their rooms and suites to their floor housekeepers Greets and assists guests whenever necessary
Public area (PA) cleaner	Cleans public areas, to include lobby, lifts, corridors, public toilets, offices and service areas Greets and assists guests whenever necessary Reports any defects to maintenance
Housekeeping porter	Assists with rooms and suites maintenance as and when required Assists floor housekeepers with the weekly and monthly stock-take Assists with floor housekeepers' and room attendants' requests Moves furniture in and out of rooms and suites as per floor housekeepers' instructions Assists with any guest room changes Delivers and collects 'special requests' to rooms (e.g. cots, blankets, extra towels) Transports dirty laundry to linen room from floors Assists room attendants during peak times Assists room attendants in deep cleaning activities

Position	Responsibilities (may differ depending on property)
Valet	Washes and irons guest laundry items Sends and receives guests' dry-cleaning items Pressing services
Linen room attendant	Sends out and receives all staff laundry and dry-cleaning items on a daily basis Organises and puts all staff laundry and dry-cleaning items in places as per departments on a daily basis Delivers all linen to the maid service on each floor as per floor housekeepers' requests
Laundry attendants	Washes and irons in-house laundry items Sends and receives in-house dry-cleaning items Organises the chute room and delivers all linen items to the laundry room Separates all types of linen and laundry items before the items are processed Receives, sorts, cleans, dries, folds and stores linen and laundry items Ensures equipment and storage areas are clean at all times Adheres to safety standards at all times
Butler (hotels) (This position is normally found only in very high-quality hotels)	For housekeeping duties only: • unpacks and packs guest belongings • sends and receives guest laundry and dry-cleaning items from the valet • communicates any issue and challenge regarding rooms and suites to housekeeping office co-coordinator and senior housekeepers • lists all guest items to and from the storage cupboards

Soil can be generated in different ways. It is the responsibility of the housekeeper to minimise the entry and build-up of soil within the operation.

There are two main types of soil.

1 **Organic (loose, dry):** commonly referred to as dust. It can usually be removed with direct mechanical action, as long as it stays dry. It can be swept, dust mopped, wiped, vacuumed or wet mopped with little or no chemical action required. Any surface that has not been cleaned in 12 hours will have dust accumulated on it. The longer it remains on a surface, the better chance it has of becoming oily, sticky soil from contamination with other substances, even from moisture in the air or from air-conditioning units.

2 **Inorganic (oily, sticky):** soil or dirt is almost always mixed with grease or other oily materials. Grease and oil make the dirt stick to a surface. The longer dirt remains on a surface, the more it tends to bond to the surface and the harder it is to remove.

Soil build-up can be prevented by:

- reducing the opportunity for soil to enter the establishment
- minimising the build-up of soil within the establishment

Soil is generated in the workplace in different ways, as outlined in Table 12.25.

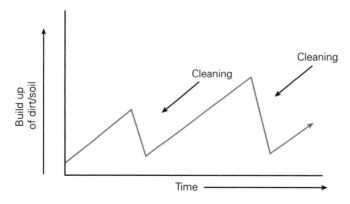

Figure 12.31 The 'theory of dirt'

Table 12.25 Soil generated in the workplace

Cause	Examples		Solutions/Prevention
Humans and employees	Poor hygiene	Poor hand washing	Signage, training, education, supervision, adequate bathing facilities
	Litter		Dustbins, signs
	Mistakes	Spillages	Training/prompt removal by cleaning
	Deliberate	Vandalism, graffiti	Code of conduct/rules
	Natural	Shedding skin, hair loss, perspiration	Personal grooming
	Disease	Sneezing, coughing	Hand-washing facilities/hand gel/disinfectant
Employees	Bringing in soil from outside	Dirt on clothing	Changing rooms, standards, employee rules and regulations
Weather	Rain/snow	Water/sludge	Doormats/temporary entry carpets/umbrella holders/umbrella disposable bags/floor mats
External matter/ foliage	Leaves, earth, dust, litter, debris	Visitors/employees bring in on footwear	Entry mats, foot grinders
Equipment	Machinery	Grease, dust, ventilation	Regular cleaning/cleaning schedules
Insects, vermin and pests	Cockroaches, rats, flies	Pests enter through the atmosphere, deliveries, luggage, cracks in maintenance, delivery areas, poor food hygiene, storage and disposal	Cover bins, keep door closed, thorough checks on delivery
The atmosphere	Smoke, exhausts, dust	The atmosphere deposits soil	Regular cleaning, good ventilation and extraction
Natural	Decay/ deterioration	Interior and exterior – buildings, paintwork, stone	Regular maintenance

Cleaning agents

To assist in the removal of soil, a selection of chemicals is available. When using cleaning agents one should remember to:

- use the right chemical for the job
- always read the label
- follow the cleaning specification
- use the correct quantity
- apply in the correct way
- apply safely and with care.

According to Raghubalan and Raghubalan (2007), examples of cleaning agents include:

- glass cleaners
- polishers
- carpet cleaners
- reagents
- organic solvents
- abrasives
- deodorisers
- toilet cleaners
- laundry aids
- floor strippers
- disinfectants and bleaches
- detergents
- water
- floor sealers.

Cleaning agents are applied using different methods, including:

- spotting
- scrubbing
- steam extraction
- buffing
- wiping
- mopping
- dusting
- vacuuming
- polishing
- laundering.

The principles of cleaning

When cleaning objects, the following principles should be applied.

- Remove all surface soil and obstructions before cleaning.
- Follow the least obtrusive and disturbing methods of cleaning, especially early in the morning.
- Restore all surfaces to as near perfect condition as soon as possible.
- Always use the simplest method of cleaning and the mildest cleaning agent.
- Beware of safety hazards.
- Remove all dust and dirt – do not transfer to another area.
- Carry out cleaning in the quickest possible time.

Safety within accommodation

When cleaning facilities employees are confronted with many risks, including:

- back problems due to bending and reaching
- defective equipment
- contamination from used needles
- stress – workload
- equipment flexes
- faulty electrics
- broken glass
- frequent lifting and moving of heavy objects
- high ladder work
- wet, slippery floors
- cleaning of high floors and balconies
- allergic reactions to chemicals
- hazardous chemicals.

Every working day in Great Britain at least one person is killed and over 6000 are injured at work. Every year three quarters of a million people take time off work because of what they regard as work-related illness. About 30 million work days are lost as a result.

(Health and Safety Executive)

Table 12.26 Cleaning equipment

Manual equipment	Mechanical equipment
Applicators	Vacuum cleaners
Brushes	Wet vacuums
Chamois leather	Wet extractors
Dusters	Rotary machines
Dustpan and brush	
Mop and bucket	
Ladders	
Trolleys	
Squeegee	
Sprayers	

Prevention and legislation

Strategies to create a healthy, safe and secure environment include:

- RIDDOR
- training
- prevention rather than cure
- good leadership at the top
- fire procedures
- goals for health and safety reduction
- penalties/warnings for non-compliance
- clear communication – reporting
- accountability
- well-executed maintenance repair
- awareness
- qualified supervision
- health and safety committees
- attend health and safety workshops and conventions
- certified, skilled employees
- adhere to and follow the law
- consult employees – bottom up!
- external health and safety consultants
- regular risk assessment
- regular health and safety audits.

Some of the legislation within the accommodation sector is listed in Table 12.28.

Table 12.27 Typical health and safety risks for housekeeping employees

Risks	Examples	Prevention
Back problems	Turning mattresses, pushing carts, bending, stretching	Training in lifting techniques, ask for assistance
Dealing with hazardous chemicals	In most cases all housekeeping employees will have to deal with chemicals at some point in time; the correct use of these chemicals is paramount and failing to do this can lead to serious injury	COSHH training, protective clothing, chemical label fact sheets
Defective equipment	Shorts in equipment	Maintenance repair/preventative maintenance programme/purchase safe, tested equipment/portable appliance testing/risk assessment
Contamination from infected needles/ blood	Use of controlled substances in rooms by customers/non-disposed used needles; hepatitis B virus or HIV are found in blood and spread when infected blood or certain body fluids get into the body	Special training and standards in the correct, safe disposal of needles/blood stains/sharps box
Work stress	All employees can be subject to additional workload and pressures, which can lead to stress	Good scheduling, regular breaks, job chats, fair distribution and allocation of work, observation, 'management by walking around' (MBWA)
Equipment flexes	Room attendants frequently use equipment with long flexes (e.g. vacuum cleaners/polishers), and can be at risk of trips and falls	Training/operating procedures
Wet/slippery floors	When floors are wet after mopping or wet weather	Non-slip work shoes, wet floor signs, grit
High floor/ladder work	Some high dusting may require the use of ladders (e.g. cleaning high balconies, artwork or chandeliers)	Training/ensure ladder is safe/colleague to hold ladder/only attempt if qualified/ Working at Height Regulations 2005/ never use chair instead of ladder
Broken glass/china	Room attendants and public area cleaners can come into contact with broken glass	Training/awareness/standards for correct disposal/broken glass containers
Office work	It is not only subordinates that face risks – managers/operators who work at computers also can suffer from back pain and repetitive strain injury (RSI)	Provide an ergonomic workplace environment

Table 12.28 Legislation within the accommodation sector

The *Reporting of Injuries, Diseases and Dangerous Occurrences Regulations* (RIDDOR) 1995 Act
Control of Substances Hazardous to Health (COSHH) 2002 Act
First Aid Regulations 1981
Manual Handling Regulations 1992 Act
Personal Protective Equipment (PPE) Regulations (1992)
Safety Signs and Signals Regulations 1996 Act
The Fire Precautions Act 1971
The Health and Safety at Work Act (HASAWA) 1974

Maintenance and facilities

Figure 12.32

Facilities are a key element of the money making aspects of the business. They serve as a location for the delivery of services, they play a role in estate appreciation and they contribute to corporate growth.

(Stipanuk and Roffman, 1996)

The objectives of the maintenance department include:

- maintain the operation's internal and surrounding facilities

- promptly repair any defective furniture, equipment or fittings
- plan and oversee any major refurbishments, renovations or redecorations
- contract external specialists to perform maintenance works as and when required
- provide a safe physical working environment for employees
- provide safe premises for visitors and customers
- actively work towards reducing energy costs.

Very few hotels employ a full team of specialised maintenance personnel. Many have general employees who work in the maintenance department, who may specialise in one area but are also cross-trained to carry out other maintenance tasks. For example, an employee who is a qualified plumber may also have had training on how to operate the energy management system. Cross-training employees provides greater flexibility. Another approach would be to have general handymen who can deal with general day-to-day tasks but when a specialised piece of work needs to be done, they employ a local contractor at an hourly rate to carry out the work.

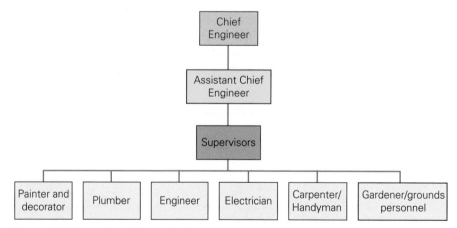

Figure 12.33 Organisational chart for the maintenance department of a large four- or five-star hotel

Security

In this section, the importance of security is presented. Both customers and employees need to feel secure while on the premises. Security may be defined as 'the condition of being protected against danger or loss'.

The size and complexity of the security department

can vary depending on the operation. City-centre hotels, hotels in volatile political locations and casinos, for example, require more security. It is common for security personnel to be outsourced from a security agency. In most cases there is one individual in the hotel who is responsible for security – this person could be the chief of security or security manager.

The key responsibilities of a security manager include:

- monitor CCTV
- escort cash-drops
- follow up
- respond rapidly to security requests
- make frequent rounds of premises
- work closely with local police

- create awareness of security issues in all employees
- escort suspicious or undesirable persons
- assist in dealing with difficult or intoxicated guests
- assist in making security checks on personnel
- complete security paperwork
- be alert at all times.

The objectives of the security department are to protect:

- guests and their assets while on the premises
- employees and their assets while on the premises
- the hotel's assets
- the data of the hotel and the customer.

Table 12.29 Security risks and prevention

Security risk example	Who is at risk?	Risk prevention
Suspicious packages	Guests, employees, assets	Visible in-house security/crisis planning/awareness by employees
Potential in-room theft from intruders	Guests	Effective in-house security/awareness by employees/educating customers/electronic locking system (ELS)/use of in-room safes/safety deposit box/CCTV surveillance system – closed-circuit television/signing in and out for all visitors
Handbag thieves in public areas	Guests	In-house security, informing guests to be aware, CCTV, handbag safety hooks
Employees attempting to defraud customers/identity theft/customer information	Guests	Employ good staff – reference/police checks/effective supervision/CCTV/standards/data protection
Employees taking cash from tills	Hotel	Reference checks, police checks, POS system, CCTV, good supervision, employee bag checks, security personnel
Harassment from customers	Employees	Visible in-house security guards
Attack on front desk reception for cash (by robber)	Employees, assets	Security training for employees on what to do in the event of such a situation, panic alarm, CCTV, security personnel, drop safe

Conclusion

The purpose of this chapter is to introduce some of the key areas of importance within accommodation management – moreover, to highlight the importance of good-quality accommodation management for guests, employees and operational profits. It has set out to detail the challenges that operators face in managing accommodation, and has provided examples of tools, systems and approaches that can be used to deal with these challenges.

The accommodation sector is highly competitive and constantly evolving, and so requires high-quality, motivated employees and managers to ensure that the delivery of the accommodation product meets the customer's expectation every time.

Some references to accommodation management elsewhere in this book:

References

Anhar, L. (2001) The definition of boutique hotels. *Hospitality Net*. Available online at http://www.hospitalitynet.org/news/4010409. print (accessed 31 April 2010).

Bardi, A.J. (2007) *Hotel Front Office Management* (2nd edn). USA: Wiley

Higgins-Desbiolles, F. (2008) Justice and alternative globalisation. *Journal of Sustainable Tourism* 16(3), pp. 345–364.

Jones, C. and Paul, V. (1996) *Accommodation Management*. London: Batsford.

Jones, T.J.A. (2008) *Professional Management of Housekeeping Operations* (5th edn). John Wiley & Sons.

Kappa, M.N., Nitschke, A. and Schappert, P.B. (1997) *Managing Housekeeping Operations* (2nd edn). Michigan: AHLA.

Kavanaugh, R.R. and Ninemeier, J.D. (2001) *Supervision in the Hospitality Industry*. Michigan: AHLA.

Knowles, T. (1994) *Hospitality Management, An Introduction*. London: Pitman.

Kotler, P. (2009) *Marketing Management* (13th edn). USA: Prentice Hall.

Nobles, H. and Thompson, C. (2001) What is a boutique hotel? *Hotel Online*. Available online at: http://www.hotel-online.com/News/PR2001_4th/Oct01_BoutiqueAttributes.html (accessed 16 May 2010).

Raghubalan, G. and Raghubalan, S. (2007) *Hotel Housekeeping*. Oxford: Oxford University Press.

Seth, P. (2006) *Successful Tourism: Vol. 1*. Sterling Publishers.

Stipanuk, D.M. and Roffmann, H. (1996) *Facilities Management*. Michigan: AHLA.

Plus:

Automobile Association (AA) hotel classification system (2010)

British Hospitality Association

Health and Safety Executive (2010)

World Tourism Organisation (WTO)

Visit Britain (2009) *Britain and Inbound Market Report*

Topics for discussion

1 Different types of accommodation attract different profiles of customers. In groups, consider the types of people who visit your city and identify the following:
   (a) their demographic profile (age, nationality, gender, occupation, etc.)
   (b) purpose of visit (business, leisure, visiting friends or family, study etc.)
   (c) length of stay
   (d) which types of accommodation in your area they would use.

2 Using a 'mind map', outline the benefits of providing quality accommodation for customers, and detail the challenges and opportunities it presents for the profits, employees and customers.

3 Consider the 'guest cycle'. Discuss and list the opportunities at each stage to 'upsell' services and products to customers.

4 Reflect and evaluate in your groups how the integration of technology on the front desk assists in achieving the following:
   (a) financial control
   (b) customer satisfaction
   (c) revenue maximisation.

5 Visit a local hotel in your town or city. Identify how the design of the hotel:
   (a) meets the needs of the target market
   (b) contributes towards sales maximisation
   (c) meets health and safety requirements.

6 Protecting the environment is at the forefront of consumers' minds. Discuss and detail what steps accommodation managers can implement to assist in achieving a more sustainable accommodation operation.

Health, safety and security

Supporting material available on Dynamic Learning Online:

> Knowledge quizzes

> Activity worksheet: health and safety

> Summary presentations

> Videos and worksheets: health and safety

Sickness and accidents in the workplace

Sickness absence costs the UK economy approximately £400–500 per employee each year. Accidents can happen in any workplace (see the section on accidents, which starts on page 380).

If an employee works on a computer, they may be at risk of:

- eye and eyesight problems
- epilepsy
- upper limb pain and discomfort
- fatigue and stress.

Stress and accidents are currently the two biggest causes of absence from work.

You can report an accident at work by:

- email
- fax
- telephone
- letter.

The average number of days taken as sick leave each year in the UK is approximately 30 million.

Table 13.1 Significant factors for the catering industry

Cause	Percentage of all injuries	Significant factor
Slips, trips	30 per cent but 75 per cent of all major injuries	88 per cent due to slippery floors due to spillage not cleared up, wet floors and buckets, etc. in passageways and uneven floors
Handling	29 per cent	33.3 per cent due to lifting pans, trays, etc.; 33.3 per cent to handling sharp objects (e.g. knives); 33.3 per cent awkward lifts from low ovens or high positions
Exposure to hazardous substances, hot surfaces, steam	16 per cent	61 per cent from splashes; 13 per cent from hot objects. Causes: poor maintenance 28 per cent of cases; steam from ovens/steamer 23 per cent; carrying hot liquids 16 per cent; misuse of cleaning materials 14 per cent; cleaning flat fryers 14 per cent; equipment failure 12 per cent; horseplay 4 per cent; hot surfaces 1 per cent
Struck by moving articles including hand tools	10 per cent	33.3 per cent most probably from knives; 25 per cent from falling articles; 10 per cent from assault
Walking into objects	4 per cent	75 per cent of cases involved walking into a fixed as opposed to a moveable object
Machinery	3 per cent	Slicers 30 per cent; mixers 16 per cent; vegetable cutting machines 9 per cent; vegetable slicing, mincing and grating attachments 10 per cent; pie and tart machines 4 per cent; dough mixer, dough moulder, mincing machine, dishwasher 2 per cent
Falls	1.8 per cent	75 per cent falls from low height (but half of the major injuries occurred on stairs)
Fire and explosion	1.6 per cent	80 per cent during manually igniting gas fire appliances, mainly ovens
Electric shock	0.5 per cent	25 per cent due to poor maintenance; 25 per cent trolley involved; 25 per cent unsafe switching and unplugging (75 per cent of these in wet conditions); 25 per cent poor maintenance
Transporter	3 per cent	50 per cent involved fork lift trucks

Reportable major injuries

- Fracture other than finger, thumb or toe
- Amputation
- Dislocation of hip, knee or spine
- Loss of sight (temporary or permanent)
- Chemical or hot metal burn to the eye or any penetration to the eye
- Injury from electric shock or burn leading to unconsciousness or requiring resuscitation or admittance to hospital for more than 24 hours
- Any other injury leading to hypothermia, heat-induced illness or unconsciousness, or requiring resuscitation or admittance to hospital for more than 24 hours
- Unconsciousness caused by asphyxia or exposure to a harmful substance or biological agent
- Acute illness requiring medical treatment, or loss of consciousness from absorption by inhalation, ingestion or through the skin
- Acute illness requiring medical treatment where there is reason to believe that this resulted from exposure to a biological agent or its toxins or infected material

RIDDOR (Reporting Injuries, Diseases and Dangerous Occurrences)

RIDDOR regulations came into effect in 1996 and require work-related accidents, diseases and dangerous occurrences to be reported by employers to the Incident Contact Centre, Caerphilly Business Park, Caerphilly CF83 3GG. Records must be kept of each occurrence.

Examples of reportable diseases include certain poisons, dermatitis, skin cancer, lung diseases such as occupational asthma, infections such as hepatitis, tuberculosis, anthrax and tetanus.

An example of a dangerous occurrence could be an overloaded electric circuit causing a major fire.

'Three-day injuries' are not major but cause the employee to be absent for more than three days consecutively (not counting the day of the injury, but including days they would not normally be at work).

Managing absence

Managing employee absence doesn't have to be difficult or complicated.

- Tell your employees what they can expect from you to help them return to work, as far as your business permits.
- Make sure they understand their own contractual duties to you, including what procedures you require for absences from work.

It is important to have a fair and consistent approach to return to work and for you, your employees and their representatives, to be honest and able to trust each other at every step of the process. The sooner you take positive action together, the more likely it will be that your sick employees can return to work successfully and get on with the job of helping you build your business.

For small employers, an instance of an employee being off work for more than 14 days is likely to be rare, but when it does happen there are considerable benefits from working in partnership with your employees, their trades union or other employee representatives, to help those off sick return to work as soon as they are able.

By doing this you will:

- keep valued staff and avoid unnecessary recruitment and training costs
- keep your business productive and, where your sick employee has built up a loyal client base, keep this as a source of income
- reduce unnecessary overheads, such as saving on lost wages and sick pay costs
- help meet your legal duties and avoid discriminating against disabled workers
- maintain and improve workplace relations by working in partnership with your employees and their workforce representatives.

Enforcement and support

In most catering businesses, health and safety law is enforced by environmental health officers (EHOs) employed by the local authority.

Control of Substances Hazardous to Health (COSHH)

The Control of Substances Hazardous to Health Regulations 1999 (COSHH) state that:

> an employer shall not carry on any work which is liable to expose any employees to any substance hazardous to health unless he has made a suitable and sufficient assessment of the risks created by work to the health of these employees.

Nature of the hazard

When considering carrying out your legal obligations under the COSHH Regulations all areas should be surveyed in order to ascertain the chemicals and substances used. Table 13.2 presents a list of areas and the likely chemicals and substances to be found in them.

COSHH Register

A COSHH register should be kept by the manager for all substances used in the establishment. Technical data sheets should be attached to the completed COSHH assessment sheet.

Substances dangerous to health are labelled 'very toxic', 'toxic', 'harmful', 'irritant' or 'corrosive'. While only a small number of such chemicals are used for cleaning catering establishments, it is necessary to be aware of the regulations introduced in 1989 and the symbols used on products.

Principles

Those persons using such substances must be made aware of their correct use and proper dilution, where appropriate, and must wear protection: goggles, gloves and face masks as appropriate. Eye goggles should be worn when using oven cleaners, gloves when hands may come into contact with any chemical cleaner, and face masks when using grease-cutting and oven degreasers. Extra protective aprons or overalls may be needed.

It is essential that staff are trained to take precautions and not to take risks.

What does COSHH require?

The basic principles of occupational hygiene underlie the COSHH Regulations.

- Assess the risk to health arising from work and what precautions are needed.
- Introduce appropriate measures to prevent or control the risk.
- Ensure that control measures are used and that equipment is properly maintained and procedures observed.
- Where necessary, monitor the exposure of the workers and carry out an appropriate form of surveillance of their health.
- Inform, instruct and train employees about the risks and the precautions to be taken.

Rules for using chemicals

- Always follow the maker's instructions.
- Always store in original containers. Decanting a chemical means you may lose its name and classification, and it may be misused.
- Keep lids tightly closed.
- Do not store in direct sunlight, near heat or naked flames.
- Read the labels. Know the product and its risk.
- Never mix chemicals.
- Know the first-aid procedure.
- Always add product to water, not water to product.
- Dispose of empty drums immediately.
- Dispose of waste chemical solutions safely.
- Wear the correct safety equipment.

Table 13.2 Work areas, and the chemicals and substances likely to be found in them

Area	Chemicals and substances
Kitchen	Cleaning chemicals including alkalis and acids, detergents, sanitisers, descalers Chemicals associated with burnishing, possibly some oils associated with machines Pest-control chemicals, insecticides and rodenticides
Restaurant	Cleaning chemicals, polishes, decalers, fuel for flame lamps including methylated spirits, LPG
Bar	Beer line cleaner, glass-washing detergent and sanitisers
Housekeeping	Cleaning chemicals including detergents, sanitisers, disinfectants, descalants, polishes, carpet-cleaning products, floor-care products
Maintenance	Cleaning chemicals, adhesives, solvents, paint, LPG, salts for water softening etc., paint stripper, varnishes etc.
Offices	Correction fluid, thinners, solvents, methylated spirits, toner for photocopier, duplicating fluids and chemicals, polishes

Other legislation

Every year in the UK 1000 people are killed at work, a million people suffer injuries, and 23 million working days are lost annually because of industrial injury and disease. As catering is one of the largest employers of labour the catering industry is substantially affected by accidents at work.

In 1974 the Health and Safety at Work Act was passed with two main aims:

1 to extend the coverage and protection of the law to all employers and employees
2 to increase awareness of safety among those at work, both employers and employees.

The law imposes a general duty on an employer 'to ensure so far as is reasonably practicable, the health, safety and welfare at work of all his employees'. The law also imposes a duty on every employee while at work to:

- take reasonable care for the health and safety of himself or herself and of other persons who may be affected by his or her acts or omissions at work
- cooperate with his or her employer so far as is necessary to meet or comply with any requirement concerning health and safety

● not interfere with, or misuse, anything provided in the interests of health, safety or welfare.

It can clearly be seen that both health and safety at work is everybody's responsibility. Furthermore, the Act protects the members of the public who may be affected by the activities of those at work.

Penalties are provided by the Act, which include improvement notices, prohibition notices and criminal prosecution. The Health and Safety Executive was set up to enforce the law, and the Health and Safety Commission issues codes of conduct and acts as an adviser.

Responsibilities of the employer

The employer's responsibilities are to:

● provide and maintain premises and equipment that are safe and without risk to health
● provide supervision, information and training

● issue a written statement of 'safety policy' to employees, to include general policy with respect to the health and safety at work of employees, the role of the organisation in ensuring the policy is carried out, how the policy will be made effective.
● consult with employees' safety representative and establish a Safety Committee.

The Workplace (Health, Safety and Welfare) Regulations 1992 require indoor workplace temperatures to be reasonable, with effective and suitable ventilation provided.

Working in extreme temperatures can cause considerable stress on staff, which could result in conditions such as hypothermia or heat exhaustion. Before these injuries occur, staff may become tired and listless, and reduced concentration could make them more prone to accidents such as cuts and burns.

Safety regulations

Six health and safety at work regulations came into force in 1993.

1 Management of Health and Safety at Work Regulations 1992:
   − risk assessment
   − control of hazardous substances
   − training.
2 Work Place (Health, Safety and Welfare) Regulations 1992:
   − floors to be of suitable construction
   − floors free from hazardous articles or substances
   − steps taken to avoid slips, trips and falls.
3 Manual Handling Operation Regulations 1992:
   − reducing incorrect handling of loads
   − preventing hazardous handling.
4 Fire Precautions in Places of Work:
   − means of firefighting
   − evacuation procedures
   − raising the alarm.
5 Provision and Use of Work Equipment:
   − ensure correct usage
   − properly maintained
   − training given.
6 Health and Safety (Display Screen Equipment):
   − to see that staff using visual display units have a suitable workplace and take regular breaks.

Risk assessment and reduction

Management of health and safety

The duties of employers, as specified by the Management of Health and Safety at Work Regulations 1999, are listed below. Employers have a duty under these regulations to carry out risk assessments and COSHH assessments.

Hazard

Means anything that can cause harm (e.g. chemicals, electricity, working from ladders).

Risk

Is the chance high or low that somebody will be harmed by the hazard?

Five steps to assessing risk

1 Look for hazards − the things that could cause harm.
2 Decide who might be harmed, and how.
3 Evaluate the risks and decide whether the existing precautions are adequate, or whether more should be done.
4 Write down your findings so you have a record that you can check back against.
5 Regularly review your assessment, and revise it if necessary.

Figure 13.1 Business protection

Managing risk

Managing risk is not a complicated procedure. To start with, a health and safety policy must be in place for the business.

Involve employees

These are people most at risk of having accidents, or experiencing ill health, and they also know the most about the jobs they do so are in the best position to help managers develop safe systems of work that are effective in practice. An actively engaged workforce is one of the foundations that support good health and safety. It ensures that all those involved with a work activity, both managers and workers, are participating in assessing risks.

Assessing risk

Assessing risk is the key to effective health and safety in the workplace. This means nothing more than a careful examination of what, in your work, could cause harm to people, so that you can weigh up whether you have taken sufficient precautions or should do more to prevent harm.

The prevention of accidents and food poisoning in catering establishments is essential; therefore it is necessary to assess the situation and decide what action is to be taken. Risk assessment can be divided into four areas, as follows.

1 Minimal risk – safe conditions with safety measures in place.
2 Some risk – acceptable risk, however attention must be given to ensure safety measures operate.
3 Significant risk – where safety measures are not fully in operation (also includes food most likely to cause food poisoning). Requires immediate action.
4 Dangerous risk – operations of process or equipment to stop immediately. The system of equipment to be completely checked and recommended after clearance.

To operate an assessment of risks the following points should be considered:

- assess the risks
- determine preventative measures
- decide who carries out safety inspections

- decide frequency of inspection
- determine methods of reporting back and to whom
- detail how to ensure inspections are effective
- see that on-the-job training in safety is related to the job.

The purpose of the exercise of assessing the possibility of risks and hazards is to prevent accidents. First, it is necessary to monitor the situation, to have regular and spasmodic checks to see that the standards set are being complied with. However, should an incident occur, it is essential that an investigation is made as to the cause or causes, and any defects in the system remedied at once. Immediate action is required to prevent further accidents. All personnel need to be trained to be actively aware of the possible hazards and risks, and to take positive action to prevent accidents occurring.

The workplace

The highest number of accidents occurring in hospitality premises are due to persons falling, slipping or tripping (see Table 13.1). Therefore, floor surfaces must be of a suitable construction to reduce this risk. A major reason for the high incidence of this kind of accident is that water and grease are likely to be spilt, and the combination of these substances is treacherous and makes the floor surface slippery. For this reason any spillage must be cleaned immediately and warning notices put in place, where appropriate, highlighting the danger of the slippery surface. Ideally a member of staff should stand guard until the hazard is cleared.

Another cause of falls is the placing of articles on the floor in corridors, passageways or between stoves and tables. Persons carrying trays and containers have their vision obstructed and items on the floor may not be visible; the fall may occur onto a hot stove and the item being carried may be hot. These falls can have severe consequences. The solution is to ensure that nothing is left on the floor that may cause a hazard. If it is necessary to have articles temporarily on the floor, then it is desirable that they are guarded so as to prevent accidents.

Kitchen personnel should be trained to think and act in a safe manner so as to avoid this kind of accident.

Managing health and safety

Employers must have appropriate arrangements in place (recorded where there are five or more employees) for maintaining a safe workplace. These should cover the usual management functions of:

- planning
- organisation
- control
- monitoring
- review.

The aim is to reduce risk and secure a progressive improvement in health and safety performance.

Health and safety information for employees

All employees, including trainees, must be provided with information on the particular risks they face, what to do in the event of a fire or other general emergency situation, and the preventative and protective measures designed to ensure their health and safety, including the identity of staff that would assist in the event of an evacuation. The information must be capable of being understood by those for whom it is intended.

Employees' duties

Employees have a duty to use correctly all work items provided by the employer in accordance with the training and instructions they have received to enable them to use the items safely.

Employees must immediately inform their employer, or person responsible for health and safety, of any work situation that might present a serious and imminent danger. Also employees should report any shortcomings in the health and safety protection arrangements in the company.

Consultation with employees

Safety Representatives and Safety Committees Regulations 1997

The employer is required to consult employee representatives in health and safety matters. The recognised trades union must notify the employer in writing of the names of the appointed persons who are the safety representatives.

The functions of a safety representative include:

- investigating potential hazards and dangerous occurrences in the workplace
- examining the cause of accidents, investigating complaints by any employee on health and safety issues
- making representations to the employer on general matters affecting the health, safety or welfare at work of employees
- attending health and safety meetings.

Safety committees

If two or more safety representatives make a request in writing for a committee, the employer must set up one within three months, after consultation with those who made the request.

Manual handling

The incorrect handling of heavy and awkward loads causes accidents, which can result in staff being off work for some time. Figure 13.2 shows how to lift heavy items in the correct way. The safest way to lift items is to bend at the knees rather than bending the back. Strain and damage can be reduced if two people do the lifting rather than one.

Handling checklist

● When goods are moved on trolleys, trucks or any wheeled vehicles, they should be loaded carefully (not overloaded) and in a manner that enables the handler to see where they are going.
● In stores, it is essential that heavy items are stacked at the bottom and that steps are used with care.
● Particular care is needed when large pots are moved containing liquid, especially hot liquid. They should not be filled to the brim.
● A warning sign that equipment handles, lids, etc. can be hot should be given; this can be indicated by a small sprinkle of flour or by wrapping an oven cloth around the handle.
● Extra care is needed when taking a tray from the oven or salamander so that the tray does not burn someone else.

Provision and Use of Work Equipment Regulations 1998 (PUWER)

'Work equipment' covers work machinery such as food processors, slicers, ovens, knives, and so on. These Regulations place duties on employers to ensure that work equipment is suitable for its intended use, and is maintained in efficient working order and in good repair, and that adequate information, instruction and training on the use and maintenance of the equipment and any associated hazards is given to employees.

Work equipment that possesses a specific risk must be used only by designated persons who have received relevant training. The Regulations' 'specific' requirements cover dangerous machinery parts, protection against certain hazards (i.e. falling objects, ejected components, overheating), the provision of certain stop and emergency stop controls, isolation from energy sources, stability and lighting, and markings and warnings.

PUWER 1998 replaces the list of prescribed dangerous machines as contained in the Prescribed Dangerous Machines Order 1964.

Need for signage

Following risk assessment under the Management of Health and Safety at Work Regulations 1992, safety signage should only be implemented to control a hazard when all other methods to reduce the risk to employees have been exhausted. Safety signs must not take the place of other risk-control methods and should significantly decrease the likelihood of an accident occurring.

The employer has a duty to:

● provide and maintain any safety sign
● give employees clear information on unfamiliar signs
● give employees instructions and training in the meaning of the signs and what to do in connection with them.

There are two main types of signage:

1 permanent – used for prohibitions, warnings and

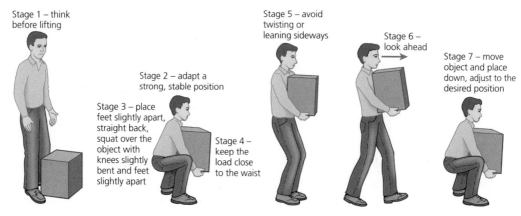

Stage 1 – think before lifting

Stage 2 – adapt a strong, stable position

Stage 3 – place feet slightly apart, straight back, squat over the object with knees slightly bent and feet slightly apart

Stage 4 – keep the load close to the waist

Stage 5 – avoid twisting or leaning sideways

Stage 6 – look ahead

Stage 7 – move object and place down, adjust to the desired position

Figure 13.2 How to lift correctly

mandatory requirements, identifying emergency escape routes, first-aid facilities and firefighting equipment

2 occasional – including acoustic signals like fire alarms, and illuminated signs (such as fire escape signs) that operate with emergency lighting systems.

Prohibition signs

Such signs prohibit behaviour that is likely to increase or cause danger. They are round with a red circular band and crossbar, featuring a black pictogram on a white background. (Red should cover at least 35 per cent of the area of the sign.) Examples include 'No Entry' and 'No Exit' signs.

Safety signs

The display and use of safety signs and other means – such as hand and acoustic signals and marking of pipework – for communicating general and specific warnings about hazards and dangers, reminders and prohibitions, as well as matters relating to road traffic in the workplace and fire safety, are dealt with in the Health and Safety (Safety Signs and Signals) Regulations 1996.

Mandatory signs

These give warning of hazard or danger, and

Figure 13.3 A prohibition sign

Figure 13.4 A warning sign

describe a behaviour. They take the form of a blue circle with a white pictogram. (Blue should take up at least 50 per cent of the area of the sign.) Examples include:

- for all fire doors, 'Fire Door – Keep Closed'
- for chemical dosing areas, 'Wear Gloves', 'Eye Protection Must Be Worn'
- for dangerous machinery, 'Guards Must Be In Position Before Starting'.

Emergency escape/first-aid signs

These are of a rectangular or square shape, with a white pictogram on a green background. (Green should take up at least 40 per cent of the area of the sign.)

Other signs

- Emergency eye wash stations: sign featuring 'Emergency Eye Wash'.
- For dangerous machinery, if applicable, sign featuring 'Emergency Stop Push Button'.

Figure 13.5 A mandatory sign

Personal protective equipment (PPE)

The Personal Protective Equipment at Work Regulations 1992 came into effect on 1 January 1993 and apply to all equipment designed to be worn or held by persons to protect them from one or more risks (e.g. uniforms, clothing required for hygiene purposes). The provision of equipment and clothing – for example, chefs' whites, safety shoes, eye protection goggles – which is intended to be worn or held by a person at work, as protection against risks to health and safety, is covered by the Personal Protective Equipment at Work Regulations 1992. The Health and Safety (Miscellaneous Amendments) Regulations 2002 added various points of detail on the provision of PPE, and instruction and training.

Information, instruction and training

Suitable information, instruction and training – including, where appropriate, demonstrations in the wearing of PPE – must be provided to guide employees on the proper use of PPE, how to correctly fit and wear it, its limitations, care and replacement. Managers and supervisors must also be aware of why PPE is being used and how it should be used. Information and instruction on the use of PPE must be kept available to them.

Health and Safety (Safety Signs and Signals) Regulations 1996

On 1 April 1996 these regulations completely revoked the previous Safety Signs and Signals Regulations 1986. They aim to standardise safety signing across the European Union, so that wherever such signs are seen, they will have the same meaning. (The labelling of dangerous substances and most machinery is not covered by these regulations.)

Due to the hazardous nature of some of the work in kitchens, it is necessary to assess the risks to employees. Provision of protective clothing and footwear, properly maintained, is essential to safety. Suitable storage, such as lockers, needs to be available for the storage of personal clothing.

Items such as oven cloths and heatproof gloves need to be provided and maintained, or replaced so that they are safe to use.

First-aid equipment must be readily available and replenished when necessary. There must be one trained first-aider for every 50 employees.

Kitchen equipment

All equipment should be safe and used correctly, properly maintained and not misused.

- Tables must be strong, easily cleaned for hygiene reasons and never used for sitting on.

- Bratt pans and tilting pans should not be able to be accidentally tilted.
- Fat fryers must not have their thermostats tampered with and must never be over-filled.
- Only step ladders should be used for reaching items stored on high shelves, not standing on boxes or a chair.
- Electrical equipment must be given special attention, particularly that listed under the Dangerous Machines Order 1964:
  - worm-type mincing machines
  - rotary bowl choppers
  - mixing machines
  - slicing/shredding machines
  - chipping/chopping machines.

Only trained people (over 18) are allowed to use and clean such machines, and warning signs and instruction in their use must be sited by the machine. (For more on electrical safety, go to: www.sgs.co.uk.)

- Gas equipment must have instructions for igniting the equipment and these must be followed. In the event of a gas leak or problems with pilot lights, maintenance personnel or the gas equipment suppliers should be contacted immediately.
- Maintenance should be regular to ensure correct function and safety of all gas and electrical equipment. This includes checking seals on microwave ovens.
- Extraction systems should function correctly, and particular care is needed to see that they are cleaned regularly as fat is liable to accumulate on filters, preventing the extractor from working properly.
- Walk-in refrigerators and deep freezers must have a door that is operable from the inside.
- Records of staff trained in the use of equipment and records of maintenance need to be kept.

Figure 13.6 Emergency/escape and first-aid signs

Computers and other display screen equipment

The employer and the person in control of the workplace, if this is different (e.g. because the user is employed by an agency or contractor, or is self-employed), must take steps to reduce the risks to health of those using a computer for work purposes under the Health and Safety (Display Screen Equipment) Regulations 1992.

The Health and Safety (Miscellaneous Amendments) Regulations 2002 widened the scope of the regulations to require all computers and other display screen workstations to meet health and safety specifications.

Electricity at work

The Electricity at Work Regulations 1989 introduced new fixed installation and portable appliance requirements, extending the general duties of the Health and Safety at Work Act 1974 to cover all workplaces and work activities.

All electrical equipment, both fixed and portable, must be maintained to ensure safety under the regulations.

The design, installation, operation, use and maintenance of all electrical systems and equipment in the workplace are covered by the Electricity at Work Regulations 1989. A whole range of specific and detailed health and safety requirements are laid down that both employers and the self-employed must have regard to.

- The design, installation and maintenance of electrical systems and equipment are carried out only by competent people.
- Equipment is suited to the job and the conditions in which it is used.
- The maker's instructions on the safe use and maintenance of equipment are followed.
- Employees use equipment safely, having been given the appropriate supervision, guidance and training, and report any faults or problems.

Arrangements are also important for checking the safety of electrical equipment at appropriate intervals, such as every six or twelve months, or at longer intervals depending on the equipment and the use to which it is put.

Health and safety training

Health and safety training is a vital, moral and legal requirement upon all employers no matter what their business activity. All staff must be aware of occupational hazards and systems developed to reduce risks and prevent accidents.

Developing a positive safety culture

It is important to develop within the organisation a safety culture to maintain health and safety, to save time and money in preventing accidents and decreased time off work. Achieving this requires time and effort to create a caring, committed and well-organised management that understands the benefits of good health and safety practice. Knowledgeable staff who understand their responsibilities and duties also contribute positively to the business.

The safety policy is the essential basic foundation on which to build. Once this policy has been developed, control of workplace hazards is possible, and this involves getting systems and procedures under way. This is a vital part of staff training.

Periodic review of systems will be necessary to further develop health and safety, which constantly changes. Reviews should be actioned on a regular

basis: when workplace systems change, when new equipment is installed, and so on.

Ten ways to reduce health and safety risk at your premises

1 **Understand the consequences:** a significant number of business owners and managers are oblivious to the sort of problems that can occur. Having at least a basic understanding of the sort of safety issues that can impact on the premises is the first and most important step.

2 **Create a competent team:** whether this is just one person or a team of people from across the business, it is vital that they have the skills, knowledge, attitude and awareness to identify and manage risks properly.

3 **Call in the experts:** look for experts that can develop the knowledge base within the team and manage functions the team is either too busy or not experienced enough to deal with.

4 **Create a clearly defined risk management system:** this should not only document all the risks that have been identified but also detail

who is responsible for dealing with them and how they will be monitored.

5 **Educate:** train as many people as possible (particularly the key personnel) in risk awareness and reduction.

6 **Monitor:** make sure that the risk management system you have developed involves obvious checkpoints that are recorded and easily identifiable when absent.

7 **Evaluate:** regularly review the risk management system to ensure that it is getting the desired results.

8 **Change:** the hospitality industry is particularly dynamic so it is important to ensure that the risk management system changes in line with the business.

9 **Tap into the knowledge base:** the problems that one hospitality business is experiencing will be similar to those of other establishments. Sharing your knowledge by communicating with hotel associations and groups can build a vital source of intelligence.

10 **A safe guest experience is a good guest experience:** poor safety standards, which could cause injury, and poor food hygiene standards, which could result in food poisoning, will deter future guests.

Staff facilities and welfare

The welfare of all employees at a place of work is the responsibility of the employer. Facilities should be provided that are both safe and beneficial. These include:

- sufficient working space (minimum 11 cubic metres per person)
- easy evacuation in an emergency
- floors and exit routes non-slip and in good repair
- proper ventilation
- temperature comfortable (normally 16°C and never below 13°C, except when foods are to be kept cold, i.e. in a cold room preparation area)
- system of maintenance put into practice
- system of cleaning in operation
- quick disposal of waste, so that is does not accumulate
- safe and non-obstructed loading and unloading bays
- provision of adequate toilets, working facilities, drinking water
- changing facilities and accommodation for outdoor clothes, separate for men and women
- provision of a rest room.

The Health Act 2006 led to smoking being banned in public places, workplaces and vehicles used for work purposes.

Enforcement policy

Enforcement officers may:

- offer information and advice, face to face and in writing, that may include a warning that you are failing to comply with the law
- serve improvement and prohibition notices, withdraw approvals, vary licence conditions or exemptions, issue formal cautions (England and Wales only)
- prosecute (or report to the Procurator Fiscal with a view to prosecution in Scotland).

Enforcement of legislation

Health and safety inspectors and local authority inspectors (environmental health officers) have the authority to enforce legal requirements. They are empowered to:

- issue a prohibition notice that immediately prevents further business until remedial action has been taken
- issue an improvement notice – whereby action must be taken to remedy the problems identified within a stated time – to an employee, employer or supplier
- prosecute any person breaking the Act; this can be instead of or in addition to serving a notice and may lead to a substantial fine or prison
- seize, render harmless or destroy anything that the inspector considers to be the cause of imminent danger.

Environmental health officers/ practitioners

The environmental health officer has two main functions: one is to enforce the law; the other aspect of the job is to act as an adviser and educator in the areas of food hygiene and catering premises. Here his or her function is to improve the existing standards of hygiene and to advise how this may be achieved. Frequently, health education programmes are organised by environmental health officers; these may include talks and free literature. If in doubt about any matter concerning food hygiene, pests, premises or legal aspects, the environmental health officer is there to be consulted.

Smoke-free premises

No smoking is allowed in an enclosed or substantially enclosed space to which members of the public have access in the course of their work, business or leisure.

Occupational health

Occupational health means remaining free from illnesses associated with conditions at work. Work-related illnesses are a major health problem in the UK today. Hazards at work may or may not be obvious. For example:

- exposure limits – many substances and environments established under COSHH regulations, exposure limits may be exceeded accidentally
- susceptibility to illness – this can vary from person to person
- workplace injuries.

Symptoms of illness

These may not appear for many years after the original contact – for example, in the case of asbestos causing asbestosis.

Action should be taken to protect employees from hazards at work. For example:

- assessments should be made and records kept of any hazards employees may face
- trained professionals should be employed to eliminate or reduce potential hazards
- safety policies should be designed to minimise the health risk to employees
- special equipment should be used to help shield employees from danger.

The employee must display the right attitude and action to safeguard their own health and safety and that of others while at work. She or he should cooperate with occupational health and safety programmes as these are designed to identify and control occupational health hazards.

Safety programmes

Training and information

Such programmes instruct staff in how to handle materials safely, use equipment correctly and detect symptoms of illness.

Medical examinations

Some problems can be detected early and before they become serious. Employees should have regular check-ups. This will depend on their age and position within the organisation.

Early treatment

If any unusual symptoms appear, the employee should inform their line manager, then report to the health and safety officer and seek medical advice. Early investigation and treatment can be most effective.

Monitoring illness patterns

Health professionals, such as occupational health nurses, record cases of illness, take samples from contaminated areas and keep medical records.

Occupational health departments

Larger employers, or groups of employers, may employ the services of an occupational health department. They will supply information and health training, and will be the first point of call for employees with health concerns. The occupational health department may also be involved in health screening of new employees.

Self-protection

Always keep a healthy frame of mind. Never assume that 'it can't happen to me' – it can! The way to help prevent illness and accidents is to take proper precautions every day you work. Treat hazardous substances and working conditions with respect. Never cut corners to get work done faster. Follow the company's health and safety policies regarding exposure limits, clean-up procedures, protective equipment, and so on. Be aware of hazards that might exist at work. For example:

- acids
- dust
- alkalis
- noise
- asbestos
- solvents
- fumes
- paints
- resins.

Take care with substances that you use or that are used around you at work. Know the generic name of all chemicals. Check whether any substances can enter the body – for example, by inhaling, swallowing or via skin contact.

Where exposure limits have been established, stick to them. Know what the potential risks are and report any health problems that are noticed. Watch for dangerous conditions that may affect your health. These include noise, heat, radiation and vibrations, as well as leaks, spills, malfunctions in protective equipment and poor safety practices on the part of colleagues.

Report any unsafe or suspicious conditions to your line manager.

Implementing a programme

Implementing health and safety measures doesn't have to be expensive, time consuming or complicated. In fact, safer and more efficient working practices can save money and greatly improve working conditions for your employees.

If you have five or more employees you will need to write down your health and safety policy. This sets out how you manage health and safety in your organisation. It needn't be overly complicated, but should be something that is meaningful and useful to you and your staff.

Accidents

It is essential that people working in practical areas are capable of using the tools and equipment in a manner that will harm neither themselves nor those with whom they work. Moreover, they should be aware of the causes of accidents and be able to deal with any that occur.

Accidents may be caused in various ways:

- excessive haste – the golden rule of the kitchen is 'never run'; this may be difficult to observe during a very busy service but excessive haste causes people to take chances, which inevitably lead to mishaps
- distraction – accidents may be caused by not concentrating on the job in hand, through lack of interest, personal worry or distraction by someone else; the mind must always be kept on the work so as to reduce the likelihood of accidents
- failure to apply safety rules and use safety equipment.

Accident prevention

It is the responsibility of everyone to observe the safety rules; in this way a great deal of pain and loss of time can be avoided.

It isn't difficult to keep your employees safe and healthy in the workplace. This will keep your profits where they belong: as profits for your company, not money paid out to cover avoidable staff absences due to ill health or injury.

When trying to establish the common causes of accidents and ill health at work, consider the following questions. They may help clarify the issues.

- What are the chances of people slipping or tripping at work?
- Do people work with, or come into contact with, asbestos?
- Do people work with hazardous substances?
- Do people perform work at height and, if so, is it done safely?
- Do people suffer from sprains, strains and pains?
- Do people use computers or other display screen equipment?
- Is your workplace noisy?
- Are employees exposed to vibration or repetitive tasks?
- How safe is electricity in your workplace?
- Do people know how to select and use your work equipment?
- What maintenance and building work takes place?
- What are the risks from transport in your workplace?
- Do you know the risks associated with pressure systems?
- Do you know how to prevent fire or explosion?
- Do you know where harmful radiation occurs?
- Are employees feeling stressed by work?
- What do you do if there's an accident at work?

Prevention of cuts and scratches

Knives

These should never be misused and the following rules should always be observed.

- The correct knife should be used for the appropriate job.
- Knives must always be sharp and clean; a blunt knife is more likely to cause a cut because excessive pressure has to be used.
- Handles should be free from grease.
- The points must be held downwards.
- Knives should be placed flat on the board or table so that the blade is not exposed upwards and the handle does not protrude over the edge of the table.
- Knives should be wiped clean, holding the edge away from the hands.
- Do not put knives in a washing-up sink.

Full name of injured person:			
Occupation:		Supervisor:	
Time of accident:	Date of accident:	Time of report:	Date of report:
Nature of injury or condition:			
Details of hospitalisation:			
Extent of injury (after medical attention):			
Place of accident or dangerous occurrence:			
Injured person's evidence of what happened (include equipment/items/or other persons): Use separate sheets if necessary			
Witness evidence (1):		Witness evidence (2):	
Supervisor's recommendations:			
Date:	Supervisor's signature:		
This form must be sent to the company health and safety officer			

Figure 13.7 Sample in-house record of accidents and dangerous occurrences

Choppers

These should be kept sharp and clean. Care should be taken that no other knives, saws, hooks or such-like can be struck by the chopper, which could cause them to splinter or fly into the air. This also applies when using a large knife for chopping.

Cutting blades on machines

Guards should always be in place when the machine is in use; they should not be tampered with nor should hands or fingers be inserted past the guards. Before the guards are removed for cleaning, the blade or blades must have stopped revolving. If the machine is electrically operated the plug should, when possible, be removed.

When the guard is removed for cleaning, the blade should not be left unattended in case someone should put a hand on it by accident. No one under 18 must do this. Training must have taken place before any employee does it.

Cuts from meat and fish bones

Jagged bones can cause cuts, which may turn septic, particularly fish bones and the bones of a calf's head that has been opened to remove the brain. Cuts of this nature, however slight, should never be neglected. Frozen meat should not be boned out until it is completely thawed because it is difficult to handle: the hands become very cold and the knife slips easily.

Prevention of burns and scalds

A burn is caused by dry heat and a scald by wet heat. Both burns and scalds can be very painful and have serious effects, so certain precautions should be taken to prevent them.

- Sleeves of jackets and overalls should be rolled down and aprons worn at a sensible length so as to give adequate protection.
- A good, thick dry cloth or gloves are most important for handling hot utensils. A cloth should never be used wet on hot objects and is best folded to give greater protection. It should not be used if thin, torn or with holes.
- Trays containing hot liquid, such as roast gravy, should be handled carefully, one hand on the side and the other on the end of the tray so as to balance it.
- A hot pan brought out of the oven should have something white, such as a little flour, placed on the handle and lid (or an oven cloth wrapped around the handle) as a warning that it is hot. This should be done as soon as the pan is taken out of the oven.
- Handles of pans should not protrude over the edge of the stove as the pan may be knocked off the stove. However, handles placed inwards over the stove will become hot.
- Large full pans should be carried correctly: when there is only one handle the forearm should run along the full length of the handle and the other hand should be used to balance the pan where the handle joins the pan. This should prevent the contents from spilling.
- Certain foods require extra care when heat is applied to them – as, for example, when a cold liquid is added to a hot roux or when adding cold water to boiling sugar for making caramel. The hot contents of the pan will bubble and spit. Extra care should always be taken when boiling sugar.
- Frying, especially deep frying, needs careful attention. When shallow or deep frying fish, for example, put the fish into the pan away from the person so that any splashes will do no harm. With deep frying, free-standing fritures should be moved with care and if possible only when the fat is cool. Fritures should not be more than two-thirds full. Wet foods should be drained and dried before being placed in the fat, and when foods are tipped out of the frying basket a spider should be to hand. Should the fat in the friture bubble over on to a gas stove then the gas taps should be turned off immediately. Fire blankets and fire extinguishers should be provided in every kitchen, conveniently sited ready for use.
- Steam causes scalds just as hot liquids do: in fact, steam is hotter than boiling water. It is important to be certain that before steamers are opened the steam is turned off, and that when the steamer door is opened no one is in the way of the escaping steam. Stand back when opening the door. The steamer should be in proper working condition; the drain hole should always be clear. The door should not be opened immediately the steam is turned off – it is better to wait for about half a minute before doing so.
- Scalds can also be caused by splashing when passing liquids through conical strainers; it is wise to keep the face well back so as to avoid getting splashed. This also applies when hot liquids are poured into containers.

Emptying and cleaning fryers

Lack of care during the emptying and cleaning of fryers is a major cause of accidents. Hazards include:

- fire
- burns from hot oil
- contact with hot surfaces
- fumes from hot cleaning chemicals
- danger of chemicals overflowing
- eye injuries from splashes
- strains and sprains while lifting and moving containers of oil.

Procedure for draining

- Switch off appliance.
- Drain only when oil is cool.
- Do not drain until oil is below 40°C.
- Follow any instructions. Remove debris.
- Clean and dry.
- Ensure that the drain-off tap cannot be turned on accidentally.
- If appropriate, eye protection should be worn.

Machinery

Accidents are easily caused by misuse of machines. The following rules should always be put into practice.

- The machine should be in correct running order before use.
- The controls of the machine should be operated by the person using the machine. If two people are involved there is the danger that a misunderstanding can occur and the machine

be switched on when the other person does not expect it.

- Machine attachments should be correctly assembled and only the correct tools used.
- When mixing machines are being used the hands should not be placed inside the bowl until the blades, whisk or hook have stopped revolving. Failure to observe this rule may result in a broken arm or severe cut.
- Electrical plugs should be removed from electric machines when they are being cleaned so they cannot be switched on accidentally.

The Gas Safety (Installation and Use) Regulations require employers to maintain gas appliances; this is distinctly separate from the duty of a landlord to maintain gas appliances in let properties. It is vital that all gas equipment, and in particular Calor gas equipment, is properly and regularly serviced and adjusted. For this reason, an agreement should be in place with a properly qualified gas installer or maintenance company.

Gas explosions

The risk of explosion from gas is considerable. To avoid this occurring it is necessary to ensure that the gas is properly lit. On ranges with a pilot on the oven it is important to see that the main jet has ignited from the pilot. If the regulo is low, sometimes the gas does not light at once – the gas collects and an explosion occurs. When lighting the tops of solid-top ranges it is wise to place the centre ring back for a few minutes after the stove is lit because the gas may go out – gas then collects and an explosion can occur.

Kitchen equipment

On 1 January 1996 a significant European Union directive concerning the design and installation of gas-fuelled catering equipment became mandatory. All gas appliances sold after that date, new or secondhand, must be fitted with a fuel cut-out mechanism should the main pilot light be extinguished. Equipment will be withdrawn from the marketplace if it does not comply. This gas directive joins other European laws

that have come into effect and are strict guidelines or explicit instructions. These rules set out safe practice on topics as diverse as electromagnetic compatibility, pressure in systems and the surface temperature of oven doors. They accompany the six sets of UK Health and Safety at Work Regulations (1992), which came into force in 1993, the legislation that implements European Union directives on Health and Safety at Work. These regulations have developed changes in the manufacture of existing equipment.

Electrical equipment is mostly covered by a non-binding European Union directive: the Low Voltage Directive. This was approved by the European Union's members in February 1973, and was passed into UK Health and Safety law in 1989, in the form of the Low Voltage Electrical Equipment Safety Regulations.

Interlocking devices: see page 388.

Floors

Accidents are also caused by grease and water being spilled on floors and not being cleaned up. It is most important that floors are always kept clean and clear; pots, pans and suchlike should never be left on the floor, nor should oven doors be left open, because anyone carrying something large may not see the door or anything on the floor, and trip over.

Many people strain themselves by incorrectly lifting or attempting to lift items that are too heavy (see Figure 13.2 for guidance). Large stock pots, forequarters and hindquarters of beef, for example, should be lifted with care. Particular attention should be paid to the hooks in the meat so that they do not injure anyone.

On no account should liquids be placed in containers on shelves above eye level, especially when hot and particularly not hot oil or fat. They may be pulled down by someone else.

Safe kitchens are those that are well lit and well ventilated, and where the staff take precautions to prevent accidents happening. When accidents do happen, however, it is necessary to know something about first aid (dealt with in the following section).

First aid

When people at work suffer injuries or fall ill, it is important that they receive immediate attention and that, in serious cases, an ambulance is called.

The arrangements for providing first aid in the

workplace are set out in the Health and Safety (First Aid) Regulations 1981. First-aiders and facilities should be available to give immediate assistance to casualties with both common injuries or illness.

As the term implies, first aid is the immediate treatment given on the spot to a person who has been injured or is ill. Since 1982 it has been a legal requirement that adequate first-aid equipment, facilities and personnel to give first aid are provided at work. If the injury is serious the injured person should be treated by a doctor or nurse as soon as possible.

Further information can be obtained from the Royal Society for the Prevention of Accidents (RoSPA) (website: www.rospa.org. uk) or the Health & Safety Executive (website: www.hse.gov.uk).

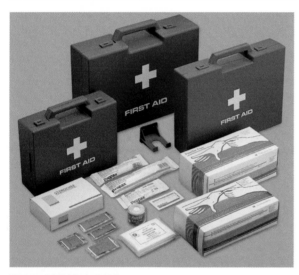

Figure 13.8 First-aid kit

First-aid equipment

A first-aid box, as a minimum, should contain:

- a card giving general first-aid guidance
- 20 individually wrapped, sterile, adhesive, waterproof dressings of various sizes
- 25 g (1 oz) cotton wool packs
- 12 safety pins
- two triangular bandages
- two sterile eye pads, with attachment
- four medium-sized sterile unmedicated dressings
- two large sterile unmedicated dressings
- two extra large sterile unmedicated dressings
- tweezers
- scissors
- plastic gloves
- report book to record all injuries.

First-aid boxes must be easily identifiable and accessible in the work area. They should be in the charge of a responsible person, checked regularly and refilled when necessary.

All establishments must have first-aid equipment. It is desirable for all establishments to have trained first-aid staff. Larger establishments must provide at least one person trained in first aid per 50 employees. Smaller companies may have instead an appointed person, who keeps the first-aid equipment topped up and contacts the emergency services if needed.

Large establishments usually have medical staff such as a nurse and a first-aid room. The room should include a bed or couch, blankets, chairs, a table, sink with hot and cold water, towels, tissues and a first-aid box. Hooks for clothing and a mirror should be provided.

After a period of three years trained first-aid staff must update their training to remain certificated.

All catering workers and students are recommended to attend a first-aid course run by St John Ambulance, St Andrew's Ambulance Association or the British Red Cross Society.

First-aid treatment

Shock

The signs of shock are faintness, sickness, clammy skin and a pale face. Shock should be treated by keeping the person comfortable, lying down and warm. Cover the person with a blanket or clothing, but do not apply hot water bottles.

Fainting

Fainting may occur after a long period of standing in a hot, badly ventilated kitchen. The signs of an impending faint are whiteness, giddiness and sweating. A faint should be treated by raising the legs slightly above the level of the head and, when the person recovers consciousness, putting them in the fresh air for a while and making sure that they have not incurred any injury in fainting.

Cuts

All cuts should be covered immediately with a waterproof dressing, after the skin round the cut has been washed. When there is considerable bleeding it should be stopped as soon as possible. Bleeding may be controlled by direct pressure, by bandaging firmly on the cut. It may be possible to stop bleeding from a cut artery by pressing the artery with the thumb against the underlying bone; such pressure may be applied while a dressing or bandage is being prepared for application, but not for more than 15 minutes.

When assisting someone with a cut, wear disposable gloves.

Nose bleeds

Sit the person down with their head forward, and loosen their clothing round the neck and chest. Ask them to breathe through their mouth and to pinch the soft part of their nose. After ten minutes release the pressure. Warn the person not to blow their nose for several hours. If the bleeding has not stopped continue for a further ten minutes. If the bleeding has not stopped then, or recurs in 30 minutes, obtain medical assistance.

Fractures

A person suffering from broken bones should not be moved until the injured part has been secured so that it cannot move. Medical assistance should be obtained.

Burns and scalds

Place the injured part gently under slowly running water or immerse in cool water, keeping it there for at least ten minutes or until the pain ceases. If serious, the burn or scald should then be covered with a clean cloth or dressing (preferably sterile) and the person sent immediately to hospital.

Do not use adhesive dressings, apply lotions or ointments, or break blisters.

Electric shock

Switch off the current. If this is not possible, free the person by using a dry insulating material such as cloth, wood or rubber, taking care not to use the bare hands otherwise the electric shock may be transmitted. If breathing has stopped, give artificial respiration and send for a doctor. Treat any burns as above.

Gassing

Do not let the gassed person walk, but carry them into the fresh air. If breathing has stopped apply artificial respiration and send for a doctor.

Artificial respiration

There are several methods of artificial respiration. The most effective is mouth to mouth (or mouth to nose) and this method can be used by almost all age groups and in almost all circumstances.

It is stressed that we would recommend all students complete a first-aid course.

Further information on first aid and emergency treatments can be obtained from the St John Ambulance Association, 27 St John's Lane, London EC1M 4BU (website: www.sja.org.uk).

Fire precautions

Fire safety

Every employer has an explicit duty for the safety of his or her employees in the event of a fire. The Regulatory Reform Fire Safety Order 2005 places a greater focus on fire prevention. It places responsibility for the fire safety of the occupants of premises and people who might be affected by fire, on a defined responsible person, usually the employer.

The responsible person must:

- make sure that the fire precautions, where reasonably practicable, ensure the safety of all employees and others in the building
- make an assessment of the risk of and from fire in the establishment; special consideration must be given to dangerous chemicals or substances, and the risks that these pose if a fire occurs
- review the preventative and protective measures.

Fire safety requires constant vigilance to reduce the risk of a fire, using the provision of detection and alarm systems, and well-practised emergency and evacuation procedures in the event of a fire.

A fire requires heat, fuel and oxygen (see the section on 'the fire triangle', below, and Figure 13.9). Without any one of these elements there is no fire. Methods of extinguishing fires concentrate on cooling (as in a water extinguisher or fire hose) or depriving the fire of oxygen (as in an extinguisher that uses foam or powder to smother it).

Although businesses no longer need a fire certificate, the fire and rescue authorities will continue to inspect premises and ensure adequate fire precautions are in place. They will also wish to be satisfied that the risk assessment is comprehensive, relevant and up to date.

An employer must consider workers' capabilities when asking them to carry out any tasks or assignments relating to fire safety. This responsibility was clarified in the Fire Safety (Employees' Capabilities) England Regulations 2010.

Fire precautions

- Identified hazards must be removed or reduced so far as is reasonable. All persons must be protected from the risk of fire and the likelihood of a fire spreading.
- All escape routes must be safe and used effectively.
- Means for fighting fires must be available on the premises.
- Means of detecting a fire on the premises and giving warning in case of fire on the premises must be available.
- Arrangements must be in place for action to be taken in the event of a fire on the premises, including the instruction and training of employees.
- All precautions provided must be installed and maintained by a competent person.

Fire risk assessment

A fire risk assessment will help determine the chances of a fire occurring and the dangers from fire that your workplace possesses for the people who use it. The assessment method suggested shares the same approach as that used in general health and safety legislation, and can be carried out either as part of a more general risk assessment or as a separate exercise.

A risk assessment is not a theoretical exercise. However, much work can be done on paper from the knowledge you, your employees or their representatives have of the workplace. A tour of the workplace will be needed to confirm, amend or add detail to your initial views.

For fire risk assessments there are five steps that you need to take.

1 Identify potential fire hazards in the workplace.
2 Decide who (e.g. employees, visitors) might be in danger in the event of a fire, in the workplace or while trying to escape from it, and note their location.
3 Evaluate the risks arising from the hazards and decide whether your existing fire precautions are adequate or whether more should be done to get rid of the hazard or to control the risks (e.g. by improving fire precautions).
4 Record your findings and details of the action you took as a result. Tell your employees about your findings.
5 Keep the assessment under review and revise it when necessary.

The fire triangle

As noted above, for a fire to start, three things are needed:

1 a source of ignition (heat)
2 fuel
3 oxygen.

If any one of these is missing, a fire cannot start. Taking steps to avoid the three coming together will therefore reduce the chances of a fire occurring.

Once a fire starts it can grow very quickly and spread from one source of fuel to another. As it grows, the amount of heat it gives off will increase and this can cause other fuels to self-ignite.

FUEL
Flammable gases
Flammable liquids
Flammable solids

OXYGEN
Always present in the air
Additional sources from oxidising substances

IGNITION SOURCE
Hot surfaces
Electrical equipment
Static electricity
Smoking/naked flames

Figure 13.9 The fire triangle

Fire detection and fire warning

You need to have an effective means of detecting any outbreak of fire and for warning people in your workplace quickly enough so that they can escape to a safe place before the fire is likely to make escape routes unusable.

In small workplaces where a fire is unlikely to cut off the means of escape (open-air areas and single-storey buildings where all exits are visible and the distances to be travelled are small), it is likely that any fire will quickly be detected by the people present and a shout of 'Fire!' may be all that is needed.

In larger workplaces, particularly multi-storey premises, an electrical fire warning system with manually operated call points is likely to be the minimum needed. In unoccupied areas, where a fire could start and develop to the extent that escape routes may become affected before it is discovered, it is likely that a form of automatic fire detection will also be necessary.

Means of fighting fire

You need to have enough firefighting equipment in place for your employees to use, without exposing themselves to danger, to extinguish a fire in its early stages. The equipment must be suitable to the risks, and appropriate staff will need training and instruction in its proper use.

In small premises, having one or two portable extinguishers in an obvious location may be all that is

Figure 13.10 Firefighting

Figure 13.11 Fire blanket

required. In larger or more complex premises, a greater number of portable extinguishers, strategically sited throughout the premises, are likely to be the minimum required. Means of fighting fire may need to be considered.

Lighting of escape routes

All escape routes, including external ones, must have sufficient lighting for people to see their way out safely. Emergency escape lighting may be needed if areas of the workplace are without natural daylight or are used at night.

Firefighting equipment

Portable fire extinguishers

Portable fire extinguishers enable suitably trained people to tackle a fire in its early stages, if they can do so without putting themselves in danger.

When you are deciding on the types of extinguisher to provide, you should consider the nature of the materials likely to be found in your workplace.

Fires are classified in accordance with British Standard EN 2 as follows.

- Class A – fires involving solid materials where combustion normally takes place with the formation of glowing embers.
- Class B – fires involving liquids or liquefiable solids.
- Class C – fires involving gases.
- Class D – fires involving metals.
- Class F – fires involving cooking oils or fats.

Fire extinguishers are red. The different types can be identified by a clearly visible, coloured rectangle.

Class A and B fires

Class A fires involve solid materials, usually of organic matter such as wood, paper, and so on. They can be dealt with using water, foam or multi-purpose powder extinguishers, with water and foam considered the most suitable.

Class B fires involve liquids or liquefiable solids such as paints, oils or fats. It would be appropriate to provide extinguishers of foam (including multi-purpose aqueous film-forming foam (AFFF) carbon dioxide, halon or dry powder types). Carbon dioxide extinguishers are also suitable for a fire involving electrical equipment.

The fire extinguishers currently available for dealing with Class A or Class B fires should not be used on cooking oil or fat fires.

Class C fires

Dry powder extinguishers may be used on Class C fires. However, you need to consider the circumstances for their use and combine this with action such as stopping the leak to remove the risk of a subsequent explosion from the build-up of unburnt gas.

Class D, E and F fires

- Class D fires involve combustible metals. Use a dry powder extinguisher (blue).
- Class E fires involve electrically energised equipment. Use a CO_2 extinguisher (black).
- Class F fires involve cooking oils and fats. Use a wet chemical fire extinguisher (yellow).

Types of portable fire extinguisher

The firefighting extinguishing medium in portable extinguishers is expelled by internal pressure, either permanently stored or by means of a gas cartridge. Generally, portable fire extinguishers can be divided into five categories according to the extinguishing medium they contain:

1 water (red)
2 foam (cream)
3 powder (blue)
4 carbon dioxide (black)
5 wet chemical (yellow).

Some fire extinguishers can be used on more than one type of fire. For instance, AFFF extinguishers can be used on both Class A fires and Class B fires. Your fire equipment supplier will be able to advise you.

The most useful form of firefighting equipment for general fire risks is the water-type extinguisher or hose reel. One such extinguisher should be provided for approximately each 200 square metres of floor space, with a minimum of one per floor. If each floor has a hose reel, which is known to be in working order and of sufficient length for the floor it serves, there may be no need for water-type extinguishers to be provided.

Areas of special risk involving the use of oil, fats or electrical equipment may need carbon dioxide, dry powder or other types of extinguisher (see above). If you are not sure what to provide in any given circumstances, your local fire authority will be able to advise you.

Fire extinguishers should conform to a recognised standard such as British Standards EN 3 for new ones and British Standard 5423 for existing ones. For extra assurance, you should look for the British Standard Kitemark, the British Approvals for Fire Equipment (BAFE) mark or the Loss Prevention Council Certification Board (LPCB) mark.

Fire extinguishers may be colour-coded to indicate their type. Previously, the entire body of the extinguisher has been colour-coded, but British Standard EN 3: Part 5 (which came into effect on 1 January 1997) requires that all new fire extinguisher bodies should be red.

Hose reels

Where hose reels are provided, they should be located where they are conspicuous and always accessible, such as in corridors.

Fire-extinguishing systems

In smaller workplaces, portable fire extinguishers will probably be sufficient to tackle small fires. However, in more complex buildings, or where it is necessary to protect the means of escape and/or the property or contents of the building, it may be necessary to consider a sprinkler system.

Sprinkler systems are traditionally acknowledged as an efficient means of protecting buildings against extensive damage from fire. They are also now acknowledged as an effective means of reducing the risk to life from fire.

A note on fire legislation: interlocking

Any completely new kitchen built after September 2002 must have interlocking in the ventilation system, and any replacement, new installation or modification to existing ventilation systems must incorporate interlocking. (Interlocking describes the mechanical link between sensors in the extraction system and the main valve of the gas supply to cooking equipment. Should the carbon monoxide level in the ventilation system go up, the interlocker will turn off.)

Gas safety

The Gas Safety (Installation and Use) Regulations 1998 require any work to a gas fitting or gas storage vessel to be carried out by a competent person. This includes installing, reconnecting, maintaining, servicing, adjusting, disconnecting, repairing and purging the equipment of gas or air.

Competence to install, repair and maintain gas appliances

Whether a contractor or in-house employee is asked to do the work, they must be Gas Safe registered (previously CORGI registered) and the operative must have a valid certificate of competence that covers the particular type of gas work to be carried out.

Security in hospitality

Security in hospitality premises is a major concern, especially with the increasing rise in crime due to fraud. All establishments should endeavour to reduce the risk of temptation. Eliminating or reducing cash handling is one measure that should be encouraged. The use of credit and debit cards, while costing a small amount in charges, reduces cash handling, thus minimising risk.

Encouraging the payment of employees through cheque or bank transfer instead of by cash means that payrolls do not have to be collected and distributed. Other such measures could include notices that no money is kept in the premises or that safes are protected by time-delay locks. Strict stock control can reduce stock levels, thereby reducing temptation and the problems of control.

A great deal of crime is of an opportunist nature. Large-scale crime is generally well planned. Reducing the amount of information available to the criminal reduces the ability for the thief to plan and thus commit the crime.

In order for a business to function it is often necessary to have cash. In order to deprive the potential criminal of knowledge make sure that only the staff that need to know actually have any information about this. For example, never have a regular routine for 'banking'. Regular and spot-check stock taking is another valuable system to identify crime.

However, in order to carry out your business efficiently it is impossible to remove all temptation. Therefore all equipment – for example, computers, fax machines, photocopiers – should be security marked.

It is important to prevent any unauthorised person entering the premises. Reception staff need to be trained to identify suspicious individuals. Everyone reporting to reception should be asked to sign in and, if they are a legitimate visitor, be given a security badge. All contract workers should be registered and given security badges; they may be restricted to working in certain areas. Staff should be made aware of the threat from terrorists.

A good security system should also be in force at the back door, with everyone delivering goods reporting to the security officer. Good lighting is also important for security reasons. Supervisors and managers should carry out regular checks of all areas.

Some companies write into employee contracts the 'right to search', so that searches can be carried out from time to time as a deterrent against theft.

However, legally, a person cannot be forced to submit to a search even if they have signed a contract to that effect. However, by refusing to submit to a search they may be in breach of their employment contract.

Closed-circuit television (CCTV) cameras are also used as a deterrent against crime.

Prevention of crime should be the main objective. With regard to staff the first step is to appoint honest staff by taking up references from previous employers.

The Health and Safety at Work Regulations now require employers to conduct a risk assessment with regard to the safety of staff in the catering business. Where staff constantly come into close contact with strangers, it is advisable to train them in anti-aggression techniques, which include the early recognition of volatile situations and how to defuse them. At the same time staff should be trained not to approach people who could pose a physical threat to them.

Staff who handle money should be trained in simple anti-fraud measures such as checking bank notes, checking signatures on plastic cards, and so on.

Security measures also include leaving lights on in some areas that can be seen by passers-by, as well as locking doors, windows and suchlike. Making sure that any suspicious person does not re-enter the building is also essential. Night-time security staff are used in some establishments.

Each business will have its own type of risk. Over time, staff become familiar with the risks and adopt the measures that the business has put in place to deal with them.

Security systems of all types should be carefully selected according to the needs of the business. Before buying into any security system agreements, seek advice from an independent security expert, who will assess the needs of the establishment. Insurance companies will have stipulated criteria to be fulfilled before they will insure the business.

Management of a security system

As with other operations a security system needs to be managed. This involves:

- developing a security policy for the establishment to cover security threats, bomb alerts, theft by customers or by employees, policy regarding prosecution
- establishing resources to cover the cost of security staff, whether in-house or contract

- developing procedures for security risk assessment, dealing with breaches of security
- understanding the legal implications of, for example, vicarious liability for false arrest or imprisonment
- seeking a proper balance between the often conflicting demands of security and safety.

The main security risks in the hotel and catering industry

- Theft: customers' property, employers' property (particularly food, drink, equipment), employees' property.

- Burglary: theft with trespass of customers' property, employers' property, employees' property.
- Robbery: theft with assault, e.g. banking cash, collecting cash.
- Fraud: false claims for damage; counterfeit currency; stolen credit cards.
- Assault: fights between customers, while staff banking/collecting cash.
- Vandalism: malicious damage to property by customers, by intruders, by employees.
- Arson: setting fire to property.
- Undesirables: drug traffickers, prostitutes.
- Terrorism: bombs, telephone bomb threats.

Catering safety management: a summary

Managers must think positively about how they can sustain and improve safety if they are to comply with legislation and minimise the risk of incidents occurring. Accidents often happen because of acts or omissions by management rather than staff neglect.

The Management of Health and Safety at Work Regulations 1999 provide the basis for safety management requirements. This legislation requires:

- all involved in safety to think positively
- competence to be established
- risk assessment to be undertaken
- implementation of effective control.

Measures to reduce risk include:

- staff training on hazard awareness and control in the workplace.

Safety management involves identifying the hazards in a business and tailoring controls through physical measures, safe systems of work, the safety policy and staff training. Safety management and supervision is a legal requirement.

Topics for discussion

1 Discuss the causes of accidents and how they may be prevented. Are some people accident prone, others naturally clumsy and others lacking in common sense? If so, how can they be 'educated' to be safe workers?
2 Do notices regarding safety have any effect? How best may people employed in the kitchen be made aware of hazards, thus making a potentially dangerous environment much safer?
3 Attendance at a first-aid course could be made obligatory for every catering employee. Do you think this would be sensible? If you do, or do not, explain why.
4 Discuss what training and the procedures following training should be provided for every person being employed in a catering establishment. Does training reduce accidents, fires and so on?
5 What provision should be made for the welfare of hospitality staff? Discuss this, bearing in

mind costs and the fact that in the industry many employees are casual or part-time.
6 Discuss the hazards that should be prevented in the kitchen.
7 Discuss the relationship between the caterer and the environmental health officer.
8 Discuss accident prevention and the responsibilities of the worker and the employer.
9 Is ample provision made for first aid?
10 What fire precautions and appropriate systems are in place for fire prevention?
11 Explain how fire extinguishers are recognised for their appropriate use.
12 How can premises be made secure and stealing be prevented?
13 If you find temperatures and food hygiene legislation complex, discuss how it could be simplified.
14 Discuss the relationship between knowing the law and implementing it.

14

Food safety and food safety legislation

Supporting material available on Dynamic Learning Online:

> Knowledge quizzes

> Activity worksheet: hygiene

> Summary presentations

> Videos and worksheets: hygiene and food safety

Why is food safety important?

Effective management of food safety is of absolute importance throughout the hospitality industry. It means putting in place all the measures needed to make sure that food and drinks are suitable, safe and wholesome through all of the processes from designing premises, selecting suppliers and delivery of food right through to serving the food to the customer.

Recorded management of food safety is now a legal requirement for *all* food businesses, but as well as ensuring compliance with the law, good standards of food safety will enable a business to:

- avoid any incidence of food poisoning
- build a good reputation locally
- give customers (and staff) confidence in the food/services provided

- incur less wastage – therefore running costs will be lower
- provide pleasant working conditions for staff, leading to staff retention and greater job security
- receive favourable press reviews
- build and retain desired levels of business.

Failure to manage food safety effectively can be extremely damaging to a business and can lead to poor reputation, serving of notices by enforcement officers, legal action, very high fines and even closure, as well as all the resulting bad publicity.

What is required under UK food safety legislation?

Legislation concerning food safety covers a wide range of topics, including:

- controlling and reducing outbreaks of food poisoning
- registration of premises/vehicles
- content and labelling of food
- preventing the manufacture and sale of food that could cause illness or injury
- monitoring of food imports
- prevention of food contamination, equipment contamination and contamination of premises
- training of food handlers
- provision of clean water, sanitary facilities and washing facilities.

The latest food safety legislation affecting all food businesses came into force in the UK in January 2006 and affects all food businesses. This new legislation originated in the European Parliament and replaced the existing 1990 Act and related regulations introduced after 1990, although most of the requirements of these earlier acts/regulations remain the same. The most important and relevant regulations for food businesses are:

- The Food Hygiene (England) Regulations 2006, The Food Hygiene (Wales) Regulations 2006, The Food Hygiene (Scotland) Regulations 2006, The Food Hygiene (Northern Ireland) Regulations 2006
- Regulation (EC) No 852/2004 on hygiene of foodstuffs; this gives details of the general hygiene requirements for all UK food businesses and all member countries of the EU.

The main difference in the laws introduced in 2006 was to provide a framework for EU legislation to be enforced in England (with similar requirements for Wales, Scotland and Northern Ireland) and the requirement for all food-related businesses to have an approved food safety management procedure in place, with up-to-date permanent records available, including staff training records. All records must be reviewed and monitored regularly, especially if there is a change in procedures.

Before the introduction of this legislation many food businesses did have a food safety management system in place as part of their operation; now it is a *legal requirement* to have a system based on the seven principles of HACCP (Hazard Analysis Critical Control Points) (see page 000). Such a system will identify, assess and monitor the critical control points in food production procedures, and ensure that corrective actions are put in place and the systems frequently verified, with accurate documentation available for inspection and ongoing review processes. (See also the information about *Safer Food Better Business* on page 421.)

Those responsible for food businesses must ensure that:

- where a full HACCP system is established, at least one person who has been trained in the principles of HACCP is involved in setting up the system
- the premises (and food vehicles) are registered with the local authority
- they can supply records of staff training commensurate with the different job roles
- policies are in place for planning and monitoring staff training
- appropriate levels of supervision are in place
- they provide adequate hygiene and welfare facilities for staff
- there is an adequate supply of materials and equipment for staff, including PPE (personal protective equipment)
- there is sufficient ventilation, potable water supplies and adequate drainage
- there are separate washing/cleaning facilities for premises, equipment and food, as well as hand-washing facilities
- there are records of suppliers used
- there are systems for accident and incident reporting.

Employees also have food safety responsibilities. They must:

- not do anything or work in such a way that would endanger or contaminate the food they work with
- cooperate with their employers and the measures they have put in place to keep food safe
- partake in planned training and instruction
- maintain high standards of personal hygiene
- report illnesses to supervisors/managers before starting work (see page 409)
- report any breakages, shortages or defects that could affect food safety.

For a business to comply with the 2006 Act, food safety records are mandatory and will always include:

- essential food business records that reputable

suppliers are used, supplier contact records, equipment and premises maintenance temperature controls, staff sickness records, cleaning schedules, pest audits, etc.

- written documentation of recruitment, supervision, ongoing training, working practices and reporting procedures.

Food safety law is outlined in more detail on Dynamic Learning. Further information is available on the website of the Food Standards Agency (www.food.gov.uk – see *Food Hygiene – A Guide For Business*, *Food Law, Inspections and Your Business*, *Food Hygiene Legislation*).

Food safety legislation under the 2006 Act and previous 1990 (1995) Acts is enforced by local authorities through inspection by Environmental Health Officers (EHOs) (Environmental Health Practitioners – EHPs), who are empowered to serve enforcement notices (e.g. hygiene improvement notice, hygiene prohibition order, hygiene prohibition notice) through criminal and civil courts. Other legislation will be in place relating to working practices, procedures and training, and may well involve Trading Standards or the Health and Safety Executive.

Environmental Health Officers (Environmental Health Practitioners)

Enforcement officers may visit food premises as a matter of routine, as a follow-up when problems have been identified, or after a complaint. The frequency of visits depends on the type of business and food being handled, possible hazards within the business, the risk rating, and any previous problems or convictions. Generally, businesses posing a higher risk will be visited more frequently than those considered low risk.

EHOs (EHPs) can enter a food business at any reasonable time without previous notice or appointment – usually, but not always, when the business is open. The main purpose of these inspections is to identify any possible risks from the food business, to assess the effectiveness of the business's own hazard controls and to identify any non-compliance with regulations so that this can be monitored and corrected.

Under the food safety acts, premises that are considered to cause an 'imminent risk to health' can be closed down by a local authority immediately, on the advice of the EHO (EHP). If it is deemed through courts of law that the proprietor of a food business is guilty of an offence under the acts, they may be liable to heavy fines and/or a term of imprisonment.

Fines and penalties for non-compliance

Magistrates courts can impose fines of up to £5000, a six-month prison sentence, or both. For serious offences (e.g. knowingly selling food dangerous to health), magistrates could impose fines of up to £20,000. In a Crown Court, unlimited fines can be imposed and/or two years' imprisonment.

When the EHO (EHP) visits food premises, they will need to see the up-to-date food safety management system, including all relevant records. Smaller businesses may use 'Safer Food Better Business' (see page 421) as their food safety system, and will still need to provide the relevant records, many of which are recorded in the SFBB pack.

The EHO (EHP) may also complete physical checks on any area of the food business, especially where they think there may be possible food safety hazards present in the operation.

Food poisoning and prevention of food poisoning

The main reason for food businesses adopting high standards of food safety is to prevent food poisoning (in 2000 the Food Standards Agency committed to reducing the incidence of food poisoning across the UK). The number of food poisoning/food-borne illness cases in the UK remains unacceptably high. While some types of food poisoning/food-borne illness caused by some specific pathogens have been reduced over the past few years, others have increased. It is also important to remember that only a very small proportion of food poisoning cases are ever reported and recorded, so no one really knows the full extent of the problem.

Most illness related to food is caused by consuming foods/drinks that are contaminated in some way or are naturally poisonous.

Food poisoning and food-borne illness: definitions

- **Food poisoning:** an acute intestinal illness that is the result of eating foods contaminated with pathogenic bacteria and/or their toxins. Food poisoning may also be caused by eating poisonous fish or plants, chemicals or metals. Symptoms of food poisoning are often similar and

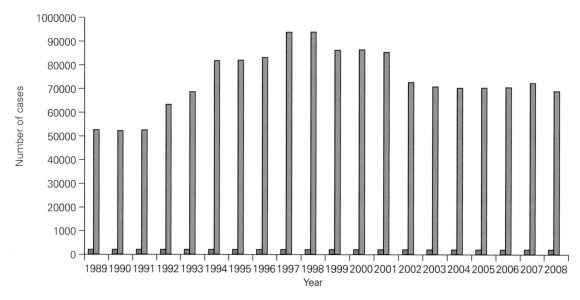

Figure 14.1 Reported food poisoning outbreaks

Source: Health Protection Agency

may include diarrhoea, vomiting, nausea, fever, headache, dehydration and abdominal pain.

- **Food-borne illness:** an illness caused by pathogenic bacteria and/or their toxins, and also viruses, but in this case pathogens do not need to multiply in the food, they just need to get into the intestine where they start to multiply. Only tiny amounts are needed and may be transmitted person to person, in water or airborne, as well as through food. Symptoms of food-borne illness are wide and varied, and include severe abdominal pain, diarrhoea, vomiting, headaches, blurred vision, flu symptoms, septicaemia and miscarriage.

At-risk groups

Food poisoning/food-borne illness can be unpleasant for anyone, but for some the illnesses can be very serious or even fatal. Extra care with food safety must be observed when providing food for these groups of people. These high-risk groups include:

- babies and the very young
- elderly people
- pregnant women
- those with an impaired immune system
- those who are already unwell.

Contamination

Contamination of food can be a major hazard in any food-related operation. A contaminant is anything that is present in food that should not be there. Food contaminants can range from the inconvenient or slightly unpleasant through to dangerous and even fatal. In any food business it is essential to protect food from contamination and remove or destroy contaminants already present (e.g. possible pathogens in raw poultry). We look in detail at some contamination hazards below.

Physical hazards

This includes physical objects such as glass, machine parts, paperclips, hair, fingernails, insects, packaging materials, coins, buttons, blue plasters and so on getting into food. Some of these could well be harmful if eaten, but they are mostly objectionable and cause for customer complaint. Good staff training, including 'clean as you go' and good general 'housekeeping', as well as planned kitchen practices recorded in the food safety management system, should help to prevent physical contamination.

Chemical hazards

Chemical hazards can arise from various chemicals such as kitchen cleaning materials, disinfectants, pesticides, degreasers, agricultural chemicals and beer line cleaners. Residues of drugs, pesticides and fertilisers may be present in raw materials. Pesticides sprayed on to fruit and vegetables just prior to harvesting may result in a toxic build-up. Chemicals can get into food by leakage, spillage or other accidents during food processing or preparation. Chemical food additives have to undergo rigorous testing before they are allowed to be used and are usually harmless. Acid foods should not be cooked or stored in equipment containing metals such as antimony, cadmium, lead, tin, zinc, aluminium or copper, unless the metal is intended for the specific purpose.

Prevention of chemical food poisoning

Chemical food poisoning can be prevented by:

- purchasing food from reliable sources, with good farming practices and suppliers with proper storage procedures
- using containers (especially metal containers) only for their intended use
- safe storage of kitchen chemicals well away from food
- accurate dilution of chemicals used in the kitchen
- not spraying chemicals such as sanitiser or fly spray around open food
- training and care in the use of substances hazardous to health – COSHH training for staff
- disposing of chemicals safely and with care according to regulations.

Allergenic hazards

These may come from various foods to which individuals may have an allergic reaction. When someone has a food allergy, their immune system mistakes certain foods – for example, wheat or nuts – for a harmful substance and a reaction takes place. This could be:

- itching and/or swelling of the lips, mouth, tongue and/or throat
- skin reactions (e.g. swelling and itching, eczema and flushing)
- diarrhoea, feeling sick, vomiting and bloating
- coughing and or runny nose
- breathlessness and wheezing
- sore, itchy eyes.

There may also be symptoms such as extreme fatigue or arthritis.

Some food allergies result in immediate, severe and even life-threatening symptoms, as happens with a severe peanut allergy. Others cause symptoms that may take longer to develop – for example, gluten allergy (coeliac disease). Some people can develop a severe allergic reaction called anaphylactic shock, which is potentially fatal. This is often linked to peanuts and other nut products. Symptoms can include dizziness, rapid pulse, a drop in blood pressure, and swelling of the airways and throat, making it difficult to breathe. This could result in loss of consciousness and can even be fatal if left untreated.

The main foods linked with allergic reactions are:

- nuts and nut products, including nut oil
- gluten, wheat and wheat products
- dairy products, including eggs
- shellfish
- mushrooms
- soft fruits, especially strawberries.

It is important to provide accurate information about ingredients in food when this is requested, or to include useful information on menus, especially when dealing with vulnerable groups such as young children. Some establishments that provide foods for such groups completely remove certain allergenic foods like nuts from their menus.

Food intolerance is different from an allergy and does not involve the immune system, though people suffering from a food intolerance may still suffer illness or discomfort after eating certain foods.

Prevention of allergenic food poisoning

Allergenic food poisoning can be avoided by:

- providing customers with accurate details of ingredients used
- providing full, useful menu information
- keeping staff fully informed of ingredients in menu dishes – a recipe file could be useful
- retaining food packaging/ingredients lists for information
- removing ingredients such as nuts from the menu
- using alternative ingredients, such as replacing nut oil with vegetable oil
- separate preparation areas and separate colour-coded equipment for allergy-related items
- staff training sessions on how to avoid problems with allergies.

Microbiological hazards

Contamination from micro-organisms includes pathogenic bacteria causing food poisoning or food-borne illness, as well as spores and toxins (see below), moulds, viruses, parasites, etc. These are of particular concern because they are often not visible on the food they are contaminating. In the case of pathogenic bacteria, very large numbers can be present in food, certainly enough to cause food poisoning but the food will smell, taste and look fine. High standards of food safety practices and awareness are needed by all food handlers to avoid contamination by micro-organisms, especially pathogens.

Contamination with pathogens can occur in many ways and particularly by:

- humans – coughing, sneezing on food; from the hands and because of poor personal hygiene
- people with illnesses or infections, or those who are 'carriers' of organisms
- animals, insects, birds getting into the kitchen and spreading pathogens from droppings, hair, saliva
- kitchen equipment – tea towels, dishcloths, knives, boards, bowls, etc.
- raw ingredients such as meat, poultry and dirty vegetables uncovered in the kitchen
- a build-up of refuse or decaying matter in the kitchen.

Good practices to avoid pathogenic food poisoning are discussed in detail below, but general measures should always include:

- food handlers practising the highest standards of personal hygiene and being meticulous about reporting any illness or infection they may have before entering the food areas
- planned processes for dealing with raw foods, especially raw meat and poultry
- planned and monitored storage, preparation, cooking and hot holding of all foods
- monitoring and supervision of temperature control and the time that food is at ambient temperatures
- recorded pest control measures and planned pest control
- planned and recorded training of staff in food safety matters.

Cross-contamination

Cross-contamination occurs when pathogenic bacteria (or other contaminants) are transferred from one place to another – for example, from contaminated food (usually raw food), equipment, areas or food handlers to ready-to-eat food. It is the cause of significant amounts of food poisoning and care must be taken to avoid it. Cross-contamination could be caused by:

- certain foods touching, e.g. raw and cooked meat
- raw meat or poultry dripping on to cooked ready-to-eat foods
- soil from dirty vegetables coming into contact with high-risk foods
- dirty cloths, staff uniforms or equipment
- equipment used for raw then cooked food, e.g. chopping boards or knives
- hands – touching raw then cooked food, not washing hands between tasks, etc.
- pests spreading bacteria from their own bodies around the kitchen

- different people touching hand-contact surfaces, e.g. fridge or cupboard doors.

To prevent the transfer of bacteria by cross-contamination, the following points should be observed:

- ensure food is obtained from reliable sources (traceability)
- handle foods as little as possible; when practicable, use tongs, palette knives, disposable plastic gloves and other suitable equipment
- ensure utensils and work surfaces are clean and sanitised
- use different colour-coded cloths for raw and cooked food areas, use disposable cloths or kitchen paper
- pay particular attention to avoid any contamination when handling raw poultry, meat and fish
- wash raw fruits and vegetables thoroughly
- clean methodically and frequently, in line with the cleaning schedule; train staff in 'clean as you go' procedures
- unpack food delivery boxes away from open food
- protect food from contamination while it is cooling in the kitchen

Figure 14.2 Chopping board colours

- keep foods covered and refrigerated as much as possible
- use colour-coded kitchen equipment (see below).
- take particular care in the defrosting of frozen raw items such as chicken, to prevent them dripping on to other items.

Colour-coded equipment

A variety of equipment is now available to help avoid cross-contamination, and can be identified by colour. The equipment used may include chopping boards, knife handles, food storage trays and bowls, food wrapping/packaging, cleaning equipment and cloths,

and staff uniforms. The most widely used of these are chopping boards; the usual colour coding of these is:

- white – dairy products
- red – raw meat and poultry
- brown – vegetables
- yellow – cooked meat
- green – fruit and salads
- blue – raw fish.

Some establishments will now have a further coloured chopping board to use for items likely to cause allergenic problems, such as nuts (these may also be prepared in a separate area).

Pathogenic bacteria, poisonous foods, food spoilage and food preservation

Bacteria are minute, single-celled organisms that can be seen only under a microscope. They are the most common cause of food poisoning and food-borne illness. Not all bacteria are harmful; some are essential to maintain good health (for example, in the digestive system), some are used in the manufacture of medicines and others in food production, as in the making of cheese and yoghurt. Others simply cause food to spoil, as in the souring of milk.

Those bacteria that can be harmful and cause food poisoning are referred to as pathogenic bacteria. These are dangerous once they get into food because they are not visible to the human eye, and the appearance, smell and taste of the food may remain unchanged. It is not possible to completely eliminate pathogenic bacteria from food premises as they are to be found widely in the environment, including in raw foods, dirty vegetables, animal pests and humans, to name just a few. They can very easily be transferred on to hands, surfaces, cooked foods, equipment and cloths; this is called cross-contamination (see above). Bacteria may be carried from one place to another in the kitchen – for example, on hands or equipment (these are referred to as 'vehicles of contamination').

The ways pathogens act

Some bacteria cause food poisoning by virtue of very large numbers of them multiplying in food then entering the digestive system, multiplying further and infecting the body. Others can form **spores**; these are often referred to as 'a resistant resting phase of bacteria'. Spores can withstand high temperatures for long periods of time, and can also withstand disinfec-

tion and dehydration. Then, on return to favourable conditions, they germinate into normal bacteria again, which can then multiply. Other bacteria produce **toxins** (poisons) outside their cells as they multiply in food. These mix with the food, making it poisonous, and symptoms of food poisoning follow. Toxins in food are resistant to heat, thus still causing illness, even if the food is heated to boiling point. Different toxins can be released by some pathogens as they multiply in the human body.

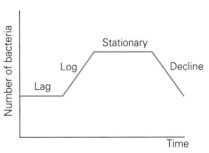

Lag[1]:	the bacteria are adjusting to the conditions before they start to multiply
Log[2]:	this is the phase of rapid growth
Stationary:	growth has stopped because their food is running out
Decline:	bacteria are dying

[1] No growth or dormant
[2] Abbreviation for logarithm, which is the means of using tables to calculate growth

Figure 14.3 How pathogens multiply

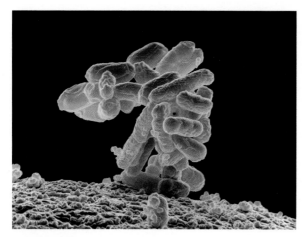

Figure 14.4 Bacteria multiplying

Some bacteria will multiply in the absence of air (anaerobes); others need it in order to multiply (aerobes). Bacteria multiply by dividing in two, under suitable conditions, once every 10–20 minutes. This is called 'binary fission'. Therefore one bacterium could multiply in 10–12 hours to between 500 million and 1000 million bacteria – enough to cause illness.

Typhoid and paratyphoid are diseases caused by harmful bacteria, and can be carried in food or water. Scarlet fever, tuberculosis and dysentery may be caused by untreated water or by drinking milk that has not been pasteurised. The time between eating the contaminated food (ingestion) to the beginning of the symptoms of the illness (onset) depends on the type of bacteria that has caused the illness.

For the multiplication of bacteria, certain conditions are necessary:

- **food** (nutrients) must be available
- **moisture** must be adequate
- **temperature** must be suitable – 5°C–63°C, with around 37°C the most favoured temperature
- **time** to allow for multiplication.

Food

Most foods can be easily contaminated; those less likely to cause food poisoning are dry or have a high concentration of vinegar, sugar or salt, or are preserved in some way. Some foods support the multiplication of bacteria more than others when given the right conditions; these are referred to as *high-risk foods*. They are usually foods that are ready to eat, have a protein and moisture content, and will not go through a cooking process that will destroy bacteria. High-risk foods include:

- stock, sauces, gravies, soups
- eggs and egg products
- meat and meat products (sausages, pâté, pies, cold meats, sandwiches)
- milk and milk products
- cooked rice
- all foods that are handled then have no further cooking
- all foods that are reheated.

The above foods are often implicated in food poisoning outbreaks, so extra care must be taken to prevent them from being contaminated and being left in conditions where bacteria can multiply.

Temperature

Food poisoning bacteria multiply most rapidly at human body temperature (37°C), but can multiply anywhere between temperatures of 5°C and 63°C. This range of temperatures is referred to as the danger zone. Warm kitchen temperatures provide ideal conditions for bacterial growth and food should be kept refrigerated wherever possible. Chilled and frozen food deliveries should be put into temperature-controlled storage within 15 minutes of delivery.

Water that is just warm is not suitable for washing crockery, cutlery or equipment as bacteria will not be destroyed. Hot water must be used for washing-up or cleaning equipment; and, where possible, use a dishwasher that will clean items thoroughly and disinfect them.

Boiling water will kill bacteria in a few seconds, but to destroy toxins prolonged boiling is needed. Spores are almost impossible to kill with normal cooking temperatures: long cooking times and/or very high temperatures are needed. Food canning processes use 'botulinum cook', which is high-heat cooking at 121°C for three minutes, or a tested alternative time/temperature combination, to kill any spores that may be present.

It is important to remember that, when cooking, food must be heated to a sufficiently high temperature and for the required amount of time, to be sure of safe food; any reheating of food must be done very thoroughly, to a minimum of 75°C. Cold foods need to be stored at temperatures below 5°C.

Bacteria are not killed by cold, although they multiply only slowly at very low temperatures; at freezer temperatures they will lie dormant for long periods. Once food is removed from cold storage, bacteria will start to multiply again as the temperature rises.

Foods that have been taken out of the refrigerator, kept in a warm kitchen and returned to the refrigerator for later use could be contaminated with a higher level of pathogenic bacteria. Food that has been

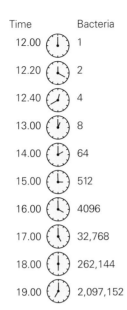

Time		Bacteria
12.00		1
12.20		2
12.40		4
13.00		8
14.00		64
15.00		512
16.00		4096
17.00		32,768
18.00		262,144
19.00		2,097,152

Figure 14.5 Under ideal conditions, bacteria can multiply by dividing into two every 20 minutes; in this way, a single bacterium could increase to 2,097,152 within 7 hours

taken from the freezer and defrosted will be susceptible to bacterial growth as the temperature rises, so food should never be re-frozen once it has defrosted.

Different organisms prefer slightly different temperature ranges for growth (multiplication) – for example, *Clostridium perfringens* grows best at 45°C, while *Listeria monocytogenes* grows most efficiently at 30°C, but can still multiply right down at refrigerator temperatures. In a refrigerator running below 5°C, bacteria would multiply very slowly or not at all, and there would be no multiplication at freezer temperatures, though these temperatures would not actually kill bacteria.

Food, time, moisture, warmth

As already noted, under ideal conditions one bacterium divides into two every 10–20 minutes if suitable moist food is available. In warm conditions, in a comparatively short time, sufficient pathogenic bacteria can be produced to cause food poisoning. Particular care is therefore required to keep foods refrigerated until they are actually being prepared or cooked, and food should certainly never be left out in a kitchen overnight.

Moisture

Bacteria need water to support their life cycle and processes. The amount of water in food is referred to as aw (water activity). Other than dried foods, most food contains some moisture, and a wide variety of foods contain enough water to support bacterial multiplication. Even dry foods such as dried pasta or rice will have water added to them in the cooking process, so once again will become vulnerable to bacterial growth. Some food preservation methods remove enough moisture to make the food safe, e.g. sundried tomatoes or food preserved with salt or sugar (osmosis).

Time

As noted above, given the conditions they need, bacteria can divide by binary fission every 10–20 minutes. Therefore foods left at ambient temperatures could contain large numbers of harmful bacteria within a few hours. Time is the element of bacterial growth that the food handler is most able to control. Make sure that food spends as little time as possible at kitchen temperatures, keep it cold in a refrigerator or hot, not in between. When heating or cooking food, take it through 'danger zone temperatures' as quickly as possible; this may mean cooking in smaller pans or in smaller batches. Do not hold food on display for long periods without proper temperature control.

A closer look at some of the main organisms causing illness

Food poisoning bacteria

Salmonella group

- Incubation period: 12–36 hours
- **Symptoms:** fever, headache, diarrhoea, vomiting
- **Prevention:** thorough cooking, correct storage, good personal hygiene, avoiding cross-contamination, exclusion of carriers

These bacteria can be present in the intestines of animals or human beings; they are excreted and anything coming into contact directly or indirectly with the excreta may be contaminated (raw meat at the slaughterhouse or the unwashed hands of an infected person). Salmonella infection is the result of human beings or animals eating food contaminated by salmonella-infected excreta, so completing a chain of infection. Faecal–oral routes are often linked with outbreaks of salmonella poisoning; for example: a chef visiting the toilet and not completing careful hand washing (salmonella on hands from intestines); high-risk food then handled by the chef, transferring the bacteria, which multiply in the food and cause food poisoning.

The foods most commonly affected by the salmonella group are poultry, meat and eggs. Contamination can be caused by:

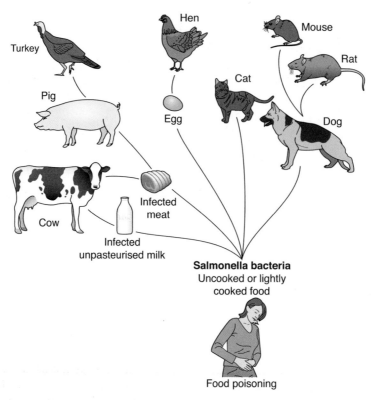

Figure 14.6 Foods contaminated by salmonella organisms if uncooked or lightly cooked may result in food poisoning

- insects and vermin, because salmonella is spread by droppings, feet, hairs or saliva
- the food itself (occasionally with eggs)
- cross-contamination (if a raw chicken is prepared on a board and the board is not properly cleaned before another food (such as cold meat) is cut on the board
- the food being infected by a human carrier (a person who does not suffer from symptoms but who carries the organism and passes it on through food they handle).

It is now highly recommended that any kitchen preparations (e.g. mayonnaise or mousses made with raw or very lightly cooked egg) are made with pasteurised egg because raw eggs can contain salmonella bacteria.

Staphylococcus aureus

- Incubation period: 1–7 hours
- **Symptoms:** severe vomiting
- **Prevention:** high standards of personal hygiene, exclusion of food handlers with illness, infections etc.

Staphylococcus will be present on humans, and will be on hands and other parts of the skin, hair and scalp, in uncovered cuts, burns and other abrasions, and also in the nose and throat. Foods affected by *Staphylococcus aureus* are often high-risk foods that have been handled and contaminated by the food handler, then left at suitable temperatures long enough for the bacteria to multiply to dangerous levels. The illness onset is rapid because *Staphylococcus aureus* produce toxins that are detected by the body as a poison and this is rejected by vomiting. Ongoing staff training in the importance of personal hygiene is crucial to the control of food poisoning from this organism.

Clostridium perfringens

- Incubation period: 12–18 hours
- **Symptoms:** diarrhoea, severe stomach cramp, little if any vomiting
- **Prevention:** thorough cooking, bringing food up to temperature quickly, and rapid cooling, prevention of cross-contamination

These bacteria are distributed from the intestines of humans and animals, and are also found in the soil. Foods affected by *Clostridium perfringens* frequently include raw meat, which is the main source of these

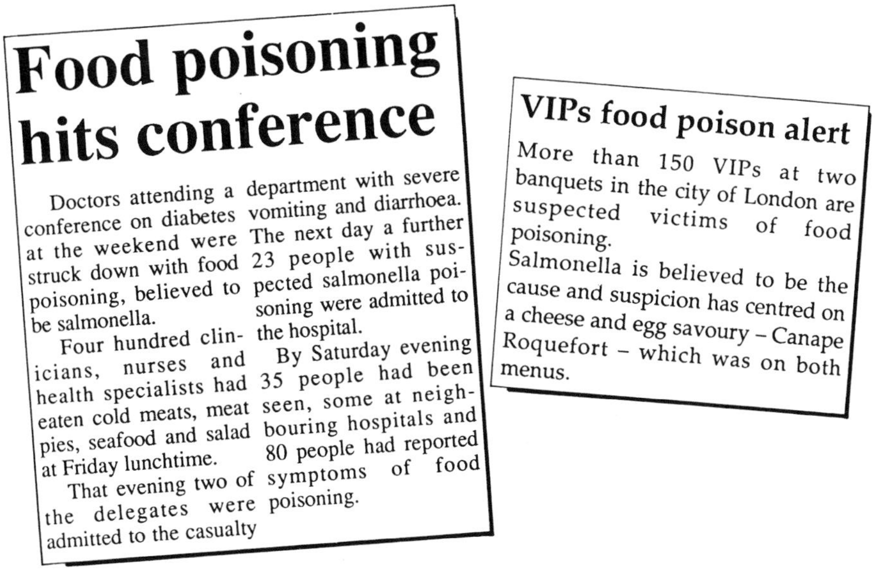

Food poisoning hits conference

Doctors attending a conference on diabetes at the weekend were struck down with food poisoning, believed to be salmonella.

Four hundred clinicians, nurses and health specialists had eaten cold meats, meat pies, seafood and salad at Friday lunchtime.

That evening two of the delegates were admitted to the casualty department with severe vomiting and diarrhoea. The next day a further 23 people with suspected salmonella poisoning were admitted to the hospital.

By Saturday evening 35 people had been seen, some at neighbouring hospitals and 80 people had reported symptoms of food poisoning.

VIPs food poison alert

More than 150 VIPs at two banquets in the city of London are suspected victims of food poisoning.

Salmonella is believed to be the cause and suspicion has centred on a cheese and egg savoury – Canapé Roquefort – which was on both menus.

Figure 14.7 Reports on salmonella food poisoning

bacteria, but dirty vegetables can also be a significant source. *Clostridium perfringens* can produce spores that may survive cooking and this organism has caused problems when large amounts of meat are cooked but take a long time to heat to boiling point (e.g. a large pan of stewing beef). During this slow heating time spores can form that may not be killed by subsequent cooking. If the food is to be cooled for later use the spores can germinate back into the organisms, which can then reproduce to dangerous levels.

Clostridium botulinum is another type of bacterium that causes food poisoning with some very serious outcomes, including death. It is found in soil and in fish intestines in some parts of the world, but fortunately is very rare in the UK.

Bacillus cereus

- **Incubation period:** 1–5 hours (common type)
- **Symptoms:** vomiting, diarrhoea
- **Prevention:** thorough cooking of rice; avoid cooking and storing rice in bulk, especially at ambient temperatures

Bacillus cereus is found in soil where vegetables and cereal crops like rice may grow. It can produce spores and can also produce two different types of toxin, making it a dangerous pathogen. It is often associated with cooking rice in large quantities (spores can form) then cooling it too slowly (spores germinate, organisms multiply, producing toxins). When the rice

is reheated, temperatures are not high enough to destroy spores and toxins. *Bacillus cereus* has also been linked with other cereal crops, spices and vegetables.

Competition

The rate at which bacteria multiply and survive may be partly dependent on other bacteria that are present as they will compete for the same conditions and nutrients.

Food-borne illness

Different organisms from those described above cause food-borne illness. These do not multiply in food, but use food to get into the human gut, where they then multiply and cause a range of illnesses, some of them very serious. They include those described in more detail below.

Campylobacter

- Incubation period: 2–5 days
- **Symptoms:** headache, fever, bloody diarrhoea, abdominal pain (mimics appendicitis)
- **Prevention:** thorough cooking, avoiding cross-contamination from raw to cooked food, treated water, pasteurised milk

Campylobacter now causes more food-related illness than any other organism. It is found in raw poultry and meat, sewage, animals, insects and birds. It has been particularly linked with raw, fresh chicken and increased chicken consumption. It is destroyed by thorough cooking.

Escherichia coli (E. coli)

- Incubation period: 10–72 hours
- **Symptoms:** vomiting, severe abdominal pain, diarrhoea (kidney failure and death with certain strains)
- **Prevention:** good personal hygiene, thorough cooking, avoiding cross-contamination from raw to cooked food, proper temperature control

Found in the intestines of humans and animals, *E. coli* is usually an indicator of faecal contamination of food or water. It has also been linked with raw meat and vegetables. Certain strains are pathogenic and produce an 'enterotoxin' in the intestine that results in abdominal pain and diarrhoea. One group of pathogenic *E. coli* is responsible for severe infantile diarrhoea, and another group causes travellers' diarrhoea. *E. coli* has been recorded at temperatures as low as 4°C.

Serious recorded outbreaks of *E. coli* occurred in Scotland in 1997, originating from a butcher selling raw and cooked meat. This resulted in 20 deaths. More recently, outbreaks have been associated with farms, takeaway food shops, other food outlets and children's animal farms.

Listeria monocytogenes

- Incubation period: 1 day–3 months
- **Symptoms:** meningitis, septicaemia, flu-like symptoms, stillbirth
- **Prevention:** thorough cooking, avoiding untreated milk/cheeses, careful temperature control

Listeria organisms can be found in soil, vegetables and animal feed. *Listeria* is a cause for concern because it can multiply (slowly) at fridge temperatures, i.e. below 5°C. *Listeria* has been linked with such chilled products as unpasteurised milk and cheeses, pâté and prepared salads, as well as cook-chill meals. It can be the cause of serious food-borne disease, particularly in the elderly, the chronically sick or babies. *Listeria* is killed by correct and thorough cooking.

Viruses

Viruses are even smaller than bacteria and can be seen only with a powerful microscope. They only multiply on living cells, not on food, though they may be transferred into the body on food or drinks, and may live for a short time on hard surfaces such as kitchen equipment. Viruses can easily be passed from person to person, and are sometimes associated with shellfish that come from contaminated water.

Sources

Food-poisoning bacteria live in:

- the soil (*bacillus cereus*, *clostridium perfringens*, *botulinum*, *listeria*)
- humans – intestines, nose, throat, saliva, skin, cuts, burns, hair, scalp, spots, cuts and burns (*salmonella*, *staphylococcus*)
- animals, rodents, domestic pets, insects and birds – intestines, skin, fur, and so on (*salmonella*, *campylobacter*, *E. coli*)
- kitchen refuse can carry a variety of pathogenic bacteria.

To prevent food poisoning, everyone concerned with food must:

- prevent bacteria from multiplying
- prevent bacteria from contaminating other areas
- destroy harmful bacteria.

This means that harmful bacteria must be isolated, the chain of infection broken and conditions favourable to their growth eliminated. It is also necessary to control the harmful bacteria being brought into premises or getting on to food. This is achieved by high standards of hygiene of personnel, premises, equipment and food handling.

Poisoning from fish, vegetable and plant items

- **Scombrotoxic fish poisoning (SFP):** associated with the consumption of contaminated fish of the Scombroid family (including tuna, mackerel, herring, marlin and sardines). The poison builds in the fish, especially in storage above 4°C. It is a chemical intoxication and symptoms occur within ten minutes to three hours after eating the affected fish. Symptoms include, rash on the face/neck/chest, flushing, sweating, nausea, vomiting, diarrhoea, abdominal cramps, headache, dizziness, palpitations and a sensation of burning in the mouth. Symptoms have usually disappeared within 12 hours. Although most cases are not serious enough for hospital attention, some are very severe and urgent medical attention is necessary, when antihistamine drugs may be used. These toxins are very heat resistant and not affected by normal cooking. Scombrotoxins are thought to be responsible for up to 70 per cent of food poisoning from fish in the UK.

- **Paralytic fish poisoning:** this is a very dangerous form of fish poisoning. It occurs when some bivalve shellfish (e.g. mussels) feed on poisonous plankton. The poison can survive normal cooking temperatures. Symptoms after eating affected shellfish may be nausea, vomiting, lowered temperature, diarrhoea, and also a numbness of the mouth, neck and arms, which can lead to paralysis and death within 2–12 hours.
- Certain **plants** are poisonous, such as some fungi, rhubarb leaves, daffodil bulbs and the parts of potatoes that are exposed to the sun above the surface of the soil.
- **Red kidney beans (black kidney beans):** every year there are a number of reported cases of mild poisoning from the toxin in red kidney beans (haemagglutin). Poisoning occurs when the beans are not boiled rapidly at temperatures that will kill the toxin (i.e. rapid boiling for ten minutes or more). After this initial rapid cooking at high temperatures, the heat can then be reduced to finish the cooking process. The symptoms of this poisoning include nausea, vomiting, pain and diarrhoea. The symptoms usually disappear within a few hours. Problems with not getting kidney beans hot enough may also occur if cooking in very large quantities or if using a 'slow cooker'.
- **Mycotoxins:** as they grow, some moulds can produce toxins – these are called mycotoxins. Mycotoxins can cause serious illness and have been linked with cancers. They are invisibly present in mouldy food over a much wider area than the visible mould. Mycotoxin-producing moulds can tolerate a wide range of acid/alkaline conditions, low water activity and temperature ranges from −6 to 35°C. They are heat resistant, so can withstand very high temperatures. A wide range of foods may be affected by mycotoxin-producing moulds, but the foods most frequently affected are cereal crops and products, nuts and fruit products such as juices, dried fruit and jams.
- **Food parasites:** a variety of parasites can live on plants or animals, from where they get their food. They present in different forms (e.g. worms, eggs, lice, grubs). They can usually be destroyed by thorough cooking or very high-temperature food preservation methods. In most cases they will also be killed by freezing.

Food spoilage and food preservation

Most foods, once removed from their natural environment, will have a limited life and will eventually deteriorate. The deterioration may be caused by *moulds, yeasts, enzymes* or *bacteria*. Spoilage of food could also be due to exposure to oxygen, moisture or chemicals, damage by pests, or poor handling and bad storage.

Unlike bacteria, moulds will grow on acid, alkaline, sugary and salty foods. They grow best between 20 and 30°C, but will also grow at refrigerator temperatures. Unlike bacterial contamination, which is impossible to detect in a normal kitchen situation, food spoilage can usually be detected by 'organaleptic observation', which means the spoilage can be observed by sight, smell, taste, touch, etc. Food spoilage includes, mouldy, slimy, dried-up, over-wet fresh foods, blown cans and vac packs, and food with freezer burn.

Over many years, different methods have been developed to prolong the natural life of various foods and keep them fresh. These include:

- use of heat – cooking, canning, sterilisation, UHT, pasteurisation, use of heat and sealing (e.g. canning, bottling, vacuum packaging)
- use of low temperatures – chilling, freezing
- exclusion of air – vacuum packaging
- changing the gases surrounding food – modified atmosphere packaging (MAP)
- removal of moisture – dehydrated foods
- use of acids, sugar or salt concentrations
- smoking – used on meat and fish (this will offer only limited preservation)
- preservatives (e.g. nitrates, nitrites).

Food preservation will often combine methods to ensure effective preservation (e.g. smoked fish may be vacuum packed and will also be refrigerated; milk is pasteurised but also stored under refrigeration). Careful use and control of temperature is essential in producing safe, high-quality food.

Keeping food safe

Methods and procedures for controlling food safety

Food delivered to food businesses will be taken through a number of stages before it reaches the customer. Careful control at each stage – known as critical control points (see page 419) – is essential to keep food safe and wholesome.

Food deliveries and storage

For food to remain in the best condition and safe to eat, it is essential that correct storage is in place and procedures fully understood by kitchen staff. Full documentation systems need to be completed for all kitchen deliveries, in line with the food safety management system. This will ensure that food is stored correctly and will be available for inspection by EHOs (EHPs) and, if necessary, as part of 'due diligence' (see page 421). Only approved suppliers should be used, who can assure that food is delivered in the best condition, in suitable packaging, properly date coded and at the correct temperature.

- All deliveries should be checked then moved to the appropriate storage area as soon as possible, and chilled/frozen food within 15 minutes of delivery.
- Use a food probe to check the temperature of food deliveries – chilled food should be below 5°C (reject it if above 8°C), frozen foods should be at or below 18°C (reject if above 15°C).
- Many suppliers will now supply a printout of temperatures at which food was delivered (save these printouts in kitchen records, they could be an important part of due diligence – see page 421).
- Dry goods should be in undamaged packaging, well within best before dates, be completely dry and in perfect condition on delivery.
- Remove food items from outer boxes before placing the products in the refrigerator, freezer or dry store. Remove outer packaging carefully, remaining fully aware of any possible pests that may have found their way into it. Avoid any possibility of physical contamination, such as staples or string getting into food.
- Segregate any unfit food from other food until it is thrown away or collected by the supplier. This is to avoid any possible contamination of other foods.

Raw meat and poultry

Wherever possible, store in refrigerators just for meat and poultry storage, running at temperatures between 1°C and 4°C (butchers' fridges −1 to 1°C). If not already packaged, place on trays, cover well with clingfilm and label. If it is necessary to store meat/poultry in a multi-use refrigerator, make sure it is covered, labelled and placed at the bottom of the refrigerator running below 5°C and is well away from other items that could be contaminated.

Fish

A specific fish refrigerator is preferable (running at 1°C). Remove fresh fish from ice containers or boxes and place on trays, cover well with clingfilm and label. If it is necessary to store fish in a multi-use refrigerator (1–4°C), make sure it is well covered, labelled and placed at the bottom of the refrigerator well away from other items. Remember that odours from fish can permeate other items, such as milk or eggs.

Dairy products/eggs

Pasteurised milk and cream, eggs and cheese should be stored in their original containers in refrigerators running at 1 to 4°C). Sterilised or UHT milk can be kept in the dry store following the storage instructions on the label, but once open treat as you would fresh milk. After delivery, eggs should be stored at a constant temperature and a refrigerator is the best place to store them. Prevent eggs from touching other items in the refrigerator.

Multi-use refrigerators.

If food needs to be stored in multi-use refrigerators it is absolutely essential that all staff know the correct procedures to store the food and this should become part of ongoing staff training. Posters, pictures and charts near the refrigerator may help with this. Ensure that the refrigerator is running at 1 to 4°C (check/monitor and record).

- store raw foods such as meat, poultry and fish at the bottom of the fridge in suitable deep containers to catch any spillage; cover with clingfilm and label with the commodity name and the date; do not allow any other foods to touch these raw foods
- store other items above raw foods – again they should be covered and labelled; keep high-risk foods well away from raw foods
- never overload the refrigerator – to operate properly, cold air must be allowed to circulate between items
- wrap strong-smelling foods very well as the smell

Figure 14.8 Food in a refrigerator

(and taste) can transfer to other foods, such as eggs and milk
- as with other foods, check date labels and use strict stock-rotation procedures.

Make sure that refrigerators are cleaned regularly. This needs to be part of the cleaning schedule. The procedure should be:

1 remove food to another refrigerator
2 clean according to cleaning schedule using a recommended sanitiser (a solution of bicarbonate of soda and water is also good for cleaning refrigerators)
3 remember to empty and clean any drip trays, and clean door seals thoroughly
4 rinse then dry with kitchen paper
5 make sure the refrigerator front and handle is cleaned and disinfected to avoid cross-contamination
6 check that the refrigerator is down to temperature (1 to 4°C), before replacing the food in the proper positions (see above)
7 check dates and condition of all food before replacing.

Frozen foods

Store in a freezer running at −18°C or below. Make sure that food is wrapped or packaged. Separate raw foods from ready-to-eat foods in the freezer and never allow food to be re-frozen once it has defrosted. In a specific ice cream freezer, ice cream can be kept at −12°C or below for up to one week before use.

Defrosting

If you need to defrost frozen food, place it in a deep tray, cover with film and label with what the item is and the date when defrosting was started. Place at the bottom of the refrigerator where thawing liquid can't drip on to anything else. Defrost food completely (no ice crystals on any part), then cook thoroughly within 12 hours. Make sure that you allow enough time for the defrosting process − it may take longer than you think! (A 2 kg chicken will take about 24 hours to defrost at 3°C.)

Fruit, vegetables and salad items

Storage conditions will vary according to type; sacks of potatoes, root vegetables and some fruit can be stored in a cool, well-ventilated storeroom, but salad items, green vegetables, soft fruit and tropical fruit would be better in refrigerated storage. If possible, a specific refrigerator running at 8–10°C would be ideal to avoid any chill damage.

Dry (ambient) food stores

A dry or ambient food store is an area to store foods that generally have a longer shelf life than those needing refrigerated or frozen storage (though the dry stores area may also have areas for refrigerated and freezer storage). Items usually kept in the dry stores include dry goods and cereal products, spices and dried herbs, packaged goods (e.g. biscuits), canned goods, bottled items, chocolate/cocoa, tea and coffee. Fruit and vegetables not requiring refrigeration (e.g. sacks of potatoes and onions) may also be stored here. Refrigerated storage may be available for items needing temperature-controlled storage. The room should be large enough to allow for the correct storage of stock. It needs to be cool (10–15°C is ideal), well ventilated, a light colour, well lit, protected to prevent entry of pests, and easy to clean/disinfect efficiently.

When fitting out the room:

- the surfaces of walls, ceilings and floors need to be smooth, impervious and easy to clean; edges where walls join the floor or ceiling should be coved if possible to prevent build-up of debris in corners
- doors should be protected by metal kick-plates and a plastic or chain curtain to prevent pests from gaining entry (but also check the packaging on deliveries for possible pests)
- windows should be well protected with wire gauze or netting, and food items should not be stored in direct sunlight from windows

- shelves/racking must be made of a non-corrosive, easy-to-clean material (e.g. tubular stainless steel); shelving must be deep enough to store the items required and the bottom shelf should be well raised from the floor to allow for ease of cleaning underneath; never store items directly on the floor as this prevents effective cleaning from taking place and packaging can get wet when the floor is cleaned, causing contamination and deterioration of the contents.

Where possible, store dry goods in covered containers or bins but make sure the stock is rotated effectively – that is, 'first in, first out' (see below); this will ensure that existing stock is always used first. When new packages of dry stock are delivered do not empty them into the container on top of what is already being stored.

To avoid any possible cross-contamination, store high-risk (ready-to-eat) foods well away from any raw foods such as dirty vegetables, and make sure all items remain covered.

Canned products

Cans are usually stored in the dry store area and, once again, rotation of stock is essential. Canned food will carry best before dates and it is not advisable to use after this. 'Blown' cans must never be used, and do not use badly dented or rusty cans. Once opened, transfer any unused canned food to a clean bowl, cover and label it, and store in the fridge for up to two days.

Cooked foods

These include a wide range of foods (e.g. pies, pâté, cream cakes, desserts and savoury flans). They will usually be high-risk foods, so correct storage is essential. For specific storage instructions see the labelling on the individual items, but generally keep items below 5°C. Store foods carefully, wrapped and labelled, where possible in a refrigerator used only for high-risk items. If a multi-use fridge needs to be used, store well away from and above raw foods to avoid any cross-contamination.

Using clingfilm

Clingfilm is a very useful product for storing food hygienically, protecting from cross-contamination and preventing food from drying out. However, because clingfilm seals in moisture it can encourage growth of moulds on food. Do not leave clingfilm-wrapped or covered foods in direct light as this can increase the temperature of the food inside. This is referred to as 'the greenhouse effect' and also applies to glass or perspex display cabinets. Because of concerns about migration of chemicals into food it is recommended that foods are never cooked or reheated when wrapped in clingfilm unless a film specifically recommended for this is used.

'First in, first out'

This term is used to describe stock rotation and is applied to all categories of food. It simply means that foods already in storage are used before new deliveries (providing stock is still within recommended dates and in sound condition). Food deliveries should be labelled with delivery date and preferably the date by which they should be used. Use this information along with food labelling codes (see below). Written stock records should form a part of a food safety management system.

Figure 14.9 Date labelling stickers

Food labelling codes

The main UK food date labelling codes to ensure the safety, quality and fitness for purpose of food are as follows.

- **Use-by dates:** these appear on perishable foods with a short life that usually need refrigerated storage. Legally, the food must be used by this date and not stored or used after it, or it could be a danger to health. The date will appear as 'use by' plus day, month and year. It is an offence to change this date.
- **Best before dates:** these apply to foods that are expected to have a longer life, e.g. dry products or canned food. A best before date advises that food is at its best before this date and to use it after the date is still legal but not advised. Dates will appear as follows:
  - three months or less – 'best before' day and month only
  - three to 18 months – 'best before' day, month and year, or 'best before end' month and year

– more than 18 months – 'best before' month and year, or 'best before end' and year only.

Some foods are exempt from date marking. These include uncut fresh vegetables, sugar or high-alcohol drinks. With both use-by and best before dates it is essential to follow the food storage advice and guidance on the packaging observed.

Food preparation

Food should not be prepared too far in advance of cooking. If food is prepared a significant time before it is to be cooked control measures must be in place to ensure that this is safe. Preparation areas for raw and cooked food should be well separated, as should dirty and clean processes. Food being prepared should only be out of temperature control (refrigeration or cooking processes) for the shortest time possible. Avoid handling food unnecessarily; use disposable gloves, tongs, slices, spoons, etc., where possible. High standards of personal hygiene are essential for those handling food; approved kitchen clothing must be worn, and changed if it becomes dirty or badly stained as this could contaminate food and equipment. It is essential to develop and monitor 'clean as you go' methods of work to help avoid microbial and physical contamination of food. Also take care when preparing food not to allow any chemical contamination from sanitiser sprays, disinfectants and so on, and be aware of allergenic contamination, whether some foods need to be prepared in a separate area or eliminated altogether. Use of colour-coded equipment is very helpful in food preparation areas, to avoid cross-contamination.

Use of temperature

Cooking is one of the best measures available to destroy and control bacteria in food. The usual recommendation is to cook to a core temperature of 75°C for at least two minutes, but cooking at a slightly lower temperature for a longer time can be as effective. In addition, dish specifications or personal preference may require lower temperatures than this, as in rare beef and some fish dishes. However, avoid undercooked dishes when dealing with groups vulnerable to the effects of food poisoning (see page 394). The usual way to check if the required core temperature (the temperature in the centre or thickest part of the food) has been achieved is with a calibrated and disinfected temperature probe, but visual checks can also be used – for example, amounts of steam and, in a cooked chicken, no part should be pink and the juices running off should be clear.

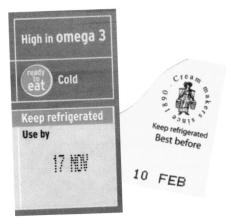

Figure 14.10 Use-by and best before dates

Staff should be aware of the danger zone temperatures (5–63°C) and the need to heat food through this temperature range quickly to avoid the formation of spores. It is also good practice to use lids on cooking pans to prevent heat escaping, and to stir food frequently to keep temperatures even. Hot food can be kept out of temperature control for up to two hours on any single occasion, such as a hot buffet. Food must be disposed of at the end of the two hours.

Low temperatures

As bacteria can multiply only very slowly at low temperatures (see Figure 14.5), good practice is to keep refrigerators running at 1–4°C. The legal requirement is at or below 8°C.

Refrigerator and freezer temperatures should be checked and recorded at least once daily, and the recorded temperatures kept as part of food safety management records. Cold food can be kept out of temperature control for up to four hours on any single occasion (e.g. a buffet). This time includes preparation time in the kitchen, and food must be disposed of at the end of the four hours.

Holding temperatures

Hot cooked food being held for service must not fall below 63°C. Make sure that there is adequate equipment to keep food above this temperature; check the temperature frequently and record it. Make sure that equipment for keeping food hot such as bains-marie or hot cabinets are pre-heated and cleaned/disinfected; do not overfill food containers and allow all of the food to be used from them before topping up. Use lids on open containers to keep the heat in.

For *cold* food being held for service or displayed there are similar rules. The food being held for service

Temperature probes

Electronic temperature probes are extremely useful in food production to measure the temperature in the centre of both hot and cold food. They are also very useful for recording the temperature of deliveries and checking the uniformity of food temperatures in fridges. Make sure the probe is clean and disinfected before use (disposable disinfectant wipes are useful for this). Place the probe into the centre of the food, making sure it is not touching bone or the cooking container. Allow the temperature to 'settle' before reading.

Check regularly that probes are working correctly (this is called calibration). This can be done electronically, but a simple and low-cost check is to place the place the probe in icy water; the reading should be within the range −1 to 1°C. To check accuracy at high levels place the probe in boiling water and the temperature reading should be in the range of 99 to 101°C. If probes read outside of these temperatures they need to be repaired or replaced. Record when temperature probes have been checked for accuracy and store this information with food safety records.

Infrared thermometers

These are also very useful in kitchen area and give instant readings as they work by measuring radiant energy. They are very hygienic to use as they do not actually touch the food, so there is no chance of cross-contamination or damaging the food.

Data loggers

These will record information about the temperatures of refrigeration over a set period. They record highs and lows of temperature in individual or different fridges/freezers, and can provide a graph of trends. Systems are available that record all refrigerator, chill units and freezer temperatures in a business and send the information to a central computer.

should not be above 5°C (legal requirement 8°C). Make sure that refrigeration/display cabinets run at the correct temperature, check the temperature and keep a record. Cold food above 8°C for four hours on one occasion must be thrown away (this includes preparation time).

Cooling cooked food

When food is cooled either to be served cold or to be reheated, this must be done carefully and quickly, to avoid the formation/germination of spores, and to reduce the risk of cross-contamination as food is cooling. It is recommended that food is cooled to 8°C within 90 minutes; this is best done in a blast-chiller. If this is not available, food in containers can be plunged into ice water baths or placed on trays and surrounded with ice or ice packs. Place cooling food in the coolest place available; fans can also be useful to speed up cooling time.

To allow food to cool more quickly it is recommended that:

- items such as soups, stews and sauces are placed in small containers; also use shallow containers – the increased surface area allows food to cool more quickly
- cook smaller joints of meat because these will cool more quickly; a maximum weight of 2.5 kg is recommended.

Reheating

Reheating should be done thoroughly and quickly to a core temperature of at least 75°C (Scottish law requires 82°C). Reheated food should also be served quickly and never reheated more than once.

Serving food

Food must also be protected when it is being served. Do not keep food unprotected and out of temperature control in service areas longer than necessary. Make sure that all service equipment and surfaces are suitable for food service and are clean. Staff training in food safety is essential for food service staff as well as for those preparing food.

High temperatures

Normal cooking temperatures of 75°C+ will kill most pathogens (but not toxins and spores). Use of heat to make food safe and to preserve it is one of the most useful procedures available in food production and manufacture. Table 14.1 shows some temperatures commonly used for this purpose.

Surplus prepared food

Some food businesses, as a matter of policy and in the interests of food safety, dispose of all unused prepared foods after set times, and always at the end of service. This is especially important when serving food to high-risk, vulnerable groups of people. Policy and procedures for using surplus food need to be planned and recorded as part of the food safety management system. Staff must be fully trained and retrained in these procedures and made aware of the potential hazards involved.

Personal hygiene

All humans are a potential source of food poisoning bacteria, and everyone working with food must be aware of the importance of personal hygiene when handling food. *Staphylococcus aureus* may be present in the nose, mouth, throat, on skin and hair, and could easily be transferred on to food where it could then multiply and cause illness. It is very important that hair, nose ears mouth, etc., are not touched while preparing food. Cuts, burns and boils are also likely to be a source of bacteria so must be covered.

Anyone suffering from or who is a carrier of any disease that could be transmitted through food must not handle food. This includes diarrhoea and/or vomiting, or any food poisoning symptom, infected cuts, burns or spots, bad cold or flu symptoms. Food handlers with any such illness, infection or wound must report this to their supervisor before starting work. They should also report any illness that has occurred on a recent holiday overseas, and illnesses suffered by other members of their family.

Table 14.1 Temperatures used to make food safe and for food preservation

Cooking 75°C for 2 minutes	This is the most common of 'heat treatments' for food. Cooked food does generally keep for longer than raw equivalents. However, treat cooked items with care as, once cooked, foods may then be in the high-risk category. Normal cooking to 75°C for 2 minutes at the core of the food will kill most pathogens but not spores and toxins.
Pasteurisation 72°C for 15 seconds	This involves heating food to a temperature similar to cooking temperatures but for a very short time, i.e. milk is heated to 72°C for 15 seconds, then rapid cooling takes place. These temperatures will kill most pathogens, bringing them to a 'safe level'. Toxins and spores will not be killed. Because relatively low temperatures are used, milk that has been pasteurised will spoil more quickly than milk preserved by some of the methods described below and must be kept at refrigerator temperatures. Pasteurisation is also used for liquid egg, cream, ice cream, some fruit juices and wine. Because of the temperatures used in pasteurisation the taste of the product remains mostly unchanged, though vitamin content is reduced by about 25%. Unpasteurised milk products can legally be sold in the UK as long as they are clearly labelled as such.
Sterilisation 100°C for 15–30 minutes	The sterilisation of milk and other food items destroys all micro-organisms. Sterilisation involves heating to 100°C for 15–30 minutes by applying steam and pressure. Because very high temperatures are used over a relatively long time some caramelisation occurs, taste is altered and vitamin content is significantly reduced. Unopened sterilised milk lasts much longer than pasteurised milk. Liquid or semi-liquid food such as soup, stock and sauces sold in pouches also go through a sterilisation process. These foods have a long shelf life and do not need refrigerated storage.
UHT 135°C for 1 second	UHT (ultra heat treatment) gives milk a long shelf life without the need for refrigeration (until the package is opened). The milk is heated under pressure to very high temperatures, i.e. 135°C, for just 1 second, then cooled rapidly and sealed in sterile containers. UHT is also used for cream.
Canning 121°C for 3 minutes	Canning is an efficient method of food preservation using very high temperatures along with sealing the food in a can, pouch or bottle. A concern with canning is the survival of anaerobic bacteria, especially *Clostridium botulinum*, which is particularly dangerous, as food poisoning from this organism can be debilitating and even fatal. This is because any surviving anaerobic bacteria could thrive inside a can where there is no oxygen; also, sources of *Clostridium botulinum* include some fish and vegetables, foods that are frequently canned. To overcome this, canned food is subjected to 'botulinum cook': a time/temperature combination – e.g. 121°C – for 3 minutes or a time/temperature combination calculated to be as effective as this, dependent upon the acidity and texture of the food.

All supervisors must be aware that food handlers can be *carriers* of dangerous pathogens that could get into the food they prepare. All known carriers must not handle food. *Convalescent carriers* are those recovering from an illness, but they still carry the bacteria and can pass it on to the food they handle. *Healthy carriers* show no signs of illness but can still contaminate the food as above; these people can remain carriers for long periods, or even all of their lives, and should not do work that involves handling food.

Before starting a job involving food handling, managers, supervisors/head chefs must make all staff aware that they must practise high standards of personal hygiene: they must always arrive at work clean (daily bath or shower) and with clean hair. They must also be aware of the following factors.

Hands

Hands can potentially be a major cause of contamination in food areas; if not kept clean they can very easily transfer harmful bacteria to food and equipment. Hands must be washed thoroughly and frequently, particularly after using the toilet, before commencing work, during the handling of food, and especially between different tasks. New staff need to be instructed in the correct procedure in washing hands properly, and existing staff will need periodic update training.

The procedure should be:

1 use a basin provided just for hand washing
2 wet hands under warm running water
3 apply liquid soap
4 rub hands together, and between fingers and thumbs
5 remember, fingertips, nails and wrists
6 rinse under the running water
7 dry hands on a paper towel and use this to turn off the tap
8 dispose of the paper towel in a foot-operated waste bin.

Staff involved in food handling must know that thorough hand washing should take place:

- when they enter the kitchen, before starting work and handling any food
- after a break (using the toilet, in contact with faeces)
- between different tasks, but especially between handling raw and cooked food
- after touching hair, nose, mouth, or using a tissue for a sneeze or cough

Figure 14.11 Drying hands on a paper towel

- after application of or changing a dressing on a cut or burn
- after cleaning preparation areas, equipment or contaminated surfaces
- after handling kitchen waste, external food packaging, money or flowers.

Jewellery/rings/watches

The wearing of jewellery is not acceptable when handling food. Jewellery can trap particles of food and provide a warm, damp environment for bacteria to grow; bacteria can then be transferred to food being prepared. This is particularly relevant to items worn on the hands such as rings and watches. Generally a plain wedding band is permissible, but be aware that this too can be a breeding ground for bacteria. Jewellery or parts of jewellery can fall into food, especially as in some food preparation hands need to be plunged into water.

Fingernails

These should always be kept clean and short as dirt can easily lodge under the nails and be transferred to food, introducing bacteria. Nails should kept neatly trimmed and nail varnish should never be worn in food areas.

The head

Hair

Hair must be washed regularly and kept covered with a suitable hat and/or net to prevent loose hair falling into food. The head/hair should never be scratched, combed or touched in the kitchen, as bacteria and loose hair could be transferred via the hands to the food, and loose hair could also fall into food.

Nose

The nose should not be touched when food is being

handled. If a handkerchief/tissue is used, the hands should be washed thoroughly afterwards. The nose is an area where there are vast numbers of harmful bacteria; it is therefore very important not to sneeze on food, other people or working surfaces. If a sneeze or cough is unavoidable, turn away and sneeze into the shoulder area.

Mouth

The mouth also harbours large numbers of bacteria, therefore the mouth or lips should not be touched when working with food. Do not use cooking utensils such as wooden spoons for tasting food, nor should fingers be used for this purpose as bacteria may be transferred to food. A clean teaspoon (or disposable plastic spoon) should be used for tasting.

Ears

Ears, too, are a source of bacteria and should not be touched when handling food.

Cuts, burns and other skin abrasions

It is particularly important to keep all cuts, burns, scratches and similar abrasions covered with a water-proof dressing (e.g. a blue plaster). Where the wound has become infected there are vast numbers of harmful bacteria that must not be permitted to get on to food; in most cases people suffering in this way should not handle food. Report this to a supervisor before handling food.

Cosmetics

Cosmetics should be used sparingly by food handlers, but ideally their use should be discouraged altogether. Cosmetics must never be applied in the kitchen and the hands should be washed thoroughly after applying them.

Smoking

Smoking is now illegal in most buildings and certainly where there is food. If food handlers smoke at break times, their hands must be washed thoroughly afterwards because when a cigarette is taken from the mouth, bacteria from the mouth can be transferred via the fingers on to food.

Use of kitchen cloths

Cloths used for holding hot dishes or removing hot items from the oven should be kept clean and dry, and should not be used for other purposes. Tea towels and dishcloths are often used in many ways, such as wiping surfaces or knives, wiping plate edges and pans. All such uses could transfer bacteria on to food and be the cause of cross-contamination. Where cloths are used, they must be clean and changed frequently; use different cloths for raw and cooked food areas (colour-coded cloths are useful for this). Do not place cloths over the shoulder because they will transfer bacteria from the neck and hair to food and equipment. Probably the best practice is to use disposable cloths or kitchen paper.

Protective clothing

Clean whites (protective clothing) and clean underwear should be worn at all times; whites should completely cover any other clothing and should be worn only in the kitchen. Dirty protective clothing can cause cross-contamination and enable multiplication of bacteria, which could then get on to food or food equipment.

Outdoor clothing, and other clothing that has been taken off before wearing whites, should be kept in a locker, away from the kitchen. Kitchen protective clothing needs to provide a barrier between the

Smoking chef fined after health check

A chef carried on smoking as he cut up meat in front of a health investigator, a court heard this week.

The senior environmental officer said that a cat was allowed to walk around while food was being prepared and that staff were wearing dirty overalls.

On a later visit he found the chef smoking a cigarette as he chopped up chicken.

TV pub 'revolting'

A picturesque pub featured in a BBC programme was fined a total of £6,750 yesterday for food hygiene breaches. The magistrate hearing the case described the kitchen as 'absolutely revolting'.

Figure 14.12 Sample newspaper reports of hygiene breaches

wearer and the food, and should protect the body from excessive heat.

- **Chefs' jackets** are usually made of cotton or a cotton mixture, are double-breasted and mostly have long sleeves; these protect the chest and arms from the heat of the stove, and prevent hot foods or liquids burning or scalding the body.
- **Aprons** are designed to protect the body from being scalded or burned, and particularly to protect the legs from any liquids that may be spilled; for this reason the apron should be of sufficient length to protect the legs.
- The main purpose of the **chef's hat** is to prevent loose hairs from falling into food and to absorb perspiration on the forehead. As well as the traditional chef's toque (tall white hat), a variety of designs is now available, some with a net incorporated to contain the hair fully. Lightweight disposable hats are now used in many establishments.

Kitchen clothing needs to be:

- **washable** – the clothing should be of an easily washable material because many frequent changes of clothing may be needed; with white clothing it is easy to see when it is stained or dirty and needs changing; kitchen clothing must be easy to wash, and cotton or a cotton mixture is preferable to enable frequent changing and laundering
- **light and comfortable** – clothing must be light in weight, comfortable and not too tight or too long
- **strong and absorbent** – clothes worn in the

A hat is essential

Clean teeth

Long hair is tied back

Men should be clean shaven

A chef's jacket, preferably with long sleeves

Keep a cloth handy

Clean hands

Use a blue plaster if you cut yourself

An apron helps to protect you from waist to knee

Chef's trousers are baggy

Safe shoes with steel toe caps

Figure 14.13 A chef in whites

kitchen must be strong enough to make them 'protective', and able to withstand the hard wear and frequent washing needed; they also need to be absorbent, to deal with perspiration caused by working in a hot kitchen.

Footwear

This should be strong, and kept in good repair so as to protect and support the feet. As kitchen staff are on their feet for many hours, suitable, clean, comfortable kitchen footwear is essential. Kitchen staff should not wear any open-top shoes or sandals, and 'trainers' are also unsuitable as they offer no protection from the spillage of hot liquids, falling knives or heavy items that could be dropped on the feet.

A clean and hygienic food environment

Cleaning and disinfection

Clean food areas play an essential part in the production of safe food. Clean premises, work areas and equipment are essential to:

- control the organisms that cause food poisoning
- reduce the possibility of physical and chemical contamination
- make accidents less likely, e.g. slips on a greasy floor
- create a positive image for customers, visitors and employees
- comply with the law
- avoid attracting pests to the kitchen

- create a pleasant and hygienic working environment that is safe and attractive, allowing for efficient and effective working methods
- assist in reducing maintenance costs and damage to equipment.

Effective cleaning uses one or more of the following:

- **physical energy**/human effort of the cleaner carrying out the task
- **chemicals**, i.e. detergents
- **mechanical methods** – machines
- **turbulence** – movement of liquids
- **thermal energy** – hot water and steam

- **CIP** (clean in place), e.g. for very large equipment.

There are different products designed to complete different tasks, as described below.

Chemicals used in cleaning and disinfection

- **Detergent** is designed to remove grease and dirt and hold them in suspension in water. Detergents may be in the form of liquid, powder, gel or foam, and usually need to be added to water to use. Detergent will not kill pathogens (although the hot water it is mixed with may help to do this), however it will clean and degrease so disinfectant can work properly. Detergents work best in hot water.
- **Disinfectant** is intended to destroy bacteria when used properly. Disinfectants must be left on a cleaned, grease-free surface for the required amount of time to be effective, and usually work best in cool water.
- **Sanitiser** cleans and disinfects, and usually comes in spray form. Sanitiser is very useful for work surfaces and equipment, especially between tasks.
- **Sterilisers** can be chemicals (or the action of extreme heat) and will kill all living micro-organisms.

When done properly, cleaning is effective in removing dirt, grease, debris and food particles. Areas will look better, be tidier and allow work to be carried out more efficiently. However, cleaning alone is not effective in the removal of micro-organisms – this will require *disinfection*. Disinfection is often carried out after the cleaning process, but sometimes the two are done together (i.e. use of sanitiser). It is unlikely that disinfection will kill all micro-organisms, but it will bring them to a safe level.

Disinfection may be completed with:

- chemicals – use only those recommended for kitchen use
- hot water – e.g. 82°C+ for 30 seconds, as occurs in a dishwasher
- steam – use of steam disinfection is good for equipment and surfaces that are difficult to dismantle or reach, e.g. clean in place (CIP).

All food contact surfaces, equipment and hand contact items (e.g. fridge handles) should be cleaned and disinfected regularly according to the cleaning schedule. Other areas and items may need thorough cleaning but not disinfection (e.g. floors and walls). It is important to clean and disinfect the actual cleaning equipment too after use.

What needs to be both cleaned and disinfected?

- **Direct food contact surfaces:** such as chopping boards, knives, work surfaces, mixing bowls, serving dishes, display counter inserts and slicing machines.
- **Hand contact surfaces:** such as taps, door handles, drawer handles, oven doors, refrigerator doors, light switches, telephones.
- **Hands:** disinfection achieved by bactericidal soap, alcohol-based disinfectant.
- **Cleaning materials and equipment:** mops, cleaning cloths, scrapers, brushes.

Disinfection needs to be carried out carefully to ensure that it is effective and safe. All chemicals in kitchens and food premises must be 'food safe' and it is important to follow manufacturers' instructions. Careless use of chemicals can be dangerous, and can cause skin irritation, respiratory problems and burns. A number of cleaning substances are regarded as hazardous to health. Therefore, a number of precautions have to be taken to control their use:

- read the label and identify the substance and its potential hazards
- follow dilution instructions carefully
- use only the right substance for the appropriate job
- use the necessary and recommended protective clothing
- do not mix different chemicals
- always store chemicals in their original containers.

Always use a fresh solution of disinfectant every time a new cleaning task is carried out. Do not top up existing solutions. Mops and cloths should not be soaked in disinfectant solutions for long periods, as the solution will weaken and can allow bacteria to grow. The disinfectant must be allowed to remain on the surface for the 'contact time' recommended by the manufacturer. Always rinse thoroughly, unless the manufacturer's instructions state that rinsing is unnecessary.

Dangers from chemicals

It is essential for all staff to be aware of the possible dangers and hazards from cleaning chemicals. Recognised COSHH (Control of Substances Hazardous to Health) training will increase staff awareness of the risks of the possible dangers from the chemicals they use as part of their job role. They must be made aware through ongoing training and supervision of the correct use of chemicals, use of PPE (personal protective equipment) and of proper chemical storage procedures. Chemicals must be kept well away from food preparation areas in separate and lockable storage; the chemicals must be kept in their original containers. Disposal of chemicals must be carried out in the correct manner according to company policy, health and safety regulations and advised COSHH procedures.

As part of kitchen training, it is important to train all staff in the importance of 'clean as you go', and not to allow waste to accumulate in the area where food preparation and cooking are being carried out. Staff need to understand that it is very difficult to keep untidy areas clean and hygienic, and it is more likely that cross-contamination will occur in untidy areas.

The cleaning of areas and equipment needs to be planned and recorded on a cleaning schedule. The cleaning schedule needs to include the following information.

- **What** is to be cleaned.
- **Who** should do it (name if possible).
- **How** it is to be done and how long it should take.
- **When**, i.e. time of day.
- **Materials** to be used, including chemicals, dilution, cleaning equipment, protective clothing to be worn.
- **Safety** precautions necessary to complete the task safely.
- **Signatures** of cleaner and supervisor checking the work; also date and time.

The cleaning process must be monitored regularly and inspected to ensure that the schedule is being followed, in order to maintain standards. Checking can include the use of rapid bacterial tests or swabbing.

Training

For effective cleaning to take place, staff involved must be properly trained, with emphasis given to use of the cleaning schedule, correct methods and use of chemicals, and use of PPE (personal protective equipment).

Kitchen waste

Kitchen waste should be placed in suitable waste bins with lids (preferably foot-operated). Bins should be made of a strong material, be easy to clean, pest-proof and lined with a suitable bin liner. They should be emptied regularly to avoid waste build-up as this could cause problems with multiplication of bacteria and attract pests. An over-full heavy bin is also much

more difficult to handle than a regularly emptied bin. Waste should never be left in kitchen bins overnight (this needs to be part of *closing checks*).

Outside waste bins also need to be strong, pest-proof and impervious, with a closely fitting lid. Bins should stand on hard surfaces that can be easily hosed down and kept clean. Planned regular emptying of the bins and cleaning of the area should be recorded in the cleaning schedule/management system.

Dishwashing

The most efficient and hygienic method of cleaning dishes and crockery is the use of a dishwasher, as this will clean and disinfect items, which will then air-dry, removing the need for cloths. The dishwasher can also be used to clean/disinfect small equipment such as bowls and chopping boards. The stages in machine dishwashing are:

- remove waste food, pre-rinse or spray
- load on to the appropriate racks
- the wash cycle will run at 50–60°C using a detergent
- the rinse cycle will run at 82–88°C.

This very high rinse temperature will disinfect items and allow them to air dry so no drying cloths will be needed. In most commercial dishwashers the wash, rinse and water-softening chemicals are fed automatically into the machine.

Dishwashing by hand

If items need to be washed by hand the recommended way to do this is:

- scrape/rinse/spray off residue food
- wash items in a sink of hot water; the temperature should be 50–60°C, which means rubber gloves need to be worn; use a dishwashing brush rather than a cloth (the brush will help to loosen food particles and is not such a good breeding ground for bacteria)
- rinse in very hot water – if rinsing can be done at 82°C for 30 seconds it will disinfect the dishes
- allow to air dry, do not use tea towels.

Before dishwashers were so widely used, a double-sink system of dishwashing was often used. Dishes were washed by hand in one sink using hot water and detergent, then loaded on to racks and plunged into a second sink of very hot rinse water (up to 80°C). The water in this sink was often heated by heating elements or pipes under the sink. Although this system

Table 14.2 Recommended methods for cleaning a kitchen surface

Six-stage	Four-stage
Remove debris and loose particles Main clean to remove soiling and grease Rinse using clean hot water and cloth to remove detergent Apply disinfectant, leave for contact time recommended on container Rinse off disinfectant if recommended Allow to air dry or use kitchen paper	Remove debris and loose particles Main clean – use hot water and sanitiser Rinse using clean hot water and cloth if recommended on instructions Allow to air dry or use kitchen paper to dry

Figure 14.14 Vacuuming

Figure 14.15 Cleaning trolley

can still be seen in some establishments it has fallen from favour because it is labour intensive, creates condensation problems, and causes health and safety concerns (open sinks of very hot water). Dishwashers are much the favoured way of cleaning and disinfecting dishes, cutlery and small equipment.

Cleaning surfaces

Because kitchen surfaces are likely to come into direct contact with food it is essential that they undergo planned and recorded cleaning and disinfection.

Avoiding hazards

Cleaning is essential to prevent food safety hazards, but if not managed properly can become a hazard in itself. Do not store cleaning chemicals in food preparation and cooking areas, and take care with their use (*chemical contamination*). Make sure that items such as cloths and paper towels, and fibres from mops, do not get into open food (*physical contamination*). *Bacterial contamination* can occur by using the same cleaning cloths and equipment in raw food areas then in high-risk food areas, or not cleaning/disinfecting cleaning equipment properly.

Pests

When there are reports of food premises being forcibly closed down, an infestation of pests is often the reason. As pests can be a serious source of contamination and disease, they must be eliminated from food premises for food safety reasons and to comply with the law. Pests can carry food poisoning bacteria into food premises on their fur/feathers or feet/paws, or in saliva, urine and droppings. Other problems caused by pests include damage to food stock and packaging, damage to buildings, equipment and wiring, and blockages in equipment and piping.

Figure 14.16 Pests

Pests can be attracted to food premises because there are food, warmth, shelter, water and possible nesting materials; kitchens and food stores provide all these conditions and, therefore, are very appealing environments to pests. All reasonable measures must be put in place to keep them out. Staff must be made aware of possible signs that pests may be present, and any sightings must be reported to the supervisor or manager immediately. Common pests that may cause problems in food areas are rats, mice, cockroaches, wasps, flies, ants (e.g. pharaoh's ants), birds and domestic pets.

Pest management needs to be planned as part of the food safety management system. Regular visits from a recognised pest control company are recommended because they will offer advice as well as deal with problems arising. Companies conducting a regular audit will provide a pest audit report, which should be kept and could be used as part of due diligence (see page 421).

Rats and mice (rodents)

Rats and mice are a dangerous source of food infection because they carry harmful bacteria on their bodies and in their droppings. Rats infest sewers and drains, and since excreta is a main source of food-poisoning bacteria, it is possible for any surface touched by rats to be contaminated.

Rats and mice like warm, dark corners and can be found in lift shafts, meter cupboards, lofts, pipe lagging, openings in walls where pipes enter, under low shelves and on high shelves. They enter premises through any holes, defective drains, open doorways and in sacks of food. Signs to look for are droppings, smears, holes, runways, gnawing marks, grease marks on skirting boards and above pipes, claw marks, damage to stock and also rat odour.

Rats spoil ten times as much food as they eat, and there are at least as many rats as human beings. They are very prolific, averaging ten offspring per litter and six litters per year. If any problem with rats or mice is suspected it is essential to contact a pest control contractor immediately.

Insect infestation

Common house flies probably spread more infection than any other insect. Flies land on animal excreta, refuse and decaying matter, and contaminate their legs, wings and bodies with harmful bacteria, which could be deposited on food. They also contaminate food with their excreta and saliva.

Wasps can also frequent dirty and decaying objects before they land on food, so should be excluded from kitchen areas.

An electronic fly killer (EFK) is an effective way to deal with flying insects: the blue light attracts the insects, which are then killed by an electrical charge. They fall into a collecting tray, which must be emptied regularly.

Cockroaches like warm, moist, dark places. They leave their droppings and a liquid that gives off a very unpleasant smell. They can carry harmful bacteria on their bodies and deposit them on anything with which they come into contact. They tend to hide away during the day and come out at night, so it is essential that no food is left out to attract them.

Silverfish are small silver-coloured insects that feed on starchy foods (among other things); they are found on moist surfaces. They thrive in badly ventilated areas, so improving ventilation will help to control them.

Beetles are found in warm places and can also carry harmful bacteria from place to place.

Insects are destroyed using an insecticide, and it is usual to employ people familiar with this work. The British Pest Control Association (see www.bpca.org. uk) has a list of member companies.

Possible diseases from pests

The presence of pests in and around kitchens and food can result in contamination and disease.

Rodents/birds	Insects
Salmonella/Typhoid	Salmonella
Clostridium perfringens	Clostridium perfringens
E. coli 0157	E. coli 0157
Leptospirosis (Weil's)	Dysentery
Cholera	
Trichinosis/parasites	
Campylobacter	
Listeria	

Pest infestations are a frequent reason for premises being closed and often lead to prosecution. Contamination of food by pests is also a common reason for prosecution.

The law (Regulation (EC) 852/2004) requires there to be pest control in premises:

- 'Effective pest control procedures must be implemented'
- 'Food must be protected from contamination'

Cats and dogs

Domestic pets should never be permitted in kitchens or any food premises as they carry harmful bacteria and may also introduce fleas.

Birds

Entry of birds into food premises must also be prevented to avoid areas being contaminated by droppings and pathogenic bacteria carried by birds.

Pest control

The role of managers and supervisors in pest control is mainly about good practice, good housekeeping and working with pest control contractors. This includes:

- reporting any damage to buildings and fittings, and organising prompt repair
- windows and other openings to the outside environment to be fitted with insect-proof screens
- keeping entrances to the building clean and clear, with undergrowth well cut back
- keeping food areas clean (especially under/behind equipment and in corners), and not leaving out any traces of food or liquids overnight (closing checks)
- making sure refuse areas are regularly checked and cleaned, and that refuse containers have tight-fitting lids and are emptied regularly
- effective stock control and regular cleaning of storage areas, dry commodities in sealed containers off the floor

Table 14.3 Signs of pest presence and how to keep them out

Pest	Signs that they are present	Ways to keep them out
Rats and mice	Sightings of rodent, droppings, unpleasant smell, fur, gnawed wires, etc. Greasy marks on lower walls, damaged food stock and packaging, paw prints and tail marks	Wherever possible, block entries, e.g. no holes around pipe work, avoid gaps and cavities where rodents could get in. Sealed drain covers, wire guards on top of pipes and soil stacks, metal kick plates on doors
Flies and wasps	Sighting of flies and wasps, hearing them, dead insects. Maggots	Make sure any damage to building, fixtures and fittings repaired quickly. Check deliveries/packaging for pests. Cut back outside vegetation. Baits and traps, inside and outside. Window/door screening/netting. Electronic fly killer. No holes around pipes, windows, etc. Sealed containers, no open food left out. Regular checks of ducting pipe lagging, etc. No build-up of waste in kitchen. Outside waste not kept too close to kitchen. Dry goods in sealed containers. No open food left in kitchen or store rooms. Effective stock control. Block entry to building, use of screens, netting, etc. Make sure outside refuse bins have close-fitting lids. Keep them out
Cockroaches	Sighting, dead or alive, also nymphs, eggs, larvae, pupae, egg cases. Live cockroaches often seen at night. Unpleasant smell	
Ants	Sightings and present in food and food stores. The tiny, pale coloured Pharaohs ants are difficult to spot but can still be the source of a variety of pathogens.	
Weevils	Sightings of weevils in stored products, e.g. flour/cornflour. Very difficult to see – tiny black insects moving in flour etc.	
Birds	Sighting, droppings, in outside storage areas and around refuse.	
Domestic pets	These must be kept out of food areas as they carry pathogens on fur, whiskers, saliva, urine, etc.	
Professional and organised pest management control, surveys and reports in place allows for organised management of pests		

Note: Pest control measures can themselves introduce food safety hazards: the bodies of dead insects or even rodents may remain in the kitchen (physical and bacterial contamination); pesticides, insecticides and baits could cause chemical contamination if not managed properly. Pest control problems are best managed by professionals.

- checking deliveries for any possible signs of pests
- discouraging suppliers from delivering items very early in the morning and leaving them outside where pests could get into them.

It is also good practice to employ a pest control contractor to inspect the site regularly and give advice as well as a written report.

Kitchen premises

Ventilation

Adequate ventilation must be provided so that fumes from stoves are taken out of kitchen areas. This is usually achieved by use of hoods over stoves and extractor fans. Hoods and fans must be kept clean; grease and dirt are drawn up by the fan and, if they accumulate, can block vents and the grease and dirt can drop on to food. Windows used for ventilation should be screened to prevent the entry of dust, insects and birds. Good ventilation makes for a much more comfortable working environment and can lead to greater staff efficiency.

Lighting

Good lighting is essential so that kitchen staff can work efficiently; it will also keep premises safer and help to prevent accidents. Natural lighting is preferable to artificial lighting. Good lighting is also necessary to enable staff to see into all areas so that the kitchen can be cleaned properly.

Plumbing

Adequate supplies of hot and cold water must be available for keeping the kitchen clean, for cleaning food and equipment, and for staff use. Hot water is essential for cleaning so the means of heating water must be capable of meeting cleaning requirements. Hand-washing facilities (separate from food preparation sinks) must also be available in the kitchen, with a suitable means of drying the hands – preferably paper towels.

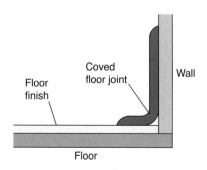

Figure 14.17 Coved floor joint

Floors

Kitchen floors have to withstand a considerable amount of wear and tear, therefore they must be:

- capable of being cleaned easily
- even, smooth and non-slip
- without cracks or open joints
- impervious (non-absorbent).

Quarry tile, vinyl sheet or epoxy resin floors, properly laid, are suitable for kitchens since they fulfil the above requirements. Where possible the join between the floor and wall should be coved, making cleaning easier and more efficient.

Walls

Walls should be strong, smooth, impervious, washable and light in colour. Suitable wall surfaces include ceramic tiles, heat-resistant plastic sheeting, stainless steel sheeting and resin-bonded fibreglass.

Clean with hot detergent water and dry. Food surface 'splash-backs' need to be cleaned/sanitised frequently; this could be done at the same time as the work surface.

Ceilings

Ceilings must be free from cracks and flaking. They should not be able to harbour dirt, condensation or grease that could fall on to food.

Doors and windows

Doors and windows should fit correctly into their frames and doors should have metal kick plates. Doors and windows need to be kept clean and glass should be clean inside and out so as to admit maximum light. Remember to include the cleaning and disinfection of door handles on the cleaning schedule as these are hand contact surfaces so could cause cross-contamination.

Hygiene of kitchen equipment

Kitchen equipment must be so designed to allow ease of cleaning and ease of inspection, to check it is clean and in good repair. Failure to do this could lead to food poisoning. Manufacturers' instructions must always be followed. Material used in the construction of equipment must be:

- hard and impervious, so that it does not absorb food particles and moisture
- smooth, so cleaning can take place easily
- resistant to rust
- resistant to chipping or cracking.

Containers, pipes and equipment made from toxic

materials, such as lead and zinc, should not be in direct contact with food or drink. Food must always be protected from machine lubricants.

Control and disposal of waste

Waste material is a potential threat to food safety because it is a source of contamination that can provide food for a variety of pests. There is a 'duty of care' under the Environmental Protection Act 1990 that makes the catering organisation responsible for its waste. It is a legal requirement to use licensed waste contractors, which must issue a *waste transfer notice*. Any special waste might need dealing with separately (e.g. chemicals, flammable substances, potentially infectious material). There is also a legal requirement that attempts to deal with the reduction of packaging. Large businesses must register with the Environmental Protection Agency and make efforts to reduce the amount of packaging they generate as waste.

Recycling

In most businesses there will be a significant amount of waste suitable for recycling, provided that the recycling meets health and safety and hygiene requirements. Separation of different items is necessary depending on local authority/contractors' policies, and regular collections by reliable collectors are essential.

HACCP and food safety management systems

Since January 2006 it has been a legal requirement for all food businesses to have a food safety management system in place. Article 5 of the Food Hygiene (England) Regulations 2005 gave effect to the EU Regulations and states that:

> Food business operators shall put into place, implement and maintain a permanent procedure based on the principles of hazard analysis critical control points (HACCP). Food handlers must receive adequate instruction and/or training in food hygiene to enable them to handle food safely. Those responsible for HACCP based procedures in the business must have enough relevant knowledge and understanding to ensure the procedures are operated effectively.

This gave strength to the Food Standards Agency's commitment to significantly reduce food poisoning cases by 2020.

Ensuring that a suitable food safety management system is in place is a management responsibility, and the HACCP approach provides a means of ensuring the provision of safe food for customers (HACCP is the cornerstone of maintaining good food safety standards). From January 2006, a documented food safety system is a legal requirement for every size of food business.

Hazard analysis identifies all the factors that could lead to harm to the consumer: all ingredients, stages in the processing of foods, environmental features and human factors that could lead to unsafe food being served. **Critical control points** (CCPs) are the points at which control is essential to reduce the risk of potential hazards and prevent them from causing harm.

The CCPs that would typically apply to a food business might be:

- selecting suppliers and delivery
- various methods of food storage
- preparation
- chilled storage
- cooking
- serving, hot holding, cooling.

All food safety systems adopted for a business must be based on the principles of HACCP. This is an internationally recognised food safety management system that looks at identifying the critical points, or stages, in any process and identifying hazards that could occur, i.e. what could go wrong, when, where, how. Controls are then put in place to deal with the risks – making possible risks safe. Controls are carried out – if something goes wrong, do staff know what to do about it? What checks are in place and what should be done to put things right? Procedures are kept up to date – confirm that they are still working. Documents and records are kept to show the system is working and is regularly reviewed – a wide range of documents are used as part of the HACCP system.

Prerequisites

Before setting up a new HACCP system, certain prerequisites need to be considered (i.e. what needs to be in place).

- **Suppliers:** these should be approved suppliers

and, wherever possible, they should provide written specifications.

- **Traceability:** systems in place along with suppliers to trace the source of all foods.
- **Premises, structure and equipment:** records that premises are properly maintained; a flow diagram needs to be produced showing the process from delivery to service, avoiding any cross-over of procedures that could result in cross-contamination.
- **Storage and stock control:** raw ingredients to finished product; effective stock control, stock rotation and temperature-controlled storage must be in place.
- **Staff hygiene:** protective clothing, hand-washing facilities, toilets and changing facilities need to be provided; a policy for personal hygiene needs to be established, with appropriate training on the standards to be achieved.
- **Pest control:** a written pest control policy, ideally as part of a pest management system and involving a recognised contractor.
- **Cleaning/disinfection/waste:** a documented system in place that includes cleaning schedules and how waste removal will be managed.
- **Staff training:** records of all staff training, with dates completed.

Setting up HACCP

- A team of people suitably trained in HACCP procedures will be established to set up the system. If the business is small, just one person may be responsible. There are also a number of specialist HACCP consultancy companies that can complete and monitor the procedure.
- The hazards identified and the controls put in place will be essential to food safety and safe production methods, e.g. core cooking temperatures, possible multiplication and survival of bacteria, time food spends in danger zone (see page 398), cooling food.
- Food handlers must receive food safety training and effective supervision commensurate with the tasks being completed. Staff training records must be kept.
- There must be awareness that physical and chemical hazards could occur at any stage in the process and controls must include these.

The stages of the HACCP system

The HACCP system involves seven stages (see Figure 14.18).

The system needs to provide a documented record of the stages *all* food will go through, right up to the time it is eaten, which is why it will need to include purchase and delivery, receipt of food, storage, prepa-

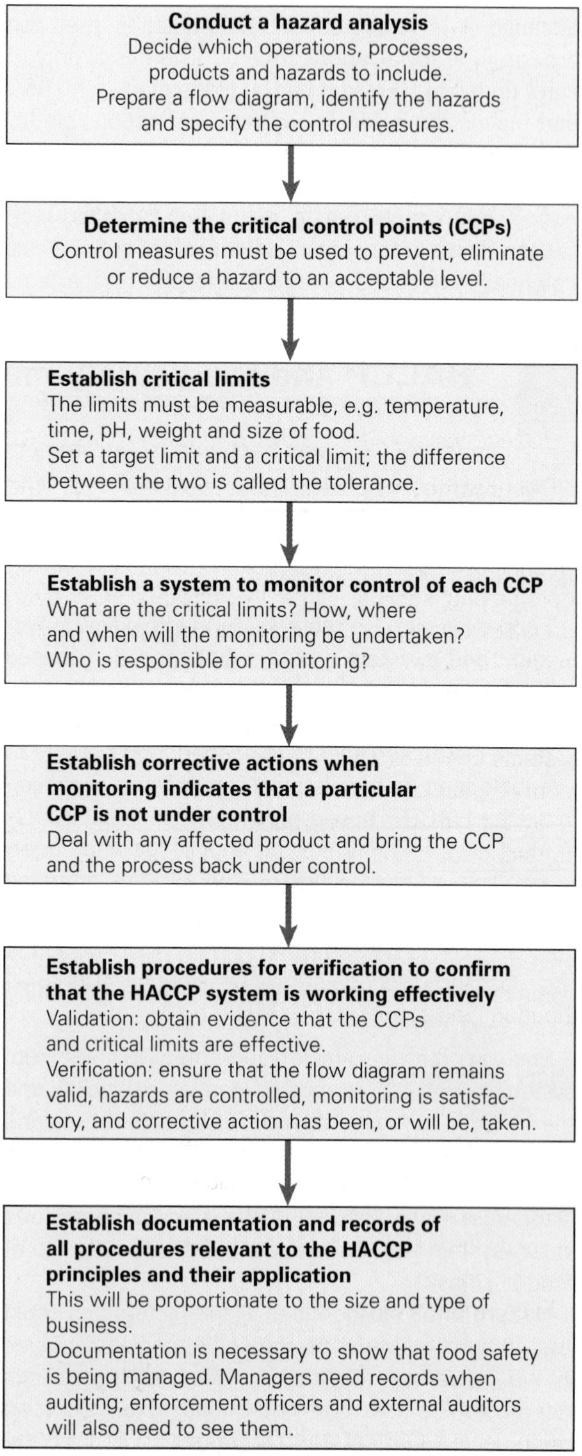

Conduct a hazard analysis
Decide which operations, processes, products and hazards to include.
Prepare a flow diagram, identify the hazards and specify the control measures.

Determine the critical control points (CCPs)
Control measures must be used to prevent, eliminate or reduce a hazard to an acceptable level.

Establish critical limits
The limits must be measurable, e.g. temperature, time, pH, weight and size of food.
Set a target limit and a critical limit; the difference between the two is called the tolerance.

Establish a system to monitor control of each CCP
What are the critical limits? How, where and when will the monitoring be undertaken?
Who is responsible for monitoring?

Establish corrective actions when monitoring indicates that a particular CCP is not under control
Deal with any affected product and bring the CCP and the process back under control.

Establish procedures for verification to confirm that the HACCP system is working effectively
Validation: obtain evidence that the CCPs and critical limits are effective.
Verification: ensure that the flow diagram remains valid, hazards are controlled, monitoring is satisfactory, and corrective action has been, or will be, taken.

Establish documentation and records of all procedures relevant to the HACCP principles and their application
This will be proportionate to the size and type of business.
Documentation is necessary to show that food safety is being managed. Managers need records when auditing; enforcement officers and external auditors will also need to see them.

Figure 14.18 Seven principles of HACCP

Possible hazards when dealing with the fresh chicken

Cooking a fresh chicken

Hazard: pathogenic bacteria are likely to be present in raw chicken

Control: the chicken needs to be cooked thoroughly to 75°C+ to ensure pathogens are killed

Monitor: check the temperature where the thigh joins the body with a calibrated temperature probe (75°C), make sure no parts of the flesh are pink and juices are running clear, not red or pink

Hot holding: before service the chicken must be kept above 63°C; this can be checked with a temperature probe

Or chill and refrigerate: chill to below 10°C within 90 minutes; cover, label and refrigerate below 5°C

Documentation: temperatures measured and recorded; hot holding equipment checked and temperature recorded; record any corrective measures necessary

For the cold storage of the chicken after cooking/chilling

Hazard: cross-contamination, multiplication of micro-organisms in cooked chicken

Control: protect from cross-contamination, store below 5°C

Monitor: check temperature of the chicken is below 5°C

Corrective action: if the chicken has been above 8°C for four hours or more it should be thrown away; investigate why the temperature control has not worked so it can be put right if there is a fault

Documentation: record temperatures at least once a day and record any corrective action

ration, cooking, cooling, hot holding, reheating, chilled storage and serving. Once the hazards have been identified, corrective measures are put in place to control the hazards and keep the food safe.

The system must be updated regularly, especially when new items are introduced to the menu or systems change (e.g. a new piece of cooking equipment). Specific new controls must be put in place to include them. A flow diagram will need to be produced for each dish or procedure showing each of the stages (CCPs) that need to be considered for possible hazards (see Figure 14.19).

As an example, when dealing with fresh chicken, it is necessary to recognise the possible hazards at all the identified stages (CCPs) (see box).

Due diligence

Due diligence is the main defence available under food safety legislation. It means that a business took all reasonable care and precautions, and did everything reasonably practicable to prevent an offence or food poisoning outbreak – that is, it exercised all due diligence.

Every food business has a responsibility to make sure that food is safe to eat. If the food is found to be unfit to eat, prosecution can take place unless it can be proved that all reasonable precautions were taken. Thus written records that are part of the food safety management system will be essential to prove **due diligence**.

To prove due diligence, the written documents necessary could include:

- staff training records, including dates completed and topics covered
- temperature records (delivery, cooking and cold storage)
- details of suppliers and contractors, and the traceability of the food they supply
- pest control policy and audits
- cleaning schedules and deep-clean reports
- maintenance schedules and records of repairs
- CCP monitoring activities (only CCPs, to avoid excessive paperwork)
- deviations, corrective actions and recalls
- modifications to the HACCP system
- customer complaints/investigation results
- calibration of instruments
- prerequisite programme records.

'Safer Food Better Business' and other systems

The HACCP system described above may seem complicated and difficult to set up for a small or fairly limited business. With this in mind, the Food Standards Agency launched its 'Safer Food Better Business' system for England and Wales. This is based on the principles of HACCP but in an easy-to-understand format with no complicated jargon. It has pre-printed pages and charts to enter the rel-

Table 14.4 Example of a HACCP control chart

Process steps	Hazards	Controls	Critical limit	Monitoring	Corrective action
Purchase	Contamination, pathogens, mould or foreign bodies present	Approved supplier			Change supplier
Transport and delivery	Multiplication of harmful bacteria	Refrigerated vehicles		Check delivery vehicles, date marks, temperatures	Reject if > 8°C or out of date
Refrigerate	Bacterial growth Further contamination – bacteria, chemicals, etc.	Store below 5°C Separate raw and cooked foods Stock rotation	Food below 5°C	Check and record temperature twice a day Check date marks	Discard if signs of spoilage or past date mark
Prepare	Bacterial growth Further contamination	No more than 30 minutes in 'danger zone' Good personal hygiene Clean equipment, hygienic premises		Supervisor to audit at regular intervals Visual checks Cleaning schedules	Discard if > 8°C for 6 hours
Cook	Survival of harmful bacteria	Thorough cooking	75°C	Check and record temperature/ time	Continue cooking to 75°C
Prepare for service	Multiplication of bacteria Contamination	No more than 20 minutes in 'danger zone'	2 hours	Supervisor to audit at regular intervals	Discard if > 8°C for 2 hours
Chill	Multiplication of bacteria Contamination	Blast chiller	90 minutes to below 10°C	Supervisor to audit at regular intervals	Discard if > 20°C for 2 hours
Refrigerate	Multiplication of bacteria Contamination	Store below 5°C Separate raw and ready-to-eat foods	8°C for 4 hours	Check and record temperature twice a day	Discard if > 8°C for 4 hours
Reheat	Survival of bacteria	Reheat to 75°C in centre	75°C (82°C in Scotland)	Check and record temperature of each batch	Continue reheating to 75°C

evant information, such as temperatures of individual dishes. There are two main parts: the first is about safe methods, such as avoiding cross-contamination, personal hygiene, cleaning, chilling and cooking; the second covers opening and closing checks, proving methods are safe, recording safe methods, training records, supervision, stock control, and the selection of suppliers and contractors.

Once the basic information has been recorded (e.g. suppliers and staff training), the actual diary pages are very easy to complete and just need confirmation that opening and closing checks have been completed, and have been dated and signed. The only other entries in the diary are the recording

of any problems occurring and what will be done about them. If no problems have occurred that day, nothing needs to be entered. This is called 'management by exception' or 'exception reporting'. A copy of 'Safer Food Better Business' is available from www.food.gov.uk.

A similar system, called CookSafe, has been developed by Food Standards Agency (Scotland), and Safe Catering in Northern Ireland.

Scores on the Doors is another strategy that has been piloted by the Food Standards Agency to raise food safety standards and help reduce the incidence of food poisoning. The piloted areas tested various schemes where a star rating of food safety was

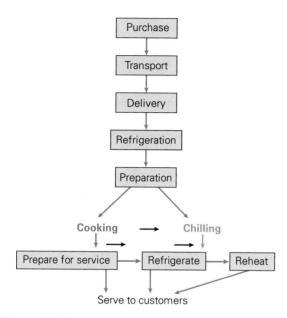

Figure 14.19 Example of a flow diagram

awarded based on the following three criteria taken from the Food Standards Agency's statutory risk rating system:

1 level of compliance of food hygiene practices and procedures
2 level of compliance relating to structure and cleanliness of premises
3 confidence in management of the business and food safety controls.

The intention is to place the given star rating in a prominent position on the door or window of premises, but it is not mandatory to do so.

After the successful pilot scheme, the Food Standards Agency decided on a standard system for England and Wales based on zero to five stars. It is expected that the Scores on the Doors scheme will have a lasting positive impact on food safety standards. No matter how good the food in a particular establishment, few people will want to eat there if the food safety score is low!

Food safety training

As well as being a legal requirement, food safety training for staff 'commensurate' to their job roles is essential in any food business. Food safety training needs to be planned, monitored and managed for staff, making sure that training records are accurate and up to date.

Before any new member of staff handles food, initial training must be carried out covering the most important food safety issues in the job role; the food handler will also need to be supervised. The initial training should then be followed up within a month with more formal training.

Specific training sessions, both formal and informal, may be delivered by supervisors and managers to meet the needs of the actual business and specific staff, as well as to satisfy legal requirements. Planned retraining/refresher sessions are also essential at all levels.

The training methods chosen will depend on the type of business, the activities carried out and any previous training staff have taken. Training could take place by:

- using food safety management companies, which undertake part or all of the food safety requirements for a business, including training at different levels
- partaking in food safety qualifications accredited by CIEH, RSPH, City & Guilds EDI, Highfield and others; courses are available at colleges and universities, through independent training providers, local authorities and adult education centres; training and testing for these can also take place in the workplace.

Food safety training at the different levels will cover all or most of the following topics with different degrees of complexity, depending on the level of the training taking place:

- food poisoning micro-organisms – sources and types, together with simple microbiology
- common food hazards – physical, chemical and microbiological
- prevention of food contamination and cross-contamination
- personal hygiene – responsibilities
- pest prevention and control
- cleaning and disinfection
- design of premises
- food storage and preparation, including temperature control
- food safety management systems
- supervision/management
- legal requirements.

The different levels for these qualifications are usually as follows.

- **Level 1:** often completed in the workplace for those new to food handling tasks or those employed on non-complex or limited tasks.
- **Level 2:** this is the most popular food safety

qualification and is designed for those handling a wide variety of foods, including 'open' and high-risk foods.

- **Level 3:** a qualification for supervisors of food premises (food operations), and for those completing more complex tasks and requiring a greater depth of knowledge.
- **Level 4:** a management-level qualification that may also be completed by more senior supervisors and anyone requiring a high-level food safety qualification.

The training can be carried out in a number of different ways. For example:

- online or computer package training, often with end tests and certification

- food safety training packs that could include books, workbooks, DVDs, activities, etc.
- as part of another qualification such as an NVQ or VRQ
- use of a variety of materials now widely available, including, posters, leaflets, films, interactive games and puzzles
- food safety consultants/trainers delivering different levels of training
- training delivered by the EHO (EHP).

Just one or a selection of these methods could be used, and some training materials are now available in a number of different languages with visual explanations. There are also training materials in the 'Safer Food Better Business' packs.

The role of management in food safety

Effective planning and management of food safety is essential to ensure that high standards are maintained, there is compliance with the 2006 food safety laws and the proceeding legislation, and to avoid the possibility of food safety-related problems. Management need to work closely with staff, taking preventative measures to protect against possible occurrences of food poisoning in connection with the business.

Managers and supervisors are crucial in implementing and managing effective food safety procedures, and provide an important link between business owners/directors and the actual food operation. In a large business, managers and supervisors may not be the actual policy-makers but it is likely that they will be involved in devising, setting and running the day-to-day food safety procedures. This will involve implementing the food safety management system (HACCP or similar) including:

- overseeing formal and informal staff training
- managing the various temperature controls, and recording
- putting measures in place to avoid contamination of food and cross-contamination
- setting required standards for personal hygiene and requirements for protective clothing
- monitoring standards for premises and equipment, and safe disposal of waste
- monitoring and managing the correct storage of food and rotation of stock
- managing cleaning and disinfection of premises and equipment, and the proactive control of pests.

Communication

Effective communication of food safety matters to staff is of great importance and can be achieved through induction procedures, ongoing staff training, supervision, mentoring, information posters, leaflets, films, and so on, information/training from the EHO (EHP), and by making food safety issues part of staff meetings, briefings and handover. Effective communication to staff of food safety standards and requirements must be ongoing and consistent.

Those managing or supervising the day-to-day food operations are in the ideal position to communicate food safety matters to business owners, senior managers, other department heads, suppliers, contractors and enforcement officers. Keeping up-to-date and accurate records is essential for effective communication.

Monitoring, control and auditing

Because food safety must be organised and planned, it is necessary to complete monitoring, control and auditing procedures.

- **Control** involves making sure that the agreed and recorded food safety policies are taking place in the day-to-day operations of the kitchen. This could be implemented by training, staff meetings, spot checks, posters and information sheets, training update sheets, short information films, etc.
- **Monitoring** involves the manager/supervisor and others checking (and recording, where appropriate) that controls are being adhered to and are working properly. Many monitoring

procedures will be part of the food safety management system (e.g. monitoring fridge temperatures or the cleaning schedule). Other methods of monitoring may include visual inspections, *organoleptic* checks of food stocks, checklists, walk-through checking procedures and checking that required tasks are completed, e.g. temperature recording. In some establishments bacterial monitoring is completed by swabbing surfaces, equipment or processes to establish specific pathogens that may be present, i.e. total viable counts – TVCs. (Swabbing kits are available from food safety management/equipment companies for checking and recording the levels of bacteria on a surface or piece of equipment. This may be done at regular intervals, and the findings used to improve cleaning and disinfection of areas. The findings also provide a good tool for staff training and meetings.)

- **Auditing** is often a more formal procedure, taking the form of an inspection. This could be done by an internal auditor (someone who is part of the organisation), or an external auditor or consultant may be used, but it should be someone who is not involved in carrying out or monitoring the day-to-day systems. Auditing is often used to verify that the HACCP or similar system is working properly.

E. coli puts ten in hospital

TEN people were in hospital last night after an E. coli outbreak. Two cases have been confirmed and up to 16 are suspected.

One of these involves a boy of ten. Health authorities are investigating a link with a supermarket. Yesterday the store closed its delicatessen counter and fresh fruit and vegetable stand.

Customers have been asked to return all meat, dairy and fresh produce bought there since 1 November. E. coli is a potentially fatal gastro-intestinal infection passed on from contaminated food.

Last night an NHS spokesman said none of those in hospital was dangerously ill.

Figure 14.20 Extract from a newspaper report on food poisoning

The Food Standards Agency

The Food Standards Agency (FSA) was established in April 2000, when it took over UK responsibility for food safety and food quality from the Department of Health (DoH) and the Ministry of Agriculture, Fisheries and Food, and the equivalent organisations in Wales, Northern Ireland and Scotland.

Its role is 'to protect public health from risks which may arise in connection with the consumption of food and otherwise to protect the interest of customers in relation to food'.

A wide variety of information can be found on the FSA website (www.food.gov.uk). This includes:

- various food safety topics
- nutritional information
- product and ingredient information (including food additives)
- information on food and products causing concern, and those that have been withdrawn from sale
- academic papers and reports linked to food safety topics
- relevant news and current information about food, including any withdrawn items.

It also has a question-answering service, and provides free leaflets, DVDs and posters for food businesses, as well as 'Safer Food Better Business' packs on request (see page 421).

Industry Guide (to good hygiene practice)

The Industry Guide to good hygiene practice gives advice (in plain, easy-to-understand English) to food businesses on how to comply with food safety law. Most industries have similar guides and, while the guides have no legal force, food authorities must give them due consideration when they enforce regulations.

It is the intention that industry guides will help business owners and managers understand and use the information to meet legal obligations and to ensure food safety. Printed industry guides are available from

HMSO Publications Offices or can be downloaded at www.archive.food.gov.uk.

More information on food safety law is available on Dynamic Learning.

Topics for discussion

1 What have been the impacts of the Food Hygiene (England) Regulations 2006 on food businesses?

2 How has the introduction of 'Safer Food Better Business' assisted smaller food businesses?

3 Apart from formal food safety training courses, how can management ensure the ongoing and up-to-date training of staff?

4 Discuss the advantages and disadvantages of the 'Scores on the Doors' scheme.

5 Discuss the implications an outbreak of food poisoning would have on: (a) a five-star hotel; (b) a takeaway food outlet; (c) a home for the elderly.

6 In food businesses, why should waste be recycled wherever possible? Are there any disadvantages to recycling?

7 Discuss the importance of time/temperature control of food in relation to food safety. How could you effectively convey this to staff?

8 What could be the implications for a food business if staff had poor/careless personal hygiene standards?

9 Why is it necessary to be able to trace back the sources, treatment and storage of food purchased from suppliers?

10 Illnesses caused by the organism E. coli have received extensive coverage in the press in recent years. Discuss why this organism has generated such interest.

Appendix: Useful websites

Ask a Chef – www.askachef.com
BBC Food Pages – www.bbc.co.uk/food
Beverage Information Group – www.beveragenet.net
British Cleaning Council –
  www.britishcleaningcouncil.org
British Dietetic Association – www.bda.uk.com
British Hospitality Association – www.bha.org.uk
British Institute of Innkeeping – www.bii.org
British Nutrition Foundation – www.nutrition.org.uk
British Standards – www.bsi-global.com or
  www.bsi-uk.com
Caterer and Hotelkeeper – www.caterersearch.com
Catering Net – www.cateringnet.co.uk
Chartered Institute of Environmental Health –
  www.cieh.org
ehotelier.com – www.ehotelier.com
Food Standards Agency – www.food.gov.uk
Foodserviceworld – www.foodserviceworld.com
Foodservice.com – www.foodservice.com
Hospitality Net – hospitalitynet.org

Induced Energy Limited – www.inducedenergy.com
Industry Guide to Hygiene Practice –
  archive.food.gov.uk/dept_health/pdf/catsec.pdf
Institute of Hospitality –
  www.instituteofhospitality.org
Into Wine – www.intowine.com
RIDDOR Incident Contact Centre –
  www.riddor.gov.uk
Royal Institute of Public Health – www.riph.org
Royal Society for the Promotion of Health –
  www.rsph.org
UK Food Law – www.fst.rdg.ac.uk/foodlaw
Unilever – www.unilever.co.uk
Webtender (online bartender) – www.webtender.com
Wine and Dine E-zine – www.dine-online.co.uk
The Wine Line – www.the-wine-line.com
Wine Spectator – www.winespectator.com
Wine.com – www.wine.com
Yahoo! food websites – www.yahoo.co.uk/
  society_and_culture/food_and_drink

Index

Page numbers in italics refer to illustrations, diagrams or charts.